Middle
E...

JAVA™

FOR ENGINEERS

AND SCIENTISTS

Gary J. Bronson

Fairleigh Dickinson University

Contributing Editor
G. J. Borse

Lehigh University

THOMSON
BROOKS/COLE

Australia • Canada • Mexico • Singapore • Spain
United Kingdom • United States

THOMSON
BROOKS/COLE

Publisher: *Bill Stenquist*
Editor: *Kallie Swanson*
Editorial Assistants: *Carla Vera, Aarti Jayaraman*
Technology Project Manager: *Burke Taft*
Executive Marketing Manager: *Tom Ziolkowski*
Director of Marketing Communications:
　Margaret Parks
Project Manager, Editorial Production: *Kelsey McGee*

Print/Media Buyers: *Vena M. Dyer, Jessica Reed*
Permissions Editor: *Sue Ewing*
Production Service: *The Book Company*
Copy Editor: *Frank Hubert*
Cover Designer: *Denise Davidson*
Cover Image: *Shinobu Hirai/Photonica*
Cover Printing, Printing, and Binding: *Webcom*
Compositor: *Pre-Press Company, Inc.*

For more information about our products,
contact us at:
Thomson Learning Academic Resource Center
1-800-423-0563
For permission to use material from this text, contact
us by:
Phone: 1-800-730-2214　　Fax: 1-800-730-2215
Web: http://www.thomsonrights.com

Library of Congress Control Number: 2002111289
ISBN 0-534-38453-6

Brooks/Cole–Thomson Learning
10 Davis Drive
Belmont, CA 94002-3098
USA

Asia
Thomson Learning
5 Shenton Way #01-01
UIC Building
Singapore 068808

Australia/New Zealand
Thomson Learning
102 Dodds Street
Southbank, Victoria
Australia 3006

Canada
Nelson
1120 Birchmount Road
Toronto, Ontario M1K 5G4
Canada

Europe/Middle East/Africa
Thomson Learning
High Holborn House
50/51 Bedford Row
London, WC1R 4LR
United Kingdom

Latin America
Thomson Learning
Seneca, 53
Colonia Polanco
11560 Mexico D.F.
Mexico

Spain/Portugal
Paraninfo
Calle Magallanes, 25
28015 Madrid
Spain

Dedicated to

Rochelle,

Matthew,

Jeremy,

and David Bronson

BRIEF CONTENTS

CONTENTS

PREFACE

Java™ is rapidly emerging as one of the preeminent applications languages for Windows®-based systems. A major reason is that Java is a true object-oriented language that now provides a complete set of visual objects that can easily be assembled into a working graphical user interface (GUI—pronounced goo-eey) and a complete set of input/output and mathematical classes.

From both a teaching and learning viewpoint, Java requires familiarity with four elements, all of which are required for object-oriented graphical-based programming. These are:

- The concept of object-oriented program class code
- The visual objects required in creating a graphical user interface
- The input, output, and mathematical classes required for creating engineering and scientific programs
- The concept of event-based programming, where the user, rather than the programmer, determines the sequence of operations to be executed

The major objective of this textbook is to introduce each of these elements, within the context of sound programming principles, in a manner that is accessible to the beginning programmer. Its purpose is both to provide you with the tools, techniques, and understanding necessary to create and maintain Java programs as well as to prepare a solid foundation for more advanced work. Thus, the basic goal of this text is that all topics be presented in a clear and unambiguous manner appropriate to a student taking an introductory course in Java programming.

In using this text, no prerequisites are assumed. The large numbers of examples and exercises in the text are drawn from basic engineering and scientific disciplines and are appropriate to an introductory language-based course.

Distinctive Features

Writing Style
I firmly believe that for a textbook to be useful it must provide a clearly defined supporting role to the leading role of the professor. Once the professor sets the stage, however, the textbook must encourage, nurture, and assist the student in acquiring and owning the material presented in class. To do this, the text must be written in a manner that makes sense to the student. Thus, first and foremost, I feel that the writing style used to convey the concepts presented is the most important and distinctive aspect of the text.

Flexibility
To be an effective teaching resource, this text is meant to provide a flexible tool that each professor can use in a variety of ways depending on *how many* programming concepts and programming techniques are to be introduced in a single course and *when* they are to be introduced. This is accomplished by partitioning the text into five parts and providing a varied number of Chapter Supplements that contain enrichment and breadth material.

Part One presents the fundamental object-oriented structure and procedural elements of Java. Additionally, both keyboard and dialog-based data entry are presented. This permits an early introduction of the swing package of visual objects as well as providing a firm grounding in basic Java Development Kit (JDK) techniques.

Once Part One is completed, the material in Parts Two, Three, Four, and Five are *interchangeable*. For example, in a more traditional introduction to programming type of course, Part One would be followed by Chapter 14 (File I/O) and Part Two, Array and String Reference Types. However, if a requirement is that the course must emphasize class design and development, Part One would be followed by Part Three. In a third instance, if the course is to have a more visual and GUI-based slant, Part One can just as easily be followed by Part Four. In each of these cases, a "pick-and-choose" approach to course structure can be implemented. This flexibility of topic introduction is illustrated by the following topic dependence chart.

Software Engineering
Although this is primarily an introduction to Java text, as opposed to a CS1 introduction to programming book, the text is meant to familiarize students with the fundamentals of software engineering from both a procedural and object-oriented viewpoint. In most cases, however, the more general programming aspects are interwoven within the text's main language component precisely because the text is meant to introduce and strengthen the *why* as well as the *how*.

Applications
Starting with Chapter 2, the majority of chapters contain an Applications section, with an average of two completed applications per chapter. Each application demonstrates effective problem solving within the context of a complete program solution. This is done both for method and class design.

Program Testing
Every single Java program in this text has been successfully entered and executed using Sun® Java 2.0 (both Versions 1.2 and 1.3). The Brooks/Cole Web site (see Appendix J)

provides all programs that are included within the text. This will permit students to both experiment and extend the existing programs and more easily modify them as required by a number of end of section exercises.

Pedagogical Features

To facilitate the goal of making Java accessible as a first-level course, the following pedagogical features have been incorporated into the text.

End-of-Section Exercises
Almost every section in the book contains numerous and diverse skill-builder and programming exercises. Additionally, solutions to selected odd-numbered exercises are provided on the Web site www.brookscole.com.

Common Programming Errors and Chapter Review
Each chapter provides a section on common programming errors. Additionally, each chapter contains an end of chapter section that reviews the main topics covered in the chapter.

Chapter Supplement Sections
Given the many different emphases that can be applied in teaching Java, a number of basic and enrichment topics have been included. These sections vary between such basic material as understanding bits and bytes, practical material, such as formatting, and theoretical material, such as insides and outsides. The purpose of these sections is to provide flexibility as to the choice of which topics to present and the timing of when to present them.

Point of Information Notes
These shaded boxes are primarily meant as a reference for commonly used tasks, for quick reference, for highlighting professional programming techniques, and to provide additional concept material.

Appendixes and Supplements

An expanded set of appendixes is provided. These include appendixes on keywords, operator precedence, Unicode codes, and packages. Additionally, the Web site www.brookscole.com contains solutions to selected odd-numbered exercises.

ACKNOWLEDGMENTS

This book began as an idea. It became a reality only due to the encouragement, skills, and efforts supplied by many people. I would like to acknowledge their contributions.

First and foremost, I wish to acknowledge and thank Kallie Swanson, my editor at Brooks/Cole, for her continuous faith and encouragement that I would complete the text no matter how many missed deadlines I went through.

As the manuscript was being developed, the skills and efforts of many other people at Brooks/Cole were required. I am very grateful and thank Carla Vera for handling numerous scheduling and review details that permitted me to concentrate on the actual writing of the text. I especially wish to express my very deep gratitude to the following individual reviewers: Sedar Kirli, University of Florida; Rubin H. Landau, Oregon State University; Chi N. Thai, University of Georgia; Guoliang (Larry) Xue, Arizona State University.

Each of these reviewers supplied extremely detailed and constructive reviews of both the original manuscript and a number of revisions. Their suggestions, attention to detail, and comments were extraordinarily helpful as the manuscript evolved and matured through the editorial process. Any errors that may now appear in the text are clearly and solely my own responsibility. Should you find any, I would very much like to hear from you through my editor, Kallie Swanson, at Brooks/Cole.

Special acknowledgement goes to G.J. Borse of Lehigh University for the material presented in Chapter 15 and the information contained within the Career Choice boxes, which Dr. Borse graciously permitted me to use from his *FORTAN 77 and Numerical Methods for Engineers,* Second Edition.*

Once the review process was completed, the task of turning the final manuscript into a textbook again required a dedicated production staff. For this I especially want to thank Kelsey McGee, the production editor at Brooks/Cole. Kelsey and I have now worked on the majority of my published books, and her attention to detail and very high standards have helped immensely to improve the quality of all of my texts. Next, I would like to thank Frank Hubert, the copyeditor, and the team at The Book Company, especially Dustine Friedman. Once this text moved to the production stage, this team of people seemed to take personal ownership of the text, and I am very grateful to them.

I would also like to gratefully acknowledge the direct encouragement and support of Fairleigh Dickinson University. Specifically, this includes the constant encouragement, support, and positive academic climate provided by my Dean, Dr. David Steele, my Associate Dean, Dr. Ron Heim, and my Chairperson, Dr. YoungBoem Kim. Without their support, this text could not have been written.

Finally, I deeply appreciate the patience, understanding, and love provided by my wife, friend, and partner, Rochelle.

Gary Bronson

*G.J. Borse, *FORTAN 77 and Numerical Methods for Engineers,* 2nd. Ed. © 1991, Brooks/Cole, an imprint of Thomson Learning.

P A R T 1

Fundamentals

CHAPTER 1

Getting

Started

In this chapter, we provide both a brief background on programming languages and a specific structure that will be used throughout the text for constructing Java programs. Additionally, we explain the concepts of methods and classes. We then describe two specific methods provided in Java, `print()` and `println()`, which are used within the context of a complete program for displaying data on a video screen. Finally, we present and use the `showMessageDialog()` method within the context of a complete program to construct a simple graphical user interface (GUI).

1.1 INTRODUCTION TO PROGRAMMING

A computer is a machine and like other machines, such as an automobile or lawn mower, it must be turned on and then driven, or controlled, to perform its intended task. In an automobile, for example, control is provided by the driver, who sits inside and directs the car. In a computer, the driver is a set of instructions, called a program. More formally, a **computer program** is a self-contained set of instructions used to operate a computer to produce a specific result. Another term for a program or set of programs is **software**, and we will use both terms interchangeably throughout the text.

The process of writing a program, or software, is called **programming,** and the set of instructions that can be used to construct a program is called a **programming language.** Available programming languages come in a variety of forms and types.

Machine Language

At its most fundamental level, the only programs that can actually operate a computer are **machine language programs**. Such programs, which are also referred to as **executable programs**, or **executables** for short, consist of a sequence of instructions composed of binary numbers such as:[1]

    11000000 000000000001 000000000010
    11110000 000000000010 000000000011

Such machine language instructions consist of two parts: an instruction part and an address part. The instruction part, which is referred to as the **opcode** (short for operation code), is usually the leftmost set of bits in the instruction. It tells the computer the operation to be performed, such as add, subtract, multiply, and so on. The rightmost bits specify the memory addresses of the data to be used. For example, assuming that the 8 leftmost bits of the first instruction just listed are the operation code to add and the next two groups of 12 bits are the addresses of the two operands to be added, this instruction would be a command to "add the data in memory location 1 to the data in memory location 2."[2] Similarly, assuming that the opcode 111100000 means multiply, the next instruction is a command to "multiply the data in memory location 2 by the data in memory location 3."

---

[1]Review the supplement at the end of this chapter if you are unfamiliar with binary numbers.

[2]To obtain the address values as decimal numbers, convert the binary values to decimal using the method presented in the chapter supplement.

Assembly Languages

Although each class of computers, such as IBM personal computers and Macintosh computers, have their own particular machine language, it is very tedious and time consuming to write machine language programs. One of the first advances in programming was the substitution of wordlike symbols, such as ADD, SUB, MUL, for the binary opcodes and both decimal numbers and labels for memory addresses. For example, using these symbols and decimal values for memory addresses, the previous two machine language instructions can be written as:

    ADD 1, 2
    MUL 2, 3

Programming languages that use this type of symbolic notation are referred to as **assembly languages.** Since computers can only execute machine language programs, the set of instructions contained within an assembly language program must be translated into a machine language program before it can be executed on a computer. Translator programs that perform this function for assembly language programs are known as **assemblers.**

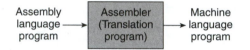

FIGURE 1.1   Assembly Programs Must Be Translated

Low- and High-Level Languages

Both machine-level and assembly languages are classified as **low-level languages.** This is because both of these language types use instructions that are directly tied to one type of computer.[3] Therefore, an assembly language program is limited to the specific computer type for which the program is written. These programs do, however, permit using special features of a computer that are different from other machines.

In contrast to low-level languages are languages that are classified as high-level. A **high-level language** uses instructions that resemble written languages, such as English, and can be run on a variety of computer types, such as an IBM, Apple, or Hewlett-Packard computer. Pascal, Microsoft® Visual Basic®, C, C++, and Java are all high-level languages. Using Java, an instruction to add two numbers and multiply by a third number can be written as:

```
result = (first + second) * third;
```

Programs written in a computer language (high or low level) are referred to interchangeably as both **source programs** and **source code.** Once a program is written in a high-level language, it must also, like a low-level assembly program, be translated into the machine language of the computer on which it will be run. This translation can be accomplished in two ways. A unique feature of Java, as you will see, is that it uses both translation techniques, one after another.

---

[3]In actuality, a low-level language is defined for the processor around which the computer is constructed. These include the Intel microprocessor chip for IBM-type personal computers, Motorola chips for Apple-based computers, and Alpha chips for many Hewlett-Packard Compaq-based computers.

When each statement in a high-level source program is translated individually and executed immediately upon translation, the programming language used is called an **interpreted language**, and the program doing the translation is called an **interpreter.**

When all of the statements in a high-level source program are translated as a complete unit before any one statement is executed, the programming language is called a **compiled language.** In this case, the program doing the translation is called a **compiler.** Both compiled and interpreted versions of a language can exist, although typically one predominates. For example, although compiled versions of BASIC do exist, BASIC is predominantly an interpreted language. Similarly, although interpreted versions of C++ exist, C++ is predominantly a compiled language.

A Java program's translation is a modification of the traditional process that uses *both* a compiler and interpreter. As shown in Figure 1.2, the output of the compilation step is a program in bytecode format. This bytecode is a machine code that *is not* geared to a particular computer's internal processor but rather to a computer referred to as a Java Virtual Machine (JVM). The Java Virtual Machine computer is not a physical machine but rather a software program that can read the bytecode produced by the compiler and execute it.

FIGURE 1.2   Translating a Java Program

The computer on which the JVM runs is referred to as the **host computer.** As shown in Figure 1.2, it is within the host computer's JVM that the bytecode is finally translated into a machine language code appropriate to the host computer. Specifically, the JVM is an interpreter that translates each bytecode instruction, as it is encountered, into a computer-specific machine code that is immediately executed by the computer.

It is this two-phase translation process that provides Java with its cross-platform capability that permits each computer, regardless of its internal processor type, to execute the same Java program. It does this by placing the machine-specific details of the final translation step within the host computer's JVM rather than on the computer under which the source code was compiled.

Procedure and Object Orientations

High-level languages are further classified as either procedure oriented or object oriented. In a **procedure-oriented language**, the available instructions are used to create self-contained units referred to as **procedures.** The purpose of a procedure is to accept data as input and transform the data in some manner to produce a specific result as an output. Until the mid-1990s, the majority of high-level languages were procedure oriented.

Within the past few years, a second orientation referred to as object oriented has taken center stage. One of the motivations for **object-oriented languages** was the development of graphical screens and support for graphical user interfaces (GUIs) capable of displaying multiple windows. In such an environment, each window on the screen can conveniently be considered an object with associated characteristics, such as color, position, and size. Using an object approach, a program must first define the objects it will be manipulating, which includes describing both the general characteristics of the objects themselves and specific units to manipulate them, such as changing size and position and transferring data between objects. Java is classified as an object-oriented language.

Application and System Software

Two logical categories of computer programs are application software and system software. **Application software** consists of programs written to perform particular tasks required by the users. Most of the examples in this book would be considered application software.

System software is the collection of programs that must be readily available to any computer system for it to operate at all. In the early computer environments of the 1950s and 1960s, a user had to initially load the system software by hand to prepare the computer to do anything. This was done with rows of switches on a front panel. Those initial hand-entered commands were said to **boot** the computer, an expression derived from "pulling oneself up by the bootstraps." Today, the so-called **bootstrap loader** is internally contained in read-only memory (ROM) and is a permanent, automatically executed component of the computer's system software.

Additionally, before the 1960s, it was not uncommon for the user to also have to load a separate set of programs necessary for reading from and writing to the input and output devices. Similarly, it was the user's responsibility to find the code that would translate an application program to the computer's internal machine language so that it could be executed. Typically, most of these **utilities** are now kept on either a hard disk or in memory and are booted into the computer either automatically when the system is turned on or on command by the user.

Various terms are used by different manufacturers for the collection of system utilities called the **operating system.** Often, the system software name ends with *OS* or *DOS* (for disk operating system). Additional tasks handled by modern operating systems include memory, input and output, and secondary storage management. Many systems handle very large programs, as well as multiple users concurrently, by dividing programs into segments or pages that are moved between the disk and memory as needed. Such operating systems create a *virtual memory*, which appears to be as large as necessary to handle any job, and a *multiuser* environment is produced that gives each user the impression that the computer and peripherals are his or hers alone. Additionally, many operating systems, including most windowed environments, permit each user to run multiple programs. Such operating systems are referred to as **multitasking** systems.

TABLE 1.1   Common Operating System Commands

Task	DOS Command	UNIX Command
Displays the directory of all files available.	DIR	ls
Deletes a specified file or group of files.	ERASE or DELETE	rm
Lists the contents of a program to the monitor.	TYPE	cat
Prints the contents of a program to the printer.	PRINT	lp or lpr
Copies a file.	COPY	cp
Renames a file.	RENAME	mv
Forces a permanent halt to a running program.	CTRL + Break or CTRL + Z or CTRL + C	Del key, CTRL + Break, or \
Forces a temporary suspension of the current operation.	CTRL + S or Pause	CTRL + S
Resumes the current operation (recover from a CTRL + S).	CTRL + S	CTRL + S

Most system operations are *transparent* to the user; that is, they take place internally without user intervention. However, some operating system commands are provided intentionally for you to interact directly with the system. The most common of these commands are those that allow the handling of data files on disk. Some of these are listed in Table 1.1.

Programming Languages

At a very basic level, the purpose of almost all programs is to process data to produce one or more specific results (Figure 1.3). In a procedure-oriented language, a program is constructed as a series of one or more sets of instructions, called **procedures**, that are individually concerned with producing a result from a set of inputs. Effectively, these languages concentrate on the processing shown in Figure 1.3, with each procedure moving the input data one step closer to the final desired output.

This implies that all computer programming languages that support a procedure orientation must provide essentially the same capabilities for performing these operations. These capabilities are provided either as specific instruction types or "prepackaged" groups of instructions that can be called to do specific tasks. Prepackaged groups of instructions in procedure-oriented languages are typically supplied in what are referred to as **function libraries**. Table 1.2 lists the fundamental set of instructions pro-

FIGURE 1.3   Basic Program Operations

TABLE 1.2 Fundamental Procedure-Oriented Language Instruction Summary

Operation	Fortran	BASIC	COBOL	Pascal	C	C++
INPUT	READ	INPUT	READ	READ	scanf()	cin
(Get the data)		READ/DATA	ACCEPT	READLN	gets()	cin.get
					getchar()	cin.getline
PROCESSING	=	LET	COMPUTE	:=	=	=
(Use the data)	IF/ELSE	IF/ELSE	IF/ELSE	IF/ELSE	if/else	if/else
	DO	FOR	PERFORM	FOR	for	for
		WHILE		WHILE	while	while
		UNTIL		REPEAT	do	do
	+	+	ADD	+	+, =+, ++	+, =+, ++
	−	−	SUBTRACT	−	-, =-, --	-, =-, --
	*	*	MULTIPLY	*	*, =*	*, =*
	/	/	DIVIDE	/	/, =/	/, =/
	**	^		**	pow()	pow()
OUTPUT	WRITE	PRINT	WRITE	WRITE	printf()	cout
(Display	PRINT	PRINT/	DISPLAY	WRITELN	puts()	
the data)		USING			putchar()	

vided by Fortran, COBOL, Pascal, C, and C++ for performing input, processing, and output tasks.

If all procedure-oriented languages provided essentially the same features, why were there so many of them? The answer is that there are vast differences in the types of input data, calculations needed, and output reports required by various applications. For example, scientific and engineering applications require high-precision numerical outputs accurate to many decimal places. In addition, these applications typically use many algebraic or trigonometric formulas to produce their results. For example, calculating the bacterial concentration level in a polluted pond, as illustrated in Figure 1.4, requires evaluating an exponential equation to a high degree of numerical accuracy. The Fortran programming language, with its algebra-like instructions, was initially developed for such applications. Fortran, whose name is derived from *for*mula *tran*slation, was introduced in 1957. It was the first commercially available high-level language and is the oldest high-level language still in use.

FIGURE 1.4 Fortran Was Developed for Scientific and Engineering Applications

Business applications usually deal in whole numbers, such as those representing inventory quantities, or dollar and cents data accurate to only two decimal places. These applications require simpler mathematical calculations than are needed for scientific applications. The outputs required from business programs frequently consist of reports containing extensive columns of neatly formatted dollar and cents numbers and totals. For these applications, the COBOL programming language, with its picture output formats, was developed. COBOL, which was commercially introduced in the 1960s, stands for COmmon Business-Oriented Language.

Part No	Description	Quantity	Price
12225	#4 Nails, common	25 boxes	1.09
12226	#6 Nails, common	30 boxes	1.09
12227	#8 Nails, common	65 boxes	1.29
12228	#10 Nails, common	57 boxes	1.35
12229	#12 Nails, common	42 boxes	
12230	#16 Nails, common		

FIGURE 1.5   COBOL Was Developed for Business Applications

Initially, teaching programming to students had its own set of requirements. Here a relatively straightforward, easy-to-understand language was initially desired that did not require detailed knowledge of a specific application. Both the BASIC and Pascal programming languages were developed for this purpose. BASIC stands for Beginners All-purpose Symbolic Instruction Code and was developed in the 1960s at Dartmouth College.

Pascal was developed in 1971 to provide students with a firmer foundation in modular and structured programming than was provided by early versions of BASIC. Modular programs consist of many small subprograms, each of which performs a clearly defined and specific task that can be tested and modified without disturbing other sections of the program. Pascal is not an acronym, as are COBOL and BASIC, but is named after 17th-century mathematician Blaise Pascal. The Pascal language was so rigidly structured, however, that there were no escapes from the structured modules when such escapes would be useful. This was unacceptable for many real-world projects and is one of the reasons Pascal did not become widely accepted in the scientific, engineering, and business fields. Instead, the C language, which is a procedure-oriented language developed in the 1970s at AT&T Bell Laboratories by Ken Thompson, Dennis Ritchie, and Brian Kernighan, became the predominant procedure language of the 1980s. This language has an extensive set of capabilities that permits it to be written as a high-level language while retaining the ability to access the machine-level features of a computer.

In the early 1980s, Bjarne Stroustrup (also at AT&T) used his simulation language background to develop C++. A central feature of simulation languages is that they model real-life situations as objects. This object orientation, which was ideal for graphical screen objects such as rectangles and circles, was combined with existing C features to form a hybrid language that was both procedure oriented and object oriented.

The next step was to create a true object-oriented language. This was accomplished by Java, which is essentially based on the object-oriented features of C++. As has already been stated, one of the prime motivations for object-oriented languages has been the development and extensive use of graphical screens and support for graphical user interfaces

(GUIs). Graphical screens are capable of displaying multiple windows that provide data entry and display capabilities that are extremely difficult to program with procedure-oriented techniques.

Java was initially designed at Sun Microsystems in 1991 by James Gosling as a language that could be embedded in consumer-electronic items to create intelligent electronic devices. At that time, the language was named Oak. In 1993, when the project for which Oak was being developed was terminated, the Internet was just beginning its phenomenal growth. Sun engineers realized that the Oak language could be easily adapted to the Internet to create dynamic Web pages. Such pages would include an executable program as an integral part of themselves rather than containing only static text and figures. Although this was always theoretically possible using other programming languages, in practice it was not feasible because of the variability of processor types. Because of its design, Oak programs would execute the same on all Web pages regardless of the computer that displays the page.

To demonstrate the feasibility of this approach, Sun created a Web browser named HotJava™, which was itself programmed using a renamed Oak language called Java. A **Web browser** is a program that is located and run on a user's computer to display Web pages. Although initially tied to the HotJava browser, it soon became apparent that Java was a very powerful general-purpose object-oriented language in its own right. In this respect, Java's development paralleled the development of C, which was used to program the UNIX® operating system developed in the late 1970s. Just as applications developers had earlier understood that C could be used as a general-purpose procedural language independently of UNIX, a similar realization quickly occurred with Java.

In Java's case, the impetus for its appeal and rapid acceptance as a general-purpose applications programming language resided in its ability to create programs that can execute on any computer, independent of the internal processor on which the computer is based, without the necessity of rewriting or retranslating the program. This capability is referred to as both **cross-platform compatibility** and **write-once-run-anywhere.** As shown in Figure 1.6, there are two main ways in which such a Java program can be created for a user's computer, which is formally referred to as both a local and Web-client computer:[4]

FIGURE 1.6   The Two Distinct Java Environments

---

[4]A third and more exotic way is as a program that is automatically executed on a Web server computer when a specific Web page is accessed. These programs are referred to as **servlets.**

1. As a small program embedded within a Web page. This type of program is referred to as an **applet**.
2. As a stand-alone program, similar to a program written in any number of high-level languages, such as C and C++. This type of program is referred to as an **application**.

Although initially Java was primarily used to create applets, this usage is now minimal because applet features are more easily created with a scripting language, such as JavaScript. Despite the similar name, JavaScript has very little relationship to the Java programming language and is not discussed further in this text.[5] This text is concerned with Java as defined in Sun's Java 2 SDK specification (Versions 1.2 and 1.3), commonly known as Java 2, and using it as a full-featured, general-purpose programming language.

EXERCISES 1.1

1. Define the following terms:
   a. computer program
   b. programming
   c. programming language
   d. high-level language
   e. low-level language
   f. machine language
   g. assembly language
   h. procedure-oriented language
   i. object-oriented language
   j. source program
   k. compiler
   l. interpreter
2. Describe the purpose and primary uses of application and system software.
3. a. Describe the difference between high- and low-level languages.
   b. Describe the difference between procedure- and object-oriented languages.
4. Describe the similarities and differences between assemblers, interpreters, and compilers.
5. a. Assume the following operation codes:

   ```
   11000000 means add the first operand to the second operand
   10100000 means subtract the first operand from the second operand
   11110000 means multiply the second operand by the first operand
   11010000 means divide the second operand by the first operand
   ```

   Translate the following instructions into English:

   ```
              Address of      Address of
    opcode   First Operand   Second Operand
   -------------------------------------
   11000000 000000000001    0000000000010
   11110000 000000000010    0000000000011
   10100000 000000000100    0000000000011
   11010000 000000000101    0000000000011
   ```

---

[5]JavaScript™ was developed by Netscape Corporation and only the name is a property of Sun Microsystems.

b. Assuming the following locations contain the following data, determine the result produced by the instructions listed in Exercise 5a.

```
                      Initial Value
                       (in Decimal)
    Address       Stored at This Address
    ------------------------------------
    00000000001             5
    00000000010             3
    00000000011             6
    00000000100            14
    00000000101             4
```

6. Rewrite the machine-level instructions listed in Exercise 5a using assembly language notation. Use the symbolic names ADD, SUB, MUL, and DIV for addition, subtraction, multiplication, and division operations, respectively. In writing the instructions, use decimal values for the addresses.

7. How does Java differ from other languages with respect to being translated from a source program to an executable program?

1.2 ALGORITHMS, METHODS, AND CLASSES

Before writing any procedural or object-oriented program, a programmer must clearly understand what data are to be used, the desired result, and the procedure that will produce this result. The procedure is referred to as an algorithm. More precisely, an **algorithm** is a step-by-step sequence of instructions that describes how the data are to be processed to produce the desired outputs. In essence, an algorithm answers the question: What method will you use to produce a specific result?

To illustrate an algorithm, we consider a simple problem. Assume that a program must calculate the sum of all whole numbers from 1 through 100. Figure 1.7 illustrates three methods to find the required sum. Each method constitutes an algorithm.

Clearly, most people do not bother to list the possible alternatives in a detailed step-by-step manner, as in Figure 1.7, and then select one of the algorithms to solve the problem. But then, most people do not think algorithmically; they tend to think intuitively. For example, if you had to change a flat tire on your car, you would not think of all the steps required; you would simply change the tire or call someone else to do the job. This is an example of intuitive thinking.

Unfortunately, computers do not respond to intuitive commands. A general statement such as "add the numbers from 1 through 100" means nothing to a computer because the computer can only respond to algorithmlike commands written in an acceptable language such as Java. To program a computer successfully, you must clearly understand this difference between algorithmic and intuitive commands. A computer is an "algorithm-responding" machine; it is not an "intuition-responding" machine. You cannot tell a computer to change a tire or to add the numbers from 1 through 100. Instead, you must give the computer a detailed step-by-step sequence of instructions that, collectively, forms an algorithm. For example, the sequence of instructions

Set n equal to 100
Set a = 1

Set b equal to 100

Calculate $sum = \dfrac{n(a + b)}{2}$

forms a detailed method, or algorithm, for determining the sum of the numbers from 1 through 100. Notice that these instructions are not a computer program. Unlike a program, which must be written in a language the computer can respond to, an algorithm can be written or described in various ways. When the algorithm (the processing steps) is written in Englishlike phrases, the description is called **pseudocode**. When mathematical equations are used, the description is called a **formula**. When diagrams that employ the symbols shown in Figure 1.8 are used, the description is referred to as a **flow-chart**. Figure 1.9 illustrates these symbols in depicting an algorithm for determining the average of three numbers.

Because flowcharts are cumbersome to revise and can easily support unstructured programming practices, they have fallen out of favor among professional programmers, except for visually describing basic programming structures. In their place, pseudocode has gained increasing acceptance. In describing an algorithm with pseudocode, short

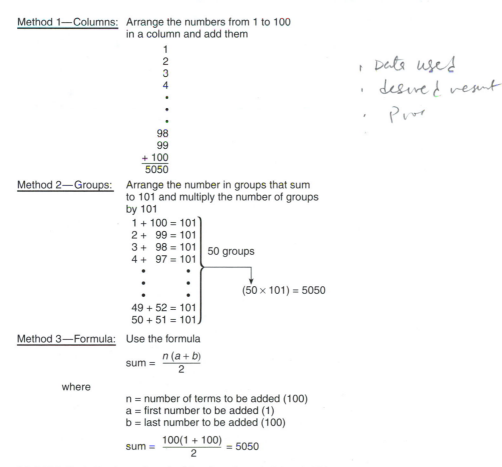

Method 1—Columns: Arrange the numbers from 1 to 100
in a column and add them

1
2
3
4
•
•
•
98
99
+ 100
5050

Method 2—Groups: Arrange the number in groups that sum
to 101 and multiply the number of groups
by 101

1 + 100 = 101
2 + 99 = 101
3 + 98 = 101
4 + 97 = 101   50 groups
•   •
•   •   (50 × 101) = 5050
•   •
49 + 52 = 101
50 + 51 = 101

Method 3—Formula: Use the formula

$sum = \dfrac{n\,(a + b)}{2}$

where

n = number of terms to be added (100)
a = first number to be added (1)
b = last number to be added (100)

$sum = \dfrac{100(1 + 100)}{2} = 5050$

FIGURE 1.7 Summing the Numbers from 1 through 100

SYMBOL	NAME	MEANING
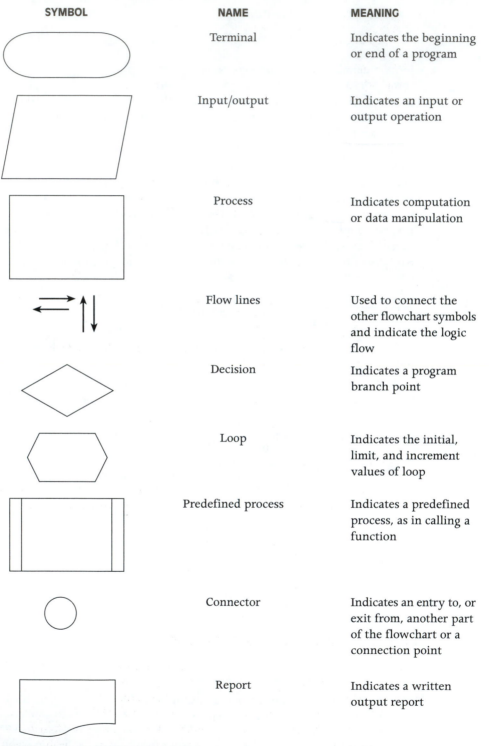	Terminal	Indicates the beginning or end of a program
	Input/output	Indicates an input or output operation
	Process	Indicates computation or data manipulation
	Flow lines	Used to connect the other flowchart symbols and indicate the logic flow
	Decision	Indicates a program branch point
	Loop	Indicates the initial, limit, and increment values of loop
	Predefined process	Indicates a predefined process, as in calling a function
	Connector	Indicates an entry to, or exit from, another part of the flowchart or a connection point
	Report	Indicates a written output report

F I G U R E 1 . 8   Flowchart Symbols

FIGURE 1.9 Flowchart for Calculating the Average of Three Numbers

English phrases are used. For example, acceptable pseudocode for describing the steps needed to compute the average of three numbers is:

Input the three numbers into the computer
Calculate the average by adding the numbers and dividing the sum by 3
Display the average

Only after an algorithm has been selected and the programmer understands the steps required can the algorithm be written using computer-language statements. The writing of an algorithm using computer-language statements is called **coding** the algorithm (Figure 1.10).

FIGURE 1.10 Coding an Algorithm

Classes and Objects: A First Look

In addition to the algorithms that you will use to manipulate data to produce outputs, classes are also central to object-oriented languages. This is because in an object-oriented language such as Java, a **class** is a single unit that defines both the data that will be used and the operations that can be performed on the data. The operations that can be performed are formally referred to as **methods**. Informally, they are known as both **procedures** and **functions**. We will use these three terms interchangeably when discussing classes. Individually, a method is an algorithm written in appropriate Java code.

Once a class is defined, a unit known as an object can be created. An **object** is a specific item from a class. The relationship of an object to a class is similar to the relationship of a specific geometric shape to a class of shapes. For example, if we define `Rectangles` as a class of four-sided shapes whose opposite sides are equal in length and whose adjacent sides are perpendicular, then a specific rectangle that measures 2 inches by 3 inches is an object of the class `Rectangles`. This particular object is a specific case, or instance, of the defined class.

In addition to defining general characteristics from which specific objects can be created, a class must be capable of providing the methods, or operations, that can be applied to objects of the class type. For example, if our class is the `Rectangle` class just described, suitable methods might be provided for calculating the area and perimeter of a specific rectangle as well as displaying and changing a rectangle object's measurements. A particular method is activated, or invoked, in object-oriented terms by sending a message to a particular object to run the desired method. The message essentially says, "Run this method on this specific object."

As an example, consider Figure 1.11, which shows two objects of the type we have called `Rectangle`. Notice that each object is not the actual rectangle but rather contains two pieces of data, the first of which is the specific rectangle's length and the second the rectangle's width. In addition, as shown, the five provided operations consist of creating a new rectangle, calculating a rectangle's area, calculating a rectangle's perimeter, changing a rectangle's measurements, and displaying a rectangle's measurements. As indicated, the methods are shared between all of the objects.

FIGURE 1.11   A Set of Rectangle Objects

To activate a specific method, we must send a message equivalent to "use this particular method on this specific object." In practice, the message is as simple as providing the name of the object and the name of the method, with the two pieces of information separated by a period. For example, the message `firstRectangle.calculateArea()` would be sufficient to tell the `calculateArea` method to determine the area of the object named `firstRectangle`. The parentheses after the method name, as you will see in the next chapter, provide the method with any additional data that might be needed to complete its operation.

A Java program is constructed as one or more classes. Although you will define your own classes and create objects as you become more fluent in Java, you can use any objects and classes that are provided by Java as long as you know the correct ways to activate the appropriate predefined methods. In fact, programming in Java requires you to become very familiar with at least a subset of the available classes provided, their respective methods, and any existing objects that have already been created for your use.

EXERCISES 1.2

1. Determine a step-by-step procedure (list the steps) to do the following tasks. (*Note:* There is no one single correct answer for each of these tasks. The exercise is designed to give you practice in converting intuitive-type commands into equivalent algorithms and making the shift between the processes involved in the two types of thinking.)
   a. Change a flat tire
   b. Make a telephone call
   c. Log on to a computer
   d. Roast a turkey

2. Are the procedures you developed for Exercise 1 algorithms? Discuss why or why not.

3. Determine and write an algorithm (list the steps) to interchange the contents of two cups of liquid. Assume that a third cup is available to hold the contents of either cup temporarily. Each cup should be rinsed before any new liquid is poured into it.

4. Write a detailed set of instructions in English to calculate the resistance of the following resistors connected in series: n resistors, each having a resistance of 56 ohms; m resistors, each having a resistance of 33 ohms; and p resistors, each having a resistance of 15 ohms. Note that the total resistance of resistors connected in series is the sum of all individual resistances.

5. Write a set of detailed, step-by-step instructions in English to find the smallest number in a group of three integer numbers.

6. a. Write a set of detailed, step-by-step instructions in English to calculate the change remaining from a dollar after a purchase is made. Assume that the cost of goods purchased is less than a dollar. The change received should consist of the smallest number of coins possible.
   b. Repeat Exercise 6a, but assume the change is given only in pennies.

7. a. Write a set of detailed, step-by-step instructions in English to calculate the fewest number of dollar bills needed to pay a bill of amount Total. For example, if Total were $98, the bills would consist of one $50 bill, two $20 bills, one $5 bill, and three $1 bills. For this exercise, assume that only $100, $50, $20, $10, $5, and $1 bills are available.
   b. Repeat Exercise 7a, but assume the bill is paid only in $1 bills.

8. a. Write an algorithm to locate the first occurrence of the name SWANSON in a list of names arranged in random order.
   b. Discuss how you could improve your algorithm for Exercise 8a if the list of names was arranged in alphabetical order.

9. Write an algorithm to determine the total occurrences of the letter *e* in any sentence.

10. Determine and write an algorithm to sort four numbers into ascending (from lowest to highest) order.

11. a. Determine the six possible step-by-step procedures (list the steps) to paint the flower in Figure 1.12, with the restriction that each color must be completed

before a new color can be started. (*Tip:* One of the algorithms is: Use yellow first, green second, black last.)

Code:
y = yellow
g = green
b = black

FIGURE 1.12   A Simple Paint-By-Number Figure

    b. Which of the six painting algorithms (series of steps) is best if you are limited to using one paintbrush and there is no way to clean the brush?

12. Define an appropriate class for each of the following specific objects:
    a. the number 5
    b. a square that is 4 inches by 4 inches
    c. this Java textbook
    d. a 2002 Ford Thunderbird car
    e. the last ballpoint pen that you used

13. **a.** What operations should the following objects be capable of doing?
      i. a 2002 Ford Thunderbird car
      ii. the last ballpoint pen that you used
    b. Do the operations determined for Exercise 13a apply only to the particular object listed, or are they more general and do they apply to a larger set of objects?

14. Using Figure 1.11, determine the response that each of the following messages should produce:
    a. `firstRectangle.calculateArea()`
    b. `firstRectangle.calculatePerimeter()`
    c. `firstRectangle.displayValues()`
    d. `secondRectangle.calculateArea()`
    e. `secondRectangle.calculatePerimeter()`
    f. `secondRectangle.displayValues()`

15. All of the messages in Exercise 14 provide the name of the object to be operated on and the method to be used. In creating a new rectangle object or changing the dimensions of an existing rectangle object, both a length and width must be provided. How can this information be included in the message?

16. Assuming that you will be using the rectangle objects shown in Figure 1.11 in a program that is capable of drawing graphical objects on a screen, what additional method or methods would be appropriate for the `Rectangle` class?

1.3 CONSTRUCTING A JAVA PROGRAM

A well-designed program is constructed with a design philosophy similar to that used in constructing a well-designed building. It doesn't just happen, but depends on careful planning and execution for the final design to accomplish its intended purpose. Just as an integral part of the design of a building is its structure, the same is true of a program.

Programs whose structure consists of interrelated segments arranged in a logical order to form an integrated and complete unit are referred to as **modular programs** (Figure 1.13). Modular programs are easier to develop, correct, and modify than programs constructed otherwise. In general programming terminology, the smaller segments used to construct a modular program are referred to as **modules.** In Java, the modules are always classes, where an individual class is defined as a unit containing a data structure and the methods that can be applied to the data structure. A method is a simpler unit that only contains a sequence of operations. It should be noted that *a Java method can only be constructed inside a class*; unlike some other object-oriented languages such as C++, a Java method cannot exist as an independent entity outside of a class.

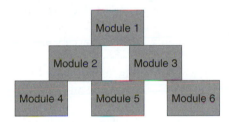

FIGURE 1.13   A Well-Designed Program Is Built Using Modules

A class, which contains both data and operations, can be thought of as a small factory that holds both raw materials, finished products, and the machines that operate on the various materials at different stages in their transformation from raw material to finished product. In computer terms, the raw materials are the data, the machines are the methods applied to the data, and the finished product are the created objects.

Typically, there will be many stages in the ultimate transformation of raw materials to finished product. At each stage, a specific machine may accomplish only one small task in this overall transformation. This analogy is applicable to a method. That is, it is useful to regard a method as a small machine that transforms its input data in some way to a desired output. For example, Figure 1.14 illustrates a method that accepts two numbers as inputs and multiplies the two numbers to produce a result.

As illustrated in Figure 1.14, the interface of the method to the outside world is its inputs and results. How the inputs are converted to results is encapsulated and hidden within the method. In this regard, the method can be thought of as a single unit that provides a special-purpose operation.

One important requirement for designing a good class or method is to give it a name that conveys to the reader some idea about what the class or method does. The names permissible for methods and classes can also name other elements of the Java

FIGURE 1.14   A Multiplying Method

language and are collectively referred to as identifiers. **Identifiers** can be made up of any combination of letters, digits, dollar signs, or underscores, _, selected according to the following rules:

1.   The first character of an identifier cannot be a digit.
2.   Only letters (both uppercase and lowercase), digits, underscores, and dollar signs may follow the initial letter. Blank spaces are not allowed. A convention is to capitalize the first letter of each succeeding word in a multiword identifier. Dollar signs are included for historical reasons and should only be used to access preexisting names in code written in versions prior to 2.0.
3.   An identifier cannot be one of the keywords listed in Table 1.3. (A *keyword* is a word that is set aside by the language for a special purpose and should only be used in a specified manner.)
4.   The maximum number of characters in an identifier name is unlimited. As a practical matter and to minimize both typing time and typing errors, a typical identifier should be limited to fewer than 14 characters, with 20 characters as an outside maximum.

Examples of valid Java identifiers are:

```
degToRad        intersect       addNums        slope
multByTwo       findMax         density        bessel
```

Examples of invalid identifiers are:

```
1ab3    (begins with a number, which violates rule 1)
e*6     (contains a special character, which violates rule 2)
while   (is a keyword, which violates rule 3)
```

Besides conforming to Java's identifier rules, a good method or class name should also be a mnemonic. A **mnemonic** is a word or name designed as a memory aid. For example, the name `degToRad` is a mnemonic if it names a method that converts degrees to radians. Here the name itself helps to identify what is being done.

Examples of valid identifiers that are not mnemonics are:

```
easy      duh      doIt      theForce     mike
```

TABLE 1.3 Java Keywords

abstract	default	if	private	this
boolean	do	implements	protected	throw
break	double	import	public	throws
byte	else	instanceof	return	transient
case	extends	int	short	try
catch	final	interface	static	void
char	finally	long	strictfp	volatile
class	float	native	super	while
const	for	new	switch	
continue	goto	package	synchronized	

Nonmnemonic identifiers should not be used because they convey no information about what their purpose is. The names you select for both classes and methods should always be descriptive and indicate the purpose or intent of the class or method being named.

Notice that all identifiers have been typed almost exclusively in lowercase letters. The convention in Java, which we will adhere to in this book, is that the names of methods begin with a lowercase letter and the first letter of a class name is always capitalized. Additionally, for both class and method names, capital letters will always be used for distinguishing words in multiword identifiers such as DateAndTime, degreesToRadians, and displayNetPay. Notice that in all three identifiers, the first letter of each word, from the second word on, has been capitalized. Furthermore, because the first letter of the identifier DateAndTime is capitalized, it indicates that this is the name of a class. Identifiers consisting of all uppercase letters are usually reserved for symbolic constants, a topic covered in Chapter 3. To separate individual words in a symbolic constant, an underscore character is sometimes used. Finally, it is important to understand that Java is a **case-sensitive** language, which means the compiler distinguishes between uppercase and lowercase letters. Thus, in Java, the names TOTAL, total, and TotaL represent three distinctly different names.

A Class Structure

A distinct advantage of using classes and their associated methods in Java is that the overall structure of the program, in general, and individual modules, in particular, can be planned in advance, including provision for testing and verifying each module's operation. Each class and method can then be written to meet its intended objective. In addition, because a very rich set of classes is provided as part of the Java language, many programs can be constructed by using these existing classes and their associated methods directly.

Every Java application program must have at least one class. A class consists of a class header line and a body. The class header line that we will use, which is always the first line of a class, contains three words:

1. The keyword public or private
2. The keyword class
3. The name of the class

The body of a class is enclosed within a set of braces, { and }, that determine the beginning and end of the class' body and enclose the data fields and methods that make up the class. Figure 1.15 illustrates the basic structure of a class that we have named

```
A class header line ----> public class DisplayHelloWorld
                      ----->{
  The class body |             class data and methods go in here
                ----->  }
```

FIGURE 1.15   The Structure of a Java Class Named `DisplayHelloWorld`

`DisplayHelloWorld`. Notice that this class name, which is programmer selectable, conforms to the rules for creating Java identifiers. Since the identifier refers to a class name, the first letter of the name has been capitalized.

The simplest body that a class can have consists of a single method. Because all executable Java applications (not applets) must contain a method named `main`, we will place such a method within our `DisplayHelloWorld` class.

The `main` Method

Figure 1.16 illustrates the basic structure for a `main` method that will be used throughout this book. Like a class, a method consists of two parts: a header line and a body. The header line is always the first line of a method. The method header line in Figure 1.16 is:

```
public static void main(String[] args)
```

As with class header lines, we will use this header line for all of the `main` methods presented in the text without an initial full understanding of what information is being provided (a full description of the parts of this header line is given in Chapter 6). Even though it is really too early in our exploration of Java to fully understand each item in this header line, it is useful to realize that this line provides five distinct pieces of information:[6]

1. A primary scope specification for the method, in this case designated by the keyword `public`, which is also referred to as a visibility modifier.
2. A secondary scope designation for the method, in this case designated by the keyword `static`, which specifies how the method is created and stored in the computer's memory. General-purpose methods, which can be used independently of any specific object, must be declared as `static`.
3. The type of data, if any, that is returned from the method. The keyword `void` designates that the method will not return any value when it has completed executing.
4. The name of the method, which is an identifier. Here the method is named `main`.
5. What type of data, if any, is sent into the method. Information within the parentheses defines the type of data that will be transmitted into the method when it is run. Such data are referred to as **arguments** of the method.

The braces in Figure 1.16 define the beginning and end of the method body, and they enclose all statements that make up the method. The statements within the braces determine what the method does. Each statement inside the method's body must end with a semicolon,;.

---

[6]Items 4 and 5, which start from the method's name to the end of the header line, are referred to as a method's signature. The importance and use of the signature are described in Section 6.1.

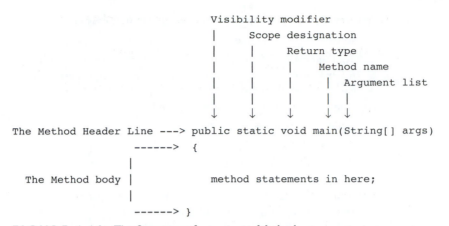

FIGURE 1.16 The Structure of a `main()` Method

You will be naming and writing many of your own Java classes and methods. In fact, the rest of this book is primarily about the statements required to construct useful methods and how to combine methods and data into useful classes and programs. Each program, however, must have a `main()` method. Until you learn how to pass data into a method and return data from a method (the topics of Section 6.2), the class and method structures illustrated in Figures 1.15 and 1.16, respectively, will serve for all the programs you need to write. At this stage, you can regard the first two lines of the `main()` method

```
public static void main(String[] args)
{
```

as stating that "the main method begins here" and regard the last line, consisting of a single brace

```
}
```

as stating that "the main method ends here." Since every Java method requires parentheses following its name, we will always include them to clearly indicate that the identifier refers to a method name. Thus, for the rest of this text, we will always refer to the main method as `main()` and follow this practice for all other method names. This will make it easier for you to clearly distinguish that a method is being discussed. So whenever you see an identifier followed by parentheses, such as `print()` and `println()`, you should understand that the identifier is the name of a method. In the next section, we will place this `main()` method structure within our class structure to produce our first working Java program.

EXERCISES 1.3

1. State whether the following are valid identifiers. If they are valid, state whether they are mnemonic names. A mnemonic identifier conveys some idea about its intended purpose. If they are invalid identifiers, state why.

power	density	m1234$	newamp	1234	abcd
total	tangent	absval	computed	b34a	34ab
volts$	a2-b3	while	minVal	sine	$sine
cosine	speed	netDistance	sum	return	stack

2. Assume that methods with the following names have been written:

    getLength(), getWidth(), calcArea(), displayArea()

  a. From the methods' names, what do you think each method might do?

  b. In what order do you think a main() method might execute these methods (based on their names)?

3. Assume that the following methods have been written:

    speed(), distance(), acceleration()

  a. From the methods' names, what do you think each method might do?

  b. In what order do you think a main() method might execute these methods (based on their names)?

4. Determine names for methods that do the following:

  a. Find the maximum value in a set of numbers.

  b. Find the minimum value in a set of numbers.

  c. Convert a lowercase letter to an uppercase letter.

  d. Convert an uppercase letter to a lowercase letter.

  e. Sort a set of numbers from lowest to highest.

  f. Alphabetize a set of names.

5. Just as the keyword void signifies that a method returns no value, the keywords int, char, float, and double signify that a method will return an integer, a character, a floating-point number, and a double-precision number, respectively. Using this information, write header lines for a main() method that will receive no arguments but will return:

  a. an integer

  b. a character

  c. a floating-point number

  d. a double-precision number

6. a. Assuming a case insensitive compiler, determine which of these program unit names are equivalent:

AVERAG	averag	MODE	BESSEL	Mode
Total	besseL	TeMp	Densty	TEMP
denSTY	MEAN	total	mean	moDE

  b. Redo Exercise 6a assuming a case-sensitive compiler.

Project Structuring Exercises

Most projects, both programming and nonprogramming, can usually be structured into smaller subtasks or units of activity. These smaller subtasks can often be delegated to different people so that when all the tasks are finished and integrated, the project or program is completed. For Exercises 7 through 11, determine a set of subtasks that, taken together, complete the project. Be aware that there are many possible solutions for each exercise. The only requirement is that the set of subtasks selected, when taken together, complete the required task.

(*Note:* The purpose of these exercises is to have you consider the different ways that complex tasks can be structured. Although there is no one correct solution to these exercises, there are incorrect solutions and solutions that are better than others. An incorrect solution is one that does not fully specify the task. One solution is better than another if it more clearly or easily identifies what must be done.)

7. You are given the task of wiring and installing lights in the attic of your house. Determine a set of subtasks that, taken together, will accomplish this. (*Tip:* The first subtask is to determine the placement of the light fixtures.)

8. You are a sophomore in college and are planning to go to graduate school for a master's degree in electrical engineering after you graduate. List a set of major objectives that you must fulfill to meet this goal. (*Tip:* One objective is: Take the right courses.)

9. You are given the job of planting a vegetable garden. Determine a set of subtasks to accomplish this. (*Tip:* One subtask is to plan the layout of the garden.)

10. You are responsible for planning and arranging the family camping trip this summer. List a set of subtasks that, taken together, accomplish this objective successfully. (*Tip:* One subtask is to select the campsite.)

11. **a.** A national medical testing laboratory desires a new computer system to analyze its test results. The system must be capable of processing each day's results. Additionally, the laboratory wants the capability to retrieve and output a printed report of all results that meet certain criteria—for example, all results obtained for a particular doctor or all results obtained for hospitals in a particular state. Determine three or four major program units into which this system could be separated. (*Tip:* One possible program unit is "Prepare Daily Results" to create each day's reports.)

    b. Suppose someone enters incorrect data for a particular test result, which is discovered after the data have been entered and stored by the system. What program unit is needed to take care of correcting this problem? Discuss why such a program unit might or might not be required by most systems.

    c. Assume a program unit exists that allows a user to alter or change data that have been incorrectly entered and stored. Discuss the need for including an "audit trail" that would allow for a later reconstruction of the changes made, when they were made, and who made them.

1.4 THE `print()` AND `println()` METHODS

Two extremely useful prewritten methods provided in Java are `print()` and `println()`. These methods are both members of the `PrintStream` class, and as their names suggest, they are print methods. Their function is to display data given to them on the standard output display device, which for most systems is the video screen. The difference between these methods is that, when the `print()` method is finished, it leaves the screen cursor positioned immediately after the last character it has sent to the monitor, whereas the `println()` method positions the cursor down to the start of a new line after it has finished operating. The cursor position determines where the next character sent to the monitor, using a new `print()` or `println()` method, is displayed. For now, we will concentrate on the `print()` method, although everything that we say about this method applies identically to the `println()` method as well.

The general syntax of the `print()` method is

```
objectName.print(data);
```

The `objectName` to the left of the required period identifies the object to which the display will be sent, and the name to the right of the period identifies the method, which in this case is `print()`. Any data that are to be displayed by this method must be enclosed in the parentheses following the method's name.

For example, if the data `Hello World!` are passed to `print()`, these data will be displayed by the method. When the data consist of characters, as in this example, they are also referred to as a string, which is short for string of characters. Sending data to a method is formally referred to as passing data to the method. A string, such as Hello World!, is passed to the `print()` method by enclosing the string in double quotation marks and placing it inside the parentheses following the method's name as follows:

```
System.out.print("Hello World!");
```

In this statement, `out` is the name of an object that is automatically created from a Java class named System whenever a Java program is executed. Specifically, the out object is referred to as the **standard output stream,** which, for most systems, connects your program's output to a video monitor. The combined term `System.out` thus uniquely identifies an object that effectively lets the `print()` method know where to display its data. Because there are a number of areas where the string could be printed, such as the video monitor, a printer, or a file, the `print()` method must be given the name of the object to which we want the output displayed. The additional period between the object's name, `System.out`, and the `print()` method's name is required.

The parentheses after the method's name provide a means by which information can be passed to the method (Figure 1.17). This is true for all methods that we will encounter and is not restricted to the `print()` methods. The items that are passed to a method through the parentheses are referred to as **parameters**, **actual arguments,** and **arguments** (the terms are used synonymously). Although these terms are interchangeable, we will generally refer to a piece of data that is passed into a method as an argument. Now let's put all this together into a working Java program that can be run on your computer. Consider Program 1.1.

```
System.out.print("Hello World!");
```

FIGURE 1.17 Passing a String to `print()`

PROGRAM 1.1

```java
// File: DisplayHelloWorld.java
// Description: Displays Hello World!
// Programmer: G. Bronson
// Date: 6/15/02

public class DisplayHelloWorld
{
  public static void main(String[] args)
  {
    System.out.print("Hello World!");
  }  // end of main() method
} // end of class
```

WHAT IS SYNTAX?

A programming language's **syntax** is the set of rules for formulating grammatically correct language statements. In practice, this means that a Java statement with correct syntax has the proper form specified for the compiler. Thus, the compiler will accept the statement and not generate an error message.

It should be noted that an individual statement or program can be syntactically correct and still be logically incorrect. Such a statement or program would be correctly structured but produce an incorrect result. This is similar to an English statement that is grammatically correct but makes no sense. For example, although the sentence "The tree is a ragged cat" is grammatically correct, it makes no sense.

The first four lines of program code, each of which begins with two slash symbols, //, are comments. We will have much more to say about comments in the next section, but for now it is important to understand that each source code program should begin with comments similar to Program 1.1. These initial comment lines, at a minimum, should provide the file name under which the source code is saved, a short program description, the name of the programmer, and the date that the program was last modified. For all of the programs in this text, the file name refers to the name of the source code file that is provided with this text. Notice that this name is the same as the class name (line 6, counting the blank line) plus the extension .java, which is a requirement of Java.

Line 6 (counting the blank) of the program is the start of the program's class, which itself includes a main() method. The main() method begins with the header line developed in the previous section, and the body of the method, enclosed in braces, consists of a single statement, which ends with a required semicolon. This statement passes the string "Hello World!" to the print() method. Because print() is a method of an existing class and is automatically made available in every Java program that we write, we can use it by activating it correctly, as is done in Program 1.1. In general, a string can consist of any number of letters, numbers, and special characters enclosed in double quotation marks ("string in here"). The double quotation marks delimit (mark) the beginning and ending of the string and are not considered part of the string.

Let us write another program to illustrate print()'s versatility. Read Program 1.2 to determine what it does.

When Program 1.2 is run, the following is displayed:

```
Computers, computers everywhere
 as far as I can see
```

You might be wondering why the \n did not appear in the output. The two characters \ and n, when used together, are called a **newline escape sequence.** They tell print() to send instructions to the display device to move to a new line. In Java, the backslash, \, character provides an "escape" from the normal interpretation of the

PROGRAM 1.2

```java
// File: DisplayTwoLines.java
// Description: Test program
// Programmer: G. Bronson
// Date: 6/15/02

public class DisplayTwoLines
{
  public static void main(String[] args)
  {
    System.out.print("Computers, computers everywhere");
    System.out.print("\n as far as I can see");
  }
}
```

character following it by altering the meaning of the next character. If the backslash was omitted from the second print statement in Program 1.2, the n would be printed as the letter n and the program would print:

```
Computers, computers everywheren as far as I can see
```

Newline escape sequences can be placed anywhere within the message passed to print. See if you can determine the display produced by Program 1.3.

PROGRAM 1.3

```java
// File: ShowEscapeSequences.java
// Description: Test program
// Programmer: G. Bronson
// Date: 6/15/02

public class ShowEscapeSequences
{
  public static void main(String[] args)
  {
   System.out.print("Computers, computers everywhere\n as far as\n\nI can see");
  }
}
```

The output for Program 1.3 is:

```
Computers, computers everywhere
 as far as

I can see
```

POINT OF INFORMATION

THE System CLASS

Java's `System` class provides a number of methods for examining system-related information, such as the name of the operating system and the Java version number, and for changing system-related information, such as a user's home directory. Additionally, and more important for our immediate purposes, this class also supports basic input and output services. In this regard, it provides a means of sending data from a program to a standard output device, which is usually a video screen. This connection is accomplished by an object named `out`, which is uniquely identified using the name `System.out`.

As you might expect, the `System` class also provides a means of sending data from a standard input device into a program. This standard device is typically a keyboard, and the connection is accomplished by an object named `in`. The use of the `System.in` object is presented in Chapter 3.

Very frequently, and especially in introductory and simple programs, you will want to display a single line of text followed by a new line. In these situations, use the `println()` method, which automatically appends a newline character to the end of the displayed data. Thus, the statement

```
System.out.println("This is a test.");
```

produces the same display as that produced by the statement

```
System.out.print("This is a test.\n");
```

You might be wondering why, if the `println()` method automatically prints a line and places the cursor at the start of the next line, you would ever need the `print()` method. The reason is that many programming situations will force you to assemble parts of a single line in sections as the data to be displayed become available. This fine control over the construction of a line ultimately makes the `print()` method valuable. For simple single-line messages, however, the `println()` method can be used more conveniently. Finally, it should be noted that you can also include newline characters within a `println()` method; the only advantage of using `println()` is that it automatically provides a newline character at the end of its output.

EXERCISES 1.4

1. a. Using `print()`, write a Java program that displays your name on one line, your street address on the second line, and your city, state, and zip code on the third line.
   b. Run the program you have written for Exercise 1a on a computer. (*Note:* You must understand the procedures for entering and running a Java program on the particular computer installation you are using.)

  2. a. Write a Java program to display the following:

```
The cosecant of an angle
    is equal to one over
        the sine of the angle.
```

     b. Run the program you have written for Exercise 2a on a computer.

  3. a. What is the minimum number of `print()` methods you need to display the following?

Degrees	Radians
0	0.0000
90	1.5708
180	3.1416
270	4.7124
360	6.2832

     b. What is the minimum number of `println()` method calls needed to display the table in Exercise 3a?

     c. What is the preferable number of either `print()` or `println()` methods you would use to display the table in Exercise 3a?

     d. Write a complete Java program to produce the output illustrated in Exercise 3a.

     e. Run the program you have written for Exercise 3d on a computer.

  4. In response to a newline escape sequence, the position of the next displayed character is at the start of a new line. This positioning of the next character actually represents two distinct cursor positioning operations. What are they?

1.5 PROGRAMMING STYLE

Because each executable Java application starts execution at the beginning of a `main()` method, you must include a `main()` method in all Java programs that you wish to run. As you have seen, all of the statements that make up the `main()` method are included within the braces, { }, following the method's name. Although the `main()` method must be present in every Java program, Java does not require that the word `main`, the parentheses, or the braces be placed in any particular form. The form used in the last section

```
public static void main(String[] args)
{
    program statements in here;
}
```

was chosen strictly for clarity and ease in reading the program. For example, the following general form of a `main()` method also works:

```
public static void main
(String[] args
) {first statement;second statement;
        third statement;fourth
statement;
}
```

Notice that more than one statement can be put on a line, or one statement can be written across lines. Except for strings, double quotation marks, identifiers, and keywords, Java ignores all whitespace (whitespace refers to any combination of one or more blank spaces, tabs, or new lines). For example, changing the whitespace in Program 1.1 while making sure not to split the string `Hello World!` across two lines and omitting all comments results in the following valid program:

```
public class DisplayHelloWorld
{
  public static void main
(String[] args
){print(
"Hello World!");
}}
```

Although this version of `main()` will work, it is an example of extremely poor programming style. It is difficult to read and understand. For readability, we will always write the `main()` method in the following form:

```
public static void main(String[] args)
{
    program statements in here;
}
```

In this form, the method header line starts in column 1 and is placed with the required parentheses on a line by itself. The opening brace of the method body follows on the next line and is placed under the first letter of the line containing the method name. Similarly, the closing method brace is placed by itself in column 1 as the last line of the method. This structure serves to highlight the method as a single unit. This same structure should also be used by the class within which it is located.

Within the method itself, all program statements are indented at least two spaces. Indentation is another sign of good programming practice, especially if the same indentation is used for similar groups of statements. Review Program 1.2 to see that the same indentation was used for both `print()` method calls.

As you progress in your understanding and mastery of Java, you will develop your own indentation standards. Just keep in mind that the final form of your programs should be consistent and should always serve as an aid to the reading and understanding of your programs.

Comments

Comments are explanatory remarks made within a program. When used carefully, comments can be very helpful in clarifying what the complete program is about, what a specific group of statements is meant to accomplish, or what one line is intended to do. Java supports two types of comments: line and block.[7] Both types of comments can be placed

---

[7]A third type of comment, referred to as a document comment, begins with the character sequence `/**` and ends with the sequence `*/`. These create HTML documents using the javadoc program.

anywhere within a program and have no effect on program execution. The compiler ignores all comments; they are strictly for the convenience of anyone reading the program.

A line comment begins with two slashes, //, and continues to the end of the line. For example, each of the following is a line comment:

```
// this is a comment
// this program prints out a message
// this program calculates a square root
```

The symbols //, with no whitespace between them, designate the start of the line comment. The end of the line on which the comment is written designates the end of the comment.

A line comment can be written either on a line by itself or at the end of a line containing a program statement. When a comment is too long to fit on one line, two solutions are possible. First, the comment can be separated into two or more line comments, with each separate comment line preceded by the double slash symbol. For example, the comment

```
// this comment is invalid because it
   extends over two lines
```

results in a Java error message when compiled. This comment is correct when written as:

```
// this comment is used to illustrate a
// comment that extends across two lines
```

Comments that span across two or more lines are, however, more conveniently written as block comments rather than as multiple single-line comments. Block comments begin with the symbols /* and end with the symbols */. For example,

```
/* This is a block comment that
   spans
   across three lines */
```

Frequently, you may see a block comment written as follows:

```
/* This is a block comment that
 * spans
 * across three lines
 */
```

In this style, the extra asterisks, *, are inserted to highlight the comment block. Note, however, that it is only the beginning, /*, and ending, */, pairs that actually delimit (i.e., mark) the comment. All of the characters within these delimiters constitute part of the comment itself.

In Java, a program's structure is intended to make the program readable and understandable, making the use of extensive comments unnecessary. This is reinforced if method, class, and variable names, which are described in the next chapter, are carefully selected to convey their meaning to anyone reading the program. However, if the purpose of a method, class, or statement is still not clear from its structure, name, or context, include comments where clarification is needed. Obscure code with no comments is a sure sign of bad programming. Excessive comments are also a sign of bad programming because they imply that insufficient thought was given to having the code itself be self-explanatory.

Typically, any program that you write should begin with a set of initial program comments that include a short program description, your name, and the date that the program was last modified. For space considerations, and because all programs in this text were written by the author, initial comments will appear only for short program descriptions when they are not provided as part of the accompanying text.

EXERCISES 1.5

1. a. Will the following program work?

```
public class TestIt
{
    public static void main(String[] args)
    {System.out.println("Hello World!"); }}
```

    b. What are the problems with the program in Exercise 1a?

2. Rewrite the following programs to conform to good programming practice.

    a.

```
public class TestIt
{
 public static void main(String[] args)
 {
    System.out.print(
    "The time has come")
   ; }
}
```

    b.

```
public class TestIt
{
  public static void main
  (String[] args)
  {System.out.println("Newark is a city");System.out.println(
   "in New Jersey"); System.out.println(
   "It is also a city")
   ; System.out.println("in Delaware")
   ; }
}
```

    c.

```
public class TestIt
{
   public static void main
   (String[] args)
```

(Continued on next page)

(Continued from previous page)

```
{System.out.print("Reading a program");System.out.print(
    " is much easier")
    ;System.out.println(" if a standard form for main is used")
    ;System.out.println(" and each statement is written")
  ;System.out.println(" on a line by itself.")
    ; }
}
```

   d.

```
public class TestIt
{
  public static void main
  (String[] args) {System.out.println("Every Java application"
  );System.out.println
  ("must have one and only one"
  );
  System.out.println("main() method."
  );
  System.out.println(
  "The escape sequence of characters"
  );System.out.println(
  "for a newline can be placed anywhere"
  );System.out.println
  ("within the message passed to System.out.println"
  ); }
}
```

3. a. When used in a message, the backslash character alters the meaning of the character immediately following it. If we wanted to print the backslash character, we would have to tell the `print()` method to escape from the way it normally interprets the backslash. What character do you think can alter the way a single backslash character is interpreted?

   b. Using your answer to Exercise 3a, write the escape sequence for printing a backslash.

4. a. A **token** of a computer language is any sequence of characters that, as a unit, with no intervening characters or whitespace, has a unique meaning. Using this definition of a token, determine whether escape sequences, method names, and the keywords listed in Table 1.3 are tokens of the Java language.

   b. Discuss whether adding whitespace to a string alters the string. Discuss whether strings can be considered tokens of Java.

   c. Using the definition of a token given in Exercise 4a, determine whether the following statement is true: Except for tokens of the language, Java ignores all whitespace.

1.6 CREATING A DIALOG BOX

Java 2 provides easily used components for producing graphical user interfaces (GUIs). These components are referred to as the "Swing" components and are contained within a set of classes that are collectively known as the `javax.swing` package. Formally, a Java

TABLE 1.4 `showMessageDialog()` Icon Types

Type	Icon	Example
WARNING_MESSAGE	An exclamation point within a triangle	Figure 1.18a
QUESTION_MESSAGE	A question mark within a box	Figure 1.18b
INFORMATION_MESSAGE	The letter i within a circle	Figure 1.18c
ERROR_MESSAGE	A hyphen within a stop sign	Figure 1.18d
PLAIN_MESSAGE	No icon	Figure 1.18e

package consists of one or more individual classes that are stored in the same directory. As you might expect, classes that are packaged, or stored together, are related in some way. For the `swing` package, the classes provide a convenient means of specifying a fully functional GUI with typical window components such as check boxes, data entry fields, push buttons, and dialogs. The first Swing component that we will discuss is a dialog. In GUI terminology, a **dialog** is a box that can present a user with information, but it always requests some type of input or response from the user.

There are two types of dialog boxes. In one type, referred to as a **modal** box, the user must respond to the dialog and close it before the application displaying the dialog can continue. The second type of dialog is a **modeless** box, which means that an application can continue without requiring a user to first close the dialog box.

The Swing method that we will use to create a dialog is named `showMessageDialog()`. For example, the boxes illustrated in Figure 1.18 were all created with the `showMessageDialog()` method. The general form of a `showMessageDialog()` method call is:

```
JOptionPane.showMessageDialog(null,"message","title",icon-type);
```

Although this method call has the same form as both `print()` and `println()` methods, it is actually quite different. Here the name `JOptionPane` is the name of a Java class and not the name of a specific object. The Point of Information Box on page 37 explains why a class name rather than an object name is being used. For now, however, we can use this syntax to create a dialog from within the `main()` method.

The `showDialogMessage()` method creates a dialog based on the four arguments it is given when the method is called. The first argument, which we will always specify as `null`, is a positioning argument that causes the dialog to be centered within the window in which the Java program is being run. The second argument is the message that will be displayed in the dialog, and the third argument is the title that is displayed at the top of the dialog. The last argument defines the icon that will be displayed within the dialog. Table 1.4 lists the five icon types that we will be using throughout the text.

For example, the statement

```
ShowMessageDialog(null,"Hello World!", "Sample", WARNING_MESSAGE);
```

produced the dialog box in Figure 1.18a. Notice that the message `Hello World!` is included within the dialog box and the title at the top of the box is `Sample`. The exclamation icon included within the box is produced by the WARNING_MESSAGE icon-type designation in the statement. (WARNING_MESSAGE is a symbolic constant provided by

Java, which is described in detail in Section 3.5.) The icons shown in Figures 1.18b through 1.18e were produced using the QUESTION_MESSAGE, INFORMATION_ MESSAGE, ERROR_MESSAGE, and PLAIN_MESSAGE icon types, respectively. That is, Figure 1.18b was produced by the statement

```
JOptionPane.showMessageDialog(null,"Hello World!", "Sample", JOptionPane.QUESTION_MESSAGE);
```

It should be noted that this statement, as with all Java statements, can spread over multiple lines. The only requirement in doing so is that the method's name and any enclosed strings are not split between lines. Thus, the preceding statement can be written as

```
JOptionPane.showMessageDialog(null,"Hello World!",
                    "Sample", JOptionPane.QUESTION_MESSAGE);
```

Because of the length of a statement that uses `showMessageDialog()`, you will usually see it split across two or more lines.

(a) WARNING_MESSAGE

(b) QUESTION_MESSAGE

(c) INFORMATION_MESSAGE

(d) ERROR_MESSAGE

(e) PLAIN_MESSAGE

FIGURE 1.18 `showMessageDialog()` Dialog Boxes

In the case of the dialog boxes in Figure 1.18, the required input from the user is either clicking the OK button, pressing the Enter or Escape (Esc) key, or clicking the Close button at the top of the dialog to close the dialog. Because all dialogs produced by the

POINT OF INFORMATION

NON-STATIC AND STATIC METHODS

Each and every method that you use in Java is contained within a class in the same manner as a `main()` method. However, within a class, there can be two fundamentally different types of methods.

Methods that must be used with objects are referred to as **non-static methods.** Two examples of such methods are `print()` and `println()`. These methods are part of the `PrintStream` class. Non-static methods are generally used with the syntax:

```
objectName.methodName(arguments);
```

An example of this syntax is `System.out.println("Hello World");`. In this example, the object is identified by a class and object name. The object is the output stream named `out`, which is an object of the `System` class (see Point of Information box on page 29). Thus, it is fully specified by the full name `System.out`. Although non-static methods are restricted to objects, they can be accessed from outside the class they are written in if their header line includes the word `public`.

The second type of method is referred to as a static method. A **static method** is one that *does not* operate on an object but receives all of its data as arguments. As with a non-static method, if a static method's header line includes the word `public`, the method can be called from outside its own class. In such a case, the method is referred to as a general-purpose method. This implies that the method is constructed to perform a general-purpose task that can be useful in a number of places, such as constructing a dialog or computing the square root of a number. An example of such a method is `showMessageDialog()`, which uses its arguments to position and display a dialog box from within any method that uses it.

In using a general-purpose method outside its class, however, you must indicate where the method is to be found. This is accomplished by listing its class name before the method's name using the syntax

```
ClassName.methodName(arguments);
```

Operationally, the syntax for both non-static and general-purpose methods look the same in that both precede the method's name with a period and either an object and/or class name. For now, simply use each method as it is given in the text. In each case, whenever a new method is presented, we will indicate its type. After a number of general-purpose mathematical methods are presented in Chapter 3 and you learn to construct your own static methods in Chapter 6 and non-static methods in Chapter 9, you will gain a much clearer understanding and appreciation of these two method types.

showMessageDialog() method are modal, a user must close the dialog before any further program execution can continue.

Program 1.4 incorporates the showMessageDialog() that produced Figure 1.18a within the context of a complete program. Although the structure of this program should be familiar, there are a number of new items that you should notice.

First, because we are using a class from the Swing package, in this case JOptionPane, we need to tell the program in which package this class can be found. This information is provided by the import statement. When the name JOptionPane is encountered, the compiler will first search a package named java.lang, which is a default package provided to all Java programs without the need for an explicit import statement. Not finding the named class in this package, the search for the class will continue with an explicitly named package provided by an import statement, which in this case specifies the javax.swing package of classes (be careful to note that the package name begins with javax and not java). Within this package, the compiler will locate the showMessageDialog() method contained within the JOptionPane class. The asterisk, *, in the import statement permits the compiler to search all classes in the package, no matter where the classes are located within the package.

The body of the main() method consists of two statements, one of which is a call to the showMessageDialog() method to create the dialog box in Figure 1.18a. The second statement is a System.exit() method that forces a closure of the program after the dialog box is closed by the user. Without the System.exit(), the underlying Java program, even though it is not doing anything, would still be active after the user closed the dialog box. Although the reason for this is presented in Chapter 12, where GUIs are discussed in detail, for now we will always use a System.exit() method whenever our application creates a graphical user interface, such as the dialog produced by Program 1.4.

PROGRAM 1.4

```java
// File: DisplayADialog.java
// Description: Construction of a dialog
// Programmer: G. Bronson
// Date: 6/15/02

import javax.swing.*;
public class DisplayADialog
{
  public static void main (String[] args)
  {
    JOptionPane.showMessageDialog(null,"Hello World!",
        "Sample",JOptionPane.WARNING_MESSAGE);
    System.exit(0);
  }
}
```

Both the message and title displayed in a dialog must be strings. Although the title string must reside on a single line, the message string follows the same rules as the strings displayed by the print() and println() methods. This means that newline escape sequences can be included within the message. For example, consider Program 1.5, which displays the same string as previously displayed by Program 1.3, but now the display is contained within a dialog box (Figure 1.19). The only difference in the displayed string is that the default font in a dialog is a proportionately spaced Times Roman font rather than the fixed-spaced Courier font used in character-based output.

PROGRAM 1.5

```java
// File: MultiLineDialog.java
// Description: Construction of a dialog
// Programmer: G. Bronson
// Date: 6/15/02

import javax.swing.*;
public class MultiLineDialog
{
  public static void main (String[] args)
  {
    JOptionPane.showMessageDialog(null,
           "Computers, computers everywhere\n as far as\n\nI can see",
           "Sample", JOptionPane.WARNING_MESSAGE);

    System.exit(0);
  }
}
```

FIGURE 1.19   The Dialog Produced by Program 1.5

EXERCISES 1.6

1. Enter and run Program 1.4 on your computer.
2. a. Modify Program 1.4 to produce the output shown in Figure 1.18c.
   b. Modify Program 1.4 to produce the output shown in Figure 1.18e.
3. Write and execute a Java program that displays your name on one line, your street address on a second line, and your city, state, and zip code on the third line within a dialog box that uses an information icon.
4. Write and execute a Java program that displays the following verse in a dialog box that uses a warning icon:

```
The cosecant of an angle
   is equal to one over
      the sine of the angle.
```

5. Write and execute a Java program that displays the following data in a dialog box that does not display any icon.

```
Degrees      Radians
0            0.0000
180          3.1416
360          6.2832
```

1.7 COMMON PROGRAMMING ERRORS

Part of learning any programming language is making the elementary mistakes commonly encountered as you begin to work with the language. These mistakes tend to be frustrating because each language has its own set of common programming errors waiting for the unwary. The more common errors made when initially programming in Java are:

1. Forgetting to save a program with the same file name as the class name used within the program.
2. Forgetting to save a program with a `.java` extension.
3. Omitting the parentheses after `main`.
4. Omitting or incorrectly typing the opening brace, {, that signifies the start of a class and the start of a method body.
5. Omitting or incorrectly typing the closing brace, }, that signifies the end of a method and the end of a class.
6. Misspelling the name of an object or method—for example, typing `pint()` instead of `print()`.
7. Forgetting to type the complete name of the `print()` and `println()` methods as `System.out.print()` and `System.out.println()`, respectively.
8. Forgetting to close a string with a double quotation mark.
9. Omitting the semicolon at the end of each statement.
10. Forgetting the `\n` to indicate a new line.
11. Misspelling the term `javax.swing` as `java.swing` when importing the `swing` package.
12. Not using a `System.exit(0)` to end a program when creating a dialog-based application.

Our experience is that errors 1, 5, 8, and 9 tend to be the most common. We suggest that you write a program and specifically introduce each of these errors, one at a time, to see what error messages are produced by your compiler. Then, when these error messages appear due to inadvertent errors, you will have had experience in understanding the messages and correcting the errors.

1.8 CHAPTER SUMMARY

1. The programs used to operate a computer are referred to as *software*.
2. Programming languages come in a variety of forms and types. *Machine language* programs, also known as *executable programs*, contain the binary codes that can be executed by a computer. *Assembly languages* permit the use of symbolic names for

mathematical operations and memory addresses. Programs written in assembly languages must be converted to machine language using translator programs called *assemblers* before the programs can be executed. Assembly and machine languages are referred to as *low-level languages*.

Compiler and *interpreter languages* are referred to as *high-level languages*. This means they are written with instructions that resemble a written language, such as English, and can be run on a variety of computer types. Compiler languages require a *compiler* to translate the program into a binary language form, whereas interpreter languages require an *interpreter* to do the translation.

3. An *algorithm* is a step-by-step procedure that must terminate and describes how a single computation or task is to be performed. An algorithm is coded as a method in Java.

4. The simplest Java program consists of a single class that contains one method named `main()` and has the form

```
public class name
{
    public static void main(String[] args)
    {
        program statements in here;
    }
}
```

This program consists of a class header line and a class body. The body of the class begins with the opening brace, {, and ends with the closing brace, }. The name of the class is programmer selected. Within the class' body is a standard header line for the `main()` method and the body of the `main()` method. As with a class body, the body of each method begins with an opening brace and ends with the closing brace.

5. The `main()` method identifies the starting execution point of a Java program. An executing Java program must have a `main()` method.

6. All single Java statements within a method body must be terminated by a semicolon.

7. Both the `print()` and `println()` methods, which are provided by the `PrintStream` class, are used to display text and numerical results. The argument to these methods can be a string of characters enclosed in double quotation marks. This string, which may also include escape sequences, such as the newline escape sequence, `\n`, is subsequently displayed within the window in which the Java program is executing. The `println()` method automatically provides a final newline escape sequence. Both `print()` and `println()`, when they are used to send a string to the standard output device connected to your program, which is typically the video screen, operate on the `System.out` object.

8. A Java *package* consists of one or more individual classes stored in the same directory. This permits classes that are related in some way to be packaged, or stored together. In also provides a way to restrict the compiler's search for classes used in the program using an `import` statement.

9. The `swing` package of classes, which can create fully functional graphical user interfaces (GUIs), is named `javax.swing`. To use the classes in the `swing` package, place the following statement at the top of your Java program: `import javax.swing.*;`

10. Along with the `javax.swing` package of classes, many other packages are provided with each Java compiler. One such set of classes, which provides language support and basic system services, is defined in the `java.lang` package. Both the `print()` and `println()` methods are part of the `PrintStream` class, which is contained in the `java.lang` package of classes. As this package of classes is automatically searched by the compiler, an `import` statement for this package is not explicitly required.

11. Dialog boxes can be created using the `showMessageDialog()` method, which is provided by the `JOptionPane` class. This class is contained in the `javax.swing` package, and thus, a Java program that creates a dialog box must import the javax.swing package of classes. The general syntax of a `showMessageDialog()` method call is

     `JOptionPane.showMessageDialog(null,"message","title",icon-type)`

     where `message` is a string that is displayed within the dialog box, `title` is a string that is displayed in the title bar of the dialog box, and `icon-type` is one of the following (see Table 1.4 for a description of each type):

     `JOptionPane.WARNING_MESSAGE`
     `JOptionPane.QUESTION_MESSAGE`
     `JOptionPane.INFORMATION_MESSAGE`
     `JOptionPane.ERROR_MESSAGE`
     `JOptionPane.PLAIN_MESSAGE`

12. A `main()` method that creates a dialog box should end with a `System.exit(0)` statement.

1.9 CHAPTER SUPPLEMENT: COMPUTER HARDWARE AND SOFTWARE

All computers, from large supercomputers costing millions of dollars to smaller desktop personal computers, must perform a minimum set of functions and provide the capability to:

1. Accept input
2. Display output
3. Store information in a logically consistent format (traditionally, binary)
4. Perform arithmetic and logic operations on either the input or stored data
5. Monitor, control, and direct the overall operation and sequencing of the system

Figure 1.20 illustrates the computer hardware components that support these capabilities. Specifically, this hardware consists of arithmetic and logic, control, memory, and input/output units.

The **arithmetic and logic unit (ALU)** performs all the arithmetic and logic functions, such as addition, subtraction, and so forth, provided by the computer.

The **control unit** directs and monitors the overall operation of the computer. It keeps track of where in memory the next instruction resides, issues the signals needed both to read data from and write data to other units in the system, and controls execution of all instructions.

The **memory unit** stores information in a logically consistent format. Typically, both instructions and data are stored in memory, usually in separate and distinct areas.

FIGURE 1.20 Basic Hardware Units of a Computer

The **input and output (I/O) unit** provides the interface to which peripheral devices such as keyboards, monitors, printers, and card readers are attached.

In the first commercially available computers of the 1950s, all hardware units were built using relays and vacuum tubes. These computers were extremely large pieces of equipment, capable of making thousands of calculations per second and costing millions of dollars.

With the introduction of transistors in the 1960s, the size and cost of computer hardware were reduced. The transistor was approximately one-twentieth the size of its vacuum tube counterpart. The transistor's small size allowed manufacturers to combine the arithmetic and logic unit with the control unit into a single new unit. This combined unit is called the **central processing unit (CPU)**. The combination of the ALU and control units into one CPU made sense because a majority of control signals generated by a program are directed to the ALU in response to arithmetic and logic instructions within the program. Combining the ALU with the control unit simplified the interface between these two units and provided improved processing speed.

The mid-1960s saw the introduction of integrated circuits (ICs), which resulted in still another significant reduction in the space required to produce a CPU. Initially, integrated circuits were manufactured with up to 100 transistors on a single 1 cm^2 chip of silicon. These devices are referred to as small-scale integrated (SSI) circuits. Current versions of these chips contain hundreds of thousands to more than a million transistors and are referred to as very large-scale integrated (VLSI) chips.

VLSI chip technology has provided the means of transforming the giant computers of the 1950s into today's desktop personal computers. The units required to form a computer (CPU, memory, and I/O) are now manufactured on an individual VLSI chip, and the single-chip CPU is referred to as a **microprocessor.** Figure 1.21 illustrates how these chips are connected internally within current personal computers, such as the IBM personal computers.

Concurrent with the remarkable reduction in computer hardware size has been an equally dramatic decrease in cost and increase in processing speeds. Equivalent computer hardware that cost more than $1 million in 1950 can now be purchased for less than $100. If the same reductions occurred in the automobile industry, a Rolls-Royce could now be purchased for $10! The processing speeds of current computers have also increased by a

FIGURE 1.21   VLSI Chip Connections for a Desktop Computer

factor of 1,000 over their 1950s predecessors, with the computational speeds of current machines measured in both millions of instructions per second (MIPS) and billions of instructions per second (BIPS).

Computer Storage

The physical components used in manufacturing a computer require that the numbers and letters inside its memory unit are not stored using the same symbols that people use. The number 126, for example, cannot be stored with the symbols 1, 2, and 6. Nor is the letter that we recognize as A stored using this symbol. In this section, you will see why this is so and how computers store numbers. In Chapter 2, you will see how letters are stored.

The smallest and most basic data item in a computer is called a **bit**. Physically, a bit is really a switch that can be either open or closed. The convention we will follow is that the open and closed positions of each switch are represented as 0 and 1, respectively.[8]

A single bit that can represent the values 0 and 1, by itself, has limited usefulness. All computers, therefore, group a set number of bits together for storage and transmission. The grouping of 8 bits to form a larger unit is an almost universal computer standard. These groups are commonly referred to as bytes. A single byte consisting of 8 bits, where each bit is either 0 or 1, can represent any one of 256 distinct patterns. These consist of the pattern 00000000 (all eight switches open) to the pattern 11111111 (all eight switches closed), and all possible combinations of 0s and 1s in between. Each of these patterns can be used to represent either a letter of the alphabet, other single characters (e.g., a dollar sign, comma, etc.), a single digit, or numbers containing more than one digit. The collection of patterns consisting of 0s and 1s that represents letters, single digits, and other single characters is called **character codes** (one such code, called Unicode, is presented in Section 2.1). The patterns that store numbers are called **number codes,** one of which is presented next.

Two's Complement Numbers

The most common number code for storing integer values inside a computer is called the **two's complement** representation. With this code, the integer equivalent of any bit pattern, such as 10001101, is easy to determine and can be found for either positive or nega-

---

[8]This convention, unfortunately, is rather arbitrary, and you will frequently encounter the reverse correspondence where the open and closed positions are represented as 1 and 0, respectively.

tive integers with no change in the conversion method. For convenience, we will assume byte-size bit patterns consisting of a set of 8 bits each, although the procedure carries directly over to larger bit patterns.

The easiest way to determine the integer represented by each bit pattern is first to construct a simple device called a value box. Figure 1.22 illustrates such a box for a single byte. Mathematically, each value in the box in Figure 1.22 represents an increasing power of 2. Because two's complement numbers must be capable of representing both positive and negative integers, the leftmost position, in addition to having the largest absolute magnitude, also has a negative sign.

```
−128| 64 | 32 | 16 |  8 |  4 |  2 |  1
----|----|----|----|----|----|----|---
    |    |    |    |    |    |    |
```

FIGURE 1.22   An 8-bit Value Box

Conversion of any binary number, for example 10001101, requires inserting the bit pattern in the value box and adding the values having 1s under them. Thus, as illustrated in Figure 1.23, the bit pattern 10001101 represents the integer number −115.

```
−128 | 64 | 32 | 16 |  8 |  4 |  2 |  1
----|----|----|----|----|----|----|---
  1  |  0 |  0 |  0 |  1 |  1 |  0 |  1
−128 +  0 +  0 +  0 +  8 +  4 +  0 +  1 = −115
```

FIGURE 1.23   Converting 10001101 to a Base-10 Number

The value box can also be used in reverse to convert a base-10 integer number into its equivalent binary bit pattern. Some conversions in fact can be made by inspection. For example, the base-10 number −125 is obtained by adding 3 to −128. Thus, the binary representation of −125 is 10000011, which equals −128 + 2 + 1. Similarly, the two's complement representation of the number 40 is 00101000, which is 32 + 8.

Although the value box conversion method is deceptively simple, the method is directly related to the underlying mathematical basis of two's complement binary numbers. The original name of the two's complement code was the weighted-sign code, which correlates directly to the value box. As the name **weighted sign** implies, each bit position has a weight, or value, of 2 raised to a power and a sign. The signs of all bits except the leftmost bit are positive, and the sign of the leftmost bit is negative.

In reviewing the value box, it is evident that any two's complement binary number with a leading 1 represents a negative number, and any bit pattern with a leading 0 represents a positive number. Using the value box, it is easy to determine the most positive and negative values capable of being stored. The most negative value that can be stored in a single byte is the decimal number −128, which has the bit pattern 10000000. Any other nonzero bit will simply add a positive amount to the number. Additionally, it is clear that a positive number must have 0 as its leftmost bit. From this, you can see that the largest positive 8-bit two's complement number is 01111111, or 127.

Words and Addresses

One or more bytes may themselves be grouped into larger units, called **words,** which facilitate faster and more extensive data access. For example, retrieving a word consisting of 4 bytes from a computer's memory results in more information than that obtained by retrieving a word consisting of 1 byte. Such a retrieval is also considerably faster than four individual byte retrievals. This increase in speed and capacity, however, is achieved by an increase in the computer's cost and complexity.

Early personal computers, such as the Apple IIe® and Commodore® machines, internally stored and transmitted words consisting of single bytes. The first IBM personal computers used word sizes consisting of 2 bytes, whereas more current personal computers store and process words consisting of 4 bytes each.

The number of bytes in a word determines the maximum and minimum values that can be represented by the word. Table 1.5 lists these values for 1-, 2-, and 4-byte words (each of the values listed can be derived using 8-, 16-, and 32-bit value boxes, respectively).

TABLE 1.5 Integer Values and Word Size

Word Size	Maximum Integer Value	Minimum Integer Value
1 Byte	127	−128
2 Bytes	32,767	−32,768
4 Bytes	2,147,483,647	−2,147,483,648

In addition to representing integer values, computers must also store and transmit numbers containing decimal points, which are mathematically referred to as real numbers. The codes for real numbers, which are more complex than those for integers, are presented in Appendix D.

CAREER CHOICES

AERONAUTICAL/AEROSPACE ENGINEERING

Among the youngest of the engineering disciplines, aeronautical/aerospace engineering is concerned with all aspects of the design, production, testing, and utilizing of vehicles or devices that fly in air (aeronautical) or in space (aerospace), from hang gliders to space shuttles. Since the science and engineering principles involved are so broad-based, aeroengineers usually specialize in a subarea that may overlap with other engineering fields such as mechanical, metallurgical/materials, chemical, civil, or electrical engineering. These subareas include the following:

1. Aerodynamics. The study of the flight characteristics of various structures or configurations. Typical considerations are the drag and lift associated with airplane design or the onset of turbulent flow. A knowledge of fluid dynamics is essential. The modeling and testing of all forms of aircraft are part of this discipline.
2. Structural design. The design, production, and testing of aircraft and spacecraft to withstand the wide range of in-flight demands on these vehicles, such as underwater vessels, are in the province of the structural engineer.
3. Propulsion systems. The design of internal combustion, jet, and liquid- and solid-fuel rocket engines and their coordination in the overall design of the vehicle. Rocket engines, especially, require innovative engineering to accommodate the extreme temperatures of storing, mixing, and burning fuels such as liquid oxygen.
4. Instrumentation and guidance. The aerospace industry has been a leader in developing and utilizing solid-state electronics in the form of microprocessors to monitor and adjust the operations of hundreds of air- and spacecraft functions. This field relies on the expertise of both electrical engineers and aeroengineers.
5. Navigation. The computation of orbits within and outside the atmosphere and the determination of the orientation of a vehicle with respect to points on the earth or in space.

CHAPTER 2

Values, Variables, and Operations

Java programs process different types of data in different ways. For example, calculating the bacteria growth in a polluted pond requires mathematical operations on numerical data, whereas sorting a list of names requires comparison operations using alphabetical data. Java has two fundamental types of data known as primitive and reference types. In this chapter, we introduce Java's primitive data types and the operations that can be performed on them. Additionally, we present the proper use of constants and variables in storing primitive data values and provide the use of print methods and dialog boxes to display the results of mathematical operations and expressions.

2.1 DATA VALUES AND ARITHMETIC OPERATIONS

Java stores and processes data as one of two general data types referred to as primitive and reference types. The primitive types, which are also referred to as built-in types, are shown in Figure 2.1. Reference types are associated either with a class, an array, or an interface (Figure 2.2). As a practical observation, the operations provided for primitive types are only provided as arithmetic symbols, such as those for addition, subtraction, multiplication, and so on, whereas for reference types, the overwhelming majority of operations are provided as methods.

In this section, we introduce all eight primitive data types, which consist of the numerical types known as integers and floating-point numbers and the character and boolean types. In addition, the String reference data type is described. We will present the specific types of values, referred to as literals, that are associated with each of these data types. A **literal** is a value that explicitly identifies itself. For example, all numbers, such as 2, 3.6, and −8.2, are referred to in computer terminology as both literals and literal values because they literally display their values. A string such as "Hello World!" is also referred to as a literal string value because the string itself is displayed. You have

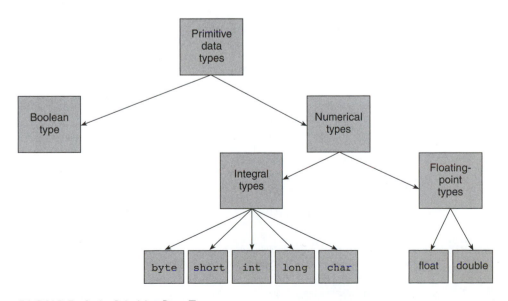

FIGURE 2.1 Primitive Data Types

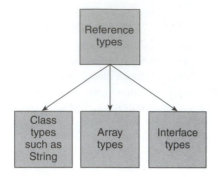

FIGURE 2.2   Reference Types

been using literal values throughout your life and commonly refer to them as numbers and words. Later in this chapter, we will see examples of nonliteral values that do not display themselves but are stored in memory locations accessed by their names.

Integer Values

An **integer literal**, which is more frequently referred to as simply an integer, is zero or any positive or negative numerical value without a decimal point. Examples of valid integer literals are:

```
0      5      -10      +25      1000      253      -26351      +36
```

As these examples illustrate, integer literals may be signed (with a leading + or − sign) or unsigned (with no leading + or − sign). No commas, decimal points, or special symbols, such as the dollar sign, are allowed. Examples of invalid integer literal values are:

```
$255.62      2,523      3.      6,243,892      1,492.89      +6.0
```

The Java language defines an integer data type as any integer value within the range −2147483648 to +2147483647 that must be stored using 4 bytes (32 bits) in two's complement form.[1] For cases in which larger integer values are required, Java also defines a long integer data type. Long integer values, which are stored as 8-byte two's complement numbers, must reside in the range −9223372036854775808 to 9223372036854775807. Long integer literals are written the same as integer literals with an L appended to the end of the value. Thus, the literal values

```
8976929L 2147483649L 62L
```

will all be stored as long integers.[2]

---

[1]It is interesting to note that the absolute value of the negative limit is 1 more than the positive limit. This is because values are stored in the two's complement format described in Section 1.9.

[2]A lowercase l can also be used, but since this letter is often confused with the digit 1, we will always use an uppercase L to indicate a long integer.

TABLE 2.1 Integer Data Types

Type	Storage	Range of Values	Comments
byte	1 byte	-128 to 127	Values are stored by assignment only. There are no byte literal values.
short	2 bytes	-32,768 to 32,767	Values are stored by assignment only. There are no short literal values.
int	4 bytes	-2,147,483,648 to 2,147,483,647	The default integer type. Literal values are permitted.
long	8 bytes	-9,223,372,036,854,775,807 to 9,223,372,036,854,775,808	Literal values are indicated by appending an L to the integer.

Java also supports both byte and short integer data types, which can store integer values in a restricted range. However, byte and short integers cannot be specified as literals (i.e., there is no notation for indicating an integer value that will be stored in byte or short integer form). For these two data types, specific values can only be stored using integer literals within assignment statements, a discussion of which is presented in the next section. Table 2.1 lists the storage requirements and range of values for the various integer number types recognized in Java.

Floating-point Values

A **floating-point literal**, which is also called a **real number**, is any signed or unsigned numerical value having a decimal point. Examples of floating-point literals are:

```
+10.625    5.    -6.2    3251.92    0.0    0.33    -6.67    +2.
```

Notice that the numbers 5., 0.0, and +2. are classified as floating-point literals, but the same numbers written without a decimal point (5, 0, +2) would be integer literal values. As with integer literals, special symbols, such as the dollar sign and the comma, are not permitted in real numbers. Examples of invalid real numbers are:

```
5,326.25    24    6,459    $10.29    7.007.645
```

Java supports two different types of floating-point data types: double and float. The difference between these types of data is the amount of storage that a Java compiler allocates for each type, which affects both the range (highest to lowest permitted numbers) and the precision (number of decimal places) of the numbers that can be stored. A double floating-point value is required to be stored using 8 bytes.[3] This is the default type assumed for floating-point numbers. The other type of floating-point value is referred to as a float.

---

[3]See Appendix I for a description of floating-point storage.

TABLE 2.2 Floating-point Data Types

Type	Storage	Absolute Range of Values (+ or −)	Comments
float	4 bytes	1.40129846432481707e−45 to 3.40282346638528860e+38	Literal values are indicated by appending either an f or F to the number.
double	8 bytes	4.94065645841246544e−324 to 1.79769313486231570e+308	The default floating-point type.

A `float` stores numbers having a decimal point using only 4 bytes. Because the storage requirement for doubles is twice that of floats, a `double` value has approximately twice the precision of a `float` (for this reason, doubles are sometimes referred to as **double-precision numbers** and floats as **single-precision numbers**). The smallest and largest values that can be stored in each floating-point data type are listed in Table 2.2.

To specifically indicate a `float` literal value, you must append either an F or f to the number. In the absence of these suffixes, a number with a decimal point is considered a double. For example:

9.234   indicates a `double` value
9.234f   indicates a `float` value
9.234F   indicates a `float` value

For numbers with more than six significant digits to the right of the decimal point, you should use a `double` value. Appendix I describes the binary storage format defined by the Institute of Electrical and Electronics Engineers (IEEE—pronounced I-triple E) standard 754 and its impact on number precision.

Exponential Notation

Floating-point literals can also be written in exponential notation, which is similar to scientific notation and is commonly used to express both very large and very small values in compact form. The following examples illustrate how numbers with decimals can be expressed in exponential and scientific notation.

Decimal Notation	Exponential Notation	Scientific Notation
1625.	1.625e3	1.625×10^3
63421.	6.3421e4	6.3421×10^4
.00731	7.31e−3	$7.31 \times 10-3$
.000625	6.25e−4	$6.25 \times 10-4$

In exponential notation, the letter e stands for exponent. The number following the e represents a power of 10 and indicates the number of places the decimal point should be moved to obtain the standard decimal value. The decimal point is moved to the right if the number after the e is positive or moved to the left if the number after the e is negative. For example, the e3 in 1.625e3 means move the decimal place three places to the right so that the number becomes 1625. The e−3 in 7.31e−3 means move the decimal point three places to the left so that 7.31e−3 becomes .00731.

WHAT IS PRECISION?

In numerical theory, the term **precision** typically refers to numerical accuracy. In this context, a statement such as "this computation is accurate, or precise, to the fifth decimal place" is used. This means that the fifth digit after the decimal point has been rounded, and the number is accurate to within ±0.00005.

In computer programming, precision can either refer to the accuracy of a number or the number of significant digits in the number, where significant digits are defined as the number of clearly correct digits plus 1. For example, if the number 12.6874 has been rounded to the fourth decimal place, it is correct to say that this number is precise (i.e., accurate) to the fourth decimal place. This statement means that all of the digits in the number are accurate except the fourth digit, which has been rounded. Similarly, it can be said that this same number has a precision of six digits, which means that the first five digits are correct and the sixth digit has been rounded. Another way of saying this is that the number 12.6874 has six significant digits.

Notice that the significant digits in a number need not have any relation to the number of displayed digits. For example, if the number 687.45678921 has five significant digits, it is only accurate to the value 687.46, where the last digit is assumed to be rounded. In a similar manner, dollar values in many very large financial applications are frequently rounded to the nearest hundred-thousand dollars. In such applications, a displayed dollar value of $12,400,000, for example, is not accurate to the closest dollar. If this value is specified as having three significant digits, it is only accurate to the hundred-thousand digit.

Character Values

The third basic type of data recognized by Java are characters. Characters include the letters of the alphabet (both uppercase and lowercase), the ten digits 0 through 9, and special symbols such as + $. , – !. A single character value is any one letter, digit, or special symbol enclosed by single quotes. Examples of valid character values are:

```
'A' '$' 'b' '7' 'y' '!' 'M' 'q'
```

Character values in Java must be stored as 16-bit unsigned values using Unicode. This code provides an extended set of 65,536 codes, which can handle multilanguage symbols. Currently, more than 35,000 different characters from diverse languages such as Arabic, Greek, and Hebrew have been defined, including the most common pictograph symbols of Chinese and Japanese. Each individual symbol and character from these languages has been assigned to a specific pattern of 0s and 1s. The bit patterns corresponding to the lowercase and uppercase letters of the English language are presented in Table 2.3.[4]

Using Table 2.3, we can determine how the characters 'J', 'E', 'A', 'N', and 'S', for example, are stored by a Java program. In Unicode, this sequence of characters requires 10 bytes of storage (2 bytes for each letter) and would be stored as illustrated in Figure 2.3.

[4]The values of the first 128 Unicode characters are identical to the values of the 128 characters in the ASCII code used by most other high-level languages.

TABLE 2.3 The English Alphabet Codes

Letter	Binary Code	Hex. Value	Decimal Value	Letter	Binary Code	Hex. Value	Decimal Value
a	00000000 01100001	0x0061	97	A	00000000 01000001	0x0041	65
b	00000000 01100010	0x0062	98	B	00000000 01000010	0x0042	66
c	00000000 01100011	0x0063	99	C	00000000 01000011	0x0043	67
d	00000000 01100100	0x0064	100	D	00000000 01000100	0x0044	68
e	00000000 01100101	0x0065	101	E	00000000 01000101	0x0045	69
f	00000000 01100110	0x0066	102	F	00000000 01000111	0x0046	70
g	00000000 01100111	0x0067	103	G	00000000 01000110	0x0047	71
h	00000000 01101000	0x0068	104	H	00000000 01001000	0x0048	72
i	00000000 01101001	0x0069	105	I	00000000 01001001	0x0049	73
j	00000000 01101010	0x006A	106	J	00000000 01001010	0x004A	74
k	00000000 01101011	0x006B	107	K	00000000 01001011	0x004B	75
l	00000000 01101100	0x006C	108	L	00000000 01001100	0x004C	76
m	00000000 01101101	0x006D	109	M	00000000 01001101	0x004D	77
n	00000000 01101110	0x006E	110	N	00000000 01001110	0x004E	78
o	00000000 01101111	0x006F	111	O	00000000 01001111	0x004F	79
p	00000000 01110000	0x0070	112	P	00000000 01010000	0x0050	80
q	00000000 01110001	0x0071	113	Q	00000000 01010001	0x0051	81
r	00000000 01110010	0x0072	114	R	00000000 01010010	0x0052	82
s	00000000 01110011	0x0073	115	S	00000000 01010011	0x0053	83
t	00000000 01110100	0x0074	116	T	00000000 01010100	0x0054	84
u	00000000 01110101	0x0075	117	U	00000000 01010101	0x0055	85
v	00000000 01110110	0x0076	118	V	00000000 01010110	0x0056	86
w	00000000 01110111	0x0077	119	W	00000000 01010111	0x0057	87
x	00000000 01111000	0x0078	120	X	00000000 01011000	0x0058	88
y	00000000 01111001	0x0079	121	Y	00000000 01011001	0x0059	89
z	00000000 01111010	0x007A	122	Z	00000000 01011010	0x005A	90

FIGURE 2.3 The Letters JEANS Stored by a Java Program

Internally, characters are stored as unsigned integers in the range of 0 to 65,535 inclusive. Since these are integer values, Java formally defines a character as an unsigned integer data type. Although strings are constructed as a sequence of one or more individual characters, strings are not a primitive type in Java. Rather, Java provides a class named String for manipulating this type of data. You have already seen how to construct a string value by enclosing individual characters within double quotation marks. The String type is a reference type. As noted at the beginning of this section, this means that the majority of operations available for strings, as reference types, will be provided as methods rather than as arithmetic symbols.

TABLE 2.4   Escape Sequences

Escape Sequence	Meaning
\b	move back one space
\f	move to next page
\n	move to next line
\r	carriage return
\t	move to next tab setting
\\	backslash character
\'	single quote
\"	double quote

Escape Sequences

When a backslash, \, is placed directly in front of a select group of characters, it tells the compiler to escape from the way these characters would normally be interpreted. For this reason, the combination of a backslash and these specific characters is called an **escape sequence**. We have already encountered an example of this in the newline escape sequence, \n. Table 2.4 lists Java's most common escape sequences.

Although each escape sequence in Table 2.4 is made up of two distinct characters, the combination of the two characters with no intervening whitespace causes the computer to store one character code. Table 2.5 on the next page lists the Unicode byte patterns for the escape sequences in Table 2.4.

Boolean Values

Boolean data are restricted to one of two value: true or false. These data are most useful when examining a specific condition and, as a result of the condition being true or false, taking a prescribed course of action. As the examination of conditions is considered in Chapter 4, we defer further discussion of boolean data until then.

Arithmetic Operations

Integers and real numbers may be added, subtracted, multiplied, and divided. Although it is usually better not to mix integers and real numbers when performing arithmetic operations, predictable results are obtained when different data types are used in the same arithmetic expression.

The operators for arithmetic operations are called **arithmetic operators.** They are as follows:

Operation	Operator
Addition	+
Subtraction	–
Multiplication	*
Division	/
Modulus	%

TABLE 2.5   The Java Escape Sequence Codes

Escape Sequence	Meaning	Unicode Code
\b	backspace	00000000 00001000
\f	form feed	00000000 00001100
\n	new line	00000000 00001010
\r	carriage return	00000000 00001101
\t	tab	00000000 00010001
\\	backslash	00000000 01011100
\'	single quote	00000000 00100111
\"	double quote	00000000 00100010

A **simple arithmetic expression** consists of an arithmetic operator connecting two operands of the form:

operand *operator* operand

where the simplest operand consists of a literal value (i.e., a number).[5] Examples of simple arithmetic expressions are:

    3 + 7
    18 − 3
    12.62 + 9.8
    .08 * 12.2
    12.6 / 2.0

The spaces around the arithmetic operators in these examples are inserted strictly for clarity and may be omitted without affecting the value of the expression. Notice that an expression in Java must be entered in a straight-line form. Thus, for example, the Java expression equivalent to 12.6 divided by 2 must be entered as 12.6 / 2 and not as the algebraic expression

$$\frac{12.6}{6}$$

When evaluating simple arithmetic expressions, the data type of the result is determined by the following rules, which are applied in the order listed:

1. If either operand is a double value, the result is a double value, else
2. If either operand is a float value, the result is a float value, else
3. If either operand is a long value, the result is a long value, else
4. The result is an integer precision (32-bit) value

An expression that contains only integer operands (long or ints) is an **integer expression**, and the result of the expression is an integer value (rules 3 and 4). Similarly, an expression containing only real-valued operands (doubles or floats) is a **floating-point** or **real expression**, and the result of the expression is a floating-point value (rules 1 and

---

[5]More formally, an operand can be either a single constant, variable (which is described in Section 2.2), function call, or any valid combination of these elements that yields a single value.

2). An arithmetic expression containing both integer and noninteger operands is a **mixed-mode** expression. The result of a mixed-mode expression is always a floating-point value (rules 1 and 2). For example, in the mixed-mode expression 16.4 + 3, the 3 is converted, internally and only for the computation, to 3.0, and the result of the expression is the floating-point number 19.4.

The value of any arithmetic expression can be displayed as character text using both the `print()` and `println()` methods or within a dialog box using the `showMessage()` method. This is done by converting the desired value to a string prior to being displayed. For example, the statement

```
System.out.println((6 + 15));
```

yields the display 21. Strictly speaking, the inner parentheses surrounding the expression 6 + 15 are not required. That is, the statement

```
System.out.println(6 + 15);
```

also displays 21. However, it is always advisable to enclose arithmetic expressions within parentheses because the final argument passed to both `print()` and `println()` is always converted to a string before being displayed. Enclosing the expression in parentheses ensures that the arithmetic operation is completed before any conversion to a string takes place. In a moment, you will see an instance where not enclosing the arithmetic expression results in a string concatenation taking place before the intended arithmetic addition is performed.

In addition to displaying a single numerical value, a string identifying the output can also be displayed by including both the string and a value to the output method. For example, the statement

```
System.out.println("The total of 6 and 15 is " +(6 + 15));
```

concatenates two items into one string, which is then passed to `println()` for display. Here the arithmetic addition is done first and then the value 21 is concatenated to the string `"The total of 6 and 15 is "`. Since the first operand is a string, the program interprets the first addition sign as a concatenation operation. To perform the concatenation, the numerical value of 21 is internally converted to the string `"21"`, which is then used in the concatenation. Finally, since a single string is obtained, it is passed to the `println()` method for display. The output produced by this statement is:

```
The total of 6 and 15 is 21
```

As far as `System.out.println()` is concerned, its input is a string of characters that is then sent on to be displayed. Also notice that the parentheses around the expression 6 + 15 are required here. Without these parentheses, because the first operand encountered is a string, the program would start concatenating all operands from left to right and produce the display

```
The total of 6 and 15 is 615
```

Notice that the space between the word is and the displayed number is caused by the space placed within the string passed to the println() method. Placing either a space, tab, or newline escape sequence into the string causes this character to be part of the output that is ultimately displayed. For example, the statement

```
System.out.println("The sum of 12.2 and 15.754 is\n" + (12.2 + 15.754));
```

yields the display

```
The sum of 12.2 and 15.754 is
27.954
```

We should mention that the final string sent to the print methods can be continued across multiple lines and contain numerous concatenations. Thus, the prior display is also produced by the statement

```
System.out.println("The sum of 12.2 and 15.754 is\n"
                    + (12.2 + 15.754)
                   );
```

The restrictions in using multiple lines are that a string contained within double quotation marks cannot be split across lines and the terminating semicolon appears only on the last line. Within a line, multiple concatenation symbols can be used.

As the last display indicates, floating-point numbers are displayed with sufficient places to the right of the decimal point to accommodate the fractional part of the number. The specification for the Java language requires that when float or double-precision values are displayed as strings, as many decimal places will be displayed as are necessary to ensure that if the numbers were input, there would be no loss of precision.[6]

Program 2.1 illustrates using System.out.println() to display the results of an expression within the statements of a complete program.

PROGRAM 2.1

```
public class ShowOperations
{
  public static void main(String[] args)
  {
    System.out.println("15.0 plus 2.0 equals " + (15.0 + 2.0) +'\n'
                    + "15.0 minus 2.0 equals " + (15.0 - 2.0) + '\n'
                    + "15.0 times 2.0 equals " + (15.0 * 2.0) + '\n'
                    + "15.0 divided by 2.0 equals " + (15.0 / 2.0) );
  }
}
```

[6]The Java specification, at the time of this writing, could be obtained at www.javasoft.com/docs/books/jls/index.html.

The output of Program 2.1 is:

```
15.0 plus 2.0 equals 17.0
15.0 minus 2.0 equals 13.0
15.0 times 2.0 equals 30.0
15.0 divided by 2.0 equals 7.5
```

In reviewing the display produced by Program 2.1, notice that only one string is ultimately passed as an argument to the `println()` method. This string is constructed by the concatenation of eleven items, four of which are the values computed from arithmetic expressions and three of which are newline escape sequences.

It is worth noting that the arithmetic operations of addition, subtraction, multiplication, and division are implemented differently for integer and floating-point values. Specifically, whether an integer or floating-point arithmetic operation is performed depends on what types of operands (integer or floating-point) are in the arithmetic expression. In this sense, the arithmetic operators are considered overloaded. More formally, an **overloaded operator** is a symbol that represents more than one operation and whose execution depends on the types of operands encountered. Although the overloaded nature of the arithmetic operators is rather simple, we will encounter the concept of overloading many more times in our journey through Java.

Integer Division

The division of two integers can produce rather strange results for the unwary. For example, the integer expression 15/2, which is the division of the integer 15 by the integer 2, will yield an integer result (from rule 4). Since integers cannot contain a fractional part, a result such as 7.5 cannot be obtained. In Java, the fractional part of the result obtained when dividing two integers is dropped (truncated). Thus, the value of 15/2 is 7, the value of 9/4 is 2, and the value of 17/5 is 3.

There are times we would like to retain the remainder of an integer division. To do this, Java provides a nonoverloaded arithmetic operator that is only implemented for integers. This operator, called both the remainder and modulus operator (the terms are synonyms), has the symbol % and captures the remainder when two integers are divided. For example,

9 % 4 is 1   (i.e., the remainder when 9 is divided by 4 is 1)
17 % 3 is 2   (i.e., the remainder when 17 is divided by 3 is 2)
14 % 2 is 0   (i.e., the remainder when 14 is divided by 2 is 0)

Negation

Besides the binary operators for addition, subtraction, multiplication, and division, Java also provides unary operators. A **unary operator** is one that operates on a single operand. One of these unary operators uses the same symbol as binary subtraction (−). The minus sign in front of a single numerical operand negates (reverses the sign of) the number.

Table 2.6 summarizes the six arithmetic operations we have described so far and lists the data type of the result produced by each operator based on the data type of the operands involved.

TABLE 2.6   *Summary of Arithmetic Operators*

Operation	Operator	Type	Operand	Result
Addition	+	Binary	Both are integers	Integer
			One operand is not an integer	Floating-point
Subtraction	−	Binary	Both are integers	Integer
			One operand is not an integer	Floating-point
Multiplication	*	Binary	Both are integers	Integer
			One operand is not an integer	Floating-point
Division	/	Binary	Both are integers	Integer
			One operand is not an integer	Floating-point
Remainder	%	Binary	Both are integers	Integer
Negation	−	Unary	Integer	Integer
			Floating-point	Floating-point

Operator Precedence and Associativity

Besides such simple expressions as 5 + 12 and .08 * 26.2, we frequently need to create more complex arithmetic expressions. Java, like most other programming languages, requires that certain rules be followed when writing expressions containing more than one arithmetic operator. These rules are:

1. Two binary arithmetic operator symbols must never be placed side by side. For example, 5 * %6 is invalid because the two operators * and % are placed next to each other.

2. Parentheses may be used to form groupings, and all expressions enclosed within parentheses are evaluated first. This permits parentheses to alter the evaluation to any desired order. For example, in the expression (6 + 4) / (2 + 3), the 6 + 4 and 2 + 3 are evaluated first to yield 10 / 5. The 10 / 5 is then evaluated to yield 2.

3. Sets of parentheses may also be enclosed by other parentheses. For example, the expression (2 * (3 + 7)) / 5 is valid and evaluates to 4. When parentheses are included within parentheses, the expressions in the innermost parentheses are always evaluated first. The evaluation continues from innermost to outermost parentheses until the expressions in all parentheses have been evaluated. The number of closing parentheses,), must always equal the number of opening parentheses, (, so that there are no unpaired sets.

4. Parentheses cannot be used to indicate multiplication. The multiplication operator, *, must be used. For example, the expression (3 + 4)(5 + 1) is invalid. The correct expression is (3 + 4) * (5 + 1).

Parentheses should specify logical groupings of operands and indicate clearly, to both the computer and programmers, the intended order of arithmetic operations. Although expressions within parentheses are always evaluated first, expressions containing multiple operators, both within and without parentheses, are evaluated by the priority, or **precedence**, of the operators, which is as follows:

5. All negations are done first.
6. Multiplication, division, and modulus operations are computed first. Expressions containing more than one multiplication, division, or modulus operator are evaluated from left to right as each operator is encountered. For example, in the expres-

TABLE 2.7 Operator Precedence and Associativity

Operator	Associativity
unary $-$	right to left
$*$ / $\%$	left to right
$+$ $-$	left to right

sion 35 / 7 % 3 * 4, the operations are all of the same priority, so the operations will be performed from left to right as each operator is encountered. Thus, the division is done first, yielding the expression 5 % 3 * 4. The modulus operation is done next, yielding a result of 2. And finally, the value of 2 * 4 is computed to yield 8.

7. Addition and subtraction are computed last. Expressions containing more than one addition or subtraction are evaluated from left to right as each operator is encountered.

Table 2.6 lists both the precedence and associativity of the operators considered in this section. As you have seen, the precedence of an operator establishes its priority relative to all other operators. Operators at the top of Table 2.6 have a higher priority than operators at the bottom of the table. In expressions with multiple operators of different precedence, the operator with the higher precedence is used before an operator with lower precedence. For example, in the expression 6 + 4 / 2 + 3, since the division operator has a higher precedence than addition (rule 6), the division is done first, yielding an intermediate result of 6 + 2 + 3. The additions are then performed, left to right, to yield a final result of 11. This ordering of computations, in the cases of the operators listed in the last two groups of Table 2.7, from left to right, is referred to as the **associativity** of the operator. Notice that the associativity of the negation operator is from right to left.

Finally, let us use either Table 2.7 or the foregoing rules to evaluate an expression containing operators of different precedence, such as 8 + 5 * 7 % 2 * 4. Because the multiplication and modulus operators have a higher precedence than the addition operator, these two operations are evaluated first (rule 6), using their left-to-right associativity, before the addition is evaluated (rule 7). Thus, the complete expression is evaluated as:

```
8 +   5 * 7 % 2 * 4 =
   8 + 35 % 2 * 4 =
      8 +  1 * 4 =
         8 + 4 = 12
```

String Concatenation

Although there are many available operations for manipulating strings, most of these operations are implemented as methods. The reason is that a string is not a primitive data type in Java but a reference type, which is defined in a class named String. One operation, however, uses the same operator symbol as for numerical addition, the + symbol.

For string data, this symbol joins two or more strings into a single string. Formally, this operation is referred to as **string concatenation**. Although string concatenation is not an arithmetic operation, it is the only operation that directly manipulates string data in a similar fashion as numerical data. For example, the expression

```
"Hot" + " Dog"
```

concatenates the two individual strings `"Hot"` and `"Dog"` into the single string `"Hot Dog"`. Notice that the space between the two words was created by the space in front of the word `Dog`.

When used with string and numerical data in the same expression, the + symbol will cause the numerical data to be converted to a string before concatenation. For example, the expression `"The result is " + 5` is a concatenation operation that results in the string `"The result is 5"`.

A worthwhile observation is that the concatenation operator has the same precedence as the addition operator, which can sometimes yield initially surprising results. For example, the expression

```
"The result is " + 15.4 * 2
```

yields the string value

```
"The result is 30.8"
```

This occurs because the multiplication operator has a higher precedence than the addition operator, which means the multiplication is done first. Then the resulting value of 30.8 is converted to the string "30.8" and appended to the first string.

Now consider the expression `"The result is " + 15.4 + 2`. Here the addition is performed from left to right, which is dictated by the associativity of the addition operator. Because the addition of a string and a numerical value is a concatenation operation, the intermediate result is `"The result is 15.4" + 2`. Now the 2 is concatenated to the first string yielding `"The result is 15.42"`. To have the two numbers accurately added first, if this was the intention, the correct expression is `"The result is " + (15.4 + 2)`. In this expression, the parentheses are required to change the default order of evaluation and ensure that the numerical values are added before any concatenation is performed.

The general rule to be taken from this discussion is that to prevent any unexpected results, *always use parentheses when performing arithmetic operations in any expression that contains a string*. We will use this rule extensively in the next section when we begin to display the results of numerical calculations using the `print()`, `println()`, and `showMessage()` methods. This is because all of these methods require a string as the item that they display.

EXERCISES 2.1

1. Determine data types appropriate for the following data:
    a. the average of four speeds
    b. the number of transistors in a circuit
    c. the length of the Golden Gate Bridge
    d. the part numbers in a machine
    e. the distance from Brooklyn, N.Y., to Newark, N.J.
    f. the single character prefix that specifies circuit components
2. Convert the following numbers into standard decimal form:

    6.34e5   1.95162e2   8.395e1   2.95e−3   4.623e−4

3. Convert the following decimal numbers into exponential notation:

    126.   656.23   3426.95   4893.2   .321   .0123   .006789

4. **a.** Using Unicode, determine the number of bytes required to store the letters KINGSLEY.
    b. Show how the letters KINGSLEY would be stored inside a computer as a sequence of Unicode codes. That is, draw a figure similar to Figure 2.3 for the letters KINGSLEY.

5. **a.** Repeat Exercise 4a using the letters of your own last name.
    b. Repeat Exercise 4b using the letters of your own last name.

6. Following are correct algebraic expressions and incorrect Java expressions corresponding to them. Find the errors and write corrected Java expressions.

Algebra	*Java Expression*
a. $(2)(3) + (4)(5)$	$(2)(3) + (4)(5)$
b. $\dfrac{6 + 18}{2}$	$6 + 18 / 2$
c. $\dfrac{4.5}{12.2 - 3.1}$	$4.5 / 12.2 - 3.1$
d. $4.6(3.0 + 14.9)$	$4.6(3.0 + 14.9)$
e. $(12.1 + 18.9)(15.3 - 3.8)$	$(12.1 + 18.9)(15.3 - 3.8)$

7. Determine the value of the following integer expressions:

    a. $3 + 4 * 6$
    b. $3 * 4 / 6 + 6$
    c. $2 * 3 / 12 * 8 / 4$
    d. $10 * (1 + 7 * 3)$
    e. $20 - 2 / 6 + 3$

    f. $20 - 2 / (6 + 3)$
    g. $(20 - 2) / 6 + 3$
    h. $(20 - 2) / (6 + 3)$
    i. $50 \% 20$
    j. $(10 + 3) \% 4$

8. Determine the value of the following floating-point expressions:

    a. $3.0 + 4.0 * 6.0$
    b. $3.0 * 4.0 / 6.0 + 6.0$
    c. $2.0 * 3.0 / 12.0 * 8.0 / 4.0$
    d. $10.0 * (1.0 + 7.0 * 3.0)$

    e. $20.0 - 2.0 / 6.0 + 3.0$
    f. $20.0 - 2.0 / (6.0 + 3.0)$
    g. $(20.0 - 2.0) / 6.0 + 3.0$
    h. $(20.0 - 2.0) / (6.0 + 3.0)$

9. Evaluate the following expressions and list the data type of the result. In evaluating the expressions, be aware of the data types of all intermediate calculations.

    a. $10.0 + 15 / 2 + 4.3$
    b. $10.0 + 15.0 / 2 + 4.3$
    c. $3.0 * 4 / 6 + 6$
    d. $3 * 4.0 / 6 + 6$
    e. $20.0 - 2 / 6 + 3$

    f. $10 + 17 * 3 + 4$
    g. $10 + 17 / 3. + 4$
    h. $3.0 * 4 \% 6 + 6$
    i. $10 + 17 \% 3 + 4$

10. Assume that `distance` has the integer value 1, v has the integer value 50, n has the integer value 10, and t has the integer value 5. Evaluate the following expressions:

    a. $n / t + 3$
    b. $v / t + n - 10 * distance$
    c. $v - 3 * n + 4 * distance$
    d. $distance / 5$
    e. $18 / t$

    f. $-t * n$
    g. $-v / 20$
    h. $(v + n) / (t + distance)$
    i. $v + n / t + distance$

11. Repeat Exercise 10 assuming that distance has the value 1.0, v has the value 50.0, n has the value 10.0, and t has the value 5.0.

12. Since most computers use different amounts of storage for integer, floating-point, double-precision, and character values, discuss how a program might alert the computer to the amount of storage needed for the various data types in the program.

13. Enter and execute Program 2.1 on your computer.

14. Determine the output of the following program:

```
public class Test1
{
  // a program illustrating integer truncation
  public static void main(String[] args)
  {
    System.out.println("answer1 is the integer " +(9/4));
    System.out.println("answer2 is the integer " +(17/3));
  }
}
```

15. Determine the output of the following program:

```
public class Test2
{
  // a program illustrating the % operator
  public static void main(String[] args)
  {
    System.out.println("The remainder of 9 divided by 4 is " +(9 % 4));
    System.out.println("The remainder of 17 divided by 3 is " +(17 % 3));
  }
}
```

16. Write a Java program that displays the results of the expressions 3.0 * 5.0, 7.1 * 8.3 − 2.2, and 3.2 / (6.1 * 5). Calculate the value of these expressions manually to verify that the displayed values are correct.

17. Write a Java program that displays the results of the expressions 15 / 4, 15 % 4, and 5 * 3 − (6 * 4). Calculate the value of these expressions manually to verify that the displayed values are correct.

    Note: For the following exercise, the reader should have an understanding of basic computer storage concepts. Specifically, if you are unfamiliar with the concept of a byte, refer to Section 1.8 before doing the next exercise.

18. Although the total number of bytes varies from computer to computer, memory sizes of 65,536 to more than several million bytes are not uncommon. In computer language, the letter K represents the number 1,024, which is 2 raised to the 10th power, and M represents the number 1,048,576, which is 2 raised to the 20th power. Thus, a memory size of 640 K is really 640 times 1,024, or 655,360 bytes, and a memory size of 4 M is really 4 times 1,048,576, which is 4,194,304 bytes. Using this information, calculate the actual number of bytes in:

    a. a memory containing 8 M bytes

    b. a memory containing 16 M bytes

    c. a memory containing 32 M bytes

d. a memory containing 96 M bytes

e. a memory consisting of 8 M words, where each word consists of 2 bytes

f. a memory consisting of 16 M words, where each word consists of 4 bytes

g. a floppy disk that specifies 1.40 M bytes

2.2 VARIABLES AND DECLARATIONS

All integer, floating-point, and other values in a computer program are stored and retrieved from the computer's memory unit. Conceptually, individual locations in the memory unit are arranged like the rooms in a large hotel. Like hotel rooms, each memory location has a unique address ("room number"). Before high-level languages such as Java existed, memory locations were referenced by their addresses. For example, storing the integer values 45 and 12 in the memory locations 1652 and 2548 (Figure 2.4), respectively, required instructions equivalent to

> *Put 45 in location 1652*
> *Put 12 in location 2548*

To add the two numbers just stored and save the result in another memory location, for example at location 3000, we need a statement comparable to

> *Add the contents of location 1652*
> *to the contents of location 2548*
> *and store the result into location 3000*

Clearly, this method of storage and retrieval is cumbersome. In high-level languages such as Java, symbolic names replace actual memory addresses. For primitive type values, such as integers, real numbers, and individual characters, the symbolic names where the values are stored are called variables. A **variable** is a name given by the programmer that refers to computer storage locations. The term *variable* is used because the value stored in the variable can change, or vary. For each name that the programmer uses, the computer keeps track of the actual memory address corresponding to that name. In our hotel room analogy, this is equivalent to putting a name on the door of a room and referring to the room by this name, such as the BLUE room, rather than by the actual room number.

In Java, the selection of variable names is left to the programmer as long as the selection follows the rules for identifiers provided in Section 1.2. Thus, the rules for selecting variable names are identical to those for selecting class and method names. As with class and method names, variable names should be mnemonics that give some indication of the variable's use. For example, a good name for a variable used to store a value that is the total of some other values would be sum or `total`. Variable names that

FIGURE 2.4 Enough Storage for Two Integers

give no indication of the value stored, such as `goForIt`, `linda`, `bill`, and `duh`, should not be selected. As with method names, variable names can be typed in uppercase and lowercase letters.

Now assume that the first memory location illustrated in Figure 2.4, which has address 1652, is given the name `num1`. Also assume that memory location 2548 is given the variable name `num2`, and memory location 3000 is given the variable name `total`, as illustrated in Figure 2.5.

FIGURE 2.5 Naming Storage Locations

Using these variable names, the operation of storing 45 in location 1652, storing 12 in location 2548, and adding the contents of these two locations is accomplished by the Java statements

```
num1 = 45;
num2 = 12;
total = num1 + num2;
```

Each of these three statements is called an **assignment statement** because it tells the computer to assign (store) a value into a variable. Assignment statements always have an equal, =, sign and one variable name immediately to the left of this sign. The value to the right of the equal sign is determined first, and this value is assigned to the variable to the left of the equal sign. The blank spaces in the assignment statements are inserted for readability. We will have much more to say about assignment statements in the next chapter, but for now we can use them to store values in variables.

A variable name is useful because it frees the programmer from concern over where data are physically stored inside the computer. We simply use the variable name and let the compiler worry about where in memory the data are actually stored. Before storing a value into a variable, however, Java requires that we clearly declare the type of data to be stored in it. We must tell the compiler, in advance, the names of the variables that will be used for characters, the names that will be used for integers, and the names that will be used to store the other Java data types.

Declaration Statements

Naming a variable and specifying the data type that can be stored in it are accomplished using **declaration statements**. A declaration statement has the general form:

dataType variableName`;`

where *dataType* designates a valid Java data type and *variableName* is a user-selected variable name. Variables that hold integer values are declared using the keyword int to specify the data type and have the form:

```
int variableName;
```

Thus, the declaration statement

```
int sum;
```

declares sum as the name of a variable capable of storing an integer value.

In addition to the reserved word int to specify an integer, the reserved word long specifies a long integer. For example, the statement

```
long datenum;
```

declares datenum as a variable that will store a long integer. Additionally, the keywords short and byte specify the remaining two integer types.

Variables that hold single-precision floating-point values are declared using the keyword float, whereas variables that hold double-precision values are declared using the keyword double. For example, the statement

```
float firstnum;
```

declares firstnum as a variable that can store a floating-point number. Similarly, the statement

```
double secnum;
```

declares that the variable secnum stores a double-precision number.

Although declaration statements may be placed anywhere within a method, declarations are typically grouped together and placed immediately after the method's opening brace or are placed at the point where the variable is first used. In all cases, however, a variable must be declared before it can be used, and declaration statements must end with a semicolon. If the declaration statements are placed after the opening method brace, a simple main() method containing declaration statements would have the general form

```
import statements;
public class ClassName
{
  public static void main(String[] args)
  {
    declaration statements;

    other statements;
  }
}
```

Program 2.2 illustrates this form in declaring and using four double-precision variables, with the `System.out.println()` method displaying the contents of one of the variables.

PROGRAM 2.2

```
public class ShowDeclarations
{
  public static void main(String[] args)
  {
    double grade1;  // declare grade1 as a double variable
    double grade2;  // declare grade2 as a double variable
    double total;   // declare total as a double variable
    double average; // declare average as a double variable

    grade1 = 85.5;
    grade2 = 97.0;
    total = grade1 + grade2;
    average = total/2.0;   // divide the total by 2.0
    System.out.println("The average grade is " + average);
  }
}
```

The placement of the declaration statements in Program 2.2 is straightforward, although you will shortly see that the four individual declarations can be combined into a single declaration. When Program 2.2 is run, the following output is displayed:

`The average grade is 91.25`

One comment with respect to the `println()` method call in Program 2.2 should be mentioned. When a variable name is one of the arguments passed to a method, as it is to `println()` in Program 2.2, the method receives only a copy of the value stored in the variable. It does not receive the variable's name. When the program sees a variable name in the method's parentheses, it first goes to the variable and retrieves the value stored. This value is then passed to the method. Thus, when a variable is included in the `println()`argument list, `println()` receives the value stored in the variable, converts it to a string, and then displays the value. Internally, `println()` does not know where the value it receives came from or the variable name under which the value was stored.

Although this procedure for passing data into a method may seem surprising to you, it is a safety procedure for ensuring that a called method does not have access to the original variable. This guarantees that the called function cannot inadvertently change data in a variable declared outside itself. We will have more to say about this in Chapter 6, when we examine and begin writing our own called methods.

Just as integer and real (single- and double-precision) variables must be declared before they can be used, a variable used to store a single character must also be declared. Character variables are declared with the reserved word `char`. For example, the declaration

```
char ch;
```

declares ch to be a character variable. Program 2.3 illustrates this declaration and the use
of System.out.println() to display the value stored in a character variable.

PROGRAM 2.3

```
public class ShowChar
{
  public static void main(String[] args)
  {
    char ch;       // this declares a character variable

    ch = 'a';      // store the letter a into ch
    System.out.println("The character stored in ch is " + ch);
    ch = 'm';      // now store the letter m into ch
    System.out.println("The character now stored in ch is "+ ch);
  }
}
```

When Program 2.3 is run, the output is:

```
The character stored in ch is a
The character now stored in ch is m
```

Notice in Program 2.3 that the first letter stored in the variable ch is a and the second letter stored is m. Because a variable can store only one value at a time, the assignment of m to the variable automatically causes a to be overwritten.

Multiple Declarations

Variables with the same data type can always be grouped together and declared using a
single declaration statement. The common form of such a declaration is:

```
dataType variable list;
```

For example, the four separate declarations in Program 2.2,

```
double grade1;
double grade2;
double total;
double average;
```

can be replaced by the single declaration statement

```
double grade1, grade2, total, average;
```

Similarly, the two character declarations,

```
char ch;
char key;
```

can be replaced by the single declaration statement

```
char ch, key;
```

Note that declaring multiple variables in a single declaration requires that the data type of the variables be given only once, that all the variables names be separated by commas, and that only one semicolon be used to terminate the declaration. The space after each comma is inserted for readability and is not required.

Declaration statements can also store an initial value into declared variables. For example, the declaration statement

```
int num1 = 15;
```

both declares the variable num1 as an integer variable and sets the value of 15 into the variable. When a declaration statement stores a value into a variable, the variable is said to be **initialized**. Thus, in this example, it is correct to say that the variable num1 has been initialized to 15. Similarly, the declaration statements

```
double grade1 = 87.0;
double grade2 = 93.5;
double total;
```

declare three double-precision variables and initialize two of them.

When initializing a single-precision variable, it is important to add either the suffix f or F to the initializing value. Failure to do so results in a compiler error and notification that an incompatible type declaration has been made. The reason is that the default for fractional numbers is double-precision, and the compiler is trying to alert you to the fact that you may be losing precision by attempting to store a double-precision value into a single-precision variable. Thus, the initialization

```
float number = 26.3; // THIS IS AN INVALID INITIALIZATION
```

is invalid, and a correct initialization is

```
float number = 26.3f; // Valid, because of the f suffix
```

When initializations are used, good programming practice dictates that each initialized variable be declared on a line by itself. Literals, expressions using only literals, such as 87.0 + 12 − 2, and expressions using literals and previously initialized variables can all be initializers within a method. For example, Program 2.2 with declaration initialization becomes Program 2.4.

PROGRAM 2.4

```
public class Initializations
{
  public static void main(String[] args)
  {
    double grade1 = 85.5;
    double grade2 = 97.0;
    double total, average;

    total = grade1 + grade2;
    average = total/2.0;   // divide the total by 2.0
    System.out.println("The average grade is " + average);
  }
}
```

Notice the blank line after the last declaration statement. Inserting a blank line after the variable declarations placed at the top of a method body is a good programming practice. It improves both a program's appearance and readability.

String Declarations

All of the declarations discussed so far have been for Java's primitive data types. Declarations can also be made for reference data types, a number of which are presented in detail starting in Chapter 7. For now, however, we will restrict ourselves to the String data type, which will serve as a general introduction to reference types.

Figure 2.6 illustrates how a value is stored in a primitive data type variable. Notice that the variable's name is effectively a mnemonic stand-in for an actual memory address and that the value is stored directly at this address.

The storage illustrated in Figure 2.6 is very different for a reference variable, an example of which is provided by Figure 2.7. Here the variable contains a memory address, and the actual string value is stored at this address. Another way of looking at this is that the variable references the location in memory where the actual value is stored. The variable is referred to as a reference variable, and the actual stored value is referred to as an object.

Assuming that the reference variable named message in Figure 2.7 has been declared as a String, a statement such as System.out.println(message); causes the program first to obtain the memory address stored in message and then to retrieve the string value stored at that address. The process of first obtaining the address from the

price

FIGURE 2.6   An Example of a Value Stored in a Primitive Data Type Variable

FIGURE 2.7   An Example of a Value Stored in a Reference Variable

reference variable, going to that address, and retrieving the correct number of bytes for the object is done automatically and is referred to as **automatic dereferencing**. For strings, the length of the string is stored with the string.

All reference types, including the String type, are derived from classes and are referred to as **objects**. The term **reference variable**, as you have seen, is applied to the identifier that stores the address of an object.

Except for String objects, which can be declared in a number of ways, most objects are declared and initialized using a two-step process that is quite different from that used in declaring primitive data type variables. We first present this general two-step declaration and then show a simpler procedure that works with String objects.

The first step in declaring a reference object is to declare a reference variable, which is identical to declaring a primitive variable. For example, the statement

```
String message;
```

declares a reference variable named `message` that will access an object of type `String`. Figure 2.8a illustrates the results produced by this declaration, which shows that a memory storage area has been reserved for the reference variable named `message` and that the value placed in this reference variable is an address designated as `null`. This `null` value means that the reference variable does not currently refer to a valid object.

The second step is to create a String object that the reference variable points to. This is done with a statement such as:

```
message = new String("Hello World!");
```

The keyword `new` in this statement is an operator that creates storage for an object of the type specified. This is done by allocating sufficient memory for the type of object specified, in this case the String value `Hello World!`. Because this allocation is done dynamically (i.e., on the fly) when the program executes, the `new` operator is referred to as the **dynamic memory allocation** operator. Also, because the process creates a specific instance of an object, the process itself is referred to as **instantiating an object**. Another way of saying this is that the dynamic memory allocation operator instantiates (i.e., creates) an object. Our particular instantiation results in the allocation of memory shown in Figure 2.8b. Notice that the string value has been placed in memory and that the location of this memory, which is an address, has been placed into the reference variable named `message`. This process is quite different from the declaration and initialization of a primitive variable, where a value is placed directly in the variable.

message

null

FIGURE 2.8A Creating a Reference Variable   **FIGURE 2.8B** Instantiating an Object

In practice, the two steps of first declaring a reference variable and then instantiating an object as we did with the two statements

```
String message;
message = new String("Hello World!");
```

can be combined into a single statement as follows:

```
String message = new String("Hello World!");
```

In your programming experience, you will find both ways of creating reference variables and objects. There are two common exceptions that do not require the new operator to actually create an object. One of these exceptions is that string literals can be created without using the new operator (the other is the declaration of arrays, which is presented in Section 8.1). For example, the declaration

```
String message = "Hello World!";
```

automatically creates a reference variable and then instantiates (creates) a String object without explicitly using the new operator. It is worthwhile to become aware, however, that this statement produces the same result as shown in Figure 2.8b, and that the string value *is not* stored in message. Rather, message is a true reference variable. Thus, it contains the first memory address of where the string value is actually stored. Because it is both simple and comparable to declarations of primitive variables, we will generally use this form of String declaration and initialization.

It should be noted that because strings are a reference data type and Java does not provide built-in operations for these types, single operator symbols and their respective operations (except for the concatenation and assignment operator) *are not* provided for strings. Extensive collections of string-handling methods, however, are available to perform string comparisons and other very useful string operations. These methods are part of the String class and are described in detail in Chapter 7.

Cleansing Memory

Although a reference variable can only contain location information for a single object, this location information can be changed. That is, the same reference variable can, in the course of a program, be used to locate many objects. For example, as shown in Figure

FIGURE 2.9   The Location of Different Strings Using the Same Reference Variable

2.9, the reference variable `message` has been used to locate three different String objects. Unfortunately, the only active object in Figure 2.9 is the last one. Because the location information for the first two objects no longer exists, the objects now take up memory space that can no longer be referenced. If too many objects are created and allowed to exist with no means of accessing them or retrieving the wasted storage they take up, the system will run out of memory and come to a halt. Formally, this is called the **memory leak problem**. Its solution is handled rather efficiently in Java and represents a major improvement in using references that was not included in Java's immediate predecessor, C++.

As a specific example of how the situation in Figure 2.9 can occur, consider Program 2.5.

PROGRAM 2.5

```
public class NoMemoryLeak
{
  public static void main(String[] args)
  {
    String message = "Hello World!";

    System.out.println(message);
    message = "This is a new and longer message";
    System.out.println(message);
    message = "shorter output";
    System.out.println(message);
  }
}
```

The output displayed by Program 2.5 is:

```
Hello World!
This is a new and longer message
shorter output
```

Let's see how this output is produced and the resulting memory allocations created by Program 2.5. Initially, the declaration statement within `main()`

```
String message = "Hello World!";
```

creates a String reference variable named message and makes this variable point to a String object containing the characters Hello World! (see Figure 2.9). When used as an argument to the println() method, the location information in message automatically locates and displays the correct string value, which produces the first line displayed by the program.[7]

Having created the message reference variable and displayed the referenced String, the location information within message is then changed by the statement

```
message = "This is a new and longer message";
```

What happens here is that the new string value is first stored in memory (along with an indication of its length), its address is placed into message, and it is internally marked as having one reference to it. The first string object temporarily remains in memory, but its internal reference count is decreased by one, which means that it now has zero references to it. At periodic times, the Java Virtual Machine automatically activates its memory cleansing program (referred to as "garbage collection"). When the garbage collection reaches the first string object and sees that it has no references pointing to it, it marks this memory as available for use. In this same manner, the second object's memory will also be reclaimed when it is no longer referenced.

Although Figure 2.9 shows three distinct object storage areas, it is possible that the memory locations used by the third string are the same as some of those that store the first string. This can happen if the garbage collection occurs after the creation of the second string object and before the creation of the third.

In practice, Java's automatic memory cleansing operation is extremely important for programs that run continuously, which is typical of many operating systems and commercial programs. It is also a safety mechanism to ensure that a single run of a program does not crash the system because it has inadvertently created too many objects that are no longer referenced. Memory leak is not a problem for a program that completes its execution because the memory allocated to such programs is automatically recaptured by the operating system independently of Java.

Specifying Storage Allocation

The declaration statements we have introduced perform two distinct tasks. From a programmer's perspective, declaration statements always provide a list of all variables and their data types. In this same role, variable declarations help to control an otherwise common and troublesome error caused by the misspelling of a variable's name within a program. For example, assume that a variable named distance is declared and initialized using the statement

```
int distance = 26;
```

Now assume that this variable is inadvertently misspelled in the statement

```
mpg = distnce / gallons;
```

---

[7]The automatic usage of a reference variable's location information to locate the related object is formally referred to as **automatic dereferencing**.

In languages that do not require variable declarations, the program would treat `distnce` as a new variable and either assign an initial value of zero to the variable or use whatever value happens to be in the variable's storage area. In either case, a value is calculated and assigned to `mpg`, and finding the error or even knowing that an error occurred could be extremely troublesome. Such errors are impossible in Java because the compiler flags `distnce` as an undeclared variable. The compiler cannot, of course, detect when one declared variable is typed in place of another declared variable.

In addition to their first role, which is a real benefit to the programmer, declaration statements also perform a distinct role needed by the compiler. Since each data type has its own storage requirements, the compiler can allocate sufficient storage for a variable only after knowing the variable's data type. When variable declarations are used to reserve sufficient physical memory storage for each variable, as they do within a method, they are also called **definition statements**.

Figure 2.10 illustrates the series of operations set in motion by declaration statements for a number of primitive data types. The figure shows that declaration statements effectively mark the first byte of each set of reserved bytes with a name. This name is, of course, the variable's name and is used by the computer to correctly locate the starting point of each variable's reserved memory area.

Within a program, after a primitive variable has been declared, it is typically used by a programmer to refer to the contents of the variable (i.e., the variable's value). Where in memory this value is stored is generally of no concern to the programmer. The compiler, however, must be concerned with where each value is stored and with correctly locating each variable. In this task, the computer uses the variable name to locate the first byte of storage previously allocated to the variable. Knowing the variable's data type then

FIGURE 2.10A   Defining the Integer Variable Named `total`

FIGURE 2.10B   Defining the Floating-point Variable Named `firstNumber`

FIGURE 2.10C Defining the Double-precision Variable Named `secondNumber`

FIGURE 2.10D Defining the Character Variable Named `key`

allows the compiler to store or retrieve the correct number of bytes. In the case of a reference variable, the same operation initially applies. Because each reference variable is of the same size, the location information in a reference variable can be accessed in the same manner as the value in a primitive data type variable.

Because a reference data type value, such as a string literal, can vary in length, actual storage for the object itself can only be allocated when a new object is instantiated. Then, when the object is actually instantiated, its location information can be loaded into a previously defined reference variable.

EXERCISES 2.2

1. Rewrite Program 2.2 so that its output is displayed in a dialog box.
2. Rewrite Program 2.3 so that each line of its output is displayed in a dialog box.
3. State whether the following variable names are valid or not. If they are invalid, state the reason.

prod_a	c1234	abcd	_c3	12345
newamp	watts	$total	new$a1	a1b2c3d4
9ab6	sum.of	average	volts1	finvolt

4. State whether the following variable names are valid or not. If they are invalid, state the reason. Also indicate which of the valid variable names should not be used because they convey no information about the variable.

current	a243	r2d2	first_num	cc_a1
harry	sue	c3p0	total	sum
maximum	okay	a	awesome	goforit
3sum	for	tot.a1	c$five	netpower

5. a. Write a declaration statement to declare that the variable `count` will be used to store an integer.
    b. Write a declaration statement to declare that the variable `volt` will be used to store a floating-point number.
    c. Write a declaration statement to declare that the variable `power` will be used to store a double-precision number.
    d. Write a declaration statement to declare that the variable `keyChar` will be used to store a character.

6. Write declaration statements for the following variables.
    a. `num1`, `num2`, and `num3` used to store integer numbers
    b. `amps1`, `amps2`, `amps3`, and `amps4` used to store floating-point numbers
    c. `volts1`, `volts2`, and `volts3` used to store double-precision numbers
    d. `codeOne`, `codeTwo`, `codeThree`, `codeFour`, and `codeFive` used to store character types

7. Write declaration statements for the following variables.
    a. `firstnum` and `secnum` used to store integers
    b. `speed`, `acceleration`, and `distance` used to store floating-point numbers
    c. `thrust` used to store a double-precision number

8. Rewrite each of these declaration statements as three individual declarations.
    a. `int month, day = 30, year;`
    b. `double hours, volt, power = 15.62;`
    c. `float price, amount, taxes;`
    d. `char inKey, ch, choice = 'f';`

9. a. Determine what each statement causes to happen in the following program:

```java
public class Test
{
  public static void main(String[] args)
  {
    int num1, num2, total;

    num1 = 25;
    num2 = 30;
    total = num1 + num2;
    System.out.println("The total of " + num1
                       + " and " + num2 + " is " + total);

  }
}
```

    b. What output is printed when the program in Exercise 9a is run?

10. Write a Java program that stores the sum of the integer numbers 12 and 33 in a variable named `sum`. Have your program display the value stored in `sum`.

11. Write a Java program that stores the integer value 16 in the variable `length` and the integer value 18 in the variable `width`. Have your program calculate the value assigned to the variable `perimeter` using the assignment statement

    `perimeter = 2 * length + 2 * width;`

    and display the value stored in the variable `perimeter`. Make sure to declare all the variables as integers at the beginning of the `main()` method.

12. Write a Java program that stores the integer value 16 in the variable num1 and the integer value 18 in the variable num2. (Make sure to declare the variables as integers.) Have your program calculate the total of these numbers and their average. Store the total in an integer variable named total and the average in an integer variable named average. (Use the statement average = total/2; to calculate the average.) Display the total and average either in a dialog box or using the println() method.

13. Repeat Exercise 12, but store the number 15 in num1 instead of 16. With a pencil, write down the average of num1 and num2. What do you think your program will store in the integer variable that you used for the average of these two numbers? How can you ensure that the correct answer will be printed for the average?

14. Write a Java program that stores the number 105.62 in the double-precision variable firstnum, 89.352 in the double-precision variable secnum, and 98.67 in the double-precision variable thirdnum. (Make sure to declare the variables as doubles.) Have your program calculate the total of the three numbers and their average. The total should be stored in the variable total and the average in the variable average. (Use the statement average = total/3.0; to calculate the average.) Display the total and average either in a dialog box or using the println() method.

15. Every variable has at least two items associated with it. What are these two items?

16. a. A statement used to clarify the relationship between squares and rectangles is: All squares are rectangles, but not all rectangles are squares. Write a similar statement that describes the relationship between definition and declaration statements.

    b. Why must a variable be defined before any other Java statement that uses the variable?

Note for Exercises 17 through 19: Remember that a character requires 2 bytes of storage, an integer 4 bytes, a floating-point number 4 bytes, a double-precision number 8 bytes and assume that variables are assigned storage in the order they are declared (review Section 1.9 if you are unfamiliar with the concept of a byte).

17. a. Refer to Figure 2.11 and assume that the variable named rate is assigned storage starting at the byte having memory address 160. Determine the addresses corresponding to each variable declared in the following statements. Also fill in the appropriate bytes with the initialization data included in the declaration statements (use letters for the characters, not the Unicode codes that would actually be stored).

```
float rate;
char ch1 = 'w', ch2 = 'o', ch3 = 'w', ch4 = '!';
double taxes;
int num, count = 0;
```

    b. Repeat Exercise 17a but substitute the actual byte patterns that a computer using the Unicode code would use to store the characters in the variables ch1, ch2, ch3, and ch4. (*Tip:* Use Table 2.3.)

18. a. Refer to Figure 2.11 and assume that the variable named cn1 is assigned storage starting at the byte having memory address 160. Determine the addresses

Addresses

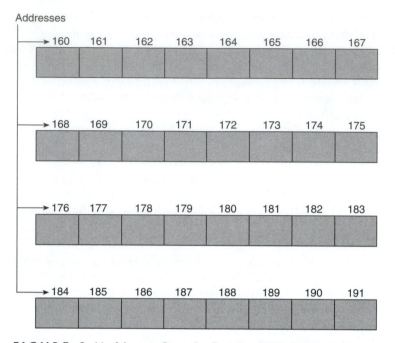

FIGURE 2.11   Memory Bytes for Exercises 17, 18, and 19

corresponding to each variable declared in the following statements. Also fill in the appropriate bytes with the initialization data included in the declaration statements (use letters for the characters, not the computer codes that would actually be stored).

```
char cn1 = 'a', cn2 = ' ', cn3 = 'b', cn4 = 'u', cn5 = 'n';
char cn6 = 'c', cn7 = 'h', key = '\\', sch = '\'', inc = 'o';
char inc1 = 'f';
```

b. Repeat Exercise 18a but substitute the actual byte patterns that a computer using the Unicode code would use to store the characters in each of the declared variables. (*Tip:* Use Table 2.3.)

19. Refer to Figure 2.11 and assume that the variable named miles is assigned to storage starting at the byte having memory address 160. Determine the addresses corresponding to each variable declared in the following statements:

```
float miles;
int count, num;
double dist, temp;
```

2.3 THE final QUALIFIER

Quite frequently, specific values within a program have a more general meaning that is recognized outside the context of the program. Examples of these types of values include 3.1416, which is π accurate to four decimal places; 32.2 ft/sec², which is the gravitational constant; and 2.71828, which is Euler's number accurate to five decimal places. The meaning of certain other constants appearing in a program are defined strictly within the context of the application being programmed. For example, in a program to determine bank interest charges, the interest rate typically appears in a number of different places throughout the program. Similarly, in a program to calculate taxes, the tax rate might appear in many individual instructions. Numbers such as these are referred to by programmers as **magic numbers**. By themselves, the numbers are ordinary, but in the context of a particular application, they have a special ("magical") meaning.

Frequently, the same magic number appears repeatedly within the same program. This recurrence of the same constant throughout a program is a potential source of error should the constant need to be changed. For example, if either the interest rate or tax rate changes, as rates are prone to do, the programmer has the cumbersome task of changing the value everywhere it appears in the program. Multiple changes, however, are subject to error; if just one rate value is overlooked and not changed, the result obtained when the program is run will be incorrect and the source of the error difficult to locate.

To avoid the problem of having a magic number spread throughout a program in many places and to permit clear identification of more universal constants, such as π, Java allows the programmer to give these constants their own symbolic names. Then the symbolic name replaces the number throughout the program. If the number ever has to be changed, the change need only be made once at the point where the symbolic name is equated to the actual number value. Equating numbers to symbolic names is accomplished using the `final` declaration qualifier. The `final` qualifier specifies that the declared identifier can only be read after it is initialized; it cannot be changed. Three examples of this qualifier are:

```
final double PI = 3.1416;
final float DENSITY = 0.238f;
final int MAXNUM = 100;
```

The first declaration statement creates the double-precision constant named PI and initializes it to 3.1416. The second declaration statement creates a floating-point constant named DENSITY and initializes it with the value 0.238f. Note that the f is required. Without this suffix, we would be attempting to initialize a float variable with a double-precision value, which results in a compiler error message. Finally, the third declaration creates an integer constant named MAXNUM and initializes it with the value 100.

Once a `final` identifier is created and initialized, *the value stored in it cannot be changed*. Thus, for all practical purposes, the name of the constant and its value are linked together for the duration of the program that declares them. An attempt to assign another value to a `final` variable results in a compiler error message equivalent to `Can't assign a value to a final variable:`.

Although we have typed the `final` identifiers in uppercase letters, lowercase letters could have been used. It is common in Java, however, to use uppercase letters for `final` identifiers to make them easy to identify. Then, whenever a programmer sees uppercase letters in a program, he or she knows the value of the constant cannot be changed within the program.

Once declared, a `final` identifier can be used in any Java statement in place of the number it represents. For example, the assignment statements

```
circum = 2 * PI * radius;
weight = DENSITY * volume;
```

are both valid. These statements must, of course, appear after the declarations for all their variables and constants. Because a `final` declaration effectively equates a constant value to an identifier, and the identifier can directly replace its initializing constant, these identifiers are commonly referred to as **symbolic constants** or **named constants**. We shall .use these terms interchangeably.

Placement of Statements

At this stage, we have introduced a variety of statement types. The general rule in Java for statement placement is that a variable or named constant must be declared before it can be used. Although this rule permits declaration statements to be placed throughout a program, doing so can result in a very poor program structure. As a general rule, with minor exceptions that will be noted throughout the text, the following statement ordering should be used:

```
public static void main (String[] args)
{
  named constants
  variable and object declarations

  other Java statements
}
```

Placing the named constant within `main()` restricts its usage to this method. If the named constant is placed before the `main()` method, it can be used in any and all methods added to the program. In this case, however, which is presented in detail in Chapter 6, the named constant should be declared using the qualifiers `public static final` rather than just `final`. Notice that these are the same qualifiers used for the `main()` method because the constant is now a class variable rather than a method variable.[8] Two such named constants, which are provided by the `java.lang.Math` class are

```
public static final double PI = 3.14159265358979323846;
public static final double E = 2.7182818284590452354;
```

These two named constants can be accessed as `Math.PI` and `Math.E` in your program. For example, the following statement displays the value of PI:

```
System.out.println("The value of PI is " + Math.PI);
```

Program 2.6 illustrates using symbolic constants to calculate the weight of a 12-inch-high steel cylinder having a radius of 3 inches. The density of the steel is 0.284 lb/inch.[3]

---

[8]The keyword `public` provides an access specification that makes the variable publicly available to all methods (whether the methods are in the class or not), whereas the keyword `static` creates a single class copy of the variable rather than reproduce the variable for each method that uses it.

PROGRAM 2.6

```java
import javax.swing.*;
public class ComputeWeight
{
  public static void main (String[] args)
  {
    final double PI = 3.1416;
    final double DENSITY = 0.284;

    double radius = 3;
    double height = 12;
    double volume, weight;
    String output;

    volume = PI * radius * radius * height;
    weight = DENSITY * volume;
    output = "For a steel cylinder of height " + height + " inches";
    output += " and radius " + radius + " inches,";
    output += "\nThe cylinder weighs " + weight + " pounds";

    JOptionPane.showMessageDialog(null,
            output, "Program 2.6",
            JOptionPane.INFORMATION_MESSAGE);

    System.exit(0);
  }
}
```

Figure 2.12 shows the output dialog displayed by Program 2.6.

FIGURE 2.12   A Sample Input for Program 2.6

In the next chapter, we will show how to format the output to display a programmer-specified number of digits after the decimal point instead of accepting the number of digits provided by the default for double-precision numerical values.

The advantage of the named constant PI in Program 2.6 is that it clearly identifies the value of 3.1416 in terms recognizable to most people. The advantage of the named constant DENSITY is that it permits a programmer to change the value of the density for another material without having to search through the program to see where the density is used. Of course, if many different materials are to be considered, the density should be changed from a named constant to a variable. A natural question arises, then, as to the difference between named constants and variables.

The value of a variable can be altered anywhere within a program. By its nature, a named constant is a constant value that must not be altered after it is defined. Naming a constant rather than assigning the value to a variable ensures that the value in the constant cannot be subsequently altered. Whenever a named constant appears in an instruction, it has the same effect as the constant it represents. Thus, DENSITY in Program 2.6 is simply another way of representing the number 0.284. Since DENSITY and the number 0.284 are equivalent, the value of DENSITY may not be subsequently changed within the program. Once DENSITY has been defined as a constant, an assignment statement such as

```
DENSITY = 0.156;
```

is meaningless and will result in the error message `Can't assign a value to a final variable: DENSITY`. This makes sense because `DENSITY` is only a stand-in for the value 0.284, and the preceding statement is equivalent to writing the invalid statement 0.284 = 0.156. In addition to using a `final` qualifier to name constants, as in Program 2.6, this statement can also be used to equate the value of an expression to a symbolic name. For example, the statement

```
final double DEGREESTORADIANS = 3.1416/180.0;
```

equates the value of the expression 3.1416/180.0 to the symbolic name DEGREESTO-RADIANS. The expression whose value is assigned to a final variable can also include other variables as long as each such variable has been initialized with a value.

Finally, any symbolic name can also be used in any subsequent statement that defines another named constant. For example, the following sequence of statements is valid:

```
final double PI = 3.1416;
final double DEGREESTORADIANS = PI / 180.0;
```

Because the constant 3.1416 has been equated to the symbolic name PI, this symbolic constant can now be used legitimately in any subsequent variable declaration, be the variable qualified with the keyword `final` or not.

EXERCISES 2.3

Determine the purpose of the methods in Exercises 1 through 3. Then rewrite each program using a symbolic constant for the appropriate literals and replace the `println()` method with a message dialog.

1.

```java
public static void main (String[] args)
{
  double radius, circum;

  radius = 6.2;
  circum = 2.0 * 3.1416 * radius;
  System.out.println("The circumference of the circle is " + circum);
}
```

2.

```java
public static void main (String[] args)
{
  float prime, amount, interest;

  prime = .08;        // prime interest rate
  amount = 2000;
  interest = prime * amount;
  System.out.println("The interest earned is " + interest);
}
```

3.

```java
public static void main (String[] args)
{
  double fahren, celsius;

  fahren = 98.6;
  celsius = (5.0/9.0) * (fahren - 32.0);
  System.out.println("The equivalent Celsius temperature is " + celsius);
}
```

4. Rewrite the following program so that the variable volts is changed to a named constant.

```java
public static void main (String[] args)
{
  double current, resistance, volts;

  volts = 12;
  resistance = 3000;

  current = volts/resistance;
  System.out.println("The current is " + current);
}
```

5. Modify Program 2.6 to handle any exceptions that can occur due to the user either providing an invalid numerical input or clicking the Cancel button.

2.4 DEVELOPING METHODS

No matter what field of work you choose or what your lifestyle may be, you will have to solve problems. Many of these, such as adding up the change in your pocket, can be solved quickly and easily. Others, such as riding a bicycle, require some practice but soon become automatic. Still others require considerable planning and forethought if the solution is to be appropriate and efficient. For example, constructing a cellular telephone network or creating an inventory management system for a department store are problems for which trial-and-error solutions could prove expensive and disastrous.

Creating a particular method is no different because a method is a solution developed to solve a particular problem. Thus, coding a method is almost the last step in a process of first determining what the method must accomplish and what steps the method will use to solve the assigned task. Each field of study has its own name for the systematic method used to solve problems by designing suitable solutions. In science and engineering, the approach is referred to as the **scientific method**, and in quantitative analysis, the approach is referred to as the **systems approach**.

One technique used by professional software developers for understanding the problem that is being solved and for creating an effective and appropriate method solution is called the **method development** procedure. This procedure consists of the four well-defined steps illustrated in Figure 2.13.

Step 1: Analyze the Problem

The analysis of a problem consists of extracting the complete input and output information required by the method. For this step, you must:

1. Determine and understand the desired output items that the method must produce
2. Determine the input items that the method must be provided with to produce the output

Together these two items are referred to as the method's input/output, or I/O for short. Only after a method's I/O has been determined is it possible to select an algorithm for transforming the inputs into the desired outputs, which can then be coded in Java to produce a working method. At this point, it is sometimes necessary and/or useful to perform a hand calculation to verify that the output can indeed be obtained from the inputs.

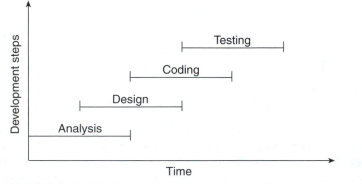

FIGURE 2.13 Steps in Developing a Method

Clearly, if there is a formula that relates the inputs to the output(s), this step can be omitted at this stage. If the required inputs are available and the desired output(s) can be produced, the problem is said to be clearly defined and can ultimately be programmed as a Java method.

Step 2: Develop a Solution

This step is frequently referred to as the design step, and we will use the terms **development** and **design** interchangeably. In this step, you must select the exact series of procedures—that is, the algorithm—for transforming the input items into the desired outputs. The algorithm must be refined as necessary so that it adequately defines all of the features that you want your method to have. If you haven't performed a hand calculation using the algorithm in the analysis step, you should do so here with specific input values.

Step 3: Code the Solution

This step, which is also referred to as writing the program and implementing the solution, consists of translating the chosen design solution into a valid method. If the analysis and solution steps have been correctly performed, the coding step becomes rather mechanical in nature. In a well-designed method, the statements making up the program will, however, conform to certain well-defined patterns or structures that have been defined in the solution step. These structures control how the program executes and consist of the following types:

1. Sequence
2. Selection
3. Iteration
4. Invocation

Sequence defines the order in which instructions are executed by the program. The specification of which instruction comes first, which comes second, and so on is essential if the program is to achieve a well-defined purpose.

Selection provides the capability to choose between different operations depending on the result of some condition. For example, the value of a number can be checked before a division is performed. If the number is not zero, it can be used as the denominator of a division operation; otherwise, the division will not be performed and the user will be issued a warning message.

Iteration, which is also referred to as looping and repetition, provides the ability for the same operation to be repeated based on the value of a condition. For example, grades might be repeatedly entered and added until a negative grade is entered. In this case, the entry of a negative grade is the condition that signifies the end of the repetitive input and addition of grades. At that point, an average for all the grades entered could be calculated.

Invocation involves invoking, or summoning, a set of statements as it is needed. For example, the computation of a person's net pay involves the tasks of obtaining pay rates and hours worked, calculating the net pay, and providing a report or check for the required amount. Each of these individual tasks would typically be coded as separate units that are called into execution, or invoked, as they are needed.

Step 4. Test and Correct the Solution

The purpose of testing is to verify that a program works correctly and actually fulfills its requirements. In theory, testing would reveal all existing program errors (in computer terminology, a program error is called a *bug*[9]). In practice, this would require checking all possible combinations of statement execution. Because of the time and effort required, this is usually an impossible goal except for extremely simple programs. (We illustrate why this is generally an impossible goal in Section 4.8.)

Because exhaustive testing is not feasible for most programs, different philosophies and methods of testing have evolved. At its most basic level, however, testing requires a conscious effort to ensure that a program works correctly and produces meaningful results. This means that careful thought must be given to what the test is meant to achieve and the data that will be used in the test. If testing reveals an error (bug), the process of debugging, which includes locating, correcting, and verifying the correction, can be initiated. It is important to realize that although testing may reveal the presence of an error, it does not necessarily indicate the absence of one. Thus, the fact that a test revealed one bug does not indicate that another one is not lurking somewhere else in the program.

To catch and correct errors in a program, it is important to develop a set of test data that determines whether the program gives correct answers. In fact, an accepted step in formal software development many times is to plan the test procedures and create meaningful test data before writing the code. This tends to help the person be more objective about what the program must do because it essentially circumvents any subconscious temptation after coding to choose test data that will not work. The procedures for testing a program should examine every possible situation under which the program will be used. The program should be tested with data in a reasonable range as well as at the limits and in areas where the program should tell the user that the data are invalid. Developing good test procedures and data for sophisticated problems can be more difficult than writing the program code itself.

Table 2.8 lists the relative amount of effort that is typically expended on each of these four development and design steps in large commercial programming projects. As this listing demonstrates, coding is not the major effort in this phase. Many new programmers have trouble because they spend the majority of their time writing a program without spending sufficient time understanding the problem or designing an appropriate solution. In this regard, it is worthwhile to remember the programming proverb: It is impossible to write a successful program for a problem or application that is not fully understood. A somewhat equivalent and equally valuable proverb is: The sooner you start coding a program, the longer it usually takes to complete.

To see how each of these steps can be implemented in practice, we now apply them to the following simple programming problem.

> *The electrical resistance of a metal wire in ohms is given by the formula* r = (ml)/a, *where m is the resistivity of the metal, l is the length of the wire in feet, and a is the cross-sectional area of the wire in circular mils. Using this information, write a Java program to calculate the resistance of a wire that is 125 feet long, has a cross-sectional area of 500 circular mils, and is copper. The resistivity of copper, m, is 10.4.*

[9]The derivation of this term is rather interesting. When a program stopped running on the Mark I at Harvard University in September 1945, Grace Hopper traced the malfunction to a dead insect that had gotten into the electrical circuits. She recorded the incident in her logbook at 15:45 hours as "Relay #70. . . . (moth) in relay. First actual case of bug being found."

TABLE 2.8 Effort Expended in Phase I

Step	Effort
Analyze the Problem	10%
Develop a Solution	20%
Code the Solution	20%
Test and Correct the Solution	50%

Step 1: Analyze the Problem The first step in developing a program for this problem statement is to perform a basic analysis. We begin by determining the required outputs. Frequently, the statement of the problem will use words such as *calculate, print, determine, find,* or *compare,* which can be used to determine the desired outputs.

For our sample problem statement, the key phrase is "to calculate the resistance of a wire." This clearly identifies an output item. Since there are no other such phrases in the problem, only one output item is required.

After we have clearly identified the desired output, the basic analysis step continues with the identification of all input items. It is essential at this stage to distinguish between input items and input values. An **input item** is the name of an input quantity, whereas an **input value** is a specific number or quantity that the input item can be. For example, in our sample problem statement, the input items are the resistivity, m, the length or the wire, l, and the cross-sectional area of the wire, a. Although these input items have specific numerical values, these values are generally not of importance at this stage.

The reason that input values are not needed at this point is that the selection of an algorithm is typically independent of specific input values. The algorithm depends on knowing what the output and input items are and if there are any special limits. Let us see why this is so.

It is clear from the problem statement that the algorithm for transforming the input items to the desired output is given by the formula $r = (ml)/a$. Notice that this formula can be used regardless of the specific values assigned to m, l, or a. Although we cannot produce an actual numerical value for the output item (resistance) unless we have numerical values for the input item, the correct relationship between inputs and outputs is expressed by the formula. Recall that this is precisely what an algorithm provides: a description of how the inputs are to be transformed into outputs that works for all inputs.

Step 2: Develop a Solution The basic algorithm for transforming the inputs into the desired output is provided by the given formula. We must now refine it by listing, in detail, how the inputs, outputs, and algorithm are to be combined to produce a solution. This listing indicates the steps that will be taken by the program to solve the problem. Thus, it constitutes an outline of the final form that will be followed by the program code. Using pseudocode, the complete algorithm for solving this problems is:

```
Assign values to m, l, and a
Calculate the resistance using the formula r = (ml)/a
Display the result
```

Notice that the structure of this algorithm conforms to the sequential control structure described earlier.

Having selected and refined the algorithm, the next step in the design (if it was not already done in the analysis step) is to check the algorithm by hand using specific data. Performing a manual calculation, either by hand or with a calculator, helps to ensure that you really do understand the problem. An added feature of doing a manual calculation is that the results can later verify program operation in the testing phase. Then, when the final program is used with other data, you will have established a degree of confidence that a correct result is being calculated.

Doing a manual calculation requires that we have specific input values that can be assigned and used by the algorithm to produce the desired output. For this problem, three input values are given: a resistivity of 10.4, a cross-sectional area of 500 circular mils, and a length of 125 feet. Placing these values into the formula, we obtain a resistance = (10.4)(125)/500 = 2.60 ohms for the copper wire.

Step 3: Code the Solution Since we have carefully developed a program solution, all that remains is to code the solution algorithm in Java. This means declaring appropriate input and output variables, initializing the input variables appropriately, computing the resistance, and printing the calculated resistance value. Program 2.7 performs these steps.

PROGRAM 2.7

```
public class ComputeResistance
{
  public static void main (String[] args)
  {
    double resistivity;
    double area;
    double length;
    double resistance;

    resistivity = 10.4;
    area = 500;
    length = 125;
    resistance = (resistivity * length) / area;

    System.out.println("The resistance of the wire (in ohms) is "
                       + resistance);
  }
}
```

When Program 2.7 is executed, the following output is produced:

```
The resistance of the wire (in ohms) is 2.6
```

Now that we have a working program that produces a result, the final step in the development process, testing the program, can begin.

Step 4: Test and Correct the Solution The purpose of testing is to verify that a program works correctly and actually fulfills its requirements. Once testing has been completed, the program can calculate outputs for differing input data without the need for retesting. This is, of course, one of the real values in writing a program; the same program can be used repeatedly with new input data.

The simplest test method is to verify the program's operation for carefully selected sets of input data. One set of input data that should always be used is the data that were selected for the hand calculation made previously in step 2 of the development procedure. In this case, the program is relatively simple and performs only one calculation. Because the output produced by the test run agrees with our hand calculation, we have a good degree of confidence that it can correctly calculate the resistance for any input values.

EXERCISES 2.4

Note: In each of these exercises, a programming problem is given. Read the problem statement first and then answer the questions pertaining to the problem. *Do not write a program to solve the problems; only answer the questions following the program specification.*

1. Assume that a Java program is to be written to calculate the total resistance of a series circuit. In such a circuit, the total resistance is the sum of all individual resistance values. Assume that the circuit consists of a number of 56 ohm, 33 ohm, and 15 ohm resistors.
    a. For this programming problem, how many outputs are required?
    b. How many inputs does this problem have?
    c. Determine an algorithm for converting the input items into output items. Assume that the number of 56-ohm resistors is m, the number of 33-ohm resistors is n, the number of 15-ohm resistors is p.
    d. Test the algorithm written for part c using the following sample data: $m = 17$, $n = 24$, and $p = 12$.

2. Assume that a program is to be written to calculate the value of *Distance* in miles given the relationship:

    *Distance = Rate * Elapsed Time*

    a. For this programming problem, how many outputs are required?
    b. How many inputs does this problem have?
    c. Determine an algorithm for converting the input items into output items.
    d. Test the algorithm written for part c using the following sample data: Rate is 55 miles per hour and Elapsed Time is 2.5 hours.
    e. How must the algorithm you determined in part c be modified if the elapsed time was given in minutes instead of hours.

3. Assume that a program is to be written to determine the value of Ergies given the relationships:

    $$Ergies = Fergies * \sqrt{Lergies}$$
    $$Lergies = 2 * n * e^{\mu}$$

    a. For this programming problem, how many outputs are required?
    b. How many inputs does this problem have?
    c. Determine an algorithm for converting the input items into output items.

    d. Test the algorithm written for part c using the following sample data: Fergies = 14.65, π = 3.1416, μ = 1.672, and e = 2.7818.

4. Assume that a program is to be written to display the following specifications:

Voltage amplification:	35
Power output:	2.5 watts
Bandwidth:	15 KHz

    a. For this programming problem, how many lines of output are required?
    b. How many inputs does this problem have?
    c. Determine an algorithm for converting the input items into output items.

5. Write a Java program to determine how far a car has traveled after 10 seconds assuming the car is initially traveling at 60 miles per hour and the driver applies the brakes to uniformly decelerate at a rate of 12 m/sec^2. Use the fact that *distance* = $s - (1/2)dt^2$, where s is the initial speed of the car, d is the deceleration, and t is the elapsed time.

    a. For this programming problem, how many outputs are required?
    b. How many inputs does this problem have?
    c. Determine an algorithm for converting the input items into output items.
    d. Test the algorithm written for part c using the data given in the problem.

6. Consider the following programming problem: In 1627, Manhattan Island was sold to the Dutch settlers for approximately $24. If the proceeds of that sale had been deposited in a Dutch bank paying 5% interest, compounded annually, what would the principal balance be at the end of 2002. A display is required as follows: Balance as of December 31, 2002 is: xxxxxx, where xxxxxx is the amount calculated by your program.

    a. For this programming problem, how many outputs are required?
    b. How many inputs does this problem have?
    c. Determine an algorithm for converting the input items into output items.
    d. Test the algorithm written for part c using the data given in the problem statement.

7. Write a program that calculates and displays the output voltages of two electrical circuits and the sum of the two voltages. The output voltage for the first circuit is given by the equation (150) $V / 0.38f$, and the output voltage for the second circuit is given by the equation

$$\frac{230V}{\sqrt{\dfrac{2}{56} + \dfrac{2}{(0.98f)}}}$$

where V is the input voltage to the circuit and f is the frequency in hertz.

    a. For this programming problem, how many outputs are required?
    b. How many inputs does this problem have?
    c. Determine an algorithm for converting the input items into output items.
    d. Test the algorithm written for part c using the following sample data: The first circuit is operated with an input voltage of 1.2 volts at a frequency of 144 hertz, and the second circuit is operated with an input voltage of 2.3 volts at 100 hertz.

8. Consider the following programming problem: The formula for the standard normal deviate, z, used in statistical applications is:

$$z = \frac{X - \mu}{\sigma}$$

where μ refers to a mean value and σ to a standard deviation. Using this formula, write a program that calculates and displays the value of the standard normal deviate when $X = 85.3$, $\mu = 80$, and $\sigma = 4$.

a. For this programming problem, how many outputs are required?
b. How many inputs does this problem have?
c. Determine an algorithm for converting the input items into output items.
d. Test the algorithm written for part c using the data given in the problem.

9. The equation of the normal (bell-shaped) curve used in statistical applications is:

$$y = \frac{-\ (1/2)\left[(x - \mu)/\sigma \right]^2}{\sigma\sqrt{2\pi}} e$$

Using this equation, assume that a Java program is to be written that calculates the value of y.

a. For this programming problem, how many outputs are required?
b. How many inputs does this problem have?
c. Determine an algorithm for converting the input items into output items.
d. Test the algorithm written for part c assuming $\mu = 90$, $\sigma = 4$, $x = 80$, and $\pi = 3.1416$.

2.5 APPLICATIONS

In this section, the software development procedure presented in the previous section is applied to two specific programming problems. Although each problem is different, the development procedure works for both situations. This procedure can be applied to any programming problem to produce a completed program, and it forms the foundation for all programs developed in this text.

Application 1: Radar Speed Traps

A common highway patrol speed-detection radar unit emits a beam of microwaves at a frequency f_0. The beam is reflected off an approaching car, and the reflected beam is picked up and analyzed by the radar unit. The frequency of the reflected beam is shifted slightly from f_0 to f_1 due to the motion of the car. The relationship between the speed of the car, v, in miles per hour and the two microwave frequencies is

$$v = (6.685 \times 10^8) x \frac{f_1 - f_0}{f_1 + f_0}$$

where the emitted waves have a frequency of $f_0 = 2 \times 10^{10}$ sec^{-1}. Using this formula, write a Java program to calculate and display the speed corresponding to a received frequency of 2.000004×10^{10} sec^{-1}.

We now apply the top-down software development procedure to this problem.

Step 1: Analyze the Problem   For this problem, a single output is required by the program: the speed of the car. The input items required to solve for the speed are the emitted frequency, f_0, and the received frequency, f_1.

Step 2: Develop a Solution   The algorithm for transforming the three input items into the desired output item is given by the formula $v = 6.685 \times 10^8 (f_1 - f_0)/(f_1 + f_0)$. Thus, the complete algorithm for our program solution is:

Assign values to f_1 and f_0.
Calculate the speed using the formula v = 6.685 x 10^8(f_1 - f_0)/(f_1 + f_0)
Display the result

A hand calculation, using the data that $f_0 = 2 \times 10^{10}$ sec^{-1} and $f_1 = 2.000004 \times 10^{10}$ sec^{-1} yields a speed of 66.85 miles per hour.

Step 3: Code the Solution   Program 2.8 provides the necessary code.

PROGRAM 2.8

```java
public class ComputeSpeed
{
  public static void main (String[] args)
  {
    double speed, f0, f1;

    f0 = 2e-10;
    f1 = 2.0000004e-10;

    speed = 6.685e8 * (f1 - f0) / (f1 + f0);

    System.out.println("The speed is " + speed + " miles/hour");
  }
}
```

Program 2.8 uses the standard class structure found in all of our Java programs. It contains a single method named `main()`. This method begins with our standard `main` header line and ends with the closing brace, }. Additionally, Program 2.8 contains one declaration statement, three assignment statements, and one output statement. The assignment statements `f0 = 2e-10` and `f1 = 2.0000004e-10` initialize the `f0` and `f1` variables, respectively. The assignment statement

```java
speed = 6.685e8 * (f1 - f0) / (f1 + f0);
```

calculates a value for the variable named `speed`. When Program 2.8 is compiled and executed, the following output is produced:

```
The speed is 66.84999331039005 miles/hour
```

In the next chapter, we will show how to explicitly format the numerical output to limit the number of displayed digits after the decimal point.

Step 4: Test and Correct the Solution The last step in the development procedure is to test the output. Because the displayed value agrees with the previous hand calculation, we have established a degree of confidence in the program. This permits us to use the program for different values of received frequencies. Note that if the parentheses were not correctly placed in the assignment statement that calculated a value for speed, the displayed value would not agree with our previous hand calculation. This would have alerted us to the fact there was an error in the program.

Application 2: Telephone Switching Networks

A directly connected telephone network is one in which all telephones in the network are directly connected and do not require a central switching station to establish calls between two telephones. For example, financial institutions on Wall Street use such a network to maintain direct and continuously open phone lines between firms.

The number of direct lines needed to maintain a directly connected network for n telephones is given by the formula

lines = $n(n - 1)/2$

For example, directly connecting four telephones requires six individual lines (Figure 2.14). Adding a fifth telephone to the network in Figure 2.14 would require an additional four lines for a total of ten lines.

Using the given formula, write a Java program that determines the number of direct lines required for 100 telephones and the additional lines required if 10 new telephones were added to the network. Use our four-step method development procedure for constructing the `main()` method.

Step 1: Analyze the Problem For this program, two outputs are required: the number of direct lines for 100 telephones and the additional number of lines needed when 10 new telephones are added to the existing network. The input item required for this problem is the number of telephones, which is denoted as n in the formula.

Step 2: Develop a Solution The first output is easily obtained using the formula

lines = $n(n - 1)/2$

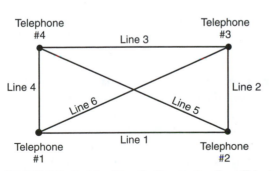

FIGURE 2.14 Directly Connecting Four Telephones

Although no formula is given for additional lines, we can use the given formula to determine the total number of lines needed for 110 subscribers. Subtracting the number of lines for 100 subscribers from the number of lines needed for 110 subscribers will then yield the number of additional lines required. Thus, the complete algorithm for our program in pseudocode is

> *Calculate the number of direct lines for 100 subscribers*
> *Calculate the number of direct lines for 110 subscribers*
> *Calculate the additional lines needed, which is the*
> *   difference between the second and first calculation*
> *Display the number of lines for 100 subscribers*
> *Display the additional lines needed*

Checking this algorithm by hand, using the data given, yields the answer: lines = $100(100 - 1)/2 = 100(99)/2 = 4,950$ for 100 telephones, and lines = 5,995 for 110 telephones. Thus, an additional 1,045 lines would be needed to directly connect the 10 additional telephones into the existing network.

Step 3: Code the Solution Program 2.9 provides the necessary code.

PROGRAM 2.9

```java
public class ComputeLines
{
  public static void main (String[] args)
  {
    int numin1, numin2, lines1, lines2;

    numin1 = 100;
    numin2 = 110;
    lines1 = numin1 * (numin1 - 1)/2;
    lines2 = numin2 * (numin2 - 1)/2;

    System.out.println("The number of initial lines is " + lines1 + ".");
    System.out.println("There are " + (lines2-lines1) + " additional lines needed.");
  }
}
```

As before, the Java program consists of one class that itself contains one `main()` method. The body of this method begins with the opening brace and ends with the closing brace. Because the number of lines between subscribers must be an integer (a fractional line is not possible), the variables `lines1` and `lines2` are specified as integer variables. The first two assignment statements initialize the variables `numin1` and `numin2`. The next assignment statement calculates the number of lines needed for 100 subscribers, and the last assignment statement calculates the number of lines for 110 subscribers. The first `println()` method displays a message and the result of the first calculation. The next output statement displays the difference between the two calculations. The following output is produced when Program 2.9 is compiled and executed:

```
The number of initial lines is 4950.
There are 1045 additional lines needed.
```

Step 4: Test and Correct the Solution As the displayed value agrees with the previous hand calculation, we have established a degree of confidence in the program.

EXERCISES 2.5

1. **a.** Modify Program 2.8 to calculate the speed of a car whose return radar frequency is $2.00000035 \times 10^{10}$ sec^{-1}.
   b. Compile and execute the program written for Exercise 1a on a computer.
2. **a.** Modify Program 2.8 to determine the frequency that will be returned by a car traveling at 55 miles per hour. Your program should produce the following display:

   ```
   The returned frequency corresponding to 55 miles per hour is: xxxxx
   ```

   where the xs are replaced by the value calculated by your program.
   b. Compile and execute the program written for Exercise 2a on a computer. Make sure to do a hand calculation so that you can verify the results produced by your program.
   c. After you have verified the results of the program written in Exercise 2a, modify the program to calculate the returned frequency of a car traveling at 75 miles per hour.
3. **a.** Modify Program 2.9 to calculate and display the total number of lines needed to connect 1,000 individual phones directly to each other.
   b. Compile and execute the program written for Exercise 3a on a computer.
4. **a.** Modify Program 2.9 so that the variable numfin is initialized to 10, which is the additional number of subscribers to be connected to the existing network. Make any other changes in the program so that the program produces the same display as Program 2.9.
   b. Compile and execute the program written for Exercise 4a on a computer. Check that the display produced by your program matches the display shown in the text.
5. **a.** Design, write, compile, and execute a Java program to convert temperature in degrees Fahrenheit to degrees Celsius. The equation for this conversion is

   Celsius = 5.0/9.0 (Fahrenheit − 32.0).

   Have your program convert and display the Celsius temperature corresponding to 98.6 degrees Fahrenheit. Your program should produce the display:

   ```
   For a Fahrenheit temperature of xxxx degrees,
   the equivalent Celsius temperature is xxxx degrees
   ```

   where appropriate values are inserted by your program in place of the xs.
   b. Check the values computed by your program by hand. After you have verified that your program is working correctly, modify it to convert 86.5 degrees Fahrenheit into its equivalent Celsius value.

6. a. Write, compile, and execute a Java program to calculate the resistance of a series circuit consisting of twelve 56-ohm resistors, twenty 39-ohm resistors, thirty-two 27-ohm, and twenty-seven 15-ohm resistors. Use the fact that the resistance of a series circuit is the sum of the resistances of all individual resistances. Your program should produce the display:

```
The total resistance, in ohms, is xxxx
```

where the xs are replaced by the value calculated by your program.

b. Check the values computed by your program by hand. After you have verified that your program works correctly, modify it to calculate the resistance of a series circuit consisting of no 56-ohm resistors, seventeen 39-ohm resistors, nineteen 27-ohm resistors, and forty-two 15-ohm resistors.

7. a. Design, write, compile, and execute a Java program to calculate the elapsed time it took to make a 183.67 mile trip. The equation for computing elapsed time is

elapsed time = total distance / average speed

Assume that the average speed during the trip was 58 miles per hour.

b. Check the values computed by your program by hand. After you have verified that your program works correctly, modify it to determine the elapsed time it takes to make a 372-mile trip at an average speed of 62 miles per hour.

8. a. Design, write, compile, and execute a Java program to calculate the sum of the numbers from 1 to 100. The formula for calculating this sum is

$$sum = (n/2)(2*a + (n - 1)d)$$

where n = number of terms to be added, a = the first number, and d = the difference between each number.

b. Check the values computed by your program by hand. After you have verified that your program works correctly, modify it to determine the sum of the integers from 100 to 1,000.

9. a. The set of linear equations

$$a_{11}X_1 + a_{12}X_2 = c_1$$
$$a_{21}X_1 + a_{22}X_2 = c_2$$

can be solved using Cramer's rule as:

$$X_1 = \frac{c_1a_{22} - c_2a_{12}}{a_{11}a_{22} - a_{12}a_{21}}$$

$$X_2 = \frac{c_2a_{11} - c_1a_{21}}{a_{11}a_{22} - a_{12}a_{21}}$$

Using these equations, write, compile, and execute a Java program to solve for the X_1 and X_2 values that satisfy the following equations

$$3X_1 + 4X_2 = 40$$
$$5X_1 + 2X_2 = 34$$

b. Check the values computed by your program by hand. After you have verified that your program works correctly, modify it to solve the following set of equations:

$$3 X_1 + 12.5 X_2 = 22.5$$
$$4.2 X_1 - 6.3 X_2 = 30$$

2.6 COMMON PROGRAMMING ERRORS

The common programming errors associated with the material presented in this chapter are:

1. Forgetting to declare all the variables used in a program. This error is detected by the compiler, and an error message is generated for all undeclared variables.
2. Attempting to store a higher precision value in a lower precision data type. Thus, integer values will be accepted for both float and double variables and are automatically converted to the correct data type, but a double value cannot be stored in a float variable. This error is detected by the compiler, and an error message equivalent to `Incompatible type for declaration` is provided (the exact error message is compiler dependent).
3. Using a variable in an expression before a value has been initially assigned to the variable. This will result in the compiler error message equivalent to `Variable . . . may not have been initialized` (the exact error message is compiler dependent).
4. Dividing integer values incorrectly. This error is usually disguised within a larger expression and can be troublesome to detect. For example, the expression

   3.425 + 2/3 + 7.9

   yields the same result as the expression

   3.425 + 7.9

   because the integer division of 2/3 is 0.
5. Mixing data types in the same expression without clearly understanding the effect produced. Since Java allows mixed-mode expressions, it is important to be clear about the order of evaluation and the data type of all intermediate calculations. When evaluating a numerical expression, the following rules are applied in the order listed:
   a. If either operand is a double value, the result is a double value, else
   b. If either operand is a float value, the result is a float value, else
   c. If either operand is a long value, the result is a long value, else
   d. The result is an integer precision (32-bit) value.
   As a general rule, it is better not to mix data types in an expression unless a specific effect is desired.
6. Forgetting to separate individual data items sent to the `showMessage()`, `print()`, and `println()` methods with the concatenation, +, symbol.
7. Failing to enclose an arithmetic expression within parentheses when the expression is meant to be evaluated and concatenated to a string. Depending on the precedence and associativity of the arithmetic operation, either the evaluation will take place without the parentheses, an inadvertent string concatenation will take place with no numerical evaluation, or an error will occur.

2.7 CHAPTER SUMMARY

1. The primitive types of data recognized by Java are numerical and boolean types. The numerical types are further classified as integer, floating-point, and character types. Each of these types of data is typically stored in a computer using different amounts of memory. A void data type cannot be instantiated.

2. Primitive type values can be displayed using `print()`, `println()`, and `showMessage()` methods.

3. Every variable in a Java program must be declared as to the type of value it can store. Declarations within a method may be placed anywhere within the method, although a variable can only be used after it is declared. Variables may also be initialized when they are declared. In addition, variables of the same type may be declared using a single declaration statement. Variable declaration statements have the general form:

```
dataType variableName(s);
```

4. A simple Java program containing declaration statements has the typical form:

```
import statements;
public class className
{
  public static void main(String[] args)
  {
    declaration statements;

    other statements;
  }
}
```

Although declaration statements may be placed anywhere within a method's body, a variable may only be used after it is declared.

5. Declaration statements always perform the task of informing both a programmer reading the program and the compiler translating the program of a method's valid variable names. A variable declaration also tells the compiler to set aside memory locations for the variable.

6. Reference variables are associated either with a class, an array, or an interface.

7. When associated with a class, a reference variable is used to locate an object of the class. Objects are declared and initialized with a two-step process. The first step declares a reference variable, which is identical to declaring a primitive variable. For example, the statement

```
String message;
```

declares a reference variable named `message`.

The second step creates an object that the reference variable points to using the keyword `new`. When an object is actually created, it is said to be instantiated. For example, the statement

```
message = new String("Hello World!");
```

instantiates a string object, initializes it with the characters `Hello World!`, and places the first memory address where this value is stored in the reference variable named `message`. This two-step process can be accomplished using either two distinct statements, as in this example, or using a single statement that both declares a reference variable and instantiates an object within the same statement.

8. The declaration of a reference variable and the creation of an object can always be accomplished using a single statement. For example, the two statements

```
String message;  // declaration of a reference variable
message = new String("Hello World!"); // creation of an object
```

can be replaced by the single statement

```
String message = new String("Hello World!");
```

9. The creation of a string object can be made by assigning a string literal to a string reference variable. Such an assignment only works for the `String` class. For example, the declaration

```
String message = "Hello World!";
```

both creates a reference variable named `message` and creates a string literal whose location is stored in the reference variable. This declaration can replace the longer declaration

```
String message = new String("Hello World!");
```

10. String values are stored along with an indication of their length.

11. Values can be equated to a single constant using the keyword `final`. This creates a named constant that is read-only after it is initialized within the declaration statement. This declaration has the syntax

```
final dataType constantName = initial value;
```

and permits the constant to be used instead of the initial value anywhere in a method after the declaration. Generally, such declarations are placed before a method's variable declarations.

12. The software development procedure consists of three phases:
    - Program development and design
    - Documentation
    - Maintenance

13. The program development and design phase consists of four well-defined steps:
    - Analyze the problem
    - Develop a solution
    - Code the solution
    - Test and correct the solution

14. The four fundamental control structures are:
    - Sequence
    - Selection
    - Iteration
    - Invocation

2.8 CHAPTER SUPPLEMENT: PROGRAMMING ERRORS

The ideal in programming is to produce readable, error-free programs that work correctly and can be modified or changed with a minimum of testing required for reverification. In this regard, it is useful to know the different types of errors that can occur, when they are detected, and how to correct them.

Compile-Time and Run-Time Errors

A program error can be detected

1. Before a program is compiled
2. While the program is being compiled
3. While the program is being run
4. After the program has been executed and the output is being examined

Or, oddly enough, it may not be detected at all. Errors detected by the compiler are formally referred to as **compile-time errors**, and errors that occur while the program is running are formally referred to as **run-time errors**.

By now, you have probably encountered numerous compile-time errors. Although beginning programmers tend to be frustrated by them, experienced programmers understand that the compiler is doing a lot of valuable checking, and it is usually quite easy to correct compiler-detected errors. In addition, because these errors happen to the programmer and not to the user, no one but the programmer generally ever knows they occurred; you fix them and they go away. For example, see if you can detect the error in Program 2.10.

The error in this program, which is not immediately obvious, is that we have not initialized the variable `rate` with any value. This omission is quickly picked up as a compile-time error, and the error message `Variable rate may not have been initialized` is displayed.

Run-time errors are much more troubling because they happen to the user executing the program, which in most commercial systems is not the programmer. For example, if a user enters data that result in an attempt to divide a number by zero, a run-time error occurs. Other examples of run-time errors are presented in Section 3.5, where exception processing is introduced. As a programmer, the only way to protect against run-time errors is to sufficiently think out what someone can do to cause errors and submit your program to rigorous testing. Although beginning programmers tend to blame a user for a run-time error caused by entering obviously incorrect data, professionals don't. They understand that a run-time error is a flaw in the final product that can damage the reputation of both program and programmer.

There are known methods for detecting errors both before a program is compiled and after it has been executed. The method for detecting errors before a program is compiled is called **desk checking**. Desk checking refers to the procedure of checking a program by hand for syntax and logic errors, at a desk or table. The method for detecting errors after a program has been executed is called **program testing**.

PROGRAM 2.10

```java
import javax.swing.*;
import java.text.*;  // needed for formatting
public class FindErrors
{
  public static void main(String[] args)
  {
    String s1, outMessage;
    double capital, amount, rate, nyrs;
    DecimalFormat num = new DecimalFormat(",###.00");

    outMessage = "This program calculates the amount of money\n"
               + "in a bank account for an initial deposit\n"
               + "invested for n years at an interest rate r.";

    JOptionPane.showMessageDialog(null, outMessage,
                                  "Program 2.10",
                                  JOptionPane.INFORMATION_MESSAGE);
    s1 = JOptionPane.showInputDialog("Enter the initial amount in the account:");
    amount = Double.parseDouble(s1);
    s1 = JOptionPane.showInputDialog("Enter the number of years:");
    nyrs = Double.parseDouble(s1);
    capital = amount * Math.pow((1 + rate/100.0), nyrs);

    outMessage = "The final amount of money is $" +num.format(capital);

    JOptionPane.showMessageDialog(null, outMessage,
                    "Program 2.10",
                    JOptionPane.INFORMATION_MESSAGE);

    System.exit(0);
  }
}
```

Syntax and Logic Errors

Computer literature distinguishes between two primary types of errors called syntax and logic errors. A **syntax** error is an error in the structure or spelling of a statement. For example, the statements

```java
if (a lt b
{
  System.out.printin("There are five syntax errors here")
  System.out.println(" Can you find tem?);
}
```

contain five syntax errors. These errors are:

1. The relational operator in the first line is incorrect and should be the symbol <.
2. The closing parenthesis is missing in the first line.
3. The method name `println` is misspelled in the third line.
4. The third line is missing the terminating semicolon.
5. The string in the fourth line is not terminated with a double quotation mark.

All of these errors will be detected by the compiler when the program is compiled. This is true of all syntax errors because they violate the basic rules of Java; if they are not discovered by desk checking, the compiler detects them and displays an error message.[10] In some cases, the error message is extremely clear and the error is obvious; in other cases, it takes a little detective work to understand the error message displayed by the compiler. Since all syntax errors are detected at compile time, the terms compile-time errors and syntax errors are frequently used interchangeably. Strictly speaking, however, compile-time refers to when the error was detected, and syntax refers to the type of error detected. Note that the misspelling of the word `them` in the last `println()` method call is not a syntax error. Although this spelling error will result in an undesirable output line being displayed, it is not a violation of Java's syntactical rules. It is a simple case of a typographical error, commonly referred to as a "typo."

Logic errors are characterized by erroneous, unexpected, or unintentional errors that are a direct result of some flaw in the program's logic. These errors, which are never caught by the compiler, may be detected by desk checking, by program testing, by accident when a user obtains an obviously erroneous output, while the program is executing, or not at all. If the error is detected while the program is executing, a run-time error occurs that results in an error message being generated and/or abnormal and premature program termination.

Because logic errors are not detected by the compiler and may go undetected at run time, they are always more difficult to detect than syntax errors. If not detected by desk checking, a logic error will reveal itself in one of two predominant ways. In one instance, the program executes to completion but produces incorrect results. Generally, logic errors of this type include:

No output: This is caused either by an omission of an output statement or a sequence of statements that inadvertently bypasses an output statement.

Unappealing or misaligned output: This is caused by an error in an output statement.

Incorrect numerical results: This is caused by incorrect values assigned to the variables in an expression, the use of an incorrect arithmetic expression, an omission of a statement, roundoff error, or the use of an improper sequence of statements.

Logic errors can cause run-time errors. Examples of this type of logic error are attempts to divide by zero or to take the square root of a negative number.

Program testing should be well thought out to maximize the possibility of locating errors. An important programming realization is that *although a single test can reveal the presence of an error, it does not verify the absence of one.* The fact that one error is revealed by a particular verification run does not indicate that another error is not lurking somewhere else in the program; *the fact that one test revealed no errors does not indicate that there are no errors.*

---

[10]They may not, however, all be detected at the same time. Frequently, one syntax error masks another error, and the second error is only detected after the first error is corrected.

Although there are no hard-and-fast rules for isolating the cause of an error, some useful techniques can be applied. The first of these is a preventive technique. Frequently, many errors are introduced by the programmer in the rush to code and run a program before fully understanding what is required and how the result is to be achieved. A symptom of this haste to get a program entered into the computer is the lack of an outline of the proposed program (pseudocode or flowcharts) or a handwritten program itself. Many errors can be eliminated by desk checking a copy of the program before it is entered or compiled.

A second useful technique is to imitate the computer and execute each statement by hand, as the computer would. This means writing down each variable as it is encountered in the program and listing the value that should be stored in the variable as each input and assignment statement is encountered. Doing this also sharpens your programming skills because it requires that you fully understand what each statement in your program causes to happen. Such a check is called **program tracing**.

A third and very powerful debugging technique is to display the values of selected variables. For example, again consider Program 2.10. If this program produces an incorrect value for `capital`, it is worthwhile displaying the value of all variables used in the computation for `capital` immediately before a value for this variable is calculated. If the displayed values are correct, then the problem is in the assignment statement that calculates a value for `capital`; if the values are incorrect, you must determine where the incorrect values were actually obtained.

In the same manner, another debugging use of output displays is to immediately display the values of all input data. This technique is referred to as **echo printing**, and it is useful in establishing that the program is correctly receiving and interpreting the input data.

The most powerful of all debugging and tracing techniques is to use a program called a **debugger**. The debugger program controls the execution of a Java program, can interrupt the Java program at any point in its execution, and can display the values of all variables at the point of interruption.

Finally, no discussion of debugging is complete without mentioning the primary ingredient needed for the successful isolation and correction of errors. This is the attitude and spirit you bring to the task. Since you wrote the program, your natural assumption is that it is correct or you would have changed it before it was compiled. It is extremely difficult to back away and honestly test and find errors in your own software. As a programmer, you must constantly remind yourself that just because you think your program is correct does not make it so. Finding errors in your own programs is a sobering experience, but one that will help you become a master programmer. It can also be exciting and fun if approached as a detection problem with you as the master detective.

CAREER CHOICES

ELECTRICAL ENGINEERING

Electrical engineering deals with the application of the principles of electricity and electromagnetism to the manufacture of all forms of machines and devices that either use electricity or produce electrical energy. The field is the largest of all engineering fields. In its beginning in the mid-1800s, it was concerned solely with generating electrical energy. It has evolved into a field with broad boundaries, encompassing devices and systems that include transistors, fiber optics, computers, and robotics.

1. Power. This area involves generation of electrical energy in large fossil-fuel, nuclear, solar, or hydroelectric plants or the efficient utilization of electrical energy by means of motors or illumination devices. Also important are the transmission and distribution of electrical energy through overhead lines, microwaves, light pipes, and superconducting lines.

2. Solid-state Electronics. In conjunction with modern physics and materials science, exotic semiconducting materials are being developed and used to construct microcircuitry that is used in monitoring and controlling the operations of all kinds of devices, from video games to assembly-line robots. The improved reliability, rapidly shrinking size, and reduced power requirements of modern miniaturized electrical components have created limitless opportunities for applications.

3. Communications. Communications involves the design and construction of equipment used in the transmission of information via electricity or electromagnetic waves (radio, light, microwaves, etc.). The use of the laser for communication is a topic of modern concern, whereas antenna characteristics and radar are somewhat older.

4. Computers and Robotics. While electronics deals with the principles associated with the functions of miniaturized components, computer engineers are concerned with designing the complex circuitry that interweaves the components into a computer. Microprocessors, or small computers, are designed to constantly monitor and control the operations of a particular piece of equipment such as a lathe or an autopilot.

CHAPTER 3

Assignment and

Interactive Input

In the last chapter, we introduced the concepts of data storage, variables, and their associated declaration using input dialog boxes for entering data interactively while a program is running. In this chapter, we complete our introduction to Java by presenting additional processing and interactive input capabilities Additionally, we present the creation and use of formatted output.

3.1 ASSIGNMENT OPERATIONS

We have already encountered simple assignment statements in the previous chapter. Assignment statements are the most basic Java statements for assigning values to variables and performing computations. This statement has the syntax:

```
variable = expression;
```

The simplest expression in Java is a single constant, which is also referred to as a **literal value**, or **literal** for short. In each of the following assignment statements, the expression to the right of the equal sign is a literal:

```
length = 25;
width = 17.5;
```

In each of these assignment statements, the value of the constant to the right of the equal sign is assigned to the variable to the left of the equal sign. It is important to note that the equal sign in Java does not have the same meaning as an equal sign in algebra. The equal sign in an assignment statement tells the computer first to determine the value of the operand to the right of the equal sign and then to store (or assign) that value in the locations associated with the variable to the left of the equal sign. In this regard, the Java statement `length = 25;` is read "length is assigned the value 25." The blank spaces in the assignment statement are inserted for readability only.

Recall that a variable can be initialized when it is declared. If an initialization is not done within the declaration statement, the variable should be assigned a value with an assignment statement before it is used in any computation. Subsequent assignment statements can, of course, change the value assigned to a variable. For example, assume the following statements are executed one after another and that `slope` was not initialized when it was declared:

```
slope = 3.7;
slope = 6.28;
```

The first assignment statement assigns the value of 3.7 to the variable named `slope`. If this were the first time a value was assigned to this variable, it would be referred to as an **initialization**. The next assignment statement causes the value of 6.28 to be assigned to `slope`. The 3.7 that was in `slope` is overwritten with the new value of 6.28 because a variable can store only one value at a time. It is sometimes useful to think of the variable to the left of the equal sign as a parking spot in a huge parking lot. Just as an individual parking spot can be used only by one car at a time, each variable can store only one value at a time. The "parking" of a new value in a variable automatically causes the computer to remove any value previously parked there.

In addition to being a constant, the operand to the right of the equal sign in an assignment statement can be a variable or any other valid Java expression. An **expression** is any combination of constants and variables that can be evaluated to yield a result. Thus, the expression in an assignment statement can perform calculations using the arithmetic operators introduced in Section 2.2. Examples of assignment statements using expressions containing these operators are:

```
sum = 3 + 7;
diff = 15 - 6;
product = 0.05 * 14.6;
tally = count + 1;
newtotal = 18.3 + total;
taxes = 0.06 * amount;
totalWeight = factor * weight;
average = sum / items;
slope = (y2 - y1) / (x2 - x1);
```

As always in an assignment statement, the value of the expression to the right of the equal sign is evaluated first, and then this value is stored in the variable to the left of the equal sign. For example, in the assignment statement `totalWeight = factor * weight;`, the arithmetic expression `factor * weight` is first evaluated to yield a result. This result, which is a number, is then stored in the variable `totalWeight`.

In writing assignment expressions, you must be aware of two important considerations. Since the expression to the right of the equal sign is evaluated first, all variables in the expression must previously have been given valid values if the result is to make sense. For example, the assignment statement `totalWeight = factor * weight;` causes a valid number to be stored in `totalWeight` only if the programmer first takes care to assign valid numbers to `factor` and `weight`. Thus, the sequence of statements

```
factor = 1.06;
weight = 155.0;
totalWeight = factor * weight;
```

ensures that we know the values that will obtain the result stored in `totalWeight`. Figure 3.1 illustrates the values stored in the variables `factor`, `weight`, and `totalWeight`.

The second consideration is that because the value of an expression is stored in the variable to the left of the equal sign, there must be a variable listed immediately to the left of the equal sign. For example, the assignment statement

```
amount + 1892 = 1000 + 10 * 5;
```

factor	weight	totalWeight
1.06	155.0	164.3

F I G U R E 3.1 Values Stored in the Variables

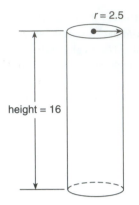

$r = 2.5$

height = 16

FIGURE 3.2 Determining the Volume of a Cylinder

is invalid. The expression on the right side of the equal sign evaluates to the integer 1050, which can be stored only in a variable. Because amount + 1892 is not a valid variable name, the program does not know where to store the calculated value. Program 3.1 illustrates assignment statements that calculate the volume of a cylinder. As illustrated in Figure 3.2, the volume of a cylinder is determined by the formula, Volume $= \pi r^2 h$, where r is the radius of the cylinder, h is the height, and π is the constant 3.1416 (accurate to four decimal places).

PROGRAM 3.1

```
//   this program calculates the volume of a cylinder,
//       given its radius and height
public class CylinderVolume
{
  public static void main(String[] args)
  {
    double radius, height, volume;

    radius = 2.5;
    height = 16.0;

    volume = 3.1416 * radius * radius * height;
    System.out.println("For a cylinder of radius " + radius);
    System.out.println("  and height " + height);
    System.out.println("The volume is " + volume);
  }
}
```

When Program 3.1 is run, the output is:

```
For a cylinder of radius 2.5
  and height 16.0
The volume is 314.16
```

Consider the computer's flow of control in executing Program 3.1. Program execution begins with the first statement in `main()` and continues sequentially, statement by statement, until the closing brace of `main()` is encountered. This flow of control is true for all programs. The computer works on one statement at a time, executing that statement with no knowledge of what the next statement will be. This explains why all operands in an expression must have values assigned to them before the expression is evaluated.

When the computer executes the statement

```
volume = 3.1416 * radius * radius * height;
```

in Program 3.1, it uses whatever value is stored in the variables `radius` and `height` at the time the assignment is executed. Therefore, to ensure a correct computation, you must assign valid values to these variables. Failure to assign any values to variables declared within a method results in a compiler error message.

It is important to realize that in Java, the equal sign in assignment statements is itself an operator, *which differs from the way most other high-level languages process this symbol.* In Java (as in C and C++), the = symbol is called the **assignment operator**, and an expression using this operator, such as `interest = principal * rate`, is an assignment expression. Because the assignment operator has a lower precedence than any other arithmetic operator, the value of any expression to the right of the equal sign is evaluated first, prior to assignment.

As always, instead of providing character-based output using the `println()` method, as is done in Program 3.1, we can just as easily provide a graphical user interface (GUI) output. Program 3.2 provides the same processing as Program 3.1 but displays the results in a dialog box.

PROGRAM 3.2

```java
import javax.swing.*;
public class GuiVolumeOutput
{
  public static void main(String[] args)
  {
    double radius, height, volume;
    String output;

    radius = 2.5;
    height = 16.0;

    volume = 3.1416 * radius * radius * height;

    output = "For a cylinder of radius " + radius
    JOptionPane.showMessageDialog(null, output, "Program 3.2",
                        JOptionPane.INFORMATION_MESSAGE);

    System.exit(0);
  }
}
```

In reviewing Program 3.2, notice that we have declared a string reference variable named `output` and then have "built up" the string using successive concatenation operations, which include newline escape sequences. The `output` variable is then passed to the `showMessageDialog()` method for display. This method retrieves the value of any variable name passed to it in the same manner as does the `println()` method. Thus, it is the characters stored in `output` that are displayed, resulting in the dialog box shown in Figure 3.3.

FIGURE 3.3   The Output Displayed by Program 3.2

Because the equal sign is an operator in Java, multiple assignments are possible in the same expression or its equivalent statement. For example, in the statement `a = b = c = 25;`, all of the assignment operators have the same precedence. Because the assignment operator has a right-to-left associativity, this statement is equivalent to

```
a = (b = (c = 25));
```

This evaluation has the effect of assigning the number 25 to each of the variables individually in the sequence

```
c = 25;
b = 25;
a = 25;
```

Coercion

In restricted cases, data type conversions will take place across assignment operators; that is, the value of the expression on the right side of the assignment operator is converted to the data type of the variable to its left. This type of forced conversion is referred to as **coercion**.

A coercion automatically occurs only when a smaller range numerical data type is assigned to a variable of a larger range type. Thus, if an integer is assigned to a variable declared as either a float or double, the integer will be converted to the variable's declared data type. For example, assigning the integer 14 to a variable defined as a double results in the value 14.0 being assigned. However, a compiler error results if an attempt is made in the reverse direction; you cannot assign a larger range numerical value to a numerical data type having a smaller range of values. The reason is that this latter type of conversion can result in a loss of precision. For example, if `temp` is an integer variable, the assignment `temp = 25.89` results in a compiler error because it would cause the loss of the fractional value 89.

A more complete example of data type coercions, which includes both mixed-mode and assignment conversions, is the evaluation of the expression

```
a = b * c
```

where a is a double-precision variable, b is an integer variable, and c is a single-precision (float) variable. When the mixed-mode expression b * c is evaluated,[1] the value of b in the expression is converted to a float for purposes of computation (it is important to note that the value stored in b remains an integer number). Finally, data type coercion across the assignment operator comes into play. Because the left side of the assignment operator is a double-precision variable, the value of the expression (b * c) is extended to a 64-bit double-precision value and stored in the variable a.

Assignment Variations

Although only one variable is allowed immediately to the left of the equal sign in an assignment expression, the variable to the left of the equal sign can also be used to the right of the equal sign. For example, the assignment expression sum = sum + 10 is valid. Clearly, as an algebra equation, sum could never be equal to itself plus 10. But in Java, the expression sum = sum + 10 is not an equation; it is an expression that is evaluated in two major steps. The first step calculates the value of sum + 10. The second step stores the computed value in sum. See if you can determine the output of Program 3.3.

PROGRAM 3.3

```java
public class ReusingAVariable
{
  public static void main(String[] args)
  {
    int sum;

    sum = 25;
    System.out.println("The number stored in sum is " + sum);
    sum = sum + 10;
    System.out.println("The number now stored in sum is " + sum);
  }
}
```

The assignment statement sum = 25; tells the computer to store the number 25 in sum (Figure 3.4).

The first println() statement in Program 3.3 causes the value stored in sum to be displayed by the message The number stored in sum is 25. The second assignment statement, sum = sum + 10;, causes the program to retrieve the 25 stored in sum and add 10 to this number, yielding 35. The number 35 is then stored in the variable to the left of

---

[1]Review the rules in Section 2.2 for the evaluation of mixed-mode expressions if necessary.

sum

```
        25
```

FIGURE 3.4   The Integer 25 Is Stored in sum

the equal sign, which is the variable sum. The 25 that was in sum is overwritten with the new value of 35, as shown in Figure 3.5.

Assignment expressions like sum = sum + 25, which use the same variable on both sides of the assignment operator, can be written with the following **shortcut assignment operators**:

```
+= -= *= /= %=
```

For example, the expression sum = sum + 10 can be written as sum += 10. Similarly, the expression price *= rate is equivalent to price = price * rate.

In using these new assignment operators, it is important to note that the variable to the left of the assignment operator is applied to the *complete* expression on the right. For example, the expression price *= rate + 1 is equivalent to the expression price = price * (rate + 1), not price = price * rate + 1.

Accumulating

Assignment expressions like sum += 10 or its equivalent, sum = sum + 10, are very common in programming. These expressions are required in accumulating subtotals when data are entered one number at a time. For example, if we want to add 96, 70, 85, and 60 in calculator fashion, the following statements could be used:

Statement	Value in sum
sum = 0;	0
sum = sum + 96;	96
sum = sum + 70;	166
sum = sum + 85;	251
sum = sum + 60;	311

The first statement initializes sum to 0. This removes any previous number ("garbage value") stored in sum that would invalidate the final total. As each number is added, the value stored in sum increases accordingly. After completion of the last statement, sum contains the total of all the added numbers.

Program 3.4 illustrates the effect of these statements by displaying sum's contents after each addition.

sum

Old value is overwritten ———————→ ⊠ ←——————— New value (35) is stored

FIGURE 3.5   sum = sum + 10; Causes a New Value to Be Stored in sum

PROGRAM 3.4

```java
public class SubTotals
{
  public static void main(String[] args)
  {
    int sum;

    sum = 0;
    System.out.println("The value of sum is initially set to " + sum);
    sum = sum + 96;
    System.out.println("  sum is now " + sum);
    sum = sum + 70;
    System.out.println("  sum is now " + sum);
    sum = sum + 85;
    System.out.println("  sum is now " + sum);
    sum = sum + 60;
    System.out.println("  The final sum is " + sum);
  }
}
```

The output displayed by Program 3.4 is:

```
The value of sum is initially set to 0
  sum is now 96
  sum is now 166
  sum is now 251
  The final sum is 311
```

Although Program 3.4 is not practical (it is easier to add the numbers by hand), it does illustrate the subtotaling effect of repeated statements having the form

```
variable = variable + newValue;
```

As we will see when we become more familiar with the repetition statements introduced in Chapter 5, we will find many uses for this type of statement. One immediately useful application, however, is the successive buildup of a single output string. For example, consider the string variable named output constructed as follows:

```
output = "The length of the rectangle is " + length
       + "\nThe width of the rectangle is " + width
       + "\nThe area of the rectangle is " + area;
```

The final string assigned to output can just as easily be assembled as follows:

```
output = "The length of the rectangle is " + length;
output += "\nThe width of the rectangle is " + width;
output += "\nThe area of the rectangle is " + area;
```

The advantage here is that the individual statements can now be separated from one another and placed within a program as needed. This permits you to initialize output with the first assignment statement and then accumulate additional pieces of the final string later in the program (clearly, each statement must be placed after values of the respective variables are assigned). For example, consider Program 3.5, which uses these statements in different parts of the program to construct the final displayed string.

PROGRAM 3.5

```java
import javax.swing.*;
public class BuildAString
{
  public static void main(String[] args)
  {
    double length, width, area;
    String output;

    length = 27.3;
    output = "The length of the rectangle is " + length;
    width = 13.4;
    output += "\nThe width of the rectangle is " + width;
    area = length * width;
    output += "\nThe area of the rectangle is " + area;

    JOptionPane.showMessageDialog(null, output, "Program 3.5",
                                 JOptionPane.INFORMATION_MESSAGE);

    System.exit(0);
  }
}
```

The output displayed by Program 3.5 is shown in Figure 3.6. The concept of building-up a single string from individually distinct pieces is so common that you should be familiar with it. In certain situations, which are presented in Chapter 5, it is in fact the only means of creating the desired string.

FIGURE 3.6   The Output Displayed by Program 3.5

Counting

An assignment statement that is very similar to the accumulating statement is the counting statement. Counting statements have the form:

```
variable = variable + fixedNumber;
```

Examples of counting statements are:

```
i = i + 1;
n = n + 1;
count = count + 1;
j = j + 2;
m = m + 2;
kk = kk + 3;
```

In each of these examples, the same variable is used on both sides of the equal sign. After the statement is executed, the value of the respective variable is increased by a fixed amount. In the first three examples, the variables i, n, and count have all been increased by 1. In the next two examples, the variables j and m have been increased by 2, and in the final example, the variable kk has been increased by 3.

For the special case in which a variable is either increased or decreased by 1, Java provides two unary operators. Using the **increment operator**, ++, the expression variable = variable + 1 can be replaced by either the expression variable++ or ++variable. Examples of the increment operator are:

Expression	**Alternative**
i = i + 1	i++ or ++i
n = n + 1	n++ or ++n
count = count + 1	count++ or ++count

Program 3.6 illustrates the use of the increment operator.

PROGRAM 3.6

```java
public class IncrementOperator
{
  public static void main(String[] args)
  {
    int count;

    count = 0;
    System.out.println("The initial value of count is "+ count);
    count++;
    System.out.println("   count is now " + count);
    count++;
    System.out.println("   count is now " + count);
    count++;
    System.out.println("   count is now " + count);
    count++;
    System.out.println("   count is now " + count);
    count++;
    System.out.println("   count is now " + count);
  }
}
```

The output displayed by Program 3.6 is:

```
The initial value of count is 0
    count is now 1
    count is now 2
    count is now 3
    count is now 4
```

When the ++ operator appears before a variable, it is called a **prefix increment operator**; when it appears after a variable, it is called a **postfix increment operator**. The distinction between a prefix and postfix increment operator is important when the variable being incremented is in an assignment expression. For example, the expression k = ++n does two things in one expression. Initially, the value of n is incremented by 1, and then the new value of n is assigned to the variable k. Thus, the statement k = ++n; is equivalent to the two statements

```
n = n + 1;    // increment n first
k = n;        // assign n's value to k
```

The assignment expression k = n++, which uses a postfix increment operator, reverses this procedure. A postfix increment operates after the assignment is completed. Thus, the statement k = n++; first assigns the current value of n to k and then increments the value of n by 1. This is equivalent to the two statements

```
k = n;        // assign n's value to k
n = n + 1;    // and then increment n
```

In addition to the increment operator, Java also provides a **decrement operator**, --. As you might expect, the expressions variable -- and --variable are equivalent to the expression variable = variable - 1. Examples of the decrement operator are:

Expression	Alternative
i = i - 1	i-- or --i
n = n - 1	n-- or --n
count = count - 1	count-- or --count

When the -- operator appears before a variable, it is called a **prefix decrement operator**. When the decrement appears after a variable, it is called a **postfix decrement operator**. For example, both of the expressions n-- and --n reduce the value of n by 1. These expressions are equivalent to the longer expression n = n - 1. As with the increment operator, however, the prefix and postfix decrement operators produce different results when used in assignment expressions. For example, the expression k = --n first decrements the value of n by 1 before assigning the value of n to k, whereas the expression k = n-- first assigns the current value of n to k and then reduces the value of n by 1.

EXERCISES 3.1

1. Write an assignment statement to calculate the circumference of a circle having a radius of 3.3 inches. The equation for determining the circumference, c, of a circle is $c = 2 \pi r$, where r is the radius and $\pi = 3.1416$.

2. Write an assignment statement to calculate the area of a circle. The equation for determining the area, *a*, of a circle is $a = \pi r^2$, where *r* is the radius and $\pi = 3.1416$.

3. Write an assignment statement to convert temperature in degrees Fahrenheit to degrees Celsius. The equation for this conversion is *Celsius = 5/9 (Fahrenheit −32)*.

4. Write an assignment statement to calculate the round trip distance, *d*, in feet of a trip that is *s* miles long one way.

5. Write an assignment statement to calculate the elapsed time in minutes that it takes to make a trip. The equation for computing elapsed time is *elapsed time = total distance / average speed*. Assume that the distance is in miles and the average speed is in miles/hour.

6. Write an assignment statement to calculate the *n*th term in an arithmetic sequence. The formula for calculating the value, *v*, of the *n*th term is $v = a + (n − 1)d$, where *a* = the first number in the sequence and *d* = the difference between any two numbers in the sequence.

7. Write an assignment statement to calculate the linear expansion in a steel beam as a function of temperature increase. The formula for linear expansion, *l*, is $l = l_o[1 + \propto(T_f − T_o)]$, where l_o is the length of the beam at temperature T_o, $\propto$ is the coefficient of linear expansion, and T_f is the final temperature of the beam.

8. Coulomb's law states that the force, *F*, acting between two electrically charged spheres is given by the formula $F = k\, q_1\, q_2/\, r^2$, where q_1 is the charge on the first sphere, q_2 is the charge on the second sphere, *r* is the distance between the centers of the two spheres, and *k* is a proportionality constant. Write an assignment statement to calculate the force, *F*.

9. Write an assignment statement to determine the maximum bending moment, *M*, of a beam. The formula for maximum bending moment is $M = XW (L − X) / L$, where *X* is the distance from the end of the beam that a weight, *W*, is placed and *L* is the length of the beam.

10. Using Program 3.1, determine the volume of cylinders having the following radii and heights.

Radius (in.)	Height (in.)
1.62	6.23
2.86	7.52
4.26	8.95
8.52	10.86
12.29	15.35

11. Determine and correct the errors in the following `main()` methods:
    a.
```
public static void main(String[] args)
{
   width = 15
   area = length * width;
   System.out.println("The area is " + area);
}
```

b. `public static void main(String[] args)`

```
{
    int length, width, area;
    area = length * width;
    length = 20;
    width = 15;
    System.out.println("The area is " + area);
```

c. `public static void main(String[] args)`

```
{
    int length = 20; width = 15, area;
    length * width = area;
    System.out.println("The area is ", area;
}
```

12. By mistake, a programmer reordered the statements in Program 3.4 as follows:

```
public class SubTotals
{
  public static void main(String[] args)
  {
    int sum;

   sum = 0;
   sum = sum + 96;
   sum = sum + 70;
   sum = sum + 85;
   sum = sum + 60;
   System.out.println("The value of sum is initially set to " + sum);
   System.out.println("   sum is now " + sum);
   System.out.println("   sum is now " + sum);
   System.out.println("   sum is now " + sum);
   System.out.println("   The final sum is " + sum);
  }
}
```

Determine the output that this program produces.

13. The area of an ellipse (Figure 3.7) is given by the formula $area = \pi\, a\, b$. Using this formula, write a Java program to calculate the area of an ellipse having a minor axis of 2.5 inches and a major axis of 6.4 inches.

FIGURE 3.7 The Minor Axis *a* and the Major Axis *b* of an Ellipse

14. Modify Program 3.1 to calculate the weight, in pounds, of the steel cylinder whose volume was found by the program. The formula for determining the weight is $weight = 0.28\,(\pi)(r^2)(h)$, where *r* is the radius in inches and *h* is the height in inches of the cylinder.

15. **a.** The combined resistance of three resistors connected in parallel, as shown in Figure 3.8, is given by the equation

$$\text{Combined resistance} = \frac{1}{\frac{1}{R_1} + \frac{1}{R_2} + \frac{1}{R_3}}$$

Write a Java program to calculate and display the combined resistance when the three resistors $R_1 = 1000$, $R_2 = 1000$, and $R_3 = 1000$ are connected in parallel. Your program should produce the display:

`The combined resistance in ohms is xxxxx`, where the xs are replaced by the value of the combined resistance computed by your program.

R_1

R_2

R_3

FIGURE 3.8 Three Resistors Connected in Parallel

   b. How do you know that the value calculated by your program is correct?
   c. Once you have verified the output produced by your program, modify it to determine the combined resistance when the resistors $R_1 = 1500$, $R_2 = 1200$, and $R_3 = 2000$ are connected in parallel.

16. **a.** Write a Java program to calculate and display the value of the slope of the line connecting the two points whose coordinates are (3,7) and (8,12). Use the fact that the slope between two points having coordinates $(x1,y1)$ and $(x2,y2)$ is slope $= (y2 - y1) / (x2 - x1)$. Your program should produce the display: `The slope is xxxx`, where the xs are replaced by the value calculated by your program.
   b. How do you know that the result produced by your program is correct?
   c. Once you have verified the output produced by your program, modify it to determine the slope of the line connecting the points (2,10) and (12,6).

17. **a.** Write a Java program to calculate and display the coordinates of the midpoint of the line connecting the two points given in Exercise 16a. Use the fact that the coordinates of the midpoint between two points having coordinates $(x1,y1)$ and $(x2,y2)$ are $((x1 + x2)/2, (y1 + y2)/2)$. Your program should produce the following display:

`The x midpoint coordinate is xxx`

`The y midpoint coordinate is xxx`

where the xs are replaced with the values calculated by your program.
   b. How do you know that the midpoint values calculated by your program are correct?
   c. Once you have verified the output produced by your program, modify it to determine the midpoint coordinates of the line connecting the points (2,10) and (12,6).

18. a. For the electrical circuit shown in Figure 3.9, the branch currents i_1, i_2, and i_3 can be determined using the formulas

$$i_1 = \frac{E_2 R_3 + E_1(R_1 + R_3)}{(R_1 + R_3)(R_2 + R_3) - (R_3)^2}$$

$$i_2 = \frac{E_1 R_3 + E_2(R_1 + R_3)}{(R_1 + R_3)(R_2 + R_3) - (R_3)^2}$$

$$i_3 = i_1 - i_2$$

FIGURE 3.9 Calculating Branch Currents

Using these formulas, write a Java program to compute the branch currents when R_1 = 10 ohms, R_2 = 4 ohms, R_3 = 6 ohms, E_1 = 12 volts, and E_2 = 9 volts. The display produced by your program should be:

```
Branch current 1 is xxxx
Branch current 2 is xxxx
Branch current 3 is xxxx
```

where the xs are replaced by the values determined in your program.

b. How do you know that the branch currents calculated by your program are correct?

c. Once you have verified the output produced by your program, modify it to determine the branch currents for the following values: R_1 = 1500, R_2 = 1200, R_3 = 2000, E_1 = 15, and E_2 = 12.

3.2 FORMATTED OUTPUT²

In addition to displaying correct results, it is important for a program to present its results attractively. In fact, most programs are judged on the perceived ease of data entry and the style and presentation of their output. For example, displaying a monetary result as 1.897000 is not in keeping with accepted reporting conventions. The display should be either $1.90 or $1.89 depending on whether rounding or truncation is used.

The precise display of both integer and floating-point numbers can be controlled by a Java-supplied `format()` method, which is a included within the `java.text.DecimalFormat` class. Formatted numbers are especially useful in printing columns with numbers in each

---

²This topic can be omitted on first reading with no loss of subject continuity.

column aligned correctly. For example, Program 3.7 illustrates how a column of integers would align in the absence of any format specification.

PROGRAM 3.7

```
public class NoFormat
{
  public static void main(String[] args)
  {
    System.out.println(6);
    System.out.println(18);
    System.out.println(124);
    System.out.println("---");
    System.out.println((6+18+124));
  }
}
```

The output of Program 3.7 is:

```
6
18
124
---
148
```

Because no explicit format specification is provided, the `println()` function allocates enough space for each number as it is received. To force the numbers to align on the units digit requires a field width large enough for the largest displayed number. For our specific example, a field width of three suffices. Program 3.8 illustrates setting the minimum field width to this size.

PROGRAM 3.8

```
import java.text.*; // this is required to access the DecimalFormat class
public class WithFormats
{
  public static void main(String[] args)
  {
      // this next statement creates the default format
    DecimalFormat num = new DecimalFormat("000");

    System.out.println(num.format(6));
    System.out.println(num.format(18));
    System.out.println(num.format(124));
    System.out.println("---");
    System.out.println(num.format(6+18+124));
  }
}
```

The output of Program 3.8 is

```
006
018
124
---
148
```

In reviewing Program 3.8 and its output, there are a number of points that need explaining. Although the displayed numbers are now aligned, the most noticeable item is the use of leading zeros within the first two numbers. A simple user-defined method is presented in Appendix E that can replace these leading zeros with spaces.[3]

Examining the program itself reveals a number of cookbook items that must be included to create a formatted output. Essentially, these items consist of the following:

1. An `import` statement for the `java.text` package of classes.
2. A statement within the `main()` method that uses the `new` operator to create the desired format string.
3. A `format()` method call that applies the format string to a numerical value.

The first item, the `import` statement, is required because we will be using format capabilities that are provided by the `DecimalFormat` class, which is contained within the `java.text` package of classes. Including the statement `import java.text.*;` within a program that uses the `DecimalFormat` class' formatting facilities means that you can call the required `format()` method as in Program 3.8.

The second item is provided by the statement

```
DecimalFormat num = new DecimalFormat("000");
```

which is placed at the top of Program 3.8's `main()` method. Except for the identifier named `num`, which is a programmer-selectable name and can be chosen by you to be any valid Java identifier, this statement is required before any explicit formatting can be done. In our particular case, this statement creates an object of the `DecimalFormat` class named `num` and a format string of "000".[4] Table 3.1 lists the acceptable symbols and what each symbol represents when it is included in a format string. In particular, the format string "000" means that an integer number with three digits should always be produced. If the number has fewer than three digits, leading zeros will be supplied, as they are in the display produced by Program 3.8. If the number has more than three digits, as you will shortly see, the integer-specified field width is ignored and the complete number is displayed.

For example, the format string in the statement

```
DecimalFormat num = new DecimalFormat(",###");
```

---

[3]Although the method presented in Appendix E can be used as is, a full understanding of how this method works requires the material presented in both Sections 5.3 (**for** loops) and 12.3 (string methods). The format "##0" does not solve the problem because of the action of the # symbol, as listed in Table 2.8.

[4]Formally, the keyword **new** in this statement is Java's *dynamic memory allocation operator*. This operator creates space for a reference object and then initializes this object with the string "000". This format string can then be accessed (i.e., referenced) by the identifier named `num`, which is formally referred to as a reference variable. This is explained in detail in Section 2.4.

TABLE 3.1 Symbols for User-Defined Format Strings

Symbol	Description
#	A digit placeholder; zero shows as absent and not as a space
0	A digit placeholder and automatic fill character
.	A decimal placeholder
,	A grouping separator
;	Separate positive and negative format strings
%	Multiply by 100 and add a % sign

specifies that an integer number is to be displayed, with no leading zeros, and that each group of three digits is to be separated by a comma. When this format string is applied to the number 12345.648, the string that results is "12,345". To format the fractional part of a number requires two format specifications separated by a decimal point; the symbols before the decimal point represent how the integer part should be formatted, and the symbols after the decimal point represent the format specification for the number's fractional part. For example, the format string in the statement

```
DecimalFormat num = new DecimalFormat(",###.##");
```

specifies that a comma separates groups of every three integer digits and that a maximum of two digits (rounded) are placed to the right of the decimal place. Using this format, a value such as 12345.648 will be converted into the string "12,345.65". Notice, however, that if the number 345.60 is formatted with this format string, the result will be the string "345.6". This result is obtained because the # placeholder does not reserve space for either leading or trailing zeros. Thus, if the # placeholder is used, and the number being formatted does not require all the places provided by the #s in the format string on either side of the decimal point, the extra #s are ignored. If the integer part of the number exceeds the number of #s to the left of the decimal point, however, additional space is allocated to accommodate the number.

The same rules apply to the 0 placeholder with one important difference: If the number does not fill the space designated by the 0s, a 0 will fill the unused spaces, as is shown by the output of Program 3.8. For example, using the format string in the following statement

```
DecimalFormat num = new DecimalFormat("0,000.00");
```

the value 12345.648 will be converted to the string value "12,345.65", and the value 345.6 will be converted to the string "0,345.60".

Because leading zeros are typically not required for numerical output, the # format symbol is frequently used to specify the integer part of a number, and the 0 format symbol is used to force a fixed number of decimal digits for the fractional part. For example, using the format string in the following statement

```
DecimalFormat num = new DecimalFormat(",###.00");
```

the value 345.6 will be converted to the string "345.60".

TABLE 3.2 Examples of Numerical Formats

Format String	Number	Returned String Value	Comments
"|##|"	3	|3|	Only one # position is used.
"|##|"	43	|43|	Both # positions are used.
"|##|"	143	|143|	# placeholders are ignored.
"|00|"	3	|03|	Leading 0 position is used.
"|00|"	43	|43|	Both 0 positions are used.
"|00|"	143	|143|	0 placeholders are ignored.
"|00|"	143.466	|143|	0 placeholders are ignored; fractional part is truncated.
"|##.00|"	2.466	|2.47|	Fractional part is rounded.
"|##.##|"	2.466	|2.47|	Fractional part is rounded.
"|00.00|"	123.4	|123.40|	Leading placeholders are ignored; fractional part is forced to two decimal places.
"|00.##|"	123.4	|123.4|	Leading placeholders are ignored; fractional part is not forced to two decimal places.

In addition to numerical placeholders, other symbols can be placed both directly before and after the numerical specification, and these symbols will be included in the string returned when a value is formatted. For example, placing a bar symbol, |, within the format string in the statement

```
DecimalFormat barform = DecimalFormat("|,###.00|");
```

will force a bar symbol to be placed before and after each number that is formatted. Notice that we have used the identifier named barform rather than the identifier named num. Again, the identifier name that you select can be any name that conforms to Java's identifier rules.

Using a bar symbol to clearly mark the beginning and end of the returned string, Table 3.2 illustrates the effect of various user formats.

Notice in the table that the specified integer part of a format string is ignored if the integer format specification is too small; thus, sufficient space is always allocated for the integer part of the number regardless of the format string. The fractional part of a number is only displayed with the number of specified digits if the 0 placeholder is used. In this case, if the fractional part contains fewer digits than specified, the number is padded with trailing zeros. For both 0 and # placeholders, if the fractional part contains more digits than specified in the format, the number is rounded to the indicated number of decimal places.

Once a format string has been defined using the DecimalFormat class, it must still be explicitly applied to all numbers that you want formatted. This is done using the DecimalFormat class' format() method. For example, the actual formatting of numerical values in Program 3.8 is done by the expression num.format() contained within each println() method used to display a numerical value. It is important to note that each of these format() method calls is preceded by a period and the identifier name, in this case num, which was selected by us when we defined the format string. It is also important to realize that the `format()` function converts each numerical value into a string, and it is the string that is displayed by the various `println()` statements.

In addition to formatting numbers for display by either a `print()` or `println()` method, as in Program 3.8, the same formatting technique is applicable to a program that creates a dialog box. For example, see if you can identify the three items necessary for creating formatted numbers in Program 3.9, which uses a `showMessageDialog()` method to create its output display.

PROGRAM 3.9

```java
import java.text.*;
import javax.swing.*;
public class GuiFormat
{
  public static void main(String[] args)
  {
    DecimalFormat num = new DecimalFormat("$,###.00");

    JOptionPane.showMessageDialog(null,
      "The result is " + num.format(25625.648),
      "Output Display",
      JOptionPane.INFORMATION_MESSAGE);

    System.exit(0);
  }
}
```

In analyzing Program 3.9 for the statements that create formatted output numbers, notice that

1. The `import java.text.*;` statement has been included.
2. The statement `DecimalFormat num = new DecimalFormat("$,###.00");` is used to create a format string.
3. The format string is applied to a numerical value using the expression `num.format(25625.648)`. Here the output of this expression, which is the string `"$25,625.65"`, is concatenated to the string `"The result is "`, and the complete string forms the message part of the `showMessageDialog()` method.

The output produced by Program 3.9 appears in Figure 3.10.

FIGURE 3.10   The Display Produced by Program 3.9

EXERCISES 3.2

1. **a.** Enter and execute Program 3.8 on your computer.
   b. Determine the output of Program 3.8 if the format string "###" is substituted for the format string "000".
2. Enter and execute Program 3.9 on your computer.
3. Determine the formatted string that results when
   a. the format string "##" is applied to the number 5
   b. the format string "####" is applied to the number 5
   c. the format string "####" is applied to the number 56829
   d. the format string "###.##" is applied to the number 5.26
   e. the format string "###.##" is applied to the number 5.267
   f. the format string "###.##" is applied to the number 53.264
   g. the format string "###.##" is applied to the number 534.264
   h. the format string "###.##" is applied to the number 534.0
4. Determine the formatted string that results when
   a. the format string "###.##" is applied the numbers 126.27, 82.3, and 1.756, and each formatted number is displayed on a line by itself
   b. the format string "###.##" is applied the numbers 26.27, 682.3, 1.968, and the expression (26.27 + 682.3 + 1.968), and each formatted number is displayed on a line by itself
   c. the format string "###.##" is applied the numbers 34.164, 10.003, and the expression (34.164 + 10.003), and each formatted number is displayed on a line by itself
5. Rewrite Program 2.6 so that the weight of the cylinder is displayed with two digits after the decimal point.
6. The combined resistance of three resistors connected in parallel, as shown in Figure 3.11, is given by the equation

$$\text{Combined resistance} = \frac{1}{\frac{1}{R_1} + \frac{1}{R_2} + \frac{1}{R_3}}$$

Using this formula, write a Java program to calculate and display the combined resistance when the three resistors $R1 = 1000$, $R2 = 1000$, and $R3 = 1000$ are connected in parallel. The output should produce the display

`The combined resistance is xxxx.xx ohms`

where `xxxx.xx` denotes that the calculated value should be placed in a field width of seven columns with two positions to the right of the decimal point.

F I G U R E 3.11 Three Resistors Connected in Parallel

7. Write a Java program to calculate and display the value of the slope of the line connecting two points with coordinates (3,7) and (8,12). Use the fact that the slope between two points having coordinates $(x1,y1)$ and $(x2,y2)$ is slope = $(y2 - y1) / (x2 - x1)$. The display produced by your program should be:
    `The value of the slope is xxx.xx`, where `xxx.xx` denotes that the calculated value should be placed in a field wide enough for three places to the left of the decimal point and two places to its right.

8. Write a Java program to calculate and display the coordinates of the midpoint of the line connecting two points with coordinates (3,7) and (8,12). Use the fact that the coordinates of the midpoint between two points having coordinates $(x1,y1)$ and $(x2,y2)$ are $((X1 + X2)/2, (Y1 + Y2)/2)$. The display produced by your program should be:

    `The x coordinate of the midpoint is xxx.xx`
    `The y coordinate of the midpoint is xxx.xx`

    where `xxx.xx` denotes that the calculated value should be placed in a field wide enough for three places to the left of the decimal point and two places to its right.

9. Write a Java program to calculate and display the maximum bending moment, M, of a beam, which is supported on both ends (see Figure 3.12). The formula for maximum bending moment is $M = X W (L - X) / L$, where X is the distance from the end of the beam that a weight, W, is placed and L is the length of the beam. The display produced by your program should be:

    `The maximum bending moment is xxxx.xxxx`

    where `xxxx.xxxx` denotes that the calculated value should be placed in a field wide enough for four places to the right and left of the decimal point.

FIGURE 3.12 Calculating the Maximum Bending Moment

10. For the electrical circuit shown in Figure 3.13, the branch currents i_1, i_2, and i_3 can be determined using the formulas

    $$i_1 = \frac{E_2 R_3 + E_1(R_1 + R_3)}{(R_1 + R_3)(R_2 + R_3) - (R_3)^2}$$
    $$i_2 = \frac{E_1 R_3 + E_2(R_1 + R_3)}{(R_1 + R_3)(R_2 + R_3) - (R_3)^2}$$
    $$i_3 = i_1 - i_2$$

    Using these formulas, write a Java program to compute the branch currents when $R_1 = 10$ ohms, $R_2 = 4$ ohms, $R_3 = 6$ ohms, $E_1 = 12$ volts, and $E_2 = 9$ volts. The display produced by your program should be:

    `Branch current 1 is xx.xxxxx`
    `Branch current 2 is xx.xxxxx`
    `Branch current 3 is xx.xxxxx`

where xx.xxxx denotes that the calculated value should be placed in a field wide enough for two places to the left of the decimal point and four places to its right.

FIGURE 3.13   Calculating Branch Currents in an Electrical Circuit

3.3 MATHEMATICAL METHODS

As you have seen, assignment statements can perform arithmetic computations. For example, the assignment statement

```
totalPrice = unitPrice * amount;
```

multiplies the value in unitPrice by the value in amount and assigns the resulting value to totalPrice. Although addition, subtraction, multiplication, and division are easily accomplished with Java's arithmetic operators, no such operators exist for raising a number to a power, finding the square root of a number, or determining trigonometric values. To facilitate such calculations, Java provides standard preprogrammed methods within a class named Math. Because these methods are general purpose, they have been written as both static, which permits their use without an object, and as public, which permits their use outside the Math class.

Before using one of Java's mathematical methods, you need to know:

• the name of the desired mathematical method
• what the mathematical method does
• the type of data required by the mathematical method
• the data type of the result returned by the mathematical method

To illustrate the use of Java's mathematical methods, consider the mathematical method named abs(), which calculates the absolute value of a number. The absolute value of a number is always positive; if the number is not negative, the absolute value is the number itself, and if the number is negative, the absolute value is the number without the negative sign. The absolute value of a number is computed with the expression

```
Math.abs(number)
```

Notice that this expression uses the same syntax as all general-purpose methods in that it provides a class name followed by a period followed by the method's name. Finally,

FIGURE 3.14 Passing Data to the Math Class' abs() Method

the method name is followed by parentheses that are used to pass data into the method. In this case, the method's name is abs, which is a method provided within the Math class. The parentheses following the method name effectively provide a funnel through which data are passed to the method (Figure 3.14). The items that are passed to the method through the parentheses, as we have noted previously in relation to the println() method, are called **arguments** of the method and constitute its input data. For example, the following expressions compute the absolute value of the arguments 4, −4, −56789L, −17.25f, 1043.29f, and −23456.78:

```
Math.abs(4)
Math.abs(-4)
Math.abs(-56789L)
Math.abs(-17.25f)
Math.abs(1043.29f)
Math.abs(-23456.78)
```

Notice that the argument to the Math.abs() method can be either an integer, long, float, or double real value. This is an example of Java's overloading capabilities. Method overloading permits the same method name to be defined for different argument data types. In this case, there are really four absolute value methods named abs—one defined for integer, long, float, and double arguments, respectively. The correct abs() method is called depending on the type of argument given it. The values returned by the previous expressions are:

Expression	Value Returned	Returned Data Type
Math.abs(4)	4	integer
Math.abs(-4)	4	integer
Math.abs(-56789L)	56789	long
Math.abs(-17.25f)	17.25	floating-point
Math.abs(1043.29f)	1043.29	floating-point
Math.abs(-23456.78)	23456.78	double-precision

In addition to the Math.abs() method, Table 3.3 lists the mathematical methods provided in Java. Although some of these mathematical methods require more than one argument, all methods can by definition directly return at most one value. Except for the abs(), min(), max(), and round() methods, which are overloaded, the other methods

TABLE 3.3 Java's Math Class Methods

Method Name	Description	Returned Value
abs(x)	absolute value	same data type as argument
pow(x1,x2)	x1 raised to the x2 power	double
sqrt(x)	square root of x	double
log(x)	natural logarithm of x	double
exp(x)	e raised to the x power	double
ceil(x)	smallest integer value that is not less than x	double
floor(x)	largest integer value that is not greater than x	double
min(x,y)	smaller of its two arguments	same data type as arguments
max(x,y)	larger of its two arguments	same data type as arguments
rint(x)	closest integer value to the argument (in case of two closest integers, the even integer is returned)	double
round(x)	rounded value	integer
random(x)	random number between 0.0 inclusive and 1.0 exclusive	double
sin(x)	sine of x (x in radians)	double
cos(x)	cosine of x (x in radians)	double
tan(x)	tangent of x (x in radians)	double
asin(x)	arcsin of x	double
acos(x)	arccos of x	double
atan(x)	arctan of x	double

convert their arguments into a double valued number and return a double. Table 3.4 illustrates the value returned by selected methods using example arguments.

It is important to remember that each Math class method is called into action by listing the name of the class, a period, the method's name, and passing any data to it within the parentheses following the method's name (Figure 3.15). The arguments that are passed to a method need not be single constants. An expression can also be an argument provided that the expression can be computed to yield a value of the required data type. For example, the following arguments are valid for the given methods:

```
Math.sqrt(4.0 + 5.3 * 4.0)      Math.abs(2.3 * 4.6)
Math.sqrt(16.0 * 2.0 - 6.7)     Math.abs(theta - phi)
Math.sqrt(x * y - z/3.2)        Math.sin(2.0 * omega)
```

The expressions in parentheses are first evaluated to yield a specific value. Thus, values have to be assigned to the variables theta, phi, x, y, z, and omega before their use in the preceding expressions. After the value of the argument is calculated, it is passed to the method.

```
Math · MethodName (data passed to the method);
```

This identifies   This identifies   This passes data
the method's   the called   to the method
class   method

FIGURE 3.15 Using and Passing Data to a Math Class Method

TABLE 3.4   Selected Math Method Examples

Example	Returned Value
`Math.abs(-7.362)`	7.362
`Math.abs(-3)`	3
`Math.pow(2.0,5.0)`	32.0
`Math.pow(10,3)`	1000
`Math.log(18.697)`	2.928363083183137
`Math.exp(-3.2)`	0.040762203978366204

Methods may also be included as part of larger expressions. For example:

```
4 * Math.sqrt(4.5 * 10.0 - 9.0) - 2.0 =
        4 * Math.sqrt(36.0) - 2.0 =
                4 * 6.0 - 2.0 =
                24.0 - 2.0 = 22.0
```

The step-by-step evaluation of an expression such as

```
3.0 * Math.sqrt(5 * 33 - 13.71) / 5
```

is:

Step	Result
1. Perform multiplication in argument	`3.0 * Math.sqrt(165 - 13.71)/5`
2. Complete argument calculation	`3.0 * Math.sqrt(151.29)/5`
3. Return a method value	`3.0 * 12.3/5`
4. Perform the multiplication	`36.9/5`
5. Perform the division	`7.38`

Program 3.10 on page 134 illustrates the use of the sqrt method to determine the time it takes a ball to hit the ground after it has been dropped from an 800-foot tower. The mathematical formula to calculate the time in seconds that it takes to fall a given distance in feet is:

*time = sqrt(2 * distance / g)*

where *g* is the gravitational constant equal to 32.2 ft/sec^2.

The output produced by Program 3.10 is:

```
It will take 7.05 seconds to fall 800 feet.
```

As used in Program 3.10, the value returned by the `Math.sqrt()` method is assigned to the variable `time`. In addition to assigning a method's returned value to a variable or using the returned value within a larger expression, it may also be used as an argument to another method. For example, the expression

```
Math.sqrt( Math.pow( Math.abs(num1),num2 ) )
```

is valid. Since parentheses are present, the computation proceeds from the inner to the outer pairs of parentheses. Thus, the absolute value of `num1` is computed first and used as

PROGRAM 3.10

```java
import java.text.*; // needed for formatting
public class FallTime
{
  public static void main(String[] args)
  {
    int height;
    double time;

    DecimalFormat df = new DecimalFormat("#.00");

    height = 800;
    time = Math.sqrt(2 * height / 32.2);
    System.out.println("It will take " + df.format(time)
            + " seconds to fall " + height + " feet.");
  }
}
```

an argument to the `Math.pow()` method. The value returned by the `Math.pow()` method is then used as an argument to the `Math.sqrt()` method.

Casts

We have already seen the conversion of an operand's data type within mixed-mode arithmetic expressions (Section 2.2) and across assignment operators (Section 3.1). In addition to these implicit data type conversions that are automatically made in mixed-mode arithmetic and assignment expressions, Java also provides for explicit user-specified type conversions. The operator that forces the conversion of a value to another type is the **cast** operator. This is a unary operator having the form (*dataType*) *expression*, where *dataType* is the desired data type of the expression following the cast. For example, the expression

```java
(int) (a * b)
```

ensures that the value of the expression a * b is converted to an integer value. It should be noted that casts between Java's built-in numerical data types and its reference types, in either direction, are not permitted. This type of conversion is accomplished with the methods presented next.

Conversion Methods

Java provides a number of extremely useful routines for converting a string to a primitive type and a primitive type to a string (Figure 3.16). These methods, among others, are in a set of classes referred to as **wrapper classes** because the classes are constructed by wrapping a class structure around the built-in integer, long, float, and double numerical data types.[5]

---

[5]There are a total of ten wrapper classes. The additional six classes are named `boolean`, `Byte`, `Character`, `Number`, `Short`, and `Void`.

FIGURE 3.16 Conversions Using a Wrapper Class Method

Each primitive data type has a corresponding wrapper class that has the same name as its equivalent built-in primitive type with the exception that the class names begin with an uppercase letter and `Character` and `Integer` are spelled out as complete words. Besides providing the conversions shown in Figure 3.16, these wrapper classes are also useful in converting a primitive type to an equivalent object type for input to any method that requires an object and not a primitive value. For our current purposes, however, these wrapper classes are of interest because of the conversion methods listed in Table 3.5.

All of the methods in Table 3.5 are `public` and `static` methods, which means that they are general-purpose methods that only operate on their arguments to produce a result. As general-purpose methods, you must list both their class and method names, separated by a period, as illustrated in all of the examples in the table. Also notice that all of the conversions from a primitive data type to a string type use the same `toString()` method. This particular method is overloaded, which means multiple versions of the method exist, and the correct version is determined by the type of argument provided when the method is invoked.

In general, we will have much more use for the methods that convert a string value to a numerical type. This is because when values are input to a Java program, which is the topic of the next two sections, the input is read in as a string of characters. This string is typically converted to an appropriate numerical type using one of the string to primitive data type conversion methods in Table 3.5. Program 3.11 on page 137 illustrates two of these methods to convert a string into both an integer and double-precision value.

The output produced by Program 3.11 is:

```
The string "12345" as an integer number is: 12345
This number divided by 3 is: 4115

The string "12345.96" as a double number is: 12345.96
This number divided by 3 is: 4115.32
```

As this output illustrates, once a string has been converted to either an integer or double-precision value, mathematical operations on the numerical value are valid. These mathematical operations could not have been performed on the original string versions of the numbers.

A number of comments need to be made with respect to the conversion methods in Table 3.5. First, it should be noted that the `toString()` methods in the table are not nearly as useful as the string to primitive type methods. This is because any numerical type can more simply be converted into a string using the concatenation operator, as is done in Program 3.11. For example, the expression `Double.toString(123.45)` can always be replaced by the simpler expression `"" + 123.45`, as is typical in practice.

TABLE 3.5 Wrapper Class Conversion Routines

Wrapper Class	Method	Description	Example	Returned Value
Integer	`parseInt(string)`	Converts a string to a primitive type int.	`Integer.parseInt("1234")`	1234 (an int value)
Integer	`toString(x)`	Converts the primitive int x value to a string object.	`Integer.toString(345)`	"345" (a string object)
Long	`parseLong(string)`	Converts a string to a primitive type long.	`Long.parseLong("128365489")`	128365489L (a long)
Long	`toString(x)`	Converts the primitive long x value to a string object.	`Long.toString(128365489)`	"128365489" (a string object)
Float	`parseFloat(string)`	Converts a string to a primitive type float.	`Float.parseFloat("345.89")`	345.89f (a float value)
Float	`toString(x)`	Converts the primitive float x value to a string object.	`Float.toString(345.873)`	"345.873" (a string object)
Double	`parseDouble(string)`	Converts a string to a primitive type double.	`Double.parseDouble("2.3456789")`	2.3456789 (a double value)
Double	`toString(x)`	Converts the primitive double x value to a string object.	`Double.toString(345.873)`	"345.873" (a string object)

PROGRAM 3.11

```
public class SampleConversions
{
  public static void main(String[] args)
  {
    String numstring = "12345";
    int num;
    double dnum;

      // convert to an integer and perform a numerical operation
    num = Integer.parseInt(numstring);
    System.out.println("The string \"" + numstring
                + "\" as an integer number is: " + num);
    System.out.println("This number divided by 3 is: " + (num / 3));

      // convert to a double and perform a numerical operation
    numstring = numstring + ".96";   // concatenate to the original string
    dnum = Double.parseDouble(numstring);
    System.out.println("\nThe string \"" + numstring
                + "\" as a double number is: " + Double.toString(dnum));
    System.out.println("This number divided by 3 is: " + (dnum / 3));
  }
}
```

Second, it is very important to realize that all of the conversion methods require valid argument values. For example, the expression `Integer.parseInt("123.56")` results in an error because the fractional part of the number cannot be converted into a legitimate integer value. From a programming standpoint, the validity of any string value being converted should, ultimately, always be checked prior to sending the string value into a conversion method. This validity check, which is referred to as **input validation**, is especially important when data are entered by a user interactively as a program is executing. This is because we have no control over what characters a user might inadvertently enter, and any characters that cannot be converted will result in a program error. Although you do not as yet have the programming tools either to input or validate user-entered data, we will have much more to say about this as you develop your Java programming expertise.

EXERCISES 3.3

1. Write valid Java statements to determine:
   a. The square root of 6.37
   b. The square root of $x - y$
   c. The smaller of the values -30.5 and -42.7
   d. The larger of the values 109 and 101
   e. The absolute value of $a^2 - b^2$
   f. The value of e raised to the power of 3

2. For $a = 10.6$, $b = 13.9$, $c = -3.42$, determine the value of:
   a. `(int) a`
   b. `(int) b`
   c. `(int) c`
   d. `(int) (a + b)`
   e. `(int) a + b + c`
   f. `(int) (a + b) + c`
   g. `(int) (a + b + c)`
   h. `(float) ( (int) a) + b`
   i. `(float) ((int) (a + b))`
   j. `Math.abs(a) + Math.abs(b)`
   k. `Math.sqrt(Math.abs(a - b))`

3. Write Java statements for the following:
   a. $b = \sin x - \cos x$
   b. $b = \sin^2 x - \cos^2 x$
   c. area $= (c * b * \sin a) / 2$
   d. $c = \sqrt{a^2 + b^2}$
   e. $p = \sqrt{|m - n|}$
   f. sum $= \dfrac{a(r^n - 1)}{r - 1}$

4. Write, compile, and execute a Java program that calculates and returns the fourth root of the number 81, which is 3. When you have verified that your program works correctly, use it to determine the fourth root of 728.896400. Your program should make use of the `sqrt()` method.

5. Write, compile, and execute a Java program that calculates the distance between two points whose coordinates are (7,12) and (3,9). Use the fact that the distance between two points having coordinates (x1,y1) and (x2,y2) is *distance* = sqrt([x1 − x2]² + [y1 − y2]²). When you have verified that your program works correctly by calculating the distance between the two points manually, use your program to determine the distance between the points (−12,−15) and (22,5).

6. Modify Program 3.10 so that the displayed time always has a maximum of four digits after the decimal point.

7. Although we have been concentrating on integer and real arithmetic, Java allows characters to be added or subtracted. This can be done because Java always converts a character to an equivalent integer value whenever a character is used in an arithmetic expression (the decimal value of each character can be found in Appendix B). Thus, characters and integers can be freely mixed in arithmetic expressions. For example, in Unicode, the expression `'a' + 1` equals 98, and `'z' - 1` equals 121. These values can be converted back into characters using the cast operator. Thus, `(char) ('a' + 1) = 'b'` and `(char) ('z' - 1) = 'y'`. Similarly, `(char)('A' + 1)` is `'B'`, and `(char)('Z' - 1)` is `'Y'`. With this as background, determine the results of the following expressions (assume that all characters are stored using Unicode):
   a. `(char) ('m' - 5)`
   b. `(char) ('m' + 5)`
   c. `(char) ('G' + 6)`
   d. `(char) ('G' - 6)`
   e. `('b' - 'a')`
   f. `('g' - 'a' + 1)`
   g. `('G' - 'A' + 1)`

8. a. The table in Appendix B lists the integer values corresponding to each letter stored using Unicode. Using this table, notice that the uppercase letters consist of contiguous codes starting with an integer value of 65 for A and ending with 90 for Z. Similarly, the lowercase letters begin with the integer

value of 97 for the letter a and end with 122 for z. With this as background, determine the character value of the expressions `(char) ('A' + 32)` and `(char) ('Z' + 32)`.

b. Using Appendix B, determine the integer value of the expression `'a' - 'A'`.

c. Using the results of Exercises 8a and 8b, determine the character value of the following expression, where `uppercase letter` can be any uppercase letter from A to Z:

```
(char) ('uppercaseletter ' + 'a' - 'A')
```

9. Modify Program 3.11 so that the following line of code is placed immediately before `main()`'s closing brace:

```
Long.parseLong(numstring);
```

Attempt to compile and run the modified program and then determine what the error is and when is it reported (at compile time or run time).

10. Complete the following program so that the average of the values represented by the strings `s1` and `s2` is computed and displayed.

```java
public class Average
{
   public static void main(String[] args)
   {
      String s1 = "15";
      String s2 = "14";
```

11. If a 20-foot ladder is placed on the side of a building at an 85-degree angle, as illustrated in Figure 3.17, the height at which the ladder touches the building can be calculated as height = 20 * sin 85°. Calculate this height by hand and then write, compile, and execute a Java program that determines and displays the value of the height. When you have verified that your program works correctly, use it to determine the height of a 25-foot ladder placed at an angle of 85 degrees.

20'

85°

FIGURE 3.17 Calculate the Height of a Ladder Against a Building

12. The maximum height reached by a ball thrown with an initial velocity v, in meters/sec at an angle of θ is given by the formula $height = (.5 * v^2 * sin^2 \theta) / 9.8$. Using this formula, write, compile, and execute a Java program that determines and displays the maximum height reached when the ball is thrown at 5 miles/hour at an angle of 60 degrees. (*Tip:* Make sure to convert the initial velocity into the correct units. There are 1,609 meters in a mile.) Calculate the maximum height manually and verify the result produced by your program. After you have verified that your program works correctly, use it to determine the height reached by a ball thrown at 7 miles/hour at an angle of 45 degrees.

13. For small values of x, the value of $sin(x)$ can be approximated by the power series:

$$x - \frac{x^3}{6} + \frac{x^5}{120}$$

As with the sin function, the value of x must be in radians. Using this power series, write, compile, and execute a Java program that approximates the sine of 180/3.1416 degrees, which equals 1 radian. Additionally, have your program use the sin function to calculate the sine and display both calculated values and the absolute difference of the two results. Verify the approximation produced by your program by hand. After you have verified your program is working correctly, use it to approximate the value of the sine of 62.2 degrees.

14. The polar coordinates of a point consist of the distance, r, from a specified origin and an angle, θ, with respect to the X axis. The x and y coordinates of the point are related to its polar coordinates by the formulas:

$x = r \cos \theta$
$y = r \sin \theta$

Using these formulas, write a Java program that calculates the x and y coordinates of the point whose polar coordinates are $r = 10$ and $= 30$ degrees. Verify the results produced by your program by calculating the results by hand. After you have verified that your program works correctly, use it to convert the polar coordinates $r = 12.5$ and $\theta = 67.8°$ into rectangular coordinates.

15. **a.** A model of worldwide population in billions of people after the year 2000 is given by the equation

   $Population = 6.0\ e^{.02\ [Year-2000]}$

   Using this formula, write, compile, and execute a Java program to estimate the worldwide population in the year 2002. Verify the result displayed by your program by calculating the answer by hand. After you have verified that your program works correctly, use it to estimate the world's population in the year 2012.

   b. Modify the program written for Exercise 15a so that the computed population estimate is displayed with a maximum of two digits after the decimal point.

16. A model to estimate the number of grams of a certain radioactive isotope left after N years is given by the formula:

   $Remaining\ material = (Original\ material)\ e^{-.00012\ N}$

   Using this formula, write, compile, and execute a Java program to determine the amount of radioactive material remaining after 1,000 years, assuming an initial amount of 100 grams. Verify the display produced by your program by hand. After you have verified that your program works correctly, use it to determine the amount of radioactive material remaining after 275 years, assuming an initial amount of 250 grams.

17. The number of years that it takes for a certain isotope of uranium to decay to one-half of an original amount is given by the formula:

Half-life = ln(2)/k

where *k* equals 0.00012. Using this formula, write, compile, and execute a Java program that calculates and displays the half-life of this uranium isotope. Verify the result produced by your program by hand. After you have verified that your program works correctly, use it to determine the half-life of a uranium isotope having *k* = 0.00026.

18. The amplification of electronic circuits is measured in units of decibels, which is calculated as:

10 LOG (P$_o$/P$_i$)

where *P$_0$* is the power of the output signal and *P$_i$* is the power of the input signal. Using this formula, write, compile, and execute a Java program that calculates and displays the decibel amplification in which the output power is 50 times the input power. Verify the result displayed by your program by hand. After you have verified that your program works correctly, use it to determine the amplification of a circuit whose output power is 4.639 watts and input power is 1 watt.

19. The loudness of a sound is measured in units of decibels, which is calculated as:

10 LOG (SL/RL)

where *SL* is intensity of the sound being measured and *RL* is a reference to sound intensity level. Using this formula, write a Java program that calculates and displays the decibel loudness of a busy street having a sound intensity of 10,000,000 *RL*. Verify the result produced by your program by hand. After you have verified that your program works correctly, use it to determine the sound level in decibels of the following sounds:

a. A whisper of sound intensity of 200 *RL*
b. A rock band playing at a sound intensity of 1,000,000,000,000 *RL*
c. An airplane taking off at a sound intensity of 100,000,000,000,000 *RL*

20. When a particular rubber ball is dropped from a given height (in meters) its impact speed (in meters/second) when it hits the ground is given by the formula *speed = sqrt(2 * g * height)*. The ball then rebounds to two thirds the height from which it last fell. Using this information, write, test, and run a Java program that calculates and displays the impact speed of the first three bounces and the rebound height of each bounce. Test your program using an initial height of 2.0 meters. Run the program twice and compare the results for dropping the ball on earth (*g* = 9.81 meters/sec²) and on the moon (*g* = 1.67 meters/sec²).

21. **a.** A balance has the following size weights: 100 lb, 50 lb, 10 lb, 5 lb, and 1 lb. The number of 100-lb and 50-lb weights required to weigh an object whose weight is WEIGHT pounds can be calculated using the following Java statements:

```
// Determine the number of 100 lb. Weights
        w100 = (int) (WEIGHT/100)
// Determine the number of 50 lb. Weights
        w50 = (int)((WEIGHT - 100 * 100)/50)
```

Using these statements as a starting point, write a Java program that calculates the number of each type of weight necessary to weigh a 789-lb object.

b. Without compiling or executing your program, check the effect by hand of each statement in the program and determine what is stored in each variable as each statement is encountered.

c. When you have verified that your algorithm works correctly, compile and execute your program. Verify that the results produced by your program are correct. After you have verified that your program works correctly, use it to determine the weights required to weigh a 626-lb object.

3.4 INTERACTIVE KEYBOARD INPUT

Data for programs that are only going to be executed once may be included directly in the program. For example, if we wanted to multiply the numbers 300.0 and 0.05, we could use Program 3.12.

PROGRAM 3.12

```java
public class MultiplyExampleOne
{
  public static void main (String[] args)
  {
    double num1, num2, product;
    num1 = 300.0;
    num2 = 0.05;
    product = num1 * num2;

    System.out.println("300.0 times 0.05 is " + product);
  }
}
```

The output displayed by Program 3.12 is:

```
300.0 times 0.05 is 15.0
```

Program 3.12 can be shortened as illustrated in Program 3.13. Both programs, however, suffer from the same basic problem in that they must be rewritten to multiply different numbers. Both programs lack the facility for entering different numbers to be operated on.

Except for the practice provided to the programmer of writing, entering, and running the program, programs that do the same calculation only once on the same set of numbers are clearly not very useful. After all, it is simpler to use a calculator to multiply two numbers than to enter and run either Program 3.12 or 3.13.

PROGRAM 3.13

```
public class MultiplyExampleTwo
{
  public static void main (String[] args)
  {
    System.out.println("300.0 times 0.05 is " + (300.0 * 0.05));
  }
}
```

This section presents the `System.in` object, which is the foundation object upon which data can be entered into a program while it is executing. Just as the `System.out` object is the connection that displays a string value on the standard output device, the `System.in` object is the connection that enters data from the standard input device, which is the keyboard (Figure 3.18). The `System.in` object is referred to as a **stream object**, or **stream** for short, because it delivers its data as a stream of individual data bytes to the program.

System.in

System.out

Keyboard

Screen

FIGURE 3.18   `System.in` Enters Data; `System.out` Displays Data

Although reading data entered from the keyboard can be constructed in a more or less cookbook manner, it is useful to understand what data are actually being sent to the program and how the program must react to process the data correctly. Table 3.6 lists the various classes and methods that accept keyboard input.

By itself, the `read()` method in Table 3.6 is not of much value to us at this stage because it returns one character at a time as an integer value. One reason for using an integer value is that the Java system must provide a means of indicating when keyboard input is over. This is accomplished with a special end-of-data value, which is formally referred to as an end-of-file (EOF) marker. Clearly, this EOF value cannot be one that could be mistaken for any character or other key typed at the keyboard, so it must have a numerical value that cannot be converted into a legitimate character value. From a user's viewpoint, in a UNIX-based system, pressing both the Ctrl and D keys at the same time generates the EOF value. On a Windows-based system, the Ctrl and Z keys produce the same effect. As shown in Figure 3.19, when the appropriate keys are pressed simultaneously, the `read()` method returns the EOF marker, which in Java has the numerical value of -1.

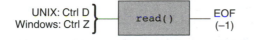

UNIX: Ctrl D
Windows: Ctrl Z   `read()`   EOF
                                            (–1)

FIGURE 3.19   Generating the EOF Value

TABLE 3.6 Keyboard Input Classes and Methods

Class	Method	Description	Example
`InputStream`	`read()`	Returns the key typed at the keyboard as an integer value.	`System.in.read();`
`InputStreamReader`	–	An object of this class converts from an integer value to a character value.	–
`BufferedReader`	`readLine()`	Returns the characters typed at the keyboard as a string.	`br.readLine();`

As a practical matter, requiring users to enter either a `Ctrl` and `D` or `Ctrl` and `Z` when they have completed entering a value is clearly unacceptable. In addition, the `read()` method requires the processing shown in Figure 3.20. This processing consists of accepting each key as it is typed, converting the received integer value into a corresponding character value, and assembling the characters into a string. Once the EOF character is detected, the string is considered complete and can be converted, if necessary, into a primitive data type using the methods in Table 3.5.

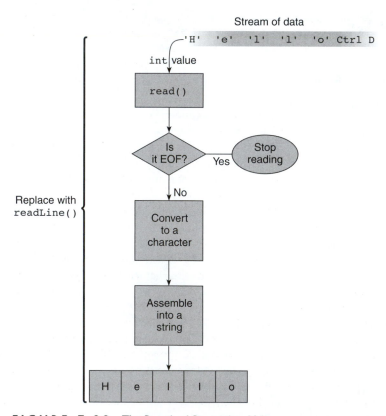

FIGURE 3.20 The Required Processing Using `system.in.read()`

Although the process shown in Figure 3.20 is far too complicated for us to achieve at this time, it can be replaced by the `readLine()` method in Table 3.6. However, to use this method, we have to construct a number of objects from `System.in`. The first object that must be constructed is an `InputStreamReader` stream object. The benefit of this object is that it automatically converts the integer values of the `System.in` stream from their integer values to character values. An `InputStreamReader` object can be constructed from the `System.in` object with the statement

```
InputStreamReader isr = new InputStreamReader(System.in);
```

In this statement, the reference variable `isr` can be changed to any valid programmer-selected Java identifier.

The next and last object that has to be constructed is a BufferedReader stream object. The benefit of this object is that it automatically constructs a string from the character values provided by the `InputStreamReader` object. This string can be read using a `readLine()` method. The desired `BufferedReader` stream object can be constructed with the statement

```
BufferedReader br = new BufferedReader(isr);
```

Although the reference variable `br` can be any valid programmer-selected name, the reference variable `isr` must be the same name that created the `InputStreamReader` object. From a strict programming aspect, then, the statements that should be included in your program to use `readLine()` are the following, where the comment lines can be omitted and the variable names changed to any valid programmer-selected name:

```
    // needed for conversion capabilities
InputStreamReader isr = new InputStreamReader(System.in);
    // needed to use readLine()
BufferedReader br = new BufferedReader(isr);
```

Program 3.14 on page 146 illustrates these declarations within the context of a complete application that accepts user input from the keyboard.

The statements related to keyboard input are boldfaced in Program 3.14. The import statement at the top of the program is required to access the `InputStreamReader` and `BufferedReader` classes in the program. The statement `throws java.io.IOException` is required when using `readLine()` and is explained fully at the end of the next section. For now, simply include this line if your program will use keyboard input. The next boldfaced lines in Program 3.14 contain the input stream declarations that we have already discussed. Now let's analyze what Program 3.14 does.

The statement `System.out.print("Enter a number: ");` displays a string that tells the person at the terminal what should be typed. When an output string is used in this manner, it is called a **prompt**. In this case, the prompt tells the user to type a number. The computer then executes the next statement, which is a call to `readLine()`. This statement puts the program into a temporary pause (or wait) state for as long as it takes the user to type in data. The user signals that the data entry is finished by pressing the Enter key after the value has been typed. The entered string value is stored in the string referenced by the name s1, and the computer is taken out of its paused state. Program execution then proceeds with the next statement, which in Program 3.14 is a call to convert the string into a value of type double.

The next print() method causes the string Great! Now enter another number: to be displayed. The second readLine() method again puts the program into a temporary wait state while the user types a second value. This second value is initially stored as the string s1, which is then converted into a double value and stored in the variable num2.

PROGRAM 3.14

```java
import java.io.*;    // needed to access input stream classes
public class MultiplyNumbers
{
  public static void main (String[] args)
  throws java.io.IOException
  {
    String s1;
    String s2;
    double num1, num2, product;

    // set up the basic input stream
      // needed for conversion capabilities
    InputStreamReader isr = new InputStreamReader(System.in);
      // needed to use readLine()
    BufferedReader br = new BufferedReader(isr);

    System.out.print("Enter a number: ");
    s1 = br.readLine();
    num1 = Double.parseDouble(s1);

    System.out.print("Great! Now enter another number: ");
    s2 = br.readLine();
    num2 = Double.parseDouble(s2);

    product = num1 * num2;
    System.out.println(num1 + " times " + num2 + " is " + product);
  }
}
```

The following is a sample run of Program 3.14:

```
Enter a number: 300.
Great! Now enter another number: 0.05
300.0 times 0.05 is 15.0
```

Notice that each time readLine() is used in Program 3.14, it retrieves a string that is then converted into a single numerical value. With the StringTokenizer class, readLine() can actually accept a string consisting of multiple values. How to do this is presented next. Before leaving Program 3.14, however, it is useful to note that the two declarations for the input streams can be combined into the single statement:

```
BufferedReader br = new BufferedReader(new InputStreamReader(System.in);
```

For clarity and to explicitly comment what each input stream does, we will continue to use the individual comments and declarations in Program 3.14.

The StringTokenizer Class[6]

In addition to accepting a single string value that is converted into one numerical value, readLine() can accept a string consisting of multiple items, each of which can be converted into an individual numerical value. To understand how this is done, consider the string in Figure 3.21. This string consists of three items, which are individually referred to as tokens. Formally, a **token** is defined as a string of characters separated by a delimiting character. In Java, the default **delimiting characters**, or **delimiters** for short, consist of the whitespace characters (space, tab, newline, and return).

F I G U R E 3.21   A String Consisting of Three Tokens

For the string in Figure 3.21, the three tokens consist of the strings "98.5", "12", and "3.25". If these three tokens could be separated from the overall string, each token could then be converted into a primitive data type value. The process of separating individual tokens from a string is formally referred to as **parsing the string** and is easily achieved using methods from the StringTokenizer class. This overall process is shown in Figure 3.22 on page 148.

As shown in Figure 3.22, the first step in the process of parsing tokens is to create an object of the class StringTokenizer from the string. Assuming that the string read from the keyboard is named inputString, the statement

```
StringTokenizer st = new StringTokenizer(inputString);
```

creates the required StringTokenizer object. Here the object's name, st, can be replaced by any valid programmer-selected identifier, and the single statement can be replaced using the two-step process of first declaring a StringTokenizer variable and then creating an actual object using the statements:

```
StringTokenizer st;
st = new StringTokenizer(inputString);
```

[6]This topic can be omitted on first reading with no loss of subject continuity.

A String object

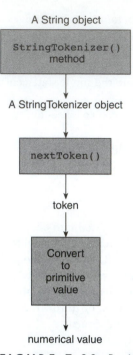

FIGURE 3.22   Parsing Tokens from a String

Once a `StringTokenizer` object has been created, the `nexttoken()` method can extract the next token in the string. For example, for the string in Figure 3.22, and assuming that the variables `s1`, `s2`, and `s3` have been declared as string variables, the three statements

```
s1 = st.nextToken();
s2 = st.nextToken();
s3 = st.nextToken();
```

consecutively "strip off" tokens from the object named `st`. Thus, after these statements have been executed, the string `s1` references the string value "98.5", the string `s2` references the string value "12", and the string `s3` references the string value "3.25". Once these individual string values have been isolated, each one can be converted to a primitive data type value.

The acceptance of the original string from the keyboard and its parsing and conversion into three individual numerical values are presented in Program 3.15. A sample run of Program 3.15 produced the following:

```
Enter three numbers: 98.5 12 3.25
The strings extracted are:
98.5
12
3.25
The value of (98.5 + 12.0)/3.25 is 34.0
```

PROGRAM 3.15

```java
import java.io.*;      // needed to read the keyboard
import java.util.*;   // needed to access the StringTokenizer class
public class MultipleLineInputs
{
  public static void main(String[] args)
  throws java.io.IOException
  {
    String inputString;
    String s1, s2, s3;
    double num1, num3;
    double num2, result;

     // set up the basic input stream
      // needed for conversion capabilities
    InputStreamReader isr = new InputStreamReader(System.in);
      // needed to use readLine()
    BufferedReader br = new BufferedReader(isr);

    System.out.print("Enter three numbers: ");
    inputString = br.readLine();

      // declare and create a StringTokenizer object from the input line
    StringTokenizer st = new StringTokenizer(inputString);

      // strip off individual items
    s1 = st.nextToken();
    s2 = st.nextToken();
    s3 = st.nextToken();

    System.out.println("The strings extracted are:  " + s1 + "  " + s2
                                     + "  " + s3);
    num1 = Double.parseDouble(s1);
    num2 = Double.parseDouble(s2);
    num3 = Double.parseDouble(s3);

    result = (num1 + num2) / num3;
    System.out.println("The value of (" + num1 +" + " + num2 +")/"
                                     + num3 +" is " + result);

  }
}
```

As shown by this output, the three tokens in the input line have been successfully parsed and converted to numerical values, which are then used within an arithmetic computation. Notice that the statement `import java.util.*;` is needed to access the `StringTokenizer` class.

The technique in Program 3.15 to parse the input line requires that we know how many items will be entered. This information, however, is not strictly necessary because the `StringTokenizer` class provides a method named `hasMoreTokens()` that returns a boolean `true` value whenever the object contains additional tokens. At this stage, however, this method is not useful to you because in practice it is used with the `while` statement presented in Chapter 5.

A First Look at User-Input Validation[7]

Validating user input and ensuring that a program does not crash due to unexpected input are signs of a well-constructed program. Programs that respond effectively to unexpected user input are formally referred to as **robust** programs and informally as "bullet-proof" programs. One of your jobs as a programmer is to produce such programs. As written, Programs 3.14 and 3.15 are not robust. Let's see why.

The first problem with both programs becomes evident when a user presses the Enter key accidentally before any value is entered. Should this happen, the entered string read by `readLine()` will contain no characters at all. The returned string is thus the zero length empty string "". Because an empty string has no tokens that can be extracted, in Program 3.15 the `next token()` method causes an error message, which is referred to as an exception in Java. In Program 3.14, this empty string also results in an error because it cannot be converted to a legitimate numerical value. Unless this error condition is correctly handled, the program will terminate. This type of termination, which occurs while a program is executing due to an error in the program, is called a **crash**.

Another error will occur whenever a user types in any other input that cannot be converted to a double-precision value. For example, entering the string `oops 12 3.25` and pressing the Enter key causes the `parseDouble ()` to fail in Program 3.15 because it cannot convert the characters `oops` to a valid double-precision number.

The first error condition is designated as a `NoSuchElementException`, and the second condition is designated as a `NumberFormatException`, which is displayed on the terminal by the program before it stops executing.[8] For example, Figure 3.23 shows the error message provided for the second condition. Notice that the exception is identified as a `NumberFormatException`.

There are two ways of handling both of these errors, and both of these error handling techniques can be applied in the same program. The first technique that should be applied is referred to as **user-input validation**, which means validating the entered data either during or immediately after the data have been entered and providing the user with a way of reentering any invalid data. User-input validation is an essential part of any commercially viable program, and if done correctly, it will protect a program from attempting to process data types that can cause a program crash. We will see

---

[7]This topic can be omitted on first reading with no loss of subject continuity.

[8]Documentation on exceptions can be found using Sun's Java documentation Web site at java.sun.com/docs, clicking on either the JAVA 2 SDK, SE1.3, or SE1.2 items, and then using the provided search engine. An equally good source of documentation is *The Java Class Libraries* (2nd ed., Vol. 1) by Chan, Lee, and Kramer (Reading, MA: Addison-Wesley, 1998). It provides a wealth of reference material, nicely organized, with many short code examples.

```
C:\jdk>
C:\jdk>
C:\jdk>
C:\jdk>
C:\jdk>
C:\jdk>
C:\jdk>

C:\jdk>java MultiplyNumbers
Exception in thread "main" java.lang.NumberFormatException: oops
        at java.lang.FloatingDecimal.readJavaFormatString(FloatingDecimal.java:
180)
        at java.lang.Double.parseDouble(Double.java:188)
        at MultiplyNumbers.main(MultiplyNumbers.java:11)

C:\jdk>
C:\jdk>
C:\jdk>
C:\jdk>

C:\jdk>

C:\jdk>

C:\jdk>
```

FIGURE 3.23 A `NumberFormatException` Notification

how to provide this type of validation after Java's selection and repetition statements have been presented in Chapters 4 and 5, respectively.[9]

The next line of defense against such errors is to provide error processing code that either corrects the problem or permits the program to terminate gracefully without reporting a run-time crash to the user. The means of providing this in Java is referred to as exception handling and is discussed at the end of the next section.

It should be noted that the expression `throws java.io.IOException` in Programs 3.14 and 3.15 is required because of the `readLine()` method and is not related to any exceptions that might occur in parsing the string or converting it to a primitive data type. The `readLine()` method requires that the programmer explicitly defines how any input error detected by it should be handled. The easiest way to satisfy this requirement is to tell the compiler to pass any related input error that occurs in `main()` up to the operating system. This is known as "throwing the error up to the operating system" and is designated by the keyword `throws` in the `throws java.io.IOException` expression. If this expression is not included, the compiler will provide the error message: `Exception java.io.IOException must be caught, or it must be declared in the throws clause of this method`. At the end of the next section, we will see how to explicitly "catch" an exception.

EXERCISES 3.4

1. Write two statements that could be used after each of the following prompts to perform the following tasks. The first statement should read a string value from the keyboard, assuming that the string is to be accessed by the string variable named `inputString`. The second statement should convert `inputString` into a

---

[9]It should be noted that `readline ()` does not permit the programmer to put the screen into "raw mode," where each character can be intercepted before it is sent to the screen. This means that validation using `readline()` is usually restricted to verification after the complete string value has been entered and not during individual character input. This is true even for the character-based `read()` method. The cause of this is that `System.in` is actually a buffered stream. The positive side is that editing, using the Backspace and Delete keys, is automatically provided.

variable of the correct primitive data type. Assume that an integer value is required for a, a long value for b, a floating-point value for c, and a double-precision value for d.

a. `System.out.println("Enter a grade: ");`

b. `System.out.println("Enter a voltage: ");`

c. `System.out.println("Enter a slope: ");`

d. `System.out.println("Enter a density: ");`

2. Enter and execute Program 3.14.

3. Enter and execute Program 3.14 but leave out the line containing the expression `throws java.io.IOException` after the `main()` header line. Record the error message provided by the compiler.

4. Write, compile, and execute a Java program that displays the following prompt:

   `Enter the radius of a circle:`

   After accepting a value for the radius, your program should calculate and display the area of the circle. (*Tip:* area = 3.1416 * radius^2.) For testing purposes, verify your program with a test input radius of 3 inches. After manually determining that the result produced by your program is correct, use your program to complete the following table:

Radius (in.)	Area (sq. in.)
1.0	
1.5	
2.0	
2.5	
3.0	
3.5	

5. a. Write, compile, and execute a Java program that displays the following prompts:

   `Enter the miles driven:`

   `Enter the gallons of gas used:`

   After each prompt is displayed, your program should use a `readLine()` method to accept data from the keyboard for the displayed prompt. After the gallons of gas used number has been entered, your program should calculate and display miles per gallon obtained. This value should be included in an appropriate message and calculated using the equation *miles per gallon = miles / gallons used*. Verify your program with the following test data:

   Test data set 1: miles = 276, gas = 10 gallons
   Test data set 2: miles = 200, gas = 15.5 gallons

   When you have completed your verification, use your program to complete the following table:

Miles driven	Gallons used	mpg
250	16.00	
275	18.00	
312	19.54	
296	17.39	

b. For the program written for Exercise 5a, determine how many verification runs are required to ensure the program is working correctly and give a reason supporting your answer.

6. a. Write a Java program that displays the following prompts:

```
Enter the length of the swimming pool:
Enter the width of the swimming pool:
Enter the average depth of the swimming pool:
```

After each prompt is displayed, your program should use a `readLine()` method to accept data from the keyboard for the displayed prompt. After the depth of the swimming pool is entered, your program should calculate and display the volume of the pool. The volume should be included in an appropriate message and calculated using the equation *volume = length * width * average depth.*

b. Check the volume displayed by the program written for Exercise 6a by calculating the result manually.

7. a. Write a Java program that displays the following prompts:

```
Enter a number:
Enter a second number:
Enter a third number:
Enter a fourth number:
```

After each prompt is displayed, your program should use a `readLine()` method to accept a number from the keyboard for the displayed prompt. After the fourth number has been entered, your program should calculate and display the average of the numbers. The average should be included in an appropriate message. Check the average displayed by your program with the following test data:

Test data set 1: 100, 100, 100, 100
Test data set 2: 100, 0, 100, 0

When you have completed your verification, use your program to complete the following table:

Numbers	Average
92, 98, 79, 85	
86, 84, 75, 86	
63, 85, 74, 82	

b. Repeat Exercise 7a making sure that you use the same variable name, `number`, for each number input. Also use the variable `sum` for the sum of the numbers. (*Tip:* To do this, you must use the statement `sum = sum + number;` after each number is accepted. Review the material on accumulating presented in Section 3.1.)

8. a. Write, compile, and execute a Java program that computes and displays the value of the second-order polynomial $ax^2 + bx + c$ for any user input values of the coefficients a, b, c, and the variable x. Have your program first display a message informing the user as to what the program will do and then display suitable prompts to alert the user to enter the desired data. (*Tip:* Use a prompt such as `Enter the coefficient of the x squared term:`)

b. Check the result produced by your program written for Exercise 8a with the following test data:

Test data set 1: $a = 0$, $b = 0$, $c = 22$, $x = 56$
Test data set 2: $a = 0$, $b = 22$, $c = 0$, $x = 2$
Test data set 3: $a = 22$, $b = 0$, $c = 0$, $x = 2$
Test data set 4: $a = 2$, $b = 4$, $c = 5$, $x = 2$
Test data set 5: $a = 5$, $b = -3$, $c = 2$, $x = 1$

When you have completed your verification, use your program to complete the following table:

a	b	c	x	polynomial value
2.0	17.0	-12.0	1.3	
3.2	2.0	15.0	2.5	
3.2	2.0	15.0	-2.5	
-2.0	10.0	0.0	2.0	
-2.0	10.0	0.0	4.0	
-2.0	10.0	0.0	5.0	
-2.0	10.0	0.0	6.0	
5.0	22.0	18.0	8.3	
4.2	-16	-20	-5.2	

9. Write, compile, and execute a program that calculates and displays the square root value of a user-entered real number. Verify your program by calculating the square roots of the following data: 25, 16, 0, and 2. When you have completed your verification, use your program to determine the square root of 32.25, 42, 48, 55, 63, and 79.

10. For the series circuit shown in Figure 3.24, the voltage drop, V_2, across resistor R_2 and the power, P_2, delivered to this resistor are given by the equations $V_2 = I R_2$ and $P_2 = I V_2$, where $I = E /(R_1 + R_2)$. Using these equations, write, compile, and execute a Java program that prompts the user for values of E, R_1, and R_2, calculates the voltage drop and power delivered to R_2, and displays the results. Check your program using the test data: $E = 10$ volts, $R_1 = 100$ ohms, and $R_2 = 200$ ohms. When you have completed your verification, use your program to complete the following table:

E (volts)	R_1 (ohms)	R_2 (ohms)	Voltage drop (volts)	Power delivered (watts)
10	100	100		
10	100	200		
10	200	200		
20	100	100		
20	100	200		
20	200	200		

11. Write, compile, and execute a Java program that computes the combined resistance of three parallel resistors. The values of each resistor should be accepted with an input statement, and the combined resistance should be computed us-

FIGURE 3.24   Calculating the Voltage Drop

ing the formula given in Exercise 6 of Section 3.2. Verify the operation of your program with the following test data:

Test data set 1: $R_1 = 1000$, $R_2 = 1000$, and $R_3 = 1000$
Test data set 2: $R_1 = 1000$, $R_2 = 1500$, and $R_3 = 500$

When you have completed your verification, use your program to complete the following table:

R1 (volts)	R2 (ohms)	R3 (ohms)	Combined Resistance (ohms)
3000	3000	3000	
6000	6000	6000	
2000	3000	1000	
2000	4000	5000	
4000	2000	1000	
10000	100	100	

12. Using input statements, write, compile, and execute a Java program that accepts the x and y coordinates of two points. Have your program determine and display the midpoint of the two points (use the formula given in Exercise 8 of Section 3.2). Verify your program with the following test data:

Test data set 1: Point 1 = (0,0) and Point 2 = (16,0)
Test data set 2: Point 1 = (0,0) and Point 2 = (0,16)
Test data set 3: Point 1 = (0,0) and Point 2 = (−16,0)
Test data set 4: Point 1 = (0,0) and Point 2 = (0,−16)
Test data set 5: Point 1 = (−5,−5) and Point 2 = (5,5)

When you have completed your verification, use your program to complete the following table:

Point 1	Point 2	Midpoint
(4,6)	(16,18)	
(22,3)	(8,12)	
(−10,8)	(14,4)	
(−12,2)	(14,3.1)	
(3.1,−6)	(20,16)	
(3.1,−6)	(−16,−18)	

13. Write, compile, and execute a Java program that calculates and displays the value of the current flowing through an *RC* circuit. The circuit consists of a battery that is connected in series to a switch, a resistor, and a capacitor. When the switch is closed the current, *i*, that flows through the circuit is given by the equation:

$$i = (E/R) \, e^{-t/\tau}$$

where *E* is the voltage of the battery (in volts), *R* is the resistance (in ohms), τ is termed the time constant, and *t* is the time (in seconds) since the switch was closed.

The program should prompt the user to enter appropriate values and use input statements to accept the data. In constructing the prompts, use statements such as `Enter the Voltage of the Battery`. Verify the operation of your program by hand calculating the current for the following test data:

Test data set 1: voltage = 20 volts, *R* = 10 ohms, τ = 0.044, *t* = 0.023 seconds
Test data set 2: voltage = 35, *R* = 10 ohms, τ = 0.16, *t* = 0.067 seconds

When you have completed your verification, use your program to determine the value of the current for the following cases:

a. voltage = 35, *R* = 10 ohms, τ = 0.16, *t* = 0.11 seconds
b. voltage = 35, *R* = 10 ohms, τ = 0.16, *t* = 0.44 seconds
c. voltage = 35, *R* = 10 ohms, τ = 0.16, *t* = 0.83 seconds
d. voltage = 15, *R* = 10 ohms, τ = 0.55, *t* = 0.11 seconds
e. voltage = 15, *R* = 10 ohms, τ = 0.55, *t* = 0.44 seconds
f. voltage = 15, *R* = 10 ohms, τ = 0.55, *t* = 0.067 seconds
g. voltage = 6, *R* = 1000 ohms, τ = 2.6, *t* = 12.4 seconds

14. Program 3.13 prompts the user to input two numbers, where the first value entered is stored in num1 and the second value is stored in num2. With this program as a starting point, write a program that swaps the values stored in the two variables.

15. Write a Java program that prompts the user to enter a number. Have your program accept the number, convert it to an integer, and display the integer value. Run your program three times. The first time you run the program enter a valid integer number, the second time enter a floating-point number, and the third time enter a character. Using the output display, see what number your program actually accepted from the data you entered.

16. Repeat Exercise 15 but have your program convert the entered string to a floating-point value and store the converted value into a floating-point variable. Run the program four times. The first time enter an integer, the second time enter a decimal number, the third time enter a decimal number with an f as the last character entered, and the fourth time enter a character. Using the output display, keep track of what number your program actually accepted from the data you entered. What happened, if anything, and why?

17. Repeat Exercise 15 but have your program convert the number to a double-precision value and store the converted value in a double-precision variable.

18. a. Why do you think that successful application programs contain extensive data input validity checks? (*Tip:* Review Exercises 15, 16, and 17.)

    b. What do you think is the difference between a data type check and a data reasonableness check?

    c. Assume that a program requests a month, day, and year from the user. What are some checks that could be made on the data entered?

19. Enter and execute Program 3.15 on your computer.

20. Enter and execute Program 3.15 on your computer, but make both of the following changes:

    a. omit the line after the `main()` header line that contains the expression

```
throws java.io.IOException
```

    b. change the statement `inputString = br.readLine();` to `inputString = "98.5 12";`

Compile and execute the program to determine what error message is provided. Discuss what occurred and why.

3.5 INTERACTIVE DIALOG INPUT

In addition to keyboard data entry, Java provides a GUI method of entering user data with a method named `showInputDialog()`, which is contained in the `JOptionPane` class. A call to this method creates a dialog box (recall from Section 1.5 that a dialog is any box that requires the user to supply additional information to complete a task) that permits a user to enter a string at the terminal. The string can then be converted to a primitive data type value, as is done for keyboard input.

The syntax for the `showInputDialog()` method is

$$\texttt{JOptionPane.showInputDialog(}string\texttt{);}$$

where the *string* argument is a prompt displayed within the input dialog box. For example, the statement

```
s = JOptionPane.showInputDialog("Enter a number:");
```

calls the `showInputDialog()` method with the argument `"Enter a number:"`, which is the prompt. When this statement is executed, the input dialog in Figure 3.25 is displayed.

Once an input dialog box is displayed, the keyboard is continuously scanned for data. As keys are pressed, the `showInputDialog()` method displays them within the input area of the dialog. When either the Enter key or the OK command button is pressed, input stops, and the entered text is returned and stored in the string variable on the left

FIGURE 3.25 A Sample `showInputDialog()` Dialog

side of the assignment statement. Program execution then continues with the next statement immediately placed after the call to `showInputDialog()`.[10]

Program 3.16 illustrates a `showInputDialog()` method within the context of a complete application.

PROGRAM 3.16

```
import javax.swing.*;
public class SampleInputDialog
{
  public static void main (String[] args)
  {
    String s1, s2;
    double num1, num2, average;

    s1 = JOptionPane.showInputDialog("Enter a number:");
    num1 = Double.parseDouble(s1);

    s2 = JOptionPane.showInputDialog("Great! Now enter another number:");
    num2 = Double.parseDouble(s2);
    average = (num1 + num2)/2.0;

    JOptionPane.showMessageDialog(null,
            "The average of " + num1 + " and " + num2 + " is " + average,
            "Program 3.16",
            JOptionPane.INFORMATION_MESSAGE);

    System.exit(0);
  }
}
```

The first input dialog displayed by Program 3.16 is shown in Figure 3.26. The 15 displayed in the input area of the dialog is the value entered from the keyboard.

Notice that the dialog's prompt tells the user to enter a number. After this dialog is displayed, the `showInputDialog()` method puts the application into a temporary pause (or wait) state for as long as it takes the user to type a value. The user signals the `showInputDialog()` method that data entry is finished by clicking one of the Command buttons. If the user clicks the OK button (or presses the Enter key), the entered value is stored in the string referenced on the left side of the assignment statement, which in this case is `s1`, and the application is taken out of its paused state. Program execution then proceeds with the next statement, which in Program 3.17 is another call to the

---

[10]If the user presses the Cancel button, a null value is returned, which cannot be converted by `parseDouble()`. This results in a program exception, and program execution comes to a halt. We show how to handle this exception correctly at the end of this section, but for now, if this button is pressed, you will have to break out of the program by either pressing the Break or Ctrl and C keys together once or twice.

FIGURE 3.26 The First Dialog After Data Are Entered

`showInputDialog()` method. This second dialog and the data entered in response to it are shown in Figure 3.27.

FIGURE 3.27 The Second Dialog After Data Are Entered

While the second dialog is displayed, the application is again put into a temporary wait state as the user types a second value. This second number is stored in the string object named `s2`. The next two statements convert the string values into double-precision numbers. Based on these converted input values, an average is computed and displayed in a message dialog (Figure 3.28).

FIGURE 3.28 A Sample Output Produced by Program 3.16

Before leaving Program 3.16, one last observation is worth making. Notice the parentheses in the statement `average = (num1 + num2)/2.0;`. The parentheses are required to produce a correct calculation. Without these parentheses, the only number that would be divided by 2 is the value in `num2` (because division has a higher precedence than addition).

To ensure that you have a good grasp of how the `showInputDialog()` method obtains user input, we provide one further example. Consider Program 3.17, which is a Fahrenheit to Celsius temperature conversion program. In this program, the user is prompted to enter a Fahrenheit temperature. Once the user enters a temperature, the program converts the entered string into a double-precision value, converts the temperature to its equivalent Celsius value, and displays the computed value.

Figure 3.29 shows the input dialog box created by the program after the user has entered a value of 212. The display produced for this input value is shown in Figure 3.30.

PROGRAM 3.17

```java
import javax.swing.*;
public class ConvertTemp
{
  public static void main (String[] args)
  {
    String fahr, output;
    double tempfahr, celsius;

    fahr = JOptionPane.showInputDialog("Enter a Fahrenheit temperature:");

    tempfahr = Double.parseDouble(fahr);
    celsius = 5.0/9.0 * (tempfahr - 32);

    output = "The equivalent Celsius temperature for " + tempfahr
           + " degrees Fahrenheit is " + celsius;
    JOptionPane.showMessageDialog(null, output, "Program 3.17",
                              JOptionPane.INFORMATION_MESSAGE);

    System.exit(0);
  }
}
```

Input

Enter a Fahrenheit Temperature:

212

OK   Cancel

FIGURE 3.29   The Input Dialog Created by Program 3.17

Notice that, within the program, a string reference named output is constructed using two assignment statements. The second assignment statement appends additional information to the string, and it is the string reference's name, output, that is passed to the showMessageDialog() method for final display.

Program 3.11

The equivalent Celsius temperature for 212.0 degrees Fahrenheit is 100.0

OK

FIGURE 3.30   A Sample Output Produced by Program 3.17

Exception Handling[11]

A feature of Java that is quite different from most high-level languages is the way in which Java handles error conditions. Most other languages have traditionally required that each method, such as `main()`, return specific values to indicate specific failures by the method. If this approach were followed by Java, the `Double.parseDouble()` method would be required to return a special value to indicate that it could not successfully complete its conversion task.

There are a number of possible problems with this traditional approach. First, it requires that the programmer actually checks the code to detect if an error did in fact occur. Next, the error handling code becomes intermixed with normal processing code, so it sometimes can be very difficult to clearly determine which part of the code is handling errors as opposed to normal program processing. And finally, returning an error condition from a method means that the condition must be of the same data type as a valid returned value; hence, the error code must be a specially identified value that can be identified as an error alert. Thus, the error code is effectively imbedded as one of the possible valid values and is only available at the point where the method returns a value. None of this is insurmountable, but Java rejected it in favor of an error handling methodology that has come to be known as exception handling.

In **exception handling**, when an error occurs while a method is executing, the method creates an object, at the point the error occurs, that contains information about the error. This exception object is then immediately passed, again at the point it was generated, to the Java Virtual Machine, which attempts to locate code to handle the exception. The process of generating and passing the exception object at the point the error was detected is referred to as **throwing an exception**. Notice that the exception is thrown from within the method while it is still executing. This permits handling the error and returning control back to the method so that it can complete its assigned task correctly.

In particular, there are two fundamental types of errors that can cause Java exceptions: those that result from an inability of the program to obtain a required resource and those that result from flawed code.

Examples of the first error type are attempts to obtain memory for a reference type, such as a string, when insufficient memory is available or an attempt to open a file for input that does not exist. Notice that these errors are the result of external resources over which the programmer has no control. To ensure that such exceptional conditions are provided for should they occur during program execution, Java checks that some mechanism is explicitly in place for receiving and processing the exception object. This check is made at compile time, and because the check is made by the compiler, it is formally referred to as a **checked exception.**

Examples of the second type of error are provided in Programs 3.16 and 3.17, where a user can either enter a string that cannot be converted to a numerical value, click the OK button without entering any string, or click the Cancel button. Because this type of error can always be prevented by programming, in this case by providing user-input

[11]This topic may be omitted on first reading with no loss of subject continuity.

TABLE 3.7   Exception Handling Terminology

Terminology	Description
Exception	An error that occurs while a program is executing.
Throw an exception	Generate an exception object.
Catch or handle an exception	Identify an exception and pass it to a handler.
Catch clause or handler	The section of code that performs the error processing.

validation, Java does not check that an exception handling mechanism is in place at compile time. As a result, this second type of exceptions is referred to as an **unchecked exception**. The fact that it is unchecked, however, does not mean that we cannot still apply Java's exception handling techniques to it. Because Java's exception handling techniques are so easy to use, we will show how they can be applied to the user-input errors that we have identified for Program 3.17.[12] Before doing so, however, review Table 3.7 to see that you are comfortable with the terminology that relates to the processing of exceptions.

The general syntax of the code required to throw and handle an exception is:

```
try
{

  // one or more statements,
  // at least one of which should
  // be capable of throwing an exception;
}
catch(exceptionName argument)
{
    // one or more statements
}
finally
{
    // one or more statements
}
```

This code uses three new keywords: `try`, `catch`, and `finally`. Let's see what each of these words does.

The keyword `try` identifies the start of an exception handling block of code. At least one of the statements within the braces defining this block of code should be capable of throwing an exception. For example, the `try` block in the following section of code

---

[12]Exception processing should generally be restricted to checked exceptions. Errors such as invalid user-entered data or attempts to divide by zero can and should be detected and handled by Java's conventional selection and repetition statements. In later sections, we will show how this is done. At this stage, however, Programs 3.16 and 3.17 provide a very easy and intuitive introduction to exception processing, and we will use them for this purpose.

THREE USEFUL EXCEPTIONS

Java provides three exceptions that you will find especially useful in your programming career. These are:

Exception	Description
ArithemeticException	Thrown whenever an attempt is made to perform an illegal arithmetic operation, such as an attempt to divide by zero.
NumberFormatException	Thrown whenever an attempt is made to convert a string that does not contain the appropriate characters for the desired number type.
NullPointerException	Thrown whenever an attempt is made to access an object that does not exist.

```
try
{
   s1 = JOptionPane.showInputDialog("Enter a number:");
   num1 = Double.parseDouble(s1);
   s2 = JOptionPane.showInputDialog("Great! Now enter another number:");

   num2 = Double.parseDouble(s2);

   average = (num1 + num2)/2.0;

   JOptionPane.showMessageDialog(null,
         "The average of " + num1 + " and " + num2 + " is " + average,
         "Program 3.18",
         JOptionPane.INFORMATION_MESSAGE);
}
```

contains six statements, only two of which may throw an exception that we want to catch. These are the two statements that use the `Double.parseDouble()` method to convert a string into a double-precision number. In particular, we want to handle the `NumberFormatException`, which is thrown when either `s1` or `s2` contains invalid characters that cannot be converted, and the `NullPointerException`, which is thrown when either `s1` or `s2` does not reference any object at all. The first exception will occur whenever the user either clicks the OK button without entering any data or enters nonnumerical characters, and the second exception will occur if the user clicks the Cancel button. Thus, from the standpoint of the `try` block, only the conversion statements are of concern. Essentially, the `try` block says, "Try all of the statements within me to see if an exception occurs."

A `try` block must be followed by one or more `catch` blocks, which serve as exception handlers for any exceptions thrown by the statements in the `try` block. For our particular case, we want to catch two specific exceptions, which is accomplished by the following section of code:

```
catch(NumberFormatException n)
{
  JOptionPane.showMessageDialog(null,
              "You must enter a number",
              "Input Data Error",
              JOptionPane.ERROR_MESSAGE);
}
catch(NullPointerException n)
{
  JOptionPane.showMessageDialog(null,
              "You Pressed the Cancel Button",
              "Program Termination",
              JOptionPane.ERROR_MESSAGE);
}
```

Here the exception handling provided by each `catch` block is simply a dialog that identifies the particular exception that has been caught. Notice the parentheses following each `catch` keyword. Listed within each set of parentheses is the name of the exception being caught and an argument identifier, which we have named n. This identifier, which is a programmer-selectable name, holds the exception object generated when the exception occurs ("is thrown").

Although we have provided two `catch` blocks, this is not required. All that is required is that at least one `catch` block be provided for each `try` block. Naturally, the more exceptions that can be caught with the same `try` block the better. The optional `finally` block provides a catchall default set of instructions that is always executed whether or not any exception occurred. For our case, we will use the code

```
finally{System.exit(0);}
```

This code ensures that the program gracefully closes down in all cases. Program 3.18 incorporates this code within the context of a complete program. Notice that the instructions within the `try` block are essentially all of the processing statements in Program 3.16. The difference in these programs is that the two exceptions that we have identified for Program 3.16 are reported to a user when they occur, and the program is terminated gracefully without reporting a run-time system error message. Figures 3.31 and 3.32 show the dialog boxes for the two exceptions that are now caught in Program 3.18.

FIGURE 3.31   Result of Catching the `NumberFormatException`

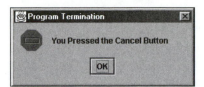

FIGURE 3.32 Result of Catching the `NullPointerException`

PROGRAM 3.18

```java
import javax.swing.*;
public class CatchingExceptions
{
  public static void main (String[] args)
  {
    String s1;
    String s2;
    double num1, num2, average;
    try
    {
      s1 = JOptionPane.showInputDialog("Enter a number:");
      num1 = Double.parseDouble(s1);
      s2 = JOptionPane.showInputDialog("Great! Now enter another number:");

      num2 = Double.parseDouble(s2);
      average = (num1 + num2)/2.0;

      JOptionPane.showMessageDialog(null,
              "The average of " + num1 + " and " + num2 + " is " + average,
              "Program 3.18",
              JOptionPane.INFORMATION_MESSAGE);
    }
    catch(NumberFormatException n)
    {
     JOptionPane.showMessageDialog(null,
              "You must enter a number",
              "Input Data Error",
              JOptionPane.ERROR_MESSAGE);
    }
    catch(NullPointerException n)
    {
     JOptionPane.showMessageDialog(null,
              "You Pressed the Cancel Button",
              "Program Termination",
              JOptionPane.ERROR_MESSAGE);
    }
    finally{System.exit(0);}
  }
}
```

EXERCISES 3.5

1. Write assignment statements that store the returned value from an input dialog box in a string variable named `test` for the following input prompts:
   a. prompt: `"Enter a grade:"`
   b. prompt: `"Enter a temperature:"`
   c. prompt: `"Enter a voltage:"`
   d. prompt: `"Enter a name:"`
   e. prompt: `"Enter a density:"`

2. Modify Program 3.17 so that the computed Celsius temperature value is always displayed with a maximum of two digits after the decimal point.

3. Write, compile, and execute a Java program that displays the following prompt in an input dialog box:

   `Enter the radius of a circle:`

   After accepting a value for the radius, your program should calculate and display the area of the circle. (*Tip: area = 3.1416 * radius²*.) For testing purposes, verify your program with a test input radius of 3 inches. After manually determining that the result produced by your program is correct, use your program to complete the following table:

Radius (in.)	Area (sq. in.)
1.0	
1.5	
2.0	
2.5	
3.0	
3.5	

4. a. Write a Java program that displays the following prompt in an input dialog box:

   `Enter the temperature in degrees Celsius:`

   Have your program accept a value entered from the keyboard and convert the temperature entered to degrees Fahrenheit using the formula *Fahrenheit = (9.0 / 5.0) * Celsius + 32.0*. Your program should then display the temperature in degrees Celsius with an appropriate output message.

   b. Compile and execute the program written for Exercise 4a. Verify your program by hand calculation and then use your program to determine the Fahrenheit equivalent of the following test data:

   Test data set 1: 0 degrees Celsius
   Test data set 2: 50 degrees Celsius
   Test data set 3: 100 degrees Celsius

   When you are sure your program is working correctly, use it to complete the following table:

Celsius	Fahrenheit
45	
50	
55	
60	
65	
70	

5. Write and execute a Java program that uses input dialog boxes to display the following prompts:

```
Enter the length of the rectangle:
Enter the width of the rectangle:
```

Your program should use the entered values to calculate and display the area of the rectangle. Verify your procedure with the following test data:

Test data set 1: length = 12.5, width = 10
Test data set 2: length = 12.4, width = 0
Test data set 3: length = 0, width = 10

6. **a.** Write and execute a Java program that uses input dialog boxes to display the following prompts:

```
Enter the miles driven:
Enter the gallons of gas used:
```

Your program should use the entered values to calculate and display the miles per gallon. Use the equation *miles per gallon = miles / gallons used.* Verify your procedure with the following test data:

Test data set 1: miles = 276, gas = 10 gallons
Test data set 2: miles = 200, gas = 15.5 gallons

When you have completed your verification, use your procedure to complete the following table:

Miles Driven	Gallons Used	mpg
250	16.00	
275	18.00	
312	19.54	
296	17.39	

   b. For the program in Exercise 6a, determine how many verification runs are required to ensure the procedure is working correctly and give a reason supporting your answer.

7. Enter and execute Program 3.16 on your computer. Record the exception message displayed when you:
   i. Click the OK button without entering any data
   ii. Enter the characters oops and click the OK button
   iii. Click the Cancel button

8. **a.** Enter and execute Program 3.17. Determine what happens when you:
   i. Click the OK button without entering any data
   ii. Enter the characters oops and click the OK button
   iii. Click the Cancel button

    b. Remove the second `catch` block in Program 3.18 and see what happens when you click the Cancel button. Determine what part of the code handles the exception that was previously taken care of by the removed `catch` code.

  9. Modify Program 3.18 so that the `try` block only contains the statements

```
num1 = Double.parseDouble(s1);
num2 = Double.parseDouble(s2);
```

10. **a.** Newton's law of cooling states that when an object with an initial temperature T is placed in a surrounding substance of temperature A, it will reach a temperature $TFIN$ in t minutes according to the formula

$$TFIN = (T - A)\, e^{-kt} + A$$

In this formula, e is the irrational number 2.71828 rounded to five decimal places, commonly known as Euler's number, and k is a thermal coefficient, which depends on the material being cooled. Using this formula, write, compile, and execute a Java program that uses an input dialog box to prompt the user for the initial temperature of the material in degrees Fahrenheit. Have your program determine the temperature reached by the object after 20 minutes assuming that it is placed in a glass of water whose temperature is 60 degrees. Assume that the object has a thermal constant of 0.0367.

  b. Check the value computed by your program by hand. After you have verified that your program works correctly, modify it to determine the temperature reached after 10 minutes when it is placed in a glass of water whose temperature is 50 degrees. To do this, modify your program so that both the temperature of the water and the time the object is left in the water are obtained from the user as input supplied using input dialog boxes.

11. **a.** The voltage gain of an amplifier is given by the formula

$$voltage\ gain = [275 / (\, 23^2 + (0.5f)^2\,)^{1/2}\,]^n$$

where f is the frequency in hertz and n is the number of stages in the amplifier. Using this formula, write, compile, and execute a Java program that determines the value of the voltage gain for a four-stage amplifier operating at a frequency that is input to the program using an input dialog box. Test your program by entering a frequency of 120 hertz. Your program should produce the display:

```
At a frequency of xxxxx hertz, the voltage gain is yyyyy
```

where the xs are replaced by the frequency and the ys by the voltage gain by your program. Check the value computed by your program by hand.

  b. After you have verified that your program works correctly, modify it to determine the voltage gain of a 12-stage amplifier operating at a frequency of 9,500 hertz. To do this, modify your program so that the number of amplification stages is also supplied using an input dialog box.

12. **a.** The electrical current, i, in amps that flows through the circuit illustrated in Figure 3.33 is given by the equation:

$$i = \frac{E[1 - e]^{-(R/L)t}}{R}$$

where E is the voltage of the battery in volts, R is the value of the resistor in ohms, L is the value of the inductor in henrys, t is the time in seconds from when the switch is closed, and e is Euler's number, which is 2.718 accurate to three decimal places. Using this formula, write, compile, and run a Java program to determine the current flowing in the circuit in Figure 3.33 when t is 0.12 seconds. The value of the resistance should be entered using an input dialog box. Initially, enter a value of 56 for the resistance.

FIGURE 3.33 A Series *RL* Circuit

    b. After you have verified that your program works correctly, modify it to determine the current in 0.12 seconds if E is 25 volts, R is 33 ohms, and L is 15 henrys.

13. a. The electrical current, i, in amps that flows through the circuit in Figure 3.34 is given by the equation:

$$i = \frac{(E)e^{-t/RC}}{R}$$

where E is the voltage of the battery in volts, R is the value of the resistor in ohms, C is the value of the capacitor in farads, t is the time in seconds from when the switch is closed, and e is Euler's number, which is 2.718 accurate to three decimal places. Using this formula, write, compile, and run a Java program to determine the current through the capacitor in Figure 3.34 when t is 0.31 seconds. The value of the resistance should be entered using an input dialog box. Initially, enter a value of 8,100 for the resistance.

FIGURE 3.34 A Series *RC* Circuit

    b. Check the value computed by your program by hand. After you have verified that your program works correctly, modify it to determine the current in 0.85 seconds if E is 25 volts, R is 220 ohms, and C is 0.00039 farads.

14. a. The electrical voltage, V, in volts across the capacitor, C, illustrated in Figure 3.35 is given by the equation:

$$V = E\,[1 - e\,]^{-t/RC}$$

where E is the voltage of the battery in volts, R is the value of the resistor in ohms, C is the value of the capacitor in farads, t is the time in seconds from when the switch is closed, and e is Euler's number, which is 2.718 accurate to three decimal places. Using this formula, write, compile, and run a Java program to determine the voltage across the capacitor in Figure 3.35 when t is 0.42 seconds. The value of the resistance should be entered using an input dialog box. Initially, enter a value of 470 for the resistance.

FIGURE 3.35   A Series *RC* Circuit

    b. Check the value computed by your program by hand. After you have verified that your program works correctly, modify it to determine the current in 0.85 seconds if E is 25 volts, R is 220 ohms, and C is 0.00039 farads.

3.6 APPLICATIONS

In this section, we present two applications to illustrate further the use of input statements to accept user input data and the use of the Math class' methods for performing calculations.

Application 1: Acid Rain

The use of coal as the major source of steam power began with the Industrial Revolution. Currently, coal is one of the principal sources of electrical power generation in many industrialized countries.

    Since the middle of the 19th century, it has been known that the oxygen used in the burning process combines with the carbon and sulfur in the coal to produce carbon dioxide and sulfur dioxide. When these gases are released into the atmosphere, the sulfur dioxide combines with the water and oxygen in the air to form sulfuric acid, which itself is transformed into separate hydronium ions and sulfates (Figure 3.36). The hydronium

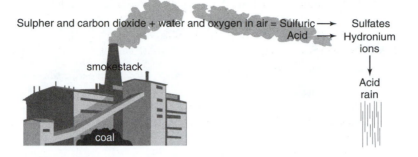

Sulpher and carbon dioxide + water and oxygen in air = Sulfuric ⟶ Sulfates
Acid ⟶ Hydronium
ions

smokestack

↓

Acid
rain

coal

FIGURE 3.36   The Formation of Acid Rain

ions in the atmosphere fall to earth, either as components of rain or as a dry deposition, and change the acidity level of lakes and forests.

The acid level of rain and lakes is measured on a pH scale with the formula

$$pH = -\log_{10}\,(Concentration\ of\ hydronium\ ions)$$

where the concentration of hydronium ions is measured in units of moles/liter. A pH value of 7 indicates a neutral value (neither acid nor alkaline), whereas levels below 7 indicate the presence of an acid, and levels above 7 indicate the presence of an alkaline substance. For example, sulfuric acid has a pH value of approximately 1, lye has a pH value of approximately 13, and water typically has a pH value of 7. Marine life usually cannot survive in water with a pH level below 4.

Using the formula for pH, we will write a Java program that calculates the pH level of a substance based on a user input value for the concentration of hydronium ions. Using the development procedure described in Section 2.4, we have:

Step 1: Analyze the Problem   Although the statement of the problem provides technical information on the composition of acid rain, from a programming viewpoint this is a rather simple problem. There is only one required output (a pH level) and one input (the concentration of hydronium ions).

Step 2: Develop a Solution   The algorithm required to transform the input to the required output is a rather straightforward use of the pH formula that is provided. The pseudocode representation of the complete algorithm for entering the input data, processing the data to produce the desired output, and displaying the output is:

Display a prompt to enter a hydronium ion concentration level
Read a value for the concentration level
Calculate a pH level using the given formula
Display the calculated value

To ensure that we understand the formula in the algorithm, we will do a hand calculation. The result of this calculation can then verify the result produced by the program. Assuming a hydronium concentration of 0.0001 (any value would do), the pH level is calculated as $-\log_{10} 10^{-4}$. Either by knowing that the logarithm of 10 raised to a power is the power itself or by referring to a log table, the value of this expressions is $-(-4) = 4$.

Step 3: Code the Solution Program 3.19 describes the selected algorithm in Java. The choice of variable names is arbitrary.

PROGRAM 3.19

```java
import java.io.*;   // needed to access input stream classes
public class ComputepHLevel
{
  public static void main (String[] args)
  throws java.io.IOException
  {
    double hydron, pHlevel;
    String s1;

    // set up the basic input stream
      // needed for conversion capabilities
    InputStreamReader isr = new InputStreamReader(System.in);
      // needed to use readLine()
    BufferedReader br = new BufferedReader(isr);

    System.out.print("Enter the hydronium ion concentration level: ");
    s1 = br.readLine();
    hydron = Double.parseDouble(s1);

    pHlevel = -Math.log(hydron)/Math.log(10);
    System.out.println("The pH level is " + Math.round(pHlevel));
  }
}
```

Within Program 3.19's `main()` method, a declaration statement declares two double variables, `hydron` and `pHlevel`, and a single string variable, `s1`. The program then displays a prompt requesting input data from the user. After the prompt is displayed, the string variable `s1` stores the entered data. This string value is immediately converted into a double-precision value, using the `parseDouble()` method, and the converted numerical value is stored in the variable `hydron`. Finally, a value for `pHlevel` is calculated using the natural logarithmic method. Because we require the base-10 logarithm of the hydronium concentration, and not the natural logarithmic value, the calculated natural logarithm is converted to a base-10 logarithm by dividing the result by the natural logarithm of 10.[13] Notice that the computed value is used as an argument to the `Math.round()` method before it is displayed. Because this method rounds a number to the closest integer, it serves our current purposes. As always, the program is terminated with a closing brace.

[13]The conversion between logarithmic values can be obtained from any elementary algebra book. Specifically, for our case, the base-10 logarithm of a number N can be computed as the natural logarithm of N divided by the natural logarithm of 10.

Step 4: Test and Correct the Solution A test run of Program 3.19 produced the following:

```
Enter the hydronium ion concentration level: 0.0001
The pH level is 4
```

Because the program performs a single calculation and the result of this test run agrees with our previous hand calculation, the program has been completely tested. It can now calculate the pH level of other hydronium concentrations with confidence that the results are accurate.

Application 2: Approximating the Exponential Function

The exponential function e^x, where e is known as Euler's number (and has the value 2.718281828459045 . . .), appears many times in descriptions of natural phenomena. For example, radioactive decay, population growth, and the normal (bell-shaped) curve used in statistical applications can all be described with this function. The value of e^x can be approximated with the series[14]

$$1 + \frac{x^1}{1} + \frac{x^2}{2} + \frac{x^3}{6} + \frac{x^4}{24} + \frac{x^5}{120} + \frac{x^6}{720} \ldots$$

Using this polynomial as a base, write a program that approximates e raised to a user input value of x using the first four terms of this series. For each approximation, display the value calculated by Java's Math class' exponential method, exp(), the approximate value, and the absolute difference between the two. Make sure to verify your program with a hand calculation. Once the verification is complete, use the program to approximate e^4. Using the top-down development procedure described in Section 2.4, we perform the following steps.

Step 1: Analyze the Problem The statement of the problem specifies that four approximations are to be made using one, two, three, and four terms of the approximating polynomial, respectively. For each approximation, three output values are required: the value of the e^x produced by the exponential method, the approximated value, and the absolute difference between the two values. Figure 3.37 illustrates in symbolic form the structure of the required output display.

The output indicated in Figure 3.37 can help you get a "feel" for what the program must look like. Realizing that each line in the display can only be produced by executing a println() statement, it should be clear that four such statements must be executed. Additionally, since each output line contains three computed values, each println() statement will have three items in its expression list.

The only input to the program consists of the value of x. This will require a single prompt and an input statement to accept the necessary value.

[14]The formula from which this is derived is

$$e^x = \frac{x^0}{0!} + \frac{x^1}{1!} + \frac{x^2}{2!} + \frac{x^3}{3!} + \ldots + \frac{x^n}{n!}$$

e^x	Approximation	Difference
-------------------------	------------------------	--------------
Math class' method value	1st approximate value	1st difference
Math class' method value	2nd approximate value	2nd difference
Math class' method value	3rd approximate value	3rd difference
Math class' method value	4th approximate value	4th difference

FIGURE 3.37 Required Output Display

Step 2: Develop a Solution Before any output items can be calculated, the program will need to prompt the user for a value of x and then accept the entered value. The actual output display consists of two title lines followed by four lines of calculated data. The title lines can be produced with two println() statements. Now let's see how the actual data being displayed are produced.

The first item on the first data output line on Figure 3.37 can be obtained using the exp() method. The second item on this line, the approximation to e^x, can be obtained by using the first term in the polynomial that was given in the program specification. Finally, the third item on the line can be calculated using the Math.abs() method on the difference between the first two items. When all of these items are calculated, a single println() statement can display the three results on the same line.

The second output line in Figure 3.37 displays the same type of items as the first line, except that the approximation to e^x requires the use of two terms of the approximating polynomial. Notice also that the first item on the second line, the value obtained by the exp() method, is the same as the first item on the first line. This means that this item does not have to be recalculated, and the value calculated for the first line can simply be displayed a second time. Once the data for the second line have been calculated, a single println() statement can display the required values.

Finally, only the second and third items on the last two output lines in Figure 3.37 need to be recalculated because the first item on these lines is the same as previously calculated for the first line. Thus, for this problem, the complete algorithm described in pseudocode is:

Display a prompt for the input value of x
Read the input value
Display the heading lines
Calculate the exponential value of x using the exp() method
Calculate the first approximation
Calculate the first difference
Print the first output line
Calculate the second approximation
Calculate the second difference
Print the second output line
Calculate the third approximation
Calculate the third difference
Print the third output line
Calculate the fourth approximation
Calculate the fourth difference
Print the fourth output line

To ensure that we understand the processing in the algorithm, we will do a hand calculation. The result of this calculation can then verify the result produced by the program. For test purposes, we will use a value of 2 for x, which causes the following approximations:

For the first term of the polynomial, the approximation is

$$e^2 = 1$$

For the first two terms of the polynomial, the approximation is

$$e^2 = 1 + 2/1 = 3$$

For the first three terms of the polynomial, the approximation is

$$e^2 = 3 + 2^2/2 = 5$$

For the first four terms of the polynomial, the approximation is

$$e^2 = 5 + 2^3/6 = 6.3333$$

Notice that in using four terms of the polynomial, it was not necessary to recalculate the value of the first three terms; instead, we used the previously calculated value.

Step 3: Code the Solution   Program 3.20 represents a description of the selected algorithm in Java.

PROGRAM 3.20

```java
// this program approximates the function e raised to the x power
// using one, two, three, and four terms of an approximating polynomial

import java.io.*;   // needed to access input stream classes
import java.text.*; // needed for formatting
public class ApproxExponential
{
  public static void main (String[] args)
  throws java.io.IOException
  {
    String s1;
    double x, actualValue, approx, difference;

    DecimalFormat df = new DecimalFormat("#.000000");

        // set up the basic input stream
        // needed for conversion capabilities
        InputStreamReader isr = new InputStreamReader(System.in);
        // needed to use readLine()
    BufferedReader br = new BufferedReader(isr);

    System.out.print("Enter a value for x: ");
    s1 = br.readLine();
    x = Double.parseDouble(s1);
```

(Continued on next page)

(Continued from previous page)

```
     // print two title lines
    System.out.println(" e to the x        Approximation        Difference");
    System.out.println("-------------        -------------        -------------");

    actualValue = Math.exp(x);     // use the Math class method

      // calculate the first approximation
    approx = 1;
    difference = Math.abs(actualValue - approx);
    System.out.println("   " + df.format(actualValue) + "             "
                        + df.format(approx) + "           "
                        + df.format(difference));

      // calculate the second approximation
    approx = approx + x;
    difference = Math.abs(actualValue - approx);
    System.out.println("   " + df.format(actualValue) + "             "
                        + df.format(approx) + "           "
                        + df.format(difference));

      // calculate the third approximation
    approx = approx + Math.pow(x,2)/2.0;
    difference = Math.abs(actualValue - approx);
    System.out.println("   " + df.format(actualValue) + "             "
                        + df.format(approx) + "           "
                        + df.format(difference));

      // calculate the fourth approximation
    approx = approx + Math.pow(x,3)/6.0;
    difference = Math.abs(actualValue - approx);
    System.out.println("   " + df.format(actualValue) + "             "
                        + df.format(approx) + "           "
                        + df.format(difference));
  }
}
```

In reviewing Program 3.20, notice that the input value of x is obtained first. The two title lines are then printed prior to any calculations being made. The value of e^x is then computed using the Math class's `exp()` method and assigned to the variable `actualValue`. This assignment permits this value to be used in the four difference calculations and displayed four times without the need for recalculation.

Since the approximation to e^x is "built up" using more and more terms of the approximating polynomial, only the new term for each approximation is calculated and added to the previous approximation. Finally, to permit the same variables to be reused, their values are immediately printed before the next approximation is made. The following is a sample run produced by Program 3.20.

```
Enter a value for x: 2

e to the x     Approximation     Difference
----------     -------------     ----------

  7.389056       1.000000         6.389056

  7.389056       3.000000         4.389056

  7.389056       5.000000         2.389056

  7.389056       6.333333         1.055723
```

Step 4: Test and Correct the Solution The first two columns of output data produced by the sample run agree with our hand calculation. A hand check of the last column verifies that it also contains the correct difference in values between the first two columns.

Because the program only performs nine calculations and the result of the test run agrees with our hand calculations, it appears that the program has been completely tested. However, it is important to understand that this is due to our choice of test data. Selecting a value of 2 for *x* forced us to verify that the program was in fact calculating 2 raised to the required powers. A choice of 0 or 1 for our hand calculation would not have given us the verification that we need. Do you see why this is so?

Using 0 or 1would not adequately test whether the program used the `Math.pow()` method correctly, or even if it used it at all! That is, an incorrect program that did not use the `Math.pow()` method could have been constructed to produce correct values for *x* = 0 and *x* = 1, but for no other values of *x*.

Our test data do adequately verify the program, and we can use it with confidence. Clearly, however, the output demonstrates that to achieve any level of accuracy with the program, more terms than four would be required.

EXERCISES 3.6

1. Enter, compile, and run Program 3.19 on your computer system.
2. a. Enter, compile, and run Program 3.20 on your computer system.
   b. Determine how many terms of the approximating polynomial should be used to achieve an error of less than 0.0001 between the approximation and the value of e^2 as determined by the `Math.exp()` method.
3. By mistake, a student wrote Program 3.20 as follows:

```
// this program approximates the function e raised to the x power
// using one, two, three, and four terms of an approximating polynomial

import java.io.*;   // needed to access input stream classes
import java.text.*; // needed for formatting
public class ApproxExponential
{
  public static void main (String[] args)
  throws java.io.IOException
  {
   String s1;
   double x, actualValue, approx, difference;
```

```java
DecimalFormat df = new DecimalFormat("#.000000");

// set up the basic input stream
  // needed for conversion capabilities
InputStreamReader isr = new InputStreamReader(System.in);
  // needed to use readLine()
BufferedReader br = new BufferedReader(isr);

// print two title lines
System.out.println(" e to the x        Approximation        Difference");
System.out.println("-------------      -------------        -------------");

System.out.print("Enter a value for x: ");
s1 = br.readLine();
x = Double.parseDouble(s1);

actualValue = Math.exp(x);    // use the Math class method

  // calculate the first approximation
approx = 1;
difference = Math.abs(actualValue - approx);
System.out.println("   " + df.format(actualValue) + "            "
                        + df.format(approx) + "           "
                        + df.format(difference));

  // calculate the second approximation
approx = approx + x;
difference = Math.abs(actualValue - approx);
System.out.println("   " + df.format(actualValue) + "            "
                        + df.format(approx) + "           "
                        + df.format(difference));

  // calculate the third approximation
approx = approx + Math.pow(x,2)/2.0;
difference = Math.abs(actualValue - approx);
System.out.println("   " + df.format(actualValue) + "            "
                        + df.format(approx) + "           "
                        + df.format(difference));

  // calculate the fourth approximation
approx = approx + Math.pow(x,3)/6.0;
difference = Math.abs(actualValue - approx);
System.out.println("   " + df.format(actualValue) + "            "
                        + df.format(approx) + "           "
                        + df.format(difference));
  }
}
```

Determine the output this program will produce.

4. The value of π can be approximated by the series

$$4 = \left(1 - \frac{1}{3} + \frac{1}{5} - \frac{1}{7} + \cdots\right)$$

   Using this formula, write a program that calculates and displays the value of π using two, three, and four terms of the series.

5. **a.** The formula for the standard normal deviate, z, used in statistical applications is

$$z = \frac{x - \mu}{\sigma}$$

   where μ refers to a mean value and σ to a standard deviation. Using this formula, write a program that calculates and displays the value of the standard normal deviate when $x = 85.3$, $\mu = 80$, and $\sigma = 4$.

   b. Rewrite the program in Exercise 5a to accept the values of x, μ, and σ as user inputs while the program is executing.

6. **a.** The equation of the normal (bell-shaped) curve used in statistical applications is:

$$y = \frac{1}{\sigma\sqrt{2\pi}}\, e^{-(1/2)[(x-\mu)/\sigma]^2}$$

   Using this equation and assuming $\mu = 90$ and $\sigma = 4$, write a program that determines and displays the value of y when $x = 80$.

   b. Rewrite the program in Exercise 6a to accept the values of x, μ, and σ as user inputs while the program is executing.

7. **a.** Write, compile, and execute a Java program that calculates and displays the voltage gain of a three-stage amplifier at a frequency of 1000 hertz. The voltage gains of the stages are:

   Stage 1 gain: $23/[2.3^2 + (0.044f)^2]^{1/2}$
   Stage 2 gain: $12/[6.7^2 + (0.34f)^2]^{1/2}$
   Stage 3 gain: $17/[1.9^2 + (0.45f)^2]^{1/2}$

   where f is the frequency in hertz. The voltage gain of the amplifier is the product of the gains of the individual stages.

   b. Redo Exercise 7a assuming that the frequency will be entered when the program is run.

8. The volume of oil stored in a underground 200-foot deep cylindrical tank is determined by measuring the distance from the top of the tank to the surface of the oil. Knowing this distance and the radius of the tank, the volume of oil in the tank can be determined using the formula Volume = π radius^2 (200 − distance). Using this information, write, compile, and execute a Java program that accepts the radius and distance measurements, calculates the volume of oil in the tank, and displays the two input values and the calculated volume. Verify the results of your program by doing a hand calculation with the following test data: radius = 10 feet and distance = 12 feet.

9. The perimeter, approximate surface area, and approximate volume of an in-ground pool are given by the following formulas:

Perimeter = 2(length + width)
*Volume = length * width * average depth*
*Underground surface area = 2(length + width)average depth + length * width*

Using these formulas as a basis, write a Java program that accepts the length, width, and average depth measurements and then calculates the perimeter, volume, and underground surface area of the pool. In writing your program, make the following two calculations immediately after the input data have been entered: length * width and length + width. The results of these two calculations should then be used, as appropriate, in the assignment statements for determining the perimeter, volume, and underground surface area. Verify the results of your program by doing a hand calculation with the following test data: length = 25 feet, width = 15 feet, and average depth = 5.5 feet. When you have verified that your program is working, use it to complete the following table:

Length	Width	Depth	Perimeter	Volume	Underground Surface Area
25	10	5.0			
25	10	5.5			
25	10	6.0			
25	10	6.5			
30	12	5.0			
30	12	5.5			
30	12	6.0			
30	12	6.5			

3.7 COMMON PROGRAMMING ERRORS

In working with the material presented in this chapter, be aware of the following possible errors:

1. Forgetting to assign or initialize values for all variables before the variables are used in an expression. Such values can be assigned by assignment statements, initialized within a declaration statement, or assigned interactively by entering values using an input dialog.
2. Applying either the increment or decrement operator to an expression. For example, the expression

`(count + n)++`

is incorrect. The increment and decrement operators can only be applied to individual variables.
3. Forgetting to precede a mathematical method with the class name `Math` and a period, as in `Math.sqrt(x)`.

4. Not understanding the difference between writing a program for your own personal use and one intended for someone else's use. Programs for your own use need not have extensive exception checking or exception handling capabilities because you will not make mistakes that a casual user will or you will know how to recover from such mistakes (e.g., by pressing the Ctrl and C keys to break out of a program). This is not true for programs that will be run by other people. Such programs should have extensive exception handling features.

5. Being unwilling to test a program in depth that is to be used by others besides yourself. After all, because you wrote the program, you assume it is correct or you would have changed it before it was completed. It is extremely difficult to back away and honestly test your own software. As a programmer, you must constantly remind yourself that just because you *think* your program is correct does not make it so. Finding errors in your own program is a sobering experience, but one that will help you become a master programmer.

3.8 CHAPTER SUMMARY

1. An *expression* is a literal, a variable, or a sequence of one or more literals and/or variables separated by operators. A value is associated with an expression.

2. Expressions are evaluated according to the precedence and associativity of the operators in the expression.

3. The assignment symbol, $=$, is an operator. Expressions using this operator assign a value to a variable; in addition, the expression itself takes on a value. Since assignment is an operation in Java, multiple uses of the assignment operator are possible in the same expression.

4. The increment operator, $++$, adds 1 to a variable, whereas the decrement operator, $--$, subtracts 1 from a variable. Both these operators can be prefixes or postfixes. In prefix operation, the variable is incremented (or decremented) before its value is used. In postfix operation, the variable is incremented (or decremented) after its value is used.

5. Java provides a Math class containing methods for calculating square root, logarithmic, and other mathematical computations. When using a Math class method, the method name should be preceded by the class name Math and a period.

6. Every Math class method operates on its arguments to calculate a single value. To use a Math class method effectively, you must know what the method does, the name of the method, the number and data types of the arguments expected by the method, and the data type of the returned value.

7. Data passed to a method are called *arguments* of the method. Arguments are passed to a library method by including each argument, separated by commas, within the parentheses following the method's name. Each method has its own requirements for the number and data types of the arguments that must be provided.

8. Methods may be included within larger expressions.

9. The Java string class provides a number of methods for converting strings into primitive numerical types. The most common of these methods, with their associated class names, are:

Method	Description
`Integer.parseInt(string object or value)`	Converts a string to an `int`
`Long.parseLong(string object or value)`	Converts a string to a `long`
`Float.parseFloat(string object or value)`	Converts a string to a `float`
`Double.parseDouble(string object or value)`	Converts a string to a `double`

10. Input from the keyboard can be accomplished with the `readLine()` method, which reads a complete line of input. This method accepts a line of data from the keyboard, which should then be assigned to a string variable. To use this method, a buffered input stream must be created. This is accomplished with the following declarations, where the variable names `isr` and `br` are programmer selectable:

    ```
    InputStreamReader isr = new InputStreamReader(System.in);
    BufferedReader br = new BufferedReader(isr);
    ```

    The first statement is required to permit access to the conversion capabilities provided by the `InputStreamReader` class. The second statement is needed to access the `readLine()` method, which is provided by the `BufferedReader` class. Once this set of declarations has been made, a statement such as

    ```
    inputString = br.readLine(isr);
    ```

    can accept a line of keyboard input and store it in the string referenced by the string variable `inputString`.

11. A Java program that uses keyboard input must include the statement `import java.io.*;`. In addition, the method within which `readLine()` is used must include the expression `throws java.io.IOException` after the method's header line.

12. When a `readLine()` method call is encountered, the program temporarily suspends statement execution until the user signals the end of data input by pressing the Enter key.

13. An input dialog box method is used for data input. This dialog accepts a string from the keyboard and assigns the characters entered to a string object. The general syntax of the statement creating an input dialog is:

    ```
    stringName = JOptionPane.showInputDialog("prompt");
    ```

    where the *prompt* is a message that is displayed in the input dialog. The characters entered by the user are stored as a string that is referenced by the *stringName*.

14. When an input dialog box is encountered, the computer temporarily suspends further statement execution until either the OK or Cancel button has been clicked.

15. An *exception* is an error condition that occurs when a program is executing and notification of which is immediately sent to the Java Virtual Machine for processing. The following is Java terminology for processing exceptions:

Terminology	Description
Exception	An error that occurs while a program is executing.
Throw an exception	Generates an exception.
Catch or handle an exception	Identifies an exception and passes it to a handler.
Catch clause or handler	The section of code that performs the error processing.

MECHANICAL ENGINEERING

Generally speaking, mechanical engineers are concerned with machines or systems that produce or apply energy. The range of technological activities that are considered part of mechanical engineering is probably broader than in any other engineering field. The field can be roughly subdivided into four categories:

1. Power. Design of power-generating machines and systems such as boiler-turbine engines for generating electricity, solar power, heating systems, and heat exchanges.
2. Design. Innovative design of machine parts or components from the most intricate and small to the gigantic. For example, mechanical engineers work alongside electrical engineers to design automatic control systems such as robots.
3. Automotive. Design and testing of transportation vehicles and the machines used to manufacture them.
4. Heating, ventilation, air conditioning, and refrigeration. Design of systems to control our environment both indoors and out and to control pollution.

Mechanical engineers usually have a thorough background in subjects like thermodynamics, heat transfer, statics and dynamics, and fluid mechanics.

16. Exceptions can be caught and processed by a `try` statement. This statement has the syntax:

```
try
{

    // one or more statements,
    // at least one of which should
    // be capable of throwing an exception;
}
catch(exceptionName argument)
{
    // one or more statements
}
finally
{
    // one or more statements
}
```

The keyword `try` identifies the start of the statement. One of the statements within the braces defining this block of code should be capable of throwing an exception.

A `try` block must be followed by at least one `catch` block, which serves as an exception handler for a specific exception thrown by the statements in the `try` block. Additional `catch` blocks are optional. Listed within the parentheses is the name of the exception being caught and a user-selectable argument name. This argument holds the exception object generated when the exception occurs. An optional `finally` block provides a catchall default set of instructions that is always executed whether or not any exception occurred.

CHAPTER 4

Selection

*The term **flow of control** refers to the order in which a program's statements are executed. Unless directed otherwise, the normal flow of control for all programs is sequential. This means that each statement is executed in sequence, one after another, in the order in which they are placed within the program.*

Both selection and repetition statements allow the programmer to alter the normal sequential flow of control. As their names imply, selection statements provide the ability to select which statement, from a well-defined set, will be executed next, whereas repetition statements provide the ability to go back and repeat a set of statements. In this chapter, we present Java's selection statements, and we present repetition statements in Chapter 5. Since selection requires choosing between alternatives, we begin this chapter with a description of Java's selection criteria.

4.1 RELATIONAL EXPRESSIONS

In the solution of many problems, different actions must be taken depending on the value of the data. Examples of simple situations include calculating an area *only if* the measurements are positive, performing a division *only if* the divisor is not zero, printing different messages *depending on* the value of a grade received, and so on.

The `if-else` statement in Java implements such a decision structure in its simplest form—that of choosing between two alternatives. The most commonly used pseudocode syntax of this statement is:

```
if (condition)
   statement executed if condition is true;
else
  statement executed if condition is false;
```

When an executing program encounters the `if` statement, the condition is evaluated to determine if it is either true or false. If the condition is true, the statement following the `if` is executed. If the condition is false, the statement following the `else` is executed. The `else` part of the statement is optional and may be omitted.

The simplest condition that can be used in an `if` statement is referred to as a relational expression. A **relational expression** consists of a relational operator connecting two variable and/or constant operands, as shown in Figure 4.1.

FIGURE 4.1 Anatomy of a Simple Relational Expression

While each operand in a relational expression can be either a variable or constant, the relational operators must be one of those listed in Table 4.1. These relational operators may be used with integer, float, double, or character operands but must be typed exactly as in Table 4.1. Thus, the following examples are all valid

TABLE 4.1   Relational Operators for Primitive Data Types

Relational Operator	Meaning	Example
<	less than	`age < 30`
>	greater than	`height > 6.2`
<=	less than or equal to	`taxable <= 20000`
>=	greater than or equal to	`temp >= 98.6`
==	equal to	`grade == 100`
!=	not equal to	`number != 250`

```
age > 40        length <= 50     temp > 98.6
  3 < 4         flag == done     idNum == 682
day != 5        2.0 > 3.3        hours > 40
```

but the following are invalid

```
length =< 50       // incorrect symbol
2.0 > 3.3          // invalid relational operator
flag = = done      // spaces between operators are not allowed
```

In this text, we will use the terms *relational expression* and *condition* interchangeably. Like all Java expressions, relational expressions are evaluated to yield a result. For relational expressions, this result is one of the boolean values, `true` or `false`. For example, the relationship 3 < 4 is always `true`, and the relationship 2.0 > 3.3 is always `false`. This can be verified using the statements

```
System.out.println( "The value of 3 < 4 is " + (3 < 4));
System.out.println( "\nThe value of 2.0 > 3.0 is " + (2.0 > 3.3));
```

which result in the displays

```
The value of 3 < 4 is true
The value of 2.0 > 3.0 is false
```

The value of a relational expression such as `hours > 40` depends on the value stored in the variable `hours`. In a Java program, a relational expression such as this is typically part of a selection statement. In these statements, which are presented in the next section, the selection of which statement to execute next is then based on the value obtained.

In addition to numerical operands, character data can also be compared with relational operators. For such comparisons, the `char` values are automatically coerced to `int`s for the comparison. For example, in Unicode, the letter 'A' is stored using a code having a lower numerical value than the letter 'B', the code for 'B' is lower in value than the code for 'C', and so on. For character sets coded in this manner, the following conditions are evaluated as listed.

Expression	Value
'A' > 'C'	false
'D' <= 'Z'	true
'E' == 'F'	false
'G' >= 'M'	false
'B' != 'C'	true

Comparing letters is essential in alphabetizing names or using characters to select a particular choice in decision-making situations. Strings of characters may also be compared, but not using the relational operators in Table 4.1. Because a string is a reference data type, the `String` class methods presented in Chapter 7 must be used for comparing String objects.

Logical Operators

In addition to simple relational expressions as conditions, more complex conditions can be created with the boolean logical operations AND, OR, and NOT. These operations are represented by the symbols &&, ||, and !, respectively.

When the AND operator, `&&`, is used with two relational expressions, the condition is `true` only if both individual expressions are `true` by themselves. Thus, the logical condition

```
(age > 40) && (term < 10)
```

is `true` only if `age` is greater than 40 and `term` is less than 10. Because relational operators have a higher precedence than logical operators, the parentheses in this logical expression could have been omitted.

The logical OR operator, `||`, is also applied between two expressions. When using the OR operator, the condition is satisfied if either one or both of the two expressions are `true`. Thus, the logical condition

```
(age > 40) || (term < 10)
```

is `true` if either `age` is greater than 40, `term` is less than 10, or both conditions are true. Again, the parentheses surrounding the relational expressions are included to make the expression easier to read. Because of the higher precedence of relational operators with respect to logical operators, the same evaluation is made even if the parentheses are omitted.

For the declarations

```
int i, j;
float a, b;
boolean complete;
```

the following represent valid conditions:

```
a > b
(a/b > 5) && (i <= 20)
(i == j) || (a < b) || complete
```

Before these conditions can be evaluated, the values of a, b, i, j, and `complete` must be known. Assuming the assignments

```
        a = 12.0;
        b = 2.0;
        i = 15;
        j = 30;
complete = false;
```

the previous expressions yield the following results:

Expression	Value
a > b	false
(a/b > 5) && (i <= 20)	true
(i == j) || (a < b) || complete	false

The NOT operation changes an expression to its opposite state; that is, if the expression is true, the value of !expression is false. If an expression is false to begin with, !expression is true. For example, assuming the number 26 is stored in the variable age, the expression (age > 40) has a boolean value of false, while the expression ! (age > 40) has a boolean value of true. Since the NOT operation is used with only one operand, it is a unary operation.

The && and || operators can only be used with boolean operands. Such operands can be either boolean literals, boolean variables, or boolean values generated by relational expressions. In addition, both of these operators use a "short-circuited evaluation." This means that the second operand is never evaluated if the evaluation of the first operand is sufficient to determine the final value of the logical operation. For the && operator, this means that if the first condition evaluates to a boolean false value, the second operand is not evaluated. The reason is that if the first operand is false and because the AND logical operation can only be true if both operands are true, the value of the operation must be false regardless of the value of the second operand. The same holds for the || operator. In this case, if the first operand yields a true, the complete OR operation must be true regardless of the value of the second operand, and the second operand need not be evaluated.

The relational and logical operators have a hierarchy of execution similar to the arithmetic operators. Table 4.2 lists the precedence of these operators in relation to the other operators we have encountered.

The following example illustrates the use of an operator's precedence and associativity to evaluate relational expressions, assuming the following declarations:

```
char key = 'm';
int i = 5, j = 7, k = 12;
double x = 22.5;
```

Expression	Equivalent Expression	Value
i + 2 == k - 1	(i + 2) == (k - 1)	false
3 * i - j < 22	((3 * i) - j) < 22	true
i + 2 * j > k	(i + (2 * j)) > k	true
k + 3 <= -j + 3 * i	(k + 3) <= ((-j) + (3*i))	false
'a' + 1 == 'b'	('a' + 1) == 'b'	true
key - 1 > 'p'	(key - 1) > 'p'	false
key + 1 == 'n'	(key + 1) == 'n'	true
25 >= x + 1.0	25 >= (x + 1.0)	true

TABLE 4.2 Operator Precedence

Operator	Associativity
++ -=	right to left
! unary -	right to left
* / %	left to right
+ -	left to right
< <= > >=	left to right
== !=	left to right
&	left to right
^	left to right
|	left to right
&&	left to right
||	left to right
= += -= *= /=	right to left

As with all expressions, parentheses can alter the assigned operator priority and improve the readability of relational expressions. By evaluating the expressions within parentheses first, the following compound condition is evaluated as:

```
(6 * 3 == 36 / 2) || (13 < 3 * 3 + 4)  && !(6 - 2 < 5)
      (18 == 18) ||     (13 < 9 + 4)   && !(4 < 5)
            true ||     (13 < 13)       && !true
            true ||     false           && false
            true ||     false
                  true
```

A Numerical Accuracy Problem

A problem that can occur with Java's relational expressions is a subtle numerical accuracy problem relating to floating-point and double-precision numbers. Because of the way computers store these numbers, tests for equality of floating-point and double-precision values and variables with the relational operator == should be avoided.

The reason is that many decimal numbers, such as 0.1, cannot be represented exactly in binary using a finite number of bits. Thus, testing for the exact equality of such numbers can fail. When equality of noninteger values is desired, it is better to require that the absolute value of the difference between operands be less than some extremely small value. Thus, for real operands, the general expression

```
operandOne == operandTwo
```

should be replaced by the condition

```
Math.abs(operandOne - operandTwo) < EPSILON
```

where EPSILON is a named constant set to any acceptably small value, such as 0.0000001 (or any other user-selected amount).[1] Thus, if the difference between the two operands is

---

[1] The comparison to EPSILON as a named constant can also fail when both operands are either extremely large or extremely small. For such cases, EPSILON should be constructed as a function of the two operands.

less than the value of EPSILON, the two operands are considered essentially equal. For example, if x and y are floating-point variables, a condition such as

```
x/y == 0.35
```

should be programmed as

```
Math.abs(x/y - 0.35) < EPSILON
```

This latter condition ensures that slight inaccuracies in representing noninteger numbers in binary do not affect evaluation of the tested condition.

EXERCISES 4.1

1. Determine the value of the following expressions. Assume a = 5, b = 2, c = 4, d = 6, and e = 3, and all variables are ints.

   a. a > b
   b. a != b
   c. d % b == c % b
   d. a * c != d * b
   e. d * b == c * e

   f. a * b < a % b *c
   g. a % b * c > c % b * a
   h. c % b * a == b % c * a
   i. b % c * a != a * b

2. Using parentheses, rewrite the following expressions to indicate their correct order of evaluation. Then evaluate each expression assuming a = 5, b = 2, and c = 4.

   a. a % b * c && c % b * a
   b. a % b * c || c % b * a
   c. b % c * a && a % c * b
   d. b % c * a || a % c * b

3. Write relational expressions to express the following conditions (use variable names of your own choosing):

   a. The distance is equal to 30 feet.
   b. The ambient temperature is 86.4.
   c. A speed is 55 mph.
   d. The current month is 12 (December).
   e. The letter input is K.
   f. A length is greater than 2 feet and less than 3 feet.
   g. The current day is the 15th day of the 1st month.
   h. An automobile's speed is 35 mph, and its acceleration is greater than 4 mph per second.
   i. An automobile's speed is greater than 50 mph, and it has been moving for at least 5 hours.
   j. The code is less than 500 characters and takes more than 2 microseconds to transmit.

4. Determine the value of the following expressions, assuming a = 5, b = 2, c = 4, and d = 5.

   a. a == 5
   b. b * d == c * c
   c. d % b * c > 5 || c % b * d < 7

4.2 THE if-else STATEMENT

The if-else structure directs the program to select a sequence of one or more instructions based on the result of a comparison. For example, suppose we are to calculate the area of a circle given the radius as an input value. If the input is a negative number, we are to print a message that the radius cannot be a negative value; otherwise, we are to calculate and print the circle's area. The if-else structure in this situation selects the correct operation based on whether the radius is negative or not. The general syntax of the if-else statement is:

```
if (condition) statement1;
else statement2;
```

The *condition*, which can be either a relational or logical expression, is evaluated first. If the value of the condition is true, statement1 is executed. If the value is false, the statement after the keyword else is executed. Thus, one of the two statements (either statement1 or statement2) is always executed depending on the boolean value of the condition. Notice that the tested relational expression must be put in parentheses, and a semicolon is placed after each statement.

For clarity, the if-else statement generally is written on four lines in the form

```
if (condition) <------------------no semicolon here
    statement1;
else <------------------no semicolon here
    statement2;
```

The form of the if-else statement that is selected typically depends on the length of statements 1 and 2. However, when using the second form, do not put a semicolon after the parentheses or the keyword else. The semicolons are placed only at the end of each statement. The flowchart for the if-else statement is shown in Figure 4.2.

As a specific example of an if-else structure, we will construct a Java program for determining the area of a circle by first examining the value of the radius. The condition to be tested is whether the radius is less than zero. An appropriate if-else statement for this situation is:

```
if (radius < 0.0)
   System.out.println("A negative radius is invalid" );
   else
   System.out.println("The area of this circle is " + Math.PI * Math.pow(radius,2) );
```

Here we have used the relational operator < to represent the relation "less than." If the value of radius is less than zero, the condition is true and the message "A negative radius is invalid" is displayed. If the condition is not true, the statement after the keyword else is executed. Program 4.1 illustrates this statement in a complete program.

A blank line was inserted before and after the if-else statement to highlight it in the complete program. We will continue to do this throughout the text to emphasize the statement being presented.

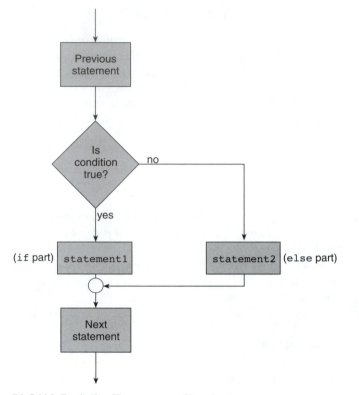

FIGURE 4.2   The `if-else` Flowchart

PROGRAM 4.1

```
import javax.swing.*;
public class AreaCalculation
{
  public static void main(String[] args)
  {
    double radius;
    String s1;

    s1 = JOptionPane.showInputDialog("Please type in the radius:");
    radius = Double.parseDouble(s1);

    if (radius < 0.0)
      System.out.println("A negative radius is invalid" );
    else
      System.out.println("The area of this circle is " + Math.PI * Math.pow(radius,2) );

    System.exit(0);
  }
}
```

To illustrate selection in action, Program 4.1 was run twice with different input data. For the input data shown in Figure 4.3, the output is

```
A negative radius is invalid
```

FIGURE 4.3 Input for First Sample Run of Program 4.1

and the input in Figure 4.4 produces the display

```
The area of this circle is 19.634954084936208
```

FIGURE 4.4 Input for Second Sample Run of Program 4.1

We will leave it as an exercise to have you format the output to reduce the number of displayed decimal places.

In reviewing this output, observe that the radius in the first run of the program was less than zero and the `if` part of the `if-else` structure correctly executed the output statement telling the user that a negative radius is invalid. In the second run, the radius is not negative, and the `else` part of the `if-else` structure yielded a correct area computation of

```
π * (2.5)²
```

where the value of π is obtained as the symbolic constant `Math.PI`, which is provided in Java's `Math` class (see Section 3.3).

Compound Statements

Although only a single statement is permitted in both the `if` and `else` parts of the `if-else` statement, this statement can be a single compound statement. A **compound statement** is any number of single statements contained between braces (Figure 4.5).

```
{
    statement1;
    statement2;
    statement3;
        .
        .
        .
    last statement;
}
```

FIGURE 4.5 A Compound Statement Consists of Individual Statements Enclosed
Within Braces

Although each single statement within the compound statement must end in a semicolon, a semicolon *is not placed* after the braces that define the compound statement.

The use of braces to enclose a set of individual statements creates a single block of statements, which may replace a single statement anywhere in a Java program. The next example illustrates a compound statement within the general form of an `if-else` statement:

```
if (condition)
{
    statement1;    // as many statements as necessary
    statement2;    // can be put within the braces
    statement3;    // each statement must end with a ;
}
else
{
    statement4;
    statement5;
        .
        .
        .
    statementn;
}
```

Program 4.2 illustrates a compound statement in an actual program. Notice the statements that have been included to facilitate keyboard input (review Section 3.4, especially Program 3.11 if necessary).

Program 4.2 checks the integer value in `tempType`. If the value is 1, the compound statement corresponding to the `if` part of the `if-else` statement is executed. Any other number results in execution of the compound statement corresponding to the `else` part. A sample run of Program 4.2 follows:

```
Enter the temperature to be converted: 212
Enter a 1 if the temperature is in Fahrenheit
 or a 2 if the temperature is in Celsius: 1

The equivalent Celsius temperature is 100.00
```

PROGRAM 4.2

```java
import java.io.*;   // needed for keyboard input
import java.text.*;  // needed for formatting
public class ConvertTemperatures
{
  public static void main(String[] args)
  throws java.io.IOException   // for keyboard input
  {
    int tempType;
    double temp, fahren, celsius;
    String s1;

      // set up format variable
    DecimalFormat num = new DecimalFormat(",###.00");

      // set up the basic input stream for keyboard entry
      // needed for conversion capabilities
    InputStreamReader isr = new InputStreamReader(System.in);
      // needed to use readLine()
    BufferedReader br = new BufferedReader(isr);

    System.out.print("Enter the temperature to be converted: ");
    s1 = br.readLine();
    temp = Double.parseDouble(s1);

    System.out.println("Enter a 1 if the temperature is in Fahrenheit");
    System.out.print(" or a 2 if the temperature is in Celsius: ");
    s1 = br.readLine();
    tempType = Integer.parseInt(s1);

    if (tempType == 1)
    {
      celsius = (5.0 / 9.0) * (temp - 32.0);
      System.out.println("\nThe equivalent Celsius temperature is "
                    + num.format(celsius));
    }
    else
    {
      fahren =  (9.0 / 5.0) * temp + 32.0;
      System.out.println("\nThe equivalent Fahrenheit temperature is "
                    + num.format(fahren));
    }
  }
}
```

POINT OF INFORMATION

THE BOOLEAN DATA TYPE

The tested condition in an `if-else` statement must always evaluate to a boolean value. Thus, the value of the condition must be either `true` and `false`. Another way of indicating this is that the syntax of the `if-else` statement is

```
if(boolean expression is true)
  execute this statement;
else
  execute this statement;
```

Although the boolean data type is generally restricted in its usage as the value of a relational expression, boolean values can be displayed, compared, and assigned. Additionally, the value of `!true` is `false` and `!false` is `true`. For example, consider the following `main()` method

```
public static void main(String[] args)
{
  boolean t1, t2, t3, t4;
  t1 = true;
  t2 = false;

  System.out.println( "The value of t1 is " + t1);
  System.out.println( "The value of t2 is " + t2);

  t3 = !t1;
  t4 = !t2;

  System.out.println( "\nThe value of t3 is " + t3);
  System.out.println( "The value of t4 is " + t4);
}
```

The output displayed by this method is:

```
The value of t1 is true
The value of t2 is false

The value of t3 is false
The value of t4 is true
```

In addition, an integer value can be converted into a boolean value using the expression `(x != 0)`, where x represents an integer value or variable. For example, if x has a value of 3, this expression results in a boolean value of `true`. This conversion "trick" follows the C language convention that any nonzero integer is considered `true` and only a zero value is considered `false`.

POINT OF INFORMATION

PLACEMENT OF BRACES IN A COMPOUND STATEMENT

A common practice for some programmers is to place the opening brace of a compound statement on the same line as the `if` and `else` statements. Using this convention, the `if-else` statement in Program 4.2 would appear as shown below. This placement is a matter of style only; both styles are used and both are correct.

```
if (tempType == 1){
  message = "The equivalent Celsius temperature is "
         + num.format(celsius);
         + num.format(celsius);
}
else{
  fahren =  (9.0 / 5.0) * temp + 32.0;
  message = "The equivalent Fahrenheit temperature is "
         + num.format(fahren);
}
```

In practice, you should use whatever style is dictated by your company's policy or your professor's instructions.

One-Way Selection

A useful modification of the `if-else` statement involves omitting the `else` part of the statement altogether. In this case, the `if` statement takes the shortened and frequently useful form:

```
if (condition)
  statement;
```

The statement following the `if (condition)` is only executed if the condition has a `true` value. This modified form of the `if` statement is called a *one-way if statement*. It is illustrated in Program 4.3, which checks a car's mileage and prints a message if the car has been driven more than 3000.0 miles. Notice that we have defined `value` as the named constant LIMIT.

As an illustration of its one-way selection criteria in action, Figure 4.6a shows the display for the case where the input data caused the statement within the `if` to be executed. Figure 4.6b shows the final message acknowledging the end of the program. For the case where the entered data are less than LIMIT, the display statement within the `if` statement is not executed, and only the final display, shown in Figure 4.6b, would be produced. This final display is especially useful when the input data do not trigger a display of the first type because it lets the user know that the program did finish executing (a program that provides no user output is not user-friendly and should be avoided).

PROGRAM 4.3

```
import javax.swing.*;
import java.text.*;  // needed for formatting
public class CheckLimit
{
  public static void main(String[] args)
  {
    final double LIMIT = 3000.0;
    String s1;
    double mileage;

    System.out.println("Please enter the mileage: ");
    mileage = Double.parseDouble(s1);

    if(mileage > LIMIT)
      JOptionPane.showMessageDialog(null, "For a mileage of " + mileage
                   + "\nThis car is over the mileage limit", "Program 4.3",
                   JOptionPane.INFORMATION_MESSAGE);

    JOptionPane.showMessageDialog(null, "End of Program", "Program 4.3",
                      JOptionPane.INFORMATION_MESSAGE);

    System.exit(0);
  }
}
```

(a) Display Produced by `if` Statement
FIGURE 4.6

(b) Closing Display

EXERCISES 4.2

1. Write appropriate `if` statements for each of the following conditions:
   a. If angle is equal to 90 degrees, print the message `"The angle is a right angle"`; otherwise, print the message `"The angle is not a right angle"`.
   b. If the temperature is above 100 degrees, display the message `"above the boiling point of water"`; otherwise, display the message `"below the boiling point of water"`.
   c. If the number is positive, add the number to `possum`; otherwise, add the number to `negsum`.
   d. If the slope is less than .5, set the variable flag to zero; otherwise, set flag to one.

   e. If the difference between `volts1` and `volts2` is less than .001, set the
      variable approx to zero; otherwise, calculate approx as the quantity
      `(volts1 - volts2) / 2.0`.
   f. If the frequency is above 60, display the message `The frequency is too
      high`.
   g. If the difference between `temp1` and `temp2` exceeds 2.3 degrees, calculate
      error as `(temp1 - temp2) * factor`.
   h. If x is greater than y and z is less than 20, read in a value for p.
   i. If distance is greater than `20` and less than `35`, read in a value for `time`.
2. Write `if` statements corresponding to the conditions illustrated by each of the
   following flowcharts.

   a.

   b.

c.

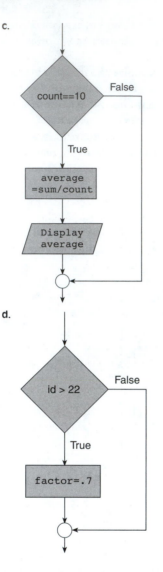

d.

3. Enter and execute Program 4.1 on your computer.

4. Program 4.1 uses a dialog box for data input and `println()` for console display. Rewrite this program to use a `readLine()` method for keyboard input. (*Tip:* Review Section 3.4.)

5. Program 4.1 uses dialog boxes for input and character data for output. Rewrite Program 4.1 to use dialog boxes for both input and output.

6. Rewrite Program 4.1 so that the output is displayed with only two digits after the decimal point. Use either a character-based or dialog box for output display.

7. Execute Program 4.2 on your computer.

8. Program 4.2 uses `readLine()` for keyboard input and `println()` for console display. Rewrite this program to use dialog boxes for both input and output.

9. Write a Java program that asks the user to input two numbers. If the first number entered is greater than the second number, the program should print the

message The first number is greater; otherwise, it should print the message The first number is smaller. Test your program by entering the numbers 5 and 8 followed by the numbers 11 and 2. What do you think your program will display if the two numbers entered are equal? Test this case.

10. a. A certain waveform is 0 volts for time less than 2 seconds and 3 volts for time equal to or greater than 2 seconds (such waveforms are referred to as step functions). Write a Java program that accepts time into the variable named time and display the appropriate voltage depending on the input value.

   b. How many runs should you make for the program written in Exercise 10a to verify that it is operating correctly? What data should you input in each of the program runs?

11. An insulation test for a wire requires that the insulation withstand at least 600 volts. Write a Java program that accepts a test voltage and prints either the message Passed Voltage Test or Failed Voltage Test, as appropriate.

12. a. Write a Java program to compute the value of pressure in pounds per square inch (psi) of a waveform described as follows:

   For time, t, equal to or less than 35 seconds, the pressure is $0.46t$ psi, and for time equal to or greater than 35 seconds, the pressure is $0.19t + 9.45$ psi.

   The program should request the time as input and should display the pressure as output.

   b. How many runs should you make for the program written in Exercise 12a to verify that it is operating correctly? What data should you input in each of the program runs?

13. a. Write a Java program that displays either the message Proceed with Takeoff or Abort Takeoff depending on the input. If the character g is entered in the variable code, the first message should be displayed; otherwise, the second message should be displayed.

   b. How many runs should you make for the program written in Exercise 13a to verify that it is operating correctly? What data should you input in each of the program runs?

14. A small factory generates its own power with a 20-kilowatt generator and a 50-kilowatt generator. The plant manager indicates which generator is required by typing a character code. Write a Java program that accepts this code as input. If code s is typed, a message directing the plant supervisor to use the smaller generator should be displayed; otherwise, a message directing the use of the larger generator should be output.

15. Enter and execute Program 4.3.

16. Rewrite Program 4.3 to use a readLine() method for keyboard input and print() or println() methods for console output.

17. The following main() method produces the output

```
The value of t1 is true
The value of t2 is false
These values are equal

    public static void main(String[] args)
    {
```

(Continued on next page)

(Continued from previous page)

```
        boolean t1, t2;
        t1 = true;
        t2 = false;

        System.out.println( "The value of t1 is " + t1);
        System.out.println( "The value of t2 is " + t2);
        if (t2 = t1)
          System.out.println( "These values are equal");
        else
          System.out.println( "These values are not equal");
    }
```

Determine why the output indicates the two boolean values are equal when they clearly are not and correct the error in the method that produces the erroneous output.

4.3 NESTED if STATEMENTS

As you have seen, an `if-else` statement can contain simple or compound statements. Any valid Java statement can be used, including another `if-else` statement. Thus, one or more `if-else` statements can be included within either part of an `if-else` statement. For example, substituting the one-way `if` statement

```
if (hours > 6)

  System.out.println("snap");
```

for `statement1` in the following if statement

```
if (hours < 9)
  statement1;
else
  System.out.println("pop");
```

results in the nested `if` statement

```
if (hours < 9)
{
  if (hours > 6)
    System.out.println("snap");
}
else
  System.out.println("pop");
```

The braces around the inner one-way `if` are essential because in their absence Java associates an `else` with the closest unpaired `if`. Thus, without the braces, the preceding statement is equivalent to

```
if (hours < 9)
  if (hours > 6)
    System.out.println("snap");
  else
    System.out.println("pop");
```

Here the `else` is paired with the inner `if`, which destroys the meaning of the original `if-else` statement. Notice also that the indentation is irrelevant as far as the compiler is concerned. Whether the indentation exists or not, the statement is compiled by associating the last `else` with the closest unpaired `if`, unless braces are used to alter the default pairing.

The process of nesting `if` statements can be extended indefinitely so that the `println( "snap");` statement could itself be replaced by either a complete `if-else` statement or another one-way `if` statement.

The `if-else` Chain

Generally, the case in which the statement in the `if` part of an `if-else` statement is another `if` statement tends to be confusing and is best avoided. However, an extremely useful construction occurs when the `else` part of an `if` statement contains another `if-else` statement. This takes the form:

```
if (condition1)
  statement1;
else
  if (condition2)
    statement2;
  else
    statement3;
```

As with all Java programs, the indentation we have used is not required. In fact, the preceding construction is so common that it is typically written in the following arrangement:

```
if (condition1)
  statement1;
else if (condition2)
  statement2;
else
  statement3;
```

This construction is called an *if-else chain*, and it is used extensively in programming applications. Each condition is evaluated in order, and if any condition is `true`, the corresponding statement is executed and the remainder of the chain is terminated. The final `else` statement is only executed if none of the previous conditions are satisfied. This serves as a default or catchall case that is useful for detecting an impossible or error condition.

The chain can be continued indefinitely by repeatedly making the last statement another `if-else` statement. Thus, the general form of an `if-else` chain is:

```
if (condition)
  statement1;
else if (condition)
  statement2;
else if (condition)
  statement3;
      .
      .
      .
else if (expression_n)
  statementn;
else
  last_statement;
```

As with all Java statements, each individual statement can be a compound statement bounded by the braces { and }. To illustrate an `if-else` chain, Program 4.4 displays an item's specification status corresponding to a numerical input. The following codes are used:

Specification Status	Input Code
Space Exploration	1
Military Grade	2
Commercial Grade	3
Toy Grade	4

PROGRAM 4.4

```
import javax.swing.*;
public class SpecStatus
{
  public static void main(String[] args)
  {
    String s1, inMessage, outMessage;
    int specCode;

    inMessage = "Enter a specification code: ";
    s1 = JOptionPane.showInputDialog(inMessage);
    specCode = Integer.parseInt(s1);

    if (specCode == 1)
      outMessage = "The item is space exploration grade.";
    else if (specCode == 2)
      outMessage = "The item is military grade.";
    else if (specCode == 3)
      outMessage = "The item is commercial grade.";
    else if (specCode == 4)
      outMessage = "The item is toy grade.";
    else
      outMessage = "An invalid code was entered.";
```

(Continued on next page)

(Continued from previous page)
```
   JOptionPane.showMessageDialog(null, outMessage,
                                 "Program 4.4",
                                 JOptionPane.INFORMATION_MESSAGE);

      System.exit(0);
    }
 }
```

As a further example illustrating an `if-else` chain, we determine the output of a digital converter using the following input/output relationships:

Input Weight	Output Reading
greater than or equal to 90 lbs	1111
less than 90 lbs but greater than 80 lbs	1110
less than 80 lbs but greater than or equal to 70 lbs	1101
less than 70 lbs but greater than or equal to 60 lbs	1100
less than 60 lbs	1011

The following statements can be used to determine the correct output reading, where the variable `inLbs` stores the input reading:

```
if (inLbs >= 90)
    digout = 1111;
else if (inLbs >= 80)
    digout = 1110;
else if (inLbs >= 70)
  digout = 1101;
else if (inLbs >= 60)
  digout = 1100;
else
  digout = 1011;
```

Notice that this example makes use of the fact that the chain is stopped once a `true` condition is found. This is accomplished by checking for the highest input weight first. If the input value is less than 90, the `if-else` chain continues checking for the next highest weight and so on until the correct weight category is obtained.

Program 4.5 uses an `if-else` chain to calculate and display the correct output reading corresponding to the weight input using an input dialog.

Figure 4.7 illustrates the display produced by Program 4.5. As indicated by the display, a digital output of 1101 was computed for an input weight of 72.5 pounds.

FIGURE 4.7 A Sample Display Produced by Program 4.5

PROGRAM 4.5

```java
import javax.swing.*;
public class DigitalOutput
{
  public static void main(String[] args)
  {
    int digout;
    String s1, outMessage;
    double inLbs;


    s1 = JOptionPane.showInputDialog("Enter the input weight:");
    inLbs = Double.parseDouble(s1);
    if (inLbs >= 90)
      digout = 1111;
    else if (inLbs >= 80)
      digout = 1110;
    else if (inLbs >= 70)
      digout = 1101;
    else if (inLbs >= 60)
      digout = 1100;
    else
      digout = 1011;

    outMessage = "For an input weight of " + inLbs
                +"\n  The digital output is " + digout;

    JOptionPane.showMessageDialog(null, outMessage,
                  "Program 4.5",
                  JOptionPane.INFORMATION_MESSAGE);

    System.exit(0);
  }
}
```

EXERCISES 4.3

1. Compile and execute Program 4.4.

2. An angle is considered acute if it is less than 90 degrees, obtuse if it is greater than 90 degrees, and a right angle if it is equal to 90 degrees. Using this information, write a Java program that accepts an angle in degrees and displays the type of angle corresponding to the degrees entered.

3. The grade level of undergraduate college students is typically determined according to the following schedule:

Number of Credits Completed	Grade Level
less than 32	Freshman
32 to 63	Sophomore
64 to 95	Junior
96 or more	Senior

Using this information, write a Java program that accepts the number of credits a student has completed, determines the student's grade level, and displays the grade level.

4. A student's letter grade is calculated according to the following schedule:

Numerical Grade	Letter Grade
greater than or equal to 90	A
less than 90 but greater than or equal to 80	B
less than 80 but greater than or equal to 70	C
less than 70 but greater than or equal to 60	D
less than 60	F

Using this information, write a Java program that accepts a student's numerical grade, converts the numerical grade to an equivalent letter grade, and displays the letter grade.

5. The tolerance of critical components in a system is determined by the application according to the following schedule:

Specification Status	Tolerance
Space Exploration	Less than 0.1%
Military Grade	Greater than or equal to 0.1% and less than 1%
Commercial Grade	Greater than or equal to 1% and less than 10%
Toy Grade	Greater than or equal to 10%

Using this information, write a Java program that accepts the tolerance reading of a component and determines the specification that should be assigned to the component.

6. Using the relationships from Program 4.5, the following set of `if` statements calculates a digital output:

```
if (inLbs >= 90) digout = 1111;
if (inLbs >= 80) && (inLbs <= 90) digout = 1110;
if (inLbs >= 70) && (inLbs <= 80) digout = 1101;
if (inLbs >= 60) && (inLbs <= 70) digout = 1100;
if (inLbs < 1000) digout = 1011;
```

a. If this set of statements replaces the `if-else` chain in Program 4.5, will a correct digital output be produced?

b. Which set of `if` statements is better and why?

7. The following `if-else` chain was written to produce the same result as Program 4.5:

```
if (inLbs < 60)
    digout = 1011;
```

(Continued on next page)

(Continued from previous page)

```
        else if (inLbs >= 60)
            digout = 1100;
        else if (inLbs >= 70)
          digout = 1101;
        else if (inLbs >= 80)
          digout = 1110;
        else if (inLbs >= 90)
          digout = 1111;
```

a. If this `if-else` chain replaces the `if-else` chain in Program 4.5, will a correct digital output be produced?

b. What does this program do?

c. For what values of input pounds does this program calculate the correct digital output?

4.4 THE switch STATEMENT

The `if-else` chain is used in programming applications where one set of instructions must be selected from many possible alternatives. The `switch` statement provides an alternative to the `if-else` chain for cases that compare the value of an integer expression to a specific value. The general form of a `switch` statement is:

```
switch (expression)
{                              // start of compound statement
  case value_1: <----------------------terminated with a colon
     statement1;
     statement2;

        .

        .

     break;
  case value_2: <----------------------terminated with a colon
     statementm;
     statementn;

        .

        .

     break;

        .

        .


  case value_n: <----------------------terminated with a colon
     statementw;
     statementx;

        .

        .

     break;
  default: <---------------------------terminated with a colon
     statementaa;
     statementbb;
}                              // end of switch and compound statement
```

There are four new keywords in the switch statement: switch, case, default, and break. Let's see what each of these words does.

The keyword switch identifies the start of the switch statement. The expression in parentheses following this word is evaluated, and the result of the expression is compared to various alternative values contained within the compound statement. The expression in the switch statement must evaluate to an integer result or a compilation error occurs.

Internal to the switch statement, the keyword case identifies or labels individual values that are compared to the value of the switch expression. The switch expression's value is compared to each of these case values in the order that these values are listed until a match is found. When a match occurs, execution begins with the statement immediately following the match. Thus, as illustrated in Figure 4.8, the value of the expression determines where in the switch statement execution actually begins.

Any number of case labels may be contained within a switch statement in any order. If the value of the expression does not match any of the case values, however, no statement is executed unless the keyword default is encountered. The keyword default is optional and operates the same as the last else in an if-else chain. If the value of the expression does not match any of the case values, program execution begins with the statement following the word default.

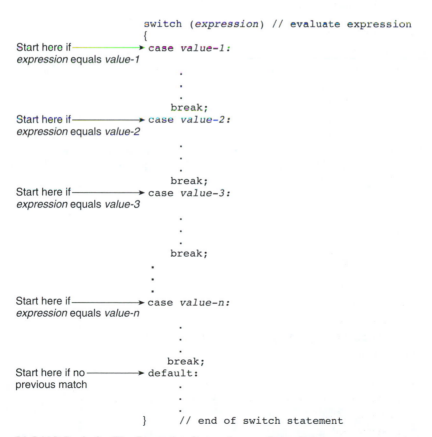

FIGURE 4.8 The Expression Determines an Entry Point

Once an entry point has been located by the `switch` statement, all further `case` evaluations are ignored, and execution continues through the end of the compound statement unless a `break` statement is encountered. This is the reason for the `break` statement, which identifies the end of a particular `case` and causes an immediate exit from the `switch` statement. Thus, just as the word `case` identifies possible starting points in the compound statement, the `break` statement determines terminating points. If the `break` statements are omitted, all cases following the matching `case` value, including the default case, are executed.

In writing a `switch` statement, multiple `case` values can refer to the same set of statements; the `default` label is optional. For example, consider the following:

```
switch (number)
{
  case 1:
    outMessage = "Have a Good Morning";
    break;
  case 2:
    outMessage = "Have a Happy Day";
    break;
  case 3: case 4: case 5:
    outMessage = "Have a Nice Evening";
}
```

If the value stored in the variable `number` is 1, the message `Have a Good Morning` is stored in the string referenced by the name `outMessage`. Similarly, if the value of `number` is 2, the message `Have a Happy Day` is assigned. Finally, if the value of `number` is 3 or 4 or 5, the last message is assigned. Because the statement to be executed for these last three cases is the same, the cases for these values can be "stacked together" as in the example. Notice that because there is no `default`, no string value is assigned if `number` is not one of the listed `case` values.[2] Although it is good programming practice to list `case` values in increasing order, this is not required by the `switch` statement. A `switch` statement can have any number of `case` values in any order; only the values being tested for need to be listed.

Program 4.6 uses a `switch` statement to select a disk drive manufacturer based on a user-entered numerical code as listed in the following table:

Code	Disk Drive Manufacturer
1	3M Corporation
2	Maxell Corporation
3	Sony Corporation
4	Verbatim Corporation

In reviewing Program 4.6, notice that each `case` statement, except for the `default`, contains a `break` statement. This ensures that the `switch` statement is exited after a

---

[2]This will result in a compiler error if the `outMessage` string is subsequently displayed within a method. Therefore, if you use this code in a program, make sure either to initialize `outMessage` or to add a default case.

PROGRAM 4.6

```java
import javax.swing.*;
public class SelectDiskMaker
{
  public static void main(String[] args)
  {
    String s1, outMessage;
    int code;

    s1 = JOptionPane.showInputDialog("Enter a number:");
    code = Integer.parseInt(s1);

    switch (code)
    {
      case 1:
        outMessage = "3M Corporation";
        break;
      case 2:
        outMessage = "Maxell Corporation";
        break;
      case 3:
        outMessage = "Sony Corporation";
        break;
      case 4:
        outMessage = "Verbatim Corporation";
        break;
      default:
        outMessage = "An invalid code was entered";
    }    // end of switch

    JOptionPane.showMessageDialog(null, outMessage,
                        "Program 4.6",
                        JOptionPane.INFORMATION_MESSAGE);

    System.exit(0);
  } // end of main()
}  // end of class
```

matching case is found. Although a break statement can be included in the default case, it serves no purpose there.

Because character data are an integer data type, a switch statement can also "switch" based on the value of a character expression. For example, assuming that choice is a character variable, the following switch statement is valid:

```
switch(choice)
{
  case 'a': case 'e': case 'i': case 'o': case 'u':
    System.out.println("The character in choice is a vowel");
    break;
  default:
    System.out.println("The character in choice is not a vowel");
}    // end of switch statement
```

EXERCISES 4.4

1. Rewrite the following `if-else` chain using a `switch` statement:

   ```
   if (letterGrade == 'A')
     System.out.println("The numerical grade is between 90 and 100");
   else if (letterGrade == 'B')
     System.out.println("The numerical grade is between 80 and 89.9");
   else if (letterGrade == 'C')
     System.out.println("The numerical grade is between 70 and 79.9");
   else if (letterGrade == 'D');
     System.out.println("How are you going to explain this one?");
   else
   {
     System.out.println("Of course I had nothing to do with my grade.");
     System.out.println("\nThe professor was really off the wall.");
   }
   ```

2. Rewrite the following `if-else` chain using a `switch` statement:

   ```
   if (factor == 1)
     pressure = 25.0
   else if (factor == 2)
     pressure = 36.0
   else if (factor == 3)
    pressure = 45.0
   else if (factor == 4) || (factor == 5) || (factor == 6)
     pressure = 49.0
   ```

3. Rewrite Program 4.4 in Section 4.3 using a `switch` statement.
4. Determine why the `if-else` chain in Program 4.5 cannot be replaced with a `switch` statement.
5. Repeat Exercise 3 in Section 4.3 using a `switch` statement instead of an `if-else` chain.
6. Write a Java program that displays a student's status based on the following codes:

Code	Student Status
1	Freshman
2	Sophomore
3	Junior
4	Senior
5	Master's Program
6	Doctoral Program

Your program should accept the code number as a user-entered input value and based on this value display the correct student status. If an incorrect code is entered, your program should display the string `"An incorrect code was entered"`.

4.5 APPLICATIONS

Two major uses of Java's selection statements are to select appropriate processing paths, such as solving for the roots of a quadratic equation based on the value of a discriminant, and to filter data to prevent an exception, such as an ArithmeticException, from occurring. Additionally, selection statements are used in conjunction with error handling exception routines, to modify inappropriate data. In this section, examples of the first two uses are provided.

Application 1: Data Filtering

An important use of Java's `if` statements is to filter data by checking for clearly invalid cases. Effectively, a filter removes inappropriate data from further data processing. For example, a date such as 5/33/86 contains an obviously invalid day. Similarly, the division of any number by zero within a program, such as 14/0, should not be allowed and should be caught before an ArithmeticException is triggered. Both of these examples illustrate the need for a technique called **defensive programming**, in which the program includes code to check for improper data before an attempt is made to process them further.

Consider the case where we are to write a Java program to calculate the square root and the reciprocal of a user-entered number. Before calculating the square root, we are to validate that the number is not negative, and before calculating the reciprocal, we are to check that the number is not zero.

Step 1: Analyze the Problem The statement of the problem requires that we accept a single number as an input, check the entered number, and based on the validation, produce two possible outputs: If the number is nonnegative, we determine its square root, and if the input number is not zero, we determine its reciprocal.

Step 2: Develop a Solution Since the square root of a negative number does not exist as a real number and the reciprocal of zero cannot be taken, our program must contain input data validation statements to screen the user input data and avoid these two cases. The pseudocode describing the processing required is:

```
Display a program purpose message
Accept a user input number
If the number is negative
  print a message that the square root cannot be taken
Else
  calculate and display the square root
EndIf
If the number is zero then
  print a message that the reciprocal cannot be taken
Else
  calculate and display the reciprocal
EndIf
```

Step 3: Code the Solution   The Java code corresponding to our pseudocode solution is listed in Program 4.7.

PROGRAM 4.7

```java
import java.io.*;    // needed to access input stream classes
public class DataCheck
{
  public static void main (String[] args)
  throws java.io.IOException
  {
    String s1;

    double usenum;

    // set up the basic input stream
       // needed for conversion capabilities
    InputStreamReader isr = new InputStreamReader(System.in);
       // needed to use readLine()
    BufferedReader br = new BufferedReader(isr);

    System.out.println("This program calculates the square root and\n"
                     + "reciprocal (1/number) of a number\n");

    System.out.print("Enter a number: ");
    s1 = br.readLine();
    usenum = Double.parseDouble(s1);

    if (usenum < 0.0)
      System.out.println("The square root of a negative number does not exist.");
    else
      System.out.println("The square root of " + usenum
                       + " is " + Math.sqrt(usenum) );
    if (usenum == 0.0)
      System.out.println("The reciprocal of zero does not exist.");
    else
      System.out.println("The reciprocal of " + usenum
                       + " is " +  (1.0/usenum) );
  }
}
```

Program 4.7 is a rather straightforward program containing two separate (nonnested) `if` statements. The first `if` statement checks for a negative input number. If the number is negative a message indicating that the square root of a negative number cannot be taken is displayed; otherwise, the square root is taken. The second `if` statement checks whether the entered number is zero. If it is zero, a message indicating that the reciprocal of zero cannot be taken is displayed; otherwise, the reciprocal is taken.

Step 4: Test and Correct the Solution Test values should include an appropriate value for the input, such as 5, and values for the limiting cases, such as a negative and zero input value. Test runs follow for two of these cases:

```
This program calculates the square root and
reciprocal (1/number) of a number

Enter a number: 5

The square root of 5.0 is 2.23606797749979
The reciprocal of 5.0 is 0.2
```

and

```
This program calculates the square root and
reciprocal (1/number) of a number

Enter a number: -6

The square root of a negative number does not exist.
The reciprocal of -6.0 is -0.16666666666666666
```

Application 2: Solving Quadratic Equations

A **quadratic equation** has the form $ax^2 + bx + c = 0$ or can be algebraically manipulated into this form. In this equation, x is the unknown variable, and a, b, and c are known constants. Although the constants b and c can be any numbers, including zero, the value of the constant a cannot be zero (if a is zero, the equation would become a **linear equation** in x). Examples of quadratic equations are:

$$5x^2 + 6x + 2 = 0$$
$$x^2 - 7x + 20 = 0$$
$$34x^2 + 16 = 0$$

In the first equation, $a = 5$, $b = 6$, and $c = 2$; in the second equation, $a = 1$, $b = -7$, and $c = 20$; and in the third equation, $a = 34$, $b = 0$, and $c = 16$.

The real roots of a quadratic equation can be calculated using the quadratic formula as:

$$\text{root } 1 = \frac{-b + \sqrt{b^2 - 4ac}}{2a}$$

and

$$\text{root } 2 = \frac{-b - \sqrt{b^2 - 4ac}}{2a}$$

Using these equations, we will write a Java program to solve for the roots of a quadratic equation.

Step 1: Analyze the Problem The problem requires that we accept three inputs—the coefficients a, b, and c—of a quadratic equation and compute the roots of the equation using the given formulas.

Step 2: Develop a Solution A first attempt at a solution would be to use the user-entered values of *a*, *b*, and *c* to calculate directly a value for each of the roots. Thus, our first solution is:

> *Display a program purpose message*
> *Accept user input values for a, b, and c*
> *Calculate the two roots*
> *Display the values of the calculated roots*

However, this solution must be refined further to account for a number of possible input conditions. For example, if a user entered a value of 0 for both *a* and *b*, the equation is neither quadratic nor linear and has no solution (this is referred to as a degenerate case). Another possibility is that the user supplies a nonzero value for *b* but makes *a* zero. In this case, the equation becomes a linear one with a single solution of $-c/b$. A third possibility is that the value of the term $b^2 - 4ac$, which is called the **discriminant**, is negative. Since the square root of a negative number cannot be taken, this case will have no real roots. Finally, when the discriminant is zero, both roots are the same (this is referred to as the repeated roots case).

Taking into account all four of these limiting cases, a refined solution for correctly determining the roots of a quadratic equation is expressed by the following pseudocode:

Display a program purpose message
Accept user input values for a, b, and c
If a = 0 and b = 0, then
> *Display a message saying that the equation has no solution*

Else if a = 0, then
> *Calculate the single root equal to -c/b*
> *Display the single root*

Else
> *Calculate the discriminant*
> *If the discriminant > 0, then*
> > *Solve for both roots using the given formulas*
> > *Display the two roots*
>
> *Else if the discriminant < 0, then*
> > *Display a message that there are no real roots*
>
> *Else*
> > *Calculate the repeated root equal to -b/(2a)*
> > *Display the repeated root*
>
> *EndIf*

EndIf

Notice the nested `if-else` structures in the pseudocode. The outer `if-else` structure validates the entered coefficients and determines that we have a valid quadratic equation. The inner `if-else` structure then determines if the equation has two real roots (discriminant > 0), two imaginary roots (discriminant < 0), or repeated roots (discriminant = 0).

Step 3: Code the Solution The equivalent Java code corresponding to our pseudocode solution is listed in Program 4.8.

PROGRAM 4.8

```java
import java.io.*;    // needed to access input stream classes
public class QuadraticEquations
{
  // this method solves for the roots of a quadratic equation
  public static void main (String[] args)
  throws java.io.IOException
  {
    String s1;
    double a, b, c, disc, root1, root2;

      // set up the basic input stream
      // needed for conversion capabilities
    InputStreamReader isr = new InputStreamReader(System.in);
      // needed to use readLine()
    BufferedReader br = new BufferedReader(isr);

    System.out.println("This program calculates the roots of a");
    System.out.println("   quadratic equation of the form");
    System.out.println("             2");
    System.out.println("          ax + bx + c = 0\n");

    System.out.print("Enter the a coefficient: ");
    s1 = br.readLine();
    a = Double.parseDouble(s1);

    System.out.print("Enter the b coefficient: ");
    s1 = br.readLine();
    b = Double.parseDouble(s1);

    System.out.print("Enter the c coefficient: ");
    s1 = br.readLine();
    c = Double.parseDouble(s1);
    System.out.println();

    if ( a == 0.0 && b == 0.0)
      System.out.println("The equation is degenerate and has no roots.\n");
    else if (a == 0.0)
      System.out.println("The equation has the single root x = " + (-c/b));
    else
    {
      disc = Math.pow(b,2.0) - 4 * a * c;    // calculate discriminant
      if (disc > 0.0)
      {
```

(Continued on next page)

(Continued from previous page)

```
        disc = Math.sqrt(disc);
        root1 = (-b + disc) / (2 * a);
        root2 = (-b - disc) / (2 * a);
        System.out.println("The two real roots are "
                           + root1 + " and " + root2);
    }
    else if (disc < 0.0)
        System.out.println("Both roots are imaginary.\n");
    else
        System.out.println("Both roots are equal to " + (-b/(2 * a)));
    }
  }
}
```

Step 4: Test and Correct the Solution Test values should include values for a, b, and c that result in two real roots, plus limiting values for a and b that result in either a linear equation ($a = 0$, $b \neq 0$), a degenerate equation ($a = 0$, $b = 0$), and a negative and zero discriminant. Two such test runs of Program 4.8 follow:

```
This program calculates the roots of a
   quadratic equation of the form
            2
         ax + bx + c = 0

Enter the a coefficient: 1
Enter the b coefficient: 2
Enter the c coefficient: -35


The two real roots are 5.0 and -7.0


This program calculates the roots of a
   quadratic equation of the form
            2
         ax + bx + c = 0

Enter the a coefficient: 0
Enter the b coefficient: 0
Enter the c coefficient: 16


The equation is degenerate and has no roots.
```

The first run solves the quadratic equation $x^2 + 2x - 35 = 0$, which has the real roots $x = 5$ and $x = -7$. The input data for the second run result in the equation

$0x^2 + 0x + 16 = 0$. Because this degenerates into the mathematical impossibility of $16 = 0$, the program correctly identifies this as a degenerate equation. We leave it as an exercise to create test data for the other limiting cases checked by the program.

EXERCISES 4.5

1. a. Write a program that accepts two real numbers from a user and a select code. If the entered select code is 1, have the program add the two previously entered numbers and display the result; if the select code is 2, the numbers should be multiplied, and if the select code is 3, the first number should be divided by the second number.

b. Determine what the program written in Exercise 1a does when the entered numbers are 3 and 0, and the select code is 3.

c. Modify the program written in Exercise 1a so that division by zero is not allowed and an appropriate message is displayed when such a division is attempted.

2. a. Write a program to display the following two prompts:

```
Enter a month (use a 1 for Jan, etc.):
Enter a day of the month:
```

Have your program accept and store a number in the variable month in response to the first prompt and accept and store a number in the variable day in response to the second prompt. If the month entered is not between 1 and 12 inclusive, print a message informing the user that an invalid month has been entered. If the day entered is not between 1 and 31, print a message informing the user that an invalid day has been entered.

b. What will your program do if the user types a number with a decimal point for the month? How can you ensure that your if statements check for an integer number?

c. In a nonleap year, February has 28 days, the months January, March, May, July, August, October, and December have 31 days, and all other months have 30 days. Using this information, modify the program written in Exercise 2a to display a message when an invalid day is entered for a user-entered month. For this program, ignore leap years.

3. a. The quadrant in which a line drawn from the origin resides is determined by the angle that the line makes with the positive X axis as follows:

Angle from the positive X axis	Quadrant
Between 0 and 90 degrees	I
Between 90 and 180 degrees	II
Between 180 and 270 degrees	III
Between 270 and 360 degrees	IV

Using this information, write a Java program that accepts the angle of the line as user input and determines and displays the quadrant appropriate to the input data. (*Note:* If the angle is exactly 0, 90, 180, or 270 degrees, the corresponding line does not reside in any quadrant but lies on an axis.) Make sure that your program accepts any positive or negative angle. (*Tip:* Use the remainder, %, operator.)

    b. Modify the program written for Exercise 3a so that a message is displayed that identifies an angle of zero degrees as the positive X axis, an angle of 90 degrees as the positive Y axis, an angle of 180 degrees as the negative X axis, and an angle of 270 degrees as the negative Y axis.

4. a. All years that are evenly divisible by 400 or are evenly divisible by 4 and not evenly divisible by 100 are leap years. For example, since 1600 is evenly divisible by 400, the year 1600 was a leap year. Similarly, since 1988 is evenly divisible by 4 but not by 100, the year 1988 was also a leap year. Using this information, write a Java program that accepts the year as user input, determines if the year is a leap year, and displays an appropriate message that tells the user if the entered year is or is not a leap year.

    b. Using the code written in Exercise 4a, redo Exercise 2c such that leap years are taken into account.

5. Based on an automobile's model year and weight, the state of New Jersey determines the car's weight class and registration fee with the following schedule:

Model Year	Weight	Weight Class	Registration Fee
1970 or earlier	Less than 2,700 lb	1	$16.50
	2,700 to 3,800 lb	2	25.50
	More than 3,800 lb	3	46.50
1971 to 1979	Less than 2,700 lb	4	27.00
	2,700 to 3,800 lb	5	30.50
	More than 3,800 lb	6	52.50
1980 or later	Less than 3,500 lb	7	19.50
	3,500 or more lb	8	52.50

Using this information, write a Java program that accepts the year and weight of an automobile and determines and displays the weight class and registration fee for the car.

6. Modify Program 4.8 so that the imaginary roots are calculated and displayed when the discriminant is negative. For this case, the two roots of the equation are:

$$x_1 = \frac{-b}{2a} + \frac{sqrt[-(b^2 - 4ac)]}{2a} i$$

and

$$x_2 = \frac{-b}{2a} - \frac{sqrt[-(b^2 - 4ac)]}{2a} i$$

where i is the imaginary number symbol for the square root of -1. (*Tip:* Calculate the real and imaginary parts of each root separately.)

7. In the game of Blackjack, the cards 2 through 10 are counted at their face values regardless of suit, all face cards (jack, queen, and king) are counted as 10, and an ace is counted as either 1 or 11 depending on the total count of all the cards in a player's hand. The ace is counted as 11 only if the resulting total value of all cards in a player's hand does not exceed 21; otherwise, it is counted as 1. Using this information, write a Java program that accepts three card values as inputs (a 1 corresponding to an ace, a 2 corresponding to a two, etc.), calculates the total value of the hand appropriately, and displays the value of the three cards with a printed message.

4.6 COMMON PROGRAMMING ERRORS

The following are programming errors that can be made using Java's selection statements:

1. Assuming the `if-else` statement is selecting an incorrect choice when the problem is really the values being tested. This is a typical debugging problem in which the programmer mistakenly concentrates on the tested condition as the source of the problem rather than the values being tested. For example, assume that the following correct `if-else` statement is part of your program:

```
if (code == 1)
{
   contemp = (5.0/9.0) * (intemp - 32.0);
   System.out.println("Conversion to Celsius was done");
}
else
{
   contemp = (9.0/5.0) * intemp + 32.0;
   System.out.println("Conversion to Fahrenheit was done");
}
```

This statement always displays `Conversion to Celsius was done` when the variable `code` contains 1. Therefore, if this message is displayed when you believe `code` does not contain 1, investigation of `code`'s value is called for. As a general rule, whenever a selection statement does not act as you think it should, make sure to test your assumptions about the values assigned to the tested variables by displaying their values. If an unanticipated value is displayed, you have at least isolated the source of the problem to the variables themselves rather than the structure of the `if-else` statement. From there, you need to determine where and how the incorrect value was obtained.

2. Using nested `if` statements without including braces to clearly indicate the desired structure. Without braces, the compiler defaults to pairing `elses` with the closest unpaired `ifs`, which sometimes destroys the original intent of the selection statement. To avoid this problem and to create code that is readily adaptable to change, it is useful to write all `if-else` statements as compound statements in the form

```
if (condition)
{
   one or more statements in here
}
else
{
   one or more statements in here
}
```

With this form, no matter how many statements are added later, the original integrity and intent of the `if` statement are maintained.

3. Inadvertently using the assignment operator, =, in place of the relational operator, ==, when comparing boolean data. For example, assuming `btrue` and `bfalse` are boolean variables with the values `true` and `false`, respectively, the statement `if(bfalse = btrue)` is the same as `if(true)`. This is because the assignment statement does not compare the values in the variables but assigns the value of `btrue` to `bfalse`. This particular error tends to be extremely rare in practice because boolean data are typically only compared in advanced engineering applications. This error cannot be made with non-boolean data because it results in a non-boolean value that is caught by the compiler. For example, if a and b are integer variables and you inadvertently use the statement `if(a = b)` instead of `if(a == b)`, the compiler provides the error message `Can't convert int to boolean`.

4. Forgetting to use a `break` statement to close off a `case` within a `switch` statement. This can be especially troubling when additional cases are added later. For example, consider the following statement:

```
switch(code)
{
  case 1: slope = 2.00;
          break;
  case 2: slope = 2.50;
}
```

Here not having a `break` for the last `case` does not immediately cause any problem. It is, however, a potential source of error later if a `case` is subsequently added. With the addition of another `case`, a `break` is necessary to prevent the new `case` 3 from always overriding `case` 2. For example, consider the following code without the `break`.

```
switch(code)
    {
      case 1: slope = 2.00;
              break;
      case 2: slope = 2.50;
      case 3: slope = 3.00;
    }
```

Because there is no `break` between `cases` 2 and 3, whenever `case` 2 is selected the code automatically "falls through" and also executes the `slope` assignment for `case` 3. To prevent this error, it is good programming practice to terminate all cases with a `break` (except where the stacking of cases is consciously desired).

4.7 CHAPTER SUMMARY

1. Relational expressions, which are referred to as conditions, compare operands. If a condition is true, the value of the expression is the boolean value `true`. If the expression is false, it has a boolean value of `false`. Relational expressions are created by the following relational operators:

Relational Operator	Meaning	Example
<	less than	age < 30
>	greater than	height > 6.2
<=	less than or equal to	taxable <=20000
>=	greater than or equal to	temp >= 98.6
==	equal to	grade == 100
!=	not equal to	number != 250

2. More complex conditions can be constructed from relational expressions using Java's logical operators, && (AND), || (OR), and ! (NOT).

3. if-else statements select between two alternative statements based on the value of a relational or logical expression. The most common form of an if-else statement is:

```
if (condition)
    statement1;
 else
    statement2;
```

This is a two-way selection statement. If the condition has a boolean true value, statement1 is executed; otherwise, statement2 is executed.

4. if-else statements can contain other if-else statements. In the absence of braces, each else is associated with the closest unpaired if.

5. The if-else chain is a multiway selection statement having the general form:

```
if (condition1)
   statement1;
else if (condition2)
   statement2;
else if (condition3)
   statement3;
               .
               .
               .
else if (conditionm)
   statementm;
else
   statementn;
```

Each condition is evaluated in the order it appears in the chain. Once a condition having a boolean true value is detected, only the statement between that condition and the next else if or else is executed, and no further conditions are tested. The final else is optional, and the statement corresponding to the final else is only executed if none of the previous conditions were true.

6. A compound statement consists of any number of individual statements enclosed within the brace pair { and }. Compound statements are treated as a single block and can be used anywhere a single statement is called for.

7. The switch statement is a multiway selection statement. The general syntax of a switch statement is:

```
switch (expression)
{                              // start of compound statement
   case value-1: <--------   terminated with a colon
      statement1;
      statement2;
          .
          .
          .
      break;
   case value-2: <-------    terminated with a colon
      statementm;
      statementn;
          .
          .
          .
      break;
          .
          .

   case value-n: <--------   terminated with a colon
      statementw;
      statementx;
          .
          .
          .
      break;
   default: <-------------   terminated with a colon
      statementaa;
      statementbb;
          .
          .
          .
} // end of switch and compound statement
```

For this statement, the value of an integer expression is compared to a number of integer constants, character constants, or expressions containing only constants and operators. Program execution is transferred to the first matching `case` and continues through the end of the `switch` statement unless an optional `break` statement is encountered. The `cases` in a `switch` statement can appear in any order, and an optional `default` case can be included. The `default` case is executed if none of the other cases is matched.

4.8 CHAPTER SUPPLEMENT: PROGRAM TESTING

In theory, a comprehensive set of test runs would reveal all logic errors and ensure that a program will work correctly for any and all combinations of input and computed data. In practice, this requires checking all possible combinations of statement executions. Due to the time and effort required, this is an impossible goal except for extremely simple programs. To see why, let's consider Program 4.9.

PROGRAM 4.9

```java
import java.io.*; // needed to access input stream classes
public class CountPaths
{
  public static void main(String[] args)
  throws java.io.IOException
  {
    String s1, outMessage;
    int  num;


    // set up the basic input stream
    // needed for conversion capabilities
    InputStreamReader isr = new InputStreamReader(System.in);
    // needed to use readLine()
    BufferedReader br = new BufferedReader(isr);


    System.out.print("Enter a number: ");
    s1 = br.readLine();
    num = Integer.parseInt(s1);


    if (num == 5)
      System.out.println("Bingo!");
    else
      System.out.println("Bongo!");
  }
}
```

Program 4.9 has two paths that can be traversed from when the program begins execution to when the program reaches its last closing brace. The first path, which is executed when the input number is 5, is in the sequence:

```java
num = Integer.parseInt(s1);
System.out.println("Bingo!");
```

The second path, which is executed when any number except 5 is input, includes the sequence of instructions:

```java
num = Integer.parseInt(s1);
System.out.println("Bongo!");
```

Testing each possible path through Program 4.9 requires two runs of the program, with a judicious selection of test input data to ensure that both paths of the if statement are exercised. The addition of one more if statement in the program increases the number of possible execution paths by a factor of 2 and requires four (2^2) runs of the program

CAREER CHOICES

CIVIL ENGINEERING

The field of civil engineering is concerned primarily with the large-scale structures and systems in a community. A civil engineer designs, constructs, and operates bridges, dams, tunnels, buildings, airports, roads, and other large-scale public works. Civil engineers are also responsible for the effects these large-scale systems have on society and the environment. Thus, civil engineers are involved in water resources, flood control, waste disposal, and overall urban planning. The field can be subdivided into three categories:

1. Structures. Design, construction, and operation of large-scale projects such as dams, buildings, and roads. The properties of materials, geology, soil mechanics, and statics and dynamics are important elements of the background training. For example, how tall a building can be constructed before it will buckle under its own weight is a question involving all of these subjects.
2. Urban planning. Planning, design, and construction of transportation systems (roads, railroads, river development, airports) and general land use. Surveying and mapmaking are necessary skills.
3. Sanitation. Waste treatment, water supply, and sewage systems. Fluid mechanics, hydrology, pollution control, irrigation, and economics are important considerations.

for complete testing. Similarly, two additional `if` statements increase the number of paths by a factor of 4 and require eight (2^3) runs for complete testing, and three additional `if` statements would produce a program that required sixteen (2^4) test runs.

Now consider a modestly sized application program consisting of only 10 methods, each method containing five `if` statements. Assuming the methods are always called in the same sequence, there are 32 possible paths through each method (2 raised to the fifth power) and more than 1,000,000,000,000,000 (2 raised to the fiftieth power) possible paths through the complete program (all methods executed in sequence). The time needed to create individual test data to exercise each path and the actual computer run time required to check each path make the complete testing of such a program impossible to achieve.

The inability to fully test all combinations of statement execution sequences has led to the programming proverb: There is no error-free program. It has also led to the realization that any testing should be well thought out to maximize the possibility of locating errors. At a minimum, test data should include appropriate values for input, illegal input values that the program should reject, and limiting values that are checked by selection statements within the program.

CHAPTER 5

Repetition

The programs examined so far have illustrated the programming concepts involved in input, output, assignment, and selection capabilities. By this time, you should have gained enough experience to be comfortable with these concepts and the mechanics of implementing them with Java. Many problems, however, require a repetition capability, in which the same calculation or sequence of instructions is repeated with different sets of data. Examples of such repetition include continual checking of user data entries until an acceptable entry, such as a valid password, is entered, counting and accumulating running totals, and constant acceptance of input data and recalculation of output values that only stops upon entry of a sentinel value.

In this chapter, we explore the different methods that programmers use in constructing repeating sections of code and how they can be implemented in Java. More commonly, a section of code that is repeated is referred to as a loop because after the last statement in the code is executed the program branches, or loops back, to the first statement and starts another repetition through the code. Each repetition is also referred to as an iteration or pass through the loop.

5.1 INTRODUCTION

The real power of a program is realized when the same type of operation must be made over and over. For example, consider Program 3.16 in Section 3.6, where the same set of instructions is repeated three times. Retyping this same set of instructions is tedious, time consuming, and subject to error. It certainly would be convenient if we could type such repeating instructions only once and then have a method of informing the program to repeat execution of the instructions three times. Such a method is available using repetitive sections of code.

Constructing a repetitive section of code requires that four elements be present. The first necessary element is a repetition statement. This **repetition statement** defines the boundaries containing the repeating section of code and controls whether the code will be executed or not. In general, there are three different forms of repetition structures, all of which are provided in Java:

1. while structure
2. for structure
3. do-while structure

Each of these structures requires a condition that must be evaluated, which is the second required element for constructing repeating sections of code. Valid conditions are identical to those in selection statements. If the condition is true, the code is executed; otherwise, it is not.

The third required element is a statement that initially sets the condition. This statement must always be placed before the condition is first evaluated to ensure correct loop execution the first time the condition is evaluated.

Finally, there must be a statement within the repeating section of code that allows the condition to become false. This is necessary to ensure that, at some point, the repetitions stop.

Pretest and Posttest Loops

The condition being tested can be evaluated at either the beginning or the end of the repeating section of code. Figure 5.1 illustrates the case where the test occurs at the be-

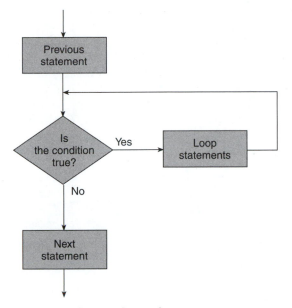

FIGURE 5.1 A Pretest Loop

ginning of the loop. This type of loop is referred to as a **pretest loop** because the condition is tested before any statements within the loop are executed. If the condition is true, the executable statements within the loop are executed. If the initial value of the condition is false, the executable statements within the loop are never executed at all and control transfers to the first statement after the loop. To avoid infinite repetitions, the condition must be updated within the loop. Pretest loops are also referred to as **entrance-controlled loops**. Both the `while` and `for` loop structures are examples of such loops.

A loop that evaluates a condition at end of the repeating section of code, as illustrated in Figure 5.2, is referred to as a **posttest** or **exit-controlled loop**. These loops always execute the loop statements at least once before the condition is tested. Since the executable statements within the loop are continually executed until the condition becomes false, there always must be a statement within the loop that updates the condition and permits it to become false. The `do-while` construct is an example of a posttest loop.

Fixed-Count Versus Variable-Condition Loops

In addition to where the condition is tested (pretest or posttest), repeating sections of code are also classified as to the type of condition being tested. In a **fixed-count loop**, the condition keeps track of how many repetitions have occurred. For example, we might want to produce a table of 10 numbers, including their squares and cubes, or a fixed design such as:

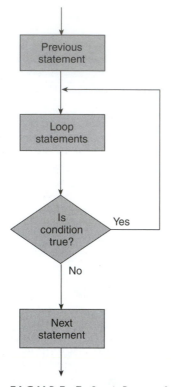

FIGURE 5.2 A Posttest Loop

In each of these cases, a fixed number of calculations is performed or a fixed number of lines is printed, at which point the repeating section of code is exited. All of Java's repetition statements can produce fixed-count loops.

In many situations, the exact number of repetitions is not known in advance or the items are too numerous to count beforehand. For example, when entering a large amount of market research data, we might not want to take the time to count the number of actual data items that are to be entered. Cases such as this call for a variable-condition loop. In a **variable-condition loop,** the tested condition does not depend on a count being achieved but rather on a variable that can change interactively with each pass through the loop. When a specified value is encountered, regardless of how many iterations have occurred, repetitions stop. All of Java's repetition statements can create variable-condition loops.[1] In this chapter, we will encounter examples of both fixed-count and variable-condition loops.

5.2 THE while STATEMENT

The while statement is a general repetition statement that can be used in a variety of programming situations. The general form of the while statement is:

---

[1]In this, Java differs from most other languages such as BASIC, Fortran, and Pascal. In each of these languages, the for structure (which is implemented using a DO statement in Fortran) can only produce fixed-count loops. Java's for structure, as you will see shortly, is virtually interchangeable with its while structure.

```
while (condition)
  statement;
```

The *condition* contained within the parentheses is evaluated in exactly the same manner as a condition contained in an if-else statement; the difference is how the condition is used. As we have seen, when the condition is true in an if-else statement, the statement following the condition is executed once. In a while statement, the statement following the condition is executed repeatedly as long as the condition remains true. This naturally means that somewhere in the while statement there must be a statement that changes the value of the tested condition to false. As we will see, this is indeed the case. For now, however, considering just the condition and the statement following the parentheses, the process used by the computer in evaluating a while statement is:

1. Test the condition
2. If the condition is true
      a. execute the statement following the parentheses
      b. go back to step 1
   else
      exit the while statement

Notice that step 2b forces program control back to step 1. This transfer of control back to the start of a while statement to reevaluate the condition is what forms the program loop. The while statement literally loops back on itself to recheck the condition until it becomes false. This naturally means that somewhere in the loop provision must be made that permits the value of the tested condition to be altered. As you will see, this is indeed the case.

This looping process produced by a while statement is illustrated in Figure 5.3. A diamond shape shows the two entry and two exit points required in the decision part of the while statement.

To make this more tangible, consider the relational condition count <= 10 and the statement System.out.print(count + "   ");. Using these, we can write the following valid while statement:

```
while (count <= 10)
  System.out.print(count + "   ");
```

Although this statement is valid, the alert reader will realize that we have created a situation in which the print() method either is called forever (or until we stop the program) or is not called at all. Let us see why this happens.

If count has a value less than or equal to 10 when the condition is first evaluated, a call to print() is made. The while statement then automatically loops back on itself and retests the condition. Since we have not changed the value stored in count, the condition is still true and another call to print() is made. This process continues forever or until the program containing this statement is prematurely stopped by the user. However, if count starts with a value greater than 10, the condition is false to begin with, and the call to print() is never made.

How do we set an initial value in count to control what the while statement does the first time the condition is evaluated? The answer, of course, is to assign values to each

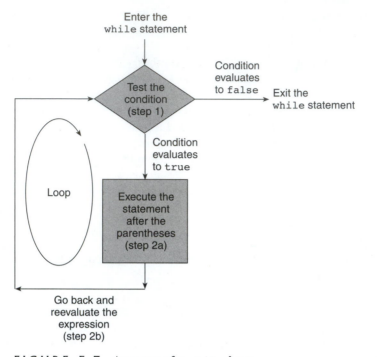

FIGURE 5.3 Anatomy of a while Loop

variable in the tested condition before the while statement is encountered. For example, the following sequence of instructions is valid:

```
count = 1;
while (count <= 10)
   System.out.print(count + "   ");
```

Using this sequence of instructions, we have ensured that count starts with a value of 1. We could assign any value to count in the assignment statement; the important thing is to assign *some* value. In practice, the assigned value depends on the application.

We must still change the value of count so that we can finally exit the while statement. This requires a condition such as count = count + 1 to increment the value of count each time the while statement is executed. The fact that a while statement provides for the repetition of a single statement does not prevent us from including an additional statement to change the value of count. All we have to do is replace the single statement with a compound statement. For example:

```
count = 1;              // initialize count
while (count <= 10)
{
   System.out.print(count + "   ");
   count++;             // increment count
}
```

Let us now analyze how this complete set of instructions works. The first assignment statement sets count equal to 1. The while statement is then entered, and the condition is evaluated for the first time. Since the value of count is less than or equal to 10, the condition is true and the compound statement is executed. The first statement in the compound statement is a call to the print() method to display the value of count followed by two spaces. The next statement adds 1 to the value currently stored in count, making this value equal to 2. The while statement now loops back to retest the condition. Since count is still less than or equal to 10, the compound statement is again executed. This process continues until the value of count reaches 11. Program 5.1 illustrates these statements.

PROGRAM 5.1

```
public class ShowWhile
{
  public static void main(String[] args)
  {
    int count;

    count = 1;                // initialize count
    while (count <= 10)
    {
      System.out.print(count + "  ");
      count++;                // increment count
    }

  }
}
```

The output for Program 5.1 is:

1   2   3   4   5   6   7   8   9   10

There is nothing special about the name count in Program 5.1. Any valid integer variable could have been used.

Before we consider other examples of the while statement, two comments concerning Program 5.1 are in order. First, the statement count++ can be replaced with any statement that changes the value of count. A statement such as count = count + 2, for example, causes every second integer to be displayed. Second, it is the programmer's responsibility to ensure that count is changed in a way that ultimately leads to a normal exit from the while loop. For example, if we replace the expression count++ with the expression count--, the value of count never exceeds 10, and an infinite loop is created. An **infinite loop** is a loop that never ends. The computer does not reach out, touch you, and say, "Excuse me, you have created an infinite loop." It just keeps displaying numbers until you realize that the program is not working as you expected. For most systems, pressing the Ctrl and C keys at the same time will break program execution.

Now that you have some familiarity with the while statement, see if you can read and determine the output of Program 5.2.

PROGRAM 5.2

```
public class CountDown
{
  public static void main(String[] args)
  {
    int i;

    i = 10;    // initialize i
    while (i >= 1)
    {
      System.out.print(i + "  ");
      i--;    // subtract 1 from i
    }


  }
}
```

The assignment statement in Program 5.2 initially sets the int variable i to 10. The while statement then checks to see if the value of i is greater than or equal to 1. While the condition is true, the value of i, followed by two spaces, is displayed by the print() method, and the value of i is then decremented by 1. When i finally reaches 0, the expression is false, and the program exits the while statement. Thus, the following display is obtained when Program 5.2 is run:

```
10   9   8   7   6   5   4   3   2   1
```

To illustrate the power of the while statement, consider the task of printing a table of numbers from 1 to 10 with their squares and cubes. This can be done with the simple while statement in Program 5.3.

When Program 5.3 is run, the following display is produced:[2]

NUMBER	SQUARE	CUBE
------	------	----
0001	0001	0001
0002	0004	0008
0003	0009	0027
0004	0016	0064
0005	0025	0125
0006	0036	0216
0007	0049	0343
0008	0064	0512
0009	0081	0729
0010	0100	1000

[2]See Appendix D for formatting statements that can replace the leading zeros with leading spaces.

PROGRAM 5.3

```java
import java.text.*;   // needed for formatting
public class CreateTable
{
  public static void main(String[] args)
  {
    int num;

    DecimalFormat df = new DecimalFormat("0000");

    System.out.println("NUMBER     SQUARE      CUBE");
    System.out.println("------     ------      ----");

    num = 1;
    while (num < 11)
    {
      System.out.print(" " + df.format(num));
      System.out.print("        " + df.format(num * num));
      System.out.println("        " + df.format(num * num * num));
      num++;            // increment num

    }
  }
}
```

Note that the expression in Program 5.3 is num < 11. For the integer variable num, this expression is exactly equivalent to the expression num <= 10. The choice of expression is entirely up to you.

If we now want Program 5.3 to produce a table of 1,000 numbers, all we do is change the expression in the while statement from num < 11 to num < 1001. Changing the 11 to 1001 produces a table of 1,000 lines—not bad for a simple eight-line while loop.

It should be noted that the spaces inserted in the print() and println() methods line up each column under its appropriate heading. The correct number of spaces can be determined by laying out the display by hand on a piece of paper and counting the required number of spaces or by making trial-and-error adjustments in the code.

All the program examples illustrating the while statement have been examples of fixed-count loops because the tested condition is a counter that checks for a fixed number of repetitions. A variation on the fixed-count loop can be made where the counter is incremented by some value other than 1 each time through the loop. For example, consider the task of producing a Celsius to Fahrenheit temperature conversion table. Assume that Fahrenheit temperatures corresponding to Celsius temperatures ranging from 5 to 50 degrees are to be displayed in increments of 5 degrees. The desired display can be obtained with the sequence of statements:

```java
celsius = 5;      // starting Celsius value
while (celsius <= 50)
{
```

(Continued on next page)

(Continued from previous page)

```
    fahren = (9.0/5.0) * celsius + 32.0;
    System.out.println(celsius + "      " + fahren);
    celsius = celsius + 5;
}
```

As before, the `while` statement consists of everything from the word `while` through the closing brace of the compound statement. Prior to entering the `while` loop, we have made sure to assign a value to the counter being evaluated, and there is a statement to alter the value of the counter within the loop (in increments of 5) to ensure an exit from the `while` loop. Program 5.4 illustrates this code in a complete program.

The following display is obtained when Program 5.4 is executed:

DEGREES CELSIUS	DEGREES FAHRENHEIT
05	041
10	050
15	059
20	068
25	077
30	086
35	095
40	104
45	113
50	122

As with Program 5.3, the spaces in both the `print()` and `println()` methods in Program 5.4 were inserted strictly to line up the output values under their appropriate headings. In addition, notice the two differing number formats: one for the Celsius temperatures that consists of two digits and a second one for the Fahrenheit temperatures that consists of three digits.

PROGRAM 5.4

```
import java.text.*;  // needed for formatting
public class ConversionTable
{
    // a method to convert Celsius to Fahrenheit
    public static void main(String[] args)
    {
        final int MAXCELSIUS = 50;
        final int STARTVAL = 5;
        final int STEPSIZE = 5;
        int celsius;
        double fahren;
```

(Continued on next page)

(Continued from previous page)

```
        DecimalFormat cf = new DecimalFormat("00");   // celsius format
        DecimalFormat ff = new DecimalFormat("000"); // fahrenheit format

        System.out.println("DEGREES    DEGREES\n"
                      +"CELSIUS   FAHRENHEIT\n"
                      +"-------   ----------");

        celsius = STARTVAL;
        while (celsius <= MAXCELSIUS)
        {
          fahren = (9.0/5.0) * celsius + 32.0;
          System.out.print("   " + cf.format(celsius));
          System.out.println("        " + ff.format(fahren));
          celsius = celsius + STEPSIZE;
        }
    }
}
```

EXERCISES 5.2

1. Rewrite Program 5.1 to print() the numbers 2 to 10 in increments of 2. The output of your program should be:

   2   4   6   8   10

2. Rewrite Program 5.4 to produce a table that starts at a Celsius value of -10 and ends with a Celsius value of 60 in increments of 10 degrees.

3. **a.** For the following main() method, determine the total number of items displayed. Also determine the first and last numbers printed.

```
public static void main(String[] args)
{
  int num = 0;

  while (num <= 20)
  {
    num++;
    System.out.print(num + "   ");
  }
}
```

   b. Enter and run the program from Exercise 3a on a computer to verify your answers to the exercise.

   c. How is the output affected if the two statements within the compound statement were reversed—that is, if the print() call were made before the num++ statement?

4. Write a Java program that converts gallons to liters. The program should display gallons from 10 to 20 in 1-gallon increments and the corresponding liter equivalents. Use the relationship that *1 gallon of liquid contains 3.785 liters.*

5. Write a Java program that converts feet to meters. The program should display feet from 3 to 30 in 3-foot increments and the corresponding meter equivalents. Use the relationship that there are *3.28 feet to 1 meter.*

6. A machine purchased for $28,000 is depreciated at a rate of $4,000 a year for 7 years. Write and run a Java program that computes and displays a depreciation table for 7 years. The table should have the form:

YEAR	DEPRECIATION	END-OF-YEAR VALUE	ACCUMULATED DEPRECIATION
1	4000	24000	4000
2	4000	20000	8000
3	4000	16000	12000
4	4000	12000	16000
5	4000	8000	20000
6	4000	4000	24000
7	4000	0	28000

7. An automobile travels at an average speed of 55 miles per hour for 4 hours. Write a Java program that displays the distance driven in miles that the car has traveled after 0.5, 1.0, 1.5, hours, and so on until the end of the trip.

8. An approximate formula for converting Fahrenheit to Celsius temperatures is

Celsius = (Fahrenheit − 30) / 2

Using this formula and starting with a Fahrenheit temperature of 0 degrees, write a Java program that determines when the approximate equivalent Celsius temperature differs from the exact equivalent value by more than 4 degrees. (*Tip:* Use a while loop that terminates when the difference between the approximate and exact Celsius temperatures exceeds 4 degrees.) The exact conversion formula is *Celsius = 5/9(Fahrenheit − 32)*.

9. Using the approximate Celsius conversion formula provided in Exercise 8, write a Java program that produces a table of Fahrenheit temperatures, exact Celsius equivalent temperatures, approximate Celsius equivalent temperatures, and the difference between the exact and approximate Celsius values. The table should begin at 30 degrees Fahrenheit, use 5-degree Fahrenheit increments, and terminate when the difference between exact and approximate values differs by more than 4 degrees.

10. The value of Euler's number, *e*, can be approximated with the formula:

$$e = 1 + \tfrac{1}{1!} + \tfrac{1}{2!} + \tfrac{1}{3!} + \tfrac{1}{4!} + \tfrac{1}{5!} + \ldots$$

Using this formula, write a Java program that approximates the value of *e* using a while loop that terminates when the difference between two successive approximations differs by less than 10 E-9.

11. The value of sin *x* can be approximated with the formula

$$\sin x = x - \frac{x^3}{3!} + \frac{x^5}{5!} - \frac{x^7}{7!} + \frac{x^9}{9!} \ldots$$

Using this formula, determine how many terms are needed to approximate the value returned by the intrinsic sin() function with an error less than 1 E-6, when *x* = 30 degrees. (*Tips:* Use a while loop that terminates when the difference between the value returned by the intrinsic sin( ) function and the approximation is less than 1 E-6. Also note that x must first be converted to radian measure and that the alternating sign in the approximating series can be determined as $(-1)^{(n+1)}$, where n is the number of terms in the approximation.)

5.3 INTERACTIVE while LOOPS

Combining interactive data entry with the repetition capabilities of the while statement produces very adaptable and powerful programs. To understand the concept involved, consider Program 5.5, where a while statement accepts and then displays four user-entered numbers one at a time. Although this is a very simple idea, the program highlights the flow of control concepts needed to produce more useful programs.

PROGRAM 5.5

```java
import javax.swing.*;
public class EnterNumbers
{
  public static void main(String[] args)
  {
    String s1, outMessage;

    final int MAXNUMS = 4;
    int count;
    double num;

    outMessage = "This program will ask you to enter "
                 + MAXNUMS + " numbers.";
    JOptionPane.showMessageDialog(null, outMessage, "Program 5.5",
                              JOptionPane.INFORMATION_MESSAGE);

    count = 1;

    while (count <= MAXNUMS)
    {
      s1 = JOptionPane.showInputDialog("Enter number " + count + ":");
      num = Double.parseDouble(s1);

      JOptionPane.showMessageDialog(null, "The number entered is " + num,
                            "Program 5.5",
                            JOptionPane.INFORMATION_MESSAGE);
      count++;
    }

    System.exit(0);
  }
}
```

Figure 5.4 illustrates the initial program message dialog box provided by Program 5.5 and the input and message dialog boxes displayed during the first execution of the loop. As shown in Figure 5.4b, the user entered 26.2 in the input dialog.

Let us review the program so we clearly understand how the output was produced. The initial program message dialog (Figure 5.4a) is the result of a call to the `showMessageDialog()`. This call is outside and before the `while` statement, so it is executed once before any statement in the `while` loop.

(a) Initial Program Message

(b) First Input Dialog

(c) First Message Dialog

FIGURE 5.4

Once the `while` loop is entered, the statements within the compound statement are executed while the tested condition is true. The first time through the compound statement, the input dialog containing the message `Enter number 1:` is displayed. The computer remains in a waiting state until a number is entered into this dialog. Once a number is typed and the Enter key is pressed, the entered string value is converted into a double-precision number that is displayed by a call to the `showMessageDialog()` method made within the `while` loop. The variable count is then incremented by 1. This process continues until four passes through the loop have been made and the value of count is 5. Each pass through the loop causes both an input dialog to be displayed for entering a value and a message dialog to display the value that was entered. Figure 5.5 illustrates this flow of control.

Rather than simply displaying the entered numbers, Program 5.5 can be modified to use the entered data. For example, let us add the numbers entered and display the total. To do this, we must be very careful about how we add the numbers because the same variable, num, is used for each number entered. Therefore, the entry of a new number in Program 5.5 automatically causes the previous number stored in num to be lost. Thus, each number entered must be added to the total before another number is entered. The required sequence is:

Enter a number
Add the number to the total

How do we add a single number to a total? A statement such as `total = total + num` does the job perfectly. This is the accumulating statement introduced in Section 3.1. After each number is entered, the accumulating statement adds the number into the total, as

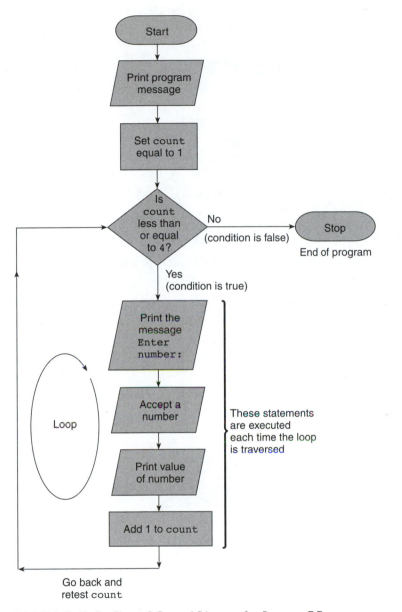

FIGURE 5.5 Flow of Control Diagram for Program 5.5

illustrated in Figure 5.6. The complete flow of control required for adding the numbers is shown in Figure 5.7.

In reviewing Figure 5.7, observe that we have made a provision for initially setting the total to zero before the `while` loop is entered. If we were to clear the total inside the `while` loop, it would be set to zero each time the loop was executed, and any value previously stored would be erased.

Program 5.6 incorporates the necessary modifications to Program 5.5 to total the numbers entered. As indicated in the flow diagram (Figure 5.7), the statement `total = total + num;` is placed immediately after a numerical value has been accepted

FIGURE 5.6   Accepting and Adding a Number to a Total

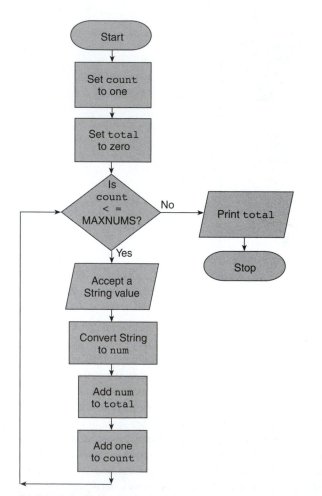

FIGURE 5.7   Accumulation Flow of Control

PROGRAM 5.6

```java
import javax.swing.*;
public class AddNumbers
{
  public static void main(String[] args)
  {
    String s1, outMessage;

    final int MAXNUMS = 4;
    int count;
    double num, total;

    outMessage = "This program will ask you to enter "
               + MAXNUMS + " numbers.";
    JOptionPane.showMessageDialog(null, outMessage, "Program 5.6",
                           JOptionPane.INFORMATION_MESSAGE);

    count = 1;
    total = 0;

    while (count <= MAXNUMS)
    {
      s1 = JOptionPane.showInputDialog("Enter number " + count + ":");
      num = Double.parseDouble(s1);

      total = total + num;
      JOptionPane.showMessageDialog(null, "The total is now "+ total,
                          "Program 5.6",
                          JOptionPane.INFORMATION_MESSAGE);
      count++;
    }

    JOptionPane.showMessageDialog(null, "The final total is " + total,
                        "Program 5.6",
                        JOptionPane.INFORMATION_MESSAGE);
    System.exit(0);
  }
}
```

from the user. Putting the accumulating statement at this point in the program ensures that the entered number is immediately "captured" into the total.

Let us review Program 5.6. The variable total was created to store the total of the numbers entered. Prior to entering the while statement, the value of total is set to zero. This ensures that any previous value present in the storage location(s) assigned to the variable total is erased. Within the while loop, the statement total = total + num; adds the value of the entered number into total. As each value is entered, it is added into the existing total to create a new total. Thus, total becomes a running subtotal of all the values entered. Only when all numbers are entered does total contain the final

FIGURE 5.8   A Sample Output Displayed by Program 5.6

sum of all the numbers. After the while loop is finished, the last message dialog, which is made by the call to showMessageDialog() after the while loop has completed execut-ing, displays this final sum. Figure 5.8 shows this last message dialog when the following data were input: 26.2, 5.0, 103.456, and 1267.89.

Having used an accumulating assignment statement to add the numbers entered, we can now go further and calculate the average of the numbers. Where do we calculate the average—within the while loop or outside it?

In this case, calculating an average requires that both a final total and the number of items in that total be available. The average is then computed by dividing the final total by the number of items. At this point, we must ask: At what point in the program is the correct total available, and at what point is the number of items available? In reviewing Program 5.6, we see that the correct total needed for calculating the average is available after the while loop is finished. In fact, the whole purpose of the while loop is to ensure that the numbers are entered and added correctly to produce a correct total. We also have the number of items used in the total contained in the named constant MAXNUMS. With this as background, see if you can read and understand Program 5.7.

PROGRAM 5.7

```
import javax.swing.*;
public class AverageNumbers
{
  public static void main(String[] args)
  {
    String s1, info, outMessage;

    final int MAXNUMS = 4;
    int count;
    double num, total, average;

    info = "This program will ask you to enter "
           + MAXNUMS + " numbers.";
    JOptionPane.showMessageDialog(null, info, "Program 5.7",
                           JOptionPane.INFORMATION_MESSAGE);
    outMessage = "The average of the numbers:\n";

    count = 1;
    total = 0;
```

(Continued on next page)

(Continued from previous page)

```
    while (count <= MAXNUMS)
    {
       s1 = JOptionPane.showInputDialog("Enter number " + count + ":");
       num = Double.parseDouble(s1);

       total = total + num;
       outMessage = outMessage + num + "   ";
       count++;
    }
    average = total / MAXNUMS;
    JOptionPane.showMessageDialog(null, outMessage + "\nis   " + average,
                        "Program 5.7",
                        JOptionPane.INFORMATION_MESSAGE);
    System.exit(0);
  }
}
```

Program 5.7 is almost identical to Program 5.6 except for the calculation of the average. We have also replaced the constant display of the total within and after the while loop with a statement that "builds up" the final message that displays the average. The primary purpose of the loop in Program 5.7 is to enter and add four numbers. After each entered number is added into the total, the same number is concatenated to the outMessage string. Immediately after the loop is exited, the average is computed, appended to the outMessage string, and the string is displayed. Figure 5.9 shows the final message dialog produced by Program 5.7, which includes both the input values and the final average.

FIGURE 5.9 A Sample Output Displayed by Program 5.7

Sentinels

All of the loops we have created thus far have been examples of fixed-count loops, where a counter controlled the number of loop iterations. By means of a while statement, variable-condition loops may also be constructed. For example, when entering grades, we may not want to count the number of grades that will be entered, but would prefer to enter the grades continuously and, at the end, type in a special data value to signal the end of data input.

In computer programming, data values that signal either the start or end of a data series are called **sentinels**. The sentinel values must be selected so as not to conflict with legitimate data values. For example, if we were constructing a program to process a student's grades, and assuming that no extra credit is given that could produce a grade higher than 100, we could use any grade higher than 100 as a sentinel value. Program 5.8 illustrates this concept. In Program 5.8, data are continuously requested and accepted until a number larger than 100 is entered. Entry of a number higher than 100 alerts the program to exit the `while` loop and display the sum of the numbers entered.

The final message dialog produced by Program 5.8 when the numbers 95, 100, 82, and 101 were input is shown in Figure 5.10. As long as values less than or equal to 100 were entered, which is the case for the first three numbers, the program continued to request and accept additional data. For each number that is less than or equal to 100, the program adds the number to the total. When the number 101 is entered, the loop is exited and the sum of the entered values is displayed (Figure 5.10).

PROGRAM 5.8

```java
import javax.swing.*;
public class Sentinels
{
  public static void main(String[] args)
  {
    final double HIGHGRADE = 100.0;
    String s1, outMessage;
    double grade, total;

    grade = 0;
    total = 0;

    outMessage = "To stop entering grades, type in any number"
               + "\n greater than 100.";
    JOptionPane.showMessageDialog(null, outMessage,
                                  "Program 5.8",
                                  JOptionPane.INFORMATION_MESSAGE);

    s1 = JOptionPane.showInputDialog("Enter a grade:");
    grade = Double.parseDouble(s1);

    while (grade <= HIGHGRADE)
    {
      total = total + grade;
      s1 = JOptionPane.showInputDialog("Enter a grade:");
      grade = Double.parseDouble(s1);
    }

    JOptionPane.showMessageDialog(null, "The total of the grades is " + total,
                                  "Program 5.8",
                                  JOptionPane.INFORMATION_MESSAGE);
    System.exit(0);
  }
}
```

FIGURE 5.10 A Sample Output Displayed by Program 5.8

The break **and** continue **Statements**

The break and continue statements are useful in connection with repetition statements. We have encountered the break statement in relation to the switch statement. The syntax of this statement is:

```
break;
```

A break statement, as its name implies, forces an immediate break, or exit, from the switch and while statements already presented and the for and do-while statements that are presented in the next sections.

For example, execution of the following while loop is immediately terminated if a number greater than 76 is entered.

```
count = 1;
while(count <= 10)
{
  s1 = JOptionPane.showInputDialog("Enter a number:");
  num = Double.parseDouble(s1);
  if (num > 76)
  {
    JOptionPane.showMessageDialog(null, "You lose!", "Test",
                                  JOptionPane.INFORMATION_MESSAGE);
    break;        // break out of the loop
  }
  else
    JOptionPane.showMessageDialog(null, "Keep on trucking!", "Test",
                                  JOptionPane.INFORMATION_MESSAGE);
  count++;
}
// break jumps to here
```

The break statement violates pure structured programming principles because it provides a second, nonstandard exit from a loop. Nevertheless, it is extremely useful and valuable for breaking out of loops when an unusual condition is detected. The break statement can also exit from a switch statement, but this is because the desired case has been detected and processed.

The continue statement is similar to the break statement but applies only to loops created with while, do-while, and for statements. The general format of a continue statement is:

```
continue;
```

When a `continue` is encountered in a loop, the next iteration of the loop begins immediately. For `while` loops, this means that execution is automatically transferred to the top of the loop, and reevaluation of the tested expression is initiated. Although the `continue` statement has no direct effect on a `switch` statement, it can be included within a `switch` statement that itself is contained in a loop. Here the effect of `continue` is the same: The next loop iteration begins.

As a general rule, the `continue` statement is less useful than the `break` statement and is not often used in practice.

The `null` Statement

All individual statements must be terminated by a semicolon. Oddly enough, a semicolon with nothing preceding it is also a valid statement called the **null statement**. Thus, the statement

```
;
```

is a `null` statement. This is a do-nothing statement that appears where a statement is syntactically required but no action is called for. A `null` statement typically is used with `while` or `for` statements. An example of a `for` statement using a `null` statement is found in Program 5.9 in the next section.

EXERCISES 5.3

1. Rewrite Program 5.6 to compute the total of eight numbers.
2. Rewrite Program 5.6 to display the prompt:

   `Please type in the total number of data values to be added:`

   In response to this prompt, the program should accept a user-entered number to control the number of times the `while` loop is executed. Thus, if the user enters 5 in response to the prompt, the program should request the input of five numbers and display the total after five numbers have been entered.

3. a. Write a Java program to convert Celsius degrees to Fahrenheit. The program should request the starting Celsius value, the number of conversions to be made, and the increment between Celsius values. The display should have appropriate headings and list the Celsius value and the corresponding Fahrenheit value. Use the relationship *Fahrenheit = (9.0 / 5.0) * Celsius + 32.0*.

   b. Run the program written in Exercise 3a on a computer. Verify that your program begins at the correct starting Celsius value and contains the exact number of conversions specified in your input data.

4. a. Modify the program written in Exercise 3 to request the starting Celsius value, the ending Celsius value, and the increment. Thus, instead of the condition checking for a fixed count, the condition checks for the ending Celsius value.

   b. Run the program written in Exercise 4a on a computer. Verify that your output starts at the correct beginning value and ends at the correct ending value.

5. Rewrite Program 5.7 to compute the average of 10 numbers.

6. Rewrite Program 5.7 to display the prompt:

   ```
   Please type in the total number of data values to be averaged:
   ```

   In response to this prompt, the program should accept a user-entered number to control the number of times the while loop is executed. Thus, if the user enters 6 in response to the prompt, the program should request the input of six numbers and display the average of the next six numbers entered.

7. By mistake, a programmer put the statement average = total / count; within the while loop immediately after the statement total = total + num; in Program 5.7. Thus, the while loop becomes:

   ```
   while (count <= MAXNUMS)
   {
       s1 = JOptionPane.showInputDialog("Enter number " + count + ":");
       num = Double.parseDouble(s1);

       total = total + num;
       average = total / count;
       count++;
   }
   ```

   Will the program yield the correct result with this while loop? From a programming perspective, which while loop is better? Why?

8. **a.** Modify Program 5.8 to compute the average of the grades entered.
   b. Run the program written in Exercise 8a on a computer and verify the results.

9. **a.** An arithmetic series is defined by

   $$a + (a + d) + (a + 2d) + (a + 3d) + \ldots + (a + (n-1)d)$$

   where a is the first term, d is the "common difference," and n is the number of terms to be added. With this information, write a Java program that uses a while loop to display each term and to determine the sum of the arithmetic series having $a = 1$, $d = 3$, and $n = 100$. Make sure that your program displays the value it has calculated.

   b. Modify the program written for Exercise 9a to permit the user to enter the starting number, ending number, and number of terms to add.

10. **a.** A geometric series is defined by

    $$a + ar + ar^2 + ar^3 + \ldots + ar^{n-1}$$

    where a is the first term, r is the "common ratio," and n is the number of terms in the series. With this information, write a Java program that uses a while loop to display each term and to determine the sum of a geometric series having $a = 1$, $r = 0.5$, and $n = 100$. Make sure that your program displays the value it has calculated.

    b. Modify the program written for Exercise 10a to permit the user to enter the starting number, common ratio, and number of terms in the series.

11. In addition to the arithmetic average of a set of numbers, both a geometric and harmonic mean can be calculated. The geometric mean of a set of n numbers x_1, $x_2, \ldots x_n$ is defined as

    $$\sqrt[n]{(x_1)(x_2)\ldots(x_n)}$$

and the harmonic mean as

$$\frac{n}{\dfrac{1}{x_1} + \dfrac{1}{x_2} + \ldots + \dfrac{1}{x_n}}$$

Using these formulas, write a Java program that continues to accept numbers until the number 999 is entered and then calculates and displays both the geometric and harmonic means of the entered numbers. (*Tip:* Your program must correctly count the number of values entered.)

12. **a.** The following data were collected on a recent automobile trip.

	Mileage	Gallons
	-------	---------
Start of trip:	22495	Full tank
	22841	12.2
	23185	11.3
	23400	10.5
	23772	11.0
	24055	12.2
	24434	14.7
	24804	14.3
	25276	15.2

Write a Java program that accepts a mileage and gallons value and calculates the miles per gallon (mpg) achieved for that segment of the trip. The miles per gallon are obtained as the difference in mileage between fill-ups divided by the number of gallons of gasoline in the fill-up.

b. Modify the program written for Exercise 12a to additionally compute and display the cumulative mpg achieved after each fill-up. The cumulative mpg is calculated as the difference between each fill-up mileage and the mileage at the start of the trip divided by the sum of the gallons used to that point in the trip.

5.4 THE for STATEMENT

The for statement performs the same functions as the while statement but in a different form. In many situations, especially those that use a fixed-count condition, the for statement format is easier to use than its while statement equivalent. The general form of the for statement is:

```
for (initializer; condition; increment)
  statement;
```

Although the for statement looks a little complicated, it is really quite simple if we consider each of its parts separately. Within the parentheses of the for statement are three items separated by semicolons. Each of these items is optional, but the semicolons must be present. As you will see, the items in parentheses correspond to the initialization, condition evaluation, and altering of condition values that we have already used with the while statement.

The middle item in the parentheses, the *condition*, is any valid Java expression that yields a boolean value, and there is no difference in the way `for` and `while` statements use this expression. In both statements, as long as the condition evaluates to a `true` value, the statement following the parentheses is executed. This means that prior to the first check of the expression, initial values for the tested condition's variables must be assigned. It also means that before the condition is reevaluated, there must be one or more statements that alter these values. Recall that the general placement of these statements in a `while` statement follows the pattern:

```
initializing statements;
while (condition)
{
  loop statements;
       .
       .
       .
  condition-altering statements;
}
```

The need to initialize variables or make some other evaluations prior to entering a repetition loop is so common that the `for` statement allows one or more initializing expressions to be grouped together as the first set of items within the `for`'s parentheses. These initializations are executed only once, before the condition is evaluated for the first time. Commas must separate multiple initializations, as in `i = 1, total = 0`.

The `for` statement also provides a single place for all condition-altering expressions, which is the last item contained within the `for`'s parentheses. These expressions, which typically increment or decrement a counter, are executed by the `for` statement at the end of each loop, just before the expression is reevaluated. Again, multiple increment expressions must be separated from each other by commas. Figure 5.11 illustrates the `for` statement's flow of control diagram.

The following section of code illustrates the correspondence between the `for` and `while` statements:

```
count = 1;
while (count <= 10)
{
  System.out.print(count + "   ");
  count++;
}
```

The `for` statement corresponding to this section of code is:

```
for (count = 1; count <= 10; count++)
  System.out.print(count + "   ");
```

As seen in these examples, the only difference between the `for` statement and the `while` statement is the placement of equivalent expressions. The grouping together of

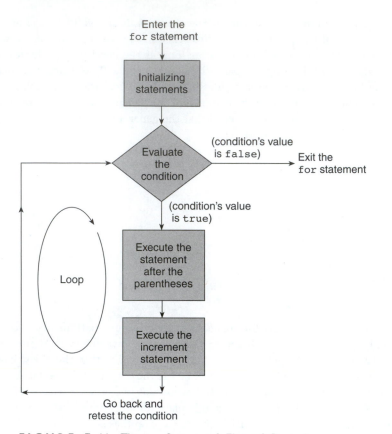

FIGURE 5.11   The for Statement's Flow of Control

initializer, condition, and increment in the for statement is very convenient, especially when it creates fixed-count loops. Consider the following for statement:

```
for (count = 2; count <= 20; count = count + 2)
  System.out.print(count + "  ");
```

In this statement, all the loop control information is contained within the parentheses. The loop starts with a count of 2, stops when the count exceeds 20, and increments the loop counter in steps of 2. Program 5.9 illustrates this for statement in an actual program. Two blanks are placed between each output value for readability.

The output of Program 5.9 is:

```
2   4   6   8   10   12   14   16   18   20
```

The for statement does not require that any of the items in parentheses be present or that they be used for initializing or incrementation purposes. However, the two semicolons must be present within the for's parentheses. For example, the construction for (; count <= 20 ;) is valid.

PROGRAM 5.9

```
public class SampleFor
{
   public static void main(String[] args)
   {
      int count;

      for (count = 2; count <= 20; count = count + 2)
         System.out.print(count + "   ");
   }
}
```

If an initializer is missing, the initialization step is omitted when the `for` statement is executed. This means, of course, that the programmer must provide the required initializations before the `for` statement is encountered. Similarly, if the increment is missing, any expressions needed to alter the evaluation of the tested expression must be included directly within the statement part of the loop. The `for` statement only ensures that all initializer expressions within the parentheses are executed once, before evaluation of the tested condition, and that all increment expressions in the parentheses are executed at the end of the loop before the tested condition is rechecked. Thus, Program 5.9 can be rewritten in any of the three ways shown in Programs 5.9a, 5.9b, and 5.9c.

In Program 5.9a, `count` is initialized outside the `for` statement, and the initializer inside the parentheses is left blank. In Program 5.9b, both the initializer and the increment are removed from within the parentheses. Program 5.9b also uses a compound statement within the `for` loop, with an incrementing statement included in the compound statement. In addition, Program 5.9c has included all items within the parentheses, so there is no need for any useful statement following the parentheses. Here the `null` statement satisfies the syntactical requirement of one statement to follow the `for`'s parentheses. Observe also in Program 5.9c that the increment part of the statement (the last set of items in parentheses) consists of two items and that a comma separates these items. The use of commas to separate items in both the initializer and increment parts of

PROGRAM 5.9a

```
public class SampleForA
{
   public static void main(String[] args)
   {
      int count;

      count = 2;     // initializer outside for statement
      for ( ; count <= 20; count = count + 2)
         System.out.print(count + "   ");
   }
}
```

PROGRAM 5.9b

```
public class SampleForB
{
  public static void main(String[] args)
  {
    int count;

    count = 2;     // initializer outside for loop
    for( ; count <= 20; )
    {
      System.out.print(count + "  ");
      count = count + 2;     // alteration statement
    }
  }
}
```

a for statement, as previously noted, is required if either of these two items contain more than one expression. Finally, note the fact that Programs 5.9a, 5.9b, and 5.9c are all inferior to Program 5.9. The for statement in Program 5.9 is much clearer because all of the expressions pertaining to the tested expression are grouped together within the parentheses.

PROGRAM 5.9c

```
public class SampleForC
{
  public static void main(String[] args)
  {
    int count;

    for (count = 2; count <= 20; System.out.print(count + "  "), count = count + 2)
      ; // null statement
  }
}
```

Although the initializer and increment items can be omitted from a for statement, omitting the tested condition results in an infinite loop unless there is a break statement that is activated somewhere within the loop. For example, the code

```
for (count = 2; ; count++)
  System.out.print(count + " ");
```

results in an infinite loop.

As with the while statement, both break and continue statements can be used within a for loop. The break forces an immediate exit from the for loop, as it does in the while loop. The continue, however, forces control to be passed to the altering list in a

POINT OF INFORMATION

WHERE TO PLACE THE OPENING BRACES

There are two styles of `for` loops that are written by professional Java programmers. These styles only come into play when the `for` loop contains a compound statement. The style illustrated and found in the text takes the form:

```
for (expression)
{
  compound statement in here
}
```

An equally acceptable style places the initial brace of the compound statement on the first line. Using this style, a `for` loop appears as:

```
for (expression) {      .
  compound statement in here
}
```

The advantage of the first style is that the braces line up under one another, making it easier to locate brace pairs. The advantage of the second style is that it makes the code more compact and saves a line, permitting more code to be viewed in the same display area. Both styles are used but are almost never intermixed. As always, the indentation within a compound statement (two or four spaces or a tab) should also be consistent throughout all of your programs. If the choice is yours, select whichever style appeals to you and be consistent. If the preferred style is dictated by the company or course in which you are programming, find out what the style is and follow it consistently.

for statement, after which the tested expression is reevaluated. This differs from the action of a `continue` in a `while` statement, in which control is passed directly to the reevaluation of the tested expression.

Finally, many programmers use the initializing list of a `for` statement both to declare and to initialize a counter variable within the `for` loop. For example, in the following `for` statement

```
for(int count = 1; count < 11; count++)
  System.out.print(count + "  ");
```

the variable `count` is declared and initialized from within the `for` statement. Being declared this way, however, restricts `count`'s usage within the bounds of the `for` loop. Attempting to declare a second variable having a different data type within the initialization part of the `for` loop results in a compiler error.

To understand the enormous power of the `for` statement, consider the task of printing a table of numbers from 1 to 10, including their squares and cubes, using this statement.

Such a table was previously produced using a while statement in Program 5.3. You may wish to review Program 5.3 and compare it to Program 5.10 to get a further sense of the equivalence between the for and while statements.

PROGRAM 5.10

```java
import java.text.*; // needed for formatting
public class ForTable
{
   public static void main(String[] args)
   {
     int num;

     DecimalFormat df = new DecimalFormat("0000");

     System.out.println("NUMBER     SQUARE     CUBE");
     System.out.println("------     ------     ----");

     for (num = 1; num < 11; num++)
     {
       System.out.print(" " + df.format(num));
       System.out.print("         " + df.format(num * num));
       System.out.println("        " + df.format(num * num * num));
     }
   }
}
```

When Program 5.10 is run, the display is:

NUMBER	SQUARE	CUBE
0001	0001	0001
0002	0004	0008
0003	0009	0027
0004	0016	0064
0005	0025	0125
0006	0036	0216
0007	0049	0343
0008	0064	0512
0009	0081	0729
0010	0100	1000

Changing the number 11 in the for statement of Program 5.10 to 101 creates a loop that is executed 100 times and produces a table of numbers from 1 to 100. As with the while statement, this small change produces an immense increase in the processing and output provided by the program. Notice also that the expression num++ replaced the equivalent num = num + 1 as the incrementing expression.

Interactive `for` Loops

A `showInputDialog()`method inside a `for` loop produces the same effect as when this method is used within a while loop. For example, in Program 5.11, an input dialog inputs a set of numbers. As each number is input, it is added to a total. When the `for` loop is exited, the average is calculated and displayed.

The `for` statement in Program 5.11 creates a loop that is executed five times. The user is prompted to enter a number each time through the loop. After each number is entered, it is immediately added to the total. Although `total` was initialized to zero before the `for` statement, this initialization could have been included with the initialization of `count` as follows:

```
for (total = 0.0, count = 0; count < 5; count++)
```

PROGRAM 5.11

```java
import javax.swing.*;
public class AverageFiveNumbers
{
   // This method calculates the average
   // of 5 user-entered numbers

   public static void main(String[] args)
   {
     final int MAXNUMS = 5;

     int count;
     double num, total, average;
     String s1;

     total = 0.0;

     for (count = 0; count < MAXNUMS; count++)
     {
       s1 =JOptionPane.showInputDialog("Enter a number:");
       num = Double.parseDouble(s1);
       total = total + num;
     }

     average = total / MAXNUMS;

     JOptionPane.showMessageDialog(null,
                 "The average of the data entered is " + average,
                 "Program 5.11",
                  JOptionPane.INFORMATION_MESSAGE);

     System.exit(0);
   }
}
```

DO YOU USE A for OR A while LOOP?

A commonly asked question by beginning programmers is which loop structure should they use: a for or a while loop? This is a good question because each of these loop structures in Java can construct both fixed-count and variable-condition loops.

In almost all other computer languages, except C, C++, and Java, the answer is relatively straightforward because the for statement can only construct fixed-count loops. Thus, in these languages (again, excepting C, C++, and Java), for statements construct fixed-count loops and while statements are generally used only when constructing variable-condition loops.

In C, C++, and Java, this easy distinction does not hold because each statement can create each type of loop. The answer for these three languages, then, is really a matter of style. Since a for and while loop are interchangeable in these languages, either loop is appropriate. Some professional programmers always use a for statement and almost never use a while statement; others always use a while statement and rarely use a for statement. Still a third group tends to retain the convention in early high-level languages—that is, use a for loop to create fixed-count loops and a while loop to create variable-condition loops. In Java, it is all a matter of style, and you will encounter all three styles in your programming career.

Note, however, that the declarations for both total and count *could not* have been included with their initializations within the for statement because they are different data types. Thus, the statement

```
for (double total = 0.0, int count = 0; count < 5; count++) // INVALID
```

is invalid because the initializing item, by itself, results in an invalid declaration statement. If both total and count were the same data type, however, they could be declared together within the for loop. For example, the statement

```
for (int total = 0, count = 0; count < 5; count++)
```

is valid because the statement int total = 0, count = 0; is a valid declaration statement. In general, and to avoid declaration problems, you should declare and initialize at most a single initializing variable within a for statement.

Nested Loops

In many situations, it is convenient or necessary to have a loop within another loop. Such loops are called **nested loops**. A simple example of a nested loop is:

```
for(i = 1; i <= 5; i++)          // start of outer loop <-----------+
{                                //                                 |
   System.out.println("\ni is now " + i);  //                      |
                                 //                                 |
   for(j = 1; j <= 4; j++)       // start of inner loop            |
      System.out.print("  j = " + j);  // end of inner loop        |
}                                // end of outer loop   <-----------+
```

The first loop, controlled by the value of i, is the **outer loop**. The second loop, controlled by the value of j, is the **inner loop**. Notice that all statements in the inner loop are within the boundaries of the outer loop and that a different variable controls each loop. For each single trip through the outer loop, the inner loop runs through its entire sequence. Thus, each time the i counter increases by 1, the inner for loop executes completely. This situation is illustrated in Figure 5.12.

Program 5.12 includes the foregoing code in a working program.

PROGRAM 5.12

```
public class NestedLoop
{
  public static void main(String[] args)
  {
    int i, j;

    for(i = 1; i <= 5; i++)          // start of outer loop <-----------+
    {                                //                                 |
      System.out.println("\ni is now " + i);  //                       |
                                     //                                 |
      for(j = 1; j <= 4; j++)        // start of inner loop            |
        System.out.print("  j = " + j);  // end of inner loop          |
    }                                // end of outer loop   <-----------+

  }
}
```

Here is the output of a sample run of Program 5.12:

```
i is now 1
  j = 1   j = 2   j = 3   j = 4
i is now 2
  j = 1   j = 2   j = 3   j = 4
i is now 3
  j = 1   j = 2   j = 3   j = 4
i is now 4
  j = 1   j = 2   j = 3   j = 4
i is now 5
  j = 1   j = 2   j = 3   j = 4
```

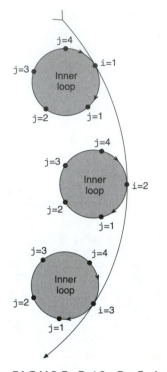

FIGURE 5.12   For Each `i,j` Loops

To illustrate the value of a nested loop, we use one to compute the average grade for each student in a class of 20. Assume that each student has taken four exams during the semester. The final grade is calculated as the average of these examination grades.

The outer loop in our program will consist of 20 passes. Each pass through the outer loop computes the average for one student. The inner loop will consist of 4 passes. One examination grade is entered in each inner loop pass. As each grade is entered, it is added to the total for the student, and at the end of the loop, the average is calculated and displayed. Program 5.13 makes the required calculations with a nested loop.

PROGRAM 5.13

```
import javax.swing.*;
public class CalculateGrade
{
  public static void main(String[] args)
  {
    final int NUMGRADES = 4;
    final int NUMSTUDENTS = 20;
    int i,j;
    double grade, total, average;
    String s1;
```

(Continued on next page)

(Continued from previous page)

```
    for (i = 1; i <= NUMSTUDENTS; i++)    // start of outer loop
    {
      total = 0;                     // clear the total for this student
      for (j = 1; j <= NUMGRADES; j++)   // start of inner loop
      {
        s1 = JOptionPane.showInputDialog(
                      "Enter an examination grade for this student:");
        grade = Double.parseDouble(s1);

        total = total + grade;    // add the grade into the total
      }                           // end of the inner for loop
      average = total / NUMGRADES;        // calculate the average

      JOptionPane.showMessageDialog(null,
                  "The average for student " + i + " is " + average,
                  "Program 5.13",
                  JOptionPane.INFORMATION_MESSAGE);
    }      // end of the outer for loop

    System.exit(0);
  }
}
```

In reviewing Program 5.13, pay particular attention to the initialization of total within the outer loop before the inner loop is entered. The variable total is initialized 20 times, once for each student. Also notice that the average is calculated and displayed immediately after the inner loop is finished. Since the statements that compute and display the average are also within the outer loop, 20 averages are calculated and displayed. The entry and addition of each grade within the inner loop use techniques you have seen before and should now be familiar.

EXERCISES 5.4

1. Write individual for statements for the following cases:
   a. Use a counter named i that has an initial value of 1, a final value of 20, and an increment of 1.
   b. Use a counter named icount that has an initial value of 1, a final value of 20, and an increment of 2.
   c. Use a counter named J that has an initial value of 1, a final value of 100, and an increment of 5.
   d. Use a counter named icount that has an initial value of 20, a final value of 1, and an increment of −1.
   e. Use a counter named icount that has an initial value of 20, a final value of 1, and an increment of −2.

f. Use a counter named `count` that has an initial value of 1.0, a final value of 16.2, and an increment of 0.2.

g. Use a counter named `xcnt` that has an initial value of 20.0, a final value of 10.0, and an increment of −0.

2. Determine the number of times that each `for` loop is executed for the `for` statements written for Exercise 1.

3. Determine the output of the following methods:

a.
```
public static void main(String[] args)
{
   int i;

   for (i = 0; i <= 20; i = i + 4)
     System.out.print(i + " ");
}
```

b.
```
public static void main(String[] args)
{
   int i;

   for (i = 1; i < 21; i = i + 3)
     System.out.print(i + " ");
}
```

c.
```
public static void main(String[] args)
{
   int i;

   for (i = 20; i >= 0; i = i - 4)
     System.out.print(i + " ");
}
```

4. Modify Program 5.10 to produce a table of the numbers 0 through 20 in increments of 2, with their squares and cubes.

5. Modify Program 5.10 to produce a table of numbers from 10 to 1 instead of 1 to 10 as it currently does.

6. Write and run a Java program that displays a table of 20 temperature conversions from Fahrenheit to Celsius. The table should start with a Fahrenheit value of 20 degrees and be incremented in values of 4 degrees. Recall that *Celsius = (5.0/9.0) * (Fahrenheit − 32.0)*.

7. Modify the program written for Exercise 4 to initially request the number of conversions to be displayed.

8. Write a Java program that converts Fahrenheit to Celsius temperature in increments of 5 degrees. The initial value of Fahrenheit temperature and the total conversions to be made are to be requested as user input during program execution. Recall that *Celsius = (5.0/9.0) * (Fahrenheit − 32.0)*.

9. Write and run a Java program that accepts six Fahrenheit temperatures, one at a time, and converts each value entered to its Celsius equivalent before the next value is requested. Use a `for` loop in your program. The conversion required is *Celsius = (5.0/9.0) * (Fahrenheit − 32.0)*.

10. Write and run a Java program that accepts 10 individual values of gallons, one at a time, and converts each value entered to its liter equivalent before the next value is requested. Use a `for` loop in your program. There are *3.785 liters in 1 gallon of liquid*.

11. Modify the program written for Exercise 10 to initially request the number of data items that will be entered and converted.

12. Is the following method correct? If it is, determine its output. If it is not, determine and correct the error so the program will run.

```java
public static void main(String[] args)
{

    for(int i = 1; i < 10; i++)
      System.out.print(i + " ");
    System.out.println();
    for (int i = 1; i < 5; i++)
      System.out.println(i + " ");


}
```

13. The expansion of a steel bridge as it is heated to a final Celsius temperature, T_F, from an initial Celsius temperature, T_0, can be approximated with the formula

Increase in length $= a * L * (T_F - T_0)$

where a is the coefficient of expansion, which for steel is 11.7 E-6, and L is the length of the bridge at temperature T_0. Using this formula, write a Java program that displays a table of expansion lengths for a steel bridge that is 7,365 meters long at 0 degrees Celsius, as the temperature increases to 40 degrees in 5-degree increments.

14. The probability that an individual telephone call will last less than t minutes can be approximated by the exponential probability function

Probability that a call lasts less than t minutes $= 1 - e^{-t/a}$

where a is the average call length and e is Euler's number (2.71828). For example, assuming that the average call length is 2 minutes, the probability that a call will last less than 1 minute is calculated as $1 - e^{-1/2} = 0.3297$.

Using this probability function, write a Java program that calculates and displays a list of probabilities of a call lasting less than 1 to less than 10 minutes in 1-minute increments.

15. **a.** The arrival rate of customers in a busy New York bank can be estimated using the Poisson probability function

$$P(x) = \frac{\lambda^x e^{-\lambda}}{x!}$$

where x = the number of customer arrivals per minute; λ = the average number of arrivals per minute, and e = Euler's number (2.71828). For example, if the average number of customers entering the bank is three customers per minute, then λ is equal to three. Thus, the probability of one customer arriving in any 1 minute equals

$$P(x = 1) = \frac{3^1 e^{-3}}{1!} = 0.149561$$

and the probability of two customers arriving in any 1 minute equals

$$P(x = 2) = \frac{3^2 e^{-3}}{2!} = 0.224454$$

Using the Poisson probability function, write a Java program that calculates and displays the probability of one to ten customer arrivals in any 1 minute when the average arrival rate is three customers per minute.

b. The formula given in Exercise 15a is also applicable for estimating the arrival rate of planes at a busy airport (here an arriving "customer" is an incoming airplane). Using this same formula, modify the program written in Exercise 15a to accept the average arrival rate as an input data item. Then run the modified program to determine the probability of zero to ten planes attempting to land in any 1-minute period at an airport during peak arrival times. Assume that the average arrival rate for peak arrival times is two planes per minute.

16. A golf ball is dropped from an airplane. The distance, d, the ball falls in t seconds is given by the equation $d = (^1\!/_2)gt^2$, where g is the acceleration due to gravity and is equal to 32 ft/sec². Using this information, write and run a Java program that displays the distance fallen in each 1-second interval for 10 seconds and the total distance the golf ball falls at the end of each interval. The output should look like the following table:

TIME	DISTANCE IN CURRENT INTERVAL	TOTAL DISTANCE
0	0.0	0.0
1	16.0	16.0
.	.	.
.	.	.
.	.	.
10	.	.

17. Assume the airplane in Exercise 16 is flying at a height of 50,000 feet. Modify the program written for Exercise 16 to determine how long it will take the golf ball to reach the ground. To increase the accuracy of your result without an undue number of calculations, decrease the time interval from 1 second to 0.1 second as the golf ball nears the ground.

18. The Fibonacci sequence is 0, 1, 1, 2, 3, 5, 8, 13, . . . , where the first two terms are 0 and 1, and each term thereafter is the sum of the two preceding terms; that is, $Fib[n] = Fib[n - 1] + Fib[n - 2]$. Using this information, write a Java program that calculates the nth number in a Fibonacci sequence, where n is interactively entered into the program by the user. For example, if $n = 6$, the program should display the value 5.

19. **Nested loops:** Four experiments are performed, each experiment consisting of six test results. The results for each experiment follow. Write a program using a

nested loop to compute and display the average of the test results for each experiment.

Experiment 1 results: 23.2 31 16.9 27 25.4 28.6
Experiment 2 results: 34.8 45.2 27.9 36.8 33.4 39.4
Experiment 3 results: 19.4 16.8 10.2 20.8 18.9 13.4
Experiment 4 results: 36.9 39 49.2 45.1 42.7 50.6

20. **a.** **Nested loops:** Modify the program written for Exercise 19 so that the number of test results for each experiment is entered by the user. Write your program so that a different number of test results can be entered for each experiment.
    b. Rewrite the program written for Exercise 20a to eliminate the inner loop. To do this, you will have to input six results for each experiment rather than one at a time.

21. **a.** **Nested loops:** An electrical manufacturer tests five generators by measuring their output voltages at three different times. Write a Java program that uses a nested loop to enter each generator's test results and then computes and displays the average voltage for each generator. Assume the following generator test results:

    Generator 1: 122.5 122.7 123.0
    Generator 2: 120.2 127.0 125.1
    Generator 3 : 121.7 124.9 126.0
    Generator 4 : 122.9 123.8 126.7
    Generator 5 : 121.5 124.7 122.6

    b. Modify the program written for Exercise 21a to calculate and display the average voltage for all the generators. (*Tip*: Use a second variable to store the total of all the generators' voltages.)

22. **Nested loops:** Rewrite the program written for Exercise 21a to eliminate the inner loop. To do this, you will have to input three voltages for each generator rather than one at a time. Each voltage must be stored in its own variable name before the average is calculated.

23. **Nested loops:** Write a program that calculates and displays values for Y when

    $$Y = XZ / (X - Z)$$

    Your program should calculate Y for values of X ranging between 1 and 5 and values of Z ranging between 2 and 6. X should control the outer loop and be incremented in steps of 1, and Z should be incremented in steps of 1. Your program should also display the message Function Undefined when the X and Z values are equal.

24. **Nested loops:** Assembly languages for some microprocessors do not have a multiply operation. Although there are sophisticated algorithms for performing multiplication in such cases, a simple method multiplies by repeated addition. In this case, the efficiency of the algorithm can be increased by using nested loops. For example, to multiply a number by 12, first add the number three times and then add the result four times. This requires only seven additions as opposed to twelve. Using this information, write a Java program that multiplies 33, 47, and 83 by 1001 using a nest of three loops and then displays the result. (*Tip*: 1001 = 7 * 11 * 13)

5.5 LOOP PROGRAMMING TECHNIQUES

In this section, we present four common programming techniques associated with pretest (`for` and `while`) loops. All of these techniques are common knowledge to experienced programmers.

Technique 1: Interactive Input within a Loop

In Section 5.2, we presented the effect of including an input dialog within a `while` loop. Interactively entering data within a loop is a general technique that is equally applicable to `for` loops. For example, in Program 5.14, an input dialog allows a user to interactively input a set of numbers. As each number is input, it is added to a total. When the for loop is exited, the average is calculated and displayed.

The `for` statement in Program 5.14 creates a loop that is executed five times. The user is prompted to enter a number each time through the loop. After each number is entered, it is immediately added to the total. Notice that `total` is initialized to zero as part of the initializing list of the `for` statement is executed. The loop in Program 5.14 is executed as long as the value in `count` is less than or equal to five and is terminated when count becomes six (the increment to six is in fact what causes the loop to end). The output produced by Program 5.14 is similar to that produced by Program 5.7.

PROGRAM 5.14

```java
import javax.swing.*;
public class InteractiveFor
{
  // This method calculates the average of MAXNUMS
  // user-entered numbers
  public static void main(String[] args)
  {
    String s1, outMessage;

    final int MAXNUMS = 4;
    int count;
    double num, total, average;

    outMessage = "This program will ask you to enter "
            + MAXNUMS + " numbers.";
    JOptionPane.showMessageDialog(null, outMessage, "Program 5.14",
                           JOptionPane.INFORMATION_MESSAGE);
```

(Continued on next page)

(Continued from previous page)

```
    total = 0;
    for(count = 1; count <= MAXNUMS; count++)
    {
      s1 = JOptionPane.showInputDialog("Enter number " + count + ":");
      num = Double.parseDouble(s1);
      total = total + num;
    }


    average = total/MAXNUMS;
    JOptionPane.showMessageDialog(null, "The average of the data entered is "
                              + average, "Program 5.14",
                              JOptionPane.INFORMATION_MESSAGE);

    System.exit(0);
  }
}
```

Technique 2: Selection within a Loop

Another common programming technique is to use either a for or while loop to cycle through a set of numbers and select those numbers that meet one or more criteria. For example, assume that we want to find both the positive and negative sum of a set of numbers. The criterion here is whether the number is positive or negative, and the logic for implementing this program is given by the pseudocode

```
While the loop condition is true
    Enter a number
    If the number is greater than zero
        add the number to the positive sum
    Else
        add the number to the negative sum
    EndIf
EndWhile
```

Program 5.15 describes this algorithm in Java for a fixed-count loop where five numbers are to be entered using keyboard input.

The following is a sample run using Program 5.15:

```
This program will ask you to enter 5 numbers.
Enter a number (positive or negative): 10
Enter a number (positive or negative): -10
Enter a number (positive or negative): 5
Enter a number (positive or negative): -7
Enter a number (positive or negative): 11
The positive total is 26.000000
The negative total is -17.000000
```

PROGRAM 5.15

```java
import java.io.*;  // needed to access input stream classes
public class PosNegTotals
{
  // This method computes the positive and negative sums of a set
  // of MAXNUMS user-entered numbers
  public static void main(String[] args)
  throws java.io.IOException
  {
    final int MAXNUMS = 5;
    int i;
    double usenum, postot, negtot;
    String s1;

      // set up the basic input stream
      // needed for conversion capabilities
    InputStreamReader isr = new InputStreamReader(System.in);
      // needed to use readLine()
    BufferedReader br = new BufferedReader(isr);

    System.out.println("This program will ask you to enter " + MAXNUMS + " numbers.");

    postot = 0; // this initialization can be done in the declaration
    negtot = 0; // this initialization can be done in the declaration

    for (i = 1; i <= MAXNUMS; i++)
    {
      System.out.print("Enter a number (positive or negative): ");
      s1 = br.readLine();
      usenum = Double.parseDouble(s1);
      if (usenum > 0)
        postot = postot + usenum;
      else
        negtot = negtot + usenum;
    }
    System.out.println("The positive total is " + postot);
    System.out.println("The negative total is " + negtot);
  }
}
```

Technique 3: Evaluating Functions of One Variable

Loops can be conveniently constructed to determine and display the values of a single-variable mathematical function for a set of values over any specified interval. For example, assume that we want to know the values of the function

$$y = 10x^2 + 3x - 2$$

for x between 2 and 6. Assuming that x has been declared as an integer variable, the following for loop can calculate the required values:

```
for (x = 2; x <= 6; x++)
{
  y = 10 * (int)Math.pow(x,2) + 3 * x - 2;
  System.out.println(x + "          " +y);
}
```

For this loop, the variable x is both the counter variable and the unknown (independent variable) in the function. For each value of x from 2 to 5, a new value of y is calculated and displayed. This for loop is contained within Program 5.16, which also displays appropriate headings for the values printed.

PROGRAM 5.16

```
public class FunctionEval
{
  public static void main(String[] args)
  {
    int x, y;

    System.out.println("x value   y value");
    System.out.println("-------   -------");
    for (x = 2; x <= 6; x++)
    {
      y = 10 * (int)Math.pow(x,2) + 3 * x - 2;
      System.out.println(x + "          " +y);
    }
  }
}
```

The following is displayed when Program 5.16 is executed:

```
x value   y value
-------   --------
2         44
3         97
4         170
5         263
6         376
```

Two items are of importance here. The first is that any equation with one unknown can be evaluated using a single for or an equivalent while loop. The method requires substituting the desired equation into the loop in place of the equation in Program 5.16 and adjusting the counter values to match the desired solution range.

The second item of note is that we are not constrained to using integer values for the counter variable. For example, by specifying a noninteger increment, solutions for fractional values can be obtained. This is shown in Program 5.17, where the equation $y = 10x^2 + 3x - 2$ is evaluated in the range $x = 2$ to $x = 6$ in increments of 0.5.

PROGRAM 5.17

```
public class FunctionDblEval
{
  public static void main(String[] args)
  {
    double x, y;

    System.out.println("x value    y value");
    System.out.println("-------    -------");
    for (x = 2.0; x <= 6.0; x = x + 0.5)
    {
      y = 10 * (int)Math.pow(x,2) + 3 * x - 2;
      System.out.println(x + "          " +y);
    }
  }
}
```

Notice that x and y have been declared as floating-point variables in Program 5.17 to allow these variables to take on fractional values. The following is the output produced by this program:

```
x value    y value
-------    -------

2.0          44.0
2.5          65.5
3.0          97.0
3.5         128.5
4.0         170.0
4.5         211.5
5.0         263.0
5.5         314.5
6.0         376.0
```

Technique 4: Interactive Loop Control

Values that control a loop may be set using variables rather than constant values. For example, the four statements

```
i = 5;
j = 10;
k = 1;
for (count = i; count <= j; count = count + k)
```

produce the same effect as the single statement

```
for (count = 5; count <= 10; count = count + 1)
```

Similarly, the statements

```
i = 5;
j = 10;
k = 1;
count = i;
while (count <= j)

  count = count + k;
```

produce the same effect as the following `while` loop

```
count = 5;
while (count <= 10)
  count = count + 1;
```

The advantage of variables in the initialization, condition, and altering expressions is that it allows us to assign values for these expressions external to either the `for` or `while` statement. This is especially useful when input statements set the actual values. To make this a little more tangible, consider Program 5.18.

PROGRAM 5.18

```
import java.io.*;     // need to access input stream classes
import java.text.*;   // needed for formatting
public class InteractiveForTable
{
  public static void main(String[] args)
  throws java.io.IOException
  {
    int num, endValue;
    String s1;

    DecimalFormat df = new DecimalFormat("0000");

      // set up the basic input stream
      // needed for conversion capabilities
    InputStreamReader isr = new InputStreamReader(System.in);
      // needed to use ReadLine()
    BufferedReader br = new BufferedReader(isr);

    System.out.print("Enter the final number for the table: ");
    s1 = br.readLine();
    endValue = Integer.parseInt(s1);
```

(Continued on next page)

(Continued from previous page)

```
      System.out.println("NUMBER     SQUARE     CUBE");
      System.out.println("------     ------     ----");
      for (num = 1; num <= endValue; num++)
      {
        System.out.print("  " + df.format(num));
        System.out.print("          " + df.format(num * num));
        System.out.println("       " + df.format(num * num * num));
      }


  }
}
```

In Program 5.18, variables control both the condition (middle) and altering expressions. Here a keyboard input statement has been placed before the loop to allow the user to decide what the final value should be. Notice that this arrangement permits the user to set the size of the table at run time rather than having the programmer set the table size at compile time. This also makes the program more general because it can now create a variety of tables without the need for reprogramming and recompiling.

EXERCISES 5.5

1. **Input within a loop:** Write and run a Java program that accepts six Fahrenheit temperatures, one at a time, and converts each value entered to its Celsius equivalent before the next value is requested. Use a for loop in your program. The conversion required is *Celsius = (5.0/9.0) * (Fahrenheit − 32)*.

2. **Input within a loop:** Write and run a Java program that accepts 10 individual values of gallons, one at a time, and converts each value entered to its liter equivalent before the next value is requested. Use a for loop in your program. There are *3.785 liters in 1 gallon*.

3. **Interactive loop control:** Modify the program written for Exercise 2 to initially request the number of data items that will be entered and converted.

4. **Interactive loop control:** Modify Program 5.15 so that the number of entries to be input is specified by the user when the program is executed.

5. **Selection:** Modify Program 5.15 so that it displays the average of the positive and negative numbers. (*Tip:* Be careful not to count zero as a negative number.) Test your program by entering the numbers 17, −10, 19, 0, −4. The positive average displayed by your program should be 18 and the negative average should be −7.

6. a. **Selection:** Write a Java program that selects and displays the maximum value of five numbers that are to be entered when the program is executed. (*Tip:* Use a for loop with both interactive input and an if statement internal to the loop.)

   b. Modify the program written for Exercise 6a so that it displays both the maximum value and the position in the input set of numbers where the maximum occurs.

7. **Selection:** Write a Java program that selects and displays the first 20 integer numbers that are evenly divisible by 3.

8. **Selection:** A child's parents promised to give the child $10 on her 12th birthday and double the gift on every subsequent birthday until the gift exceeded $1,000. Write a Java program to determine how old the girl will be when the last amount is given and the total amount she received, including the last gift.

9. **Mathematical functions:** Modify Program 5.17 to produce a table of Y values for the following:

   a. $y = 3x^5 - 2x^3 + x$

   for x between 5 and 10 in increments of 0.2.

   b.
   $$y = 1 + x + \frac{x^2}{2} + \frac{x^3}{6} + \frac{x^4}{24}$$

   for x between 1 and 3 in increments of 0.1.

   c. $y = 2e^{.8t}$ for t between 4 and 10 in increments of 0.2.

10. **Mathematical functions:** A model of worldwide population in billions of people is given by the equation

    $$Population = 6.0\ e^{0.02\ [Year - 2000]}$$

    Using this formula, write a Java program that displays a yearly population table for the years January 2000 though January 2010.

11. **Mathematical functions:** The x and y coordinates, as a function of time, t, of a projectile fired with an initial velocity v at an angle of θ with respect to the ground is given by:

    $x = v\ t\ cos(\theta)$
    $y = v\ t\ sin(\theta)$

    Using these formulas, write a Java program that displays a table of x and y values for a projectile fired with an initial velocity of 500 ft/sec at an angle of 22.8 degrees. (*Tip*: Remember to convert to radian measure.) The table should contain values corresponding to the time interval 0 to 10 seconds in increments of 0.5 seconds.

5.6 THE do-while STATEMENT

Both the while and for statements evaluate an expression at the start of the repetition loop. In some cases, however, it is more convenient to test the expression at the end of the loop. For example, suppose we have constructed the following while loop to add a set of numbers:

```
s1 = JOptionPane.showInputDialog("Enter a value:");
value = Double.parseDouble(s1);
while (value != SENTINEL)
{
  total = total + value;
  s1 = JOptionPane.showInputDialog("Enter a value:");
  value = Double.parseDouble(s1);
}
```

This while statement requires either duplicating the input dialog and conversion calls before the loop and then within the loop, as we have done, or resorting to some other artifice to force initial execution of the statements within the while loop.

The do-while statement, as its name implies, allows us to execute statements before an expression is evaluated. In many situations, this can eliminate the duplication illustrated in the previous example. The syntax of the do-while statement is:

```
do statement;
while(condition);
```

In practice, however, the statement following the keyword do is usually a compound statement, and the do statement takes the more general form:

```
do
{
   any number of statements in here;
}
while(condition); <------------don't forget the final  ;
```

A flow-control diagram illustrating the operation of the do-while statement is shown in Figure 5.13.

As illustrated in Figure 5.13, all statements within the do-while statement are executed at least once before the expression is evaluated. Then, if the condition has a true

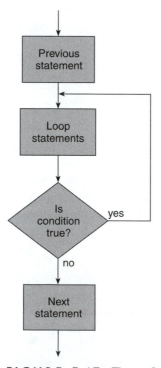

FIGURE 5.13   The do Statement's Flow of Control

value, the statements are executed again. This process continues until the condition evaluates to false. For example, consider the following do-while statement:

```
do
{
  s1 = JOptionPane.showInputDialog("Enter a value:");
  value = Double.parseDouble(s1);
  if ( abs(value - SENTINEL) < 0.0001 ) break;
  total = total + value
}
while(price != SENTINEL);
```

Observe that only one showInputDialog() and conversion statement are used here because the tested condition is evaluated at the end of the loop.

As with all repetition statements, the do-while statement can always replace or be replaced by an equivalent while or for statement, although the exact replacement is not always immediately obvious. The choice of statement depends on the application and the style preferred by the programmer. In general, the while and for statements are preferred because they clearly let anyone reading the program know what is being tested "right up front" at the top of the program loop.

Validity Checks

The do-while statement is particularly useful in filtering user-entered input and providing data validity checks. For example, assume that an operator is required to enter a valid customer identification number between 100 and 1999. Any number outside this range is to be rejected, and a new request for a valid number is made. The following section of code provides the necessary data filter to verify the entry of a valid identification number:

```
do
{
  s1 = JOptionPane.showInputDialog("Enter a value:");
  idNum = Integer.parseInt(s1);
}
while (idNum < 100 || idNum > 1999);
```

Here a request for an identification number is repeated until a valid number is entered. This section of code is "bare bones" in that it neither alerts the operator to the cause of the new request for data nor allows premature exit from the loop if a valid identification number cannot be found. An alternative that removes the first drawback is:

```
do
{
  s1 = JOptionPane.showInputDialog("Enter a value:");
  idNum = Integer.parseInt(s1);
  if (idNum < 100 || idNum > 1999)
  {
```

(Continued on next page)

(Continued from previous page)

```
        JOptionPane.showMessageDialog(null,
                    "Please check the ID number and re-enter",
                    "An invalid number was just entered",
                    JOptionPane.ERROR_MESSAGE);
    }
    else
      break;    // break if a valid id num was entered
} while(true);  // this expression is always true
```

Here we have used a break statement to exit from the loop. Because the expression being evaluated by this do-while statement is always true, an infinite loop has been created that is only exited when the break statement is encountered.

EXERCISES 5.6

1. **a.** Using a do-while statement, write a Java program to accept a grade. The program should request a grade continuously as long as an invalid grade is entered. An invalid grade is any grade less than 0 or greater than 100. After a valid grade has been entered, your program should display the value of that grade.

   b. Modify the program written for Exercise 1a so that the user is alerted when an invalid grade has been entered.

   c. Modify the program written for Exercise 1b so that it allows the user to exit the program by entering the number 999.

   d. Modify the program written for Exercise 1b so that it automatically terminates after five invalid grades are entered.

2. **a.** Write a Java program that continuously requests a grade to be entered. If the grade is less than 0 or greater than 100, your program should display an appropriate message informing the user that an invalid grade has been entered; a valid grade should be added to a total. When a grade of 999 is entered, the program should exit the repetition loop and compute and display the average of the valid grades entered.

   b. Run the program written in Exercise 2a on a computer and verify the program with appropriate test data.

3. **a.** Write a Java program to reverse the digits of a positive integer number. For example, if the number 8735 is entered, the number displayed should be 5378. (*Tip:* Use a do-while statement and continuously strip off and display the units digit of the number. If the variable num initially contains the number entered, the units digit is obtained as (num % 10). After a units digit is displayed, dividing the number by 10 sets up the number for the next iteration. Thus, (8735 % 10) is 5 and (8735 / 10) is 873. The do-while statement should continue as long as the remaining number is not zero.)

   b. Run the program written in Exercise 3a on a computer and verify the program with appropriate test data.

4. **a.** Write a program to reverse the digits of a positive integer number. For example, if the number 8735 is entered, the number displayed should be 5378. (*Tip:* Use a do statement and continuously strip off and display the units digit

of the number. If the variable num initially contains the number entered, the units digit is obtained as (num % 10). After a units digit is displayed, dividing the number by 10 sets up the number for the next iteration. Thus, (8735 % 10) is 5 and (8735 / 10) is 873. The do statement should continue as long as the remaining number is not zero.)

    b. Run the program written in Exercise 4a on a computer and verify the program using appropriate test data.

5. Repeat any of the exercises in Section 5.3 using a do statement rather than a for statement.

6. Given a number n and an approximation for its square root, a closer approximation to the actual square root can be obtained using the formula:

$$\text{new approximation} = \frac{(n/\text{previous approximation}) \; + \; \text{previous approximation}}{2}$$

Using this information, write a Java program that prompts the user for a number and an initial guess at its square root. With this input data, your program should calculate an approximation to the square root that is accurate to 0.00001. (*Tip:* Stop the loop when the difference between two approximation is less than 0.00001.)

7. Here is a challenging problem for those who know a little calculus. The Newton-Raphson method can find the roots of any equation $y(x) = 0$. In this method, the $(i + 1)st$ approximation, x_{i+1}, to a root of $y(x) = 0$ is given in terms of the *ith* approximation, x_i, by the formula

$$x_{i+1} = x_i - y(x_i) / y'(x_i)$$

For example, if $y(x) = 3x^2 + 2x - 2$, then $y'(x) = 6x + 2$, and the roots are found by making a reasonable guess for a first approximation x_1 and iterating using the equation

$$x_{i+1} = x_i - (3x_i^2 + 2x_i - 2) / (6x_i + 2)$$

    a. Using the Newton-Raphson method, find the two roots of the equation $3x^2 + 2x - 2 = 0$. (*Tip:* There is one positive root and one negative root.)

    b. Extend the program written for Exercise 6a so that it will find the roots of any function $y(x) = 0$, when the function for $y(x)$ and the derivative of $y(x)$ are placed in the code.

5.7 COMMON PROGRAMMING ERRORS

Five errors are commonly made by beginning Java programmers when using repetition statements.

1. Creating a loop that is "off by one," where the loop executes either one too many or one too few times. For example, the loop created by the statement for(i = 1; i < 11; i++) executes 10 times, not 11, even though the number 11 is in the statement. Thus, an equivalent loop can be constructed using the statement for(i = 1; i <= 10; i++). However, if the loop is started with an initial value of i = 0, using the statement for(i = 0; i < 11; i++), the loop will be executed 11 times, as will a loop constructed with the statement for(i = 0; i <= 10; i++). Thus, in

constructing loops, you must pay particular attention to both initial and tested conditions that control the loop to ensure that the number of loop repetitions is not off by one too many or one too few executions.

2. As with the `if` statement, repetition statements should not test for equality when testing floating-point or double-precision operands. For example, the condition `fnum == 0.01` should be replaced by a test requiring that the absolute value of `fnum - 0.01` be less than an acceptable amount. One reason is that all numbers are stored in binary form. Using a finite number of bits, decimal numbers such as 0.01 have no exact binary equivalent so that tests requiring equality with such numbers can fail.

3. Placing a semicolon at the end of either the `while`'s or `for`'s parentheses, which frequently produces a do-nothing loop. For example, consider the statements

```
for(count = 0; count < 10; count++);
   total = total + num;
```

Here the semicolon at the end of the first line of code is a null statement. This has the effect of creating a loop that is executed 10 times with nothing done except the incrementing and testing of `count`. This error tends to occur because Java programmers are accustomed to ending most lines with a semicolon.

4. Using commas to separate the items in a `for` statement instead of the required semicolons. An example is the statement

```
for (count = 1, count < 10, count++)
```

Commas should separate items within the initializing and altering lists, and semicolons must be used to separate these lists from the tested condition.

5. Omitting the final semicolon from the `do-while` statement. This error is usually made by programmers who have learned to omit the semicolon after the parentheses of a `while` statement and carry over this habit when the reserved word `while` is encountered at the end of a `do-while` statement.

5.8 CHAPTER SUMMARY

1. A section of repeating code is referred to as a **loop**. The loop is controlled by a repetition statement that tests a condition to determine whether the code will be executed. Each pass through the loop is referred to as a *repetition* or *iteration*. The tested condition must always be explicitly set prior to its first evaluation by the repetition statement. Within the loop, there must always be a statement that permits altering of the condition so that the loop, once entered, can be exited.

2. There are three basic type of loops:
   a. `while`
   b. `for`
   c. `do-while`

The `while` and `for` loops are *pretest* or *entrance-controlled loops*. In this type of loop, the tested condition is evaluated at the beginning of the loop, which requires that the tested condition be explicitly set prior to loop entry. If the condition is true, loop repetitions begin; otherwise, the loop is not entered. Iterations continue as long as the condition remains true. In Java, while and for loops are constructed using while and for statements, respectively.

The do-while loop is a *posttest* or *exit-controlled loop,* where the tested condition is evaluated at the end of the loop. This type of loop is always executed at least once. A do-while loop continues to execute as long as the tested condition remains true.

3. Loops are also classified as to the type of tested condition. In a *fixed-count loop,* the condition keeps track of how many repetitions have occurred. In a *variable-condition loop,* the tested condition is based on a variable that can change interactively with each pass through the loop.

4. In Java, a while loop is constructed using a while statement. The most common form of this statement is:

```
while(condition)
{
    any number of statements in here;
}
```

The condition contained within parentheses is the condition tested to determine if the statement following the parentheses, which is generally a compound statement, is executed. The expression is evaluated in exactly the same manner as that contained in an if-else statement; the difference is how the expression is used. In a while statement, the statement following the expression is executed repeatedly as long as the condition retains a boolean true value rather than just once, as in an if-else statement. An example of a while loop is:

```
count = 1;   // initialize count
while (count <= 10)
{
    System.out.print(count + "   ");
    count++;   // increment count
}
```

The first assignment statement sets count equal to 1. The while statement is then entered, and the expression is evaluated for the first time. Because the value of count is less than or equal to 10, the condition has a true value and the compound statement is executed. The first statement in the compound statement displays the value of count followed by two blank spaces. The next statement adds 1 to the value currently stored in count, making this value equal to 2. The while statement now loops back to retest the expression. Because count is still less than or equal to 10, the compound statement is again executed. This process continues until the value of count reaches 11.

The while statement always checks its expression at the top of the loop. This requires that any variables in the tested condition must have values assigned before the while is encountered. Within the while loop, there must be a statement that alters the tested condition's value.

5. In Java, a for loop is constructed using a for statement. This statement performs the same functions as the while statement but in a different form. In many situations, especially those that use a fixed-count condition, the for statement format

is easier to use than its `while` statement equivalent. A common form of a `for` statement is:

```
for(initializingExpression; condition; incrementExpression)
{
    any number of statements in here;
}
```

Initializing expressions (including declarations), the tested condition, and expressions affecting the tested condition can all be included in parentheses at the top of a `for` loop. In addition, any other loop statement can be included within the `for`'s parentheses as part of its altering list.

The initializing list sets any initial values before the loop is entered; generally, it initializes a counter. Statements within the initializing list are only executed once. The condition being tested in the `for` statement is tested at the start of the loop and prior to each iteration. The altering list contains loop statements that are not contained within the compound statement; generally, it increments or decrements a counter each time the loop is executed.

6. The `for` statement is extremely useful in creating fixed-count loops. This is because the initializing statements, the tested condition, and a statement affecting the tested condition can all be included in parentheses at the top of a `for` loop for easy inspection and modification.

7. The `do-while` statement creates posttest loops because it checks its expression at the end of the loop. This ensures that the body of a `do` loop is executed at least once. Within a `do` loop, there must be at least one statement that alters the tested expression's value. The most common form of a loop constructed with a `do-while` statement is:

```
do
{
    any number of statements in here;
}while(condition);
```

INDUSTRIAL ENGINEERING

Each of the traditional engineering disciplines (civil, mechanical, electrical, chemical, and metallurgical/mining) relies on a particular area of natural science for its foundation. Industrial engineering, however, incorporates the knowledge of the social sciences into designing improvements in human-machine systems. Industrial engineers are responsible for designing, installing, and evaluating machines and systems and also for monitoring their interface with people to improve overall productivity. This job may involve understanding human behavioral characteristics and their effects on the design of machines or the workplace. Industrial engineers draw heavily on knowledge in economics, business management, and finance as well as in the natural sciences. The areas of specialization of the industrial engineer may be divided into four categories:

1. Operations research. This area involves the application of analytical techniques and mathematical models to phenomena such as inventory control, simulation, decision theory, and queuing theory to optimize the total systems necessary for the production of goods.
2. Management or administrative engineering. The increasingly complex interplay of management and production skills in modern industrial operations has resulted in a need for technically trained managers. These managers evaluate and plan corporate ventures and interact with labor, engineering departments, and subcontractors. A management engineer may also participate in the financial operations of a company, drawing on knowledge in economics, business management, and law.
3. Manufacturing and production engineering. Before a product is produced, the complete manufacturing process must be designed and set up to optimize the economics involved and the final quality of the item. This task requires a broad knowledge of process design, plant layouts, tool design, robotics, and human-machine interactions.
4. Information systems. This area involves the use of computers to gather and analyze data for decision making and planning and to improve human-machine activity.

The following list includes the most common responsibilities of industrial engineers who responded to a recent survey by the American Institute of Industrial Engineers:

Facilities planning and design	Cost control
Methods engineering	Inventory control
Work systems design	Energy conservation
Production engineering	Computerized process control
Management information and control systems	Product packaging, handling, and testing
Organization analysis and design	Tool and equipment selection
Work measurement	Production control
Wage administration	Product improvement study
Quality control	Preventive maintenance
Project management	Safety programs
	Training programs

CHAPTER 6

General-Purpose

Methods

Each and every method in Java must be contained within a class in the same manner as a `main()` *method. However, within a class, there can be two fundamentally different types of methods: static and nonstatic. Although the term static is a holdover from C++ and is not very descriptive, its purpose is well defined: A* `static` *method is meant to receive its data as arguments and access or modify a variable that is shared by all objects of a class. Chapter 10 presents how to accomplish this. In addition, if a* `static` *method's header line includes the keyword* `public`*, the method can be used by methods outside its own class.*

Together, the `static` *and* `public` *designations permit the construction of general-purpose methods that are not restricted to operating on objects of a specific class. Examples of such methods are the mathematical methods presented in Chapter 3. In this chapter, you learn how to write such general-purpose methods, pass data to them, process the passed data, and return a result. Almost all of the information learned about these methods is directly applicable to the nonstatic class methods presented in Chapter 9.*

6.1 METHOD AND PARAMETER DECLARATIONS

In creating a general-purpose method, we must be concerned with both the method itself and how it interacts with other methods, such as `main()`. This includes correctly passing data into a method when it is called, having the method process the passed data, and returning one or more values when it has finished executing. In this section, we describe the first two parts of the interface: passing data to a general-purpose method and having the method correctly receive, store, and process the transmitted data.

As you have already seen with mathematical methods, a general-purpose method is called, or used, by giving the method's name and passing any data to it as arguments in the parentheses following the method name (Figure 6.1). As also shown in Figure 6.1, if a general-purpose method is called from outside its class, it must also be preceded by its class name and a period.

```
MethodName (data passed to Method);
```
This identifies   This passes data
the called   to the method
method

FIGURE 6.1 Calling and Passing Data to a Method

The called method must be able to accept the data passed to it by the method doing the calling. Only after the called method successfully receives the data can the data be manipulated to produce a useful result.

To clarify the process of sending and receiving data, consider Program 6.1, which calls a method named `findMaximum()`. The class, as shown, is not yet complete. Once the method `findMaximum()` is written and included in Program 6.1, the completed class, consisting of the methods `main()` and `findMaximum()`, can be compiled and executed.[1]

---

[1] The `findMaximum()` method could also be included in a separate class, as is demonstrated in Exercise 12 on page 295. In practice, however, only one class would be used because one of the purposes of a class is to contain methods (and data) that are logically related.

PROGRAM 6.1

```java
import javax.swing.*;
public class ShowTheCall
{
  public static void main(String[] args)
  {
    String s1;

    double firstnum, secnum;

    s1 = JOptionPane.showInputDialog("Enter a number:");
    firstnum = Double.parseDouble(s1);
    s1 = JOptionPane.showInputDialog("Great! Please enter a second number:");
    secnum = Double.parseDouble(s1);


    findMaximum(firstnum, secnum); // the method is called here

    System.exit(0);
  }  // end of method
}  // end of class
```

Let us examine the calling of the `findMaximum()` method from `main()`. We will then write `findMaximum()` to accept the data passed to it and determine the largest, or maximum, value of the two passed values.

The `findMaximum()` method is referred to as the **called method** because it is called, or summoned, into action by its reference in `main()`. The method that does the calling, in this case `main()`, is referred to as the **calling method.** The terms *called* and *calling* come from standard telephone usage, where one person calls another on a telephone. The person initiating the call is referred to as the calling party, and the person receiving the call is the called party. The same terms describe method calls.

Calling a general-purpose method is a rather easy operation. If the method is located in the same class as the method from which it is called, all that is required is that the name of the method be used and that any data passed to the method be enclosed within the parentheses following the method name; otherwise, the name of the called method must be preceded by its class name and a period. The items enclosed within the parentheses are called **arguments** of the called method (Figure 6.2). Other terms for arguments are **actual arguments** and **actual parameters.** All of these terms refer to the actual data values supplied to a method when the call is made.

`findMaximum` `(firstnum, secnum);`

This identifies   This causes two
the `findMaximum()`   values to be
method   passed to
                             `findMaximum()`

FIGURE 6.2   Calling and Passing Two Values to `findMaximum()`

If a primitive data type variable is one of the arguments in a method call, the called method receives a copy of the value stored in the variable. For example, the statement `findMaximum(firstnum, secnum);` calls the method `findMaximum()` and causes the values currently residing in the variables `firstnum` and `secnum` to be passed to `findMaximum()`. The variable names in parentheses are arguments that provide values to the called method. After the values are passed, control is transferred to the called method.

As illustrated in Figure 6.3, the method `findMaximum()` *does not receive the variables named* `firstnum` *and* `secnum` *and has no knowledge of these variables' names.*[2] The method simply receives the values in these variables and must itself determine where to store these values before it does anything else.

Let us now begin writing the `findMaximum()` method to process the values passed to it.

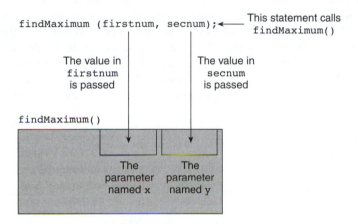

FIGURE 6.3   `findMaximum()` **Receives Actual Values**

Like the `main()` method, every Java method consists of two parts: a **method header** and a **method body** (Figure 6.4). The purpose of the method header is to specify access privileges (where the method can be called), identify the data type of the value returned by the method, provide the method with a name, and specify the number, order, and type of arguments expected by the method. The purpose of the method body is to operate on the passed data and directly return at most one value back to the calling method. (In Section 6.2, you will see how a method can be made to return multiple values.)

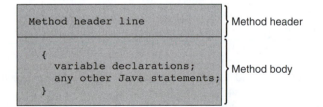

FIGURE 6.4   **General Format of a Method**

---

[2]This is significantly different from earlier high-level languages such as Fortran, where called methods received access to these variables and could directly alter the variables from within the called method. In Section 6.2, you will see how, using reference variables, Java permits direct access to the objects being referenced.

The header must contain the two access keywords, `public` and `static`, a mandatory return type, a name, and a set of parentheses.

```
public static returnType methodName (parameter list) <--- Required Parentheses
```

FIGURE 6.5   The Structure of a Method's Header Line

Except for the `parameter list`, this header line should be very familiar because it is the one we have used throughout the text for our `main()` methods. To review, a general-purpose method's header must contain the keywords `public` and `static`. The keyword `public` means that the method can be used both within and outside the class that includes the method, which is appropriate for a general-purpose method. As you will see in Chapter 9, we can restrict access to a class' methods using the keywords `protected` and `private`. The keyword `static` allows the method to be used without reference to a specific object constructed from a class. The `parameter list` in the header line provides the data types and names that will hold the values passed to the method when it is called. Among other things, this list, which we will describe in detail shortly, specifies the number, sequence, and data types of the argument values that the called method expects to receive.

Using this generic header line, let us now construct a specific header line for our `findMaximum()` method. Because `findMaximum()` will not formally return any value and is to receive two double-precision values, the following header line can be used:

```
public static void findMaximum(double x, double y) <---- no semicolon
```

The identifier names within the parentheses in the header are referred to as **formal parameters** of the method. You will also see them referred to as formal arguments, arguments, and parameters. Thus, the parameter x will store the first value passed to `findMaximum()`, and the parameter y will store the second value passed at the time of the method call. All parameters, such as x and y, receive values from the calling method, be they built-in or reference data types. The called method does not know where the values come from when the call is made from `main()`. The first part of the call procedure executed by the program involves going to the variables `firstnum` and `secnum` and retrieving the stored values. These values are then passed to `findMaximum()` and ultimately stored in the parameters x and y (see Figure 6.3).

The method name and all parameter names in the header, in this case `findMaximum`, x, and y, are chosen by the programmer. Any names selected according to the rules for choosing variable names can be used. All parameters listed in the method header line must be separated by commas and must have their individual data types declared separately.

Notice that as far as the method `findMaximum()` is concerned, the parameters x and y are dealt with exactly as variables. Parameter declarations declare the data type of the values expected by the method, and the order of declarations is important. The parameter declarations are identical to variable declarations. The only difference between parameter declarations and variable declarations is their placement in the method. Parameter declarations are always placed within the parentheses following the method's name, whereas method variable declarations are placed within the method's body. From a programming viewpoint, parameters can be considered as variables whose initialization occurs from outside the method. The number, order (sequence), and data types of the arguments passed to a method must agree in number, order, and data type with the parameters declared in the method's header line. If the values passed to a method do not agree with the data types declared for a parameter and would result in a possible loss of precision (e.g., attempting to send a double-precision argument into an integer parameter), the compiler error message `Incompatible type for method. Explicit cast needed to convert ...` or its equivalent appears. If the number of passed arguments does not agree with the number of declared parameters, compiler error message equivalent to `Wrong number of arguments in method` appears.

Now that we have written the method header for `findMaximum()`, we can construct its body. Let us assume that the `findMaximum()` method selects and displays the larger of the two numbers passed to it.

As illustrated in Figure 6.6, a method body begins with an opening brace, contains any necessary declarations and other Java statements, and ends with a closing brace. Again, this should look familiar because it is the same structure found in all the `main()` methods we have written. This should not be a surprise because `main()` is itself a method and must adhere to the rules required for constructing all legitimate methods.

```
{
    variable declarations
    and other Java statements
}
```

FIGURE 6.6 The Structure of a Method Body

In the body of the `findMaximum()` method, we will declare one variable to store the maximum of the two numbers passed to it. We will then use an `if-else` statement to find the maximum of the two numbers.[3] Finally, a message dialog will display the maximum. The complete method definition for the `findMaximum()` method is:

```
// following is the findMaximum() method
public static void findMaximum(double x, double y)
{                       // start of method body
    double maxnum;        // variable declaration

    if (x >= y)          // find the maximum number
        maxnum = x;
    else
        maxnum = y;


    JOptionPane.showMessageDialog(null,
                    "The maximum of " + x + " and " + y + " is " + maxnum,
                    "Maximum Value", JOptionPane.INFORMATION_MESSAGE);

}   // end of method body and end of method
```

---

[3]Alternatively, we could have used the `Math.max()` method (see Exercise 3 on page 293).

Notice that the parameter declarations are within the header line, and the variable declaration is placed immediately after the opening brace of the method's body. This is in keeping with the concept that parameter values are passed to a method, from outside the method, and method variables are declared and assigned values from within the method's body.

Program 6.2 includes the `findMaximum()` method within the program code previously listed in Program 6.1.

Program 6.2 selects and displays the maximum of any two double-precision numbers entered by the user. Figure 6.7 illustrates the output displayed by Program 6.2 when the values 97.6 and 45.3 were accepted as user-entered data.

PROGRAM 6.2

```java
import javax.swing.*;
public class CompleteTheCall
{
  public static void main(String[] args)
  {
    String s1;

    double firstnum, secnum;

    s1 = JOptionPane.showInputDialog("Enter a number:");
    firstnum = Double.parseDouble(s1);
    s1 = JOptionPane.showInputDialog("Great! Please enter a second number:");
    secnum = Double.parseDouble(s1);


    findMaximum(firstnum, secnum); // the method is called here

    System.exit(0);
  }  // end of main() method

   // following is the findMaximum() method
  public static void findMaximum(double x, double y)
  {                   // start of method body

 double maxnum;       // variable declaration
    if (x >= y)       // find the maximum number
      maxnum = x;
    else
      maxnum = y;

    JOptionPane.showMessageDialog(null,
              "The maximum of " + x + " and " + y + " is " + maxnum,
              "Maximum Value", JOptionPane.INFORMATION_MESSAGE);

  }  // end of method body and end of method
}  // end of class
```

FIGURE 6.7 A Sample Output Displayed by Program 6.2

The placement of the `findMaximum()` method after the `main()` method in Program 6.2 is a matter of choice. We will always list `main()`as the first `public static` method. How the processing gets "stitched together" can then be ascertained by referring to the `main()` method before the details of each method are encountered. In Part Two, when nonstatic class methods are introduced, these methods will always be written before `main()`.[4]

With one notable exception, nesting of methods is not permitted in Java, and each method must be written by itself outside any other method. Thus, the definition of `findMaximum()` cannot be placed inside `main()`. The one exception, which is presented in detail in Part Three, is that classes can be nested within classes and can even be contained within a method. So although a Java method can never be directly nested within another method, it can be indirectly nested when it is contained within a nested class. For now, however, since we are only dealing with a single class in each of our programs, make sure to construct each Java method as a separate and independent entity with its own parameters and variables.

Placement of Statements

Java does not impose a rigid statement ordering structure on the programmer. The general rule for placing statements in a Java method is simply that all named constants and variables must be declared before they can be used. As we have noted previously, although this rule permits declaration statements to be placed throughout a method, doing so results in very poor program structure.

As a matter of good programming style, the following statement ordering should form the basic structure around which all of your general-purpose Java methods are constructed. With a minor modification to the header line, this is the same structure in the nonstatic methods presented in Chapter 9.

```
public static returnType methodName(parameter declarations)
{
  named constants
  variable declarations

  other statements
  return value
}
```

---

[4]This is done because most of an object-oriented program's work should be defined by nonstatic class methods that are carefully thought out and listed first, which gives anyone reading the program an idea of what the class and its processing are all about. In these cases, the `main()` method may do no more than create an instance of the class within which it is contained.

As always, comment statements can be freely intermixed anywhere within this basic structure.

Method Stubs

An alternative to completing each method required in a complete program is to write the `main()` method first and add other general-purpose methods later as they are developed. The problem that arises with this approach, however, is the same problem that occurred with Program 6.1; that is, the program cannot be run until all of the methods are included. For convenience, we reproduce the code for Program 6.1 here:

PROGRAM 6.1

```java
import javax.swing.*;
public class ShowTheCall
{
  public static void main(String[] args)
  {
    String s1;

    double firstnum, secnum;

    s1 = JOptionPane.showInputDialog("Enter a number:");
    firstnum = Double.parseDouble(s1);
    s1 = JOptionPane.showInputDialog("Great! Please enter a second number:");
    secnum = Double.parseDouble(s1);


    findMaximum(firstnum, secnum); // the method is called here


    System.exit(0);
  }  // end of method
}  // end of class
```

This program would be complete if there were a method defined for `findMaximum()`. But we really don't need a *correct* `findMaximum()` method to test and run what has been written; we only need a method that *acts* like it is. A "fake" `findMaximum()` that accepts the proper number and types of parameters and returns a value of the proper form for the method call is all we need to allow initial testing. This fake method is called a stub. A **stub** is the beginning of a method that serves as a placeholder for the final method until the method is completed. A stub for `findMaximum()` is as follows:

```java
public static void findMaximum(double x, double y)
{
  String outMessage;
```

```
outMessage = "In findMaximum()"
            + "\nThe value of x is " + x
            + "\nThe value of y is " + y;

JOptionPane.showMessageDialog(null, outMessage, "Maximum Value",
                            JOptionPane.INFORMATION_MESSAGE);
}
```

This stub method can now be compiled and linked with the previously completed `main()` method to obtain an executable program. The code for the stub method can then be further developed, with the real code, when it is completed, replacing the stub portion.

The minimum requirement of a stub method is that it compile and link with its calling module. In practice, it is a good idea to have a stub display its received parameters, as in the stub for `findMaximum()`. As the method is refined, you let it do more and more, perhaps allowing it to return intermediate or incomplete results. This incremental, or stepwise, refinement is an important concept in efficient program development that provides you with the means of running a program that does not yet meet all of its final requirements.

Methods with Empty Parameter Lists

Although useful general-purpose methods having an empty parameter list are extremely limited (one such method is provided in Exercise 11 on page 294), they can occur. In any case, to indicate that there are no parameters requires writing nothing at all between the parentheses following the method's name. For example, the header line

```
public static int display()
```

indicates that the `display()` method takes no parameters and returns an integer. A method with an empty parameter list is called by its name with nothing written within the required parentheses following the method's name. For example, the statement `display();` correctly calls the `display()` method whose header line was just given.

Reusing Method Names (Overloading)[5]

Java provides the capability of using the same method name for more than one method, which is referred to as **method overloading.** The only requirement in creating more than one method with the same name is that the compiler must be able to determine which method to use based on the data types of the parameters (not the data type of the return value, if any). For example, consider the three following methods, all named `calcAbs()`:

---

[5]This topic can be omitted on first reading with no loss of subject continuity.

POINT OF INFORMATION

ISOLATION TESTING

One of the most successful software testing methods known is always to embed the code being tested within an environment of working code. For example, assume you have two untested methods that are called in the order shown and the result returned by the second method is incorrect.

From the information in the figure, one or possibly both of the methods could be operating incorrectly. The first order of business is to isolate the problem to a specific method.

One of the most powerful methods of performing this code isolation is to decouple the methods. This is done either by testing each method individually or by testing one method first and, only when you know it is operating correctly, reconnecting it to the second method. Then, if an error occurs, you have isolated the error to either the transfer of data between methods or the internal operation of the second method.

This specific procedure is an example of the *basic rule of testing*, which states that each method should only be tested in a program in which all other methods are known to be correct. This means that one method must first be tested by itself, using stubs if necessary for any called methods, that a second tested method should be tested either by itself or with a previously tested method, and so on. This ensures that each new method is isolated within a test bed of correct methods, with the final program effectively built up of tested method code.

```java
public static void calcAbs(int x)  // compute and display the
{                                  // absolute value of an integer
  if ( x < 0 )
    x = -x;
  System.out.println("The absolute value of the integer is  " + x);
}


public static void calcAbs(float x)  // compute and display the
{                                    // absolute value of a float
  if ( x < 0 )
    x = -x;
  System.out.println("The absolute value of the float is  " + x);
}


public static void calcAbs(double x)  // compute and display the
{                                     // absolute value of a double
  if ( x < 0 )
    x = -x;
  System.out.println("The absolute value of the double is  " + x);
}
```

Which of the three methods named `calcAbs()` is called depends on the argument types supplied at the time of the call. Thus, the method call `calcAbs(10);` would cause the compiler to use the method named `calcAbs()` that expects an integer argument, and the method call `calcAbs(6.28f);` would cause the compiler to use the method named `calcAbs()` that expects a floating-point argument.

Notice that overloading a method's name simply means using the same name for more than one method. Each method that uses the name must still be written and exists as a separate entity. The use of the same method name does not require that the code within the methods be similar, although good programming practice dictates that methods with the same name should perform similar operations.

Clearly, overloading a method requires that the compiler can distinguish which method to select based on the method's name and its parameter list. The part of a header line that contains this information (i.e., name and parameter list) is referred to as the method's **parameter signature**. For a class to compile correctly, each method must have a unique parameter signature. This terminology is derived from everyday usage where it is expected that each individual has a unique signature that can identify that individual. From a compiler's viewpoint, unless each method has a unique parameter signature, the compiler cannot correctly determine which method is being referenced.

EXERCISES 6.1

1. For the following method headers, determine the number, type, and order (sequence) of the values that must be passed to the method:
   a. `public static void factorial(int n)`
   b. `public static void volts(int res, double induct, double cap)`
   c. `public static void power(int type, double induct, double cap)`
   d. `public static void flag(char type, double current, double time)`
   e. `public static void total(double amount, double rate)`
   f. `public static void roi(int a, int b, char c, char d, double e, double f)`
   g. `public static void getVal(int item, int iter, char decflag, char delim)`

2. Enter and execute Program 6.2 on your computer.

3. Rewrite the `findMaximum()` method in Program 6.2 to use the `Math.max()` method in place of the `if-else` statement used currently. Note that `Math.max(a, b)` returns the maximum of the values stored in the variables a and b.

4. a. Write a general-purpose method named `check()` that has three parameters. The first parameter should accept an integer number, the second parameter a floating-point number, and the third parameter a double-precision number. The body of the method should display only the values of the data passed to the method when it is called.

   (*Note:* When tracing errors in methods, it is helpful to have the method display the values it has been passed. Quite frequently, the error is not in what the body of the method does with the data but in the data received and stored.)

   b. Include the method written in Exercise 4a in a working program. Make sure your method is called from `main()`. Test the method by passing various data to it.

5. a. Write a general-purpose method named `findAbs()` that accepts a double-precision number passed to it, computes its absolute value, and displays the absolute value. The absolute value of a number is the number itself if the number is positive or zero and the negative of the number if the number is negative.

b. Include the method written in Exercise 5a in a working program. Make sure your method is called from `main()`. Test the method by passing various data to it.

6. a. Write a general-purpose method named `squareIt()` that computes the square of the value passed to it and displays the result. The method should be capable of squaring numbers with decimal points.

b. Include the method written in Exercise 7a in a working program. Make sure your method is called from `main()`. Test the method by passing various data to it.

7. a. Write a general-purpose method named `powfun()` that raises a long integer number passed to it to a positive integer power (also passed as an argument) and displays the result. The positive integer should be the second value passed to the method. Additionally, declare the variable that stores the result as a long integer data type to ensure sufficient storage for the result.

b. Include the method written in Exercise 8a in a working program. Make sure your method is called from `main()`. Test the method by passing various data to it.

8. a. Write a general-purpose method that produces a table of the numbers from 1 to 10, their squares, and their cubes. The method should produce the same display as Program 5-10.

b. Include the method written in Exercise 9a in a working program. Make sure your method is called from `main()`. Test the method by passing various data to it.

9. a. Modify the method written for Exercise 9 to accept the starting value of the table, the number of values to be displayed, and the increment between values. If the increment is not explicitly sent, the method should use a default value of 1. Name your method `selTable()`. A call to `selTable(6,5,2)` should produce a table of five lines, the first line starting with the number 6 and each succeeding number increasing by 2.

b. Include the method written in Exercise 10a in a working program. Make sure your method is called from `main()`. Test the method by passing various data to it.

10. a. Write a Java method that accepts an integer argument, determines whether the passed integer is even or odd (*Tip:* Use the `%` operator), and displays the results of the determination.

b. Include the method written for Exercise 11a in a working Java program. Make sure your method is called from `main()` and correctly displays whether the passed value is an even or odd number.

11. A useful general-purpose method that uses no parameters can be constructed to return a value for π that is accurate to the maximum number of decimal places allowed by your computer. This value is obtained by taking the arcsine of 1.0, which is π/2, and multiplying the result by 2. In Java, the required expression is *2.0 * Math.asin(1.0)*, where the `asin()` method is provided by the Java Math class. Using this expression, write a Java method named `Pi()` that calculates and displays the value of π.

12. The following program provides the same functionality as Program 6.2 but places each method in its own class. Enter and store each class in a separate file and then compile each class. Execute `class One` to determine if it produces the same result as Program 6.2. Notice that because the called method is in a different class, its class name is included when the `findMaximum()` method is called.

```java
import javax.swing.*;
public class One
{
  public static void main(String[] args)
  {
    String s1, outMessage;

    double firstnum, secnum;

    s1 = JOptionPane.showInputDialog("Enter a number:");
    firstnum = Double.parseDouble(s1);
    s1 = JOptionPane.showInputDialog("Great! Please enter a second number:");
    secnum = Double.parseDouble(s1);

    Two.findMaximum(firstnum, secnum); // the method is called here

    System.exit(0);
  }
} // end of first class

import javax.swing.*;
public class Two
{
    // following is the method findMaximum()

  public static void findMaximum(double x, double y)
  {                   // start of method body
    double maxnum;       // variable declaration

    if (x >= y)       // find the maximum number
      maxnum = x;
    else
      maxnum = y;

    JOptionPane.showMessageDialog(null,
                  "The maximum of " + x + " and " + y + " is " + maxnum,
                  "Maximum Value", JOptionPane.INFORMATION_MESSAGE);

  }  // end of method body and end of method
} // end of second class
```

6.2 RETURNING A SINGLE VALUE

Using the method of passing arguments into a method presented in the previous section, the called method only receives copies of the values contained in the arguments at the time of the call (review Figure 6.3 if this is unclear). This is true for both built-in and reference arguments. Although this procedure for passing data to a method may seem surprising, it is really a safety procedure for ensuring that a called method does not inadvertently change data stored in the variables of the calling method. The called method gets a copy of the data. It may change its copy and change any variables declared inside itself or an object referenced by a passed reference value.[6] This procedure, where only values are passed to a called method, is formally referred to as **pass by value** (or **call by value**).

The method receiving the passed by value arguments may process the data sent to it in any fashion desired and directly return at most one, and only one, "legitimate" value to the calling method (Figure 6.8). In this section, we first see how such a value is returned to the calling method when primitive data types are the arguments. As you might expect, given Java's flexibility, there is a way of returning more than a single value. How to do this is presented at the end of this section after the passing and processing of reference variables are discussed.

A method can receive many values

Only one value can
be directly returned

FIGURE 6.8 A Method Directly Returns at Most One Value

As with the calling of a method, directly returning a value requires that the interface between the called and calling methods be handled correctly. From its side of the return transaction, the called method must provide the following items:

• the data type of the returned value
• the actual value being returned

A method returning a value specifies the data type of the value that will be returned in its header line. As a specific example, consider the `findMaximum()` method written in the last section. It determined the maximum value of two numbers passed to the method. For convenience, the `findMaximum()` code is listed here again:

```
public static void findMaximum(double x, double y)
{                       // start of method body
  double maxnum;        // variable declaration
```

---

[6]Except, of course, for strings, which are immutable and, therefore, cannot be modified.

```
if (x >= y)       // find the maximum number
  maxnum = x;
else
  maxnum = y;

JOptionPane.showMessageDialog(null,
             "The maximum of the two numbers is " + maxnum,
             "Maximum Value", JOptionPane.INFORMATION_MESSAGE);

}  // end of method body and end of method
```

As written, the method's header line is

```
public static void findMaximum(double x, double y)
```

where x and y are the names chosen for the method's parameters. The keyword void in the header line specifies that the method will return no value. If findMaximum() is now to return a value, this keyword must be changed to indicate the data type of the value being returned. For example, if a double-precision value is to be returned, the proper method header line is[7]

```
public static double findMaximum(double x, double y)
```

Observe that this is the same as the original method header line for findMaximum() with the substitution of the keyword double for the keyword void. Similarly, if the method is to receive two integer values and return an integer value, the correct method header line is

```
public static int findMaximum(int x, int y)
```

and if the method is to receive two single-precision values and return a single-precision value, the header line is

```
public static float findMaximum(float x, float y)
```

Because findMaximum() will return a double-precision value, which is the maximum value of the two double-precision numbers passed to it, the appropriate header line is

```
public static double findMaximum(double x, double y)
```

Having declared the data type that findMaximum() will return, we must now alter the method's body by including a statement that will force the return of the correct

---

[7]The return data type is only related to the parameter data types inasmuch as the returned value is computed from parameter values. In this case, because the method is used to return the maximum value of its parameters, it makes little sense to return a data type that does not match the method's parameter types.

value. To return a value from a method requires a `return` statement, which has the syntax:[8]

```
return expression;
```

When the return statement is encountered, the *expression* is evaluated first, and this value is sent back to the calling method. After the value is returned, program control reverts to the calling method. Because the maximum value determined by `findMaximum()` is stored in the double-precision variable `maxnum`, it is the value of this variable that should be returned. To return this value, all we need to do is add the statement `return maxnum;` before the closing brace of the `findMaximum()` method. The complete method code is:

```
                      -------------------
                      |                 |
                      |                 V
These         |       public static double findMaximum(double x, double y)  // header line
should        |       {                      // start of method body
be            |          double maxnum;      // variable declaration
the           |
same          |          if (x >= y)
data          |             maxnum = x;
type          |          else
              |             maxnum = y;
              |
              |          return maxnum;   // return statement
              |       }              ^
              |                      |
                      ---------------
```

In this new code for the `findMaximum()` method, note that the data type of the expression contained in the `return` statement correctly matches the data type indicated for the returned type in the method's header line. It is up to the programmer to ensure that this is so for every method returning a value. Failure to match the return value exactly with the method's declared data type results in an error when your program is compiled. If you attempt to return a value that has more precision than the return type declared in the header line, the compiler will alert you with the error message `Incompatible type for return. Explicit cast needed to convert ...` (For example, you will receive this error message if you attempt to return a double-precision value when an integer has been declared as the return type.) However, attempting to return a value that has less precision than that declared in the header line is permitted. For example, if you attempt to return an integer value from a method that has been declared as returning a double-precision value, the integer is automatically promoted to a double-precision value and there is no compiler error message.

---

[8]Some programmers place the expression within parentheses, yielding the statement `return (expression);`. The parentheses are not required.

POINT OF INFORMATION

PRECONDITIONS AND POSTCONDITIONS

Preconditions are any set of conditions required by a method to be true if it is to operate correctly when it is called. Thus, preconditions are primarily concerned with conditions that must be true at run time. On the other hand, a postcondition is a condition that will be true after the method is executed, assuming that the preconditions are met.

Pre- and postconditions are typically written as user comments. For example, consider the following method header line and comments:

```
boolean leapyr(int year)
/* Precondition: the parameter year must be a year as a four-digit
     integer, such as 2003
   Postcondition: a true is returned if the year is a leap year;
     otherwise a false is returned
*/
```

Pre- and postcondition comments should be included with both class and method definitions whenever clarification is needed.

Having taken care of the sending side of the return transaction, we must now prepare the calling method to properly receive the returned value. To do so, the calling program must either provide a variable to store the returned value or use the value directly in an expression. Storing the returned value in a variable is accomplished with a standard assignment statement. For example, the statement

```
max = findMaximum(firstnum, secnum);
```

can store the value returned by `findMaximum()` in the variable named `max`. This assignment statement does two things. First the right side of the assignment statement calls `findMaximum()`, and then the result returned by this method is stored in the variable `max`. Since the value returned by `findMaximum()` is a double-precision value, the variable `max` must also be declared as a double-precision variable within the calling method's variable declarations.

The value returned by a method need not be stored directly in a variable, but can be used wherever an expression is valid. For example, the expression

```
2 * findMaximum(firstnum, secnum)
```

multiplies the value returned by `findMaximum()` by 2, and the statement

```
System.out.println(findMaximum(firstnum, secnum));
```

displays the returned value.

Program 6.3 illustrates the inclusion of an assignment statement for main() to correctly call and store a returned value from findMaximum(). As before and in keeping with our convention of placing the main() method first, we have placed the findMaximum() method after main().

In reviewing Program 6.3, it is important to note the four items we have introduced in this section. The first item to notice in main() is the use of an assignment statement to store the returned value from the findMaximum() call into the variable max. Second, we have also made sure to correctly declare max as a double within main()'s variable declarations so that it matches the data type of the returned value.

PROGRAM 6.3

```
import javax.swing.*;
public class FindTheMaximum
{
  public static void main(String[] args)
  {
    String s1, outMessage;

    double firstnum, secnum, max;

    s1 = JOptionPane.showInputDialog("Enter a number:");
    firstnum = Double.parseDouble(s1);
    s1 = JOptionPane.showInputDialog("Great! Please enter a second number:");
    secnum = Double.parseDouble(s1);

    max = findMaximum(firstnum, secnum); // the method is called here

    JOptionPane.showMessageDialog(null,
            "The maximum of the two numbers is " + max,
            "Maximum Value", JOptionPane.INFORMATION_MESSAGE);

    System.exit(0);
  }


    // following is the method findMaximum()
  public static double findMaximum(double x, double y)
  {                       // start of method body
    double maxnum;        // variable declaration
    if (x >= y)        // find the maximum number
      maxnum = x;
    else
      maxnum = y;

    return maxnum;
  } // end of method body and end of method
}
```

The last two items concern the coding of the findMaximum() method. The header line for findMaximum() declares that the method will return a double, and the expression in the return statement evaluates to a matching data type. Thus, findMaximum() is internally consistent in sending a double-precision value back to main(), and main() has been correctly written to receive and use the returned double-precision value.

In writing your own general-purpose methods, you must always keep these four items in mind. For another example, see if you can identify these items in Program 6.4.

PROGRAM 6.4

```java
import javax.swing.*;
public class CheckItems
{
  public static void main(String[] args)
  {
    final int CONVERTS = 4;   // number of conversions to be made
    String s1;
    int count;
    double fahren;

    for(count = 1; count <= CONVERTS; count++)
    {
      s1 = JOptionPane.showInputDialog("Enter a Fahrenheit temperature:");
      fahren = Double.parseDouble(s1);
      JOptionPane.showMessageDialog(null,
            "The Celsius equivalent is " + convertTemp(fahren),
            "Program 6.4", JOptionPane.INFORMATION_MESSAGE);
    }

    System.exit(0);
  }


  // convert Fahrenheit to Celsius

  public static double convertTemp(double inTemp)
  {
    return 5.0/9.0 * (inTemp - 32.0);
  }
}
```

In reviewing Program 6.4, let us first analyze the convertTemp() method. The complete definition of the method begins with the method's header line and ends with the closing brace after the return statement. The method is declared as returning a double; this means the expression in the method's return statement should evaluate to a double-precision number, which it does.

On the receiving side, main() correctly calls convertTemp() and uses its returned value. No variable is declared in main() to store the returned value from convertTemp() because the returned value is immediately passed to a showMessage() method for display.

Passing a Reference Value

Java passes the value that is stored in both a primitive data type variable and a reference variable in the same manner: A copy of the value in the variable is passed to the called method and stored in one of the method's formal parameters. A consequence is that any change to the parameter's value has no effect on the argument's value. From a programming viewpoint, this means that an argument's value can never be altered from within a called method.

Passing arguments by value in a method call has its advantages. It allows methods to be written as independent entities that can use any variable or parameter name without concern that other methods may also have the same name. It also alleviates any concern that altering a parameter or variable in one method may inadvertently alter the value of a variable in another method. Under this approach, parameters can be considered as variables that are initialized from the calling method.

Although both primitive and reference variable values are passed in the same way, passing a reference value does have implications that passing a primitive value does not. With respect to primitive values, the best a called method can do is receive values from the calling method, store and manipulate the passed values, and directly return at most a single value. With respect to reference values, however, the called method gets to access the exact same object as is referenced by the calling method. This situation is illustrated in Figure 6.9, where the calling method's reference variable and the called method's parameter reference the same object.

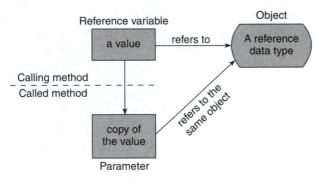

FIGURE 6.9   Passing a Reference Value

Program 6.5 illustrates how a reference value is passed in practice. Notice that the method call and parameter declaration are essentially the same as for primitive data types.

The output produced by Program 6.5 is:

```
From within display(): Original Message
```

As seen by this output, we have successfully passed a reference value as an argument to a called method and used the passed value to access a string created in the calling method. Because both the value in the reference variable named s1 in main() and the value passed to the parameter named msg in display() are the same, the display()

method now has direct access to the string created in `main()`. What the `display()` method has been programmed to do with this access is simply to obtain the string value and display it.

PROGRAM 6.5

```
public class PassAReference
{
  public static void main(String[] args)
  {
    String s1 = "Original Message";

    display(s1);    // call the method
  }  // end of main() method

  public static void display(String msg)
  {
    System.out.println("From within display(): " + msg);
  }
}  // end of class
```

Having obtained a reference value, any change to the object being referenced in the called method will be reflected whenever the object is referenced in the calling method. However, if the parameter is assigned to a completely new object, the change in reference value in the parameter will not affect the reference value in the calling method. Thus, if a new object is created within the called method, the originally referenced argument is not affected, and no change is made to the original object's value. This is in keeping with the basic Java philosophy that a called method cannot alter the value of a calling method's arguments.

The ability to alter a referenced object from within a method can be used in cases where a method must return more than one primitive value. For these cases, the primitive data type must first be converted into an equivalent object type, such as a `StringBuffer` (see Section 9.3), and then the reference to this object is passed to the called method. The called method can then compute a new value and, using its parameter, place the computed value into the referenced location, as illustrated in Figure 6.9. This new value is then accessed in the calling method using its reference variable and, if necessary, converted back to a primitive data type. An example of this procedure is provided as Program 9.7 in Section 9.3.

It should be noted that this will not work with a string value because the `String` class only creates immutable objects. This means that once a string object is initialized, its contents cannot be changed, and you actually create a new string object each time you assign a string constant to a string variable. Thus, for example, if the string referenced by `msg` in Program 6.5 is changed in `display()` by a statement such as `msg = "Have a happy day";`, the change will not be accessible from within `main()`. Creating a new string breaks the correspondence between the reference value stored in `s1` within `main()`, which still refers to the original string, and the reference value in the parameter `msg`. The value in `msg` will be changed to refer to the new string.

EXERCISES 6.2

1. a. Rewrite Program 6.3 to have the method `findMaximum()` accept two integer values and return an integer value. Make sure to modify `main()` so that it passes two integer values to `findMaximum()` and accepts and stores an integer value from `findMaximum()`.

b. Modify the `findMaximum()` method written for Exercise 1a so that it attempts to return a double-precision value, even though its header line declares it as returning an integer. Determine the error message generated by the compiler.

2. For the following method headers, determine the number, type, and order (sequence) of values that should be passed to the method when it is called and the data type of the value returned by the method.

a. `public static int factorial(int n)`

b. `public static double price(int type, double yield, double maturity)`

c. `public static double yield(int type, double price, double maturity)`

d. `public static char interest(char flag, double price, double time)`

e. `public int total(double amount, double rate)`

f. `public static double roi(int a, int b, char c, char d, double e, double f)`

g. `public static void getVal(int item, int iter, char decflag)`

3. Write method headers for the following:

a. A general-purpose method named `check()`, that has three parameters. The first parameter should accept an integer number, the second parameter a floating-point number, and the third parameter a double-precision number. The general-purpose returns no value.

b. A general-purpose method named `findAbs()` that accepts a double-precision number passed to it and returns its absolute value.

c. A general-purpose method named `mult()` that accepts two floating-point numbers as parameters, multiplies these two numbers, and returns the result.

d. A general-purpose method named `square()` that computes and returns the square of the integer value passed to it.

e. A general-purpose method named `powfun()` that raises an integer number passed to it to a positive integer (also passed as an argument) power and returns the result as a long integer.

f. A general-purpose method named `table()` that produces a table of the numbers from 1 to 10, their squares, and their cubes. No arguments are to be passed to the method and the method returns no value.

4. a. Write a general-purpose Java method named `findAbs()` that accepts a double-precision number passed to it, computes its absolute value, and returns the absolute value to the calling method. The absolute value of a number is the number itself if the number is positive or zero and the negative of the number if the number is negative.

   b. Include the method written in Exercise 4a in a working program. Make sure your method is called from `main()` and correctly returns a value to `main()`. Have `main()` display the value returned. Test the method by passing various data to it.

5. a. Write a general-purpose Java method called `mult()` that uses two double-precision numbers as parameters, multiplies these two numbers, and returns the result to the calling method.

   b. Include the method written in Exercise 5a in a working program. Make sure your method is called from `main()` and correctly returns a value to `main()`. Have `main()` display the value returned. Test the method by passing various data to it.

6. a. Write a general-purpose method named `hypotenuse()` that accepts the lengths of two sides of a right triangle as the parameters a and b, respectively. The method should determine and return the hypotenuse, c, of the triangle. (*Tip:* Use the Pythagorean theorem, $c^2 = a^2 + b^2$.)

   b. Include the method written in Exercise 6a in a working program. Make sure your method is called from `main()` and correctly returns a value to `main()`. Have `main()` display the value returned. Test the method by passing various data to it.

7. A second-degree polynomial in x is given by the expression $ax^2 + bx + c$, where a, b, and c are known numbers and a is not equal to zero. Write a general-purpose Java method named `polyTwo(a,b,c,x)` that computes and returns the value of a second-degree polynomial for any passed values of a, b, c, and x.

8. a. Rewrite the method `convertTemp()` in Program 6.4 to accept a temperature and an integer as arguments. If the integer passed to the method is 1, the method should convert the passed temperature from Fahrenheit to Celsius; otherwise, the method should convert the passed temperature from Celsius to Fahrenheit.

   b. Modify the `main()` method in Program 6.4 to call the method written for Exercise 8a. Your `main()` method should ask the user for the type of temperature being entered and pass the type (*f* or *c*) into `convertTemp()`.

9. a. Write a general-purpose method named `distance()` that accepts the rectangular coordinates of two points (x_1, y_1) and (x_2, y_2) and calculates and returns the distance between the two points. The distance, d, between two points is given by the formula

$$d = \sqrt{(x_2 - x_1)^2 + (y_2 - y_1)^2}$$

   b. Include the method written for Exercise 9a in a working Java program. Make sure your method is called from `main()` and correctly returns a value to `main()`. Have `main()` display the value returned and test the method by passing various data to it and verifying the returned value. In particular, make sure your method returns a value of zero when both points are the same—for example, $(x_1, y_1) = (5,2)$ and $(x_2, y_2) = (5,2)$.

10. a. Write a general-purpose Java method that accepts an integer argument and determines whether the passed integer is even or odd. (*Tip:* Use the % operator.) Make sure your method is called from `main()` and correctly returns a value to `main()` to indicate whether the integer is even or odd.

    b. Include the method written for Exercise 10a in a working Java program. Have `main()` display the value returned and test the method by passing various data to it and verifying the returned value.

11. **a.** The volume of a cylinder, v, is given by the formula

$$v = \pi r^2 l$$

    where r is the cylinder's radius and l is its length. Using this formula, write a general-purpose method named `cylvol()` that accepts the radius and length of a cylinder and returns its volume.

    b. Include the method written in Exercise 11a in a working program. Make sure your method is called from `main()` and correctly returns a value to `main()`. Have `main()` display the value returned. Test the method by passing various data to it.

12. **a.** The volume of a right circular cylinder is given by its radius squared times its height times π. Write a general-purpose method that uses two double-precision parameters corresponding to the cylinder's radius and height, respectively, and returns the cylinder's volume.

    b. Include the method written for Exercise 12a in a working Java program. Make sure your method is called from `main()` and correctly returns a value to `main()`. Have `main()` display the value returned. Test the method by passing various data to it and verifying the returned value.

13. **a.** The surface area, s, of a cylinder is given by the formula

$$s = 2\pi r l$$

    where r is the cylinder's radius and l is its length. Using this formula, write a general-purpose method named `surfarea()` that accepts the radius and length of a cylinder and returns its surface.

    b. Include the method written in Exercise 13a in a working program. Make sure your method is called from `main()` and correctly returns a value to `main()`. Have `main()` display the value returned. Test the method by passing various data to it.

14. **a.** The load, P_{cr}, in units of kips applied to a column that will cause the column to buckle is referred to as the critical buckling load. This load can be determined using the equation

$$P_{cr} = \pi^2 E A / (L/r)^2$$

    where E is the modulus of elasticity of the material in the column, A is the cross-sectional area, L is the length of the column, and r is its radius of gyration. Using this formula, write a Java method named `cLoad()` that accepts values of E, A, L, and r and returns the critical load.

    b. Include the method written in Exercise 14a in a working program. Make sure your method is called from `main()` and correctly returns a value to `main()`. Have `main()` display the value returned. Test the method by passing various data to it.

15. **a.** The maximum allowable deflection of a beam depends on its method. For a floor, the typical maximum allowable deflection in inches is $D_{max} = L / 240$, while for a roof beam $D_{max} = L / 180$, where L is the length of the beam in inches. Using these formulas, write and test a method named `maxDeflect()`

that accepts the length of a beam in feet and the type of beam (floor or roof) as a character code and returns the maximum allowable deflection.

  b. Include the method written in Exercise 15a in a working program. Make sure your method is called from `main()` and correctly returns a value to `main()`. Have `main()` display the value returned. Test the method by passing various data to it.

16. All years that are evenly divisible by 400 or evenly divisible by 4 and are not evenly divisible by 100 are leap years. For example, since 1600 is evenly divisible by 400, the year 1600 was a leap year. Similarly, since 1988 is evenly divisible by 4 but not by 100, the year 1988 was also a leap year. Using this information, write a Java method that accepts the year as a user input and returns a one if the passed year is a leap year or a zero if it is not.

17. a. Write a general-purpose Java method named `whole()` that returns the integer part of any number passed to the method. (*Tip:* Assign the passed argument to an integer variable.)

  b. Include the method written in Exercise 17a in a working program. Make sure your method is called from `main()` and correctly returns a value to `main()`. Have `main()` display the value returned. Test the method by passing various data to it.

18. a. Write a Java method named `fracPart()` that returns the fractional part of any number passed to the method. For example, if the number 256.879 is passed to `fracPart()`, the number .879 should be returned. Have the method `fracPart()` call the method `whole()` that you wrote in Exercise 17. The number returned can then be determined as the number passed to `fracPart()` less the returned value when the same argument is passed to `whole()`. The completed program should consist of `main()` followed by `fracPart()` followed by `whole()`.

  b. Include the method written in Exercise 18a in a working program. Make sure your method is called from `main()` and correctly returns a value to `main()`. Have `main()` display the value returned. Test the method by passing various data to it.

19. a. An extremely useful programming algorithm for rounding a real number to n decimal places is:

Step 1: Multiply the number by 10^n
Step 2: Add 0.5
Step 3: Delete the fractional part of the result
Step 4: Divide by 10^n

For example, using this algorithm to round the number 78.374625 to three decimal places yields:

Step 1: $78.374625 \times 10^3 = 78374.625$
Step 2: $78374.625 + 0.5 = 78375.125$
Step 3: Retaining the integer part $= 78375$
Step 4: 78375 divided by $10^3 = 78.375$

Use this information to write a Java method named `round()` that rounds the value of its first parameter to the number of decimal places specified by its second parameter.

b. Incorporate the `round()` method written for Exercise 19a into a program that accepts a user-entered amount of money, multiplies the entered amount by an 8.675 percent interest rate, and displays the result rounded to two decimal places. Enter, compile, and execute this program and verify the result for the following test data:

Amount: $1,000, $0, $100, $10

6.3 APPLICATIONS

Preparing a well-designed computer method is very much like preparing a well-designed term paper in that both should start with an outline. This outline can either be written down or, for very small methods, may simply be kept in mind as the method is being developed. As with a term paper, however, which lists the paper's main topics, a computer method's initial outline must list the primary tasks that the method will accomplish.

In written form, a method's initial outline is typically either a pseudocode description (see Section 1.3) or a diagram showing the method's internal structure. Such a diagram is referred to as a structure diagram. A general outline applicable to many engineering and scientific tasks is the following algorithm:

> *Get the required inputs*
> *Calculate the desired result*
> *Report the results of the calculation*

These three tasks are the primary responsibilities of every method, and an equivalent structure diagram of this algorithm is shown in Figure 6.10.

We now apply this basic structure to two programming problems. The first is a coin toss simulation that uses a single method. For this simulation, however, we will first need to construct a series of random numbers. The second application uses a series of methods to perform a Cartesian to polar coordinate conversion.

Random Numbers

There are many commercial and scientific simulation problems in which probability must be considered or statistical sampling techniques must be used. In simulating automobile traffic flow or telephone usage patterns, statistical models are required. In addition, applications such as simple computer games and more involved gaming scenarios can only be described statistically. All of these statistical models require the generation of **random numbers**—that is, a series of numbers whose order cannot be predicted.

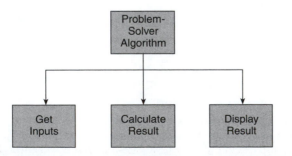

FIGURE 6.10 Initial Structure Diagram of the Problem-Solver Algorithm

In practice, it is hard to find truly random numbers. Dice are never perfect, cards are never shuffled completely randomly, and digital computers can handle numbers only within a finite range and with limited precision. The best one can do in most cases is generate *pseudorandom* numbers, which are sufficiently random for the task at hand.

Some computer languages contain a library method that produces random numbers; others do not. All Java compilers provide a general-purpose method for creating random numbers named random() that is defined in the Math class. This method produces a series of double-precision random numbers in the range 0.0 up to, but not including, 1.0.

The general procedure for creating a series of *N* random numbers using Java's library methods is illustrated in Program 6.6, which uses the Math.random() method to generate a series of 10 random numbers:

PROGRAM 6.6

```java
public class RandomNumbers
{
  public static void main(String[] args)
  {
    final int NUMBERS = 10;

    double randValue;
    int i;

    for (i = 1; i <= 10; i++)
    {
      randValue = Math.random();
      System.out.println(randValue);
    }

  }
}
```

The following is the output produced by one run of Program 6.6:

```
0.9332932472758279
0.6655689601942523
0.9368189009265464
0.3030248315838068
0.6346712906930385
0.27545891900300157
0.028702213952233935
0.3854898736878013
0.3519811183758321
0.4604059714098424
```

Each time Program 6.6 is executed, it will create a different series of 10 random numbers.

Scaling

One modification to the random numbers produced by the `random()` method typically, but not always, must be made in practice. In many applications, the random numbers are required as integers within a specified range, such as 1 to 100. The method for adjusting the random numbers produced by a random number generator to reside within specified ranges is called **scaling**.

Scaling a random number as an integer value between 0 and N - 1 is accomplished using the expression `(int)(Math.random() * N)`. For example, the expression `int(Math.random() * 100)` produces a random integer between 0 and 99. The expression `1 + (int)(Math.random() * N)` produces an integer random number between 1 and N. For example, in simulating the roll of a die, the expression `1 + (int)(Math.random() * 6)` produces a random integer between 1 and 6. The more general scaling expression `a + (int)(Math.random() * (b + 1 - a)` produces a random integer between the numbers a and b.

Application 1: Coin Toss Simulation

A common use of random numbers is to simulate events using a method rather than going through the time and expense of constructing a real-life experiment. For example, statistical theory tells us that the probability of having a single tossed coin turn up heads is 50 percent. Similarly, there is a 50 percent probability of having a single tossed coin turn up tails.

Using these probabilities, we would expect a single coin that is tossed 1,000 times to turn up heads 500 times and tails 500 times. In practice, however, this is seldom exactly realized for a single experiment consisting of 1,000 tosses. Instead of actually tossing a coin 1,000 times, we can use a random number generator to simulate these tosses. In particular, we will use the random number method developed in the previous sections.

Step 1: Analyze the Problem   For this problem, two outputs are required: the percentage of heads and the percentage of tails that result when a simulated coin is tossed 1,000 times. No input item is required for the random number method provided by the Math class.

Step 2: Develop a Solution   The percentage of heads and tails is determined as:

```
                    Number of heads
Percentage of heads = --------------- x 100%
                          1000


                    Number of tails
Percentage of tails = --------------- x 100%
                          1000
```

To determine the number of heads and tails, we need to simulate 1,000 random numbers in such a manner that we can define a result of "heads" or "tails" from each generated number. There are a number of ways to do this.

One way is to scale the `random()` method generated numbers to be integers between 1 and 100. Knowing that any single toss has a 50 percent chance of being either a head or a tail, we could designate a head as an even random number and a tail as an odd random number. Another approach would be to use the generated values as is and define a head as any number greater than 0.5 and any other result as a tail. This is the approach we will adopt.

Having defined how we will create a single toss that has a 50 percent chance of turning up heads or tails, the generation of 1,000 tosses is rather simple: A fixed-count loop generates 1,000 random numbers. For each generation, we identify the result as either a head or tail and accumulate the results in a heads and tails counter. Thus, the complete simulation algorithm is given by the pseudocode:

```
Initialize a heads count to zero
For 1000 times
  Generate a random number between 0 and 1
  If the random number is greater than 0.5
    add one to the heads count
EndFor
Calculate the tails count as 1000 minus the heads count
Calculate the percentage of heads as the number of heads divided by 1000 x 100%
Calculate the percentage of tails as the number of tails divided by 1000 x 100%
Print the percentage of heads and tails obtained
```

Step 3: Code the Solution Program 6.7 codes this algorithm in Java.

PROGRAM 6.7

```java
public class CoinToss
{
  public static void main(String[] args)
  {
    int tosses = 1000;

    percentages(tosses);
  }

  // a method to simulate the multiple tossing of a coin
  public static void percentages(int tosses)
  {
    double randValue;
    int i;
    int heads = 0;
    int tails;
    double perheads, pertails;
    for (i = 1; i <= tosses; i++)
    {
      randValue = Math.random();
      if (randValue > 0.5)
        heads = heads + 1;
    }
```

(Continued on next page)

```
(Continued from previous page)
        tails = tosses - heads;


         // calculate the percentages
        perheads = ((double)heads/(double)tosses * 100.0);
        pertails = ((double)tails/(double)tosses * 100.0);


        System.out.println("Heads came up " + perheads +
                          " percent of the time.");
        System.out.println("Tails came up " + pertails +
                          " percent of the time.");

    }
 }
```

Following are two sample runs using Program 6.7.

```
Heads came up 47.5 percent of the time.
Tails came up 52.5 percent of the time.
```

and

```
Heads came up 50.7 percent of the time.
Tails came up 49.3 percent of the time.
```

Writing and executing Program 6.7 are certainly easier than manually tossing a coin 1,000 times. It should be noted that the validity of the results produced by the method depends on how random the numbers produced by `random()` actually are.

Step 4: Test and Correct the Solution   There are really two tests that Program 6.7 must pass. The more important test concerns the randomness of each generated number. This, of course, is really a test of the random number method. For our purposes, we have used a previously written method using an algorithm that ensures generating a series of 50,000 random numbers before the sequence of numbers repeats. So at this point, we accept the "randomness" of the generator (see Exercise 7 on page 324 for a method of verifying the method's randomness).

Once the question of the random number generator has been settled, the second test requires that we correctly generate 1,000 numbers and accumulate a head and tail count. That this is correctly accomplished is adequately verified by a simple desk check of the `for` loop within Program 6.7. Also, we do know that the result of the simulation must be close to 50 percent heads and 50 percent tails. The results of the simulation verify this to be the case.

Application 2: Rectangular to Polar Coordinate Conversion

Assume that we must write a Java program to convert the rectangular (x,y) coordinates of a point into polar form. That is, given an x and y position on a Cartesian coordinate sys-

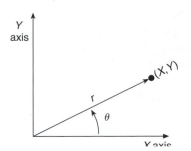

Y axis

Y axis

FIGURE 6.11   Correspondence Between Polar (Distance and Angle) and Cartesian (x,y) Coordinates

tem, as illustrated in Figure 6.11, we must calculate the distance from the origin, d, and the angle from the x axis, θ, specified by the point. The values of d and θ are referred to as the point's *polar coordinates*.

Step 1: Analyze the Problem   When the x and y coordinates of a point are known, the equivalent r and θ coordinates can be calculated with the formulas:

$$d = \sqrt{x^2 + y^2}$$
$$\theta = \tan^{-1}(y/x), \qquad x \neq 0$$

Step 2: Develop a Solution   We begin the development of our method with an outline of what the method is to accomplish. For this application, the required inputs are an x and y coordinate. Two calculations are required: one to determine a distance, d, and an angle, θ, which are polar coordinates. The output consists of the display of the calculated polar coordinates. Thus, the initial pseudocode description is:

> **Get the x and y coordinate values**
> **Calculate the polar (r and θ) coordinate values**
> **Display the polar coordinate values**

The equivalent structure diagram for this algorithm is illustrated in Figure 6.12.

Step 3: Code the Solution   As this is a relatively simple method and each task described by the algorithm is well defined, coding each task can begin. To illustrate that any task may be coded independently of any other task, we will arbitrarily start coding the

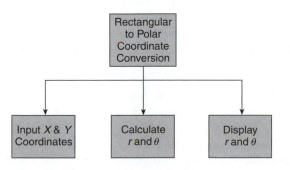

FIGURE 6.12   Structure Diagram

methods that perform the calculations of the polar coordinates. Starting with the distance method, the calculation requires the input of both *x* and *y* coordinates and returns a distance. Naming this method `getDistance()`, the following code performs the necessary calculation and return of a distance coordinate:

```
public static double getDistance(double x, double y)
{
    return Math.sqrt(x * x + y * y);
}
```

This method is rather straightforward. The method's header line declares that the method returns a double-precision value, and each of its parameters is declared as a double-precision data type. These two parameters can accept an *x* and *y* value, which are used in the calculation of the distance value returned by the method. Notice that the calculation of the distance is performed directly within the `return` statement. An equally acceptable alternative is first to assign the calculated value to a variable and then use this variable in the `return` statement, as for example in:

```
double distance = Math.sqrt(x * x + y * y);
return distance;
```

The calculation of θ requires the same two inputs used in computing the distance coordinate. As an added feature, we will have the method that calculates the angle θ return the angle in degrees rather than the radian measure returned by the Math class' `atan()` method. The following method, named `getAngle()`, performs the necessary input, calculation, and output of the angle coordinate:

```
public static double getAngle(double x, double y)
{
    final double TODEGREES = 180.0/Math.PI;

    return Math.atan(y/x) * TODEGREES;
}
```

Within the method's body, a named constant TODEGREES is defined as the factor $180.0 / \pi$. The return statement uses the two parameter values, *x* and *y*, to compute the angle value. Within this statement, the symbolic constant named TODEGREES converts the returned radian value from the `atan()` method into degrees. As written, both the `getDistance()` and `getAngle()` methods may be included in a functioning Java program to check for any syntax and logic errors.

Step 4: Test and Correct the Solution Once the two conversion methods are written, they can be tested independently of any other method. This is done by writing a program that calls these methods, as in Program 6.8.

Notice that in `main()` we pass the constants 3.0 and 4.0 into each conversion method. Each method accepts these inputs as the parameters *x* and *y* and uses these parameters in calculating corresponding values for the polar distance and angle coordinates. Within main(), the return values are known as distance and angle, and their values are displayed immediately after the respective method calls. The output produced by Program 6.8 is:

```
The polar coordinates are:
  Distance from origin: 5.25
  Angle (in degrees) from x-axis: 53.13
```

These are the same results that would be obtained from a hand calculation. As each method performs a single calculation, and the results displayed by our test program agree with those from a hand calculation, each method can be considered completely tested.

PROGRAM 6.8

```java
import java.text.*; // needed for formatting
public class ConvertXY
{
  public static void main(String[] args)
  {
    double x = 3.0, y = 4.0;
    double distance, angle;

    DecimalFormat num = new DecimalFormat("###.00");

     // convert to Polar coordinates
    distance = getDistance(x,y);
    angle = getAngle(x,y);

    System.out.println("\nThe polar coordinates are:");
    System.out.println("  Distance from origin: " + num.format(distance));
    System.out.println("  Angle (in degrees) from the x-axis: "
                        + num.format(angle));
  }

  public static double getDistance(double x, double y)
  {
    return Math.sqrt(x * x + y * y);
  }

  public static double getAngle(double x, double y)
  {
    final double TODEGREES = 180.0/Math.PI;

    return Math.atan(y/x) * TODEGREES;
  }
}
```

Completing the Application The structure diagram for our complete program (Figure 6.11) requires that methods also be written for accepting *x* and *y* rectangular coordinates and displaying the calculated polar coordinates. The following method, getCoordinate(), can accept each coordinate as an individually entered double-precision value.

```
public static double getCoordinate(String prompt)
throws java.io.IOException
  {
    String s1;
    double coordinate;

    // set up the basic input stream
     // needed for conversion capabilities
    InputStreamReader isr = new InputStreamReader(System.in);
     // needed to use readLine()
    BufferedReader br = new BufferedReader(isr);

    System.out.print(prompt);
    s1 = br.readLine();
    coordinate = Double.parseDouble(s1);
    return coordinate;
  }
```

The getCoordinate() method provides a simple and quick procedure for accepting keyboard input that is converted into a double-precision value.[9] This method accepts a string as an input, which is subsequently used to prompt the user for a desired value. The input method can be tested by itself with a small Java program, as in Program 6.9. This program also includes a method named display() that outputs a message describing the conversion that is being performed.

PROGRAM 6.9

```
import java.io.*;    // needed to access input stream classes
public class GetXYCoords
{
  public static void main(String[] args)
  throws java.io.IOException
  {
    double x, y;

    display();

    x = getCoordinate("Enter the x coordinate: ");
    y = getCoordinate("Enter the y coordinate: ");
```
(Continued on next page)

[9]A more robust method that incorporates exception handling and error correction is the readDouble() method that is listed as the last method in the keyboard input class provided in Appendix G.

(Continued from previous page)

```java
System.out.println("The entered value for x is " + x);
    System.out.println("The entered value for y is " + y);
}

public static void display()
{
    System.out.println("Rectangular to Polar Coordinate"
                    + "Conversion Program\n");
}

public static double getCoordinate(String prompt)
throws java.io.IOException
{
    String s1;
    double coordinate;

    // set up the basic input stream
     // needed for conversion capabilities
    InputStreamReader isr = new InputStreamReader(System.in);
     // needed to use readLine()
    BufferedReader br = new BufferedReader(isr);

    System.out.print(prompt);
    s1 = br.readLine();
    coordinate = Double.parseDouble(s1);
    return coordinate;
}
}
```

The following output produced by Program 6.9 verifies the correct operation of the getCoordinate() method:

```
Rectangular to Polar Coordinate Conversion Program

Enter the x coordinate: 3
Enter the y coordinate: 4
The entered value for x is 3.0
The entered value for y is 4.0
```

The method for displaying a set of polar coordinates is constructed in a similar manner. Program 6.10 contains both the method, which we have named showPolar(), and a main() method that tests the method. Notice that the parameter names in the header line for showPolar() need not be the same as those in any other method. The showPolar()

method is constructed to display the values in its two parameters, which in this case have been named `distance` and `angle`.

PROGRAM 6.10

```java
import java.text.*; // needed for formatting
public class ShowPolar
{
  public static void main(String[] args)
  {
    showPolar(5.247, 53.1301);
  }

  public static void showPolar(double distance, double angle)
  {
    DecimalFormat num = new DecimalFormat("###.00");

    System.out.println("\nThe polar coordinates are:");
    System.out.println("  Distance from origin: " + num.format(distance));
    System.out.println("  Angle (in degrees) from the x-axis: "
                        + num.format(angle));

  }
}
```

The output of Program 6.10 verifies that `showPolar()` correctly displays the values passed to it:

```
The polar coordinates are:
  Distance from origin: 5.25
  Angle (in degrees) from the x-axis: 53.13
```

It now remains to create one `main()` method that calls each of the developed methods in the correct order. This is done in Program 6.11, which also includes the methods `display()`, `getCoordinate()`, `getDistance()`, `getAngle()`, and `showPolar()`.

The following output was produced from one run of Program 6.11:

```
Rectangular to Polar Coordinate Conversion Program

Enter the x coordinate: 3
Enter the y coordinate: 4

The polar coordinates are:
  Distance from origin: 5
  Angle (in degrees) from the x-axis: 53.1301
```

PROGRAM 6.11

```
// This program converts rectangular coordinates to polar coordinates
// Methods used:
//              display() - display a program message
 //             getCoordinate() - obtain a rectangular coordinate
//              getDistance() - convert rectangular coordinates to a polar distance value
//              getAngle() - convert rectangular coordinates to a polar angle value
//              showPolar() - display the polar coordinates
//
import java.io.*;   // needed to access input stream classes
import java.text.*; // needed for formatting

public class RecToPolar
{
  public static void main(String[] args)
  throws java.io.IOException
  {
    double x, y;
    double distance, angle;

    display();

      // input the x and y Cartesian coordinates
    x = getCoordinate("Enter the x coordinate: ");
    y = getCoordinate("Enter the y coordinate: ");

      // convert to Polar coordinates
    distance = getDistance(x,y);
    angle = getAngle(x,y);

      // display the Polar coordinates
    showPolar(distance, angle);
  }

  public static void display()
  {
    System.out.println("Rectangular to Polar Coordinate"
                       + "Conversion Program\n");
  }

  public static double getCoordinate(String prompt)
  throws java.io.IOException
  {
    String s1;
    double coordinate;
```

(Continued on next page)

(Continued from previous page)

```java
     // set up the basic input stream
     // needed for conversion capabilities
  InputStreamReader isr = new InputStreamReader(System.in);
     // needed to use readLine()
  BufferedReader br = new BufferedReader(isr);

  System.out.print(prompt);
  s1 = br.readLine();
  coordinate = Double.parseDouble(s1);
  return coordinate;
}

public static double getDistance(double x, double y)
{
   return Math.sqrt(x * x + y * y);
}

public static double getAngle(double x, double y)
{
  final double TODEGREES = 180.0/Math.PI;

  return Math.atan(y/x) * TODEGREES;
}

public static void showPolar(double distance, double angle)
{
  DecimalFormat num = new DecimalFormat("###.00");

  System.out.println("\nThe polar coordinates are:");
  System.out.println("  Distance from origin: " + num.format(distance));
  System.out.println("  Angle (in degrees) from the x-axis: " + num.format(angle));
}
}
```

EXERCISES 6.3

1. Enter and execute Program 6.7 on your computer.
2. Modify Program 6.7 so that it requests the number of tosses from the user. (*Tip:* Make sure to have the program correctly determine the percentages of heads and tails obtained.)
3. Enter and execute Program 6.11 on your computer.
4. Modify Program 6.11 to accept the rectangular coordinates of two points (x_1, y_1) and (x_2, y_2), calculate the distance of each point from the origin, and calculate

the distance between the two points. The distance, d, between two points is given by the formula

$$d = \sqrt{(x_2 - x_1)^2 + (y_2 - y_1)^2}$$

5. Modify Program 6.11 so that it uses the readDouble() method in Appendix G in place of the getCoordinate() method.

6. The viscosity of three common fluids are:

	Viscosity (foot-pound-sec /ft²)
Ethyl alcohol	2.29×10^5
Methyl alcohol	1.17×10^5
Propyl alcohol	4.01×10^5

Using these data, write and test a Java method named Viscosity() that returns the viscosity of a selected fluid. The type of fluid should be passed to the method as a character.

7. The density of three common fluids are:

	Density (slug/ft³)
Ethyl alcohol	1.527
Methyl alcohol	1.531
Propyl alcohol	1.556

Using these data, write and test a Java method named Density() that returns the density of a selected fluid. The type of fluid should be passed to the method as a character.

8. a. Fluid flowing in a pipe will either flow in a smooth pattern known as *laminar flow* or in a turbulent pattern known as *turbulent flow*. The velocity that produces a laminar flow pattern can be determined with the formula:

$$V_{lam} = 2100\mu/\rho D$$

where:

V_{lam} is the velocity of the fluid in ft/sec that produces a definite laminar flow
μ is the viscosity of the fluid in foot-pound-sec /ft²
ρ is the density of the fluid in slug/ft³
D is the inside diameter of the pipe in feet

Using this formula, write and test a Java method named laminarFlow() that returns the laminar flow velocity, V_{lam}. The method should calculate this velocity for water, which has a viscosity, μ, of 1.9×10^5 foot-pound-sec /ft² and a density, ρ, of 1.94 slug/ft³. A pipe diameter of 0.1 foot should also be passed into the laminarFlow() method.

b. Write a Java method that determines the turbulent flow velocity of a liquid. The turbulent flow velocity is given by the formula $V_{tur} = 4000\mu / \rho D$. Use your method to calculate the turbulent flow velocity for water using the data given in Exercise 8a.

9. Many algorithms have been developed for generating pseudorandom numbers. Some of these algorithms utilize a counting technique, such as counting bits

beginning at some arbitrary location in a changing memory. Another technique, which creates pseudorandom numbers by performing a calculation, is the *power residue method.*

The power residue method begins with an odd *n*-digit integer, which is referred to as the "seed" number. The seed is multiplied by the value $(10^{n/2} - 3)$. The lowest *n* digits of the result (the "residue") produce a new seed. Continuing this procedure produces a series of random numbers, with each new number serving as the seed for the next number. If the original seed has four or more digits (*n* equal to or greater than 4) and is not divisible by either 2 or 5, this procedure yields $5 \times 10^{(n-2)}$ random numbers before a sequence of numbers repeats itself. For example, starting with a six-digit seed (*n* = 6), such as 654321, a series of $5 \times 10^4 = 50,000$ random numbers can be generated.

As an algorithm, the specific steps in generating pseudorandom numbers with a power residue procedure consist of the following:

Step 1: Have a user enter a six-digit integer seed that is not divisible by 2 or 5; this means the number should be an odd number not ending in 5.

Step 2: Multiply the seed number by 997, which is $10^3 - 3$.

Step 3: Extract the lower six digits of the result produced by step 2. Use this random number as the next seed.

Step 4: Repeat steps 2 and 3 for as many random numbers as needed.

Thus, if the user-entered seed number is 654321 (step 1), the first random number generated is calculated as follows:

Step 2: 654321 * 997 = 652358037

Step 3: Extract the lower six digits of the number obtained in step 2. This is accomplished using a standard programming "trick."

The trick involves:

Step 3a: Divide the number by $10^6 = 1000000$.
    For example, 652358037 / 1000000 = 652.358037

Step 3b: Take the integer part of the result of step 3a.
    For example, the integer part of 652.358037 = 652

Step 3c: Multiply the previous result by 10^6.
    For example, $652 \times 10^6 = 652000000$

Step 3d: Subtract this result from the original number.
    For example, 652358037 − 652000000 = 358037

The integer part of a floating-point number can be taken either by assigning the floating-point number to an integer variable or by a Java *cast* (see Section 3.3). In our procedure, we will use the cast mechanism. Thus, the algorithm for producing a random number can be accomplished with the following code:

```
i = int(997.0 * x / 1.E6);    // take the integer part
x = 997.0 * x - i * 1.E6;
```

Using this information:

a. Create a method named `randnum()` that accepts a floating-point seed as a parameter and returns a floating-point random number between 0 and 1.E6.

b. Incorporate the `randnum()` method created in Exercise 9a into a working Java program that produces 10 random numbers between 0 and 1.E6.

c. Test the randomness of the `randnum( )` method created in Exercise 9a using the method described in [Exercise 14]. Try some even seed values and some odd seed values that end in 5 to determine whether these affect the randomness of the numbers.

10. Write a Java method that determines the quadrant that a line drawn from the origin resides in. The determination of the quadrant is made using the angle that the line makes with the positive X axis as follows:

Angle from the positive X axis	Quadrant
Between 0 and 90 degrees	1
Between 90 and 180 degrees	2
Between 180 and 270 degrees	3
Between 270 and 360 degrees	4

Note: If the angle is exactly 0, 90, 180, or 270 degrees, the corresponding line does not reside in any quadrant but lies on an axis. For this case, your method should return zero.

11. Write a program to simulate the rolling of two dice. If the total of the two dice is 7 or 11 you win; otherwise, you lose. Embellish this program as much as you like, with betting, different odds, different combinations for win or lose, stopping play when you have no money left or reach the house limit, displaying the dice, and so forth (*Tip:* Calculate the dots showing on each die by the expression dots = (int)(6.0 ∗ random number + 1), where the random number is between 0 and 1.)

12. A value that is sometimes useful is the greatest common divisor (gcd) of two integers $n1$ and $n2$. A famous mathematician, Euclid, discovered an efficient method to do this more than 2,000 years ago. Right now, however, we'll settle for a stub. Write the integer method stub gcd($n1$,$n2$). Have it return a value that suggests it received its parameters correctly. (*Tip:* N1 + N2 is a good choice of return values. Why isn't N1 / N2 a good choice?)

13. Euclid's method for finding the greatest common divisor of two positive integers consists of the following steps:

Step 1: Divide the larger number by the smaller and retain the remainder.
Step 2: Divide the smaller number by the remainder, again retaining the remainder.
Step 3: Continue dividing the prior remainder by the current remainder until the remainder is zero, at which point the last nonzero remainder is the greatest common divisor.

For example, assuming the two positive integers are 84 and 49, we have:

Step 1: 84/49 yields a remainder of 35
Step 2: 49/35 yields a remainder of 14
Step 3: 35/14 yields a remainder of 7
Step 3: 14/7 yields a remainder of 0

Thus, the last nonzero remainder, which is 7, is the greatest common divisor of 84 and 49. Using Euclid's algorithm, replace the stub method written for Exercise 12 with an actual method that determines and returns the gcd of its two integer parameters.

14. Write a program that tests the effectiveness of the math random ( ) method. Start by initializing 10 counters, such as zerocount, onecount, twocount, . . . , ninecount to 0. Then generate a large number of pseudorandom integers between 0 and 9. Each time a 0 occurs, increment zerocount, when a 1 occurs increment onecount, and so on. Finally, print out the number of 0s, 1s, 2s, and so on that occurred and the percentage of the time they occurred.

15. The following program uses the same variable names in both the calling and called method. Determine if this causes any problem for the compiler.

```
import java.io.*;    // needed to access input stream classes
public class SameNames
{
  public static void main (String[] args)
  throws java.io.IOException
  {
    String s1;
    String s2;
    double minutes, hours, seconds;
    // set up the basic input stream
      // needed for conversion capabilities
    InputStreamReader isr = new InputStreamReader(System.in);
      // needed to use readLine()
    BufferedReader br = new BufferedReader(isr);

    System.out.print("Enter a number: ");
    s1 = br.readLine();
    minutes = Double.parseDouble(s1);

    System.out.print("Enter another number: ");
    s2 = br.readLine();
    hours = Double.parseDouble(s2);

    seconds = time(minutes, hours);
    System.out.println("The total number of seconds is " + seconds);
  }

  public static double time(double minutes, double hours)
  {
    double seconds;

    seconds = (hours * 60 + minutes) * 60;
    return seconds;
  }
}
```

16. The determinant of the 2 by 2 matrix

$$\begin{vmatrix} a_{11} & a_{12} \\ a_{21} & a_{22} \end{vmatrix}$$

is $a_{11}a_{22} - a_{21}a_{12}$.

Similarly, the determinant of a 3 by 3 matrix

$$\begin{vmatrix} a_{11} & a_{12} & a_{13} \\ a_{21} & a_{22} & a_{23} \\ a_{31} & a_{32} & a_{33} \end{vmatrix} =$$

$$a_{11}\begin{vmatrix} a_{22} & a_{23} \\ a_{32} & a_{33} \end{vmatrix} - a_{21}\begin{vmatrix} a_{12} & a_{13} \\ a_{32} & a_{33} \end{vmatrix} + a_{31}\begin{vmatrix} a_{12} & a_{13} \\ a_{22} & a_{23} \end{vmatrix}$$

Using this information, write and test two methods named `det2()` and `det3()`. The `det2()` method should accept the four coefficients of a 2 by 2 matrix and return its determinant. The `det3()` method should accept the nine coefficients of a 3 by 3 matrix and return its determinant by calling `det2()` to calculate the required 2 by 2 determinants.

6.4 VARIABLE SCOPE

Now that we have begun to write programs containing more than one method, we can look more closely at the variables and parameters declared within each method and their relationship to variables and parameters declared in other methods.

By their very nature, Java methods are constructed to be independent modules. As you have seen, values are passed to a method using the method's argument list, and a value is returned from a method using a `return` statement. Seen in this light, a method can be thought of as a closed box with slots at the top to receive values and a single slot at the bottom to return a value (Figure 6.13).

The metaphor of a closed box is useful because it emphasizes the fact that what goes on inside the method, including all variable declarations within the method's body, are hidden from the view of all other methods. Since the variables created inside a method are conventionally available only to the method itself, they are said to be local to the method, or **local variables.** A local variable is one that has had storage locations set aside for it by a declaration statement made within a method body. Local variables are only meaningful when used in expressions or statements inside the method that declared them. This means that the same variable name can be declared and used in more than one method. For each method that declares the variable, a separate and distinct variable is created.

Values into the method

A single value directly
returned by the method

FIGURE 6.13   A Method Can Be Considered a Closed Box

All the variables we have used until now have been local variables. This is a direct result of placing our declaration statements inside methods and using them as definition statements that cause the compiler to reserve storage for the declared variable. The same is true for all parameters declared within a method's header line; method parameters can only be used within the method that declares them. Thus, parameter names are also local to their declaring methods.

Formally, the section of a program within which an identifier is valid or "known" is referred to as its **scope**. This section of the program is also referred to as where the variable is visible, which means that it can be legitimately accessed and will cause no compiler errors. In Java, two predominant types of scope are defined: block scope and class scope.

Except for variables declared in a `for` statement, local variables and parameters of a method all have **block scope,** where a block is defined as any code within a method that begins with an opening brace and terminates with a brace. Variables or parameter with block scope can be used from their point of declaration until the end of the block of code within which they are declared. Variables declared in a `for` statement are only visible within the structure defined by the `for` statement.

In contrast to block scope, **class scope** begins at the opening brace that starts a class definition and continues to the closing brace that ends the class definition. Thus, all method names within a class have class scope, as do any class variables. A **class variable** is any variable that is declared within a class, outside any method. In addition, a class variable that is designated as static can be modified without being constructed as part of an object. As a specific example of both class and block scope using static class variables, consider Program 6.12.

The variable `firstnum` in Program 6.12 has class scope because it is declared by a statement located outside any one method. It is also a `private` and `static` variable, which means that it can be changed by any method subsequently defined in the class without being incorporated into an object. Because both methods, `main()` and `changeValues()`, are in the same class, they can use this private class variable with no further declaration needed. Notice that the access specification designated by the keyword `private` in `firstnum`'s declaration restricts this variable's usage to those methods in the class. If the keyword `public` had been used, `firstnum` could also be used by methods in all other classes. The keyword `static` ensures that only one copy of the variable will be created and that a specific object need not be created using the keyword `new` for a method to use this variable (access specifications and object creation considerations are presented in detail in Chapter 9).

In addition to the class variable `firstnum`, Program 6.12 also contains two separate local variables, both named `secnum`. Storage for the `secnum` variable named in `changeValues()` is created by the declaration statement located in `changeValues()`. A different storage area for the `secnum` variable in `main()` is created by the declaration statement located in the `main()` method. Figure 6.14 on page 328 illustrates the three distinct storage areas reserved by the three declaration statements in Program 6.12.

Each of the variables named `secnum` is local to the method in which its storage is created, and each can only be used from within the appropriate method. Thus, when `secnum` is used in `main()`, the storage area reserved by `main()` for its `secnum` variable is accessed, and when `secnum` is used in `changeValues()`, the storage area reserved by `changeValues()` for its `secnum` variable is accessed. The following output is produced when Program 6.12 is run:

PROGRAM 6.12

```java
public class ShowScope
{

  private static int firstnum;  // this has class scope

    // all variables in this method have block scope
  public static void main(String[] args)
  {
    int secnum;            // create a local variable named secnum

    firstnum = 10; // store a value into the class variable
    secnum = 20;    // store a value into the local variable

    System.out.println("From main(): firstnum = " + firstnum);
    System.out.println("From main(): secnum =   " + secnum);

    changeValues();       // call the method changeValues

    System.out.println("\nFrom main() again: firstnum = " + firstnum);
    System.out.println("From main() again: secnum = " + secnum);
  }
      // all variables declared in this method have block scope
  public static void changeValues()    // no values are passed to this method
  {                                    // and no value is returned
    int secnum;  // create a local variable named secnum

    secnum = 30; // this only affects this local variable's value

    System.out.println("\nFrom changeValues(): firstnum = " + firstnum);
    System.out.println("From changeValues(): secnum = " + secnum);

    firstnum = 40;    // this changes firstnum for both methods
  }
}  // end of class
```

```
From main(): firstnum = 10
From main(): secnum = 20

From changeValues(): firstnum = 10
From changeValues(): secnum = 30

From main() again: firstnum = 40
From main() again: secnum = 20
```

Let's analyze this output. Since firstnum is a static class variable, both the main() and changeValues() methods can use and change its value. Initially, both methods

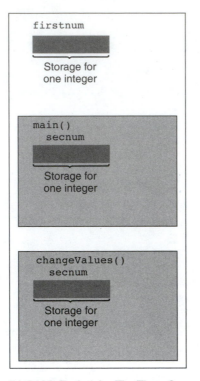

FIGURE 6.14   The Three Storage Areas Created by Program 6.12

display the value of 10 that `main()` stored in `firstnum`. Before returning, `changeValues()` changes the value of `firstnum` to 40, which is the value displayed when the variable `firstnum` is next displayed from within `main()`.

Because each method only "knows" its own local variables, `main()` can only display the value of its `secnum` variable, and `changeValues()` can only display the value of its `secnum`. Thus, whenever `secnum` is obtained from `main()`, the value 20 is displayed, and whenever `secnum` is obtained from `changeValues()`, the value 30 is displayed.

Java does not confuse the two `secnum` variables. While a method is executing, only those variables and parameters that are "in scope" for that method (static and local) can be accessed.

The scope of a variable in no way influences or restricts the data type of the variable. Just as a local variable can be a character, integer, float, double, boolean, or any of the other data types (long/short) we have introduced, so can class variables be of these data types. The scope of a variable is determined by the placement of the declaration statement that reserves storage for it, whereas the data type of the variable is determined by placing the appropriate keyword (`char`, `int`, `float`, `double`, `boolean`, etc.) before the variable's name in a declaration statement.

The length of time that storage locations remain reserved for an identifier is referred to as both an identifier's **lifetime** and **duration.** All identifiers with class scope come into being when the class within which they are declared is loaded into memory and remain until the program finishes execution. Because static variables can only have class scope, such variables always have the same duration as their defining class. Variables with block scope exist only while the block within which they are defined is in scope. Once the block goes out of scope, the storage areas for these variables are released back to the operating system. Should the block come back into scope, new storage areas are reserved and reinitialized as defined by the code within the block.

Scope Resolution

When a variable with block scope (a local variable) has the same name as a variable with class scope, all references to the variable name made within the scope of the local variable refer to the local variable. This situation in illustrated in Program 6.13, where the variable name number is defined as both a class and local variable.

PROGRAM 6.13

```java
public class ScopeCover
{

  private static double number = 42.8;   // this variable has class scope

  public static void main(String[] args)
  {
    double number = 26.4;     // this variable has local scope

    System.out.println("The value of number is " + number);

  }
} // end of class
```

When Program 6.13 is executed, the following output is displayed:

```
The value of number is 26.4
```

As shown by this output, the local variable name takes precedence over the class variable having the same name. In these cases, we can still access the class variable by prefacing it with its class name. The class name tells the compiler to use the variable having class scope rather than the method's local variable. For an example of this notation, consider Program 6.14.

The output produced by Program 6.14 is:

```
The value of number is 42.8
```

As indicated by this output, the class variable rather than the local variable is now accessed. This naming problem cannot occur between a parameter and local variable name. This is because a method's parameters have the same block scope as the method's local variables. Attempting to subsequently declare a local variable with the name of a parameter that is already in local scope results in a compiler error message equivalent to `Variable ... is already defined in this method.`

PROGRAM 6.14

```java
public class ScopeResolution
{
  private static double number = 42.8;    // this variable has class scope

  public static void main(String[] args)
  {
    double number = 26.4;       // this is a local variable

    System.out.println("The value of number is " + ScopeResolution.number);

  }
}  // end of class
```

Inner and Outer Blocks

Compound statements also define a single block of code, and any variable declared within a compound statement has a block scope restricted from its point of declaration to the closing brace of the block. What this means practically is that variables declared in an outer block can be accessed within all inner blocks because the variable is in scope throughout the outer block, which also includes all inner blocks. However, variables that are declared within an inner block *cannot be accessed* in any enclosing outside block because the inner block goes out of scope once its closing brace is reached. For example, consider the following main() method, which consists of three blocks of code:

```java
public static void main (String[] args)
  // start of outer block
{
  double a = 42.25;
    // start of inner block
  {
    int b = 50;
    System.out.println("a = " + a);  // this is okay
    System.out.println("b = " + b);  // this is okay
  } // end of inner block
  System.out.println("a = " + a);  // this is okay
  System.out.println("b = " + b);  // NOT OKAY - SEE EXPLANATION

  for(int i = 1; i < 10; i++) // this also constitutes an inner block
    System.out.print(i + "  "); // this is okay

  System.out.println("i is now " + i);  // NOT OKAY - SEE EXPLANATION


} // end of outer block
```

Because the variable a is declared in the outer block, it remains in scope for the complete outer block, which also includes the inner block. This means it can legitimately be accessed from within the inner block. This is not true, however, for the variable b. This variable is declared inside the inner block, which means that its scope is limited to this block, and the variable is not "known" outside the block. Attempting to display its value outside the block in which it has been declared results in the compiler error message Undefined variable: b. Interestingly enough, and sometimes more troublesome, is that the same scope rule applies to variables declared within the parentheses of a for statement. Thus, the attempt to display i's value once the for loop in the preceding code has completed executing results in the compiler error message Undefined variable: i. Thus, variables declared within the for statement are local to their respective blocks of code.

Because an inner block variable goes out of scope when the end of the block is reached, the same variable name can be declared again *after* the inner block is out of scope. An example of this is shown in the next section of code, where the variable b is declared twice, once within an inner block and then after this block goes out of scope. However, the name of any variable declared in an outer block *before* an inner block is defined cannot be declared again within an inner block. An example of this is shown in the following section of code where the variable a is first declared in the outer block and then an attempt is made to declare it within an inner block. The second declaration produces the compiler error message Variable 'a' is already defined in this method. This, of course, is the same error as attempting to declare a local variable with the same name that has been used for a parameter.

```
public static void main (String[] args)
  // start of outer block
{
  double a = 42.25; // this variable is "in scope" within both the outer
                    // and inner blocks
    // start of inner block
  {
    double a = 76.5;    // PRODUCES THE COMPILER ERROR MESSAGE
                        // Variable 'a' is already defined in this method.
    double b = 10.5;
    System.out.println("a = " + a);
  } // end of inner block

  double b = 20.75;    // this is okay, because the inner block
                       // is now "out of scope"
}
```

EXERCISES 6.4

1. a. For the following section of code, determine the data type and scope of all declared constants and variables. To do this, list the three column headings that follow on a sheet of paper (we have filled in the entries for the first variable):

Identifier	Data Type	Scope
flag	integer	class scope

```
public class Test
{
  private static int flag;
  private static long date;
  private static double thrust;


    public static void main(String[] args)
    {
      int flag;
      double factor, watts;
        .
        .
    }

    public static double resistance(int r1, int r2)
    {
      int count;
      double impedance;
        .
        .
      return impedance;
    }

    public static int step(double first, double last)
    {
      int numofyrs;
      double fracPart;
        .
        .
      return 10*numofyrs;
    }
}
```

    b. Draw boxes around the appropriate section of the foregoing code to enclose the scope of each variable.

    c. Determine the data type of the arguments that the methods `resistance()` and `step()` expect and the data type of the value returned by these methods.

2. a. For the following section of code, determine the data type and scope of all declared constants and variables. To do this, list the three column headings that follow on a sheet of paper (we have filled in the entries for the first variable):

Identifier	Data Type	Scope
key	char	class scope

```
public class Test
{
```

```
        private static char key;
        private static long number;

        public static void main(String[] args)
        {
          int a,b,c;
          double x,y;
              .

              .

        }

        public static int method1(int num1, int num2)
        {
          int o,p;
          double q;
              .

              .

          return p;
        }

        double method2(double first, double last)
        {
          int a,b,c,o,p;
          double r;
          double s,t,x;
              .

              .

          return s * t;
        }
      }
```

b. Draw a box around the appropriate section of the foregoing code to enclose the scope of the variables key, num1, y, and r.

c. Determine the data type of the arguments that the methods method1() and method2() expect and the data type of the value returned by these methods.

3. Besides speaking about the scope of a variable, we can also apply the term to a method's parameters. What is the scope of all method parameters?

4. Determine the values displayed by the following program:

```
public class Test
{
  private static int firstnum = 10;  // declare and initialize a class variable

  public static void main(String[] args)
  {
    int firstnum = 20;    // declare and initialize a local variable
```

(Continued on next page)

(Continued from previous page)

```
System.out.println("\nThe value of firstnum is " + firstnum;

display();
}


public static void display()
{
  System.out.println("\nThe value of firstnum is now " + firstnum;
}


}
```

5. What is the difference between the values displayed by the following two classes?

```
public class Test1
{
  private static double years = 1;

  public static void main(String[] args)
  {
    int i;

    for(i = 1; i < 4; i++)
      init1();
  }

  public static void init1()
  {
    System.out.println("\nThe value of years is "  +  years);
    years = years + 2;
  }

}
```

```
public class Test2
{
  private static double years;

  public static void main(String[] args)
  {
    int i;

    for(i = 1; i < 4; i++)
      init2();
  }
```

```
      public static void init2()
      {
        years = 1;
        System.out.println("\nThe value of years is " +  years);
        years = years + 2;
      }
    }
```

6. Determine the values displayed by the following program:

```
public class Test
{
  private static boolean a;

  public static void main(String[] args)
  {
    int count;       // count is a local variable

    for(count = 1; count <= 3; count++)
      switchBoolean();
  }

  public static void switchBoolean()
  {

    System.out.println("The value of the variable a is " + a);
    a = !a;
  }


} // end of class
```

6.5 COMMON PROGRAMMING ERRORS

1. Attempting to pass incorrect data types is an extremely common programming error related to methods. The values passed to a method must correspond to the data types of the parameters declared for the method. One way to verify that correct values have been received is to display all passed values within a method's body before any calculations are made. Once this verification has taken place, the display can be dispensed with.[10]

2. Declaring the same variable locally within both the calling and called methods and assuming a change in one variable affects the other variable. Even though the variable name is the same, a change to one local variable *does not* alter the value in the other local variable.

3. Terminating a method's header line with a semicolon.

4. Forgetting to include the data type of a method's parameters within the header line.

---

[10]In practice, a good debugger program should be used.

6.6 CHAPTER SUMMARY

1. A method is called by giving its name and passing any data to it in the parentheses following the name. If a variable is one of the arguments in a method call, the called method receives a copy of the variable's value.

2. The common form of a general-purpose user-written method is:

```
public static returnType methodName(parameter list)
{
  declarations and other Java statements;
  return  expression;
}
```

    The first line of the method is called the *method header*. The opening and closing braces of the method and all statements between these braces constitute the method's *body*. The parameter list is a comma-separated list of parameter declarations.

3. A method's return type declares the data type of the value returned by the method. If the method does not return a value, it should be declared as a void type.

4. Methods can directly return at most a single value to their calling methods. This is the value of the expression in the `return` statement.

5. A called method cannot alter either a primitive data type argument's value or a reference variable's value by changing the value of the equivalent parameter.

6. Reference values are passed to a called method in the same manner as primitive data types; the called method receives a copy of the reference value. Thus, both the called and calling method initially have a reference value that references the same object. If the called method alters the object being referenced, the changed object value will be accessible to both the called and calling methods. However, if the called method's parameter references a newly created object, the change in parameter value will not be reflected in the calling method. That is, in no case can a change in a called method's parameter value change the corresponding argument in the calling method.

7. The section of a program within which an identifier is valid or "known" is referred to as its *scope*. This section of the program is also referred to as where the variable is visible, which means that it can be legitimately accessed and will cause no compiler errors.

8. Except for variables declared in a `for` statement, variables and parameters of a method all have *block scope*, where a block is defined as any code within a method that begins with an opening brace and terminates with a closing brace. Variables or parameters with block scope can be used from their point of declaration until the end of the block of code within which they are declared. Variables having block scope are also referred to as *local variables*. Variables declared in a `for` statement are also local variables whose scope is limited to the loop defined by the `for` statement.

9. *Class scope* begins at the opening brace that starts a class definition and continues to the closing brace that ends the class definition. Thus, all methods within a class have class scope, as do any class variables. A *class variable* is any variable that is declared within a class, outside any method.

10. Class variables that are declared as static can be accessed without being constructed into an object. If no explicit initialization is defined, a primitive data type numerical static variable is initialized to zero, a boolean static variable is initialized to false, and a reference static variable is initialized to null.

CHEMICAL ENGINEERING

Chemical engineering is the application of the knowledge and techniques of science, particularly chemistry, to industry. Chemical engineers are responsible for the design and operation of large-scale manufacturing plants for all those materials that undergo chemical changes in their production. These materials include all the new and improved products that have so profoundly affected society, such as petrochemicals, rubbers and polymers, new metal alloys, industrial and fine chemicals, foods, paints, detergents, cements, pesticides, industrial gases, and medicines. Chemical engineers also play an important role in pollution abatement and the management of existing energy resources. Because the field of chemical engineering has grown to be so broad, it is difficult to classify the activities of chemical engineers. A rough subdivision is into large-scale production systems, or chemical processing, and smaller scale, or molecular, systems.

CHEMICAL PROCESSING

Chemical processing concerns all aspects of the design and operation of large chemical-processing plants. It includes the following areas:

1. Petrochemicals. The distillation and refinement of fuels such as gasoline, synthetic natural gas, coal liquefaction and gasification, and the production of an infinite variety of products made from petroleum, from cosmetics to pharmaceuticals.
2. Synthetic materials. The process of polymerization, a joining of simpler molecules into large complex molecules, is responsible for many modern materials such as nylon, synthetic rubbers, polystyrene, and a great variety of plastics and synthetic fibers.
3. Food and biochemical engineering. The manufacture of packaged food, improved food additives, sterilization, and the utilization of industrial bacteria, fungi, and yeasts in processes like fermentation.
4. Unit operations. The analysis of the transport of heat or fluid, such as the pumping of chemicals through a pipeline or the transfer of heat between substances. This area also includes the effect of heat transfer on chemical reactions such as oxidation, chlorination, and so on.
5. Cryogenic engineering. The design of plants operating at temperatures near absolute zero.
6. Electrochemical engineering. The use of electricity to alter chemical reactions, such as electroplating, or the design of batteries and energy cells.
7. Pollution control. A rapidly growing field that seeks to monitor and reduce the harmful effects of chemical processing on the environment. Topics of concern are wastewater control, air pollution abatement, and the economics of pollution control.

(Continued on next page)

(Continued from previous page)

MOLECULAR SYSTEMS

This field involves the application of laboratory techniques to large-scale processes. It includes the following areas:

1. Biochemical engineering. Application of enzymes, bacteria, and so on to improve large-scale chemical processes.
2. Polymer synthesis. Molecular basis for polymer properties and the chemical synthesis of new polymers adapted for large-scale production.

Preparation for a career in chemical engineering requires a thorough background in physics, chemistry, and mathematics and a knowledge of thermodynamics and physical, analytic, and organic chemistry. Although extensively trained in chemistry, chemical engineers differ from chemists in that their main concern is the adaptation of laboratory techniques to large-scale manufacturing plants.

PART 2

Array and String

Reference Types

C H A P T E R 7

Arrays

The primitive data type variables that we have discussed so far have all had one common characteristic: Each variable can only store a single value at a time. For example, although the variables key, count, *and* grade *declared in the statements*

```
char key;
int count;
double grade;
```

are of different data types, each variable can only store one value of the declared built-in data type. These types of variables are called scalar variables. A **scalar variable** *is a variable whose value is a single built-in data type value, such as a single integer, character, or double.*

Frequently, we may have a set of values, all of the same data type, that forms a logical group. For example, Figure 7.1 illustrates three groups of items. The first group is a list of five floating-point slopes, the second is a list of four character codes, and the last is a list of six integer voltages.

Slopes	Codes	Voltages
3.25	x	98
-7.0	a	87
10.625	m	92
12.317	n	79
5.4		85
		72

FIGURE 7.1 Three Lists of Items

A simple list containing individual items of the same data type is called a one-dimensional array. In this chapter, we describe how one-dimensional arrays are declared, initialized, stored, and used. Because arrays are reference data types, we will see that they are also declared differently from the built-in data types that we have predominantly been using.

7.1 ONE-DIMENSIONAL ARRAYS

A **one-dimensional array**, which is also referred to as either a **single-dimensional array** or a **vector**, is a list of related values with the same data type that is stored using a single group name.[1] In Java, as in other computer languages, the group name is referred to as the array name. For example, consider the list of temperatures in Figure 7.2.

Temperatures
98.75
83.3
97.625
72.5
85.25
90.7

FIGURE 7.2 A List of Temperatures

[1]Lists can be implemented in a variety of ways. An array is simply one implementation of a list in which all of the list elements are of the same type and each element is stored consecutively in a set of contiguous memory locations.

All the temperatures in the list are double-precision numbers and must be declared as such. However, the individual items in the list do not have to be declared separately. The items in the list can be declared as a single unit and stored under a common reference variable name, referred to as the array name. For convenience, we will choose `temperature` as the array name for the list in Figure 7.2. The specification that `temperature` is to store six individual double-precision values can be accomplished using the two statements[2]

```
double temperature[];    // declare the array's type
temperature = new double[6];   // allocate space for the array
```

The first statement is a declaration statement that declares the data type of the items that will be stored in the array and the array name. As shown in Figure 7.3, this statement causes a reference variable to be created and initialized with a null address. The second statement, which uses the `new` operator, forces the program to create an array object consisting of six double-precision storage locations and to store the location of this array object into the reference variable named `temperature`. The resulting allocation provided by this statement is shown in Figure 7.4.

temperature

```
      null value
```

A reference variable

FIGURE 7.3 The Results of the Declaration `double temperature[];` (Declaring an Array Creates a Reference Variable)

When the `new` operator allocates actual storage space for an array, the individual array elements are automatically initialized to zero for numerical built-in types, to `false` for boolean built-in types, and to `null` for reference types (an example of an array of reference types is provided at the end of this section).

FIGURE 7.4 The Results of the Allocation `temperature = new double[6];`

[2]An alternative and less common declaration syntax, except for `main`'s argument, is to place the array's name after the brackets rather than before them. Thus, the declarations `double temperature[];` and `double []temperature;` are equivalent.

As always with reference types, the declaration and allocation statements can be combined into a single statement. Thus, the previous declaration and allocation of the `temperature` array can also be accomplished with the single statement

```
double temperature[] = new double[6];
```

Although `temperature` is truly a reference variable distinct from the array it locates, common usage refers to the array by its reference variable name. Thus, although not technically correct, conventional usage would refer to the newly created array as the `temperature` array. We will frequently adhere to this convention.

A common programming practice is to define the number of array items as a symbolic constant before allocating the array. Using this convention, the declaration and allocation of the `temperature` array would appear as either

```
final int NUMELS = 6;   // define a constant for the number of items
double temperature[];  // declare the array
temperature = new double[NUMELS];    // allocate the array
```

or

```
final int NUMELS = 6;    // define a constant for the number of items
double temperature[] = new double[NUMELS]  // declare and allocate the array
```

Further examples of array declarations using symbolic constants are:

```
final int ARRAYSIZE = 4; // this creates the symbolic constant
char code[] = new char[ARRAYSIZE];    // declare and allocate the array

final int NUMELS = 5;
int volts[] = new int[NUMELS];

final int SIZE = 100;
float amount[] = new float[SIZE];
```

In these examples, the reference variable named `code` has been declared and refers to an array capable of holding four characters, the array referenced by the variable `volts` has storage reserved for five integer numbers, and the array referenced by the variable `amount` has storage reserved for 100 double-precision numbers. The symbolic constants ARRAYSIZE, NUMELS, and SIZE are programmer-selected names. Figure 7.5 illustrates the storage reserved for the arrays referenced by `volts` and `code`.

Each item in an array is called an **element** or **component** of the array. The individual elements in the arrays in Figure 7.5 are stored sequentially, with the first array element stored in the first reserved location, the second element stored in the second reserved location, and so on until the last element is stored in the last reserved location. This contiguous storage allocation for the list is a key feature of arrays because it provides a mechanism for easily locating any single element in the list.

Since elements in the array are stored sequentially, any individual element can be accessed by giving the name of the array and the element's position. This position is called

FIGURE 7.5   The Arrays Referenced by `volts` and `code`

the element's **index** or **subscript** value (the terms are synonymous). For a one-dimensional array, the first element has an index of 0, the second element has an index of 1, and so on. In Java, the array name and index of the desired element are combined by listing the index in brackets after the array name. For example, for the `volts` illustrated in Figure 7.5

> `volts[0]` refers to the first value stored in the `volts` array
> `volts[1]` refers to the second value stored in the `volts` array
> `volts[2]` refers to the third value stored in the `volts` array
> `volts[3]` refers to the fourth value stored in the `volts` array
> `volts[4]` refers to the fifth value stored in the `volts` array

Figure 7.6 illustrates the `volts` array in memory with the correct designation for each array element. Each individual element is referred to as an **indexed variable** or a **subscripted variable** because both a variable name and an index or subscript value must be used to reference the element. Remember that the index or subscript value gives *the position* of the element in the array.

The subscripted variable, `volts[0]`, is read as "volts sub zero." This is a shortened way of saying "the volts array subscripted by zero" and distinguishes the first element in an array from a scalar variable that could be declared as `volts0`. Similarly, `volts[1]` is read as "volts sub one," `volts[2]` as "volts sub two," and so on.

Although it may seem unusual to designate the first element with an index of zero, doing so increases the computer's speed when it accesses array elements. Internally, unseen by the programmer, the program uses the index as an offset from the array's starting position. As illustrated in Figure 7.7, the index tells the computer how many elements to skip, starting from the beginning of the array, to reach the desired element. The location of the beginning of the array, as has been noted, is the value stored in the reference variable created when the array is allocated.

FIGURE 7.6   Identifying Individual Array Elements

FIGURE 7.7　Accessing an Individual Array Element: Element 3

Subscripted variables can be used anywhere that scalar variables are valid. Examples using the elements of the volts array are:

```
volts[0] = 95.75;
volts[1] = volts[0] - 11.0;
volts[2] = 5.0 * volts[0];
volts[3] = 79.0;
volts[4] = (volts[1] + volts[2] - 3.1) / 2.2;
sum = volts[0] + volts[1] + volts[2] + volts[3] + volts[4];
```

The subscript contained within brackets need not be an integer constant; any expression that evaluates to an integer may be a subscript. In each case, of course, the value of the expression must be within the valid subscript range defined when the array is declared. For example, assuming that i and j are int variables, the following subscripted variables are valid:

```
volts[i]
volts[2*i]
volts[j-i]
```

One extremely important advantage of integer expressions as subscripts is that they allow sequencing through an array by using a loop. This makes statements such as

```
sum = volts[0] + volts[1] + volts[2] + volts[3] + volts[4];
```

unnecessary. The subscript values in this statement can be replaced by a for loop counter to access each element in the array sequentially. For example, the code

```
sum = 0;                    // initialize the sum to zero
for (i = 0; i < NUMELS; i++)
   sum = sum + volts[i];    // add in a volt
```

sequentially retrieves each array element and adds the element to sum. Here the variable i is both the counter in the for loop and a subscript. As i increases by 1 each time through the loop, the next element in the array is referenced. The symbolic constant

NUMELS, which in this case is 5, is typically the same symbolic constant used when the array was allocated. This procedure for adding the array elements within the for loop is similar to the accumulation procedure you have seen many times before.

The advantage of using a for loop to sequence through an array becomes apparent when working with larger arrays. For example, if the volts array contained 100 values rather than only 5, setting the constant NUMELS to 100 is sufficient to allocate the larger array and to have the for statement sequence through all 100 elements and add each volts value to the sum.

A very useful consequence of array storage in Java is that the size of the array is automatically stored in a variable named length. Thus, the exact size of any array can be obtained by prefixing this variable with the name of the desired array. For example, if temperature is an array containing five elements, the identifier temperature.length will have the value 5 stored in it. Using this variable, the previous loop used to sum all of the values of the temperature array can be written as:

```
sum = 0;                        // initialize the sum to zero
for (i = 0; i < temperature.length; i++)
  sum = sum + temperature[i];     // add in a temperature
```

As another example of using a for loop to sequence through an array, assume that we want to locate the maximum value in an array of 1000 elements named temperature. Our procedure to locate the maximum value is to assume initially that the first element in the array is the largest number. Then, as we sequence through the array, the maximum is compared to each element. When an element with a higher value is located, that element becomes the new maximum. The following code does the job:

```
maximum = temperature[0];            // set the maximum to element zero
for (int i = 1; i < temperature.length; i++)  // cycle through the rest of the array
  if (temperature[i] > maximum)        // compare each element to the maximum
    maximum = temperature[i];     // capture the new high value
```

In this code, the for statement consists of one if statement. The search for a new maximum value starts with the element 1 of the array and continues through the last element. Assuming that temperature is a 1000-element array, the variable temperature.length will have the value 1000. This is the length of the array whose first element is designated as temperature[0] and last element is temperature[999]. In this code, each element is compared to the current maximum, and when a higher value is encountered, it becomes the new maximum.

Performance Note

An expression such as

```
for (i = 0; i < temperature.length; i++)
```

forces a repeated call to obtain the value temperature.length each time the loop is traversed. For most arrays, the additional time in obtaining this value is negligible. However, for very large arrays, performance can be enhanced by removing the repeated reference to a single reference outside the loop. For example, the sequence of statements

```
size = temperature.length;
for (i = 0; i < size; i++)
```

obtains the value of `temperature.length` only once and then uses this value repeatedly throughout the loop. When the size of the array is known to be small, the more compact single-line code that includes the length reference within the `for` statement is acceptable. However, if the array is either known to be very large or the size is not known beforehand, the second two-line code is preferred. You will see both in your programming career.

Removing the reference to an array's size within the `for` statement follows a more general programming rule that you should be aware of. This rule is: Wherever it is possible to remove a repeated computation or call from within a loop that has a significant number of repetitions (generally, more than 50) and place a single computation or call before the start of the loop, this should be done. For loops with small numbers of repetitions, this rule is generally of no concern because the increased performance obtained is so negligible as not to warrant increasing the lines of code necessary for its adherence.

Input and Output of Array Values

Individual array elements can be assigned values interactively in the same manner as scalar variables, using either a keyboard `readLine()` or `showInputDialog()` method. For example, the statements

```
s1 = JOptionPane.showInputDialog("Enter a temperature");
temperature[0] = Integer.parseInt(s1);
```

cause a single value to be read and stored in the variable named `temperature[0]`.

Alternatively, a `for` loop can cycle through the array for interactive data input. For example, the code

```
for (int i = 0; i < temperature.length; i++)
{
  JOptionPane.showInputDialog("Enter a temperature: ");
  temperature[i] = Integer.parseInt(s1);
}
```

prompts the user for five temperatures.[3] The first temperature entered is stored in `temperature[0]`, the second in `temperature[1]`, and so on until five temperatures have been input.

It should be noted that when accessing an array element, Java does check the value of the index being used at run time (called a **bounds check**). Thus, if an array has been declared as consisting of five elements, for example, and you use an index of 5, which is outside the bounds of the array (remember, the index goes from 0 to 4), Java will notify you of an `ArrayIndexOutOfBounds` exception when the offending index is used to access the nonexistent element at run time.

---

[3]An equivalent statement is `for (int i = 0; i <= temperature.length - 1; i++)`. Which statement you use is a matter of choice.

AGGREGATE DATA TYPES

An array object is considered an aggregate data type. This type, which is also referred to as a **structured type** and a **data structure**, is any type whose individual elements are other data types and whose elements are related by some defined structure. In addition, operations must be available for retrieving and updating individual values in the data structure.

In a one-dimensional array, such as an array of integers, the array is composed of individual integer values where integers are related by their position in the list. Indexed variables provide the means of accessing and modifying values in the array.

During output, individual array elements can be displayed by the `print()` and `println()` methods, or complete sections of the array can be displayed by these methods within a `for` loop. Examples of a `println()` method to display subscripted variables are:

```
System.out.println(temperature[5]);
```

and

```
System.out.println("The value of element " + i + " is "
                + temperature[i]);
```

and

```
for (int k = 5; k < 21; k++)
   System.out.println("index = " k + "    value = " + amount[k]);
```

The first `println()` call displays the value of the subscripted variable `temperature[5]`. The second `println()` call displays the value of the subscript `i` and the value of `temperature[i]`. Before this statement can be executed, `i` needs to have an assigned value. The final example includes a `println()` call within a `for` loop. Both the value of the index and the value of the elements from 5 to 20 are displayed.

Program 7.1 illustrates these input and output techniques using an array named `temperature` that is defined to store five integer numbers. Two `for` loops are in the program. The first `for` loop cycles through each array element and allows the user to input individual array values. After five values have been entered, the second `for` loop displays the stored values. Assuming that the temperatures 85, 90, 78, 75, and 92 are entered when Program 7.1 is executed, the following output is produced:

```
temperature[0] is 85
temperature[1] is 90
temperature[2] is 78
temperature[3] is 75
temperature[4] is 92
```

PROGRAM 7.1

```java
import javax.swing.*;
public class ElementInputAndDisplay
{

  public static void main(String[] args)
  {
    final int NUMELS = 5;

    String s1;
    int i;
    int temperature[];              // declare the array
    temperature = new int[NUMELS]; // allocate the array

    for (i = 0; i < NUMELS; i++)     // enter the temperatures
    {
      s1 = JOptionPane.showInputDialog("Enter a temperature: ");
      temperature[i] = Integer.parseInt(s1);
    }

    for (i = 0; i < NUMELS; i++)     // print() the temperatures
      System.out.println("temperature[" +i +"] is " + temperature[i]);

    System.exit(0);
  }
}
```

In reviewing the output produced by Program 7.1, pay particular attention to the difference between the subscript value displayed and the numerical value stored in the corresponding array element. The subscript value refers to the location of the element in the array, whereas the subscripted variable refers to the numerical value stored in the designated location.

In addition to displaying the values stored in each array element, the elements can also be processed by appropriately referencing the desired element. For example, in Program 7.2, the value of each element is accumulated in a total, which is displayed upon completion of the individual display of each array element. Again assuming temperatures of 85, 90, 78, 75, and 92, the following output is displayed when Program 7.2 is executed:

```
The total of the temperatures  85   90   78   75  92  is   420
```

Notice that in Program 7.2, unlike Program 7.1, only the values stored in each array element are displayed. Although the second for loop accumulates the total of each element, the accumulation could also have been accomplished in the first loop by placing the statement total = total + temperature[i]; after the call to showInputDialog() enters a value. Also notice that the System.out.print() call that displays the total is made outside

PROGRAM 7.2

```java
import javax.swing.*;
public class AccumulateElements
{
  public static void main(String[] args)
  {
    final int NUMELS = 5;

    String s1;
    int i;
    int total = 0;
      // declare and allocate the array
    int temperature[] = new int[NUMELS]; // allocate the array

    for (i = 0; i < NUMELS; i++)    // enter the temperatures
    {
      s1 = JOptionPane.showInputDialog("Enter a temperature: ");
      temperature[i] = Integer.parseInt(s1);
    }

    System.out.print("The total of the temperatures");

    for (i = 0; i < NUMELS; i++)     // display and total the temperatures
    {
        System.out.print("  " + temperature[i]);
        total =  total + temperature[i];
    }

    System.out.print(" is " + total);

    System.exit(0);
  }
}
```

the second for loop so that the total is displayed only once, after all values have been added to the total. If this System.out.print() call is placed inside the for loop, five totals would be displayed, with only the last displayed total containing the sum of all the array values.

String Arrays[4]

In addition to arrays of primitive data types, such as arrays of ints and doubles, arrays of reference data types may also be constructed. For example, the declaration and alloca-

---

[4]This topic can be omitted on first reading without loss of subject continuity.

tion of an array of four strings named names can be constructed with either the declaration and allocation statements

```
String names[];
names = new String[4];
```

or the single statement

```
String names[] = new String[4];
```

Once the array has been allocated, individual elements can be assigned values by specifying an element name and supplying it with a string value. For example, the statements

```
names[0] = "Joe";
names[1] = "Harriet";
names[2] = "Allyn";
names[3] = "Roberta";
```

would assign the string values "Joe", "Harriet", "Allyn", and "Roberta" to the respective names' elements. The declaration and allocation of a string array and the use of the previous four assignment statements to initialize values into the array elements are illustrated in Program 7.3.

PROGRAM 7.3

```
public class StringArray
{
  public static void main(String[] args)
  {
    int i;
    String names[];          // declare the array
    names = new String[4]; // allocate the array

       // assign values to each array element
    names[0] = "Joe";
    names[1] = "Harriet";
    names[2] = "Allyn";
    names[3] = "Roberta";

       // display the names
    for (i = 0; i < names.length; i++)
      System.out.println("names[" + i + "] is " + names[i]);
  }
}
```

The output displayed by Program 7.3 is:

```
names[0] is Joe
names[1] is Harriet
names[2] is Allyn
names[3] is Roberta
```

It should be noted that arrays of reference types, such as strings, are stored differently from arrays of built-in data types. For example, Figures 7.8a through 7.8c illustrate how the array of four strings created in Program 7.3 is stored in memory. As shown, the declaration statement `String names[];` defines a reference variable named names that will store the address of an array. This first step is identical to that performed for an array of a built-in data type. The actual allocation of the array, which is performed by the statement `names = new String[4];`, is where the process for reference types differs from that for built-in types. As shown in Figure 7.8b, an array is created that is capable of storing four references, each of which initially contains a null address. Only when we assign an actual string value, as shown in Figure 7.8c, is the storage for the string created and the address of the string stored in the array. If the array were an array of built-in data types, the actual values would be stored directly in the array rather than a reference to the value, as in Figure 7.8c.

Although each value referenced in the string array in Figure 7.8c is accessed in an identical manner as a built-in data type by giving the array name and index value, as in

names

A reference variable

FIGURE 7.8a   The Declaration String names[]; Creates a Single Reference Variable

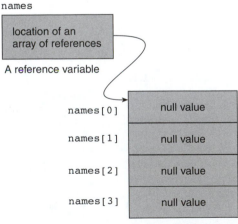

FIGURE 7.8b   The Allocation names = new String[4] Creates an Array of References

names

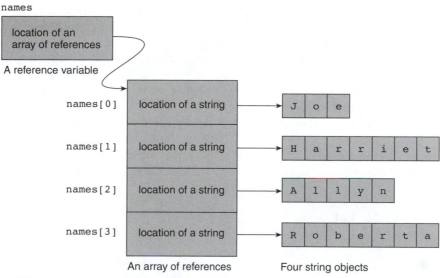

FIGURE 7.8c   The Assignment of Values Creates Actual Array Objects

names[2], it is worthwhile being aware that the actual allocation of storage is different. The reason for this storage is that each element can have a different length, which can only be determined when a string value is actually assigned.

Once a string value has been assigned to an array element, a subsequent assignment can replace the existing string with a new string. For example, assuming the four string assignments have been made in Program 7.3, resulting in the storage allocation shown in Figure 7.8c, the assignment

```
names[2] = "Louisa"
```

creates a new string and replaces the reference value in names[2] to correctly reference this new string value. Also notice that, from a strictly programming standpoint, a reference type is accessed in an identical manner as a built-in data type by using the array's name and an index value (Figure 7.9). Thus, the additional level of internal storage required when using arrays of references is in effect hidden from a programming perspective and does not affect the way individual elements are accessed.

Run-Time Dimensioning

In addition to specifying the size of an array at compile time, as has been done in all of the example programs presented so far, the size of the array can also be entered interactively

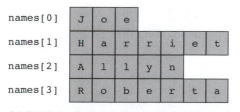

FIGURE 7.9   A Programming View of the names Array

at run time. The entered value can then allocate space for the array using the new operator. Because the size of an array is referred to as its dimension, sizing an array at run time is also referred to as run-time dimensioning.

As a specific example of run-time dimensioning, consider the sequence of instructions

```
s1 = JOptionPane.showInputDialog("Enter the number of temperatures to be processed: ");
numtemps = Integer.parseInt(s1);
int temperature[] = new int[numtemps]; // declare and allocate the array
```

In this sequence of instructions, the actual dimension of the allocated temperature array depends on the value input by the user. Program 7.4 illustrates this sequence of code in the context of a complete program.

PROGRAM 7.4

```
import javax.swing.*;
public class RunTimeDimension
{
  public static void main(String[] args)
  {
    inti, numtemps;
    String s1;

    s1 = JOptionPane.showInputDialog("Enter the number of temperatures to be processed: ");
    numtemps = Integer.parseInt(s1);

    int temperature[] = new int[numtemps]; // allocate the array

    System.out.println("An array was created for " + numtemps + " integers.");
    System.out.println(" The values stored in the array have been initialized to:");
    for (i = 0; i < numtemps; i++)
      System.out.println("temperature[" +i +"] is " + temperature[i]);

    System.exit(0);
  }
}
```

Following is a sample display produced by Program 7.4 in response to a user input of 10 when the program was run:

```
An array was created for 10 integers.
 The values stored in the array have been initialized to:
temperature[0] is 0
temperature[1] is 0
temperature[2] is 0
temperature[3] is 0
temperature[4] is 0
```

```
temperature[5] is 0
temperature[6] is 0
temperature[7] is 0
temperature[8] is 0
temperature[9] is 0
```

EXERCISES 7.1

1. Write array declarations and allocation statements for the following:
   a. a list of 100 integer voltages
   b. a list of 50 floating-point temperatures
   c. a list of 30 characters, each representing a code
   d. a list of 100 integer years
   e. a list of 32 floating-point velocities
   f. a list of 1000 floating-point distances
   g. a list of 6 integer code numbers

2. Write appropriate notation for the first, third, and seventh elements of the following arrays:
   a. `int grades[20]`
   b. `double volts[10]`
   c. `double amps[16]`
   d. `int dist[15]`
   e. `double velocity[25]`
   f. `double time[100]`

3. a. Using a `showInputDialog()` method and suitable parsing method, write statements that can enter values into the first, third, and seventh elements of each of the arrays declared in Exercises 2a through 2f.
   b. Write a `for` loop that can enter values for the complete array declared in Exercise 2a.

4. a. Write individual statements that can display the values from the first, third, and seventh elements of each of the arrays declared in Exercises 2a through 2f.
   b. Write a `for` loop that can display values for the complete array declared in Exercise 2a.

5. List the elements that will be displayed by the following sections of code:
   a. ```
   for (m = 1; m <= 5; m++)
       System.out.print(a[m] + " ");
   ```
   b. ```
   for (k = 1; k <= 5; k = k + 2)
       System.out.print(a[k] + " ");
   ```
   c. ```
   for (j = 3; j <= 10; j++)
       System.out.print(b[j] + " ");
   ```
   d. ```
   for (k = 3; k <= 12; k = k + 3)
       System.out.print(b[k] + " ");
   ```
   e. ```
   for (i = 2; i < 11; i = i + 2)
       System.out.print(c[i] + " ");
   ```

6. a. Write a Java program to input the following values into an array named `volts`: 10.95, 16.32, 12.15, 8.22, 15.98, 26.22, 13.54, 6.45, 17.59. After the data are entered, have your program output the values.
   ```

b. Repeat Exercise 6a, but after the data are entered, have your program display them in the following form:

```
10.95       16.32       12.15
 8.22       15.98       26.22
13.54        6.45       17.59
```

7. Write a Java program to input eight integer numbers into an array named `temp`. As each number is input, add the number to a total. After all numbers are input, display the numbers and their average.

8. **a.** Write a Java program to input 10 integer numbers into an array named `fmax` and determine the maximum value entered. Your program should contain only one loop, and the maximum should be determined immediately after array element values are input. (*Tip:* Set the maximum equal to the first array element, which should be input before the loop used to input the remaining array values.)

   b. Repeat Exercise 8a, keeping track of both the maximum element in the array and the index number for the maximum. After displaying the numbers, display these two messages:

   ```
   The maximum value is: xxx
   This is element number xx in the list of numbers
   ```

   Have your program display the correct values in place of the xs in the messages.

   c. Repeat Exercise 8b, but have your program locate the minimum value of the data entered.

9. **a.** Write a Java program to input the following integer numbers into an array named `grades`: 89, 95, 72, 83, 99, 54, 86, 75, 92, 73, 79, 75, 82, 73. As each number is input, add the numbers to a total. After all numbers are input and the total is obtained, calculate the average of the numbers and use the average to determine the deviation of each value from the average. Store each deviation in an array named `deviation`. Each deviation is obtained as the element value less the average of all the data. Have your program display each deviation alongside its corresponding element from the `temperature` array.

   b. Calculate the variance of the data in Exercise 9a. The variance is obtained by squaring each individual deviation and dividing the sum of the squared deviations by the number of deviations.

10. Write a Java program that specifies three one-dimensional arrays named `current`, `resistance`, and `volts`. Each array should be capable of holding 10 elements. Using a `for` loop, input values for the `current` and `resistance` arrays. The entries in the `volts` array should be the product of the corresponding values in the `current` and `resistance` arrays (thus, `volts[i]` = `current[i]` * `resistance[i]`). After all the data have been entered, display the following output:

    ```
    Current        Resistance      Volts
    -------        ----------      -----
    ```

    Display the appropriate value under each column heading.

11. **a.** Write a program that inputs 10 double-precision numbers into an array named `raw`. After 10 user-input numbers are entered into the array, your program should cycle through `raw` 10 times. During each pass through the

array, your program should select the lowest value in `raw` and place the selected value in the next available slot in an array named `sorted`. Thus, when your program is complete, the `sorted` array should contain the numbers in `raw` in sorted order from lowest to highest. (*Tip:* Make sure to reset the lowest value selected during each pass to a very high number so that it is not selected again. You will need a second `for` loop within the first `for` loop to locate the minimum value for each pass.)

    b. The method in Exercise 11a to sort the values in the array is very inefficient. Can you determine why? What might be a better method of sorting the numbers in an array?

12. a. Write declaration statements to store the string `"Input the Following Data"` in an array named `message1`, the string `"------------------------"` (24 dashes) in an array named `message2`, the string `"Enter the Date: "` in an array named `message3`, and the string `"Enter the Account Number: "` in an array named `message4`.

    b. Include the arrays constructed in Exercise 12a in a program that uses `println()` methods to display the messages. For example, the statement `System.out.println(message1);` causes the string stored in the `message1` array to be displayed. Your program will require four such statements to display the four individual messages.

13. Program 7.4 uses a single statement both to declare and to allocate space for the `temperature` array. Many programmers prefer to place all declarations at the top of a method to make them immediately visible to anyone reading the program. To accomplish this, modify Program 7.4 by placing the declaration statement `int temperature[];` with the other declarations at the top of the program and change the statement `int temperature[] = new int[numtemps];` so that it only allocates space for the `temperature` array. Compile and execute your program to ensure that it operates correctly.

14. Modify Program 7.4 to enable a user to enter values into each element of the `temperature` array after the array has been created.

7.2 ARRAY INITIALIZATION

Array elements can be initialized within their declaration statements in the same manner as scalar variables, but the initializing elements must be included in braces and the size of the array *must not* be specified. When an initializing list of values is supplied, the array's size is automatically determined by the number of values in the initializing list. Examples of such initializations are:

```
int temperature[] = {98, 87, 92, 79, 85};
char codes[] = {'s', 'a', 'm', 'p', 'l', 'e'};
double slopes[] = {10.96, 6.43, 2.58, .86, 5.89, 7.56, 8.22};
```

As shown, an initializing list consists of a set of comma-separated values that are enclosed in braces. Values within the braces are applied in the order they are written, with the first value used to initialize element 0, the second value used to initialize element 1, and so on until all values have been used. Thus, in the declaration

```
int temperature[] = {98, 87, 92, 79, 85};
```

temperature[0] is initialized to 98, temperature[1] is initialized to 87, temperature[2] is initialized to 92, temperature[3] is initialized to 79, and temperature[4] is initialized to 85. Notice that declarations that include an initializing list do not require explicit allocation using the new operator in a similar manner as a string is initialized when it is declared.

Since Java ignores whitespace, initializations may be continued across multiple lines. For example, in the declaration

```
int gallons[] = {19, 16, 14, 19, 20, 18,   // initializing values
                 12, 10, 22, 15, 18, 17,   // may extend across
                 16, 14, 23, 19, 15, 18,   // multiple lines
                 21, 5};
```

four lines are used to initialize all of the array elements.

Unfortunately, there is no method of either indicating repetition of an initialization value or initializing later array elements without first specifying values for earlier elements. Thus, when supplying an initializing list, all elements must be supplied with a specific value, and the final size of the array is determined by the number of values in the list. Also, as noted previously, the size of the array must not be included within the brackets, [] if a specific size is included, the compiler will provide the error message Can't specify array dimension in a declaration.

An array of characters cannot be initialized with a string. Thus, the valid Java declaration

```
char code[] = {'s', 'a', 'm', 'p', 'l', 'e'};
```

cannot be replaced by the declaration

```
char code[] = "sample";    // THIS IS INVALID
```

Attempting to initialize a character array with a string results in the compiler error message Can't convert java.lang.String to char[]. An array of strings, however, is valid, and such arrays can be initialized by string values when they are declared. For example, the declaration

```
String names[] ={"Joe", "Harriet", "Allyn", "Roberta"};
```

creates an array of four strings and initializes the four string elements with the string values Joe, Harriet, Allyn, and Roberta, respectively. Program 7.5 uses this declaration statement within the context of a complete program. The output produced by Program 7.5 is:

```
names[0] is Joe
names[1] is Harriet
names[2] is Allyn
names[3] is Roberta
```

PROGRAM 7.5

```java
public class InitializeNames
{
  public static void main(String[] args)
  {
    int i;
    String names[] = {"Joe", "Harriet", "Allyn", "Roberta"};

      // display the names
    for (i = 0; i < names.length; i++)
      System.out.println("names[" + i + "] is " + names[i]);
  }
}
```

Once values have been assigned to array elements, either through initialization within the declaration statement, assignment, or using interactive input, the array elements can be processed as described in the previous section. For example, Program 7.6 illustrates element initialization within the declaration of the array and then uses a for loop to locate the maximum value stored in the array.

PROGRAM 7.6

```java
public class FindMaxValue
{
  public static void main(String[] args)
  {
    int i, max;
    int nums[] = {2, 18, 1, 27, 16};

    max = nums[0];

    for (i = 1; i < nums.length; i++)
      if (max < nums[i])
        max = nums[i];

    System.out.println("The maximum value is " + max);
  }
}
```

The output produced by Program 7.6 is:

```
The maximum value is 27
```

Deep and Shallow Copies[5]

In addition to allocating and initializing arrays using the various methods presented, an array can be allocated and initialized using the `System.arraycopy()` method. This method copies a user-specified number of elements from one array, referred to as the **source array**, to a second array, referred to as the **target array**. The method requires five arguments and has the syntax

```
System.arraycopy(source array name, starting source element index,
                 target array name, starting target element index,
                 number of elements to be copied);
```

For example, the statement

```
System.arraycopy(nums, 1, newnums, 2, 3);
```

causes three elements (this is the last argument) to be copied from an array named `nums` (the source array name, which is the first argument) into the `newnums` array (the target array, which is the third argument). The copy will begin at `nums[1]`, which will be copied to `newnums[2]`, and proceed sequentially until three elements have been copied. Similarly, the statement

```
System.arraycopy(nums, 0, newnums, 0, nums.length);
```

will cause all elements in `nums` to be copied and stored into the array named `newnums`. The only restriction in using the `System.arraycopy()` method is that the target array must be allocated as sufficiently large to accommodate the copied elements. Failure to do so will result in a run-time `ArrayIndexOutOfBoundsException` error message. Program 7.7 illustrates an `arraycopy()` method within the context of a complete program.

In analyzing Program 7.7, first notice that the declaration statement for `newnums` uses the `new` operator to allocate the same number of elements as exist in `nums`. Figure 7.10 illustrates the storage allocation provided by the declaration statements for both `nums`

FIGURE 7.10   Initial Allocation for the Arrays Declared in Program 7.7

[5]This topic can be omitted on first reading with no loss of subject continuity.

PROGRAM 7.7

```java
public class DeepCopy
{
  public static void main(String[] args)
  {
    int i, max;
    int nums[] = {2, 18, 1, 27, 16};
    int newnums[] = new int[nums.length];

    // copy all elements from nums to newnums
    System.arraycopy(nums, 0, newnums, 0, nums.length);

    newnums[2] = 50;  // this only affects newnums
    // display newnums
    for (i = 0; i < newnums.length; i++)
      System.out.println("newnums[" + i + "] is " + newnums[i]);

    System.out.println();

    // display nums
    for (i = 0; i < nums.length; i++)
      System.out.println("nums[" + i + "] is " + nums[i]);
  }
}
```

and newnums. As shown in this figure, two distinct arrays have been constructed, with all of the elements in newnums initialized to zero.

Immediately after the call to arraycopy(), the storage allocation for the two arrays is as shown in Figure 7.11. In this figure, notice that each individual array value in nums has been copied to newnums. This type of complete, element-by-element copy is referred to as a **deep copy.**

nums[0]   nums[1]   nums[2]   nums[3]   nums[4]

| 2 | 18 | 1 | 27 | 16 |

| 2 | 18 | 1 | 27 | 16 |

newnums[0] newnums[1] newnums[2] newnums[3] newnums[4]

FIGURE 7.11   After the Call to System.arraycopy()

The display produced by Program 7.7 is:

```
newnums[0] is 2
newnums[1] is 18
newnums[2] is 50
newnums[3] is 27
newnums[4] is 16

nums[0] is 2
nums[1] is 18
nums[2] is 1
nums[3] is 27
nums[4] is 16
```

In reviewing this output, notice that the assignment to `newnums[2]`, which is made after the copy, has no effect on the values in `nums`. This is what we would expect because the deep copy provided by the `arraycopy()` method preserves the distinct nature of the two arrays created within the program.

In contrast to a deep copy, a **shallow copy** is produced when an array assignment is executed. As an example of a shallow copy, consider Program 7.8.

PROGRAM 7.8

```java
public class ShallowCopy
{
  public static void main(String[] args)
  {
    int i;
    int nums[] = {2, 18, 1, 27, 16};
    int newnums[] = new int[nums.length];

    // this produces a shallow copy
    newnums = nums;  // this only copies the address
    newnums[2] = 50;  // this affects both newnums and nums, because
                      // they are the same array

    // display newnums
    for (i = 0; i < newnums.length; i++)
      System.out.println("newnums[" + i + "] is " + newnums[i]);
    System.out.println();

    // display nums and note the change
    for (i = 0; i < nums.length; i++)
      System.out.println("nums[" + i + "] is " + nums[i]);
  }
}
```

In analyzing Program 7.8, pay attention to the assignment statement `newnums =` `nums;`. All that this statement accomplishes is to copy the address that is stored in `nums` into the reference variable `newnums`. Once this statement is executed, the storage allocation for the two arrays will be that shown in Figure 7.12.

As seen in Figure 7.12, both reference variables, `nums` and `newnums`, now refer to the same array. In effect, all that we have accomplished by this statement is to force `newnums` to be an alias for `nums`, and we now have two array names for the same array. The output produced by Program 7.8 is:

```
newnums[0] is 2
newnums[1] is 18
newnums[2] is 50
newnums[3] is 27
newnums[4] is 16

nums[0] is 2
nums[1] is 18
nums[2] is 50
nums[3] is 27
nums[4] is 16
```

The equivalence between the two array names illustrated in Figure 7.12 is verified by this output that shows the new value assigned to `newnums[2]` is displayed when the value of `nums[2]` is displayed. The storage area initially allocated for the array object referenced by `newnums`, now that this area no longer has any reference variables pointing to it, will be automatically erased when Java's automatic memory cleansing program is run or when Program 7.8 finishes executing, whichever comes first. As an aside, because

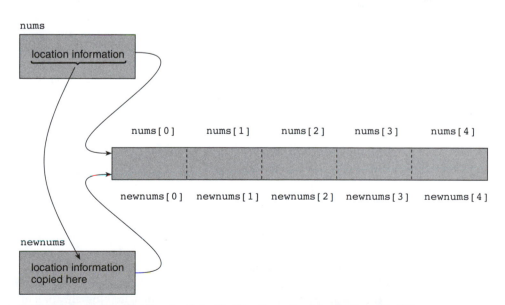

FIGURE 7.12 The Result of the Shallow Copy Provided by Program 7.8

Program 7.8 never uses the storage allocated to the array initially located by newnums and simply assigns the address in nums to the reference variable newnums, the declaration statement for newnums did not need to use the new operator to allocate space for the array. In this program, the declaration int newnums[];, which creates the newnum reference variable, is sufficient for the program to compile and run.

Although shallow, as opposed to deep, array copies are not frequently used in programming practice, there is one programming situation that does make good use of such a copy. Where this situation can occur is explored in Exercise 10.

EXERCISES 7.2

1. Write array declarations, including initializers, for the following:
   a. a list of the ten integer voltages: 89, 75, 82, 93, 78, 95, 81, 88, 77, 82
   b. a list of the five double-precision slopes: 10.62, 13.98, 18.45, 12.68, 14.76
   c. a list of the six double-precision interest distances: 6.29, 6.95, 7.25, 7.35, 7.40, 7.42
   d. a list of the ten floating-point temperatures: 78.2, 69.6, 68.5, 83.9, 55.4, 67.0, 49.8, 58.3, 62.5, 71.6
   e. a list of the seven character codes: f, j, m, q, t, w, z

2. Write an array declaration statement that stores the following values in an array named volts: 16.24, 18.98, 23.75, 16.29, 19.54, 14.22, 11.13, 15.39. Include these statements in a program that displays the values in the array.

3. Write a program that uses an array declaration statement to initialize the following numbers in an array named slopes: 17.24, 25.63, 5.94, 33.92, 3.71, 32.84, 35.93, 18.24, 6.92. Your program should locate and display the maximum and minimum values in the array.

4. Write a program that stores the following numbers in an array named resistance: 16, 27, 39, 56, and 81. Your program should also create two arrays named current and power, each capable of storing five double-precision numbers. Use a for loop and have your program accept five user-input numbers into the current array when the program is run. Your program should store the product of the corresponding values of the square of the current and resistance array in the power array—for example, power[1] = resistance[1] * Math.pow(current[1],2)—and display the following output (fill in the table appropriately):

```
Resistance      Current      Power
----------      -------      ------
16                 .            .
27                 .            .
39                 .            .
56                 .            .
81                 .            .

                              ------
Total:                          .
```

5. Enter and execute Program 7.6 on your computer.
6. The characters Good Morning are to be stored in a character array named stringChars. Write the declaration, allocation, and initialization of this array using both one and two statements.

7. Enter and execute Program 7.7 on your computer.

8. Enter and execute Program 7.8 on your computer.

9. Change the declaration statement for `newnums` in both Programs 7.7 and 7.8 to `int newnums[];`. Explain why this modification results in a run-time error for Program 7.7 but does not affect the execution of Program 7.8.

10. Java does not provide an explicit redimensioning statement that can change an array's dimension at run time. When such an array redimensioning becomes necessary, it can be accomplished by the following steps:

    a. Allocating an array of the desired new size

    b. Performing a deep copy of array elements from the original array to the new array

    c. Performing a shallow copy of the new array's name to the original array's name

    This last step makes the reference variable name for the original array reference the newly dimensioned array. Construct a Java program that initially creates and stores the integer values 10, 20, 30, and 40 into an array named `original`. Then permit a user to enter a value greater than 4. Once a value has been entered, use the foregoing steps to dynamically allocate a new array named `bigarray`, copy the values from `original` to `bigarray`, and change `new`'s value to point to the new array. Finally, display the values in the expanded `original` array.

7.3 APPLICATIONS

Arrays are extremely useful in any application that requires multiple passes through the same set of data elements. Two such applications are presented in this section. The first application is a statistical data analysis requiring two passes through the data. The first pass inputs the list and determines the average of the data, and the second pass uses the average to determine a standard deviation.

The second application deals with sorting a list of data items and then searching the sorted list for a particular item. Although it is generally not necessary to sort a list before searching it, as you will see in Section 7.7, much faster searches are possible if the list is in sorted order. In this section, we introduce the fundamentals of both sorting and searching lists using the Java Arrays class' `sort()` and `search()` methods. Use of Java's `search()` method does require that the array elements be in sorted order.

Application 1: Statistical Analysis

For this application, a Java program is to be developed that accepts a list of user-entered voltages as input, determines both the average and standard deviation of these voltages, and then displays the results.

Step 1: Analyze the Problem   The statement of the problem indicates that two output values are required: an average and a standard deviation. In step 2, we will verify that we know how these values are to be calculated. The input item defined in the problem statement is a set of user-entered voltages. This means that any number of voltages could be input by the user when the program is executed. To accommodate for this, we will have to ask the user how many voltages he or she intends to input. Thus, the first input will be the number of voltages that will subsequently be entered.

Step 2: Develop a Solution   The I/O specification determined in step 1 defines that the user will enter two types of input: the number of voltages followed by the actual data. Based on this input, the program is to calculate and display the average and standard deviation of the data. These output items are determined as follows:

> *Calculate the average by adding the voltages and dividing by the number of voltages that were added.*
> *Determine the standard deviation by:*
>   *1. Subtracting the average from each individual voltage. This results in a set of new numbers, each of which is called a deviation.*
>   *2. Square each deviation found in the previous step.*
>   *3. Add the squared deviations and divide the sum by the number of deviations.*
>   *4. The square root of the number found in the previous step is the standard deviation.*

Notice that the calculation of the standard deviation requires the average, which means that the standard deviation can only be calculated after the average has been computed. This is the advantage of specifying the algorithm in detail before any coding is done; it ensures that all necessary inputs and requirements are discovered early in the programming process.

To ensure that we understand the required processing, we will do a hand calculation. For this calculation, we will assume that the average and standard deviation of the following 10 voltages are to be determined: 98, 82, 67, 54, 78, 83, 95, 76, 68, and 63.

The average of these data is determined as:

$$Average = (98 + 82 + 67 + 54 + 78 + 83 + 95 + 76 + 68 + 63)/10$$
$$= 76.4$$

The standard deviation is calculated by first determining the sum of the squared deviations. The standard deviation is then obtained by dividing the resulting sum by 10 and taking its square root.

$$
\begin{aligned}
\textit{Sum of squared deviations} = &(98 - 76.4)^2 \\
+ &(82 - 76.4)^2 \\
+ &(67 - 76.4)^2 \\
+ &(54 - 76.4)^2 \\
+ &(78 - 76.4)^2 \\
+ &(83 - 76.4)^2 \\
+ &(95 - 76.4)^2 \\
+ &(76 - 76.4)^2 \\
+ &(68 - 76.4)^2 \\
+ &(63 - 76.4)^2 \\
= &\ 1730.4007
\end{aligned}
$$

$$
\begin{aligned}
\textit{Standard deviation} &= \sqrt{1730.4007/10} \\
&= \sqrt{173.04007} \\
&= 13.154470
\end{aligned}
$$

Having specified the required algorithms, we are now in a position to code them.

Step 3: Code the Solution Program 7.9 presents the Java version of the selected algorithm. Notice that the program uses one `for` loop to enter and sum the individual voltages and a second `for` loop to determine the sum of the squared deviations. Because calculation of the squared deviations requires the average, the standard deviation only can be calculated after the average has been computed. Notice also that the termination value of the loop counter in both `for` loops is `numvolts`, which is the number of voltages input by the user. The use of this argument gives the program its generality and allows it to be used for lists of any number of voltages.

PROGRAM 7.9

```java
import java.io.*;    // needed to access input stream classes
import java.text.*; // needed for formatting
public class StandardDeviation
{
  public static void main (String[] args)
  throws java.io.IOException
  {
    String s1;
    int i, numvolts;
    double volt[];    // declare the array
    double average, stddev;
    double sumvolts = 0.0, sumdevs = 0.0;

    DecimalFormat df = new DecimalFormat("00.000000");
    // set up the basic input stream
      // needed for conversion capabilities
    InputStreamReader isr = new InputStreamReader(System.in);
      // needed to use readLine()
    BufferedReader br = new BufferedReader(isr);

    System.out.print("Enter the number of voltages to be analyzed: ");
    s1 = br.readLine();
    numvolts = Integer.parseInt(s1);

    // allocate the array
    volt = new double[numvolts];
    // read the input voltages and total them
    for (i = 0; i < numvolts; i++)
    {
      System.out.print("Enter voltage " + (i+1) + ": ");
      s1 = br.readLine();
      volt[i] = Double.parseDouble(s1);
      sumvolts = sumvolts + volt[i];
    }
```

(Continued on next page)

```
(Continued from previous page)
      // calculate and display the average
      average = sumvolts / numvolts;
      System.out.println("\nThe average of the voltages is "
                          + df.format(average));


      // calculate and display the standard deviation
      for (i = 0; i < numvolts; i++)
       sumdevs = sumdevs + Math.pow((volt[i] - average),2);
      stddev = Math.sqrt(sumdevs/numvolts);
      System.out.println("The standard deviation of the voltages is "
                          + df.format(stddev));

   }

  }
```

Step 4: Test and Correct the Program A test run of Program 7.9 produced the following display:

```
Enter the number of voltages to be analyzed: 10
Enter voltage 1: 98
Enter voltage 2: 82
Enter voltage 3: 67
Enter voltage 4: 54
Enter voltage 5: 78
Enter voltage 6: 83
Enter voltage 7: 95
Enter voltage 8: 76
Enter voltage 9: 68
Enter voltage 10: 63


The average of the voltages is   76.400000
The standard deviation of the voltages is 13.154467
```

Although this result agrees with our previous hand calculation, testing is really not complete without verifying the calculation at the boundary points. In this case, such a test consists of checking the calculation with all of the same values, such as all 0s and all 100s. Another simple test would be to use five 0s and five 100s. We leave these tests as an exercise.

Application 2: The `sort()` and `binarySearch()` Methods

A common requirement of many programs is to search a list for a given element. For example, in a list of names and telephone numbers, we might search for a specific name so that the corresponding telephone number can be printed, or we might wish to search the list simply to determine if a name is there.

Java provides two methods, named sort() and binarySearch(), that can conveniently sort and search an array. The sort() method, which uses a modified quicksort algorithm (described in Section 7.7) arranges the elements of an array into ascending (increasing) order, whereas the binarySearch() method searches an array for a specified value. Because binarySearch() uses a binary search algorithm (also described in Section 7.7), it requires a sorted array. Thus, in practice, the sort() method is typically called immediately before the binarySearch() method is invoked. Both methods are members of the Arrays class and, unless fully qualified names are used, require the import statement import java.util.*;.

In this application, we demonstrate these methods within the context of a complete program. As a specific example, consider Program 7.10, which permits keyboard entry of a user-specified number of integer values. Immediately after the values are entered, the program calls the sort() method to rearrange the elements into ascending order. Once the sort has been completed, the program requests the entry of a value that is subsequently an argument to the binarySearch() method. If this value is found in the array, binarySearch() returns its position in the array; otherwise, it returns a negative number. Because the search algorithm does not necessarily locate the first occurrence of a value that has multiple occurrences, a returned positive index number can be that of any of the duplicate values. The statements in Program 7.10 that use the sort() and binarySearch() methods have been boldfaced for easy identification.

PROGRAM 7.10

```java
import java.io.*;    // needed to access input stream classes
import java.util.*; // needed for sort() and binarySearch()
public class SearchSort
{
  public static void main (String[] args)
  throws java.io.IOException
  {
    String s1;
    int i, numels;
    int variousNums[];
    int item, location;

    // set up the basic input stream
      // needed for conversion capabilities
    InputStreamReader isr = new InputStreamReader(System.in);
      // needed to use readLine()
    BufferedReader br = new BufferedReader(isr);

    System.out.print("Enter the number of array values: ");
    s1 = br.readLine();
    numels = Integer.parseInt(s1);
```

(Continued on next page)

(Continued from previous page)

```java
        // allocate the array
        variousNums = new int[numels];
        // read the array values
        for (i = 0; i < numels; i++)
        {
          System.out.print("Enter element " + (i+1) + ": ");
          s1 = br.readLine();
          variousNums[i] = Integer.parseInt(s1);
        }

        // sort the array
        Arrays.sort(variousNums);

        // display the sorted array
        System.out.print("The values in sorted order are:");
        for (i = 0; i < numels; i++)
           System.out.print("  " + variousNums[i]);

        // now locate a desired element
        System.out.print("\n\nEnter the item you are searching for: ");
        s1 = br.readLine();
        item = Integer.parseInt(s1);

        location = Arrays.binarySearch(variousNums, item);

        if (location > 0)
          System.out.println("This item is at location "
                        + (location + 1) + " in the sorted array.");
        else
          System.out.println("This item is not in the list.");
    }
  }
```

Following is a sample run of Program 7.10, where the user enters five values into the array and then requests that the sorted array values be searched for a value of 80.

```
Enter the number of array values: 5
Enter element 1: 101
Enter element 2: 50
Enter element 3: 70
Enter element 4: 2
Enter element 5: 80
The values in sorted order are:  2  50  70  80  101
```

```
Enter the item you are searching for: 80
This item is at location 4 in the sorted array.
```

In reviewing Program 7.10, the following items should be considered. First, the sort() method arranges array elements into increasing numerical order for primitive data types only. When applied to arrays whose elements are strings, this will result in the strings being arranged in alphabetical order. For other types of objects, the sort is done by a comparison of object reference values, which effectively results in a random ordering of objects.

When the binarySearch() method is used to locate a specified value, the method returns the index of the located element, with 0 referring to the first array position. This is in keeping with the Java indexing convention. If the element is not found, binarySearch() returns a negative number. The magnitude of the negative number is obtained as the position that the value would be inserted into the array less 1. Also notice that both sort and search methods use the array's name as an argument, while the search method requires an additional argument, which is the searched for value. Additionally, both method names are preceded by the class name, Arrays, and a period.

EXERCISES 7.3

1. Enter and run Program 7.9 on your computer.
2. Run Program 7.9 to determine the average and standard deviation of the following list of 15 voltages: 68, 72, 78, 69, 85, 98, 95, 75, 77, 82, 84, 91, 89, 65, 74.
3. When the switch illustrated in Figure 7.13 is closed at time $t = 0$, the voltage, V, across the capacitor is given by the equation $V = E[1 - e^{t/(RC)}]$, where E is the voltage of the battery, R is the circuit resistance, C is the value of the capacitance, and t is in seconds. Assuming that $E = 50$, $R = 4000$, and $C = 0.005$, modify Program 7.9 to plot the voltage across the capacitor from $t = 0$ to $t = 30$ in increments of 1 second.

FIGURE 7.13 A Simple *RC* Circuit

4. Figure 7.14 illustrates a *harmonic oscillator*, which consists of an object of mass m fastened to one end of a spring. The other end of the spring is attached to a wall, and the object is free to slide over a frictionless surface. Assuming the object is initially at rest (i.e., the spring is neither stretched or compressed) and then pulled to position A at time $t = 0$, the position of the mass at any other time, t, is described by the equation

$$X = A \cos[(\sqrt{k / m}) t]$$

where k is the spring constant in newtons/meter, m is the mass in units of kilograms, and A is the initial displacement in units of centimeters. Assuming A is

FIGURE 7.14 A Harmonic Oscillator

10 centimeters, k is 2000 newtons/meter, and m is 200 kilograms, modify Program 7.9 to display the displacement of the mass from $t = 0$ to $t = 25$ seconds in increments of 1 second.

7.4 ARRAYS AS ARGUMENTS

Individual array elements are passed to a called method in the same manner as individual scalar variables; they are included as subscripted variables when the method call is made. For example, the method call

```
findMaximum(temperature[2], temperature[6]);
```

passes the values of the elements `temperature[2]` and `temperature[6]` to the method `findMaximum()`. When individual array elements are passed to a method, they are always passed by value. This means that the called method receives a copy of the stored value, can use the value in any manner it needs to, but cannot directly change the value in the original array.

Passing a complete array of values to a method is in many respects an easier operation than passing individual elements. When a complete array is passed, it is passed by reference. This means the called method receives access to the actual array rather than a copy of the values in the array. The called method can thus not only use the values stored in the array but can also modify any array value. First, however, let's see how to pass an array to a called method.

An array is passed to a method by including the array's name as an argument to the called method. For example, if `temperature` is a reference to an array, the call statement `findMaximum(temperature);` makes the complete `temperature` array available to the `findMaximum()` method. Assuming the following array declarations

```
int nums[] = new int[5];           // an array of five integers
char keys[] = new char[256];       // an array of 256 characters
double volts[] = new volts[500]    // an array of 500 doubles
```

examples of method calls using these array names are

```
findMaximum(nums);
findCharacter(keys);
calcTotal(nums, volts);
```

On the receiving side, the called method must be alerted that an array is being made available. For example, suitable method header lines for the previous methods are:

```
int findMaximum(int vals[])
char findCharacter(char inKeys[])
void calcTotal(int array1[], double array2[])
```

In each of these method header lines, the names in the parameter list are chosen by the programmer. However, the parameter names used by the methods still refer to the original array created outside the method. This is made clear in Program 7.11.

PROGRAM 7.11

```
public class ArrayArgument
{
  public static void main(String[] args)
  {
    int nums[] = {2, 18, 1, 27, 16};

    // the call is made here
    System.out.println("The maximum value is " + findMaximum(nums));

  }

  // this is the called method
  // it is used to find the maximum value
  // stored in an array of integers
  public static int findMaximum(int vals[])
  {
    int i, max = vals[0];

    for (i = 1; i < vals.length; i++)
      if (max < vals[i]) max = vals[i];

    return max;
  }
}
```

First, it is important to understand that only one array is created in Program 7.11. In main(), this array is referenced by the nums variable, and in findMaximum(), the array is referenced by the vals parameter. Because the vals parameter contains a location value,

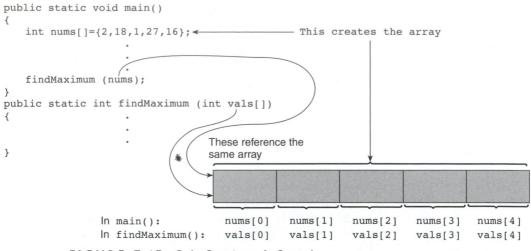

```
public static void main()
{
    int nums[]={2,18,1,27,16};                        This creates the array
              .
              .
              .
    findMaximum (nums);
}
public static int findMaximum (int vals[])
{                      .
                       .
                       .
}
```

These reference the
same array

```
In main():        nums[0]   nums[1]   nums[2]   nums[3]   nums[4]
In findMaximum(): vals[0]   vals[1]   vals[2]   vals[3]   vals[4]
```

FIGURE 7.15   Only One Array Is Created

it is referred to as a **reference parameter**. As illustrated in Figure 7.15, both nums and vals locate the same array. Thus, in Figure 7.15, vals[3] is the same element as nums[3].

All that findMaximum() must specify in its header line is that the parameter vals refers to an array of integers. Since the actual array has been created in another method, in this case main(), and no additional storage space is needed in findMaximum(), the declaration for vals omits the size of the array. This header line makes sense when you realize that only one item is actually passed to findMaximum() when the method is called, which is the location information (i.e., the memory address) of the array. This is illustrated in Figure 7.16.

Since only an array location is passed to findMaximum(), the number of elements in the array is not included in the declaration for vals and in fact must be omitted. In Java, the array referenced by nums is an object that contains certain attributes. One of these attributes, as you have already seen, is the size of the array, which is stored in the object's length variable. Within the findMaximum() method, the array must be accessed by its parameter name, which in this case is vals.

As is seen in the program, the header line for findMaximum() declares that the method returns an integer value. Using the length attribute variable as a boundary for

```
nums[0]   nums[1]   nums[2]   nums[3]   nums[4]
```

Starting location
of the array
is passed to
the method

```
findMaximum(nums);
```

FIGURE 7.16   The Location of the Array Is Passed

its search, the method's for loop causes each array element to be examined in sequential order to locate the maximum value. The output displayed by Program 7.11 is:

```
The maximum value is 27
```

As we have already noted, an important consequence of the way arrays are passed is that the method has direct access to each array element. For arrays, this avoids making duplicate copies of the array for each method call and permits a method to make multiple element changes. As an example, consider Program 7.12, in which the changeValues() method replaces each element by 10 times itself.

PROGRAM 7.12

```java
public class MultiplyElements
{
  public static void main(String[] args)
  {
    int i;
    int nums[] = {2, 18, 1, 27, 16};

    changeValues(nums);  // call the method

    // display the values
    System.out.print("The values in the nums array are");
    for (i = 0; i < nums.length; i++)
      System.out.print("  " + nums[i]);
  }

  // multiply each element by 10
  public static void changeValues(int vals[])
  {
    int i;

    for (i = 0; i < vals.length; i++)
      vals[i] = 10*vals[i];
  }
}
```

In reviewing Program 7.12, notice that the array is referenced as nums in main() and is referenced as vals in changeValues(). Because both references refer to the same array, any changes made from within changeValues() using the vals parameter will be reflected in the array referenced as nums in main(). This is verified by the program's output, which is

```
The values in the nums array are 20 180  10  270  160
```

As this output shows, the values stored in the nums array have all been multiplied by 10 after the call to changeValues() has been made.

EXERCISES 7.4

1. The following statements created an array referenced by the variable `volts`:

   ```
   final int NUMVOLTS = 500;
   double volts[] = new double[NUMVOLTS];
   ```

   Write a method header line for a method named `sortArray()` that accepts `volts` as a parameter named `inArray` and returns no value.

2. The following statements created an array referenced by the variable `factors`.

   ```
   final int NUMFACTORS = 256;
   char factors[] = new char[NUMFACTORS];
   ```

   Write a method header line for a method named `findKey()` that accepts `factors` as a parameter named `select` and returns a character.

3. The following statements created an array referenced by the variable `power`:

   ```
   final int NUMELS = 256;
   double power[][ = new double[NUMELS];
   ```

   Write a method header line for a method named `power()` that accepts `rates` as a parameter named `power` and returns a floating-point number.

4. **a.** Rename the `findMaximum()` method in Program 7.11 to `findMinimum()` and modify it to locate the minimum value of the passed array.

   b. Include the method written in Exercise 4a in a complete program and run the program on a computer.

5. Write a program that has a declaration in `main()` to store the following numbers into an array referenced by a variable named `temps`: 6.5, 7.2, 7.5, 8.3, 8.6, 9.4, 9.6, 9.8, 10.0. There should be a call to `show()`. The `show()` method should accept `temps` as a parameter named `temps` and then display the numbers in the array.

6. Write a program that declares three one-dimensional arrays referenced by the variables named `volts`, `current`, and `resistance`. Each array should be declared in `main()` and should be capable of holding 10 double-precision numbers. The numbers that should be stored in `current` are 10.62, 14.89, 13.21, 16.55, 18.62, 9.47, 6.58, 18.32, 12.15, 3.98. The numbers that should be stored in `resistance` are 4, 8.5, 6, 7.35, 9, 15.3, 3, 5.4, 2.9, 4.8. Your program should pass references to these three arrays to a method named `calcVolts()`, which should calculate the elements in the `volts` array as the product of the corresponding elements in the `current` and `resistance` arrays (e.g., `volts[1]` = `current[1] * resistance[1]`). After `calcVolts()` has put values into the `volts` array, the values in the array should be displayed from within `main()`.

7. Write a program that includes two methods named `calcAverage()`and `variance()`. The `calcAverage()` method should calculate and return the average of the values stored in an array named `testvals`. This array should be declared in `main()` and include the values 89, 95, 72, 83, 99, 54, 86, 75, 92, 73, 79, 75, 82, 73. The `variance()` method should calculate and return the variance of the data. The variance is obtained by subtracting the average from each value in `testvals`, squaring the differences obtained, adding their squares, and dividing by the number of elements in `testvals` (see Program 7.9). The values returned from `calcAverage()` and `variance()` should be displayed from within `main()`.

7.5 COMMON PROGRAMMING ERRORS

Four common errors associated with declaring, creating, and using arrays are:

1. Forgetting the empty bracket pairs when declaring an array's name. Without the brackets, the array name will simply be considered as a scalar variable.
2. Declaring an array reference variable using explicit dimension sizes. A Java array declaration must only specify the type of elements that will be stored by the array being referenced, the array reference name, and one set of empty brackets for each dimension. Thus, a one-dimensional array will be declared by one empty set of bracket pairs. Attempting to include a dimension size results in a compiler error message equivalent to `Can't specify array dimension in a type expression`.
3. Using a subscript that references a nonexistent array element—for example, declaring the array to be of size 20 and using a subscript value of 25. This error results in a run-time `ArrayIndexOutOfBoundsException` error.
4. Not using a large enough counter value in a `for` loop to cycle through all the array elements. This error usually occurs when an array is initially specified to be of size n and there is a `for` loop within the program of the form `for (int i = 0; i < n; i++)`. The array size is then expanded, but the programmer forgets to change the interior `for` loop parameters. In practice, this error is eliminated either by using the same named constant for both the array size and loop parameter or by employing the length attribute of the array as the checked condition in the `for` statement.

7.6 CHAPTER SUMMARY

1. A one-dimensional array is a data structure that can store a list of values of the same data type. Such arrays must be declared by giving the data type of the values that will be stored in the array, a reference variable name, and a set of empty brackets. For example, the declaration:

   ```
   int num[];
   ```

   declares that the reference variable named `num` will reference a one-dimensional array consisting of integer values. In practice, the reference variable is commonly referred to as the array's name.

2. Once a reference variable has been declared for it, a one-dimensional array must be allocated memory space. This can be done using the `new` operator in an allocation statement. For example, the statement

   ```
   num = new int[25];
   ```

   will cause an integer array of 25 elements to be created with the location of the array stored in the previously declared reference variable (the array name) named `num`. All array elements are set to zero for numerical data type elements and to null for arrays of references. Alternatively, a declaration and allocation statement can be combined into a single statement. For example, the statement `int num[] = new int[25];` both declares an array referenced by the name `num` and allocates space for 25 integer values.

3. Array elements are stored in contiguous locations in memory and referenced using the array name and a subscript, such as `num[22]`. Any nonnegative integer value expression can be used as a subscript, and the subscript 0 always refers to the first element in an array.

4. Arrays can be initialized when they are declared. For one-dimensional arrays, this is accomplished by including all array values within braces, starting from element zero. For example, the declaration

    ```
    int num[] = {10, 20, 30, 40, 50};
    ```

    declares, creates, and initializes a one-dimensional array of five integers.

5. Arrays are reference data types that provide an attribute named `length`. This attribute, preceded by the array's name and a period, provides the number of array elements. For example, if an array is referenced by the variable named `vals` and is created with 10 elements, the number 10 will automatically be stored in the variable `vals.length`.

6. Arrays are passed to a method by passing the reference variable name of the array as an argument. The value actually passed is the location of the array as it is stored in memory. Thus, the called method receives direct access to the array and not a copy of the array's elements.

7.7 CHAPTER SUPPLEMENT: SEARCH AND SORT ALGORITHMS

Most programmers encounter the need both to sort and search a list of data items at some time in their programming careers. For example, experimental results might have to be arranged in either increasing (ascending) or decreasing (descending) order for statistical analysis, lists of names may have to be sorted in alphabetical order, or a list of dates may have to be rearranged in ascending date order. Similarly, a list of names may have to be searched to find a particular name in the list, or a list of dates may have to be searched to locate a particular date.

Although the `Arrays` class' `sort()` and `binarySearch()` methods, which were introduced in Section 7.3, work very well for many applications, you may encounter applications in which you will want to write your own methods. Also, an understanding of search and sort algorithms is considered part and parcel of a programmer's basic knowledge. In this section, we present these fundamentals.

Search Algorithms

A common requirement of many programs is to search a list for a given element. The two most common methods of performing such searches are the linear and binary search algorithms.

Linear Search

In a **linear search**, which is also known as a **sequential search**, each item in the list is examined in the order in which it occurs in the list until the desired item is found or the end of the list is reached. This is analogous to looking at every name in the phone directory, beginning with the first name, which might be Aardvark, Aaron, until you find the one you want or until you reach the last name, such as Zzxgy, Zora. Obviously, this is not the most efficient way to search a long alphabetized list. However, a linear search has these advantages:

1. The algorithm is simple.
2. The list need not be in any particular order.

A linear search begins at the first item in the list and continues sequentially, item by item, through the list. The pseudocode for a method performing a linear search is:

```
For all the items in the list
  Compare the item with the desired item
  If the item was found
      Return the index value of the current item
  EndIf
EndFor
Return -1 because the item was not found
```

Notice that the method's return value indicates whether the item was found or not. If the returned value is −1, the item was not in the list; otherwise, the returned value provides the index of where the item is located within the list.

The method `linearSearch()` illustrates this procedure as a Java method:

```
// this method returns the location of key in the list
// a -1 is returned if the value is not found
public static int linearSearch(int list[], int key)
{
  int i;
  int size;

  size = list.length;
  for (i = 0; i < size; i++)
  {
    if (list[i] == key)
      return i;
  }

  return -1;
}
```

In reviewing `linearSearch()`, notice that the `for` loop accesses each element in the list, from first element to last, until a match is found with the desired item. If the desired item is located, the index value of the current item is returned, which causes the loop to terminate; otherwise, the search continues until the end of the list is encountered.

To test this method, we have written a `main()` method to call `linearSearch()` and display the returned result. The complete test program is illustrated in Program 7.13.

PROGRAM 7.13

```
import java.io.*;    // needed to access input stream classes
public class LinearSearch
{
```

(Continued on next page)

(Continued from previous page)

```java
    public static void main (String[] args)
    throws java.io.IOException
    {
      String s1;
      int nums[] = {5,10,22,32,45,67,73,98,99,101};
      int item, location;

      // set up the basic input stream
        // needed for conversion capabilities
      InputStreamReader isr = new InputStreamReader(System.in);
        // needed to use readLine()
      BufferedReader br = new BufferedReader(isr);

      System.out.print("Enter the item you are searching for: ");
      s1 = br.readLine();
      item = Integer.parseInt(s1);

      location = linearSearch(nums, item);

      if (location > -1)
      System.out.println("The item was found at index location "
                         + location);
      else
       System.out.println("The item was not found in the list");
    }

    // this method returns the location of key in the list
    // a -1 is returned if the value is not found
    public static int linearSearch(int list[], int key)
    {
      int i;
      int size;

      size = list.length;
      for (i = 0; i < size; i++)
      {
        if (list[i] == key)
          return i;
      }

      return -1;
    }
}
```

Sample runs of Program 7.13 follow.

```
Enter the item you are searching for: 101
The item was found at index location 9
```

and

```
Enter the item you are searching for: 65
The item was not found in the list
```

As has already been pointed out, an advantage of a linear search is that the list does not have to be in sorted order to perform the search. Another advantage is that if the desired item is toward the front of the list, only a small number of comparisons will be done. The worst case occurs when the desired item is at the end of the list. On average, however, and assuming that the desired item is equally likely to be anywhere within the list, the number of required comparisons will be $N/2$, where N is the list's size. Thus, for a 10-element list, the average number of comparisons needed for a linear search is 5, and for a 10,000 element list, the average number of comparisons needed is 5,000. As we show next, this number can be significantly reduced using a binary search algorithm.

Binary Search

In a **binary search**, the list *must be* in sorted order. Starting with an ordered list, the desired item is first compared to the element in the middle of the list (for lists with an even number of elements, either of the two middle elements can be used). Three possibilities present themselves once the comparison is made: The desired item may be equal to the middle element, it may be greater than the middle element, or it may be less than the middle element.

In the first case, the search has been successful, and no further searches are required. In the second case, since the desired item is greater than the middle element, if it is found at all it must be in the second half of the list. This means that the first half of the list consisting of all elements from the first to the midpoint element can be discarded from any further search. In the third case, since the desired item is less than the middle element, if it is found at all it must be found in the first half of the list. For this case, the second half of the list containing all elements from the midpoint element to the last element can be discarded from any further search.

The algorithm for implementing this search strategy is illustrated in Figure 7.17 and defined by the following pseudocode:

```
Set the lower index to 0
Set the upper index to 1 less than the size of the list
Begin with the first item in the list
While the lower index is less than or equal to the upper index
    Set the midpoint index to the integer average of the lower and
    upper index values
    Compare the desired item to the midpoint element
    If the desired element equals the midpoint element
```

> *Return the index value of the current item*
> *Else If the desired element is greater than the midpoint*
> *element*
> *Set the lower index value to the midpoint value plus 1*
> *Else if the desired element is less than the midpoint element*
> *Set the upper index value to the midpoint value less 1*
> *EndIf*
EndWhile
Return -1 because the item was not found

As illustrated by both the pseudocode and the flowchart in Figure 7.17, a while loop controls the search. The initial list is defined by setting the lower index value to 0 and the upper index value to 1 less than the number of elements in the list. The midpoint element is then taken as the integerized average of the lower and upper values. Once the comparison to the midpoint element is made, the search is subsequently restricted by moving either the lower index to one integer value above the midpoint or by moving the upper index to one integer value below the midpoint. This process is continued until the desired element is found or the lower and upper index values become equal. The method binarySearch() presents the Java version of this algorithm:

```java
// this method returns the location of key in the list
// a -1 is returned if the value is not found
public static int binarySearch(int list[], int key)
{
  int left, right, midpt, size;

  size = list.length;
  left = 0;
  right = size - 1;
  while (left <= right)
  {
    midpt = (int) ((left + right) / 2);
    if (key == list[midpt])
    {
      return midpt;
    }
    else if (key > list[midpt])
      left = midpt + 1;
    else
      right = midpt - 1;
  }

  return -1;
}
```

For purposes of testing this method, Program 7.14 on page 384 is used.

A sample run using Program 7.14 yielded the following:

```
Enter the item you are searching for: 99
The item was found at index location 9
```

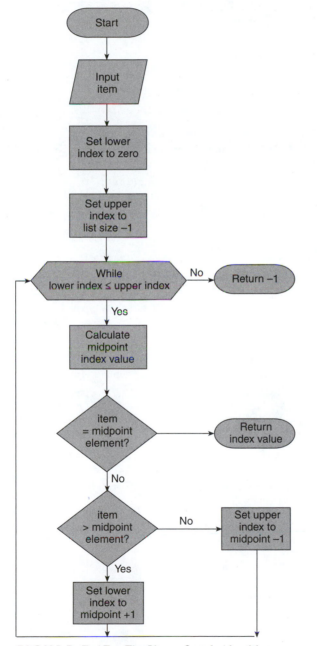

FIGURE 7.17   The Binary Search Algorithm

PROGRAM 7.14

```java
import java.io.*;   // needed to access input stream classes
public class BinarySearch
{
  public static void main (String[] args)
  throws java.io.IOException
  {
    String s1;
    int nums[] = {5,10,22,32,45,67,73,98,99,101};
    int item, location;

    // set up the basic input stream
      // needed for conversion capabilities
    InputStreamReader isr = new InputStreamReader(System.in);
      // needed to use readLine()
    BufferedReader br = new BufferedReader(isr);

    System.out.print("Enter the item you are searching for: ");
    s1 = br.readLine();
    item = Integer.parseInt(s1);

    location = binarySearch(nums, item);

    if (location > -1)
    System.out.println("The item was found at index location "
                       + location);
    else
     System.out.println("The item was not found in the list");
  }

  // this method returns the location of key in the list
  // a -1 is returned if the value is not found
  public static int binarySearch(int list[], int key)
  {
    int left, right, midpt, size;

    size = list.length;
    left = 0;
    right = size - 1;
    while (left <= right)
    {
      midpt = (int) ((left + right) / 2);
      if (key == list[midpt])
      {
        return midpt;
```

(Continued on next page)

```
(Continued from previous page)
      }
      else if (key > list[midpt])
        left = midpt + 1;
      else
        right = midpt - 1;
    }


    return -1;
  }
}
```

The value of a binary search algorithm is that the number of elements that must be considered is cut in half each time through the `while` loop. Thus, the first time through the loop, N elements must be searched; the second time through the loop, N/2 of the elements have been eliminated and only N/2 remain. The third time through the loop another half of the remaining elements have been eliminated and so on.

In general, after p passes through the loop, the number of values remaining to be searched is $N/(2^p)$. In the worst case, the search can continue until there is less than or equal to 1 element remaining to be searched. Mathematically, this can be expressed as $N/(2^p) \le 1$. Alternatively, this may be rephrased as p is the smallest integer such that $2^p \ge N$. For example, for a 1,000-element array, N is 1,000 and the maximum number of passes, p, required for a binary search is 10. Table 7.1 compares the number of loop passes needed for a linear and binary search for various list sizes.

As illustrated, the maximum number of loop passes for a 50-item list is almost 9 times more for a linear search than for binary search and even more spectacular for larger lists. As a rule of thumb, 50 elements are usually taken as the switchover point: For lists smaller than 50 elements, linear searches are acceptable; for larger lists, a binary search algorithm should be used.

Big-O Notation

On average, over a large number of linear searches with N items in a list, we would expect to examine half (N/2) of the items before locating the desired item. In a binary search, the maximum number of passes, p, occurs when $N/2^p = 1$. This relationship can be algebraically manipulated to $2^p = N$, which yields $p = \log_2 N$, which approximately equals $3.33 \log_{10} N$.

For example, finding a particular name in an alphabetical directory with $N = 1000$ names would require an average of 500 (i.e., N/2) comparisons using a linear search. With a binary search, only about 10 (which is $\approx 3.33 * \log_{10} 1000$) comparisons would be required.

A common way to express the number of comparisons required in any search algorithm using a list of N items is to give the order of magnitude of the number of comparisons required on average to locate a desired item. Thus, the linear search is said to be of order N and the binary search of order $\log_2 N$. This is expressed in big-O notation as O(N) and O($\log_2 N$). The O is read as "the order of."

TABLE 7.1   A Comparison of `while` Loop Passes for Linear and Binary Searches

	Array Size	10	50	500	5,000	50,000	500,000	5,000,000	50,000,000
Average Linear Search Passes		5	25	250	2,500	25,000	250,000	2,500,000	25,000,000
Maximum Linear Search Passes		10	50	500	5,000	50,000	500,000	5,000,000	50,000,000
Maximum Binary Search Passes		4	6	9	13	16	19	23	26

Sort Algorithms

For sorting data, two major categories of sorting techniques exist called internal and external sorts, respectively. **Internal sorts** are used when the data list is not too large and the complete list can be stored within the computer's memory, usually in an array. **External sorts** are used for much larger data sets that are stored in large external disk or tape files and cannot be accommodated within the computer's memory as a complete unit. Here we present three internal sort algorithms. For sorting lists with less than approximately 50 elements, either of the first two algorithms is appropriate. For larger lists, a more sophisticated sorting algorithm, such as the quicksort, which is the third algorithm presented, is typically employed.

Selection Sort

One of the simplest sorting techniques is the selection sort. In a **selection sort**, the smallest value is initially selected from the complete list of data and exchanged with the first element in the list. After this first selection and exchange, the next smallest element in the revised list is selected and exchanged with the second element in the list. Since the smallest element is already in the first position in the list, this second pass need only consider the second through the last elements. For a list consisting of N elements, this process is repeated $N - 1$ times, with each pass through the list requiring one less comparison than the previous pass.

For example, consider the list of numbers in Figure 7.18. The first pass through the initial list results in the number 32 being selected and exchanged with the first element in the list. The second pass, made on the reordered list, results in the number 155 being selected from the second through fifth elements. This value is then exchanged with the second element in the list. The third pass selects the number 307 from the third through fifth elements in the list and exchanges this value with the third element. Finally, the fourth and last pass through the list selects the remaining minimum value and exchanges it with the fourth list element. Although each pass in this example resulted in an exchange, no exchange would have been made in a pass if the smallest value were already in the correct location.

Initial List	Pass 1	Pass 2	Pass 3	Pass 4
690	32	32	32	32
307	690	155	144	144
32	307	690	307	307
155	155	307	690	426
426	426	426	426	690

FIGURE 7.18   A Sample Selection Sort

In pseudocode, the selection sort is described as:

```
Set interchange count to zero (not required, but done just to keep
track of the interchanges)
For each element in the list from first to next-to-last
  Find the smallest element from the current element being refer
  enced to the last element by:
   Setting the minimum value equal to the current element
   Saving (storing) the index of the current element
  For each element in the list from the current element + 1 to the
  last element in the list
     If element[inner loop index] < minimum value
        Set the minimum value = element[inner loop index]
        Save the index the new found minimum value
     EndIf
  EndFor
  Swap the current value with the new minimum value
  Increment the interchange count
EndFor
Return the interchange count
```

The method `selectionSort()` incorporates this procedure into a Java method:

```java
public static int selectionSort(int num[])
{
  int i, j, size;
  int min, minidx, temp, moves = 0;

  size = num.length;
  for ( i = 0; i < (size - 1); i++)
  {
    min = num[i];    // assume minimum is the first array element
    minidx = i;      // index of minimum element
    for(j = i + 1; j < size; j++)
    {
      if (num[j] < min)    // if we've located a lower value
      {                        // capture it
        min = num[j];
        minidx = j;
      }
    }
    if (min < num[i])  // check if we have a new minimum
    {                      // and if we do, swap values
      temp = num[i];
      num[i] = min;
      num[minidx] = temp;
      moves++;
```

(Continued on next page)

(Continued from previous page)

```
      }
    }

    return moves;
  }
```

The `selectionSort()` method expects one argument: the list to be sorted. As specified by the pseudocode, a nested set of `for` loops performs the sort. The outer `for` loop causes one less pass through the list than the total number of data items in the list. For each pass, the variable `min` is initially assigned the value `num[i]`, where `i` is the outer `for` loop's counter variable. Because `i` begins at 0 and ends at one less than the number of elements in the array, each element in the list, except the last, is successively designated as the current element.

The method's inner loop cycles through the elements below the current element to select the next smallest value. Thus, this loop begins at the index value `i + 1` and continues through the end of the list. When a new minimum is found, its value and position in the list are stored in the variables named `min` and `minidx`, respectively. Upon completion of the inner loop, an exchange is made only if a value less than that in the current position was found.

For purposes of testing `selectionSort()`, Program 7.15 was constructed. This program implements a selection sort for the same list of 10 numbers that was previously used to test our search algorithms. For later comparison to the other sorting algorithms that will be presented, the number of actual moves made by the program to place the data into sorted order is counted and displayed.

PROGRAM 7.15

```java
import java.io.*;
public class SelectionSort
{
  public static void main(String[] args)
  throws java.io.IOException
  {
    int nums[] = {22,5,67,98,45,32,101,99,73,10};
    int i, moves, size;

    moves = selectionSort(nums);

    System.out.println("The sorted list, in ascending order, is:");
    size = nums.length;
    for (i = 0; i < size; i++)
      System.out.print("  " + nums[i]);
    System.out.println("\n" + moves + " moves were made to sort this list");
  }

  public static int selectionSort(int num[])
  {
    int i, j, size;
    int min, minidx, temp, moves = 0;
```

(Continued on next page)

```
(Continued from previous page)
      size = num.length;
      for ( i = 0; i < (size - 1); i++)
      {
         min = num[i];    // assume minimum is the first array element
         minidx = i;      // index of minimum element
         for(j = i + 1; j < size; j++)
         {
            if (num[j] < min)   // if we've located a lower value
            {                   // capture it
            min = num[j];
            minidx = j;
            }
         }
         if (min < num[i])   // check if we have a new minimum
         {                   // and if we do, swap values
            temp = num[i];
            num[i] = min;
            num[minidx] = temp;
            moves++;
         }
      }

      return moves;
   }
}
```

The output produced by Program 7.15 is:

```
The sorted list, in ascending order, is:
  5   10   22   32   45   67   73   98   99   101
8 moves were made to sort this list
```

Clearly, the number of moves displayed depends on the initial order of the values in the list. An advantage of the selection sort is that the maximum number of moves that must be made is $N - 1$, where N is the number of items in the list. Further, each move is a final move that results in an element residing in its final location in the sorted list.

A disadvantage of the selection sort is that $N(N - 1)/2$ comparisons are always required, regardless of the initial arrangement of the data. This number of comparisons is obtained as follows: The last pass always requires one comparison, the next-to-last pass requires two comparisons, and so on to the first pass, which requires $N - 1$ comparisons. Thus, the total number of comparisons is:

$$1 + 2 + 3 + \ldots + N - 1 = N(N - 1)/2 = N^2/2 - N/2.$$

For large values of N, the N^2 dominates, and the order of the selection sort is $O(N^2)$.

Exchange ("Bubble") Sort

In an **exchange sort**, contiguous elements of the list are exchanged with one another in such a manner that the list becomes sorted. One example of such a sequence of exchanges is provided by the **bubble sort**, where successive values in the list are compared beginning with the first two elements. If the list is to be sorted in ascending (from smallest to largest) order, the smaller value of the two being compared is always placed before the larger value. For lists sorted in descending (from largest to smallest) order, the smaller of the two values being compared is always placed after the larger value.

For example, assuming that a list of values is to be sorted in ascending order, if the first element in the list is larger than the second, the two elements are interchanged. Then the second and third elements are compared. Again, if the second element is larger than the third, these two elements are interchanged. This process continues until the last two elements have been compared and exchanged, if necessary. If no exchanges were made during this initial pass through the data, the data are in the correct order and the process is finished; otherwise, a second pass is made through the data, starting from the first element and stopping at the next-to-last element. The reason for stopping at the next-to-last element on the second pass is that the first pass always results in the most positive value "sinking" to the bottom of the list.

As a specific example of this process, consider the list of numbers in Figure 7.19. The first comparison results in the interchange of the first two element values, 690 and 307. The next comparison, between elements two and three in the revised list, results in the interchange of values between the second and third elements, 690 and 32. This comparison and possible switching of adjacent values are continued until the last two elements have been compared and possibly switched. This process completes the first pass through the data and results in the largest number moving to the bottom of the list. As the largest value sinks to its resting place at the bottom of the list, the smaller elements slowly rise, or "bubble," to the top of the list. This bubbling effect of the smaller elements is what gave rise to the name "bubble" sort for this sorting algorithm.

Because the first pass through the list ensures that the largest value always moves to the bottom of the list, the second pass stops at the next-to-last element. This process continues with each pass stopping at one higher element than the previous pass, until either $N - 1$ passes through the list have been completed or no exchanges are necessary in any single pass. In both cases, the resulting list is in sorted order. The pseudocode describing this sort is:

```
Set interchange count to zero (not required, but done
just to keep track of the interchanges)
For the first element in the list to one less than the
last element (i index)
  For the second element in the list to the last element
  (j index)
    If num[j] < num[j - 1]
        Swap num[j] with num[j - 1]
        Increment interchange count
    EndIf
  EndFor
EndFor
Return interchange count
```

690	307	307	307	307
307	690	32	32	32
32	32	690	155	155
155	155	155	690	426
426	426	426	426	690

FIGURE 7.19   The First Pass of an Exchange Sort

This sort algorithm is coded in Java as the method `bubbleSort()`, which in included within Program 7.16 for testing purposes. This program tests `bubbleSort()` with the same list of 10 numbers found in Program 7.15 to test `selectionSort()`. For comparison to the earlier selection sort, the number of adjacent moves (exchanges) made by `bubbleSort()` is also counted and displayed. Here is the output produced by Program 7.16:

```
The sorted list, in ascending order, is:
    5   10   22   32   45   67   73   98   99   101
    18 moves were made to sort this list
```

As with the selection sort, the number of comparisons using a bubble sort is $O(N^2)$, and the number of required moves depends on the initial order of the values in the list. In the worst case, when the data are in reverse sorted order, the selection sort performs better than the bubble sort. Here both sorts require $N(N-1)/2$ comparisons, but the selection sort needs only $N-1$ moves, whereas the bubble sort needs $N(N-1)/2$ moves. The additional moves required by the bubble sort result from the intermediate exchanges between adjacent elements to "settle" each element into its final position. In this regard, the selection sort is superior because no intermediate moves are necessary. For random data, such as those in Programs 7.18 and 7.19, the selection sort generally performs equal to or better than the bubble sort. A modification to the bubble sort that causes the sort to terminate as soon as the list is in order, regardless of the number of passes made, can make the bubble sort operate as an $O(N)$ sort in specialized cases.

Quicksort

The selection and exchange sorts both require $O(N^2)$ comparisons, which make them very slow for long lists. The **quicksort** algorithm, which is also called a **partition sort**, divides a list into two smaller sublists and sorts each sublist by partitioning into smaller sublists and so on.[6] The order of a quicksort is $N\log_2 N$. Thus, for a 1,000-item list, the total number of comparisons for a quicksort is on the order of $1,000(3.3 \log_{10}1,000) = 1,000(10) = 10,000$ compared to $1,000(1,000) = 1,000,000$ for a selection or bubble sort.

The quicksort puts a list into sorted order by a partitioning process. At each stage, the list is partitioned into sublists so that a selected element, called the pivot, is placed in its correct position in the final sorted list. To understand the process, consider the list in Figure 7.20.

The original list consists of seven numbers. Designating the first element in the list, 98, as the pivot element, the list is rearranged as shown in the first partition. Notice that

---

[6]This algorithm was developed by C.A.R. Hoare and first described by him in an article entitled "Quicksort" in *Computer Journal* (vol. 5, pp. 10–15) in 1962. This sorting algorithm was so much faster than previous algorithms that it became known as *the* quicksort.

PROGRAM 7.16

```java
import java.io.*;
public class BubbleSort
{
  public static void main(String[] args)
  throws java.io.IOException
  {
    int nums[] = {22,5,67,98,45,32,101,99,73,10};
    int i, moves, size;

    moves = bubbleSort(nums);

    System.out.println("The sorted list, in ascending order, is:");
    size = nums.length;
    for (i = 0; i < size; i++)
      System.out.print("   " + nums[i]);

    System.out.println("\n" + moves + " moves were made to sort this list");
  }

  public static int bubbleSort(int num[])
  {
    int i, j, size;
    int temp, moves = 0;

    size = num.length;
    for (i = 0; i < (size - 1); i++)
    {
      for(j = 1; j < size; j++)
      {
        if (num[j] < num[j-1])
        {
        temp = num[j];
        num[j] = num[j-1];
        num[j-1] = temp;
        moves++;
        }
      }
    }

    return moves;
  }
}
```

this partition results in all values less than 98 residing to its left and all values greater than 98 to its right. For now, disregard the exact order of the elements to the left and right of the 98 (in a moment, you will see how the arrangement of the numbers came about).

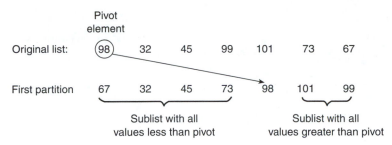

FIGURE 7.20   A First Quicksort Partition

The numbers to the left of the pivot constitute one sublist, and the numbers to the right form another sublist, which individually must be reordered by a partitioning process. The pivot for the first sublist is 67, and the pivot for the second sublist is 101. Figure 7.21 shows how each of these sublists is partitioned using their respective pivot elements. The partitioning process stops when a sublist has only one element. In the case in Figure 7.21, a fourth partition is required for the sublist containing the values 45 and 32 because all other sublists have only one element. Once this last sublist is partitioned, the quicksort is completed and the original list is in sorted order.

As we have illustrated, the key to the quicksort is its partitioning process. An essential part of this process is that each sublist is rearranged in place; that is, elements are rearranged within the existing list. This rearrangement is facilitated by first saving the value of the pivot, which frees its slot for use by another element. The list is then examined from the right, starting with the last element in the list, for a value less than the pivot; when one is found, it is copied to the pivot slot. This copy frees a slot at the right of the list for use by another element. The list is now examined from the left for any value greater than the pivot; when one is found, it is copied to the last freed slot. This right-to-left and left-to-right scan is continued until the right and left index values meet. The saved pivot element is then copied into this slot. At that point, all values to the left of the index are smaller than the pivot value, and all values to the right are greater. For an understanding of how a quicksort is accomplished in practice, we will show all of the steps required to complete one partition using our previous list of numbers.

Consider Figure 7.22, which shows our original list of Figure 7.20 and the positions of the initial left and right indexes. As shown in the figure, the pivot value has been saved into a variable named `pivot`, the right index points to the last list element and is the active index. Using this index, the scan for elements less than the pivot value of 98 begins.

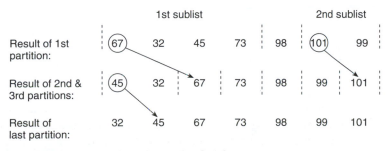

FIGURE 7.21   Completing the Quicksort

FIGURE 7.22   Start of the Scanning Process

Since 67 is less than the pivot value of 98, the 67 is moved into the pivot slot (the pivot value is not lost because it has been assigned to the variable pivot) and the left index is incremented. This results in the arrangement shown in Figure 7.23.

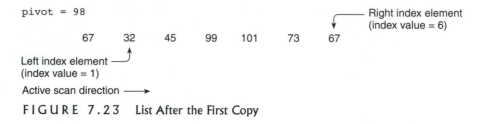

FIGURE 7.23   List After the First Copy

Notice in Figure 7.23 that the element pointed to by the right index is now available for the next copy because its value, 67, has been reproduced as the first element. (This will always be the case; when a scan stops, its index will indicate the position available for the next move.)

Scanning of the list in Figure 7.23 continues from the left for a search of all values greater than 98. This occurs when 99 is reached. Since 99 is greater than the pivot value of 98, the scan stops and 99 is copied into the position indicated by the right index. The right index is then decremented, which produces the situation in Figure 7.24.

FIGURE 7.24   Start of Second Right-Side Scan

Scanning of the list shown in Figure 7.24 now continues from the right in a search for values less than the pivot. Since 73 qualifies, the right scan stops, 73 is moved into the position indicated by the left index, and the left index is incremented. This results in the list shown in Figure 7.25.

Scanning of the list in Figure 7.25 now resumes from the left in a search for values greater than 98. Since 101 qualifies, this scan stops, 101 is moved into the slot indicated by the right index, and the right index is incremented. This results in the list in Figure 7.26.

FIGURE 7.25   Start of Second Left-Side Scan

Notice in this figure that left and right indexes are equal. This is the condition that stops all scanning and indicates the position where the pivot should be placed. Doing so results in completion of this partition with the list in the order

| 67 | 32 | 45 | 73 | 98 | 101 | 99 |

Compare this list with the one previously shown for the first partition in Figure 7.20. As is seen, they are the same. Here the pivot has been placed so that all elements less than it are to its left and all values greater than it are to its right.

The quicksort algorithm uses the returned pivot value to recursively determine whether additional partitions are required for each sublist defined by the list segments to the left and right of the pivot index. The code implemented by the `Arrays` class' `sort()` method is a modified version of the quicksort algorithm.

FIGURE 7.26   Position of List Elements After 101 Is Moved

CHAPTER 8

Multidimensional Arrays

In addition to one-dimensional arrays, Java provides the capability of defining and using larger array sizes. In this chapter, we present such arrays, with the emphasis on two-dimensional arrays. We then introduce matrices, which are the mathematical equivalent of one- and two-dimensional arrays. After describing standard matrix operations, we show their use with array processing techniques to solve systems of linear equations. The applications illustrating these techniques include Gaussian elimination and the method of least-squares straight-line curve fitting.

8.1 TWO-DIMENSIONAL ARRAYS

A **two-dimensional array,** which is sometimes referred to as a **table,** consists of both rows and columns of elements. For example, the array of numbers

8	16	9	52
3	15	27	6
14	25	2	10

is a two-dimensional array of integers. This array consists of three rows and four columns. To reserve storage for this array, both the number of rows and the number of columns must be included when the array is created. As with a one-dimensional array, however, a reference variable to the array must first be declared. For example, the following statement declares a reference variable named `val` that can subsequently create a two-dimensional array of integers.

```
int val[][];
```

Similarly, the declarations

```
double temperatures[][];
char code[][];
```

declare that the reference variables named `temperatures` and `code` are available to reference two-dimensional arrays of double-precision and character values, respectively.

Once a reference variable has been declared, the actual two-dimensional array object can be allocated space using the `new` operator. For example, the allocation statement `val = new int[3][4];` allocates sufficient memory space for a two-dimensional array of integers having three rows and four columns. This allocation statement may be combined with the declaration statement as the single statement `int val[][] = new int[3][4];`. Although `val` is truly a reference variable, it is common to refer to the array by its associated reference variable name, as is the case for one-dimensional arrays.

To locate each element in a two-dimensional array, an element is identified by its position in the array. As illustrated in Figure 8.1, the term `val[1][3]` uniquely identifies the element in row 1, column 3. Also, as indicated in the figure, the first row has a row index of 0, and the first column has a column index of 0. As with one-dimensional array variables, two-dimensional array variables can be used anywhere scalar variables are valid. Examples using elements of the `val` array are:

FIGURE 8.1 Each Array Element Is Identified by Its Row and Column Position

```
price = val[2][3];
val[0][0] = 62;
newnum = 4 * (val[1][0] - 5);
sumRow = val[0][0] + val[0][1] + val[0][2] + val[0][3];
```

The last statement causes the values of the four elements in row 0 to be added and the sum to be stored in the scalar variable sumRow.

As with one-dimensional arrays, two-dimensional arrays can be initialized from within their declaration statements. This is done by listing the initial values for each row within braces and separating them by commas. For example, the declaration

```
int val[][] = {{8,16,9,52}, {3,15,27,6}, {7,25,2,10}};
```

creates an array of integers with three rows and four columns, with the initial values given in the declaration. The first set of internal braces contains the values for row 0 of the array, the second set of braces contains the values for row 1, and the third set contains the values for row 2. Because whitespace is ignored in Java, this declaration can also be made across multiple lines as:

```
int val[][] = {{8,16,9,52},
               {3,15,27,6},
               {7,25,2,10}};
```

The commas in the initialization braces are always required, and the inner braces cannot be omitted because doing so would not provide the compiler with sufficient information for allocating the values into rows and columns. Note that because the left side of this statement is a declaration, the statement must omit any array dimensions, which are only specified if the new operator is used to allocate space for the array without an initializing list. An interesting feature of two-dimensional arrays is that the number of columns need not be the same for each row. This feature, which is not often seen in practice, is presented at the end of this section.

As with one-dimensional arrays, two-dimensional arrays may be displayed by individual element notation or by using loops. This is illustrated by Program 8.1, which displays all the elements of a three-by-four two-dimensional array using two different techniques. Notice in Program 8.1 that the variable val.length provides the number of rows in the array referenced by val and the variable val[i].length provides the number of columns in the ith row. For almost all of the programs you will encounter, the number of columns in each row will be the same, but because Java does provide for arrays in which each row can have a different number of columns, it also provides a distinct `length` attribute for each row. Thus, `val[1].length` provides the number of columns in row 1, which is 4, `val[2].length` provides the number of columns in row 2, which is also 4, and so on.

PROGRAM 8.1

```
public class TableDisplay
{
   public static void main(String[] args)
   {
     int i, j;
     int val[][] = {{8,16,9,52}, {3,15,27,6}, {7,25,2,10}};

     System.out.print("\nDisplay of val array by explicit element"
                      +'\n' + val[0][0] + "   " + val[0][1] + "   "
                      + val[0][2] + "   " + val[0][3]
                      +'\n' + val[1][0] + "   " + val[1][1] + "   "
                      + val[1][2] + "   " + val[1][3]
                      +'\n' + val[2][0] + "   " + val[2][1] + "   "
                      + val[2][2] + "   " + val[2][3]);

     System.out.print("\n\nDisplay of val array using a nested for loop");

     for (i = 0; i < val.length; i++)
     {
       System.out.print('\n');        // print() a new line for each row
       for (j = 0; j < val[i].length; j++)
         System.out.print(val[i][j] + "   ");
     }

     System.out.println();
   }
}
```

Following is the display produced by Program 8.1:

```
Display of val array by explicit element
8   16   9   52
3   15   27   6
7   25   2   10

Display of val array using a nested for loop
8   16   9   52
3   15   27   6
7   25   2   10
```

The first display of the array produced by Program 8.1 is constructed by explicitly designating each array element. The second display of array element values, which is identical to the first, is produced using a nested for loop. Nested loops are especially useful when dealing with two-dimensional arrays because they allow the programmer to designate each element easily. In Program 8.1, the variable i controls the outer loop, and the variable j controls the inner loop. Each pass through the outer loop corresponds to a single row, with the inner loop supplying the appropriate column elements. After a complete row is printed, a new line is started for the next row. The effect is a display of the array in a row-by-row fashion.

Once two-dimensional array elements have been assigned values, array processing can begin. Typically, for loops process two-dimensional arrays because they allow the programmer to cycle through each array element easily. For example, the nested for loop in Program 8.2 multiplies each element in the val array by the scalar number 10 and displays the resulting value.

PROGRAM 8.2

```java
public class MultiplyByTen
{
   public static void main(String[] args)
   {
      int i, j;
      int val[][] = {{8,16,9,52}, {3,15,27,6}, {7,25,2,10}};

       // multiply each element by 10 and display it
      System.out.print("\nDisplay of multiplied elements");
      for (i = 0; i < val.length; i++)
      {
         System.out.println();    // start each row on a new line
         for (j = 0; j < val[i].length; j++)
         {
            val[i][j] = val[i][j] * 10;
            System.out.print(val[i][j] + "  ");
         }  // end of inner loop
      }  // end of outer loop

      System.out.println();
   }
}
```

The output produced by Program 8.2 is:

```
Display of multiplied elements
80   160   90   520
30   150   270   60
70   250   20   100
```

Two-Dimensional Arrays as Arguments

Passing a two-dimensional array into a method is a process identical to passing a one-dimensional array. Because a reference is passed, the called method receives access to the entire array. For example, assuming that `val` references a two-dimensional array, the method call `display(val);` makes the referenced array available to the method named `display()`. Thus, any changes made by `display()` are made directly to the `val` array. As further examples, assume that the following two-dimensional arrays are referenced by the names `test`, `code`, and `mass` , which are declared as:

```
int test[] = new int[7][9];
char code[] = new char[26][10];
double mass[] = new double[256][52];
```

Then the following method calls are valid:

```
findMaximum(test);
obtain(code);
weight(mass);
```

On the receiving side, the called method must be alerted that a reference to a two-dimensional array is being made available. For example, assuming that each of the previous methods returns an integer, character, and double-precision value, respectively, suitable method header lines for these methods are:

```
public static int findMaximum(int nums[][])
public static char obtain(char key[][])
public static double weight(double values[][])
```

In each of these method header lines, no values are included for either row or column dimensions. This information will be supplied by the array object that is passed at the time of the call. Although the parameter names are local to each method, the names used by the method still refer to the original array that is created outside the method and passed to it. Program 8.3 illustrates passing a two-dimensional array into a method that displays the array's values.

Only one array is created in Program 8.3. This array is referenced as `val` in `main()` and as `nums` in `display()`. Thus, `val[0][2]` refers to the same element as `nums[0][2]`. As in Programs 8.1 and 8.2, a nested `for` loop in Program 8.3 cycles through each array element. The effect is a display of the array in a row-by-row fashion:

```
8   16   9    52
3   15   27   6
7   25   2    10
```

The parameter declaration for `nums` in `display()` does not (and must not) contain information about the array's size. This is because each array object "knows" its own size. If any array dimension is inadvertently included in a method's header line, the compiler error `Can't specify array dimension in a declaration` will be issued.

PROGRAM 8.3

```java
public class PassTwoDimensional
{
  public static void main(String[] args)
  {
    int val[][] = {{8,16,9,52},
                   {3,15,27,6},
                   {7,25,2,10}};

    display(val);
  }

  public static void display(int nums[][])
  {
    int i, j;

    for (i = 0; i < nums.length; i++)
    {
      for(j = 0; j < nums[i].length; j++)
        System.out.print(nums[i][j] + "  ");
      System.out.println();
    }
  }
}
```

Advanced Dimensioning Capabilities[1]

Java provides the capability to create two-dimensional arrays in which each row can have a different number of columns. There are two procedures for creating such arrays. In one procedure, the differing numbers of columns are created by an initializing list that explicitly lists values for each row when a reference variable is declared for the array. For example, the declaration

```java
int nums[][] = {{12, 14, 16}, {20, 40}, {6, 7, 8, 9}};
```

will create a two-dimensional array that has three rows, where row 0 contains three elements, row 1 has two elements, and row 3 has four elements. Alternatively, this same array can be created dynamically using the new operator and then values placed into the newly created array.

The following statements can create the nums array dynamically:

```java
int nums[][]; // declare the array
nums = new int[3][];  // allocate three rows
```

---

[1]This topic can be omitted on first reading with no loss of subject continuity.

```
nums[0] = new int[3]; // allocate three columns for row 0
nums[1] = new int[2]; // allocate two columns for row 1
nums[2] = new int[4]; // allocate four columns for row 2
```

As is suggested by this allocation, each row element is actually a reference variable that contains location information for an array of values that constitutes the column elements for that row. These allocations will automatically initialize all values to zero. Once allocated, however, each element can be accessed using its appropriate row and column index value. For row 0, there are three valid column indexes, namely, 0, 1, and 2. For row 1, the valid column indexes are 0 and 1. Row 3 can use the four index values 0, 1, 2, and 3.

Larger Dimensional Arrays[2]

Although arrays with more than two dimensions are not overly common in applications, Java does allow any number of dimensions to be created. This is done in a manner similar to creating and allocating two-dimensional arrays. For example, the declaration statement

```
int val[][][];    // declare a three-dimensional array
```

declares `val` to be a three-dimensional array, and the statement

```
val = new int[3][2][2];   // allocate the array
```

actually creates storage for an array having dimensions $3 \times 2 \times 2$. As with one- and two-dimensional arrays, the declaration and allocation statements for a three-dimensional array can be combined into a single statement. Thus, the previous two statements can be replaced by the single statement

```
int val[][][] = new int[3][2][2];
```

The first element in the array created by this statement is accessed as `val[0][0][0]`, and the last element as `val[3][2][2]`.

In addition, a three-dimensional array can be created using an initializing list. For example, the statement

```
int val[][][] = {{{1,2},{3,4}}, {{5,6},{7,8}}, {{9,10},{11,12}}};
```

declares a reference variable, creates a three-dimensional array, and initializes all of its elements. Notice in this statement that the outer braces contain three sets of inner braces, each of which contains two sets of additional brace pairs. The first set of inner braces, `{{1,2},{3,4}}`, corresponds to all the elements in row 0. Within these braces, the next set of braces consists of the elements corresponding to column 0, and the second set of braces contains the elements corresponding to column 1. To see this connection more clearly, a declaration containing this initializing list is included within Program 8.4.

---

[2]This topic can be omitted on first reading with no loss of subject continuity.

PROGRAM 8.4

```
public class MultiDimensional
{
   public static void main(String[] args)
   {
     int i, j, k;
     int val[][][] = {{{1,2},{3,4}}, {{5,6},{7,8}}, {{9,10},{11,12}}};

     for (i = 0; i < 3; i++)
     {
       for (j = 0; j < 2; j++)
       {
         for (k = 0; k < 2; k++)
           System.out.println("val[" + i + "][" + j + "][" + k + "] = " + val[i][j][k]);
       }
     }

     System.out.println();
   }
}
```

When Program 8.4 is executed, the following output is produced, which shows the assignment of values in the initializing list to their respective index values:

```
val[0][0][0] = 1
val[0][0][1] = 2
val[0][1][0] = 3
val[0][1][1] = 4
val[1][0][0] = 5
val[1][0][1] = 6
val[1][1][0] = 7
val[1][1][1] = 8
val[2][0][0] = 9
val[2][0][1] = 10
val[2][1][0] = 11
val[2][1][1] = 12
```

Conceptually, as illustrated in Figure 8.2, a three-dimensional array can be viewed as a book of data tables. Using this visualization, the first index value can be thought of as the location of the desired row in a table, the second index value as the desired column, and the third index value, which is often called the *rank*, as the page number of the selected table. Similarly, arrays of any dimension can be declared. Conceptually, a four-dimensional array can be represented as a shelf of books, where the first dimension declares a desired book on the shelf, and a five-dimensional array can be viewed as a bookcase filled with books, where the first dimension refers to a selected shelf in the bookcase. Using the same

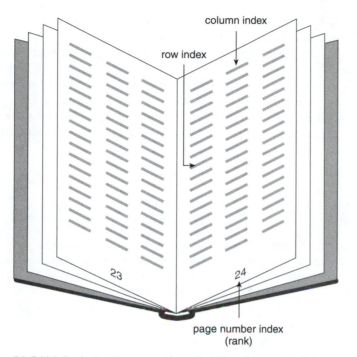

column index

row index

23

24

page number index
(rank)

FIGURE 8.2 Representation of a Three-Dimensional Array

analogy, a six-dimensional array can be considered as a single row of bookcases, where the first dimension refers to the desired bookcase in the row, a seven-dimensional array can be considered as multiple rows of bookcases, where the first dimension refers to the desired row, and so on. Alternatively, arrays of three, four, five, six, or more dimensions can be viewed as mathematical *n*-tuples of order three, four, five, six, and so on, respectively.

EXERCISES 8.1

1. Write a single declaration and allocation statement for:
   a. an array of integers with 6 rows and 10 columns
   b. an array of integers with 2 rows and 5 columns
   c. an array of characters with 7 rows and 12 columns
   d. an array of characters with 15 rows and 7 columns
   e. an array of double-precision numbers with 10 rows and 25 columns
   f. an array of double-precision numbers with 16 rows and 8 columns
2. Determine the output produced by the following method:

```
public static void main(String[] args)
{
   int i, j, val[][] = {{8,16,9,52},{3,15,27,6},{7,25,2,10}};

   for (i = 0; i < val.length; i++)
     for (j = 0; j < val[i].length; j++)
       System.out.print(val[i][j]+"  ");
}
```

3. **a.** Write a Java program that adds the values of all elements in the `val` array in Exercise 2 and displays the total.

   b. Modify the program written for Exercise 3a to display the total of each row separately.

4. Write a Java program that adds equivalent elements of the two-dimensional arrays named `first` and `second`. Both arrays should have two rows and three columns. For example, element `[1][2]` of the resulting array should be the sum of `first[1][2]` and `second[1][2]`. The `first` and `second` arrays should be initialized as follows:

First				Second		
-----------				-----------		
16	18	23		24	52	77
54	91	11		16	19	59

5. **a.** Write a Java program that finds and displays the maximum value in a two-dimensional array of integers. The array should be declared as a four-by-five array of integers and initialized with these data: {{16, 22, 99, 4, 18}, {−258, 4, 101, 5, 98}, {105, 6, 15, 2, 45}, {33, 88, 72, 16, 3}}.

   b. Modify the program written in Exercise 5a so that it also displays the maximum value's row and column subscript values.

6. Write a Java program to select the values in a four-by-five array of positive integers in increasing order and store the selected values in the one-dimensional array referenced by the name `sort`. Use the data given in Exercise 5a to initialize the two-dimensional array.

7. **a.** An engineer has constructed a two-dimensional array of double-precision numbers having three rows and five columns. This array currently contains the test voltages of an amplifier. Write a Java program that permits user entry of the 15 array values and then determine and display the total number of voltages in the ranges less than 60, greater than or equal to 60 and less than 70, greater than or equal to 70 and less than 80, greater than or equal to 80 and less than 90, and greater than or equal to 90.

   b. It is cumbersome to enter 15 voltages each time the program written for Exercise 7a is run. What method is appropriate for initializing the array during the testing phase?

   c. How might the program you wrote for Exercise 7a be modified to include the case of no voltage being present? That is, what voltage could indicate an invalid voltage and how would you modify your program to exclude counting such a voltage?

8. **a.** Write a method named `findMaximum()` that finds and displays the maximum value in a two-dimensional array of integers. The array should be declared as a 10-row by 20 column array of integers in `main()`.

   b. Modify the method written in Exercise 8a so that it also displays the row and column number of the element with the maximum value.

9. Write a method to sort the elements of a 10 by 20 two-dimensional array of integers. (*Tip:* You will need to develop a procedure to exchange two array elements.)

8.2 MATRIX OPERATIONS

A **matrix** is mathematically defined as a rectangular array of elements arranged in horizontal rows and vertical columns that is enclosed within straight lines or brackets. Examples of matrices are:

$$\mathbf{A} = \begin{vmatrix} 100 \\ 50 \\ 200 \end{vmatrix} \qquad \mathbf{B} = \begin{vmatrix} 21 & 0 & 0 & 5 & 4 \end{vmatrix}$$

$$\mathbf{C} = \begin{vmatrix} 1 & 2 & 3 \\ 4 & 5 & 6 \\ 7 & 8 & 9 \end{vmatrix} \qquad \mathbf{D} = \begin{vmatrix} 2 & 4 \\ 0 & 8 \\ 1.7 & 1 \end{vmatrix} \qquad \mathbf{E} = \begin{vmatrix} 1 & 0 & 0 & 1 & 0 & 0 \\ 0 & 1 & 1 & 0 & 0 & 1 \\ 0 & 0 & 0 & 0 & 1 & 0 \end{vmatrix}$$

In this text, we designate matrices by uppercase, boldface, sans serif letters.

A matrix per se is nothing more than a table in which the horizontal and vertical lines usually used to separate the rows and columns have been deleted. Only the numbers themselves appear. Thus, matrices are simply arrays that have been enclosed in straight lines. When a matrix, such as **B**, consists of a single row, it is referred to as a **row vector.** Similarly, when a matrix consists of a single column, such as **A**, it is called a **column vector.** Thus, row and column vectors represent one-dimensional arrays, and all other matrices represent two-dimensional arrays.

By convention, the number of rows is given before the number of columns when discussing the size, or *order*, of a matrix. Matrix **A** contains three rows and one column, so we say it has order 3×1 (read "three by one"). Matrix **B** has one row and five columns, so we say it has order 5×1. The orders of **C**, **D**, and **E**, are 3×3, 3×2, and 3×6, respectively.

As with arrays, the entries in a matrix are called **elements.** Since it is confusing to discuss elements in terms of their values (after all, if the zero element in matrix **E** was referred to, which element would be meant?), we identify them by their positions in the matrix. We designate these elements by lowercase letters and use subscripts to pinpoint their positions. The first subscript denotes the row, and the second subscript denotes the column. Accordingly, c_{23} represents the element in **C** located in the second row and third column, whereas e_{32} designates the element in **E** found in the third row and second column. For the particular matrices given, $a_{31} = 200$, $b_{14} = 5$, $d_{22} = 8$, but c_{37} does not exist because **C** does not have a seventh column.

The **main diagonal** of a matrix is made up of all the elements whose row position equals their column position. Included on the main diagonal are the 1-1 element, the 2-2 element, the 3-3 element, and so on. Examples of main diagonals, indicated here by diagonal lines, are:

$$\begin{vmatrix} 1 & 2 & 3 \\ 4 & 5 & 6 \\ 7 & 8 & 9 \end{vmatrix} \qquad \begin{vmatrix} 1 & 2 & 3 & 4 & 5 \\ 6 & 7 & 8 & 9 & 0 \end{vmatrix} \qquad \begin{vmatrix} 1 & 2 & 3 & 4 \\ 0 & 1 & 0 & 1 \\ 2 & 1 & 0 & 1 \\ 3 & 4 & 1 & 1 \\ 7 & 8 & 9 & 1 \end{vmatrix}$$

As you will see in the next section, a particularly important matrix is the identity matrix. An **identity matrix** is a square matrix having its diagonal elements equal to 1 and all other elements equal to 0. For example, the 3×3 and 4×4 identity matrices are, respectively:

$$\begin{vmatrix} 1 & 0 & 0 \\ 0 & 1 & 0 \\ 0 & 0 & 1 \end{vmatrix} \quad \text{and} \quad \begin{vmatrix} 1 & 0 & 0 & 0 \\ 0 & 1 & 0 & 0 \\ 0 & 0 & 1 & 0 \\ 0 & 0 & 0 & 1 \end{vmatrix}$$

Elementary Matrix Operations

Just as scalar numbers can be compared for equality, added, subtracted, and multiplied, similar operations are defined for matrices (matrix division is not defined). By extension, since matrices are really single and multidimensional arrays, these operations can be implemented using array processing techniques. Before seeing how these operations are applied, however, we must understand what they mean.

Two matrices are equal if they have the same order and if their corresponding elements are equal. It follows from this that two conditions must be satisfied before two matrices can be called equal. First, they must have exactly the same size, and second, every set of corresponding elements must match. In particular, the matrices

$$\begin{vmatrix} 1 & 2 \\ 3 & 4 \end{vmatrix} \quad \begin{vmatrix} 1 & 2 & 0 \\ 3 & 4 & 0 \end{vmatrix}$$

are not equal because they do not have the same order. The matrices

$$\begin{vmatrix} 1 & 2 \\ 3 & 4 \end{vmatrix} \quad \begin{vmatrix} 2 & 3 \\ 1 & 4 \end{vmatrix}$$

have the same order but are still not equal because their corresponding elements do not match.

The sum of two matrices of the same order is obtained by adding corresponding elements. For example, if

$$\mathbf{A} = \begin{vmatrix} 2 & 4 & -1 \\ 0 & 7 & 2 \\ 3 & 5 & 6 \end{vmatrix} \quad \text{and} \quad \mathbf{B} = \begin{vmatrix} -1 & 0 & -1 \\ 1 & 2 & .5 \\ 4 & -3 & 7 \end{vmatrix}$$

then

$$\mathbf{C} = \mathbf{A} + \mathbf{B} = \begin{vmatrix} 1 & 4 & -2 \\ 1 & 9 & 2.5 \\ 7 & 2 & 13 \end{vmatrix}$$

Notice that the order of **C** is the same as that of **A** and **B** and that element $c_{ij} = a_{ij} + b_{ij}$, where i denotes the row subscript and j is the column subscript. Thus, $c_{11} = a_{11} + b_{11}$, $c_{12} = a_{12} + b_{12}$, and so on. Program 8.5 illustrates how the addition of two matrices can be implemented in Java.

PROGRAM 8.5

```java
public class AddMatrices
{
  public static void main(String[] args)
  {
    int i, j;
    int matrixA[][] = {{10,20,30}, {40,50,60}, {70,80,90}};
    int matrixB[][] = {{2,-4,6},   {8,1,-3},   {-5,7,9}};
    int matrixC[][] = new int[3][3];

      // add the corresponding matrix elements
    for (i = 0; i < matrixA.length; i++)
      for (j = 0; j < matrixB[i].length; j++)
        matrixC[i][j] = matrixA[i][j] + matrixB[i][j];

      // display the resulting matrix elements
    System.out.print("\nDisplay of added matrix elements");
    for (i = 0; i < matrixA.length; i++)
    {
      System.out.println();    // start each row on a new line
      for (j = 0; j < matrixC[i].length; j++)
        System.out.print(matrixC[i][j] + "  ");
    }
  }
}
```

Following is the output provided by Program 8.5:

```
Display of added matrix elements
12  16  36
48  51  57
65  87  99
```

Matrix subtraction is defined similarly to matrix addition; the matrices must be of the same order, and the subtraction is performed on the corresponding elements. Thus,

$$\begin{vmatrix} 1 & 2 \\ 3 & 4 \end{vmatrix} - \begin{vmatrix} -1 & 2 \\ 0.5 & -2.1 \end{vmatrix} = \begin{vmatrix} 1-(-1) & 2-2 \\ 3-0.5 & 4-(-2.1) \end{vmatrix} = \begin{vmatrix} 2 & 0 \\ 2.5 & 6.1 \end{vmatrix}$$

In defining multiplication of matrices, there are two possibilities. The first is called *scalar multiplication* in which a matrix is multiplied by a number. The product of a number c with a matrix $\mathbf{A}$ is obtained by multiplying each element of $\mathbf{A}$ by c. Thus,

$$3\begin{vmatrix} 2 & 1 \\ -1 & 3 \\ 4 & 5 \end{vmatrix} = \begin{vmatrix} 6 & 3 \\ -3 & 9 \\ 12 & 15 \end{vmatrix}$$

and

$$-\frac{1}{2}\begin{vmatrix} 1 & -2 \\ -3 & 4 \end{vmatrix} = \begin{vmatrix} -\dfrac{1}{2} & 1 \\ 1\dfrac{1}{2} & -2 \end{vmatrix}$$

The method named scalarMultiply() illustrates the multiplication of a matrix by a scalar number.

```
public static void scalarMultiply(double matrix[][], double multiplier)
{
  int i, j;

  for (i = 0; i < matrix.length; i++)
    for (j = 0; j < matrix[i].length; j++)
      matrix[i][j] = multiplier * matrix[i][j];
}
```

Program 8.6 incorporates this method within the context of a complete program. A sample run using Program 8.6 is as follows:

```
Enter the number of rows in the matrix: 3
Enter the number of columns in the matrix: 4
Enter the value for row 1 col 1: 8
Enter the value for row 1 col 2: 16
Enter the value for row 1 col 3: 9
Enter the value for row 1 col 4: 52
Enter the value for row 2 col 1: 3
Enter the value for row 2 col 2: 15
Enter the value for row 2 col 3: 27
Enter the value for row 2 col 4: 6
Enter the value for row 3 col 1: 5
Enter the value for row 3 col 2: 25
Enter the value for row 3 col 3: 2
Enter the value for row 3 col 4: 10
Enter the scalar multiplier: 10

Display of multiplied matrix elements
80.0   160.0   90.0   520.0
30.0   150.0   270.0   60.0
50.0   250.0   20.0   100.0
```

As is seen by this output, the final matrix elements are the initial matrix elements multiplied by the scalar number.

As the previous examples show, the operations of matrix addition, subtraction, and scalar multiplication are simple extensions of the analogous operations for real numbers. The situation changes drastically, however, when we consider the multiplication of two

PROGRAM 8.6

```java
import java.io.*;    // needed for keyboard input
public class ScalarMultiply
{
  public static void main(String[] args)
  throws java.io.IOException
  {
    String s1;
    int i, j, rows, cols;
    double matrix[][];    // declare the array
    double num;           // declare the scalar multiplier

    // set up the basic input stream
      // needed for conversion capabilities
    InputStreamReader isr = new InputStreamReader(System.in);
      // needed to use readLine()
    BufferedReader br = new BufferedReader(isr);

      // enter the dimension of the matrix
    System.out.print("Enter the number of rows in the matrix: ");
    s1 = br.readLine();
    rows = Integer.parseInt(s1);

    System.out.print("Enter the number of columns in the matrix: ");
    s1 = br.readLine();
    cols = Integer.parseInt(s1);
      // allocate the array
    matrix = new double[rows][cols];
      // enter the matrix elements
    for (i = 0; i < rows; i++)
      for (j = 0; j < cols; j++)
      {
        System.out.print("Enter the value for row " + (i+1)
                       + " col " + (j+1) + ": ");
        s1 = br.readLine();
        matrix[i][j] = Double.parseDouble(s1);
      }

    // input the scalar
    System.out.print("Enter the scalar multiplier: ");
    s1 = br.readLine();
    num = Integer.parseInt(s1);

    scalarMultiply(matrix, num);  // perform the scalar multiplication
```

(Continued on next page)

(Continued from previous page)

```
        // display the resulting multiplied matrix elements
    System.out.print("\nDisplay of multiplied matrix elements");
    for (i = 0; i < matrix.length; i++)
    {
        System.out.println();    // start each row on a new line
        for (j = 0; j < matrix[i].length; j++)
            System.out.print(matrix[i][j] + "  ");
    }
  }


  public static void scalarMultiply(double matrix[][], double multiplier)
  {
    int i, j;

    for (i = 0; i < matrix.length; i++)
      for (j = 0; j < matrix[i].length; j++)
        matrix[i][j] = multiplier * matrix[i][j];
  }
}
```

matrices. No longer is the operation performed on corresponding elements. Additionally, not all matrices of the same order can be multiplied together, and even those that can often have a product with a different order. Other differences, some startling, will become apparent as we proceed.

At first, matrix multiplication appears complicated and unmotivated. It is neither. It is precisely this operation that makes matrices useful as tools in engineering and scientific problems. The motivation comes from the applications we investigate in the next section. As a means of uncomplicating the operation itself, we present the multiplication of two matrices as a two-step process: (1) determining those matrices that can be multiplied and (2) giving the rule for performing the multiplication. The first step simplifies the second.

A simple method for determining whether or not two matrices can be multiplied is first to write their respective orders next to each other. For example, consider the product **AB** if

$$\mathbf{A} = \begin{vmatrix} 0 & 1 & 0 \\ -3 & 4 & 2 \end{vmatrix} \quad \text{and} \quad \mathbf{B} = \begin{vmatrix} 6 \\ 7 \\ 8 \end{vmatrix}$$

Matrix **A** has order 2 × 3, and **B** has order 3 × 1. We write

$$(2 \times 3) \; (3 \times 1)$$

Next consider the adjacent numbers, indicated in this expression by the curved arrow. If the adjacent numbers are the same, the multiplication can be performed. If the adjacent numbers are not the same, the multiplication cannot be performed. In this example, the adjacent numbers are both 3, so the product **AB** is defined.

The order of the product (when the multiplication is defined) is obtained by canceling the adjacent numbers. In the preceding example, we cancel the adjacent 3s, leaving 2×1 as the order of **A** times **B**. For example, consider the following matrices:

$$\mathbf{C} = \begin{vmatrix} 0 & 1 & 2 \\ 3 & 4 & 5 \end{vmatrix} \qquad \mathbf{D} = \begin{vmatrix} 6 & 7 \\ 8 & 9 \\ -1 & -2 \end{vmatrix} \quad \text{and} \quad \mathbf{E} = \begin{vmatrix} 1 & 0 \\ 2 & -1 \\ 3 & -2 \end{vmatrix}$$

The product **CD** is defined because

$$(2 \times 3) \ (3 \times 2) = (2 \times 2)$$

Similarly, for the product **DC**, we have

$$(3 \times 2) \ (2 \times 3) = (3 \times 3)$$

For the product **DE**, we write

$$(3 \times 2) \ (3 \times 2)$$

Now, the adjacent numbers are not equal, and the multiplication cannot be performed. Notice that $\mathbf{CD} \neq \mathbf{DC}$; the order of **CD** is 2×2, and the order of **DC** is 3×3. In general, the product of two matrices is not commutative. That is, interchanging the sequence of the matrices being multiplied usually changes the answer. Thus, we must be extremely careful to write the orders of matrices in the correct sequence when we use the method given here.

Knowledge of the size of a product is useful in computing the product. For example, for the matrices

$$\mathbf{C} = \begin{vmatrix} 0 & 1 & 2 \\ 3 & 4 & 5 \end{vmatrix} \quad \text{and} \quad \mathbf{D} = \begin{vmatrix} 6 & 7 \\ 8 & 9 \\ -1 & -2 \end{vmatrix}$$

we know that

$$\mathbf{CD} = \begin{vmatrix} 0 & 1 & 2 \\ 3 & 4 & 5 \end{vmatrix} \begin{vmatrix} 6 & 7 \\ 8 & 9 \\ -1 & -2 \end{vmatrix} = \begin{vmatrix} \text{---} & \text{---} \\ \text{---} & \text{---} \end{vmatrix}$$

The product **CD** will have a 1-1 element, a 1-2 element, a 2-1 element, and a 2-2 element. The determination of these elements is defined as follows:

> The i-j *element (where* i *is the row and* j *is the column) of a product is obtained by multiplying the elements in the* ith *row of the first matrix by the corresponding elements (the first with the first, the second with the second, etc.) in the* jth *column of the second matrix and adding the result.*

Thus, for the product **CD**, the 1-1 element ($i = 1, j = 1$) is obtained by multiplying the elements in the *first row* of **C** by the corresponding elements in the *first column* of **D** and adding the results. This yields:

$$\begin{vmatrix} 0 & 1 & 2 \end{vmatrix} \begin{vmatrix} 6 \\ 8 \\ -1 \end{vmatrix} = (0)(6) + (1)(8) + (2)(-1) = 0 + 8 - 2 = 6$$

The 1-2 element ($i = 1, j = 2$) in **CD** is obtained by multiplying the elements in the first row of **C** by the corresponding elements in the second of **D** and adding the results. It is:

$$\begin{vmatrix} 0 & 1 & 2 \end{vmatrix}\begin{vmatrix} 7 \\ 9 \\ -2 \end{vmatrix} = (0)(7) + (1)(9) + (2)(-2) = 0 + 9 - 4 = 5$$

The 2-1 element ($i = 2, j = 1$) in **CD** is obtained by multiplying the elements in the second row of **C** by the corresponding elements in the first column of **D** and summing the results. It is:

$$\begin{vmatrix} 3 & 4 & 5 \end{vmatrix}\begin{vmatrix} 6 \\ 8 \\ -1 \end{vmatrix} = (3)(6) + (4)(8) + (5)(-1) = 18 + 32 - 5 = 45$$

Finally, the 2-2 element ($i = 2, j = 2$) in **CD** is obtained by multiplying the elements in the second row of **C** by the corresponding elements in the second column of **D** and summing the results. It is:

$$\begin{vmatrix} 3 & 4 & 5 \end{vmatrix}\begin{vmatrix} 7 \\ 9 \\ -2 \end{vmatrix} = (3)(7) + (4)(9) + (5)(-2) = 21 + 36 - 10 = 47$$

Thus, putting the individual elements back into matrix form, we have:

$$\mathbf{CD} = \begin{vmatrix} 6 & 5 \\ 45 & 47 \end{vmatrix}$$

When the multiplication of two matrices is defined (i.e., the number of columns in the first matrix equals the number of rows in the second matrix), the procedure for multiplying two matrices that has just been illustrated is:

```
For each row, designated by the row index i, in the first matrix
    For each column, designated by the column index j, in the second matrix
        Set a sum variable equal to zero
        For each element in the first matrix's ith row (i goes from 0 to one less than the
        number of columns)
            Multiply the row element by the corresponding element in the second matrix's column
                (j goes from 0 to one less than the number of rows)
            Add the result of the multiplication to the sum variable
        EndFor
        Set the value of the product matrix's element [i][j] equal to the calculated sum
    EndFor
EndFor
```

The `matrixMultiply()` method illustrates how this matrix multiplication algorithm can be implemented in Java. In practice, this method would only be invoked after a check has been made to ensure that its two matrices' arguments have the appropriate orders for matrix multiplication to take place.

```
// method to multiply two matrices
   public static void matrixMultiply(double matrixA[][], double matrixB[][], double matrixC[][])

   {
   int i, j, k;
   double sum;

   for (i = 0; i < matrixA.length; i++)
     for (j = 0; j < matrixB[i].length; j++)
     {
        sum = 0.0;
        for (k = 0; k < matrixA[i].length; k++)
          sum = sum + matrixA[i][k] * matrixB[k][j];
        matrixC[i][j] = sum;
     }
   }
```

EXERCISES 8.2

1. Determine the order of the following matrices:

$$\mathbf{A} = \begin{vmatrix} 2 & -1 \\ 0 & 3 \end{vmatrix} \qquad \mathbf{B} = \begin{vmatrix} 1 & 2 & 0 & 0 & 1 \end{vmatrix}$$

$$\mathbf{C} = \begin{vmatrix} 2 & 1 & 3 \\ -4 & 5 & 6 \end{vmatrix} \qquad \mathbf{D} = \begin{vmatrix} 3 & 2 & 1 \\ 4 & 1 & 7 \\ 0 & 0 & 0 \\ 0 & 0 & 0 \end{vmatrix} \qquad \mathbf{E} = \begin{vmatrix} -1 \\ 1 \\ -1 \end{vmatrix}$$

2. List the 1-1 and 2-2 element, if they exist, for the matrices in Exercise 1.

3. Find $\mathbf{A} + \mathbf{B}$ and $\mathbf{A} - \mathbf{B}$, if they exist, for

a. $\mathbf{A} = \begin{vmatrix} 1 & 3 \\ 0 & -1 \end{vmatrix} \qquad \mathbf{B} = \begin{vmatrix} 1 & -2 \\ 0 & 1 \end{vmatrix}$

b. $\mathbf{A} = \begin{vmatrix} 1 \\ 2 \\ -1 \end{vmatrix} \qquad \mathbf{B} = \begin{vmatrix} 0 \\ 1 \\ 2 \end{vmatrix}$

c. $\mathbf{A} = \begin{vmatrix} 1 & 0 & 3 \\ 2 & 1 & 1 \end{vmatrix} \qquad \mathbf{B} = \begin{vmatrix} 2 & 1 \\ 4 & -1 \end{vmatrix}$

d. $\mathbf{A} = \begin{vmatrix} 1 & 2 & 3 \\ 4 & 5 & 6 \\ 7 & 8 & 9 \end{vmatrix} \qquad \mathbf{B} = \begin{vmatrix} 9 & 8 & 7 \\ 6 & 5 & 4 \\ 3 & 2 & 1 \end{vmatrix}$

e. $\mathbf{A} = \begin{vmatrix} 1 \\ 3 \\ 5 \\ 7 \end{vmatrix} \qquad \mathbf{B} = \begin{vmatrix} 2 & 4 & 6 & 8 \end{vmatrix}$

4. Find $5\mathbf{A} + 2\mathbf{B}$ if

$$\mathbf{A} = \begin{vmatrix} 1 & 3 \\ 0 & -1 \end{vmatrix} \qquad \mathbf{B} = \begin{vmatrix} -2 & 3 \\ 7 & 4 \end{vmatrix}$$

5. Find a, b, c, and d if

$$\begin{vmatrix} 1 & a & 3 & b \\ 2 & 1 & 0 & -1 \\ c & 1 & 4 & d \end{vmatrix} = \begin{vmatrix} 1 & 2 & 3 & 4 \\ 2 & 1 & 0 & -1 \\ 4 & 1 & 4 & -5 \end{vmatrix}$$

6. Enter and compile Program 8.5 on your computer.

7. The order of **A** is 3×4, the order of **B** is 4×1, the order of **C** is 1×3, the order of **D** is 4×3, and the order of **E** is 3×3. Determine the order of:
   a. **AB**
   b. **BA**
   c. **CA**
   d. **AD**
   e. **DA**
   f. **BCE**
   g. **CEA**
   h. **ABCD**
   i. **DABCE**

8. Enter and compile Program 8.6 on your computer.

9. Write a Java program that tests the `matrixMultiply()` method presented at the end of this section.

10. The **transpose** of a matrix is defined as a new matrix that is obtained from the original matrix by converting all the rows to columns. That is, the first row of the original matrix becomes the first column of the transposed matrix, the second row of the original matrix becomes the second column of the transposed matrix, and so on. Using this information, write a Java program that computes and displays the transpose of a user-input matrix.

11. A certain electronic circuit board manufactured by an electronics company is made in three grades: military, commercial, and toy. Each circuit board uses the same number of components, one CPU, four memory chips, ten resistors, and five capacitors. Due to the much closer tolerances required for the military version as compared to the commercial and toy versions, however, the manufacturer uses completely different sets of components for the three versions it sells. The cost of individual components in each version is:

Component	Military	Commercial	Toy
CPU	$100	$45	$15
Memory	$50	$30	$10
Resistors	$5	$2	$1
Capacitors	$8	$3.50	$2

Using these data, write a Java program that determines the cost of these components for each version of the circuit board.

8.3 APPLICATIONS

In this section, we present two classical applications of matrix methods. The first application uses matrices to determine the solution of a system of linear equations using a Gaussian elimination algorithm. The second application applies this algorithm in determining the linear equation that best fits a set of data points using the method of least squares.

Application 1: Solving Simultaneous Linear Equations Using Gaussian Elimination

A **system of simultaneous linear equations** is a set of equations in two or more variables where each variable is raised only to the first power and multiplied only by a known number. Examples of such systems are

$$x + 2y = 5$$
$$5x - y = 3$$

and

$$3r + 2s + t = 10$$
$$4r + s + 3t = 15$$

and

$$x + y - 2z = -3$$
$$-x - y + z = 0$$
$$2x + 3y - 2z = 2$$

The first set of equations is a linear system of two equations in the two unknowns, x and y. The second set is a linear system of two equations in three unknowns, r, s, and t, and the last set is an example of a system of three linear equations in three unknowns, x, y, and z. An example of a system of equations that is not linear is:

$$x + 3y^2 + 4z = 2$$
$$x - \sqrt{y} + 2z = 1$$
$$3x + 2y + xz = 4$$

In the first equation, y appears squared, and in the second equation, it appears to the one-half power; to be linear, each variable must be raised only to the first power. In the third equation, z is multiplied by x; to be linear, each variable can be multiplied only by a number. A system is **nonlinear** if any one of its equations is not linear.

For engineering and scientific purposes, linear systems of equations are important because they model a large number of engineering and scientific applications. From a mathematical viewpoint, linear systems are important because they can be solved.

Whenever one deals with systems of equations, the primary objective is to find a solution. In general, a **solution** to a system of equations is a set of numbers for the variables that together satisfy *all* of the equations in the system.

Some systems of equations have many different solutions, but other systems have none. In particular, a system of simultaneous linear equations has either one, infinitely many, or no solutions. We now develop a straightforward matrix method for determining which systems have solutions and how to obtain the solutions. The first step in this process is to transform the system of linear equations into matrix notation. Let's see how to do this.

Consider the system of linear equations:

$$2x + 4y + 6z = 46$$
$$3x + 12y + 12z = 102$$
$$4x + 5y + z = 28$$

We first collect all the unknowns, here x, y, and z, and place them together in the same vector. We then collect the coefficients of these unknowns and place them together in their own matrix. Similarly, we combine the right sides of each equation into one vector. Doing so results in:

$$\begin{vmatrix} 2 & 4 & 6 \\ 3 & 12 & 12 \\ 4 & 5 & 1 \end{vmatrix} \begin{vmatrix} x \\ y \\ z \end{vmatrix} = \begin{vmatrix} 46 \\ 102 \\ 28 \end{vmatrix} \quad \text{(Eq. 8.1)}$$

Multiplying the left two matrices using the matrix multiplication operation defined in Section 8.2 yields the original system of equations. This same procedure can convert any system of simultaneous linear equations into one matrix equation: Collect all the numerical coefficients of the unknown variables into one matrix denoted as **A**. Then collect all the unknown variables into a column vector denoted as **X**. Finally, collect all the numbers on the right side of the equations into a column vector denoted by **B**. Then the system of equations will be equivalent to the one matrix equation:

AX = **B**

In this system, **A** is referred to as the **coefficient matrix, X** is the **unknown vector,** and **B** is the **known vector.**

Solving the matrix equation **AX** = **B** is accomplished by transforming the equations so that **A** becomes the identity matrix; that is, it has 1s on its diagonal elements and 0s in all other positions. For example, consider the matrix equation:

$$\begin{vmatrix} 1 & 0 & 0 \\ 0 & 1 & 0 \\ 0 & 0 & 1 \end{vmatrix} \begin{vmatrix} x \\ y \\ z \end{vmatrix} = \begin{vmatrix} 2 \\ 3 \\ 5 \end{vmatrix}$$

Multiplying the left side of this equation yields:

$$\begin{vmatrix} x \\ y \\ z \end{vmatrix} = \begin{vmatrix} 2 \\ 3 \\ 5 \end{vmatrix}$$

By the property of matrix equality, this is equivalent to:

$x = 2$
$y = 3$
$z = 5$

One method of transforming a matrix equation so that the coefficient matrix becomes the identity matrix is to use Gaussian elimination. To use this method, we must first combine the coefficient matrix **A** and the known vector **B** into an **augmented matrix.** For matrix Equation 8.1, the corresponding augmented matrix is:

$$\begin{vmatrix} 2 & 4 & 6 & | & 46 \\ 3 & 12 & 12 & | & 102 \\ 4 & 5 & 1 & | & 28 \end{vmatrix}$$

We can now proceed to transform the coefficient matrix part of the augmented matrix, which lies to left of the straight line, into the desired form having 1s and 0s. This, however, must be accomplished in a manner that does not affect the original solution. The operations that are permitted are referred to as **row operations.** There are three such row operations, which are:

1. **Any two rows of the augmented matrix may be interchanged**
2. **Any row of the augmented matrix may be multiplied or divided by a nonzero number**

3. *Any row of the augmented matrix may be multiplied by a constant and added to another row of the matrix*

Let's apply these operations to our example augmented matrix to achieve the desired result. The procedure is to start with the 1-1 element, get it to 1, and then use this element to obtain zeros below it. We then move to the 2-2 element, get it to 1, and use this element to get zeros above and below it. We then move to the 3-3 element and do the same, and so on down the diagonal, until we have transformed the coefficient matrix elements to the desired form.

To transform the 1-1 element in the augmented matrix to the number 1, we divide the complete first row by the value 2 (this is permitted by the second row operation), which yields:

$$\begin{vmatrix} 1 & 2 & 3 & | & 23 \\ 3 & 12 & 12 & | & 102 \\ 4 & 5 & 1 & | & 28 \end{vmatrix}$$

To obtain zeros in both positions below the 1-1 element, we apply the third row operation twice; that is, we multiply the first row by -3 and add it to the second row and then multiply the first row by -4 and add it to the third row. Doing so yields:

$$\begin{vmatrix} 1 & 2 & 3 & | & 23 \\ 0 & 6 & 3 & | & 33 \\ 0 & -3 & -11 & | & -64 \end{vmatrix}$$

Whenever one element transforms a second element to zero using a row operation, the first element is called the **pivot element**, or simply the **pivot**. In the previous operations, the 1-1 element was the pivot.

Having gotten zeros below the 1-1 element, we now move on to the 2-2 element and make it the pivot. This element is transformed to 1 by dividing the complete second row by 6. Doing so yields:

$$\begin{vmatrix} 1 & 2 & 3 & | & 23 \\ 0 & 1 & .5 & | & 5.5 \\ 0 & -3 & -11 & | & -64 \end{vmatrix}$$

We now use this element, which is our new pivot, to obtain zeros in the position immediately above it by multiplying the second row by -2 and adding it to the first row and then multiplying the second row by 3 and adding it to the third row. This yields:

$$\begin{vmatrix} 1 & 0 & 2 & | & 12 \\ 0 & 1 & .5 & | & 5.5 \\ 0 & 0 & -9.5 & | & -47.5 \end{vmatrix}$$

The process is completed by now making the 3-3 element the pivot and using it to obtain zeros above it. The 3-3 element is first set to 1 by dividing the third row by -9.5:

$$\begin{vmatrix} 1 & 0 & 2 & | & 12 \\ 0 & 1 & .5 & | & 5.5 \\ 0 & 0 & 1 & | & 5 \end{vmatrix}$$

To obtain zeros in the positions immediately above the 3-3 element, the third row is multiplied by $-.5$ and added to the second row and then multiplied by -2 and added to the first row. Doing so results in:

$$\begin{vmatrix} 1 & 0 & 0 & | & 2 \\ 0 & 1 & 0 & | & 3 \\ 0 & 0 & 1 & | & 5 \end{vmatrix}$$

From this transformed augmented matrix, the solution vector, **X**, is given as:

$$\mathbf{X} = \begin{vmatrix} 2 \\ 3 \\ 5 \end{vmatrix}$$

From the property of matrix equality, this matrix equation can be written as the three single equations:

$x = 2$

$y = 3$

$x = 5$

These, as we have seen, are the solution to the original set of linear equations.

In reviewing the procedure we have used to solve the original system of linear equations, two points should be noted. Mathematically, only those system of linear equations having the same number of equations as unknowns can have a unique solution. This fact implies that the coefficient matrix must have the same number of rows (which corresponds to the number of equations) as columns (which corresponds to the number of unknowns). Second, even with the same number of equations as unknowns, a unique solution is not guaranteed. If at any point in the process a nonzero pivot cannot be found, the system does not have a unique solution. In this case, the coefficient matrix is said to be **singular,** and either no solutions exist or an infinity of solutions exist. (Exercise 2 explores this point in more depth.) The pseudocode for the algorithm we have used, which is called the **Gaussian elimination algorithm,** is:

```
Enter the number of equations
Enter the coefficient matrix
Enter the known vector
Form the augmented matrix
Do for each row in the augmented matrix
   If the diagonal element (the pivot) for the current row is 0
       Interchange it with a row below it that does not have a 0 in the same column
       If there is no nonzero element below the pivot that can be interchanged
       Return with an indication that no unique solution exists
       EndIf
   Else
       Divide the pivot row by the value of the diagonal element - this sets the pivot to 1
   EndIf
   Do for each row in the augmented matrix above and below the pivot row
      Set a factor variable equal to the negative of the element in the current row
      corresponding to the pivot element in the pivot row
```

Generate a 0 in the columns above and below the pivot by multiplying each
element in the pivot row by the factor variable's value adding it to the
corresponding element in the current row is the value of the element
　　EndDo
EndDo
Return an indication that the augmented matrix has been successfully converted

　　　　Program 8.7 illustrates how the Gaussian elimination algorithm can be implemented
in Java.

PROGRAM 8.7

```java
import java.io.*;   // needed for keyboard input
public class SolveLinear
{
  public static void main(String[] args)
  throws java.io.IOException
  {
    String s1;
    int i, j, rows, cols;
    double augmented[][];   // declare the augmented matrix
    boolean solution;

    // set up the basic input stream
      // needed for conversion capabilities
    InputStreamReader isr = new InputStreamReader(System.in);
      // needed to use readLine()
    BufferedReader br = new BufferedReader(isr);

      // enter the number of equations
    System.out.print("Enter the number of linear equations: ");
    s1 = br.readLine();
    rows = Integer.parseInt(s1);
    cols = rows + 1;
      // allocate the array
    augmented = new double[rows][cols];

      // enter coefficient values
    for (i = 0; i < rows; i++)
      for (j = 0; j < (cols - 1); j++)
      {
        System.out.print("Enter the coefficients for equation " + (i+1)
                    + " variable " + (j+1) + ": ");
        s1 = br.readLine();
        augmented[i][j] = Double.parseDouble(s1);
      }
```

(Continued on next page)

(Continued from previous page)

```
    // enter known (right-hand) values
  for (i = 0; i < rows; i++)
  {
    System.out.print("Enter the known coefficients for equation " + (i+1) + ": ");
    s1 = br.readLine();
    augmented[i][cols-1] = Double.parseDouble(s1);
  }


    // perform the gaussian elimination
  solution = gaussian(augmented);
  if (solution)
    display(augmented);
  else
   System.out.println("\nA unique solution does not exist for these equations.");
}


// gaussian elimination method
public static boolean gaussian(double matrix[][])
{
  int i, j, k, row, numeqs;
  double pivot, factor, temp;
  boolean solution;

  numeqs = matrix.length;
  for(i = 0; i < numeqs; i++)
  {
    // make sure we have a non-zero pivot element
    pivot = matrix[i][i];
    row = i + 1;
  if(pivot == 0.0)
   {
     // loop until we find a non-zero pivot for this row
    while(pivot == 0.0 && row < numeqs)
    {
    if(matrix[row][i] != 0.0)
      pivot = matrix[row][i];
    else
       row++;
    }
       // check that a non-zero pivot was found
    if (pivot == 0.0)
      return false;  // no solution
      else
```

(Continued on next page)

(Continued from previous page)

```
            // interchange this row with the new pivot row
        for(j = 1; j <= numeqs; j++)
          {
             temp = matrix[i][j];
           matrix[i][j] = matrix[row][j];
           matrix[row][j] = temp;
           }
      }

        // use gaussian elimination on the rows above
        // and below the pivot
        // first, get the pivot to a 1
      pivot = matrix[i][i];
      for(j = 0; j <= numeqs; j++)
        matrix[i][j] = matrix[i][j] / pivot;
         // get zeros above and below the pivot
      for(k = 0; k < numeqs; k++)
      {
        factor = -matrix[k][i];
      if (k != i)
          for (j = 0; j <= numeqs; j++)
          matrix[k][j] = matrix[k][j] + factor * matrix[i][j];
      }
    }
  return true;  // solution found
}


// method to display matrix elements
public static void display(double matrix[][])
{
  int i;

  System.out.println("\nThe solution is:");
  for (i = 0; i < matrix.length; i++)
     System.out.println("X" + (i+1) + " = " + matrix[i][matrix.length]);
 }
}
```

Following is a sample run of Program 8.7:

```
Enter the number of linear equations: 3
Enter the coefficients for equation 1 variable 1: 2
Enter the coefficients for equation 1 variable 2: 4
Enter the coefficients for equation 1 variable 3: 6
```

```
Enter the coefficients for equation 2 variable 1: 3
Enter the coefficients for equation 2 variable 2: 12
Enter the coefficients for equation 2 variable 3: 12
Enter the coefficients for equation 3 variable 1: 4
Enter the coefficients for equation 3 variable 2: 5
Enter the coefficients for equation 3 variable 3: 1
Enter the known coefficients for equation 1: 46
Enter the known coefficients for equation 2: 102
Enter the known coefficients for equation 3: 28


The solution is:
X1 = 2.0
X2 = 3.0
X3 = 5.0
```

This result agrees with the solution of the system of linear equations that we previously calculated by hand.

Application 2: Linear Least-Squares Curve Fit

An extremely common data problem is illustrated by Figure 8.3. Here either experimental or empirical data are obtained, and although a straight line appears to be a reasonable approximation to the data, no single line of the form $y = mx + b$ contains all of the given data points. Nevertheless, we would like to obtain the equation of the straight line that best fits the data.

Any straight-line approximation that we derive will have one y-value on the line for each value of x. This y-value may or may not agree with the given data. Thus, for the values of x at which data are available, we generally have two values of y: one value from the original data and a second value from the straight-line approximation to the data. This situation is illustrated in Figure 8.4. The error at each x is the difference between the y-value of the data point and the y-value obtained from the straight-line approximation. We designate this error as $e(x)$.

The concept illustrated in Figure 8.4 can be extended to the more general situation involving N data points. Let (x_1,y_1), (x_2,y_2), (x_3,y_3), . . . , (x_N,y_N) be a set of N data points. Any straight-line approximation to these data generates errors $e(x_1)$, $e(x_2)$, $e(x_3)$, . . . , $e(x_N)$ that individually can be positive, negative, or zero. This latter case occurs when the approximation agrees with the data at a particular point. For this situation, the overall **squared error**, E, is defined as the sum of the squares of the individual errors. That is,

$$E = [e(x_1)]^2 + [e(x_2)]^2 + [e(x_3)]^2 + \ldots + [e(x_N)]^2$$

Using calculus, it can be shown (although not considered here) that the straight line that minimizes the squared error, which is called the **least-squares straight line**, is given by the equation $y = mx + b$, where m and b simultaneously satisfy the two equations:

$$\begin{aligned} Nb + \sum x_i\, m &= \sum y_i & \text{(Eq. 8.2)} \\ \sum x_i\, b + \sum (x_i)^2\, m &= \sum x_i y_i & \text{(Eq. 8.3)} \end{aligned}$$

FIGURE 8.3   Experimental Data

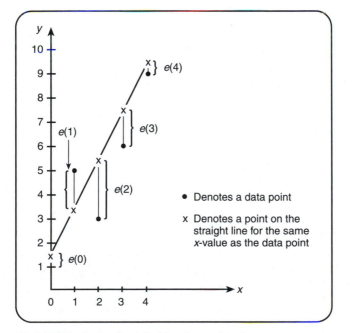

FIGURE 8.4   Straight-Line Approximation

Here x_i and y_i denote the values of the ith data point, N is the total number of data points being considered, and Σ is the sigma notation for "the sum of." Thus, once the coefficients of the b and m terms in Equations 8.2 and 8.3 are calculated from the data points, Program 8.7 can solve for the unknowns b and m.

As an example of how the coefficients required in Equations 8.2 and 8.3 can be calculated, we will find the least-squares straight line for the following data:

x:	0	1	2	3	4
y:	1	5	3	6	9

Here we have five data points ($N = 5$). The required sums indicated in Equations 8.2 and 8.3 are calculated as follows:

X_i	Y_i	$(X_i)^2$	X_iY_i
0	1	0	0
1	5	1	5
2	3	4	6
3	6	9	18
4	9	16	36
$\Sigma x_i = 10$	$\Sigma y_i = 24$	$\Sigma(x_i)^2 = 30$	$\Sigma x_iy_i = 65$

Substituting the appropriate sums into Equations 8.2 and 8.3 with $N = 5$ because there are five data points, we have:

$$5b + 10m = 24$$
$$10b + 30m = 65$$

Using Program 8.7 to solve these two simultaneous equations yields:

```
Enter the number of linear equations: 2
Enter the coefficients for equation 1 variable 1: 5
Enter the coefficients for equation 1 variable 2: 10
Enter the coefficients for equation 2 variable 1: 10
Enter the coefficients for equation 2 variable 2: 30
Enter the known coefficients for equation 1: 24
Enter the known coefficients for equation 2: 65

The solution is:
X1 = 1.4
X2 = 1.7
```

From this output, we have $b = x1 = 1.4$ and $m = x2 = 1.7$. Thus, the equation of the least-squares line is $y = 1.7x + 1.4$, which is graphed with the original data in Figure 8.5.

Program 8.8 illustrates a Java program for calculating the required coefficients for Equations 8.2 and 8.3. We leave it as an exercise for this program to be combined with either Program 8.7 or another procedure (see Exercise 4) to yield the slope, m, and y-intercept, b, of the least-squares straight line directly from the input data points.

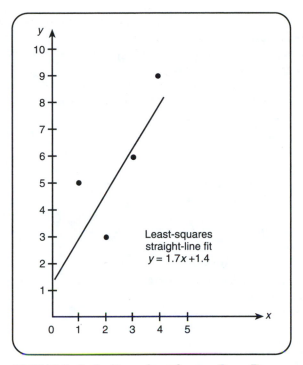

FIGURE 8.5 Linear Least-Squares Curve Fit

PROGRAM 8.8

```java
import java.io.*;    // needed for keyboard input
public class CalculateLLSums
{
  public static void main(String[] args)
  throws java.io.IOException
  {
    String s1;
    int i, j, numpoints;
    double x[], y[];    // declare the arrays
    double xsums =0.0;
    double ysums =0.0;
    double xxsums =0.0;
    double xysums =0.0;

    // set up the basic input stream
      // needed for conversion capabilities
    InputStreamReader isr = new InputStreamReader(System.in);
      // needed to use readLine()
    BufferedReader br = new BufferedReader(isr);
```

(Continued on next page)

```
(Continued from previous page)
        // enter the number of data points
    System.out.print("Enter the number of data points: ");
    s1 = br.readLine();
    numpoints = Integer.parseInt(s1);


      // allocate the x and y arrays
    x = new double[numpoints];
    y = new double[numpoints];


      // enter the x and y values and calculate the sums
    for (i = 0; i < numpoints; i++)
    {
      System.out.print("Enter the x value " + (i+1) + " : ");
      s1 = br.readLine();
      x[i] = Double.parseDouble(s1);
      System.out.print("Enter the y value " + (i+1) + " : ");
      s1 = br.readLine();
      y[i] = Double.parseDouble(s1);
       // caclulate the sums
      xsums += x[i];
      ysums += y[i];
      xxsums += Math.pow(x[i],2);
      xysums += x[i]*y[i];
    }


    System.out.println("\nThe required sums are:");
    System.out.println("Sum of the x values = " + xsums);
    System.out.println("Sum of the y values = " + ysums);
    System.out.println("Sum of the x squared values = " + xxsums);
    System.out.println("Sum of the x times y values = " + xysums);
  }
}
```

Following is a sample run of Program 8.8 with the five data points from our previous hand calculation.

```
Enter the number of data points: 5
Enter the x value 1 : 0
Enter the y value 1 : 1
Enter the x value 2 : 1
Enter the y value 2 : 5
Enter the x value 3 : 2
Enter the y value 3 : 3
Enter the x value 4 : 3
```

```
Enter the y value 4 : 6
Enter the x value 5 : 4
Enter the y value 5 : 9

The required sums are:
Sum of the x values = 10.0
Sum of the y values = 24.0
Sum of the x squared values = 30.0
Sum of the x times y values = 65.0
```

EXERCISES 8.3

1. a. Compile and run Program 8.7 on a computer. Enter the data necessary to solve the linear equations:

$$2x + 3y = 57.4$$

$$4x + 6y = 93.6$$

   b. Using Program 8.7, solve the linear equations:

$$2x + 3y + 4z = 11$$
$$5x + 6y \qquad = 12$$
$$7x - 8y - 9z = 13$$

2. Modify Program 8.7 to display the intermediate results—that is, the transformed augmented matrix after each pivot has been converted to 1 and the other elements in the pivot column have been transformed to 0s.

3. a. Determine why the following equations have no solution:

$$2x + y = 7$$
$$2x + y = 14$$

   b. Determine why the following equations have many solutions:

$$2x + y = 10$$
$$6x + 3y = 30$$

4. a. An alternative method of determining the solution of systems of linear equations is provided by Cramer's rule. For two equations of the form

$$ax + by = c$$
$$dx + ey = f$$

Cramer's rule provides the solution as:

$$x = \frac{ce - bf}{ae - bd}$$

$$y = \frac{af - cd}{ae - bd}$$

     Notice that when the denominators of these two equations are zero, the equations are singular and no unique solution exists. Using these equations, write a Java program that calculates and displays the solution for systems of two linear equations.

b. Combine the program written for Exercise 4a with Program 8.8 to determine the slope and y-intercept of the least-squares straight line directly from the input data points.

5. Determine the equation of the straight line that best fits the following data points: $(1,3)$, $(2,1)$, $(3,2)$, $(4,1)$, $(6,2)$, $(8,5)$.

6. Experimental results on an unknown resistor produced the following table of voltages and currents.

Voltage (volts)	Current (amps)
1	0.018
2	0.043
3	0.056
4	0.085
5	0.092
6	0.100
7	0.102

The equation relating voltage, V, current, I, and resistance, R, is given by Ohm's law, which states that $V = R * I$. Using this information, find the "best" guess at the resistance value, R. (*Tip*: Use a least-squares curve fit.)

7. Fitting a quadratic curve to a set of N data points, denoted as (x_1,y_1), (x_2,y_2), (x_3,y_3), ... (x_n,y_n), requires determining the values of a, b, and c for the equation $y = a + bx + cx^2$ that fits the data in some best manner. One technique for determining the values of a, b, and c is called the **quadratic least-squares** fit. For such a fit, the unknowns a, b, and c are related by the set of equations:

$$Na + b\sum_{i=1}^{N}x_i + c\sum_{i=1}^{N}x_i^2 = \sum_{i=1}^{N}y_i$$

$$a\sum_{i=1}^{N}x_i + b\sum_{i=1}^{N}x_i^2 + c\sum_{i=1}^{N}x_i^3 = \sum_{i=1}^{N}x_iy_i$$

$$a\sum_{i=1}^{N}x_i^2 + b\sum_{i=1}^{N}x_i^3 + c\sum_{i=1}^{N}x_i^4 = \sum_{i=1}^{N}x_i^2y_i$$

Using Program 8.7 as a starting point, write a Java program that accepts the given x and y values as inputs, determines the coefficients of the three equations, and then solves for the values of a, b, and c. (*Tip*: Accept the number of data points as the first input and store the actual data points in two arrays named X and Y, respectively.) Test your program using these data points: $(1,0.5)$, $(2,1.5)$, $(3,1)$, $(4,2)$.

8. **a.** The official U.S. population for each census taken since the year 1900 follows. The population figures are in millions of people and are rounded off to one fractional digit.

Year	U.S. Population
1900	76.2
1910	92.2
1920	106.0
1930	123.2
1940	132.2
1950	151.3
1960	179.3
1970	203.3
1980	226.5
1990	248.7
2000	281.4

Using the program developed for Exercise 7, determine the equation of the least-squares quadratic curve for these data.

    b. Using your equation from Exercise 8a, determine an estimate for the population of the United States in the year 2020.

8.4 COMMON PROGRAMMING ERRORS

The common errors associated with multidimensional arrays are almost identical to those for one-dimensional arrays. These errors are:

1. Forgetting the empty bracket pairs when declaring an array's name. Without the brackets, the array name will simply be considered as a scalar variable.
2. Declaring an array reference variable using explicit dimension sizes. A Java array declaration must only specify the type of elements that will be stored by the array being referenced, the array reference name, and one set of empty brackets, [ ], for each dimension. Thus, a one-dimensional array will be declared by one empty set of bracket pairs, a two-dimensional array by two empty sets of bracket pairs, and so on for larger dimensional arrays. Attempting to include a dimension size results in a compiler error message equivalent to `Can't specify array dimension in a type expression`.
3. Using a subscript that references a nonexistent array element; for example, declaring the array to be of size 20 and using a subscript value of 25. This error results in a run-time ArrayIndexOutOfBoundsException error.
4. Not using a large enough counter value in a `for` loop counter to cycle through all an array's elements.

8.5 CHAPTER SUMMARY

1. A two-dimensional array is declared by providing a data type, a reference variable name, and two sets of empty bracket pairs after the array's name. For example, the declaration:

```
int voltages[][];
```

creates a reference variable that can access a two-dimensional array. The reference variable is commonly referred to as the name of a two-dimensional array.

2. The number of rows and columns in a two-dimensional array can be specified when the array is allocated memory space using the new operator. For example, assuming that `voltages` has been declared as a reference to a two-dimensional array, the allocation statement `voltages = new int[3][4];` creates a three-by-four integer array in memory, initializes each array value to zero, and stores the array's location into the reference variable named `voltages`.

3. Multidimensional arrays may be initialized when they are declared. For two-dimensional arrays, this type of initialization is accomplished by listing the initial values in a row-by-row manner within braces pairs separated by commas. For example, the declaration:

    `int vals[][] = {{1, 2}, {3, 4}, {5, 6}};`

    produces the following three-row-by-two-column array:

    1   2
    3   4
    5   6

    In no case can these inner braces be omitted. Arrays that are initialized when they are declared are automatically created and must not be allocated further space using an allocation statement.

4. The *length* attribute, when applied to two-dimensional arrays, provides the number of array elements in each row. For example, if an array is referenced by the variable named `vals`, the syntax `vals[i].length` provides the number of elements in the ith array row.

5. The number of columns in a multidimensional array need not be the same for each row.

6. Multidimensional arrays are passed to a method by passing the reference variable name of the array as an argument in an identical manner as one-dimensional arrays. Because the value actually passed is the location of the array as it is stored in memory, the called method receives direct access to the array and not a copy of the array's elements.

7. A *matrix* is a rectangular array of elements arranged in horizontal rows and vertical columns enclosed within either straight lines or brackets. For example,

$$\begin{vmatrix} 2 & 1 & \sqrt{5} & 0 \\ -3 & 0 & -2 & 4 \end{vmatrix}$$

8. A matrix with only one row or column is referred to as a *vector* and is equivalent to a one-dimensional array. All other matrices are equivalent to two-dimensional arrays.

9. The *size* or *order* of a matrix is the number of rows followed by the number of columns in the matrix. For example, the order of the matrix:

$$\begin{vmatrix} 0 & 1 & 2 \\ 3 & 4 & 5 \end{vmatrix}$$

    is 2×3 (read "two-by-three").

10. The main diagonal of a matrix is made up of all the elements whose row position equals their column position.

11. An *identity matrix* is a square matrix having its diagonal elements equal to 1 and all other elements equal to 0. The 3 × 3 identity matrix is:

$$\begin{vmatrix} 1 & 0 & 0 \\ 0 & 1 & 0 \\ 0 & 0 & 1 \end{vmatrix}$$

12. Two matrices are *equal* if they have the same order and if their corresponding elements are equal.

13. The product of a number c with a matrix **A** is obtained by multiplying each element of **A** by c. This is referred to as *scalar multiplication*.

14. The multiplication of two matrices, called *matrix multiplication*, is only defined when the number of columns of the first matrix is equal to the number of rows of the second matrix. The order of the product matrix is the number of rows of the first matrix by the number of columns of the second matrix. The *i-j* element of the product matrix is obtained by multiplying the elements in the *i*th row of the first matrix by the corresponding elements in the *j*th column of the second matrix and adding the results.

CHAPTER 9

Strings and Characters

A string in Java is an object that is created from either the `String` or `StringBuffer` class. Each class has its own set of methods for both initially creating and manipulating strings. The main difference between these two classes is that a string created from the `String` class cannot be changed; if a modification is desired, such as adding or changing characters in the original string, a new String object must be created. This is not the case for a string created from the `StringBuffer` class. Strings created from this class can be altered, either by adding, changing, or deleting characters within the string, and the string will dynamically expand or contract as necessary.

In general, the `String` class is more commonly used for constructing strings for input and output purposes, such as for prompts and displayed messages. In addition, because of the provided capabilities, this class is used when strings need to be compared, searched, or individual characters in a string need to be examined or extracted as a substring. The `StringBuffer` class is used in more advanced situations when characters within a string need to be replaced, inserted, or deleted on a relatively regular basis.

9.1 THE `String` CLASS

A **string literal** is any sequence of characters enclosed in double quotation marks. A string literal is also referred to as a string value, a string constant, and more conventionally, as a string. Examples of strings are `"This is a string"`, `"Hello World!"`, and `"xyz 123 *!#@&."` The double quotation marks indicate the beginning and ending points of the string and are never stored with the string.

Figure 9.1 shows how the string `Hello` is stored. By convention, the first character in a string is designated as position 0, not 1. This position value is also referred to as both the character's index value and its offset value.

In Java, a string value is always created as an object of either the `String` or `StringBuffer` class. In this and the next section, we describe how strings are stored as objects rather than variables, how they are created, and how they are processed using `String` class methods; this is followed by a similar presentation of the `StringBuffer` class. The main difference between the two classes is that strings created as String objects cannot be modified without constructing a new String object, whereas StringBuffer objects can be modified.

Creating a String

Although a string can be created in a number of different ways, each creation results in taking the same set of steps. For example, in Section 2.4, strings were constructed either using a single declaration and initialization statement of the form

FIGURE 9.1 The Storage of a String as a Sequence of Characters

```
         String identifier = new String(string-value);
```

or using the equivalent two-statement form

```
      String identifier;
      Identifier = new String(string-value);
```

or using the shorter single statement form

```
      String identifier = string-value;
```

For example, all of the following store the characters H,e,l,l,o into a newly created string.

```
String message = new String("Hello");
```

and

```
String message;
message = new String("Hello");
```

and

```
String message = "Hello";
```

Unlike the declaration of a built-in data type, however, the declared variable, in this case `message`, *does not* store the value of the declared data type, which in this case is a string. This makes sense because each string can consist of a different number of characters so that a fixed variable length capable of storing all string values cannot realistically be defined. Rather, storage for the string is created in memory when the string is created, and the location of where this string is stored is placed in the variable `message`. The memory storage allocation that is used is shown in Figure 9.2. Also included in the storage of the string, but not shown in the figure, is the string's length. This value tells Java how many characters to retrieve when the string is accessed.

It is important to understand that although the value in the created string in Figure 9.2 can be displayed with a statement such as `System.out.println(message);`, the contents of `message` are not displayed. Rather, the Java system knows that `message` should be used to locate the actual string and displays the contents of this string. Because the variable `message` references where the actual string is stored, it is formally called a **reference variable.** The actual stored data value, which in this case consists of a set of char-

FIGURE 9.2 Storage Allocation for Both `message` and the String `Hello`

acters stored together as a single string entity, as well as other information about the string, such as its length, is formally referred to as a **String object.**

Notice that, as a programmer, you did not get the choice of creating message as either a reference or nonreference variable; the choice is automatically made by the Java compiler based on the data type being declared. For the built-in data types presented in Chapter 2, the compiler automatically creates a nonreference variable having the correct size to store a data value of the designated type. For nonbuilt-in data types, a reference variable and an object are automatically created. In Chapters 10 and 11, we will see how to define our own data types, which by definition are not built-in types. Such user-defined data types are always created from classes. In creating strings, however, we are using a class named String that has been provided by the Java compiler. It should be noted that in addition to reference variables created when an object from a class is used, reference variables are also created from array types, which were presented in the last chapter.

To recap, when a data value such as a string is created from a class, such as the String class, the following steps are always taken:

1. A variable, referred to as a reference variable, is declared.
2. An object of the correct data type is created.
3. The location of the object created in step 2 is stored in the reference variable declared in step 1.

Although it is common to refer to a reference variable, such as message, as a string variable with the implication that, as a variable, it contains a string value, it is again important to understand that this is technically incorrect. *A string variable is always a reference variable that provides access to a String object.* The characters making up the string are stored in the memory allocated to the object, not in the memory allocated to the reference variable.

Constructors

The actual storage allocation for a String object and the initialization of this storage with specific characters are created by the new operator. This is true even for the shorter form of a string declaration, which implicitly uses this operator. As described in Section 2.4, the process of creating a new object is referred to as **instantiating an object.**

The instantiation of a String object always requires the calling of a String method. This call is more clearly seen in a statement such as

```
String message = new String("Have a great day!");
```

Specifically, in this statement, the expression String("Have a great day!") is a call to a method named String() to which the argument "Have a great day!" is passed. It is no accident that the method name in this call is the same as the data type being declared. In Java, as in most object-oriented languages, the name of the method or methods that can instantiate a new object of a designated class type must be the same name as the class. So in this case, we are declaring a String object and using a method named String() to actually create an object of this type. Methods that have the same name as their class are formally referred to as **constructor methods,** or **constructors** for short, because they are specifically used to construct an object of the declared class.

The `String` class provides nine different constructors for creating String objects, two of which have been deprecated and should be avoided.[1] Table 9.1 provides the syntax of the nondeprecated constructors and an example of each.

Program 9.1 uses each of the examples listed in Table 9.1 in the context of a complete program.

PROGRAM 9.1

```java
import java.io.*;
public class StringConstructors
{
  public static void main (String[] args)
  {

    String str1 = new String();
    String str2 = new String("Good Morning");
    char data []= {'H', 'o', 't', ' ', 'D', 'o', 'g'};
    String str3 = new String(data);
    String str4 = new String(data, 4 ,3);
    byte bytedata[]= {(byte) 'l', (byte) 'i',
                      (byte) 'n', (byte) 'e',
                      (byte) 'a', (byte) 'r'};
    String str5 = new String(bytedata);
    String str6 = new String(bytedata, 3, 3);
    StringBuffer sb = new StringBuffer("Have a great day!");
    String str7 = new String(sb);

    System.out.println("str1 is: " + str1);
    System.out.println("str2 is: " + str2);
    System.out.println("str3 is: " + str3);
    System.out.println("str4 is: " + str4);
    System.out.println("str5 is: " + str5);
    System.out.println("str6 is: " + str6);
    System.out.println("str7 is: " + str7);

  }
}
```

The output created by Program 9.1 is:

```
str1 is:
str2 is: Good Morning
str3 is: Hot Dog
str4 is: Dog
str5 is: linear
str6 is: ear
str7 is: Have a great day!
```

[1]A deprecated method is one that is still supported for consistency with older versions but may be removed in future releases.

TABLE 9.1 String Constructors

Constructor	Description	Example
`String()`	Creates and initializes a String object to represent an empty character sequence. The length of the string is 0.	`String str1 = new String();`
`String(string-value)`	Creates and initializes a String object to represent the sequence of characters provided as the argument. The argument can be a string constant or string reference variable. The newly created string is a copy of the argument string.	`String str2 = new String("Good Morning");`
`String(char[] charArray)`	Creates and initializes a new String object to represent the sequence of characters currently contained in the character array argument.	`char data[]= {'H', 'o', 't', ' ', 'D', 'o', 'g'};` `String str3 = new String(data);`
`String(char[] charArray, int offset, int count)`	Creates and initializes a new String object to represent a subarray of the characters currently contained in the character array argument.	`char data[]= {'H', 'o', 't', ' ', 'D', 'o', 'g'};` `String str4 = new String(data, 4 ,3);`

`String(byte[] byteArray)`	Creates and initializes a new String object using the bytes currently contained in the byte array argument. Converts bytes to characters using the platform's default character encoding.	`byte bytedata[]= {(byte) 'l', (byte) 'i',`
		`                   (byte) 'n', (byte) 'e',`
		`                   (byte) 'a', (byte) 'r'};`
		`String str5 = new String(bytedata);`

`String(byte[] bytes, int offset, int length)`	Creates and initializes a new String object using a subarray of the bytes currently contained in the byte array argument. Converts bytes to characters using the platform's default character encoding.	`byte bytedata[]= {(byte) 'l', (byte) 'i',`
		`                   (byte) 'n', (byte) 'e',`
		`                   (byte) 'a', (byte) 'r'};`
		`String str6 = new String(bytedata, 3, 3);`

`String(StringBuffer buffer)`	Creates and initializes a new String object using the characters currently contained in the string buffer argument.	`StringBuffer sb =`
		`    new StringBuffer("Have a great day!");`
		`String str7 = new String(sb);`

Although this output is straightforward, two comments are in order. First, notice that str1 is an empty string consisting of no characters. Next, because the first character in a string is designated as position zero, not one, the character position of the D in the string Hot Dog is located at position four (Figure 9.3).

String objects of the String class are always created as immutable objects. An **immutable object** is one whose stored values cannot be changed or altered in any way. For a string, this means that any characters comprising the string are specified when the string is created, and these characters cannot subsequently be changed.

Because the string concatenation operator introduced in Chapter 2 can make it appear that a String object can be altered, which violates the immutability of the string, we will take a moment to revisit this operator. As you will see, the concatenation operator actually creates a new string and changes the location information stored in the reference variable that accesses the string. As an example, consider the following sequence of statements:

```
  // create a string and display its value
String message = "Start";
System.out.println("The string is: " + message);
  // use the concatenation operator and display the new string
message = message + "le";
System.out.println("The string is now: " + message);
```

The output produced by this sequence of statements is:

```
The string is: Start
The string is now: Startle
```

Although it might look like we have changed the string from Start to Startle, what is created here is actually two separate String objects. After the first statement is executed, the storage allocation shown in Figure 9.4a is created. When the first println() call is executed, it displays the string currently referenced by message, which is Start. The next assignment to message creates the storage allocation shown in Figure 9.4b. Notice that the concatenation creates a new String object and changes the address in message to now reference the second object, which contains the string Startle. The last println() call then displays this second string, which is located by the reference variable message. The reference to the first string is lost, and the storage used by this string will eventually be reclaimed either by Java's automatic memory recovery mechanism or by the operating system when the program containing these statements has completed execution. Thus, although it appears that the concatenation operator alters an existing string, this is not the case. String objects are always immutable and cannot be changed in any way once they have been created.

Character position: 0   1   2   3   4   5   6

F I G U R E 9 . 3   The Character Positions of the String Hot Dog

FIGURE 9.4a   The Original String and Its Associated Reference Variable

FIGURE 9.4B   The New String Uses the Previous Reference Variable

String Input and Output

In addition to initializing a string using the constructors in Table 9.1, strings can be input from the keyboard and displayed on the screen. Table 9.2 lists the basic string input and output methods provided in Java.

The print() and println() methods are extremely useful and have been used throughout the text to display output from Java programs. Essentially, these two methods are interchangeable with their only difference being that the println() method automatically positions the cursor at the start of the next line after it has displayed the value of its string argument. This same effect can always be produced with a print() method and displaying a newline escape sequence '\n' as the last character.

TABLE 9.2   Basic String Input and Output Methods

Method	Description	Example
print()	General-purpose output, typically to the standard output stream System.out, which is the screen.	System.out.print("Have a Good Day");
println()	General-purpose screen output that provides an automatic carriage return and new line, typically sent to the standard output stream, System.out, which is the screen.	System.out.println("Have a Good Day");
read()	Restricted-purpose input that reads each character in integer format, typically from the standard input stream System.in, which is the keyboard.	int inchr; inchr = System.in.read()

For input, the `read()` method is generally not as useful by itself because it reads a character at a time from the keyboard, and each character is input in integer format. In general, it is much easier to use the keyboard and dialog input methods presented in Sections 3.3 and 3.4, respectively, which permit input of strings as a completed unit, than to assemble a string from individual characters input using the `read()` method.

9.2 STRING PROCESSING

Strings can be manipulated using either standard `String` class methods or character-at-a-time methods provided by the `Character` class. Both techniques are presented in this section.

String **Class Methods**

Because strings are created from a class, except for concatenation using the addition operator, +, and initialization using the equal operator, =, operations on strings are performed using `String` class methods. This means that assignment and relational operations, as they apply to primitive types, *are not* provided for strings.[2] Extensive collections of `String` class methods, however, that supply string comparison and other very useful string operations are provided. The more common are listed in Table 9.3.

The most common methods listed in Table 9.3 are those that are shaded at the beginning of the table. The concatenation method is not included in this group because this operation is almost always implemented using the concatenation operator, +, rather than the `concat()` method. Exactly like its operator counterpart, however, the `concat()` method appends one string onto the end of another string. For example, if the contents of a string referenced by `string1` is `"Hello"`, then the method call `string1.concat(" there World!")` results in the string value `"Hello there World!"`

The `length()` method returns the number of characters in the string, which is referred to as the string's length. For example, the value returned by the method call `"Hello World!".length()` is 12. As always, the double quotation marks surrounding a string value are not considered part of the string. Similarly, if the string referenced by `string1` contains the value `"Have  a  good  day."`, the value returned by the call `string1.length()` is 16.

Notice that there is no string copy method that copies one string to another. Because String objects cannot be changed, the only way a string can be copied is to create a new string using the string to be copied as an argument to the constructor. For example, the statement `String s2 = new String(s1)` effectively copies the String object referenced by `s1` into a string referenced by the variable `s2`.

Finally, two string expressions may be compared for equality using either the `compareTo()` and `equals()` methods and their variations that ignore case (upper or lower). In Unicode, a blank precedes (is less than) all letters and numbers, the letters of the alphabet are stored in order from A to Z, and the digits are stored in order from 0 to 9. In this sequence, the lowercase letters come before (are less than) the uppercase letters, unless case is ignored, and the letter codes come before (are less than) the digit codes.

---

[2]Although the equality operator, ==, can be used, it does not always operate as you might expect, which is explained later in this section.

TABLE 9.3 string Class Methods

Method	Description
int length()	Returns the length of the string.
boolean equals(String anotherString)	Compares two strings for equality.
boolean equalsIgnoreCase(String anotherString)	Compares two strings for equality, ignoring whether characters are upper- or lowercase.
char charAt(int index)	Returns the character at the specified index.
int compareTo(String anotherString)	Compares two strings.
int compareToIgnoreCase(String anotherString)	Compares two strings, ignoring case considerations.
String toLowerCase()	Returns a new string with all characters in lowercase.
String toUpperCase()	Returns a new string with all characters in uppercase.
String trim()	Removes whitespace from the beginning and end of the string.
String concat(String anotherString)	Concatenates str to the end of a string.
static String copyValueOf(char[] data)	Returns the string equivalent of the character array.
static String copyValueOf(char[] data, int offset, int count)	Returns the string equivalent of a subarray of the character array.
boolean endsWith(String suffix)	Tests if the string ends with the specified string.
void getChars(int srcBegin, int srcEnd, char[] dst, int dstBegin)	Copies characters from a string into a character array.
int hashCode()	Returns an integer number derived from the string.
int indexOf(int ch)	Returns the position of the first occurrence of the specified character.
int indexOf(int ch, int fromPos)	Returns the position of the first occurrence of the specified character, starting the search at the specified position.
int indexOf(String str)	Returns the position of the first occurrence of the specified substring.
int indexOf(String str, int fromPos)	Returns the position of the first occurrence of the specified substring, starting at the specified position.

(Continued on next page)

(Continued from previous page)

TABLE 9.3 String Class Methods

Method	Description
`int lastIndexOf(int ch)`	Returns the position of the last occurrence of the specified character.
`int lastIndexOf(int ch, int fromIndex)`	Returns the position of the last occurrence of the specified character, searching backward starting at the specified position.
`int lastIndexOf(String str)`	Returns the position of the last occurrence of the specified substring.
`int lastIndexOf(String str, int fromPos)`	Returns the position of the last occurrence of the specified substring, searching backward starting from the specified position.
`String replace(char oldChar, char newChar)`	Returns a new string with all occurrences of `oldChar` replaced with `newChar`.
`boolean startsWith(String prefix)`	Tests if the string starts with the specified prefix.
`boolean startsWith(String prefix, int startPos)`	Tests if the string starts with the specified prefix, starting at the specified position.
`String substring(int start)`	Returns a new string that is a substring of the original string. The substring starts at the specified position and extends to the end of the string.
`String substring(int start, int end)`	Returns a new string that is a substring of the original string. The new string starts at the specified position and ends at one character position less than the end argument.

When two strings are compared, their individual characters are compared a pair at a time (both first characters, then both second characters, etc.). If no differences are found, the strings are equal; if a difference is found, the string with the first lower character is considered the smaller string. The `equals()` methods tell if two strings are equal or not by returning either a boolean `true` or `false`. The `compareTo()` methods provide additional information indicating the smaller or larger string and the character position that determined the result. If the two strings are equal, the `compareTo()` methods return a 0. When using the `ignoreCase` versions of these methods, the result of the comparison is independent of a letter's case. Thus, if case is ignored, the letters 'h' and 'H' are considered equal. Following are examples of string comparisons when case is not ignored:

"Hello" is greater than "Good Bye" because the first H in Hello is greater than the first G in Good Bye.

"hello" is less than "Hello" because the first h in hello is less than the first H in Hello.

"SMITH" is greater than "JONES" because the first S in SMITH is greater than the first J in JONES.

"123" is greater than "1227" because the third character, the 3 in 123, is greater than the third character, the 2 in 1227.

"Behop" is greater than "Beehive" because the third character, the h in Behop, is greater than the third character, the e in Beehive.

Program 9.2 uses these string methods within the context of a complete program.

PROGRAM 9.2

```java
import java.io.*;
public class StringMethods
{
  public static void main (String[] args)
  {

    String string1 = new String("Hello");
    String string2 = new String("Hello there");
    int n;

    System.out.println("string1 is the string " + string1);
    System.out.println("string2 is the string " + string2);
    System.out.println();   // blank line


    n = string1.compareTo(string2);


    if (n < 0)
      System.out.println(string1 + " is less than " + string2);
    else if (n == 0)
      System.out.println(string1 + " is equal to " + string2);
    else
```

(Continued on next page)

(Continued from previous page)

```
        System.out.println(string1 + " is greater than " + string2);

    if (string1.equalsIgnoreCase("HELLO"))
        System.out.println("string1 equals (ignoring case) HELLO");
    else
        System.out.println("string1 does not equal (ignoring case) HELLO");

    System.out.println("\nThe number of characters in string1 is " + string1.length());
    System.out.println("The number of characters in string2 is " + string2.length());

    string1 = string1.concat(" there world!");
    System.out.println("\nAfter concatenation, string1 contains the characters " +string1);
    System.out.println("The length of this string is " + string1.length());

    string1 = string1.toLowerCase();
    System.out.println("\nIn lowercase this string is " + string1);

    string1 = string1.toUpperCase();
    System.out.println("In uppercase this string is " + string1);


    }
}
```

Following is a sample output produced by Program 9.2:

```
string1 is the string Hello
string2 is the string Hello there

Hello is less than Hello there
string1 equals (ignoring case) HELLO

The number of characters in string1 is 5
The number of characters in string2 is 11

After concatenation, string1 contains the characters Hello there world!
The length of this string is 18

In lowercase this string is hello there world!
In uppercase this string is HELLO THERE WORLD!
```

In reviewing this output, refer to Figure 9.5, which shows how the characters in `string1` and `string2` are stored in memory. Note that the length of each string refers to the total number of characters in the string and that the first character in each string is located at index position 0. Thus, the length of a string is always one more than the index number of the last character's position in the string.

String1

String2

FIGURE 9.5   The Initial Strings in Program 9.2

Caution

When comparing two strings for equality, you should never use the equality operator, ==. The reason is that while the String class' compareTo() and equals() methods compare the actual characters in the strings being compared, the == operator compares the values stored in the reference variables that access the strings. This can lead to seemingly incorrect results. For example, assuming that s1 is declared as String s1 = "Help";, the expression(s1 == "Help") is true. However, if the characters H,e,l,p are instantiated in any other way, such as String s2 = "Helpless".substring(0,4);, the expression (s1 == s2) is false. The reason is that, although the strings referenced by both s1 and s2 consist of the same characters, the reference variables s1 and s2, as shown in Figure 9.6, reference two different strings. Thus, even though the characters in each string are the same, the reference variables themselves are different.

The important point to bring away from this is that equality of strings should not be tested using the equality operator, ==, that is used for comparing primitive data types. Rather, when testing for string equality, you should use either a compareTo() or equals() String class method.

FIGURE 9.6   Different Reference Variables Can Reference Equal Strings

Other String Methods

Although you will predominantly be using the shaded `String` class methods listed in Table 9.3, there are times when you will find the other string methods in this table useful. One of the more useful of these is the `charAt()` method, which permits you to retrieve individual characters in a string. Program 9.3 uses this method to select one character at a time from the string, starting at string position zero and ending at the position of the last character in the string. This last position is always one less than the number of characters in the string.

PROGRAM 9.3

```java
import java.io.*;
public class CountVowels
{
  public static void main (String[] args)
  {

    String str = new String("Counting the number of vowels");
    int i, numChars;
    int vowelCount = 0;

    System.out.println("The string: " + str);

    numChars = str.length();
    for (i = 0; i < numChars; i++)
    {
      switch(str.charAt(i))    // here is where a character is retrieved
      {
        case 'a':
        case 'e':
        case 'i':
        case 'o':
        case 'u':
           vowelCount++;
      }
    }

    System.out.println("has " + vowelCount + " vowels.");
  }
}
```

The expression `str.charAt(i)` in Program 9.3's `switch` statement retrieves the character at position `i` in the string. This character is then compared to five different character values. The `switch` statement uses the fact that selected cases "drop through" in the absence of `break` statements. Thus, all selected cases result in an increment to `vowelCount`. The output displayed by Program 9.3 is:

```
The string: Counting the number of vowels
has 9 vowels.
```

In programming practice, the remaining string methods listed in Table 9.3 usually center around locating specific characters in a string and creating substrings. Program 9.4 illustrates a number of examples of some of these other methods.

PROGRAM 9.4

```java
public class OtherMethods
{
  public static void main(String[] args)
  {

    String string1 = "LINEAR PROGRAMMING THEORY";
    String s1, s2, s3;
    int j, k, l;

    System.out.println("The original string is " + string1);

    j = string1.indexOf('I');
    System.out.println("  The first position of an 'I' is " + j);
    k = string1.indexOf('I', (j+1));
    System.out.println("  The next position of an 'I' is " + k);

    l = string1.lastIndexOf('I');
    System.out.println("  The last position of an 'I' is " + l);

    j = string1.indexOf("THEORY");
    System.out.println("  The first location of \"THEORY\" is " + j);

    k = string1.lastIndexOf("ING");
    System.out.println("  The last index of \"ING\" is " + k);

    s1 = string1.substring(2,6);
    s2 = string1.substring(18,22);
    s3 = string1.substring(6,14);

    System.out.println(s1.concat(s2).concat(s3));
  }
}
```

The output produced by Program 9.4 is:

```
The original string is LINEAR PROGRAMMING THEORY
  The first position of an 'I' is 1
  The next position of an 'I' is 15
  The last position of an 'I' is 15
  The first location of "THEORY" is 19
  The last index of "ING" is 15
NEAR THE PROGRAM
```

TABLE 9.4 Character Class General-Purpose Methods

Method	Description
`public static boolean isDigit(char ch)`	Returns a `true` if `ch` is a digit; otherwise, it returns a `false`.
`public static boolean isLetter(char ch)`	Returns a `true` if `ch` is a letter; otherwise, it returns a `false`.
`public static boolean isLowerCase(char ch)`	Returns a `true` if `ch` is a lowercase letter; otherwise, it returns a `false`.
`public static boolean isSpaceChar(char ch)`	Returns a `true` if `ch` is a space character; otherwise, it returns a `false`.
`public static boolean isUpperCase(char ch)`	Returns a `true` if `ch` is an uppercase letter; otherwise, it returns a `false`.
`public static boolean isWhitespace(char ch)`	Returns a `true` if `ch` is a Java-defined white-space; otherwise, it returns a `false`.
`public static char toLowerCase(char ch)`	Returns the lowercase equivalent of `ch` if the character is lowercase; otherwise, it returns the character unchanged.
`public static char toUpperCase(char ch)`	Returns the uppercase equivalent of `ch` if the character is lowercase; otherwise, it returns the character unchanged.
`public static char toString(char ch)`	Returns the string representation of `ch`.

The main point illustrated by Program 9.4 is that both individual characters and sequences of characters can be located in an existing string and extracted from a string. In extracting a substring, however, it is important to realize that the second argument in the `substring()` method is the position of the character one after the last character that is to be extracted. And as can be clearly seen, the concatenation operator, $+$, is preferable to the more complicated expression that uses the `concat()` method in the program's last executable statement.

Character **Class Methods**

In addition to the string methods provided by the `string` class, the Java language provides a number of very useful `Character` class general-purpose methods. A common subset of these methods is listed in Table 9.4.

Because all of the methods in Table 9.4 are `public` and `static`, which makes them general-purpose methods that are used independently of any object created from the class, each of these methods is preceded with its class name when it is invoked. Also notice that, except for the last three methods, each of the other methods return a boolean value of `true` if the character meets the desired condition and a value of `false` if the condition is not met. These methods that return a boolean value are generally used directly within an `if` statement. For example, consider the following code segment, which assumes that `ch` is a character variable:

```
if(Character.isDigit(ch))
  System.out.println("The character is a digit");
```

```
else if(Character.isLetter(ch))
  System.out.println("The character is a letter");
```

Here, if the ch contains a digit character, the first println() method is executed; if the character is a letter, the second println() statement is called. In both cases, however, the character to be checked is included as an argument to the appropriate method, which itself is preceded by the class name, Character, and a period. Program 9.5 illustrates this type of code within a program that counts the number of letters, digits, and other characters in a string. The individual characters to be checked are obtained using the String class' charAt() method in the same manner as was previously illustrated in Program 9.3. As in Program 9.3, this method is in a for loop that cycles through the string from the first to the last.

PROGRAM 9.5

```java
import java.io.*;
public class CharMethods
{
  public static void main (String[] args)
  {
    String str = new String("This –123/ is 567 A ?<6245> Test!");
    char nextChar;
    int i, numChars;
    int numLetters = 0, numDigits = 0, numOthers = 0;

    System.out.println("The original string is: " + str);

    numChars = str.length();
    System.out.println("This string contains " + numChars + " characters,"
                      + " which consist of");
      // check each character in the string
    for (i = 0; i < numChars; i++)
    {
      nextChar = str.charAt(i);   // get a character
      if (Character.isLetter(nextChar))
        numLetters++;
      else if (Character.isDigit(nextChar))
        numDigits++;
      else
        numOthers++;
    }

    System.out.println("    " + numLetters + " letters");
    System.out.println("    " + numDigits + " digits");
    System.out.println("    " + numOthers + " other characters.");

  }
}
```

The output produced by Program 9.5 is:

```
The original string is: This -123/ is 567 A ?<6245> Test!
This string contains 33 characters, which consist of
        11 letters
        10 digits
        12 other characters.
```

As indicated by this output, each of the 33 characters in the string has correctly been categorized as either a letter, digit, or other character.

Conversion Methods

The last group of string methods, which are listed in Tables 9.5 and 9.6, convert strings to and from primitive numerical data types. The methods in Table 9.5 are both `public` and `static` members of the `String` class, which means they are general purpose and are typically invoked by preceding the method name with the `String` class name and a period. In each case, the value to be converted is provided as a primitive data type argument, and the converted string value is returned from the method. For example, the statement `String str = String.valueOf(42689.65);` causes the string `"42689.65"` to be created from the double-precision number 42689.65 (recall that the default for values with a decimal point is double), and this string value can now be referenced by the variable named `str`.

For computational purposes, the conversion methods listed in Table 9.6, which provide conversions from string types to primitive types, are more useful. These methods have been divided into four categories that represent conversions from strings to integers, longs, floats, and doubles. Within each category of conversion types, there are three methods. In practice, either the first method alone converts from a string to a primitive type, or the last two methods are combined to produce the same conversion. For example, assuming the following declarations

```
String str = "42689.65";
double dvalue;
```

each of the following statements will convert the `str` string to the double-precision number 42689.65.

```
dvalue = Double.parseDouble(str);
```

and

```
dvalue = Double.valueOf(str).doubleValue()
```

Throughout this text, we have consistently used the conversion technique represented by the first statement because it is simpler. Because this conversion uses the general-purpose `parseDouble()` method, it is always invoked by preceding the method's name with the class name `Double` and a period. It is worthwhile examining how the second conversion technique works because you will also see it in your programming career.

TABLE 9.5 Primitive Type to String Conversion Methods (All Methods Are Members of the `String` Class)

Method	Description
`public static String valueOf(boolean b)`	Returns the string representation of its `boolean` argument.
`public static String valueOf(char c)`	Returns the string representation of its `char` argument.
`public static String valueOf(char[] data)`	Returns the string representation of its `char` array argument.
`public static String valueOf(char[] data, int offset, int count)`	Returns the string representation of a specific subarray of its `char` array argument.
`public static String valueOf(double d)`	Returns the string representation of its `double` argument.
`public static String valueOf(float f)`	Returns the string representation of its `float` argument.
`public static String valueOf(int i)`	Returns the string representation of its `int` argument.
`public static String valueOf(long l)`	Returns the string representation of its `long` argument.

TABLE 9.6 String to Primitive Type Conversion Methods (All Methods Are Members of the `String` Class)

Method	Class	Description
`public static integer parseInt(String str)`	`Integer`	Returns the integer representation of `str`.
`public static valueOf(String str)`	`Integer`	Returns the Integer value of `str`.
`integer integerValue()`	`Integer`	Returns the integer value of an Integer object.
`public static long parseLong(String str)`	`Long`	Returns the long representation of `str`.
`public static valueOf(String str)`	`Long`	Returns the Long value of `str`.
`long value()`	`Long`	Returns the long value of a Long object.
`public static float parseFloat(String str)`	`Float`	Returns the float representation of `str`.
`public static valueOf(String str)`	`Float`	Returns the Float value of `str`.
`float floatValue()`	`Float`	Returns the float value of a Float object.
`public static double parseDouble(String str)`	`Double`	Returns the double representation of `str`.
`public static valueOf(String str)`	`Double`	Returns the Double value of `str`.
`double doubleValue()`	`Double`	Returns the double value of a Double object.

First, the expression `Double.valueOf(str)` invokes the `Double` class' static method `valueOf()` to convert its string argument into an object of type `Double`. Once this object has been created, the `doubleValue()` method, which is a nonstatic method, is applied to it. Thus, a longer equivalent to the second conversion that more clearly shows how the conversion is accomplished is:

```
Double tempval = Double.valueOf(str);
dvalue = tempval.doubleValue();
```

Here the first statement uses the general-purpose method `valueOf()` to convert the `str` string to an object of type `Double`, which is then further converted to a double value in the second statement by applying a class method to the `Double` object.

EXERCISES 9.2

1. Enter and execute Program 9.2 on your computer.
2. Modify Program 9.2 to accept a string entered by the user.
3. Determine the value of `text.charAt(0)`, `text.charAt(3)`, and `text.charAt(10)`, assuming that `text` is the following string of characters:
   a. now is the time
   b. rocky raccoon welcomes you
   c. Happy Holidays
   d. The good ship
4. The following program illustrates the problems associated with the `==` operator when comparing strings. Enter and execute this program and then discuss why the second comparison did not indicate that the strings referenced by `s1` and `s3` were equal.

```
public class Caution
{
  public static void main(String[] args)
  {
    String s1 = "Help";
    String s2 = "Helpless";
    String s3;

    System.out.println("The string s1 is: " + s1);
    System.out.println("The string s2 is: " + s2);

    s3 = s2.substring(0,4);
    System.out.println("The string s3 is: " + s3);

    if (s1 == "Help")
     System.out.println("The first comparison returned a true.");
    else
      System.out.println("The first comparison returned a false.");
    if (s1 == s3)
      System.out.println("The second comparison returned a true.");
```

```
        else
          System.out.println("The second comparison returned a false.");
    }
}
```

5. Enter and execute Program 9.3 on your computer.

6. Modify Program 9.3 to count and display the individual numbers of each vowel contained in the string.

7. Modify Program 9.3 to display the number of vowels in a user-entered string.

8. Using the `charAt()` method, write and execute a Java program that reads in a string and prints the string out in reverse order. (*Tip:* Once the string has been entered and saved, retrieve and display characters starting from the end of the string.)

9. Write and execute a Java program that retrieves each character in a string, converts the character to uppercase form, and displays the character.

10. Assuming that the string variable `str` references the string `"1234"`, write two different statements that can convert this string into an integer number that is stored in the integer variable named `intnum`.

11. Assuming that the string variable `str` references the string `"1234"`, write two different statements that can convert this string into a long number that is stored in the long variable named `longnum`.

12. Assuming that the string variable `str` references the string `"1234.52"`, write two different statements that can convert this string into a floating-point number that is stored in the floating-point variable named `floatnum`.

13. Write and execute a Java program that counts the number of words in a string. A word is encountered whenever a transition from a blank space to a nonblank character is encountered. Assume that the string contains only words separated by blank spaces.

14. Generate 10 random numbers in the range 0 to 127. If the number represents a printable Unicode character, print the character with an appropriate message that:

    ```
    The character is a lowercase letter
    The character is an uppercase letter
    The character is a digit
    The character is a space
    ```

    If the character is none of these, display its value in integer format.

15. **a.** Write a general-purpose method named `countlets()` that returns the number of letters in a string passed as an argument. Digits, spaces, punctuation, tabs, and newline characters should not be included in the returned count.

    b. Include the `countlets()` method written for Exercise 15a in an executable Java program and test the method with the program.

9.3 THE `StringBuffer` CLASS

Although strings created from the `String` class can be manipulated using both `String` and `Character` class methods, the strings are immutable, which means that characters cannot be inserted, replaced, or added to the string once it is created. When this restric-

Table 9.7 `StringBuffer` Initializing (constructor) Class Methods

Method	Description	Example
`StringBuffer()`	Constructs a string having no characters and an initial capacity of 16 characters.	`StringBuffer str = new StringBuffer();`
`StringBuffer(int length)`	Constructs a string having no characters and an initial capacity specified by length.	`StringBuffer str = new StringBuffer(64);`
`StringBuffer(String str)`	Constructs a string having the same characters as `str` with a capacity of an additional 16 characters. The stored string is a copy of `str`, and the constructor effectively provides a conversion from a String to a StringBuffer object.	`StringBuffer str1 =new StringBuffer("Hello");`

tion becomes a problem, a better choice for implementing a string is as a StringBuffer object. Because StringBuffer strings are implemented as a mutable sequence of characters, these strings *can be* modified in a way that alters the total number of characters, replaces existing characters, and inserts or deletes characters within an existing string. The disadvantage is that the `StringBuffer` class does not provide a set of methods for comparing strings or locating characters and substrings within a string. Thus, the `string` class is the preferred class for displaying or comparing strings that tend to remain constant, whereas the `StringBuffer` class is preferred for applications that require individual character additions, modifications, and multiple text edits. Because String and StringBuffer conversion methods exist, one object type can always be converted into its other class counterpart when a particular method is required.

Initially, every StringBuffer string is created and stored in a buffer having a set character capacity. Because StringBuffer objects are stored in expandable buffer areas, and to distinguish them from their string counterparts, StringBuffer strings are frequently referred to as **string buffers.** In this text, we will use the terms string and string buffer interchangeably whenever it is clear to which class type we are referring.

As long as the number of characters in a string buffer, either because characters were inserted or appended, does not cause the buffer's capacity to be exceeded, the same buffer area is retained. However, if additions exceed the string's capacity, a new string buffer area is automatically allocated. Reducing the number of characters in a string buffer due to deletions does not decrease the capacity of the buffer.

From a user's standpoint, we would expect the `StringBuffer` class to provide all of the processing currently available using the `string` class, plus the additional methods that permit modifying a string buffer. This is, indeed, the case. Table 9.7 lists the methods provided by the `StringBuffer` class to create an initial String object of this data type, and Table 9.8 lists all of the available class methods.

As is seen in Table 9.8, the majority of the provided methods have to do with appending and inserting characters into an existing string. Both the `append()` and `insert()` methods are overloaded to accommodate a number of different data types. In all cases, the data are first converted to a StringBuffer and appended or inserted into the existing StringBuffer. The StringBuffer `append()` methods always add characters to the

str

FIGURE 9.7 Initial Storage of a StringBuffer Object

end of the string, and the insert() methods insert characters within a string at the designated position.

To illustrate some of the more common methods in Table 9.8, assume that we start with a string buffer type string created by the statement

```
StringBuffer str = new StringBuffer("This cannot be");
```

Figure 9.7 illustrates how this string is stored in the buffer created for it. As indicated in Table 9.7, the initial capacity of the buffer is the length of the string plus 16 characters.

Now assume that the following statement is executed:

```
str.insert(4, " I know");
```

This statement causes the designated seven characters, beginning with a blank, to be inserted starting at index position 4 in the existing string. The resulting string buffer, after the insertion, is shown in Figure 9.8 on page 461.

If the statement str.replace(12, 18, "to"); is now executed, the existing characters in index positions 12 through 17, which is one less than the designated ending index position, will be deleted, and the two characters t and o will be inserted starting at index position 12. Thus, the net effect of the replacement is as shown in Figure 9.9 on page 461. It is worthwhile noting that the number of replacement characters, which in this particular case is two, can be less than, equal to, or greater than the characters being replaced, which in this case is six.

Finally, if we append the string " correct" to the string in Figure 9.9 using the statement str.append(" correct");, the string illustrated in Figure 9.10 (page 461) is obtained.

Program 9.6 (page 462) illustrates the statements we have just examined within the context of a complete program. In addition, after the append() method is called, which results in the string shown in Figure 9.10, the program invokes the reverse() method to show how this string can be reversed.

T A B L E 9.8 StringBuffer Class Methods

Method	Description
Append Methods	
StringBuffer append(boolean b)	Appends the string representation of the boolean value b.
StringBuffer append(char c)	Appends the string representation of the char value c.
StringBuffer append(char[] str)	Appends the string representation of the char array str.
StringBuffer append(char[] str, int offset, int len)	Appends the string representation of the designated subarray.
StringBuffer append(int i)	Appends the string representation of the int value i.
StringBuffer append(long l)	Appends the string representation of the long value l.
StringBuffer append(double d)	Appends the string representation of the double value d.
StringBuffer append(float f)	Appends the string representation of the float value f.
StringBuffer append(String str)	Appends the string value str.
StringBuffer append(Object obj)	Appends the string representation of the Object obj.
Capacity Methods	
int capacity()	Returns the current string's capacity.
void ensureCapacity(int minCap)	Ensures the capacity of the string is at least equal to minCap. If the current capacity is less than minCap, the capacity is increased; otherwise, the capacity remains the same.
int length()	Returns the number of characters currently in the string.
void setLength(int newLength)	Increases or decreases the maximum length of the string. If the current length is greater than newLength, characters are discarded from the end of the string. If newLength is greater than the current length, null characters (\0) are added to the string.
Character Manipulation Methods	
char charAt(int index)	Returns the character at the specified index.
void setCharAt(int position, char ch)	Sets the character at the specified position to the value ch.
StringBuffer reverse()	Reverses the characters in the string.
void getChars(int srcBegin, int srcEnd, char[] dst, int dstBegin)	Copies the designated characters from the src string into the dst character array.

(Continued on next page)

TABLE 9.8 StringBuffer Class Methods

Method	Description
Replacement Method	
StringBuffer replace(int start, int end, String str)	Replaces the characters starting at position start and ending at one less than position end with the characters in the string str. The number of characters in str need not be the same as those being replaced.
Delete Methods	
StringBuffer delete(int start, int end)	Removes the specified characters starting at position start and ending at one position less than end. Start must be greater than zero and less than the length of the string or an exception error is generated.
StringBuffer deleteCharAt(int index)	Removes the character at the designated position and closes up the string around the deleted characters.
Insert Methods	
StringBuffer insert(int offset, Boolean b)	Inserts the string representation of the boolean value b into the string at the designated position.
StringBuffer insert(int offset, char c)	Inserts the string representation of the char value c into the string at the designated position.
StringBuffer insert(int offset, char[] str)	Inserts the string representation of the char array str into the string at the designated position.
StringBuffer insert(int index, char[] str, int offset, int len)	Inserts the string representation of the designated subarray into the string at the designated position.
StringBuffer insert(int offset, int i)	Inserts the string representation of the int value i into the string at the designated position.
StringBuffer insert(int offset, long l)	Inserts the string representation of the long value l into the string at the designated position.
StringBuffer insert(int offset, double d)	Inserts the string representation of the double value d into the string at the designated position.

(Continued on next page)

(Continued from previous page)

TABLE 9.8 `StringBuffer` Class Methods

Method	Description
`StringBuffer insert(int offset, float f)`	Inserts the string representation of the `float` value `f` into the string at the designated position.
`StringBuffer insert(int offset, String str)`	Inserts the string `str` into the string at the designated position.
`StringBuffer insert(int offset, Object obj)`	Inserts the string representation of the `Object` `obj` into the string.
`String substring(int start)`	Returns a new string that is a substring of the original string. The substring starts at the specified position and extends to the end of the string.
`String substring(int start, int end)`	Returns a new string that is a substring of the original string. The substring starts at the specified position and ends at one character position less than the end argument.

Conversion Method

`String toString()`	Converts the StringBuffer string into a string.

str

FIGURE 9.8   The String After the Insertion

str

FIGURE 9.9   The String After the Replacement

str

FIGURE 9.10   The String After the Append

PROGRAM 9.6

```java
import java.io.*;
public class StringBufferMethods
{
  public static void main (String[] args)
  {
    StringBuffer str = new StringBuffer("This cannot be");
    int i, numChars;

    System.out.println("The original string is: " + str);

    numChars = str.length();
    System.out.println("  This string has " + numChars + " characters.");

      // insert characters
    str.insert(4, " I know");
    System.out.println("The string, after insertion, is now: " + str);
    numChars = str.length();
    System.out.println("  This string has " + numChars + " characters.");

      // replace characters
    str.replace(12, 18, "to");
    System.out.println("The string, after replacement, is: " + str);
    numChars = str.length();
    System.out.println("  This string has " + numChars + " characters.");

      // append characters
    str.append(" correct");
    System.out.println("The string, after appending, is: " + str);
    numChars = str.length();
    System.out.println("  This string has " + numChars + " characters.");

      // reverse the characters
    str.reverse();
    System.out.println("The string, after being reversed, is: " + str);


  }
}
```

The following output is produced by Program 9.6. Except for the final reversal of string characters, it matches the individual strings shown in Figures 9.8 to 9.10.

```
The original string is: This cannot be
  This string has 14 characters.
The string, after insertion, is now: This I know cannot be
  This string has 21 characters.
```

```
The string, after replacement, is: This I know to be
   This string has 17 characters.
The string, after appending, is: This I know to be correct
   This string has 25 characters.
The string, after being reversed, is: tcerroc eb ot wonk I sihT
```

It is worthwhile noting that the concatenation operation provided for `String` class strings is actually implemented using the `StringBuffer` class' `append()` method. This is accomplished by first creating a new, initially empty StringBuffer object, applying as many `append()` methods as necessary to construct the final string value, and then converting the StringBuffer representation to a `String` class value. For example, the statement

```
String message = "Result = " + 2.04 + " feet.";
```

is implemented as:

```
String message = new StringBuffer().append("Result = ").append(2.04).append(" feet.").toString();
```

The conversion to a StringBuffer value is necessary because `String` class objects are immutable, which means they cannot be changed. StringBuffer objects permit implementation of a concatenation using an expandable StringBuffer object as an intermediary. Thus, if your program is going to require extensive concatenations, you are better off using StringBuffer objects directly, which removes the implicitly invoked conversion from String to StringBuffer at the beginning of each concatenation and the conversion back from StringBuffer to String at the completion of the concatenation.

Returning Multiple Values[3]

As was noted in Chapter 6, every Java method is restricted to returning at most one declared value to a calling method. As was also noted in Section 6.2, reference arguments can circumvent this restriction by passing multiple values back through their parameter list if a reference argument is used and the reference argument does not refer to an immutable object, such as a string. Now that we have introduced StringBuffer types, which are specifically designed to be mutable (i.e., object values can be changed), we can illustrate passing values from a called method to its calling method through the parameter list.

To understand how this is accomplished, reconsider Figure 6.9, which has been redrawn as Figure 9.11. Notice in the figure that both the calling and called method have access to the exact same object via the same reference value. Thus, if the called method changes the object's value, the change will be accessible by the called method. This implies that as many values can be returned to a calling program as there are reference arguments in the called method's parameter list.

To see how this works in practice, consider Program 9.7, in which the `main()` method passes a single reference argument named `stringArg` when the method named `changeArgValue()` is called. Although the called method is formally declared as returning

---

[3]This topic can be omitted on first reading with no loss of subject continuity.

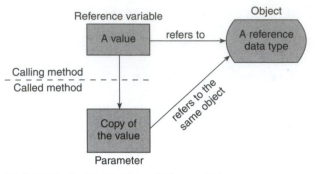

FIGURE 9.11   Passing a Reference Value

no value (`void`), a value is returned through its single reference parameter. The mechanism for doing this relies on the correspondence between the reference argument, named `stringArg`, used when the method is called and the reference parameter, named `stringBufRef`, declared in the method's header line.

In calling the `changeArgValue()` method within Program 9.7, it is necessary to understand the connection between the calling method's reference argument and the called method's reference parameter. As shown in Figure 9.12, *both reference the same object*. The calling method refers to the object using the name `stringArg`, while the called method refers to the object as `stringBufRef`. Thus, a change by either the called or calling method to the value stored in the referenced object will be reflected in both methods.

Specifically, the called method in Program 9.7 converts its StringBuffer value into an integer number, multiplies the number by 2, and returns the value as a StringBuffer object. To verify this, the output produced by Program 9.7 is:

```
The StringBuffer value sent into the method is: 10
The StringBuffer value sent back through the argument is: 20
```

Although the method `changeArgValue()` in Program 9.7 is more complicated than it needs to be for illustrating how to return a StringBuffer value through the parameter list, it was also constructed to illustrate all of the conversions required in manipulating and

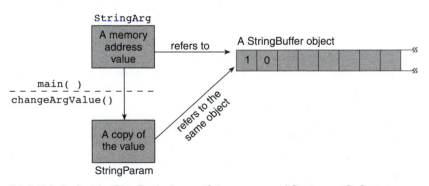

FIGURE 9.12   The Equivalence of Argument and Parameter References

PROGRAM 9.7

```java
public class ChangeArg
{
  public static void main(String[] args)
  {
    StringBuffer stringArg = new StringBuffer("10");

    System.out.println("The StringBuffer value sent into the method is: "
                       + stringArg);
    changeArgValue(stringArg);
    System.out.println(
        "The StringBuffer value sent back through the argument is: "
        + stringArg);
  }

  public static void changeArgValue(StringBuffer stringParam)
  {
    int num;

    num = Integer.parseInt(stringParam.toString());
    num = 2 * num;
    stringParam.delete(0,stringParam.length()); // clear the StringBuffer
    stringParam.append(num);    // set the new value into the StringBuffer
  }
}
```

returning values that have a numerical equivalent. As seen, these conversions require a StringBuffer to string to numerical conversion before the multiplication by 2 can take place and then a numerical to StringBuffer conversions within the called method for the returned value. If the calling method needed to use the returned value as a number, individual conversions from a StringBuffer to a string to a numerical type would also be required. As you might expect, this much data manipulation might indicate that there is a better procedure for effectively returning multiple values from a called method, which indeed is the case.

For cases where multiple numerical values need to be returned from a method, the values should be incorporated into an object with appropriate class methods that can directly manipulate numerical values. One such case, where a method is required to swap the values contained in two variables, is presented in Section 11.3.

EXERCISES 9.3

1. Enter and execute Program 9.6 on your computer.
2. a. Write a Java method to count the total number of characters, including blanks, contained in a string.
   b. Include the method written for Exercise 2a in a complete working program.

3. Write a program that accepts a string of characters from a terminal and displays the hexadecimal equivalent of each character.

4. Write a Java program that accepts a string of characters from a terminal and displays the string one word per line.

5. Write a method that reverses the characters in a string.

6. Write a method named `remove()` that returns nothing and deletes all occurrences of its character argument from a StringBuffer value. The method should take two arguments: the StringBuffer name and the character to be removed. For example, if the StringBuffer object named `message` contains the string `Happy Holidays`, the method call `remove(message,'H')` should place the string `appy olidays` into the message.

7. a. Write a general-purpose Java method named `toUpper()` that converts all lowercase letters in a string into uppercase letters. The original string should be passed as an argument to the method, and the uppercase equivalent string should be returned.

   b. Add a data input check to the method written in Exercise 7a to verify that a valid lowercase letter is passed to the method. A character in Unicode is lowercase if it is greater than or equal to a and less than or equal to z. If the character is not a valid lowercase letter, have the method `toUpper()` return the passed character unaltered.

8. Write a Java program that accepts a string from a terminal and converts all lowercase letters in the string to uppercase letters. (*Tip:* See Exercise 7.)

9. Write a Java program that counts the number of words in a StringBuffer. A word occurs whenever a transition from a blank space to a nonblank character is encountered. Assume the string contains only words separated by blank spaces.

10. Write a general-purpose method named `trimfrnt()` that deletes all leading blanks from a StringBuffer and returns a String.

11. Write a general-purpose method named `trimrear()` that deletes all trailing blanks from a StringBuffer and returns a String.

12. Write a method named `addchars()` that adds n occurrences of a character to a StringBuffer. For example, the call `addchars(message, 4, '!')` should add four exclamation points at the end of `message`.

13. Write a general-purpose method named `extract()` that accepts a String, referenced as `s1`, and two integer numbers, n1 and n2, as arguments. The method should extract n2 characters from the string referenced by `s1`, starting at position n1, and return the extracted characters as a string. For example, if string s1 contains the characters `05/18/95 D169254 Rotech Systems`, the method call `extract(s1, 18, 6)` should return the string `Rotech` in s2.

14. A word or phrase in which the letters spell the same message (with changes in the whitespace permitted and punctuation not considered) when written both forward and backward is a palindrome. For example, Madam I'm Adam and A man, a plan, a canal: Panama! are both palindromes. Write a Java program that accepts a line of text as input and examines the entered text to determine if it is a palindrome. If the entered text is a palindrome, display the message `This is a palindrome`. If a palindrome was not entered, the message `This is not a palindrome` should be displayed.

9.4 APPLICATIONS

In this section, we present two applications. The first application deals with string objects and the second is about StringBuffer objects. In the first application, we construct a word counting algorithm and method. Such methods are particularly useful when the number of words in an article or paper must be known.

The second application presents a simple but elegant method of plotting data on either a video screen or standard line printer. Here a first pass initializes an array with the data points to be plotted and determines maximum and minimum values. These values are then used to calculate an appropriate scaling factor to ensure that the final plot fits within the area of the video screen or paper. Finally, a second pass through the data converts each data point into a StringBuffer object and produces the plot.

Application 1: Word Counting

In writing a paper, it is often desirable to have a count of the number of words in the paper. The computer can aid in this task. For this application, we develop a general-purpose method that counts the number of words in a string that is passed to it.

Step 1: Analyze the Problem Since each word in a sentence is followed by a blank space, it would seem that we could determine the number of words in a line of text by counting the number of blanks it contains. However, we should look at an example to be sure that this method works. The sentence "This is a sentence." has three blank spaces and four words; so far, the number of words is not equal to the number of blanks. However, if we were to store that sentence (or string) in a string variable named `line`, the characters would look like Figure 9.13. Notice that each word is followed by at least one blank, but one or more blanks could be inserted between words. So if the program counted blank spaces, the number of blanks would give us an incorrect word count.

A more elegant approach would be to count the number of transitions from a blank space to a nonblank character. This is the approach we will take. Then, no matter how many blank spaces separate words, we will obtain an accurate word count. However, there is one modification. The first word in a sentence may or may not be preceded by a blank. So we will have to take this boundary value case into consideration.

Step 2: Develop a Solution The basis of our solution will be to make use of a boolean variable that will be set to `false` whenever a blank space is encountered and will be set and remain as `true` whenever a nonblank character is encountered. Using this approach, whenever a blank space is detected, we will set the boolean variable to indicate that we

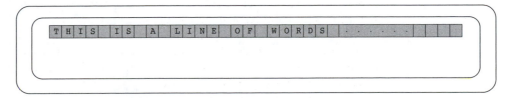

FIGURE 9.13 A Sample Line of Words

are not in a word. Then, only when there is a transition of the variable from a `false` state, which indicates the detection of a blank character, to a `true` state, which indicates the detection of a nonblank character, will we add one to the word count. This approach, with one modification for the first word, works because each word *must be preceded* by at least one blank space. To handle the first word in a sentence, which may or may not be preceded by a blank space, we can simply initialize our boolean variable to `false`. Then, if the first character in the word is nonblank, the transition to a `true` state will also be triggered, and the word count will be set to one. The algorithm describing this is:

```
Set a boolean variable to false
Set a word count to zero
Enter the string to be checked
For each character in the string
  If the character is a blank character
      Set the boolean variable to false
  Else If the boolean variable is false
      Add one to the word counter
      Set the  boolean variable to true
Display the value of the word counter
```

There are two key points that are necessary to understand this algorithm. The first is that the boolean variable that keeps track of whether we are in a word or not is set to `false` *each and every time* a blank character is detected, but it is set to `true` *only on the first occurrence* of a new word. Thus, if five blank characters in a row are detected, for example, the boolean variable will be set `false` five times. Once a new word has been detected, however, and the boolean variable is set to `true`, it will not reset until a blank is encountered, and then it will be set `false`. The second point to note is that the `else-if` statement is executed every time a nonblank character has been detected. Each time this happens, we test whether or not we were in a word. If we were not in a word (boolean variable is `false`), we have successfully detected a transition to a new word, and the word counter is incremented. Then, to prevent the next character in the same word from incrementing the counter, the boolean variable is set to `true`.

Step 3: Code the Solution The following method presents Java code for our algorithm. Notice that the name selected for the boolean variable is `inAWord`. When this variable is false, indicating that a blank character has been detected, we are clearly not in a word, but when this variable is true, indicating that a nonblank character has been detected, we are clearly within a word. It is the transitions for not in a word to in a word that increment the word counter.

```java
public static int countWords(String line)
{
  int i, count = 0;
  boolean inAWord = false;

  // search the string for a transition from a blank
  // to a non-blank - initially, the first non-blank
  // character will signify the start of a new word.
  for(i = 0; i < line.length(); i++)
```

```
  {
    if(Character.isSpaceChar(line.charAt(i)))
      inAWord = false;
    else if(inAWord == false)
    {
      inAWord = true;
      count++;
    }
  }
  return count;

}
```

Program 9.8 implements this method within the context of a complete program.

PROGRAM 9.8

```
import java.io.*;    // needed to access input stream classes
public class WordCount
{
  public static void main (String[] args)
  throws java.io.IOException
  {
    String s1;
    int wordCount;

    // set up the basic input stream
      // needed for conversion capabilities
    InputStreamReader isr = new InputStreamReader(System.in);
      // needed to use readLine()
    BufferedReader br = new BufferedReader(isr);

    System.out.println("Enter a sentence to be checked");
    s1 = br.readLine();

    wordCount = countWords(s1);
    System.out.println("\nThe number of words entered is " + wordCount);
  }

  public static int countWords(String line)
  {
    int i, count = 0;
    boolean inAWord = false;

    // search the string for a transition from a blank
    // to a non-blank - initially, the first non-blank
```

(Continued on next page)

```
(Continued from previous page)
     // character will signify the start of a new word.
     for(i = 0; i < line.length(); i++)
     {
       if(Character.isSpaceChar(line.charAt(i)))
         inAWord = false;
       else if(inAWord == false)
       {
         inAWord = true;
         count++;
       }
     }
     return count;
   }
 }
```

Step 4: Test and Correct the Solution: A test run of Program 9.8 produced the following result:

```
Enter a sentence to be checked
This is the sentence that I would like checked.

The number of words entered is 9
```

Further tests should now include sentences with multiple blank spaces before each word and the final period.

Application 2: Curve Plotting

Two basic constraints must be considered when graphing data on either a video screen or printer. The first constraint is that both devices automatically move in a forward direction, which means that our graphs should avoid the need to "back up" (although there are methods for reversing the cursor motion on a video screen, all of our programs will be constructed to work for both printers and screens). The second constraint is that both printer paper and video displays are restricted in the horizontal direction to displaying a maximum of either 80 or 132 characters. No such restriction exists in the vertical direction because the paper length is effectively unlimited and the video display scrolls forward. For this reason, our plots will always be constructed "sideways" with the y axis horizontal and the x axis vertical. This means that the values must always be checked, and scaled if necessary, to fit across a page or screen. With these two constraints in mind, consider the plot in Figure 9.14.

As illustrated in Figure 9.14, the graph is plotted sideways with the y axis displayed across the top of the graph and the x axis displayed down the side. Omitting, for the moment, the two header lines,

y axis

+ – →

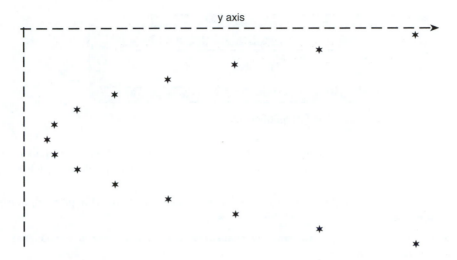

FIGURE 9.14

the actual graph of the data points consists of 15 individual lines, as follows:

```
line  1: |                                                    *
line  2: |                                          *
line  3: |                                   *
line  4: |                           *
line  5: |                 *
line  6: |           *
line  7: |      *
line  8: |     *
line  9: |      *
line 10: |         *
line 11: |              *
line 12: |                    *
line 13: |                          *
line 14: |                                 *
line 15: |                                              *
```

Notice that individually, each line consists of only two printed symbols: a bar, |, and an asterisk, *. The bar is always displayed in column one and the asterisk is positioned to indicate an appropriate *y* value. With these points in mind, it is rather easy to construct these 15 lines. To do this, we will first construct an exact image of the first line to be printed as a StringBuffer value. After the StringBuffer is constructed and printed, it will be used to construct an image of the second line. After the second image is displayed, the same array is used to construct an image of the third line and so on until all 15 lines have been displayed. This is the reason for using a StringBuffer; the value in the StringBuffer can be changed for each line that is to be displayed. To ensure that the elements in the StringBuffer can be displayed on a page, the length of the StringBuffer should be the same size as the width of either the paper or video screen being used for the display.

FIGURE 9.15   The StringBuffer line

As illustrated in Figure 9.15, the array, called line, is filled with blanks, except for the first element, which stores the bar symbol, and one other element, which stores an asterisk.

Using a StringBuffer to store the image of each line before it is printed, our graphing algorithm is:

Step 1. Store an asterisk in the desired character position of the StringBuffer
Step 2. Print the StringBuffer
Step 3. Reset the character set in step 1 to a blank
Step 4. Repeat steps 1 through 3 until the required number of lines have been displayed

Assuming that the name of the StringBuffer is line, the four steps in the graphing algorithm are easily implemented with a for loop having the form:

```
for (x = 1; x <= 15; x++)
{
   calculate a value for y
   line[y] = '*';      // set character to an asterisk
   System.out.println(line);
   line[y] = ' ';      // reset character to a blank
}
```

The calculation of the y value, which is then used as an index into the StringBuffer, depends on the graph being plotted. For the graph in Figure 9.14, the equation $y = (x - 8)^2 + 3$ was used.[4] Incorporating this into the for loop yields the executable code

```
for (x = 1; x <= 15; ++x)
{
   y = pow((x-8),2.0) + 3;
   line[y] = '*';      // set character to an asterisk
   System.out.println(line);
   line[y] = ' ';      // reset character to a blank
}
```

Program 9.9 includes this code within a working program.

[4]To use the y value as a subscript for the line array requires that this value be an integer between the numbers 0 and 72, inclusive. The curve $y = (x - 8)^2 + 3$ was selected precisely because it yielded y values within this range. Once the plotting algorithm is understood, an algorithm is presented for scaling all y values into the required range.

PROGRAM 9.9

```java
import java.io.*;
public class LineOne
{
  public static void main(String[] args)
  throws java.io.IOException
  {
    int x, y;
    StringBuffer line =
      new StringBuffer("|                                    ");
    for (x = 1; x <= 15; x++)
    {
      y = (int)Math.pow((x-8),2.0) + 3;
      line.setCharAt(y,'*');        // set character to an asterisk
      System.out.println(line);
      line.setCharAt(y,' ');        // reset character to a blank
    }
  }
}
```

Notice in Program 9.9 that the StringBuffer named line is declared and initialized with a bar symbol and the remaining characters with blanks. The for loop then calculates a y value, uses this value as an index to locate where the asterisk should be placed in the StringBuffer, displays the StringBuffer's value, and restores a blank in place of the asterisk. This process is repeated 15 times, resulting in the plot illustrated in Figure 9.16.

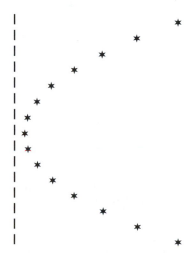

FIGURE 9.16　The Display Produced by Program 9.9

In reviewing Program 9.9, two observations must be made. First, y axis header lines have not been explicitly included on the output. This is a minor omission that is rectified by Program 9.10.

PROGRAM 9.10

```java
import java.io.*;
public class PlotTwo
{
  public static void main(String[] args)
  throws java.io.IOException
  {
    int x, y;
    String label =
      new String("                        y axis");
    String axis =
      new String("+----------------------------------------------------------->");
    StringBuffer line =
      new StringBuffer("|                                                        ");

    System.out.println(label);
    System.out.println(axis);

    for (x = 1; x <= 15; x++)
    {
      y = (int)Math.pow((x-8),2.0) + 3;
      line.setCharAt(y,'*');       // set character to an asterisk
      System.out.println(line);
      line.setCharAt(y,' ');       // reset character to a blank
    }
  }
}
```

Notice that Program 9.10 is essentially the same as Program 9.9 with the addition of two StringBuffer declarations for the y axis and two `println()` calls to display the label and y axis strings. These statements are placed before the `for` loop to display the header lines. Program 9.10 produces the completed plot shown in Figure 9.17.

A more serious problem with both Programs 9.10 and 9.11 is that negative y values and y values greater than the length of the `line` StringBuffer cannot be accommodated as a subscript to the line array. To accommodate graphs with such values requires scaling of the y values to fit within the initial StringBuffer's length. The scaling algorithm to do this, which ensures that our plotting program works for any y value, requires the use of an array, which is presented next.

Equation 9.1 provides a scaling formula that ensures that all plotted data will fit within the width of a paper or video screen. Thus, it should be used before a plotting routine is employed.

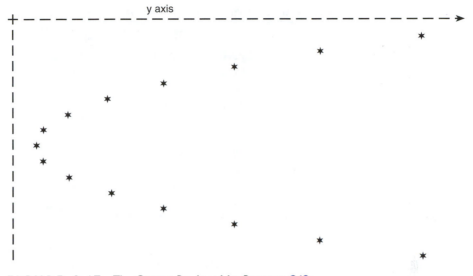

FIGURE 9.17   The Output Produced by Program 9.10

$$
\textit{(Eq. 9.1)} \quad \text{Scaled y value} = \frac{\textit{Original value} - \textit{Minimum value}}{\textit{Maximum value} - \textit{Minimum value}} \times \textit{(W - 1)}
$$

where the *Maximum* and *Minimum* values are the respective maximum and minimum values for the complete set of data values being plotted and *W* is the desired width of the paper or video display.

The term

$$
\frac{\textit{Original value} - \textit{Minimum value}}{\textit{Maximum value} - \textit{Minimum value}}
$$

in Equation 9.1 forces each original *y* value to lie within the range 0 to 1, with the minimum data value corresponding to 0 and the maximum data value to 1. Multiplying this result by the term $(W - 1)$ produces values between 0 and $(W - 1)$, for a total width of *W*.

For example, the second column in Table 9.9 lists *y* values of the equation $y = -x^3$ for values of *x* between -5 and 5 in increments of 0.5. As shown in column two, the maximum and minimum *y* values are $+125$ and -125, respectively.

For purposes of illustration, assume that the width of the display area for plotting each *y* value in column 2 is 55 characters. Also assume that a single character of this display area is to be used for an axis symbol, such as the bar. This leaves a total width, *W*, of 54 for the actual data display. Applying Equation 9.1 to the data of column two with $W = 54$, and using the correct minimum and maximum values of -125 and 125, respectively, yields the values listed in column three of the table. Notice that the minimum value of -125 is converted to the value 0.000 and the maximum value of 125 is converted to the value 53.000. The last column in the table is the rounded and integerized values of the scaled numbers listed in the third column. Notice that the values in column four range from 0 to 53, for a total range of 54 possible *y* values. These values can be used directly by the curve plotting routine presented in Program 9.10 to create a graph similar to that in Figure 9.18.

TABLE 9.9   Values of the Equation $y = -x^3$

x	y	Scaled y	Rounded
−5 0	−125.000	0.000	0
−4.5	−91.125	7.186	7
−4.0	−64.000	12.932	13
−3.5	−42.875	17.411	17
−3.0	−27.000	20.776	21
−2.5	−15.625	23.188	23
−2.0	−8.000	24.804	25
−1.5	−3.375	25.786	26
−1.0	−1.000	26.288	26
−0.5	−0.125	26.473	26
0.0	0.000	26.500	27
0.5	0.125	26.527	27
1.0	1.000	26.712	27
1.5	3.375	27.216	27
2.0	8.000	28.196	28
2.5	15.625	29.813	30
3.0	27.000	32.224	32
3.5	42.875	35.590	36
4.0	64.000	40.068	40
4.5	91.125	45.819	46
5.0	125.000	53.000	53

Program 9.11, which created Figure 9.18, includes the data scaling algorithm for the equation $y = -x^3$ and the curve plotting routine in Program 9.10.

PROGRAM 9.11

```
import java.io.*;
public class PlotThree
{
  public static void main(String[] args)
  throws java.io.IOException
  {
    final int MAXPOINTS = 100;
    int i, npts;
    int nval[] = new int[MAXPOINTS];
    double x, xinc, fval, ymin, ymax, width;
    double sval[] = new double[MAXPOINTS];

    String label =
      new String("                    y axis");
    String axis =
```

(Continued on next page)

(Continued from previous page)

```java
      new String("+--------------------------------------------------------->");
   StringBuffer line =
      new StringBuffer("|                                                    ");

   System.out.println(label);
   System.out.println(axis);

   ymax = 1.0e-5;
   ymin = 1.0e+5;
   x = -5.0;
   xinc = 0.5;
   npts = 21;
   width = 53;

   // load up the data to be plotted and find the max and min values
   for (i = 1; i <= npts; i++)
   {
    sval[i] = Math.pow(x,3.0);
    if (sval[i] > ymax)
      ymax = sval[i];
    if (sval[i] < ymin)
      ymin = sval[i];
    x = x + xinc;
    }

   // scale all y values to be plotted
   for (i = 1; i <= npts; ++i)
   {
      fval = ( (sval[i] - ymin)/(ymax - ymin) ) * width;
      nval[i] = (int) (fval + 0.5);   // convert to an integer value
   }

   // produce the plot
   System.out.println("Minimum Y Value: " + ymin);
   System.out.println("Maximum Y Value: " + ymax);
   System.out.println(label);
   System.out.println(axis);
   for (i = 1; i <= npts; ++i)
   {
      line.setCharAt(nval[i] + 2,'*');     // set character to an asterisk
      System.out.println(line);
      line.setCharAt(nval[i] + 2,' ');     // reset character to a blank
   }
  }
}
```

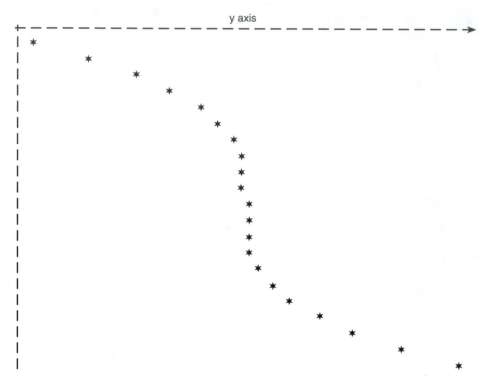

```
Minimum Y Value: -125.000000
Maximum Y Value: 125.000000
```

FIGURE 9.18   The Output Produced by Program 9.11

EXERCISES 9.4

1. Enter and execute Program 9.8 on your computer.
2. Modify Program 9.8 so that it counts the number of nonblank and blank characters as well as words.
3. Modify Program 9.8 so that it uses any whitespace (blanks, tabs, and new lines) as word delimiters.
4. Modify Program 9.8 to count sentences as well as words in a string. Assume that each sentence ends in a period. Then have the program compute and display the total number of words in all of the sentences and the average number of words per sentence.
5. Modify Program 9.8 so that it counts the number of letters in each word of a sentence. Have the program then compute the average word length of the sentence.
6. Write a Java program to read in a name having the form *first name last name* and display it the form *last name, first name*. (*Tip:* Check for one or more blank spaces after the first word.)

7. Write a Java program that converts numbers written in a base other than 10 to their base-10 value. The program should accept two numbers: the base and a value in the given base. The output of the program should be the equivalent base-10 value of the input. Test your program with the following data:

Base	Value
2	11101
5	231024
8	2760
12	3B07
16	9A3

8. Write a Java program to convert positive integers written in one base to their equivalent value in a second base. The program must permit both bases in the range of base 2 to base 16. Test your program with the following data:

34_{10} to base 16

110111_2 to base 4

$EF23_{16}$ to base 8

3211_5 to base 6

2512_7 to base 16

2347_8 to base 2

3490_{10} to base 8

9. Enter and run Program 9.11 on your computer.

10. Modify Program 9.11 to plot the curve $y = x^3 - 4x^2 + 3x + 2$ for x equal to 0, 1, 2, 3, 4, 5, and 6.

11. Modify Program 9.11 to plot the curve $y = x^3 - 4x^2 + 3x + 2$ for x between -8 and $+8$ in increments of 0.5.

12. Modify Program 9.11 to plot the curve $y = 4x^3 - x^4$ for x between -10 and $+10$ in increments of 0.5.

9.5 COMMON PROGRAMMING ERRORS

1. Breaking a string across two or more lines. For example, the statement

```
System.out.println("The result of the computation
                    is: ");
```

results in a compiler error. The correct way to separate a string across multiple lines is to concatenate two or more strings. Thus, the previous statement can be written as:

```
System.out.println("The result of the computation"
                    + " is: ");
```

2. Not remembering that the first character in a string is located at position 0, not 1.

3. Not remembering that the number returned by the `length()` method is one more than the position number of the string's last character. For example, the length of the string `"Hello"` is 5, but the position of the last character is 4. The length of a string is simply the number of characters in the string.

4. Using the == operator to compare two strings rather than the `compareTo()` or `equals()` methods. Because the comparison methods compare strings on a character-by-character basis, but the == operator does not, you should not use the == operator when comparing strings.

5. Not specifying one position beyond the desired character to be extracted using the `substring()` method. For example, to extract the characters near from the string `"Linear"` requires the statement `"Linear".substring(2,6);`.

9.6 CHAPTER SUMMARY

1. A *string literal* is any sequence of characters enclosed in double quotation marks. A string literal is also referred to as a string value, a string constant, or more conventionally, as a string.

2. String literals can be constructed from either String or StringBuffer objects.

3. Strings constructed from the `String` class are *immutable*. This means that characters cannot be inserted, replaced, or added to an existing string without creating a new string.

4. The `String` class is more commonly used for constructing strings for input and output purposes, such as for prompts and displayed messages. In addition, because of the provided capabilities, this class is also used when strings need to be compared, searched, or individual characters in a string need to be examined or extracted as a substring.

5. The `StringBuffer` class is used in more advanced situations when characters within a string need to be replaced, inserted, or deleted on a relatively regular basis.

6. String and StringBuffer objects are accessed using reference variables.

7. Because a string is constructed as an object of either the `String` or `StringBuffer` class, it must first be created by allocating space for the object. The methods that initially allocate memory space for a new object, be it a string or some other type of object, are referred to as *constructors*.

8. Strings can be manipulated using either the methods of the class they are objects of or by using general-purpose string and character methods.

PART 3

Creating Classes

481

CHAPTER 10

Introduction
to Classes

In addition to providing a rich set of prewritten classes, Java provides the capabilities of creating one's own set of classes. Although for most initial applications the Java-provided packages of classes are more than sufficient, as you progress in your programming experience you may need to begin constructing your own library of classes. An additional benefit is that once you understand how to do this, you will have invaluable insight into how the Java classes are themselves constructed and a much better understanding of how to use and extend existing classes for your own purposes.

In its most fundamental form, a class is defined as an abstract data type, which is simply a programmer-defined data type. In this chapter, we explore the implications of permitting programmers to define their own data types and then present Java's mechanism for constructing classes and incorporating multiple classes into a single package. As you will see, the construction of a data type is based on variables and methods; the variables provide the means for creating new data configurations, and the methods provide the means for performing operations on these class variables. A complete Java class provides a unique way of combining variables and methods together into a self-contained, cohesive unit from which objects can be created.

10.1 OBJECT-BASED PROGRAMMING

We live in a world full of objects: planes, trains, cars, telephones, books, computers, and so on. Until the mid-1990s, however, programming techniques had not reflected this at all. The primary programming paradigm[1] had been procedural, where a program is defined as an algorithm written in a machine-readable language. The reasons for this emphasis on procedural programming are primarily historical.

When computers were developed in the 1940s, they were used by mathematicians for military purposes such as computing bomb trajectories, decoding enemy orders, and diplomatic transmissions. After World War II, computers were still primarily used by mathematicians for mathematical computations. This reality was reflected in the name of the first commercially available high-level language, introduced in 1957. The language's name is Fortran, which was derived from *for*mula *tran*slation. Further reflecting this predominant mathematical usage was the fact that in the 1960s almost all computer courses were within mathematics departments. Even the term **computer science** was not yet in common use.

This situation has changed dramatically, primarily for two reasons. One of the reasons for disenchantment with procedural-based programs was the failure of traditional procedural languages to provide an adequate means of containing software costs. Software costs include all costs associated with initial program development and subsequent program maintenance. As illustrated in Figure 10.1, the major cost of most computer projects today, whether technical or commercial, is for software.

Software costs contribute so heavily to total project costs because they are directly related to human productivity (they are labor intensive), whereas the equipment associated with hardware costs is related to manufacturing technologies. For example, microchips that cost more than $500 ten years ago can now be purchased for less than $1.

It is far easier, however, to increase manufacturing productivity 1,000-fold with the consequent decrease in hardware costs, than it is for programmers to double either the

---

[1]A paradigm is a standard way of thinking about or doing something.

FIGURE 10.1   Software Is the Major Cost of Most Computer Projects

quantity or quality of the code they produce. So as hardware costs have plummeted, software productivity and its associated costs have remained relatively constant. Thus, the ratio of software costs to total system costs (hardware plus software) has increased dramatically.

One way to significantly increase programmer productivity is to create code that can be reused without extensive revision, retesting, and revalidation. The inability of procedurally structured code to provide this type of reusability led to the search for other software approaches.

The second reason for disenchantment with procedural-based programming was the emergence of graphical screens and the subsequent interest in window applications. Programming multiple windows on the same graphical screen is virtually impossible using standard procedural programming techniques.

The solution to producing programs that efficiently manipulate graphical screens and provide reusable windowing code was found in artificial intelligence-based and simulation programming techniques. Artificial intelligence contained extensive research on geometric object specification and recognition. Simulation contained considerable background on simulating items as objects with well-defined interactions between them. This object-based paradigm fit well in a graphical windows environment, where each window can be specified as a self-contained object.

An object is also well suited to a programming representation because it can be specified by two basic characteristics: a current **state,** which defines how the object appears at the moment, and a **behavior,** which defines how the object reacts to external inputs. To make this more concrete, consider a geometric object, such as a rectangle. A rectangle's current state is defined by its shape and location. The shape is traditionally specified by its length and width, while its location can be specified in a number of ways. One simple way is to list the values of two diagonal corner positions. The behavior we provide a rectangle depends on what we are willing to have our rectangle do. For example, if we intend to display the rectangle on a screen, we might provide it with the ability to move its position and change either its length or width.

It is worthwhile distinguishing here between an actual rectangle, which might exist on a piece of paper or a computer screen, and our description of it. Our description is more accurately termed a model. By definition, a **model** is only a representation of a real object; it is not the object itself. Very few models are ever complete; that is, a model typically does not reveal every aspect of the object it represents. Each model is defined for a

POINT OF INFORMATION

PROCEDURAL, HYBRID, AND PURE OBJECT-ORIENTED LANGUAGES

Most high-level programming languages can be placed into one of three main categories: procedural, object-based, or object-oriented. Fortran, which was the first commercially available high-level programming language, is procedural. This makes sense because Fortran was designed to perform mathematical calculations that used standard algebraic formulas. Formally, these formulas were described as algorithms, and then the algorithms were coded using method and subroutine procedures. Other procedural languages that followed Fortran include BASIC, COBOL, and Pascal.

The first requirement of an object-oriented language is that it contain three specific features: classes, inheritance, and polymorphism (each of these features is described in this and the next chapter). Because Java provides these three features, it is categorized as object-oriented.

In a pure object-oriented language, all data types would be constructed as classes, all data values would be objects, all operators could be overloaded, and every data operation could only be executed using a class member method. Thus, in a pure object-oriented language, it would be impossible not to use object-oriented features throughout a program. Currently, only Eiffel and Smalltalk qualify as pure object-oriented languages.

Languages that use classes but do not provide inheritance and polymorphic features are referred to as *object-based* languages rather than *object-oriented*. An example of an object-based language was any version of Visual Basic prior to Version 4. None of these earlier versions of Visual Basic provided inheritance features.

The distinguishing feature of a hybrid language is that it is possible to write a complete program using procedural code and no classes. C++ is an example of this type of language.

particular purpose that usually requires representing only the part of an object's state or behavior that is of interest. To clarify this point further, consider another common object, an elevator.

Like all objects, an elevator can be modeled in terms of a state and a behavior. Its state might be given in terms of its size, location, interior decoration, or any number of attributes. Likewise, its behavior might be specified in terms of its reaction when one of its buttons is pushed. Constructing a model of an elevator, however, requires that we select those attributes and behavior that are of interest to us. For purposes of a simulation, for example, we may only be concerned with the current floor position of the elevator and how to make it move to another floor location. Other attributes and behavior of the elevator may be left out of the model because they do not affect the aspects of the elevator that we are interested in studying. At the end of this chapter, we will see how to model an elevator and make our model elevator "move" in Java using a very simple representation.

It is also important to distinguish between the attributes we choose to include in our model and the values that these attributes can have. For example, an attribute of all automobiles is their color. The value of this attribute for a specific car is its specific color, such as blue, black, white, silver, and so on. The attributes and behavior together define a category or type of object out of which many individual objects can be designated. In object-based programming, the category of objects defined by a given set of attributes and behavior is called a **class**. Only when specific values have been assigned to the attributes is a particular object defined.

For example, the attributes length and width can define a general type of shape called a rectangle. Only when specific values have been assigned to these attributes have we represented a particular rectangle. This distinction carries over into Java: The attributes and behavior we select are said to define a general class, or type, of object. An object itself only comes into existence when we assign specific values to the attributes.

As you might expect, attributes in Java are defined by variables, and behaviors are constructed from methods. The set of attributes and behavior defining a class is frequently referred to as the class' **interface.** Once the interface has been specified, creating a particular object is achieved by assigning specific values to the appropriate variables. How all of this is constructed is the topic of the remaining sections.

EXERCISES 10.1

1. Define the following terms:
   a. attribute
   b. behavior
   c. state
   d. model
   e. class
   f. object
   g. interface

2. a. In place of specifying a rectangle's location by listing the position of two diagonal corner points, what other attributes could be used?
   b. What other attributes, besides length and width, might describe a rectangle if the rectangle is to be drawn on a color monitor?
   c. Describe a set of attributes that could define circles that are to be drawn on a black-and-white monitor.
   d. What attributes would you add to those selected in response to Exercise 2c if the circles were to be drawn on a color monitor?

3. a. For each of the following, determine what attributes might be of interest to someone considering buying the item.

   i. a book
   ii. a can of soda
   iii. a pen
   iv. a cassette tape
   v. a cassette tape player
   vi. an elevator
   vii. a car

   b. Do the attributes you used in Exercise 3a model an object or a class of objects?

4. For each of the following, what behavior might be of interest to someone considering buying the item?
   a. a car
   b. a cassette tape player

5. All of the examples of classes considered in this section have consisted of inanimate objects. Do you think that animate objects such as pets and even human beings could be modeled in terms of attributes and behavior? Why or why not?

6. a. The attributes of a class represent how objects of the class appear to the outside world. The behavior represents how an object of a class reacts to an external stimulus. Given this, what do you think is the mechanism by which one object "triggers" the designated behavior in another object? (*Tip:* Consider how one person typically gets another person to do something.)

   b. If behavior in Java is constructed by defining an appropriate method, how do you think the behavior is activated in Java?

10.2 CLASSES

Although all of the programs we have written to this point have been constructed as classes, they have not used the full capabilities provided in Java. In its most general form, a **class** is a programmer-defined data type.[2] To understand the full implications of this more clearly, consider three of the built-in data types supplied by Java: integers, doubles, and characters. In using these data types, we typically declare one or more variables of the desired type, use them in their accepted ways, and avoid using them in ways that are not specified. Because the modulus operator makes no sense for double-precision numbers, this operation is not supplied for this data type in Java.

In computer terminology, the combination of data and their associated operations constitutes a class. That is, a class defines *both* the types of data and the types of operations that may be performed on the data. Such a definition conveys that both a type of data and specific operational capabilities are being supplied. In a simplified form, this relationship can be described as:

Class = Allowable Data + Operational Capabilities

Before seeing how to construct our own classes, let's take a moment to list some of the operational capabilities supplied with Java's built-in classes. The reason is that we will have to provide the same type of capabilities as part of our own classes. The minimum set of the capabilities provided by Java's built-in classes appears in Table 10.1.

Although we don't normally think of these capabilities individually when we use them, the designers of Java clearly needed to when they created the Java compiler. Since Java allows us to create our own classes, we must now be aware of these capabilities and provide appropriate ones with the classes that we construct.

Construction of a class is inherently easy, and we already have all the necessary tools in variables and methods. In Java, various combinations of variables provide the means of defining new data types, and methods provide the means of defining operational capabilities. Using this information, we can now extend our equation definition of a class to its Java representation as follows:

Java Class = Data + Methods

Thus, in Java, a class provides a mechanism for packaging data and methods together in a self-contained unit. In this chapter, we describe how classes are constructed and how class variables and objects are declared and initialized.

---

[2]More generally, a programmer-defined data type is referred to as an **abstract data type**.

TABLE 10.1   Built-in Data Type Capabilities

Capability	Example
Define one or more variables.	`int a, b;`
Initialize a variable at definition.	`int a = 5;`
Assign a value to a variable.	`a = 10;`
Assign one variable's value to another variable.	`a = b;`
Perform mathematical operations.	`a + b;`
Convert from one data type to another.	`a = (int)(7.2);`

Class Construction

A class defines both data and methods. This is usually accomplished by constructing a class in two parts consisting of a declaration section and a definition section. As illustrated in Figure 10.2, the declaration section declares the class variables. The definition section then defines the methods that can operate on the class variables plus any additional general-purpose methods that are not directly associated with processing class variables.

```
// class variable declaration section
variable declarations

// class method definition section
method definitions
```

FIGURE 10.2   Format of a Class Definition

The variables and methods contained within a class are collectively referred to as **class members**. Individually, the variables are referred to as both **data members** and as **instance variables** (the terms are synonymous), and the methods are referred to as **member methods**. Although a member method name can be the same as a data member name, it is generally not a good idea to give the same name to both a data and method member.

As a specific example of a class, consider the following definition of a class named `Date`.

```
public class Date:
{
  // class variable declaration section
  private int month;
  private int day;
  private int year;

  // class method definition section
  Date()    // this is a constructor method because it has the same
  {         // name as the class
    month = 7;
    day = 4;
    year = 2001;
```

```
  }

  public void setDate(int mm, int dd, int yyyy)
  {
    month = mm;
    day = dd;
    year = yyyy;
  }

  public void showDate()
  {
    DecimalFormat df = new DecimalFormat("00");

    System.out.println("The date is " + df.format(month) + '/'
            + df.format(day) + '/'
            + df.format(year % 100)); // extract the last 2 year digits
  }
}
```

The name of this class is Date. Although the initial capital letter is not required, it is conventionally used to designate a class. The body of the Date class, which is enclosed within braces, consists of variable declarations and method definitions. In this case, the variable members month, day, and year are declared as integers. The keywords private and public, referred to as both **visibility modifiers** and **access specifiers,** define access rights. The keyword private specifies that the class members following—in this case, the variable members month, day, and year—may only be accessed using Date class methods. Thus, the private designation specifically enforces data security by requiring all access to private data members through the provided member methods. This type of access, which restricts a user from seeing how the data are actually stored, is referred to as **data hiding.**

Specifically, we have chosen to store a date using three integers: one for the month, day, and year, respectively. We will also always store the year as a four-digit number. Thus, for example, we will store the year 1998 as 1998 and not as 98. Making sure to store all years with their correct century designation will eliminate a multitude of problems that can crop up if only the last two digits, such as 98, are stored. For example, the number of years between 2002 and 1999 can be quickly calculated as $2002 - 1999 = 3$ years, but this same answer is not so easily obtained if only the year values 02 and 99 are used. In addition, we are sure of what the year 2000 refers to, while a two-digit value such as 00 could refer to either 1900 or 2000.

The **definition section** follows the declaration of the class data members and is where the member methods are written. Notice that the methods defined in the Date class have been declared as public. This means that these class methods *can* be called by any objects and methods not in the class (outside). In general, all class methods should be public; as such, they furnish capabilities to manipulate the class variables from outside the class. For our Date class, we have initially provided three methods named Date(), setDate(), and showDate(). Notice that one of these member methods has the same name, Date, as the class name. This particular method is referred to as a **constructor** method, and it has a specially defined purpose: It can initialize class data members with values.

Figure 10.3 illustrates the general form of methods included in the definition section. This format is correct for all methods except the constructor, which has no return type.

```
visibilityModifier returnType methodName(parameter declarations)
{
  method body
}
```

FIGURE 10.3 Format of a Member Method

As shown in Figure 10.3, member methods have the same format as all user-written Java methods. Let us now reconsider the definition section of our Date class, which is repeated below for convenience:

```
// class method definition section
Date()    // this is a constructor method because it has the same
{         // name as the class
  month = 7;
  day = 4;
  year = 2001;
}

public void setDate(int mm, int dd, int yyyy)
{
  month = mm;
  day = dd;
  year = yyyy;
}

public void showDate()
{
  DecimalFormat df = new DecimalFormat("00");

  System.out.println("The date is " + df.format(month) + '/'
          + df.format(day) + '/'
          + df.format(year % 100)); // extract the last 2 year digits
}
```

Notice that the first method in this definition section has the same name as the class, which makes it a constructor method. Thus, it has no return type. The empty parentheses following the Date() header define the method as having no parameters. The body of this method assigns the data members month, day, and year with the values 7, 4, and 2001, respectively. The next method header line

```
public void setDate(int mm, int dd, int yyyy)
```

defines the setDate() method. This method returns no value (void) and expects three integer parameters, mm, dd, and yyyy. The body of this method assigns the class' data members, month, day, and year, with the values of its parameters.

Finally, the last method header line in the definition section defines a method named showDate(). This method has no parameters, returns no value, and is a member of the Date class. The body of this method, however, needs a little more explanation.

Although we have chosen to internally store all years as four-digit values that retain century information, users are accustomed to seeing dates with the year represented as a two-digit value, such as 12/15/99. To display the last two digits of the year value, the expression year % 100 is initially used. For example, if the year is 1999, the expression 1999 % 100 yields the value 99, and if the year is 2001, the expression 2001 % 100 yields the value 1. Notice that if we had used an assignment such as year = year % 100;, we would actually be altering the stored value of year to correspond to the last one or two digits of the year. Since we want to retain the year as a four-digit number, we must be careful only to manipulate the displayed value using the expression year % 100 . The formatting ensures that the displayed values correspond to conventionally accepted dates. For example, a date such as December 9, 2002, will appear as 12/09/02 and not as 12/9/2.

To see our Date class within the context of a complete program, consider Program 10.1. To make the program easier to read, it has been shaded in lighter and darker areas. The lighter area contains the class declaration and definition sections that we have already considered for the Date class. The darker area contains a main() method that we will use to test the class. For convenience, we will retain this shading for all programs using multiple classes.[3] In addition, because we will be making a number of modifications to the Date class, and to avoid naming the classes as Date_1, Date_2, and so on to distinguish each class, the programs in this and the next chapter will be stored using their program designations, such as Program10_1.java.[4]

First consider the lighter shaded region, which includes the Date class. The declaration and definition sections should look familiar, as they contain the class declaration and definition sections that we have already discussed. Notice, however, that these sections do not actually create any class variables; they only declare a set of variables. This is true of all Java types, including the built-in types such as integers and floats. Just as a variable of an integer type must be defined (recall that this means actually reserving memory storage for the variable), actual storage areas must also be created for class variables. Storage areas created for class values are referred to as **objects.**

Using this terminology, the first two statements in Program 10.1's main() method define two objects of type Date. The variables named a and b are reference variables that can access the values stored in these objects. In Java, a new object is created using the new operator. As you saw in Chapter 7, this operator creates an object of the specified type by obtaining sufficient memory to store the required values. In this particular case, enough memory to store three integer values would be obtained. Because this memory is dynamically allocated while the program is executing, the new operator is referred to as the **dynamic memory allocation operator.** Formally, the process of creating a new object using the dynamic memory allocation operator is referred to as both **creating an instance** and **instantiating an object.** As part of this instantiation process, the new

[3]This shading is not accidental. In practice, the lighter shaded region containing the Date class would be placed in its own source file named Date.java and constructed as a package (see Appendix F). In addition, the code in main() would be placed in a separate class with its own corresponding source code file. As long as both files are in the same directory, the Date class will be correctly located when the main() method is executed. If the Date class were constructed as a package, any class using it could gain access to it using an import statement.

[4]The implication of this is that you must rename each program as Date.java to compile it.

PROGRAM 10.1

```
import java.text.*;   // needed for formatting

public class Date
{
  // class variable declaration section
  private int month;
  private int day;
  private int year;

  // class method definition section
  Date()   // this is a constructor method because it has the same
  {        // name as the class
    month = 7;
    day = 4;
    year = 2001;
  }

  public void setDate(int mm, int dd, int yyyy)
  {
    month = mm;
    day = dd;
    year = yyyy;
  }

  public void showDate()
  {
    DecimalFormat df = new DecimalFormat("00");

    System.out.println("The date is " + df.format(month)
            + '/' + df.format(day) + '/'
            + df.format(year % 100)); // extract the last 2 year digits
  }

  public static void main(String[] args)
  {
    Date a = new Date();  // declare 2 objects of type Date
    Date b = new Date();

    b.setDate(12,25,2002);  // assign values to b's data members
    System.out.println( );

    a.showDate();  // display object a's values
    b.showDate();  // display object b's values
  }
}
```

operator returns the address of where the object's values are located, and this address is stored into the declared reference variable. From that point on, the reference variable is required to access the object. As part of this process, the object's data values can be automatically initialized. This can be achieved because a call is automatically made to the class' constructor method when the instantiation is done. For example, consider the statement `Date a = new Date();` contained in `main()`. Here both the reference variable named a is defined and the constructor method `Date()` is called. This constructor has been defined to assign the default values 7, 4, and 2001 to an object's month, day, and year variables, respectively, resulting in the initialization:

```
a.month = 7
a.day = 4
a.year = 2001
```

Notice the notation here. It consists of an object's reference name and a variable name separated by a period. This syntax is standard for referring to an object's data members, namely,

objectReferenceName.dataMemberName

where *objectReferenceName* is the name of a reference variable for a specific object and *dataMemberName* is the name of a class variable.

Thus, the notation `a.month = 7` refers to the fact that the object referenced by variable a has its month data member set to the value 7. In common usage, this is usually shortened to read "object a's month value is 7," but it is important to realize that a is not the object itself but only a reference to an object. Similarly, the notation `a.day = 4` and `a.year = 2001` refers to the fact that a's day and year data members have been set to the values 4 and 2001, respectively. In the same manner, when the object named b is defined, the same default values are used (again, although b is referred to as an object, it is important to realize that b is really a reference to the object and not the object itself), resulting in the initialization of b's data members as:

```
b.month = 7
b.day = 4
b.year = 2001
```

The next statement in `main()`, `b.setDate(12,25,2002)`, causes the class' `setDate()` method to operate on b's value, which assigns the argument values 12, 25, 2002 to b's data members and results in the assignment:

```
b.month = 12
b.day = 25
b.year = 2002
```

Notice the syntax in `main()` for invoking a class method. This syntax is

objectReferenceName.methodName(arguments)

where *objectReferenceName* is the name of a specific object and *methodName* is the name of one of the methods defined for the object's class. Since we have defined all class methods as `public`, a statement such as `b.setDate(12,25,2002)` is valid inside the `main()` method and is a call to the class' `setDate()` method. This statement tells the `setDate()` method to operate on the `b` object with the arguments 12, 25, and 2002. It is important to understand that because all class data members were specified as `private`, a statement such as `b.month = 12` would be invalid from outside the class because it would allow a method in one class to directly access another class' data members. Declaring the `Date` class' data members as `private` forces us to rely on its member methods for all data access.

The last two statements in `main()` call the `showDate()` method to operate on the `a` and `b` objects. The first call results in the display of `a`'s data values and the second call in the display of `b`'s data values. Thus, the output displayed by Program 10.1 is:

```
The date is 02/04/10
The date is 12/25/02
```

Notice that a statement such as `System.out.println(a);` is invalid within `main()` because the `println()` method does not know how to handle an object of class `Date`. Thus, we have supplied our class with a method that can access and display an object's internal values.

Before leaving Program 10.1's `main()` method, one important comment about the definition of the reference variables `a` and `b` is worth restating. The statement `Date a = new Date();` is a frequently used construction that actually incorporates the following two individual statements into a single statement:

```
Date a;          // this is a declaration statement for a reference variable
a = new Date();  // this statement creates an object of type Date
```

The first statement creates a reference variable to a `Date` object. Because no actual `Date` object has yet been created, the address stored into the reference variable is the `null` address. The second definition statement reserves actual storage locations for a `Date` object, uses the constructor method to initialize these memory locations with the values 7, 4, and 2001, and stores the first reserved memory address into the reference variable `a`. In your programming careers, you will encounter both ways of defining class objects.

Terminology

As there is sometimes confusion about the terms classes, objects, and other terminology associated with object-oriented programming, we will take a moment to clarify and review the terminology.

A **class** is a programmer-defined data type out of which objects can be created. **Objects** are created from classes; they have a similar relationship to classes as variables do to Java's built-in data types. For example, in the declaration

```
int a;
```

`a` is said to be a variable, while in Program 10.1's declaration

POINT OF INFORMATION

U S E R   I N T E R F A C E S ,
D E F I N I T I O N S ,   A N D
I N F O R M A T I O N   H I D I N G

The terms user interface and definition are used extensively in object-oriented programming literature. Each of these terms can be equated to specific parts of a class' declaration and definition sections.

A *user interface* consists of a class' public member method declarations and any supporting comments. Thus, the interface should be all that is required to tell a programmer
how to use the class.

The *definition* consists of both the class' definition section, which consists of both
private and public member definitions, *and* the class' private data members that are in a
class declaration section.

The definition is the essential means of providing information hiding. In its most
general context, *information hiding* refers to the principle that *how* a class is internally
constructed is not relevant to any programmer who wishes to use the class. That is, the
definition can and should be hidden from all class users precisely to ensure that the class
is not altered or compromised in any way. All that a programmer needs to know to use
the class correctly should be provided by the interface.

```
Date a;
```

a is said to be a reference variable. A variable for a built-in data type contains an actual
data value, whereas a reference variable contains the memory address of an object.

Objects are also referred to as **instances** of a class, and the process of creating a new
object is frequently referred to as an **instantiation** of the object. Each time a new object
is instantiated (created), a new set of data members belonging to the object is created.[5]
The particular values contained in these data members determine the object's **state.**

Seen in this way, a class can be thought of as a blueprint out of which particular instances (objects) can be created. Each instance (object) of a class will have its own set of
particular values for the set of data members specified in the class declaration section.

In addition to the data types allowed for an object, a class also defines **behavior**—
that is, the methods that are permitted on an object's data members. Users of the object
need to know *what* these methods can do and how to activate them through method calls,
but unless run time or space implications are relevant, they do not need to know *how* the
operation is done. The actual definition details of an object's operations are contained in
the class definition, which can be hidden from the user. Other names for the methods defined in a class definition section are **procedures, operations,** and **services.** We will use
these terms interchangeably throughout the remainder of the text.

---

[5]Note that only one set of class methods is created. These methods are shared between objects.

EXERCISES 10.2

1. Define the following terms:

   a. class
   b. object
   c. declaration section
   d. definition section
   e. instance variable
   f. member method
   g. data member
   h. constructor
   i. class instance
   j. services
   k. methods
   l. user interface

2. Write a class declaration and definition section for each of the following specifications. In each case, include a constructor and a member method named `showdata()` that can display member values.

   a. A class named `Time` that has integer data members named `secs`, `mins`, and `hours`.

   b. A class named `Complex` that has floating-point data members named `real` and `imaginary`.

3. Write a class declaration and definition section for each of the following specifications. In each case, include a constructor and a member method named `showdata()` that can display member values.

   a. A class named `Circle` that has integer data members named `xcenter` and `ycenter` and a floating-point data member named `radius`.

   b. A class named `Computer` that has string data members named `computer`, `printer`, and `screen`, each capable of referencing a String, and double-precision data members named `compPrice`, `printPrice`, and `screenPrice`.

4. a. Include the class declaration and definition sections prepared for Exercise 2a in a complete working program.

   b. Include the class declaration and definition sections prepared for Exercise 2b in a complete working program.

5. a. Include the class declaration and definition sections prepared for Exercise 3a in a complete working program.

   b. Include the class declaration and definition sections prepared for Exercise 3b in a complete working program.

6. Determine the errors in the following class:

   ```
   public class Employee
   {
   public int empnum;
   public char code;

   private void showemp(int, char)
   {
      .

      .

   }
   }
   ```

7. a. Add another member method named `convert()` to the `Date` class in Program 10.1 that does the following: The method should access the month, year, and day data members and display and then return a long integer that is calculated as *year* * *10000* + *month* * *100* + *day*. For example, if the date is

4/1/2002, the returned value is 20020401 (dates in this form are useful when performing sorts because placing the numbers in numerical order automatically places the corresponding dates in chronological order).

    b. Include the modified Date class constructed for Exercise 7a in a complete Java program.

8. a. Add a member method to the Date class in Program 10.1 named leapyr() that returns true when the year is a leap year and false if it is not. A leap year is any year that is evenly divisible by 4 but not evenly divisible by 100, with the exception that all years evenly divisible by 400 are leap years. For example, the year 1996 is a leap year because it is evenly divisible by 4 and not evenly divisible by 100. The year 2000 was a leap year because it is evenly divisible by 400.

    b. Include the class constructed for Exercise 8a in a complete Java program. The main() method should display the message The year is a leap year or The year is not a leap year depending on the date object's year value.

9. a. Add a member method to the Date class in Program 10.1 named dayOfWeek() that determines the day of the week for any date object of the form mm/dd/yyyy. An algorithm for determining the day of the week, known as Zeller's algorithm, is the following:

```
If the month is less than 3
    month = month + 12
    year = year - 1
EndIf
    Set century = int(year/100)
    Set year = year % 100
    Set T = dd + int(26 * (month + 1) / 10) + year + int(year / 4)
        + int(century / 4) - 2 * century
Set dayOfWeek = T % 7
If dayOfWeek is less than 0
    Set dayOfWeek = dayOfWeek + 7
EndIf
```

Using this algorithm, the variable dayOfWeek will have a value of 1 if the date is a Sunday, 2 if a Monday, and so on.

    b. Include the class definition constructed for Exercise 9a in a complete Java program. The main() method should display the name of the day (Sun., Mon., Tues., etc.) for the Date object being tested.

10. a. Construct a class named Rectangle that has floating-point data members named length and width. The class should have member methods named perimeter() and area() to calculate the perimeter and area of a rectangle, a member method named getdata() to set a rectangle's length and width, and a member method named showdata() to display a rectangle's length, width, perimeter, and area.

    b. Include the Rectangle class constructed in Exercise 10a within a working Java program.

11. a. Modify the Date class defined in Program 10.1 to include a nextDay() method that increments a date by one day. Test your method to ensure that it correctly increments days into a new month and into a new year.

b. Modify the Date class in Program 10.1 to include a priorDay() method that decrements a date by one day. Test your method to ensure that it correctly decrements days into a prior month and into a prior year.

12. Modify the Date class in Program 10.1 to contain a method that compares two Date objects and returns the larger of the two. The method should be written according to the following algorithm:

```
Comparison method:
    Accept two Date values as parameters
    Determine the later date using the following procedure:
        Convert each date into an integer value having the form yyyymmdd
        (This can be accomplished using the formula year * 100000 + month * 100 + day)
        Compare the corresponding integers for each date
        The larger integer corresponds to the later date
    Return the later date
```

10.3 CONSTRUCTORS

A **constructor** method is any method that has the same name as its class. Multiple constructors can be defined for each class as long as they are distinguishable by the number and types of their parameters (which is an example of method overloading).

The intended purpose of a constructor is to initialize a new object's data members. Thus, depending on the number and types of supplied arguments, one constructor method is automatically called each time an object is created. If no constructor method is written, the compiler supplies a default constructor in which all numerical data values are initialized to zeros and all strings are initialized to nulls. In addition to its initialization role, a constructor method may also perform other tasks when it is called and can be written in a variety of ways. In this section, we present the possible variations of constructor methods.

Figure 10.4 illustrates the general format of a constructor. As shown in this figure, a constructor:

- Must have the same name as the class to which it belongs
- Must have no return type (not even void)

```
optionalVisibilityModifier className(parameter list)
{
    method body
}
```

FIGURE 10.4 Constructor Format

For example, consider the following class declaration:

```
public class Date
{
    private int month;
    private int day;
    private int year;

    public void setDate(int mm, int dd, int yyyy)
```

```
   {
      month = mm;
      day = dd;
      year = yyyy;
   }

   public void showDate()
   {
      DecimalFormat df = new DecimalFormat("00");
      System.out.println("The date is " + df.format(month)
                + '/' + df.format(day) + '/'
                + df.format(year % 100)); // extract the last 2 year digits
   }
}
```

Because no user-defined constructor has been declared here, the compiler creates a default constructor that sets the month, day, and year data members to 0. For our Date class, this default constructor is equivalent to the definition

```
Date()
{
   month = 0;
   day = 0;
   year = 0;
}
```

Although the compiler-provided default constructor may or may not be useful in a particular application, it does provide a known state for each instantiated object if no other constructor is declared. In its more general usage, the term **default constructor** refers to any constructor that does not require any arguments when it is called. For example, the constructor in Program 10.1, which is repeated here for convenience, is considered a default constructor. Whenever an explicit user-defined default constructor is supplied, the compiler will not provide one.

```
Date()
{
   month = 7;
   day = 4;
   year = 2001;
}
```

Here each data member is assigned a default value, and an object can be declared as type Date without supplying any arguments. Using such a constructor, the declaration Date a = new Date(); both initializes the newly created object with the default values 7, 4, and 2001 and sets the address of this object into the reference variable named a.

To verify that a constructor method is automatically called whenever a new object is created, consider Program 10.2. Notice that in the class' definition section we have added

PROGRAM 10.2

```java
import java.text.*;   // needed for formatting

public class Date
{
  // class variable declaration section
  private int month;
  private int day;
  private int year;

  // class method definition section
  Date()    // this is a constructor method because it has the same
  {         // name as the class
    month = 7;
    day = 4;
    year = 2001;
    System.out.println("From the default constructor:"
        + "\n  Created a new Date object with data values"
        + "\n    month = " + month + "  day = " + day + "  year = " + year);
  }

  public void setDate(int mm, int dd, int yyyy)
  {
    month = mm;
    day = dd;
    year = yyyy;
  }

  public void showDate()
  {
    DecimalFormat df = new DecimalFormat("00");

    System.out.println("The date is " + df.format(month)
            + '/' + df.format(day) + '/'
            + df.format(year % 100)); // extract the last 2 year digits
  }

  public static void main(String[] args)
  {
    Date a = new Date();    // declare an object
    Date b = new Date();    // declare an object
  }
}
```

a call to `println()` within the constructor that displays a message whenever the constructor is called. Because the `main()` method creates two objects, the constructor is automatically called twice and the message is displayed twice. The following output is produced when Program 10.2 is executed:

```
From the default constructor:
  Created a new Date object with data values
    month = 7  day = 4  year = 2001
From the default constructor:
  Created a new Date object with data values
    month = 7  day = 4  year = 2001
```

Although any legitimate Java statement can be used within a constructor method, such as the `println()` method call in Program 10.2, it is best to keep constructors simple and use them only for initialization purposes.

Overloaded Constructors

The primary difference between a constructor and other user-written methods is how the constructor is called: Constructors are called automatically each time an object is created, whereas other methods must be explicitly called by name. As a method, however, a constructor must still follow all of the rules applicable to a user-written method. This means that constructors may be overloaded.

Recall from Section 6.1 that method overloading permits the same method name to be used with different parameter lists. Based on the supplied parameter types, the compiler determines which method to use when the call is encountered. Let's see how this can be applied to our `Date` class. For convenience, the default constructor in Program 10.2 is repeated here:

```
Date()    // this is a constructor method because it has the same
{         // name as the class
  month = 7;
  day = 4;
  year = 2001;
  System.out.println("From the default constructor:"
     + "\n  Created a new Date object with data values"
     + "\n    month = " + month + "  day = " + day + "  year = " + year);
}
```

Instead of always accepting the default values provided by this constructor, we typically would also want the ability to initialize each `Date` object with values of our own choosing. Doing this with the classes defined in either Program 10.1 or 10.2 would first require instantiating a `Date` object with the default initializing values and then using the `setDate()` method to reset the variables to the desired values. An alternative is to provide a second constructor that accepts and uses argument values to initialize a newly instantiated object. The code for one such a constructor is:

```
Date(int mm, int dd, int yyyy)  // this is an overloaded constructor
{
  month = mm;
  day = dd;
  year = yyyy;
  System.out.println("From the first overloaded constructor:"
    + "\n  Created a new Date object with data values"
    + "\n    month = " + month + "  day = " + day + "  year = " + year);
}
```

Here the constructor is declared as receiving three integer arguments, which then initialize the month, day, and year data members. In addition, we have included a println() method to display the values immediately. Program 10.3 contains this overloaded constructor within the context of a complete Date class.

PROGRAM 10.3

```
import java.text.*;   // needed for formatting

public class Date
{
  // class variable declaration section
  private int month;
  private int day;
  private int year;

  // class method definition section
  Date()    // this is a constructor method because it has the same
  {         // name as the class
    month = 7;
    day = 4;
    year = 2001;
    System.out.println("From the default constructor:"
      + "\n  Created a new Date object with data values"
      + "\n    month = " + month + "  day = " + day + "  year = " + year);
  }

  Date(int mm, int dd, int yyyy)  // this is an overloaded constructor
  {
    month = mm;
    day = dd;
    year = yyyy;
    System.out.println("From the first overloaded constructor:"
      + "\n  Created a new Date object with data values"
      + "\n    month = " + month + "  day = " + day + "  year = " + year);
  }
```

(Continued on next page)

(Continued from previous page)

```java
public void setDate(int mm, int dd, int yyyy)
{
  month = mm;
  day = dd;
  year = yyyy;
}


public void showDate()
{
  DecimalFormat df = new DecimalFormat("00");

  System.out.println("The date is " + df.format(month)
           + '/' + df.format(day) + '/'
           + df.format(year % 100)); // extract the last 2 year digits
}

public static void main(String[] args)
{
  Date a = new Date();    // declare an object
  Date b = new Date(5,1,2004);   // declare an object
}
}
```

The output produced by Program 10.3 is:

```
From the default constructor:
  Created a new Date object with data values
    month = 7   day = 4   year = 2001
From the first overloaded constructor:
  Created a new Date object with data values
    month = 5   day = 1   year = 2004
```

Two objects are created in Program 10.3's main() method. The first object, which is referenced by the variable named a, is initialized with the default constructor. The second object, which is initialized with the arguments 5, 1, and 2004, uses the second, overloaded, constructor. The compiler knows to use this second constructor because three integer arguments are specified, and there is only one constructor that accepts three integer arguments. It is worthwhile pointing out that a compiler error would occur if two constructors for the same class had the same number and types of arguments. In such a case, the compiler would not be able to determine which constructor to use. A method's name and the name, number, and type of its arguments are referred to as its **parameter signature.** Thus, in each class, only one constructor can be written as the default, and each overloaded constructor must have a unique parameter signature.

CONSTRUCTORS

A *constructor* is any method that has the same name as its class. The primary purpose of a constructor is to initialize an object's member variables when an object is created. A constructor is automatically called when an object is declared.

A class can have multiple constructors provided that each constructor is distinguishable by having a different formal parameter list. A compiler error results when unique identification of a constructor is not possible. If no constructor is provided, the compiler supplies a default constructor that initializes all numerical data members to zero and all string data members to `null`.

Every constructor method must be declared *with no return type* (not even void). Even though they are methods, constructors *may not* be explicitly called in nondeclarative statements.

Adding a Second Overloaded Constructor

An alternative method of specifying a date is to use a `long` integer in the form *year * 10000 + month * 100 + day*. For example, the date 12/24/1998 in this form would be 19981224, and the date 2/5/2002 is 20020205.[6] A suitable header line for a constructor that has dates of this form is:

```
Date(long)
```

This header line declares the constructor as receiving one `long` integer argument. The code for this new `Date` method must, of course, correctly convert its single argument into a month, day, and year. The actual code for such a constructor is:

```
Date(long yyyymmdd)    // a second constructor
{
  year = int(yyyymmdd/10000.0);     // extract the year
  month = int( (yyyymmdd - year * 10000.0) / 100.00 ); // extract the month
  day = int(yyyymmdd - year * 10000.0 - month * 100.0); // extract the day
  System.out.println("From the second overloaded constructor:"
    + "\n  Created a new Date object with data values"
    + "\n    month = " + month + "  day = " + day + "  year = " + year);
}
```

Do not be overly concerned with the actual conversion code within the constructor's body. The important point here is the concept of overloading the `Date()` method to accept a `long` integer. In addition, we have provided a `println()` method to display the initialized values. Program 10.4 contains this second overloaded constructor within the context of a complete `Date` class.

---

[6]The reason for specifying dates in this manner is that only one number is needed per date, and sorting the numbers automatically puts the corresponding dates into chronological order.

PROGRAM 10.4

```java
import java.text.*;    // needed for formatting

public class Date
{
  // class variable declaration section
  private int month;
  private int day;
  private int year;

  // class method definition section
  Date()   // this is a constructor method because it has the same
  {         // name as the class
    month = 7;
    day = 4;

   year = 2001;
   System.out.println("From the default constructor:"
      + "\n  Created a new Date object with data values"
      + "\n    month = " + month + "  day = " + day + "  year = " + year);
  }

  Date(int mm, int dd, int yyyy)  // this is an overloaded constructor
  {
    month = mm;
    day = dd;
    year = yyyy;
    System.out.println("From the first overloaded constructor:"
       + "\n  Created a new Date object with data values"
       + "\n    month = " + month + "  day = " + day + "  year = " + year);
  }

  Date(long yyyymmdd)    // here is the second overloaded constructor
  {
    year = (int)(yyyymmdd/10000.0);    // extract the year
    month = (int)( (yyyymmdd - year * 10000.0)/100.00 );  // extract the month
    day = (int)(yyyymmdd - year * 10000.0 - month * 100.0); // extract the day
    System.out.println("From the second overloaded constructor:"
       + "\n  Created a new Date object with data values"
       + "\n    month = " + month + "  day = " + day + "  year = " + year);
  }

  public void setDate(int mm, int dd, int yyyy)
  {
```

(Continued on next page)

(Continued from previous page)

```
      month = mm;
      day = dd;
      year = yyyy;
    }
    public void showDate()
    {
      DecimalFormat df = new DecimalFormat("00");

      System.out.println("The date is " + df.format(month)
              + '/' + df.format(day) + '/'
              + df.format(year % 100)); // extract the last 2 year digits
    }

    public static void main(String[] args)
    {
      Date a = new Date();    // declare an object
      Date b = new Date(5,1,2004);    // declare an object
      Date c = new Date(20050915L);   // declare an object
    }
  }
```

The output provided by Program 10.4 is:

```
From the default constructor:
  Created a new Date object with data values
    month = 7   day = 4   year = 2001
From the first overloaded constructor:
  Created a new Date object with data values
    month = 5   day = 1   year = 2004
From the second overloaded constructor:
  Created a new Date object with data values
    month = 9   day = 15   year = 2005
```

Three objects are created and initialized in Program 10.4's `main()` method. The first object is initialized with the default constructor using the default values 7, 4, and 2001. The second object uses an overloaded constructor and is initialized with the three integer values 5, 1, and 2004. Finally, the third object, `c`, uses an overloaded constructor and is initialized with a `long` integer. For this initialization, the compiler knows to use the second overloaded constructor because the argument specified, 20050915L, is clearly designated as a `long` integer.[7] Because of the display produced by the `println()` methods included within each constructor, we can clearly identify the constructor in each ini-

---

[7]Because there is only one constructor with a single parameter, the compiler will call the correct constructor even if the L suffix is omitted.

ACCESSOR AND MUTATOR METHODS

An *accessor method* is any nonconstructor class member method that accesses an object's data members. For example, the method showDate() in the Date class is an accessor method. Such methods are extremely important because they provide a means of displaying private data member's stored values.

When you construct a class, make sure to provide a complete set of accessor methods. Each accessor method does not have to return a data member's exact value, but it should return a useful representation of the value. For example, assume that a date such as 12/25/2002 is stored as a long integer in the form 20022512. Although an accessor method could display this value, a more useful representation would typically be either 12/25/02 or December 25, 2002.

A *mutator method* is any nonconstructor class method that changes an object's data values. For example, the setDate() method in the Date class is an example of a mutator method. Constructors, whose primary purpose is to initialize an object's member variables, are not considered mutator methods.

tialization. These displays are included purely for instructional purposes. In practice, a constructor only initializes data members, and displays such as those provided by Programs 10.2 through 10.4 are not necessary.

EXERCISES 10.3

1. Determine whether the following statements are true or false:
   a. A constructor method must have the same name as its class.
   b. A class can have only one constructor method.
   c. A class can have only one default constructor method.
   d. A default constructor can only be supplied by the compiler.
   e. A default constructor can have no parameters.
   f. A constructor must be declared for each class.
   g. A constructor must be declared with a return type.
   h. A constructor is automatically called each time an object is created.

2. For Program 10.4, what date would be initialized for object c if the declaration Date c = new Date(15); replaced the declaration Date c = new Date(20050915L); ?

3. Modify Program 10.4 so that the only data member of the class is a long integer named yyyymmdd. Do this by substituting the declaration

   private long yyyymmdd;

   for the existing declarations

   private int month;
   private int day;
   private int year;

Then, using the same constructor method header lines currently in the class declaration section, rewrite each method to correctly initialize the single class data member.

4. a. Construct a `Time` class containing integer data members seconds, minutes, and hours. Have the class contain two constructors: The first should be a default constructor that initializes each data member with a default value of 0. The second constructor should accept a `long` integer representing a total number of seconds and disassemble the long integer into hours, minutes, and seconds. The final method member should display the class data members.

    b. Include the class written for Exercise 4a within the context of a complete program.

5. a. Construct a class named `Student` consisting of an integer student identification number, an array of five floating-point grades, and an integer representing the total number of grades entered. The constructor for this class should initialize all `Student` data members to zero. Included in the class should be member methods to (1) enter a student ID number, (2) enter a single test grade and update the total number of grades entered, and (3) compute an average grade and display the student ID followed by the average grade.

    b. Include the class constructed in Exercise 5a within the context of a complete program. Your program should declare two objects of type `Student` and accept and display data for the two objects to verify operation of the member methods.

6. a. In Exercise 4, you were asked to construct a `Time` class. For such a class, include a `tick()` method that increments the time by 1 second. Test your method to ensure that it correctly increments into a new minute and into a new hour.

    b. Modify the `Time` class written for Exercise 6a to include a `detick()` method that decrements the time by 1 second. Test your method to ensure that it correctly decrements time into a prior hour and into a prior minute.

10.4 APPLICATIONS

Now that you have an understanding of how classes are constructed and the terminology used in describing them, let us apply this knowledge to two new applications using user-defined classes.

Application 1: Constructing an Elevator Object

In this application, we will simulate the operation of an elevator. Specifically, what is required is an output that describes the current floor that the elevator is either stationed at or passing by and an internal elevator request button that is pushed as a request to move to another floor. The elevator can travel between the 1st and 15th floors of the building.

Step 1: Analyze the Problem For this application, we have one object, which is an elevator. The only attribute of interest is the location of the elevator. The single service is the

ENCAPSULATION

The term *encapsulation* refers to the inclusion of a number of items into a single unit. For example, a method encapsulates the details of an algorithm. Similarly, a class encapsulates both variables and methods together in a single unit.

Although the term encapsulation sometimes refers to the process of information hiding, this usage is technically not accurate. The correct relationship between terms is that information hiding refers to the encapsulation and hiding of all definition details from a user of a class.

ability to request a change in the elevator's position (state). Additionally, we must be able to establish the initial floor position when a new elevator is put in service.

Step 2: Develop a Solution The location of the elevator, which corresponds to its current floor position, can be represented by an integer member variable. The value of this variable, which we will name `currentFloor`, effectively represents the current state of the elevator. The services that we will provide for changing the state of the elevator will be an initialization method to set the initial floor position when a new elevator is put in service and a request method to change the elevator's position (state) to a new floor. Putting an elevator in service is accomplished by declaring a single class instance (i.e., declaring an object of type `Elevator`), and requesting a new floor position is equivalent to pushing an elevator button. To accomplish this, a suitable data member declaration is:

```
private int currentFloor;
```

This data member, `currentFloor`, will store the current floor position of the elevator. As a private member, it can only be accessed through member methods. The external services provided by each `Elevator` object will be handled by two member methods, `Elevator()` and `request()`. The `Elevator()` method will be the constructor method for our class. Thus, our class will be named `Elevator`. We will provide two constructor methods: The first will be a default constructor that initializes the starting floor to 1, and the second will be an overloaded constructor that permits initialization with a programmer-supplied value. The `request()` method will alter the position of the elevator.

Step 3: Code the Solution From the design considerations, a suitable method definition section is:

```
// class method definition section
public Elevator()  // this is the default constructor
{
  currentFloor = 1;
}
```

(Continued on next page)

(Continued from previous page)

```java
public Elevator(int cfloor)   // an overloaded constructor
{
  currentFloor = cfloor;
}

private void request(int newfloor)
{
  if (newfloor < 1 || newfloor > MAXFLOOR || newfloor == currentFloor)
    ;   // do nothing
  else if ( newfloor > currentFloor)   // move elevator up
  {
    System.out.println("\nStarting at floor " + currentFloor);
    while (newfloor > currentFloor)
    {
      currentFloor++;     // add one to current floor
      System.out.println("   Going Up - now at floor " + currentFloor);
    }
    System.out.println("Stopping at floor " + currentFloor);
  }
  else  // move elevator down
  {
    System.out.println("\nStarting at floor " + currentFloor);
    while (newfloor < currentFloor)
    {
      currentFloor--;     // subtract one from current floor
      System.out.println("   Going Down - now at floor " + currentFloor);
    }
    System.out.println("Stopping at floor " + currentFloor);
  }
}
```

The constructor methods are straightforward. When an `Elevator` object is declared, it can either be initialized to the floor specified, or if no floor is explicitly given, a default value of 1 will be used. For example, the declaration

```java
Elevator a = new Elevator(7);
```

uses the overloaded constructor to initialize a newly created `Elevator` object's single data member `currentFloor` to 7, and the declaration

```java
Elevator a = new Elevator();
```

uses the default constructor and initializes its data member `currentFloor` to 1.

The `request()` method defined in the definition section is more complicated and provides the class' primary service. Essentially, this method consists of an `if-else` statement having three parts: If an incorrect service is requested, no action is taken; if a floor above the current position is selected, the elevator moves up; and if a floor below the current position is selected, the elevator moves down. For movement up or down, the method uses a `while` loop to increment the position one floor at a time and report the elevator's movement using a `println()` method call.

Step 4: Test and Correct the Solution Testing the `Elevator` class entails testing each class operation. To do this, we first include the `Elevator` class within the context of a working program, which is listed in Program 10.5.

The lightly shaded portion of Program 10.5 contains the class construction that we have already described. To see how this class is used, concentrate on the darker shaded section of the program. The `main()` method includes three statements. The first statement creates an object of type `Elevator` that can be accessed using the reference variable named a. Since no explicit floor has been given, this elevator will begin at floor 1, which is provided by the default constructor.

A request is then made to move the elevator to floor 6, which is followed by a request to move to floor 3. The output produced by Program 10.5 is:

```
Starting at floor 1
   Going Up - now at floor 2
   Going Up - now at floor 3
   Going Up - now at floor 4
   Going Up - now at floor 5
   Going Up - now at floor 6
Stopping at floor 6

Starting at floor 6
   Going Down - now at floor 5
   Going Down - now at floor 4
   Going Down - now at floor 3
Stopping at floor 3
```

PROGRAM 10.5

```java
public class Elevator
{
  // class variable declaration section
  private int currentFloor;
  private static final int MAXFLOOR = 15;

  // class method definition section
  public Elevator()  // this is the default constructor
  {
    currentFloor = 1;
  }
```

(Continued on next page)

(Continued from previous page)

```java
    public Elevator(int cfloor)  // an overloaded constructor
    {
      currentFloor = cfloor;
    }


    public void request(int newfloor)
    {
      if (newfloor < 1 || newfloor > MAXFLOOR || newfloor == currentFloor)
        ;  // do nothing
      else if ( newfloor > currentFloor)  // move elevator up
      {
        System.out.println("\nStarting at floor " + currentFloor);
        while (newfloor > currentFloor)
        {
          currentFloor++;    // add one to current floor
          System.out.println("  Going Up - now at floor " + currentFloor);
        }
        System.out.println("Stopping at floor " + currentFloor);
      }
      else  // move elevator down
      {
        System.out.println("\nStarting at floor " + currentFloor);
        while (newfloor < currentFloor)
        {
          currentFloor--;    // subtract one from current floor
          System.out.println("  Going Down - now at floor " + currentFloor);
        }
        System.out.println("Stopping at floor " + currentFloor);
      }
    }

    public static void main(String[] args)
    {
      Elevator a = new Elevator();    // declare 1 object of type Elevator

      a.request(6);
      a.request(3);
    }
  }
```

The basic requirements of constructing a user-defined class and programming with an object-oriented design are evident in even as simple a program as Program 10.5. Before the main() method can be written, a useful class must be constructed from which objects can be instantiated. This is typical of programs that use objects. For such programs, the design process is front-loaded with the requirement that careful consideration of the class—its declaration and definition—be given. Code contained within the class' methods effectively removes code that would otherwise be part of `main()`'s responsibility. Thus, any program that uses objects created from the class does not have to repeat the definition details within its `main()` method. Rather, the `main()` method and any method called by `main()` are only concerned with sending messages to their objects to activate them appropriately. How the object responds to the messages and how the state of the object is retained are not `main()`'s concern. These details are hidden within the class' construction.

One further point concerning Program 10.5 is the control provided by the `main()` method. Notice that this control is sequential, with two calls made to the same object operation, using different argument values. This control is perfectly correct for testing purposes. However, by incorporating calls to `request()` within a `while` loop and using the random number method `Math.random()` to generate random floor requests, a continuous simulation of the elevator's operation is possible (see Exercise 3).

Application 2: A Single Class Gas Pump Simulation

We have been requested to write a program that simulates the operation of a gas pump. At any time during the simulation, we should be able to determine, from the pump, the price per gallon of gas and the amount remaining in the supply tank from which the gas is pumped. If the amount of gas in the supply tank is greater than or equal to the amount of gas requested, the request should be filled; otherwise, only the available amount in the supply tank should be used. Once the gas is pumped, the total price of the gallons pumped should be displayed and the amount of gas in gallons that was pumped should be subtracted from the amount in the supply tank.

For the simulation, assume that the pump is randomly idle between 1 to 15 minutes between customer arrivals and that a customer randomly requests between 3 and 20 gallons of gas. Although the default supply tank capacity is 500 gallons, assume that the initial amount of gas in the tank for this simulation is only 300 gallons. Initially, the program should simulate a one-half hour time frame.

Additionally, for each arrival and request for gas, we want to know the idle time before the customer arrived, how many gallons of gas were pumped, and the total price of the transaction. The pump itself must keep track of the price per gallon of gas and the amount of gas remaining in the tank. Typically, the price per gallon is $1.25, but the price for the simulation should be $1.00.

For this part of the simulation, we will construct a gas-pump class that can be used in the final simulation, which is completed in Section 11.3.

Step 1: Analyze the Problem This problem involves two distinct object types. The first is a person who can arrive randomly between 1 and 15 minutes and can randomly request between 3 and 20 gallons of gas. The second object type is the gas pump. For this part of the problem, our goal is to create a suitable gas pump class.

The model for constructing a gas pump class that meets the requirements of the simulation are easily described in pseudocode as:

```
Put Pump in Service
  Initialize the amount of gas in the supply tank
  Initialize the price per gallon of gas

Display Values
  Display the amount of gas in the supply tank
  Display the price per gallon

Pump an Amount of Gas
  If the amount in the supply tank is greater than or equal to the requested amount
      Set the pumped amount of gas equal to the requested amount
  Else
      Set the pumped amount equal to the amount in the tank
  EndIf
  Subtract the pumped amount from the amount in the tank
  Calculate the total price as the price per gallon * pumped amount
  Display the gallons of gas pumped
  Display the amount remaining in the supply tank
  Display the total price for the pumped amount of gas
```

Step 2: Develop a Solution From the pseudocode description, the implementation of a Pump class is rather straightforward. The attributes of interest for the pump are the amount of gallons in the supply tank and the price per gallon. The required operations include supplying initial values for the pump's attributes, interrogating the pump for its attribute values, and satisfying a request for gas.

Since the two attributes, the amount in the tank and the price per gallon, can have fractional values, it is appropriate to make them floating-point values. Additionally, three services need to be provided. The first consists of initializing a pump's attributes, which consists of setting values for the amount in the supply tank and the price per gallon. The second consists of satisfying a request for gas, and the third service provides a reading of the pump's current attribute values.

Step 3: Code the Solution A suitable class definition is:

```java
public class Pump
{
  // class variable declaration section
  private double amtInTank;
  private double price;
  private static final double AMOUNT_IN_TANK = 500.0;
  private static final double DEFAULT_PRICE = 1.25;

  // class method definition section
  public Pump()  // this is the default constructor
  {
    amtInTank = AMOUNT_IN_TANK;
    price = DEFAULT_PRICE;
```

```
}

public Pump(double start, double todaysPrice)   // an overloaded constructor
{
   amtInTank = start;
   price = todaysPrice;
}

public void values()
{

   DecimalFormat num = new DecimalFormat("$##.00");

   System.out.println("\nThe gas tank has " + amtInTank
                        + " gallons of gas.");
   System.out.println("The price per gallon of gas is "
                        + num.format(price));
}

public void request(double pumpAmt)
{
   double pumped;

   DecimalFormat num = new DecimalFormat("$##.00");

   if (amtInTank >= pumpAmt)
      pumped = pumpAmt;
   else
      pumped = amtInTank;

   amtInTank -= pumped;
   System.out.println();
   System.out.println(pumpAmt + " gallons were requested.\n"
                        + pumped + " gallons were pumped.\n"
                        + amtInTank + " gallons remain in the tank.");
   System.out.println("The total price for the pumped gas is "
                        + num.format(pumped * price) + ".");
}
```

Let's analyze this class by individually inspecting both its data and member methods. First, notice that we have declared four data members and four member methods. As private members, the data attributes can only be accessed through the class' member methods: Pump(), values(), and request(). These methods provide the external services available to each Pump object.

The two Pump() methods, which have the same name as their class, are the constructor methods, one of which will be automatically called when an object of type Pump is created. For both constructors, when a Pump object is declared, it will be initialized to a given amount of gas in the supply tank and a given price per gallon. If no values are given, the default constructor will use the default values of 500 gallons and $1.25 per gallon.

The `values()` method defined in the implementation section provides a readout of the current attribute values. The `request()` method is the most complicated because it provides the primary `Pump` service. The code follows the requirement that the pump provides all of the gas required unless the amount remaining in the supply tank is less than the requested amount. Finally, it subtracts the amount pumped from the amount in the tank and calculates the total dollar value of the transaction.

Step 4: Test and Correct the Solution Testing the `Pump` class entails testing each class operation. To do this, we first include the `Pump` class within the context of a working program, which is listed as Program 10.6.

PROGRAM 10.6

```
public class TestPump
{
  public static void main(String[] args)
  {
    Pump a = new Pump(300,1.00);
    Pump b = new Pump();    // use the default constructor's values
    a.values();
    a.request(30);
    a.request(280);
    b.values();
  }
}
```

Notice that in Program 10.6, unlike Program 10.5, we have constructed the test program as its own class, separate from the class being tested. For testing purposes, either approach is acceptable. Assume that the `Pump` class has been compiled and resides in the same folder as the `TestPump` class. If this were not the case, we would have to include an `import` statement for the `Pump` class at the top of the program (see Appendix F for how this can be accomplished using packages).

The `main()` method includes six statements. The first two statements create two objects of type `Pump`. The supply tank for the first pump object contains 300 gallons and the price per gallon is set to $1.00, while the second `Pump` object uses the default values AMOUNT_IN_PUMP and DEFAULT_PRICE, which are 500 and 1.25, respectively.

A call is then made to `values()` to display the first pump's attribute values, which are correctly displayed as 300 gallons and $1.00.

The next statement is a request for 30 gallons of gas from the first `Pump` object. This is followed by a request for 280 gallons, which exceeds the remaining gas in the supply tank. Finally, the attribute values for the second pump are displayed. The output produced by Program 10.6 is:

The gas tank has 300.0 gallons of gas.
The price per gallon of gas is $1.00

30.0 gallons were requested.
30.0 gallons were pumped.
270.0 gallons remain in the tank.
The total price for the pumped gas is $30.00.

280.0 gallons were requested.
270.0 gallons were pumped.
0.0 gallons remain in the tank.
The total price for the pumped gas is $270.00.

The gas tank has 500.0 gallons of gas.
The price per gallon of gas is $1.25

EXERCISES 10.4

1. Enter Program 10.5 in your computer and execute it.
2. a. Modify the `main()` method in Program 10.5 to put a second elevator in service starting at the 5th floor. Have this second elevator move to the 1st floor and then move to the 12th floor.
   b. Verify that the constructor method is called by adding a message within the constructor that is displayed each time a new object is created. Run your program to ensure its operation.
3. Modify the `main()` method in Program 10.5 to use a `while` loop that calls the `Elevator`'s request method with a random number between 1 and 15. If the random number is the same as the elevator's current floor, generate another request. The `while` loop should terminate after five valid requests have been made and satisfied by movement of the elevator. (*Tip:* Review Section 6.4 for the use of random numbers.)
4. a. Modify the `main()` method in Program 10.6 to use a `while` loop that calls the `Pump`'s request method with a random number between 3 and 20. The `while` loop should terminate after five requests have been made.
   b. Modify the `main()` method written for Exercise 4a to provide a 30-minute simulation of the gas pump's operation. To do this, you will have to modify the `while` loop to select a random number between 1 and 15 that represents the idle time between customer requests. Have the simulation stop once the idle time exceeds 30 minutes.
5. a. Construct a class definition of a `Person` object type. The class is to have no attributes, a single constructor method, and two additional member methods named `arrive()` and `gallons()`. The constructor method should be an empty, do-nothing method. The `arrive()` method should provide a random number between 1 and 15 as a return value, and the `gallons()` method should provide a random number between 3 and 20.
   b. Test the `Person` class methods written for Exercise 5a in a complete working program.

    c. Use the `Person` class method to simulate a random arrival of a person and a random request for gallons of gas within the program written for Exercise 5b.

6. Modify Program 10.6 so that the `Pump` class definition resides in a directory named pumpclass. Then have Program 10.6 use an `import` statement to include the class definition within the program.

7. Construct a class named `Light` that simulates a traffic light. The color attribute of the class should change from green to yellow to red and then back to green by the class' `change()` method. When a new `Light` object is created, its initial color should be red.

8. a. Construct a class definition that can represent an employee of a company. Each employee is defined by an integer ID number, a floating-point pay rate, and the maximum number of hours the employee should work each week. The services provided by the class should be the ability to enter data for a employee, the ability to change data for an employee, and the ability to display the existing data for a new employee.

    b. Include the class definition created for Exercise 8a in a working Java program that asks the user to enter data for three employees and displays the entered data.

10.5 COMMON PROGRAMMING ERRORS

The more common programming errors associated with the construction of classes are:

1. Including a return type in a constructor's header line.
2. Failing to include a return type in a nonconstructor member method's header line.
3. Defining more than one default constructor for a class.

All of these errors result in a compiler error message.

10.6 CHAPTER SUMMARY

1. A *class* is a programmer-defined data type. *Objects* of a class may be defined and have the same relationship to their class as variables do to Java's built-in data types.

2. A class is defined using a class variable declaration section and a class method definition section. The most common form of a class definition is:

```
public className
{
  // class variable declaration section
     variables typically declared as private;

  // class method definition section
     methods typically declared as public
}
```

    The variables are individually referred to as *class data members*, and the methods are referred to as *class member methods*. The terms private and public are referred to as both *visibility modifiers* and *access specifiers*. The keyword private specifies that the class members following it are `private` to the class and can only be accessed by member methods. The keyword `public` specifies that the class members following may be accessed from outside the class. Generally, all data members should be specified as `private` and all member methods as `public`.

3. Except for constructor methods, all class methods defined in the class definition section typically have the header line syntax

    ```
    public returnType  methodName(parameter list)
    ```

4. A *constructor* is a special method that is automatically called each time an object is declared. It must have the same name as its class and cannot have any return type. Its purpose is to initialize each declared object.

5. If no constructor is declared for a class, the compiler will supply a default constructor. The compiler-provided constructor initializes all numerical data members to zero and all string data members to a `null`.

6. The term *default constructor* refers to a constructor that does not require any arguments when it is called.

7. Each class may only have one default constructor. If a user-defined default constructor is provided, the compiler will not create its default constructor.

8. Objects are created with either a single- or double-statement declaration. The double-statement style of declaration has the form:

    ```
    className objectName;
    objectName = new className(optional list of arguments);
    ```

    An example of this style of declaration, including initializers, for a class named `Date` is:

    ```
    Date a; // declare an object of type date
    a = new Date(12, 25, 2003); // instantiate the object
    ```

    Although the variable `a` is commonly referred to as an object, it is actually a reference variable. The `new` operator then creates an actual object in memory that can be accessed using this reference variable. When an object is created with the `new` operator, it is also said to be *instantiated*.

    The single-statement declaration and instantiation, including the optional list of initializers, has the form:

    ```
    className objectName = new className(list of initializers);
    ```

    An example of this style of declaration is:

    ```
    Date a = new Date(12,25,2002);
    ```

9. Constructors can be overloaded in the same manner as any other user-written Java method.

10.7 CHAPTER SUPPLEMENT: INSIDES AND OUTSIDES

Just as the concept of an algorithm is central to methods, the concept of encapsulation is central to objects. In this section, we provide a way of looking at encapsulation using an inside-outside analogy that should help in your understanding of what object-oriented programming is all about.

In programming terms, an object's attributes are described by data, such as the length and width of a rectangle, and the operations that can be applied to the attributes are described by methods. As a practical example, assume that we will be writing a program that can deal a hand of cards. From an object-oriented approach, one of the objects that we must model is clearly a deck of cards. For our purposes, the attribute of interest for the card deck is that it contains 52 cards consisting of four suits (hearts, diamonds, spades, and clubs), with each suit consisting of 13 pip values (ace to ten, jack, queen, and king).

Now consider the behavior of our deck of cards, which consists of the operations that can be applied to the deck. At a minimum, we will want the ability to shuffle the deck and deal single cards. Let's now see how this simple example relates encapsulation using an inside-outside concept.

A useful visualization of the inside-outside concept is to consider an object as a boiled egg (Figure 10.5). Notice that the egg consists of three parts: a very inside yolk, a less inside white surrounding the yolk, and an outer shell, which is the only part of the egg visible to the outside world.

FIGURE 10.5   The Boiled Egg Object Model

In terms of our boiled egg model, the attributes and behavior of an object correspond to the yolk and white, respectively, which are inside the eggshell. That is, the innermost protected area of an object, its data attributes, can be compared to the egg yolk.

Surrounding the data attributes, in a similar manner as an egg's white surrounds its yolk, are the operations that we choose to incorporate within an object. Finally, the interface to the outside world, which is represented by the shell, is how a user gets to invoke the object's internal procedures.

The egg model, with its eggshell interface separating the inside of the egg from the outside, is useful precisely because it so clearly depicts the separation between what should be contained inside an object and what should be seen from the outside. This separation forms an essential element in object-oriented programming. Let's see why this is so.

From an inside-outside perspective, an object's data attributes, the selected algorithms for the object's operations, and how these algorithms are actually implemented are always inside issues that are hidden from the view of an object user. What remains—how a user or another object can actually activate an inside procedure—is an outside issue.

Now let's apply this concept to our card deck example. First, consider how we might represent cards in the deck. Any of the following attributes (and there are others) could represent a card:

1.   Two integer variables, one representing a suit (a number from 1 to 4) and one representing a value (a number from 1 to 13).
2.   One character value and one integer value. The character represents a card's suit, and the integer represents a card's value.

3. One integer variable having a value from 0 to 51. The expression `(int) (number / 13 + 1)` provides a number from 1 to 4, which represents the suit, and the expression `(number % 13 + 1)` represents a card value from 1 to 13.

Whichever representation we choose, however, is not relevant to the outside. The specific way we choose to represent a card is an inside issue to be decided by the designer of the `Deck` class. From the outside, all that is of concern is that we have access to a deck consisting of 52 cards having the necessary suits and pip values.

The same is true for the operations we decide to provide as part of our card `Deck` class. Consider just the shuffling for now.

There are a number of algorithms for producing a shuffled deck. For example, we could use Java's random number method, `Math.random()`, or create our own random number generator. Again, the selected algorithm is an inside issue to be determined by the designer of the `Deck` class. The specifics of which algorithm is selected and how it is applied to the attributes we have chosen for each card in the deck are not relevant from the object's outside. For purposes of illustration, assume that we decide to use Java's `Math.random()` method to produce a randomly shuffled deck.

If we select the first attribute set previously given, each card in a shuffled deck is produced using `Math.random()` at least twice: once to create a random number from 1 to 4 for the suit and then again to create a random number from 1 to 13 for the card's pip value. This sequence must be done to construct 52 different attribute sets with no duplicates allowed.

On the other hand, if we choose the second attribute set previously given, a shuffled deck can be produced in exactly the same fashion just described with one modification: The first random number (from 1 to 4) must be changed into a character to represent the suit.

Finally, if we choose the third representation for a card, we need to use `math.random()` once for each card to produce 52 random numbers from 0 to 51 with no duplicates allowed.

The important point here is that the selection of an algorithm and how it will be applied to an object's attributes are definition issues, *and definition issues are always inside issues*. A user of the card deck, who is outside, does not need to know how the shuffling is done. All the user of the deck must know is how to produce a shuffled deck. In practice, this means that the user is supplied with sufficient information to correctly instantiate a deck object and invoke the shuffle method. This corresponds to the interface, or outer shell of the egg.

Abstraction and Encapsulation

The distinction between insides and outsides relates directly to the concepts of abstraction and encapsulation. **Abstraction** means concentrating on what an object is and does before making any decisions about how the object will be implemented. Thus, abstractly, we define a deck and the operations we want to provide. (Clearly, if our abstraction is to be useful, it had better capture the attributes and operations of a real-world deck.) Once we have decided on the attributes and operations, we can actually implement them.

Encapsulation means incorporating the definition details of the chosen abstract attributes and behavior inside a class. The external side of an object should provide only the necessary interface to users of the object for activating internal procedures. Imposing a strict inside-outside discipline when creating classes is really another way of saying that the class successfully encapsulates all definition details. In our deck of cards example, encapsulation means that users need never be concerned with how we have internally modeled the deck or how an operation, such as shuffling, is performed; they only need to know how to activate the given operations.

Code Reuse and Extensibility

A direct advantage of an inside-outside approach is that it encourages both code reuse and extensibility. This is a direct result of having all interactions between objects centered on the outside interface and restricting all definition details within the object's inside.

For example, consider the object shown in Figure 10.6. Here any of the two object's operations can be activated by correctly stimulating either the circle or square on the outside. In practice, the stimulation is simply a method call. We have used a circle and square to emphasize that two different methods are provided for outside use. In our card deck example, activation of one method might produce a shuffled deck, while activation of another method might result in a card suit and pip value being returned from the object.

The Interface

FIGURE 10.6   Using an Object's Interface

Now assume that we want to alter the definition of an existing operation or add more functionality to our class. *As long as the existing outside interface is maintained, the internal definition of any and all operations can be changed without the user ever being aware that a change took place.* This is a direct result of encapsulating the attribute data and operations within a class.

In addition, as long as the interface to existing operations is not changed, new operations can be added as they are needed. Essentially, from the outside world, all that is being added is another method call that accesses the inside attributes and modifies them in a new way.

CHAPTER 11

Additional Class

Capabilities

The creation of a class requires that we provide the capability to declare, initialize, assign, manipulate, and display data members. In the previous chapter, we presented the declaration, initialization, and display of methods. In this chapter, we continue our construction of classes by providing the ability to create copy instructors and extend existing classes using Java's inheritance features. With these additions, we can use existing classes to easily create extended classes that meet our exact needs.

11.1 MEMBERWISE ASSIGNMENT

In Chapter 3, we saw how Java's assignment operator, =, performs assignment between variables. In this section, we see how assignment works when it is applied to objects. For a specific assignment example, consider the main() method of Program 11.1. Notice that the Date class' method definition section contains no assignment method. Nevertheless, we would expect the assignment statement a = b; in main() to assign b's data member values to their counterparts in a. This is in fact the case and is verified by the following output, which is produced when Program 11.1 is executed:

```
The date stored in a is originally 04/01/99
After assignment the date stored in a is 12/18/01
```

The type of assignment illustrated in Program 11.1 is referred to as **memberwise assignment.** In the absence of any specific instructions to the contrary, the Java compiler builds this type of default assignment operator for each class. If the class *does not* contain any reference data members, this default assignment operator is adequate and can be used without further consideration. Before considering the problems that can occur with reference data members, let's see how to construct our own explicit assignment methods.

An assignment method, like all class methods, must be defined in the class' method definition section. For our specific purposes, we will name our method setEqual() and provide it with a Date parameter. Using this information, a suitable method definition is:

```java
public void setEqual(Date newdate)
{
  day = newdate.day;        // assign the day
  month = newdate.month;    // assign the month
  year = newdate.year;      // assign the year
}
```

In the header line for this method, the keyword void indicates that the method will not return a value, and the parameter name that we have arbitrarily given to newdate has been correctly declared as a Date object type. Within the body of the method, the day member of the newdate object is assigned to the day member of the object that is referenced when the method is called, which is then repeated for the month and year members. A statement such as a.setEqual(b); can then call the method and assign b's member values to the Date object named a. Program 11.2 contains our assignment method within the context of a complete program.

PROGRAM 11.1

```java
import java.text.*;  // needed for formatting
public class Date
{
  // class variable declaration section
  private int month;
  private int day;
  private int year;

  // class method definition section
  public Date(int mm, int dd, int yyyy) // constructor
  {
    month = mm;
    day = dd;
    year = yyyy;
  }

  public void showDate()
  {
    DecimalFormat df = new DecimalFormat("00");

    System.out.print(df.format(month)
                    + '/' + df.format(day) + '/'
                    + df.format(year % 100));
  }

  public static void main(String[] args)
  {
    Date a = new Date(04,01,1999); // create two Date methods
    Date b = new Date(12,18,2001);

    System.out.print("\nThe date stored in a is originally ");
    a.showDate();  // display the original date
    a = b;         // assign b's value to a
    System.out.print("\nAfter assignment the date stored in a is ");
    a.showDate();  // display a's values
    System.out.println();
  }
}
```

Except for the addition of the `setEqual()` method, Program 11.2 is identical to Program 11.1 and produces the same output. It is useful because it illustrates how we can explicitly construct our own assignment methods.

Two potential problems exist with the `setEqual()` method as it is currently written. As constructed, our simple assignment method returns no value, which precludes using it in making multiple assignments, such as `a.setEqual(b.setEqual(c))`. To provide for

PROGRAM 11.2

```java
import java.text.*;  // needed for formatting
public class Date
{
  // class variable declaration section
  private int month;
  private int day;
  private int year;

  // class method definition section
  public Date(int mm, int dd, int yyyy) // constructor
  {
    month = mm;
    day = dd;
    year = yyyy;
  }

  public void setEqual(Date newdate)
  {
    day = newdate.day;        // assign the day
    month = newdate.month;    // assign the month
    year = newdate.year;      // assign the year
  }

  public void showDate()
  {
    DecimalFormat df = new DecimalFormat("00");

    System.out.print(df.format(month)
                     + '/' + df.format(day) + '/'
                     + df.format(year % 100));
  }

  public static void main(String[] args)
  {
    Date a = new Date(04,01,1999); // create two Date objects
    Date b = new Date(12,18,2001);

    System.out.print("\nThe date stored in a is originally ");
    a.showDate();      // display the original date
    a.setEqual(b);     // assign b's value to a
    System.out.print("\nAfter assignment the date stored in a is ");
    a.showDate();  // display a's values
    System.out.println();
  }
}
```

this type of method call, which is referred to as both a **cascading** and **concatenated call,** our method must return a reference to a Date type. Providing this type of return must be postponed until we introduce the this reference in the next section. The second problem with our setEqual() method is that it provides what is called a **shallow copy.** What this means, why it is only a problem when an object contains a reference variable, and how to deal with it are presented in Section 11.4.

EXERCISES 11.1

1. Enter and run Program 11.2 on your computer.

2. **a.** Construct a class named Time that contains three integer data members named hrs, mins, and secs, which will store hours, minutes, and seconds. The class methods should include a constructor that provides default values of 0 for each data member, a constructor that permits initialization of a Time object to a programmer-selected value when it is created, a display method that prints an object's data values, and an assignment method that performs a member-wise assignment between two Time objects.

   b. Include the Time class developed in Exercise 2a in a working Java program that creates and displays two Time objects, the second of which is assigned the values of the first object.

3. **a.** Construct a class named Complex that contains two double-precision data members named real and imag, which will store the real and imaginary parts of a complex number. The class methods should include a constructor that provides default values of 0 for each member method, a constructor that permits initialization of a Complex object to a programmer-selected value when it is created, a display method that prints an object's data values, and an assignment operator that performs a memberwise assignment between two Complex number objects.

   b. Include the class written for Exercise 3a in a working Java program that creates and displays the values of two Complex objects, the second of which is assigned the values of the first object.

4. **a.** Construct a class named Car that contains the following three data members: a double-precision variable named engineSize, a String variable named bodyStyle, and an integer variable named colorCode. The class methods should include a constructor that permits a user to initialize a Car object when it is created; a display method that prints the engine size, body style, and color code; and an assignment method that performs a memberwise assignment between two car objects for each instance variable.

   b. Include the class written for Exercise 4a in a working Java program that creates and displays two Car objects, the second of which is assigned the values of the first object.

5. **a.** Construct a class named Cartesian that contains two floating-point data members named x and y, which will store the x and y values of a point in rectangular coordinates. The class methods should include a constructor that initializes the x and y values of an object to 0, a constructor that permits initialization of a Cartesian object to programmer-selected values when it is created, and methods to input and display an object's x and y values. In addition, there should be an assignment method that performs a memberwise assignment between two Cartesian objects.

b. Include the class written for Exercise 5a in a working Java program that creates and displays the values of two `Cartesian` objects, the second of which is assigned the values of the first object.

6. a. Construct a class named `RecCoord` that contains two double-precision data members named `xval` and `yval`, which will store the x and y values of a point in rectangular coordinates. The class methods should include appropriate constructor and display methods and a method named `convertToPolar()`. The `convertToPolar()` method should accept a `RecCoord` object and convert its rectangular coordinates into polar coordinates. For conversion from rectangular to polar coordinates, use the formulas:

$$r = \sqrt{x^2 + y^2}$$
$$\theta = arctan \ (y/x)$$

b. Include the program written for Exercise 6a in a working Java program.

7. a. Construct a class named `PolCoord` that contains two double-precision data members named `distance` and `angle`, which will store the distance and angle values of a point represented in polar coordinates. The class methods should include appropriate constructor and display methods and a method named `convertToXandY()`. The `convertToXandY()` method should accept a `PolCoord` object and convert its polar coordinates into rectangular coordinates. For conversion from polar to rectangular coordinates, use the formulas:

$$x = r \ cos \ \theta$$
$$y = r \ sin \ \theta$$

b. Include the class written for Exercise 7a in a working Java program.

8. a. Construct a class named `RecCoord` that contains two double-precision data members named `xval` and `yval`, which will store the x and y values of a point in rectangular coordinates. The class methods should include appropriate constructor and display methods and a method named `distance()`. The `distance()` method should accept two `RecCoord` objects and determine the distance between the points. Use the conversion formula:

$$distance = \sqrt{(x2 - x1)^2 + (y2 - y1)^2}$$

b. Include the program written for Exercise 8a in a working Java program.

9. a. Construct a class named `Savings` that contains three floating-point data members named `balance`, `rate`, and `interest` and a constructor that initializes each of these members to 0. In addition, there should be a member object that inputs values for `balance` and `rate` and then calculates `interest`. The `rate` value should be stored as a percentage, such as 6.5 for 6.5 percent, and the interest computed as *interest = balance × rate/100*. In addition, there should be a class method to display the values stored in all the class variables.

b. Include the class written for Exercise 9a in a working Java program that tests each member method.

11.2 ADDITIONAL CLASS FEATURES

This section presents additional features pertaining to classes. These include class scope and visibility, creating static class data members, and the special reference variable named `this`. Each of these topics may be read independently of the others.

Class Scope and Visibility

As you saw in Section 6.3, the scope of a variable defines the portion of a class where the variable can be used. Variables that are declared within a method are formally said to have **block scope,** where the block starts at the opening brace, {, that begins the method and stops at the closing brace, }, that ends the method. In addition, all parameters of a method are considered to have the same block scope. Thus, within a method, any variables declared inside an inner block have a block scope restricted by the brace pair that defines the block.

Class scope starts at the opening brace that begins the class' definition and stops at the closing brace that ends the class. Thus, class scope includes both variables declared in the class' variable declaration section and all methods contained within the class' method definition section. Figure 11.1 illustrates the scope of the variables and methods for the following class definition:

```
public class Test
{
  // class variable declaration section
  private double amount;
  private float price;

  // class method definition section
  public double calcTotal(float amt, float pr);
  {
    double total;

    amount = amt;
    price = pr;

    total = amt * pr;
    return total;
  }
}
```

FIGURE 11.1 Example of Scopes

VALUES AND IDENTITIES

Apart from any behavior that an object is supplied with, a characteristic feature that objects share with variables is that they always have a unique identity. It is an object's identity that permits distinguishing one object from another. This is not true of a value, such as the number 5, because all occurrences of 5 are indistinguishable from one another. Thus, values are not considered as objects in object-oriented programming languages such as Java. A value is an entity that stands for itself.

Now consider a string such as "Chicago". As a string, this is a value. However, since Chicago could also be a specific and identifiable object of type City, the context in which the name is used is important. Notice that if the string "Chicago" were assigned to an object's name attribute, it reverts to being a value.

In addition to scope, as shown in Figure 11.1, classes and their members have **visibility,** which determines whether the member can be accessed from outside the class in which it is declared. Visibility is set using one or none of the following access modifiers: public, private, or protected. Regardless of these access modifiers, all class variables and methods are accessible everywhere within their class and conform to the following visibility rules, examples of which will be presented later in this section:

1. A class variable declared as private cannot be accessed outside its class.
2. A class variable declared as public can be accessed outside its class by prefixing the variable's name with its class name and a period.
3. If a class variable has the same name as a method variable, the class variable effectively becomes hidden within the method, and any use of the variable's name will refer to the method variable. In such cases, the class variable can still be accessed within the scope of the method variable having the same name by prefixing the class variable's name with the class' name for static variables and with the object's name or the keyword this (as demonstrated at the end of this section) for nonstatic object instantiated data members. In all cases, the prefixed name must be separated from the variable's name with a period.
4. A class method declared as public can be accessed outside its class. In general, such methods present the services that the class provides to the outside world.
5. A class method declared as public and static is a general-purpose method that can perform a task not related to any specific object created from the class.
6. A class method declared as private can only be accessed by other methods in the same class that contains the private method.

In addition to the visibility of methods and variables defined within a class, the class itself has a visibility. When the keyword class is preceded by the keyword public, the class can be accessed by other classes. If the class is preceded by the keyword private, it can only be accessed by other classes within the same source file that it is located. Finally, if the class has no visibility modifier, it has **package visibility.** This means that the class can be used by any class within the same package that the class is located (see Appendix F).

THE KEYWORD static

In Java, a class variable declared as static creates a member variable that belongs to the class as a whole. Thus, a static class variable is created only once, no matter how many objects of the class are created, and it exists even if no objects are created. Each object shares the same static variable, and a change of value by one object effectively changes the value of the static variable for all objects. This is because only one static variable is actually created, and the same variable is shared by all subsequently instantiated objects.

Because static variables can exist independently of any specific object, there had to be some means of accessing such variables precisely when no object existed. This was the original purpose of a static method. A very useful side effect of the fact that static methods could be invoked independently of any object is that it also permitted such methods to perform any general-purpose task not associated with an object. One such task is to start program processing with a main() method before any object has had a chance to be created.

From within both static and nonstatic class methods, a static variable is accessed by simply using the variable's name. When it is accessed as a data member of a specific object, it can be prefixed with the object's name and a period. Finally, a static variable can be accessed by prefixing it with its class name and a period.

Static Variable Members

We have already encountered static methods. As we have seen, when the keyword static is applied to a method, it creates a general-purpose method that can be used independently of any individual object. These methods are never prefixed with the name of a specific object when they are invoked.

When the term static is applied to a class variable, it performs a different function. To understand what this function is, it is first necessary to see how class objects are actually created.

As each class object is created, it gets its own block of memory for its data members. In some cases, however, it is convenient for every object to share the *same* memory location for a specific variable. For example, consider a class consisting of employee records, where each employee is subject to the same state income tax rate. Clearly, we could declare the tax rate as a class variable, in which case it would be included with every employee object that is created. But this solution is wasteful of computer storage and can result in an error if the tax rate changes and the change is not made in all existing employee objects.

This type of situation is handled in Java by declaring a class variable to be static. A static class variable is created only once when a class comes into scope and is shared by all objects created from the class. Thus, a static data member is effectively a global variable for the class that exists even if no object is instantiated.

Java requires that static variables be declared within the class' declaration section. For example, consider the Employee class definition within Program 11.3.

PROGRAM 11.3

```java
public class Employee
{
  // class variable declaration section
  private static double taxRate = 0.0025;
  private int idNum;

  // class method definition section
  public Employee(int num)  // constructor
  {
    idNum = num;
  }

  public void display()
  {
    System.out.println("Employee number " + idNum
              + " has a tax rate of " + taxRate);
  }

  public static void main(String[] args)
  {
    Employee BSMITH = new Employee(11122);
    Employee JJONES = new Employee(11133);

    BSMITH.display();
    JJONES.display();
  }
}
```

In Program 11.3, both the definition and initialization of the `static` variable `taxRate` are accomplished by the statement

```java
private static double taxRate = 0.0025;
```

The storage sharing produced by the `static` data member and the methods created in Program 11.3 are illustrated in Figure 11.2.

The output produced by Program 11.3 is:

```
Employee number 11122 has a tax rate of 0.0025
Employee number 11133 has a tax rate of 0.0025
```

To verify that a `static` variable exists independently of any specific object, consider Program 11.4, which displays the value of the `Employee` class' `static taxRate` variable without any objects being created.

FIGURE 11.2 **Sharing the** `static` **Data Member** `taxRate`

It was precisely to provide a means of accessing `static` variables in the absence of, and independently of, any specific objects that `static` member methods are provided in Java. Such methods are restricted to accessing `static` variables, other `static` methods, objects, and values passed as arguments when the method is called. Because a `static` method is independent of any specific object, it can also construct general-purpose methods, as was done in Chapter 6.

PROGRAM 11.4

```java
public class Employees
{
  // class variable declaration section
  private static double taxRate = 0.0025;
  private int idNum;

  // class method definition section
  public Employees(int num)  // constructor
  {
    idNum = num;
  }

  public static void main(String[] args)
  {
    System.out.print("The tax rate is " + taxRate);
  }
}
```

The `this` Reference

Except for `static` data members, which are shared by all class objects, each object maintains its own set of class variables. This permits each object to have its own clearly defined state as determined by the values stored in its set of class variables. For example, consider the `Date` class defined in Program 11.1 and repeated here for convenience:

```
public class Date
{
   // class variable declaration section
   private int month;
   private int day;
   private int year;

   // class method definition section
   public Date(int mm, int dd, int yyyy) // constructor
   {
      month = mm;
      day = dd;
      year = yyyy;
   }

   public void showDate()
   {
      DecimalFormat df = new DecimalFormat("00");

      System.out.print(df.format(month)
                     + '/' + df.format(day) + '/'
                     + df.format(year % 100));
   }
}
```

Each time an object is created from this class, a distinct area of memory is set aside for its data members. For example, if two objects referenced by the variable names a and b are created from this class, the memory storage for these objects is as shown in Figure 11.3. Notice that two sets of class variables are created, and each set has its own storage in memory.

This replication of data storage is not implemented for member methods. In fact, for each class *only one copy of each member method is retained in memory*, and each and every object uses these same methods.

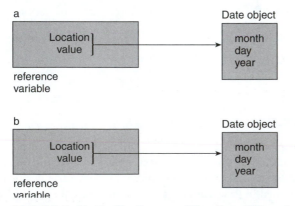

FIGURE 11.3   The Storage of Two Date Objects in Memory

Sharing member methods requires providing a means of identifying which specific object a member method should be operating on. This is accomplished by providing information to the method indicating where in memory a specific object is located. This information is provided by the reference variable used to identify each object. For example, again using our `Date` class and assuming a is a reference variable of this class, the statement `a.showDate()` passes the memory location information stored in a to the `showDate()` method. This information tells the method which object to locate and operate on.

An obvious question at this point is how this reference to the stored object is actually passed to `showDate()` and where this referencing information is stored. The answer is that the location information for the object is stored in a special reference variable named `this`, which is automatically supplied as a hidden argument to each nonstatic member method when such a method is called. That is, each member method actually receives an extra argument that permits it to locate the particular object it is to operate on. Although it is usually not necessary to do so, this "hidden" reference argument can be explicitly used in member methods. For example, consider Program 11.5, which incorporates the `this` reference in each of its member methods to access the appropriate object.

PROGRAM 11.5

```java
import java.text.*;   // needed for formatting
public class Date
{
  // class variable declaration section
  private int month;
  private int day;
  private int year;

  // class method definition section
  public Date(int mm, int dd, int yyyy) // constructor
  {
    this.month = mm;
    this.day = dd;
    this.year = yyyy;
  }

  public void showDate()
  {
    DecimalFormat df = new DecimalFormat("00");

    System.out.print(df.format(this.month)
                        + '/' + df.format(this.day) + '/'
                        + df.format(this.year % 100));
  }
```

(Continued on next page)

(Continued from previous page)

```
    public static void main(String[] args)
    {
      Date a = new Date(04,01,1999); // create two Date objects
      Date b = new Date(12,18,2001);

      System.out.print("\nThe date stored in a is originally ");
      a.showDate();  // display the original date
      a = b;              // assign b's value to a
      System.out.print("\nAfter assignment the date stored in a is ");
      a.showDate();  // display a's values
      System.out.println();
    }
  }
```

The output produced by Program 11.5 is:

```
The date stored in a is originally 04/01/99
After assignment the date stored in a is 12/18/01
```

This is the same output produced by Program 11.1, which omits using the this reference to access the data members. Clearly, the this reference in Program 11.5 is unnecessary and clutters the class methods' code. There are times, however, when an object must pass its address on to other methods. These occur in more advanced situations when it is necessary for a method to return a reference to the current object being processed, when it is necessary to have one constructor call another, and more generally, when it is necessary to have cascading method calls where one method calls another. In these last two situations, the called method must return a reference to the current object it has operated on, and the statement return this; provides the correct return type.

EXERCISES 11.2

1. Enter and run Program 11.3 on your computer.
2. a. Rewrite Program 11.3 to include an integer static data member named numemps. This variable should act as a counter that is initialized to zero and is incremented by the class constructor each time a new object is created. Write a static method named disp() to display the value of this static data member.
   b. Test the class written for Exercise 2a. Have the main() method call disp() after each Employee object is created.
3. a. Construct a class named Circle that contains two integer data members named xCenter and yCenter and a double-precision data member named radius. In addition, the class should contain a static data member named scaleFactor. Here the xCenter and yCenter values represent the center point of a circle, radius represents the circle's actual radius, and scaleFactor

represents a scale factor that will scale the circle to fit on a variety of display devices.

    b. Include the class written for Exercise 3a in a working Java program.

4. Enter and exit Program 11.5.

5. Modify Program 11.3 to explicitly use the `this` reference in all member methods.

6. Modify Program 11.2 so that it returns a reference to a `Date`.

11.3 APPLICATIONS
Application 1: A MultiClass Gas Pump Simulation

In Application 2 of Section 10.4, we presented a requirement to construct a Java program that simulated a gas pump's operation over the course of one-half hour. In that section, we constructed a gas `Pump` class to model the operation of a gas pump. In this section, we use this gas `Pump` class within the context of a complete simulation. For convenience, we repeat the complete program requirement here:

> *We have been requested to write a program that simulates the operation of a gas pump. At any time during the simulation, we should be able to determine, from the pump, the price per gallon of gas and the amount remaining in the supply tank from which the gas is pumped. If the amount of gas in the supply tank is greater than or equal to the amount of gas requested, the request should be filled; otherwise, only the available amount in the supply tank should be used. Once the gas is pumped, the total price of the gallons pumped should be displayed and the amount of gas in gallons that was pumped should be subtracted from the amount in the supply tank.*
>
> *For the simulation, assume that the pump is randomly idle between 1 to 15 minutes between customer arrivals and that a customer randomly requests between 3 and 20 gallons of gas. Although the default supply tank capacity is 500 gallons assume that the initial amount of gas in the tank for this simulation is only 300 gallons Initially, the program should simulate a one-half hour time frame.*
>
> *Additionally, for each arrival and request for gas, we want to know the idle time before the customer arrived, how many gallons of gas were pumped, and the total price of the transaction. The pump itself must keep track of the price per gallon of gas and the amount of gas remaining in the tank. Typically, the price per gallon is $1.25, but the price for the simulation should be $1.00.*

In Section 10.4, we constructed a `Pump` class that can be used for this simulation. In this problem, we complete the simulation by providing a `Customer` class and the controlling code within a `main()` method to create an actual multiobject simulation program consisting of both `Customer` and `Pump` objects.

Step 1: Analyze the Problem As specified, the problem entails two types of objects: a gas pump and a customer. Let's consider these object types separately.

THE PUMP

A `Pump` class was designed and implemented in Section 10.4 and is repeated here for convenience.

```java
import java.text.*;    // needed for formatting
public class Pump
{
  // class variable declaration section
  private double amtInTank;
  private double price;
  private static final double AMOUNT_IN_TANK = 500.0;
  private static final double DEFAULT_PRICE = 1.25;

  // class method definition section
  public Pump()  // this is the default constructor
  {
    amtInTank = AMOUNT_IN_TANK;
    price = DEFAULT_PRICE;
  }

  public Pump(double start, double todaysPrice)  // an overloaded constructor
  {
    amtInTank = start;
    price = todaysPrice;
  }

  public void values()
  {

    DecimalFormat num = new DecimalFormat("$##.00");

    System.out.println("\nThe gas tank has " + amtInTank
                       + " gallons of gas.");
    System.out.println("The price per gallon of gas is "
                       + num.format(price));
  }

  public void request(double pumpAmt)
  {
    double pumped;

    DecimalFormat num = new DecimalFormat("$##.00");

    if (amtInTank >= pumpAmt)
      pumped = pumpAmt;
    else
      pumped = amtInTank;

    amtInTank -= pumped;
    System.out.println();
    System.out.println(pumpAmt + " gallons were requested.\n"
                       + pumped + " gallons were pumped.\n"
                       + amtInTank + " gallons remain in the tank.");
```

```
        System.out.println("The total price for the pumped gas is "
                        + num.format(pumped * price) +".");
  }
}
```

You should review Application 2 in Section 10.4 if either the data or method members of this `Pump` class are not clear. For later convenience in writing the required simulation program, assume that the code for the `Pump` class is being stored in the same directory as all remaining classes written for this simulation. Once this is done and the `Pump` class has been compiled, it will automatically be accessed by any program in the same directory that attempts to use it. For documentation purposes, the statement `import Pump;` can be included at the top of the program.

THE CUSTOMER

For this problem, there are multiple instances of customers arriving randomly between 1 and 15 minutes and requesting gas in amounts that vary randomly between 3 and 20 gallons. From an object viewpoint, however, we are not interested in storing the arrival and number of gallons requested by each customer. We simply need a customer object to present us with an arrival time and a request for gas in gallons.

Notice that our `Customer` object type will have no attributes and will consist of two operations. The first operation, called `arrival()`, will provide a random arrival time between 1 and 15 minutes. The second operation, called `gallons()`, will provide a random request of between 3 and 20 gallons of gas. This class is relatively simple, and its design and implementation are coded as:

```
public class Customer
{
  // class variable declaration section
  // no class variables needed

  // class method definition section
  public Customer() {} // this is a default do-nothing constructor

  public int arrive()
  {
    return (1 + (int)(Math.random() * 15));
  }

  public int gallons()
  {
    return (3 + (int)(Math.random() * 18));
  }
}
```

In reviewing this code, notice that the class constructor is a do-nothing constructor that can be omitted with no effect on the class. The real purpose of the class is to provide the two member methods, `arrive()` and `gallons()`, which create a random arrival time for a new customer and a request for a random number of gallons to be dispensed (review

Section 6.3 if you are unfamiliar with the `Math.random()` method). The `arrive()` method returns a random integer between 1 and 15, and the `gallons()` method returns a random integer between 3 and 20 (we leave it as an exercise for you to rewrite the `gallons()` method to return a floating-point value).

Again, for later convenience in writing the complete simulation program, assume that the code for the `Customer` class is placed in the same directory as the `Pump` class.

PROGRAM LOGIC

Having analyzed and defined the two classes that we will be using, we still need to analyze and define the logic to correctly control the interaction between these two objects for a valid simulation.

In this particular case, the only interaction between a `Customer` object and the single `Pump` object is that a customer's arrival, followed by a request, determines when the pump is activated and how much gas is requested. Thus, each interaction between a `Customer` and the `Pump` can be expressed by the pseudocode

> *Obtain a Customer arrival time*
> *Obtain a Customer request for gas*
> *Activate the Pump with the request*

Although this repetition of events takes place continuously over the course of a day, we are only interested in a one-half hour period. Therefore, we must place these three events in a loop that is executed until the required simulation time has elapsed.

Step 2: Develop a Solution We have already developed and coded the two required classes, `Pump` and `Customer`, for the simulation. What remains to be developed is the control logic within the `main()` method for correctly activating class events. From the analysis, we know that a loop controlled by the total arrival time for all customers is required. A suitable control structure for `main()` is described by the algorithm:

```
Create a Pump object with the required initial gallons of gas
Display the values in the initialized Pump
Set the total time to 0
Obtain a Customer arrival time    // first arrival
Add the arrival time to the total time
While the total time does not exceed the simulation time
  Display the total time
  Obtain a Customer request for gas
  Activate the Pump with the request
  Obtain a Customer arrival time   // next arrival
  Add the arrival time to the total time
EndWhile
Display a message that the simulation is over
```

Step 3: Code the Solution The Java code corresponding to our design is in Program 11.6.

Step 4: Test and Correct the Solution Assuming that the `Pump` and `Customer` classes have been thoroughly tested and debugged, testing and debugging Program 11.6 is really restricted to testing and debugging the `main()` method. This specificity of testing is precisely

PROGRAM 11.6

```java
public class PumpSimulation
{
  private final static double SIMTIME = 0.5;    // simulation time in hours
  private final static int MINUTES = 60;         // number of minutes in an hour

  public static void main(String[] args)
  {
    Pump a = new Pump(300, 1.00);    // declare 1 object of type Pump
    Customer b = new Customer();     // declare 1 object of type Customer

    int totalTime = 0;
    int idleTime;
    int amtRequest;
    int SimMinutes;   // simulation time in minutes

    SimMinutes = (int) (SIMTIME * MINUTES);
    System.out.println("\nStarting a new simulation - simulation time is "
                    + SimMinutes + " minutes.");
    a.values();

      // get the first arrival
    idleTime = b.arrive();
    totalTime += idleTime;

    while (totalTime <= SimMinutes)
    {
      System.out.println("\nThe idle time is " + idleTime + " minutes,"
                    + " and we are " + totalTime
                    + " minutes into the simulation.");
      amtRequest = b.gallons();
      a.request((double)(amtRequest));

        // get the next arrival
      idleTime = b.arrive();
      totalTime += idleTime;
    }
    System.out.println("\nThe idle time is " + idleTime + " minutes."
              + "\nAs the total time now exceeds the simulation time, "
              + "this simulation run is over.");
  }
}
```

one of the advantages of an object-oriented approach. Using previously written and tested class definitions allows us to focus our attention on the remaining code that controls the flow of events between objects, which in Program 11.6 centers on the `main()` method.

By itself, the main( ) method in Program 11.6 is a straightforward while loop where the Pump idle time corresponds to the time between customer arrivals. The output of a sample run, shown below, verifies that the loop is operating correctly:

```
Starting a new simulation - simulation time is 30 minutes.

The gas tank has 300.0 gallons of gas.
The price per gallon of gas is $1.25

The idle time is 9 minutes, and we are 9 minutes into the simulation.

6.0 gallons were requested.
6.0 gallons were pumped.
294.0 gallons remain in the tank.
The total price for the pumped gas is $7.50.

The idle time is 10 minutes, and we are 19 minutes into the simulation.

4.0 gallons were requested.
4.0 gallons were pumped.
290.0 gallons remain in the tank.
The total price for the pumped gas is $5.00.

The idle time is 2 minutes, and we are 21 minutes into the simulation.

7.0 gallons were requested.
7.0 gallons were pumped.
283.0 gallons remain in the tank.
The total price for the pumped gas is $8.75.

The idle time is 1 minutes, and we are 22 minutes into the simulation.

16.0 gallons were requested.
16.0 gallons were pumped.
267.0 gallons remain in the tank.
The total price for the pumped gas is $20.00.

The idle time is 6 minutes, and we are 28 minutes into the simulation.

9.0 gallons were requested.
9.0 gallons were pumped.
258.0 gallons remain in the tank.
The total price for the pumped gas is $11.25.

The idle time is 9 minutes. As the total time now exceeds the simulation
time, this simulation run is over.
```

POINT OF INFORMATION

PROGRAM AND CLASS LIBRARIES

The concept of a program library began with Fortran, which was the first commercial high-level language introduced in 1954. The Fortran library consisted of a group of completely tested and debugged mathematical routines that were provided with the compiler. Since that time, every programming language has provided its own library of methods. In Java, this library includes such general-purpose methods as sqrt(), pow(), abs(), and random(). The advantage of such methods is that they significantly enhance program development and design by providing code that is known to work correctly without the need for additional testing and debugging.

With the introduction of object-oriented languages, the concept of a program library has been extended to include class libraries. A *class library* is a library of tested and debugged classes.

One of the key practical features of class libraries is that they help realize the goal of code reuse in a significant way. By providing tested and debugged code consisting of both data and function members, class libraries furnish large sections of prewritten and reusable code ready for incorporation within new applications. This shifts the focus of writing application programs from the creation of new code to understanding how to use predefined objects and stitch them together in a cohesive and useful way. A prime example of this is the visual object classes consisting of check boxes, list boxes, dialogs, command buttons, and option buttons provided in the Java swing package.

Application 2: Swapping Values

The need to exchange the values stored in two variables occurs frequently in programming when either lists of numbers or names need to be sorted. To illustrate how such an exchange of values is constructed in practice, using an object-oriented approach we will develop a class containing appropriate data members and a method named swap() that can exchange the values of two double-precision class variables.

Step 1: Analyze the Problem The swapping of values between two variables always requires the use of a temporary variable. The most common procedure is the following three-step exchange algorithm:

Step 1. Store the first variable's value in a temporary location (see Figure 11.4a)
Step 2. Store the second variable's value in the first variable (see Figure 11.4b)
Step 3. Store the temporary value in the second variable (see Figure 11.4c)

FIGURE 11.4a   Save the First Value

b

FIGURE 11.4b   Replace the First Value with the Second Value

c

FIGURE 11.4c   Change the Second Value

The reason for step 1, which uses the temporary variable to hold the first variable's value, is immediately obvious once you consider what happens if this variable were not used. For example, if the value of the second variable were initially moved into the first variable (step 2) before temporarily saving the first value (step 1), the first value would be lost.

Step 2: Develop a Solution Because any change to a method's parameters has no effect on the calling method, the desired exchange cannot be constructed by passing two values into a method and having the method perform the exchange. Similarly, because the values of two variables are affected, a swapping procedure cannot be provided by any method that returns a single value.

Although it is possible to construct a static method that accepts two references and exchanges their values, which would be reflected on the values in the calling method, this is a cumbersome process. To perform the exchange this way requires an initial translation of the double type to an object type, such as a StringBuffer, and then a retranslation into a double type after the swap has occurred.[1]

A class-based approach is the correct strategy to take when programming a swapping procedure in Java precisely because of the language's object orientation. The key to such an approach is to create a user-defined class that supports appropriate data members and methods that can be used to swap values in these data members. For our immediate application, this translates into creating a class that supports objects having two class data members, which we will refer to as x and y. These will be our class variables. Our class methods will consist of a constructor that permits us to initialize the two values of each object, accessor methods to alter and retrieve individual x and y values, and a swap() method that will interchange x and y values. This approach works precisely because class methods are permitted to alter the value of any number of designated class variables.

Step 3: Code the Solution The following class, xyvalues, provides the required two data members, x and y, and class methods to initialize, alter, display, and swap values for the data members.

---

[1]An example of a method that changes the value of a single StringBuffer argument was presented in Section 9.3.

```
public class XYValues
{

    private double x;    // first value is stored in this variable
    private double y;    // second value is stored in this variable

    public XYValues(double xVal, double yVal)    // constructor
    {
      x = xVal;
      y = yVal;
    }


      // methods to set and retrieve individual values
    public void setX(double xVal) {x = xVal;}
    public void setY(double yVal) {y = yVal;}
    public double getX() {return x;}
    public double getY() {return y;}

    public void swap()
    {
      double temp;

      temp = x;    // Step 1. Store the first variable's value in a temporary location
      x = y;       // Step 2. Store the second variable's value in the first variable
      y = temp;    // Step 3. Store the temporary value in the second variable
    }
}
```

Except for the swap() method, the other member methods are all straightforward constructor and accessor methods. In reviewing swap(), notice that its three assignment statements identically mirror the three steps previously listed for the exchange algorithm and illustrated in Figure 11.4.

Step 4: Test and Correct the Solution Program 11.7 uses the TestSwap class to test the XYValues class' methods. The following output was obtained using Program 11.7:

```
Before the call to swap():
  The value stored in firstnum is: 20.5
  The value stored in secnum is: 6.25

After the call to swap():
  The value stored in firstnum is: 6.25
  The value stored in secnum is: 20.5
```

As illustrated in this output, the values stored in main()'s variables have been modified from within swap(), which was made possible by the use of an object of type XYValues.

PROGRAM 11.7

```java
public class TestSwap
{
  public static void main(String[] args)
  {
    double firstnum = 20.5, secnum = 6.25;
    XYValues xyPair;

    System.out.println("Before the call to swap():");
    System.out.println("  The value stored in firstnum is: " + firstnum);
    System.out.println("  The value stored in secnum is: "  + secnum);

    xyPair = new XYValues(firstnum, secnum);
    xyPair.swap();  // apply the swap() method to the object

    firstnum = xyPair.getX();
    secnum = xyPair.getY();

    System.out.println("\nAfter the call to swap():");
    System.out.println("  The value stored in firstnum is: " + firstnum);
    System.out.println("  The value stored in secnum is: " + secnum);
  }
}
```

EXERCISES 11.3

1. Enter Program 11.6 on your computer and execute it.

2. In place of the main() method in Program 11.6, a student proposed the following:

```java
public static int main(String[] args)
{
  Pump a = new Pump(300, 1.00);   // declare 1 object of type Pump
  Customer b = new Customer();     // declare 1 object of type Customer
  int totalTime = 0;
  int idleTime;
  int amtRequest;
  int SimMinutes;  // simulation time in minutes

  SimMinutes = (int) (SIMTIME * MINUTES);
  System.out.println("\nStarting a new simulation - simulation time is "
                     + SimMinutes + " minutes.");
  a.values();

  while (true)  // always true
  {
    idleTime = b.arrive();
    totalTime += idleTime;
```

```
      if (totalTime > (SIMTIME * MINUTES))
      {
        System.out.println("\nThe idle time is " + idleTime + " minutes.,"
              + "\nAs the total time now exceeds the simulation time, "
              + "this simulation run is over.");
        break;
      }
      else
      {
        System.out.println("\nThe idle time is " + idleTime + " minutes"
                          + " and we are " + totalTime
                          + " minutes into the simulation.");
        amtRequest = b.gallons();
        a.request((double)(amtRequest));
      }
    }
  }
}
```

Determine if this `main()` method produces a valid simulation. If it does not, discuss why not. If it does, discuss which version you prefer and why.

3. Using the `Elevator` class defined in Section 10.4 and defining a new class named `Person`, construct a simulation whereby a `Person` randomly arrives at any time from 1 to 10 minutes on any floor and calls the elevator. If the elevator is not on the floor that the person is on, it must move to that floor. Once inside the elevator, the person can select any floor except the current one. Run the simulation for three randomly arriving people and have the simulation display the movement of the elevator.

4. Compile and execute Program 11.7. Make sure to also compile the `XYValues` class code.

5. Rewrite Program 11.7 to include a static swap method named `swapOne()` that accepts an `XYValue` object as a parameter. The `swapOne()` method should then exchange the two values contained within this parameter. The method header should be `public static void swapOne(XYValue xypair)`.

6. Rewrite Program 11.7 to include a static swap method named `swapTwo()` that accepts two variables and returns an `XYValue` object whose x and y values have been swapped. The method header should be `public static XYValue swapTwo(int x, int y)`.

11.4 CLASS INHERITANCE

The ability to create new classes from existing ones is the underlying motivation and power behind class and object-oriented programming techniques. Doing so facilitates reusing existing code in new ways without the need for retesting and validation. It also permits the designers of a class to make the class available to others for additions and extensions without relinquishing control over the basic class' features.

Constructing one class from another is accomplished using a capability called inheritance. Related to this capability is an equally important feature named polymorphism. Polymorphism provides the ability to redefine how methods of related classes operate based on the object being referenced. In fact, for a programming language to be classified as an object-oriented language, it must provide the features of classes, inheritance, and polymorphism. In this section, we describe the inheritance and polymorphism features provided in Java.

Inheritance

Inheritance is the capability of deriving one class from another class. The initial class that forms the basis for the derived class is referred to as either the **base, parent,** or **superclass.** The derived class is referred to as either the **derived, child,** or **subclass.**

A derived class is a completely new class that incorporates all of the variables and methods of its base class. It can, and usually does, however, add its own new data and method members and can override any base class method. As an example of inheritance, consider three geometric shapes consisting of a circle, cylinder, and sphere. For these shapes, we can make the circle a base type for the other two shapes (Figure 11.5). Reformulating these shapes as class types, we would make the circle the base class and derive the cylinder and sphere classes from it.

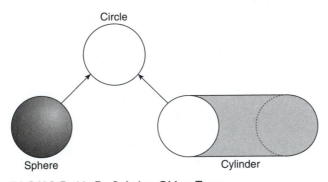

Circle

Sphere   Cylinder

FIGURE 11.5 Relating Object Types

The relationships illustrated in Figure 11.5 are examples of simple inheritance. In **simple inheritance,** each derived type has only one immediate base type. The complement to simple inheritance is multiple inheritance. In **multiple inheritance,** a derived type has two or more base types. Figure 11.6 presents an example of multiple inheritance, which is not supported in Java.

The class derivations in both Figures 11.5 and 11.6 are formally referred to as **class hierarchies** because they illustrate the hierarchy, or order, in which one class is derived from another. Let's now see how to derive one class from another.

FIGURE 11.6 An Example of Multiple Inheritance

OBJECT-BASED VERSUS OBJECT-ORIENTED LANGUAGES

An object-based language is one in which data and operations can be incorporated together in a class, such that data values can be isolated and accessed through the specified methods. The ability to combine the data members with operations into a single unit is referred to as *encapsulation*. For a language to be classified as object-oriented, it must not only provide encapsulation but also inheritance and polymorphism.

Inheritance is the capability of deriving one class from another. A derived class is a completely new class that incorporates all of the variables and methods of the original class plus any new variables and methods unique to itself. The class used as the basis for the derived type is referred to as the *parent*, *superclass*, or *base* type, and the derived data type is referred to as the *derived*, *subclass*, or *child* type.

Polymorphism permits the same method name to invoke one set of operations on objects created from the parent class and a different set of operations in objects created from the derived class.

A derived class has the same form as any other class in that it consists of both variable and method members. The only difference is in the header line for the class. For a derived class, this line is extended to include a base class name and has the syntax:

```
public class  derivedClassName extends baseClassName
```

For example, if `Circle` is the name of an existing class, a new class named `Cylinder` can be derived as follows:

```
public class Cylinder extends Circle
{
   // add any additional variable declarations and
   // method definitions in here
}
```

Except for the keyword `extends` and the base class name, there is nothing inherently new or complicated about the construction of the `Cylinder` class. Before providing a description of the `Circle` class and adding data and method members to the derived `Cylinder` class, we need to reexamine visibility specifications and how they relate to derived classes.

Visibility Specifications

Until now, we have only used `private` and `public` visibility specifications within a class. Giving all class variables `private` visibility ensures that they can only be accessed by a class' methods. This restricted access prevents access by any nonclass methods, which also precludes access by any derived class' methods. This is a sensible restriction because if it did not exist, anyone could "jump around" the `private` designation simply by deriving a class.

To retain a restricted type of access across derived classes, Java provides a third visibility specification: `protected`. Protected visibility behaves identically to `private` visibility within a class, but it permits this restriction to be inherited by any derived class. Thus, a `protected` visibility is essentially a `private` visibility that can be extended into a derived class.

An Example

To illustrate the process of deriving one class from another, we will derive a `Cylinder` class from a base `Circle` class. The definition of the `Circle` class is:

```
public class Circle
{
  // class variable declaration section
  public final static double PI = 2.0 * Math.asin(1.0);
  protected double radius;

  // class method definition section
  public Circle(double r)   // constructor
  {
    radius = r;
  }

   public double calcval()    // this calculates an area
  {
    return(PI * radius * radius);
  }
}
```

Except for the substitution of the visibility specifier `protected` in place of the usual `private` specification for the class' variables, this is a standard class definition. Notice also the declaration of the constant `PI`, which is used later in the `calcval()` method. This is defined as:

```
public final static double PI = 2.0 * Math.asin(1.0);
```

This is a "trick" that forces the computer to return the value of `PI` accurate to as many decimal places as allowed by your computer. This value is obtained by taking the arcsin of 1.0, which is $\pi/2$, and multiplying the result by 2. The keyword `static` ensures that this value is calculated and stored only once per class, and the keyword `final` ensures that the value cannot be changed by any subsequent method. Finally, the keyword `public` makes this value accessible by any and all methods within or external to the class.

Having defined our base class, we can now extend it by a derived class. The definition of the derived class is:

```
public class Cylinder extends Circle  // Cylinder is derived from Circle
{

  // class variable declaration section
```

```
    protected double length;   // add an additional data member


    // class method definition section
    public Cylinder(double r, double l)
    {
       super(r);
       length = l;
    }


    public double calcval()    // this calculates a volume
    {
       return (length * super.calcval()); // note the base method call
    }
}
```

This definition encompasses several important concepts relating to derived classes. First, as a derived class, `Cylinder` contains all of the variable and method members of its base class, `Circle`, plus any additional members that it may add. In this particular case, the `Cylinder` class consists of a `radius` data member, inherited from the `Circle` class, plus an additional `length` member. Thus, each `Cylinder` object contains *two* data variables, as illustrated in Figure 11.7. As a `public` class, `Cylinder` must be stored in its own source file named `Cylinder.java`.

FIGURE 11.7 Relationship Between `Circle` and `Cylinder` Data Members

In addition to having two data members, the `Cylinder` class also inherits both `Circle`'s symbolic constant PI and its method members. This is illustrated in the `Cylinder` constructor, which uses the keyword `super`. When this keyword is used by itself and with zero or more arguments, it refers to a base class' constructor having the matching argument list. Notice that the `Cylinder`'s `calcval()` method also makes a call to one of its base class' methods using the keyword `super`. Here the expression `super.calcval()` refers to the base class version of the `calcval()` method.

In both classes, the same method name, `calcval()`, has been specifically used to illustrate the overriding of a base method by a derived method. When a `Cylinder` object calls `calcval()`, it is a request to use the `Cylinder` version of the method, whereas a `Circle` object call to `calcval()` is a request to use the `Circle` version. In this case, the `Cylinder` class can still access the `Circle` class' version of `calcval()` using the keyword `super`. Program 11.8 uses the `Cylinder` class within the context of a complete program. Assuming that the `Circle` class source file exists in the same directory as the `Cylinder` class source file and that both classes have been compiled, the output produced by Program 11.8 is:[2]

[2]If the `Circle` class source file does not exist in the same directory, an `import` statement, as described in Appendix F, must be included in the `Cylinder` source code.

```
The area of circleOne is 3.141592653589793
The area of circleTwo is 12.566370614359172
The volume of cylinderOne is 113.09733552923255
```

This output is straightforward and is produced by the first three println() calls in the program. As the output shows, a call to calcval() using a Circle object activates the Circle version of this method, while a call to calcval() using a Cylinder object activates the Cylinder version.

PROGRAM 11.8

```java
public class Cylinder extends Circle  // Cylinder is derived from Circle
{

  // class variable declaration section
  protected double length;  // add an additional data member

  // class method definition section
  public Cylinder(double r, double l)
  {
    super(r);
    length = l;
  }

  public double calcval()    // this calculates a volume
  {
    return (length * super.calcval()); // note the base method call
  }

  public static void main(String[] args)
  {
    Circle circleOne = new Circle(1);  // create two Circle objects
    Circle circleTwo = new Circle(2);
    Cylinder cylinderOne = new Cylinder(3,4);       // create one Cylinder object

    System.out.println("The area of circleOne is " + circleOne.calcval());
    System.out.println("The area of circletwo is " + circleTwo.calcval());
    System.out.println("The volume of cylinderOne is " + cylinderOne.calcval());
  }
}
```

Polymorphism

The overriding of a base member method using an overloaded derived member method, as illustrated by the calcval() method in Program 11.8, is an example of polymorphism. **Polymorphism** permits the same method name to invoke one response in objects of a base class and another response in objects of a derived class. The determination of which overloaded method is actually called is made at run time, when the call statement is encountered, and is based on the object making the call. This type of selection is referred to as **run-time binding, late binding,** and **dynamic binding** (the terms are synonymous). By default, Java uses late binding in all method calls. This type of binding means that the object being operated on ultimately determines the appropriate method to be called and is required for a language to implement true polymorphic behavior.

In contrast to late binding is **early binding,** in which the method that will actually be called is set at compile time. This type of binding, which is also referred to as both **static** and **compile-time binding,** is the default binding technique in languages that do not support true polymorphic behavior. Such early binding can be forced in Java by making a method `final`.

Inheritance Diagrams

An inheritance diagram illustrates the relationship between a base class and one or more derived classes. As shown in Figure 11.8, these diagrams can be drawn in a number of ways, but *a base class is always drawn at the top of the diagram and a derived class is drawn under its parent class*. In this sense, the figure can be slightly misleading because the base class, upon which all other classes are built, is placed at the top of the figure rather than at its bottom, or base.

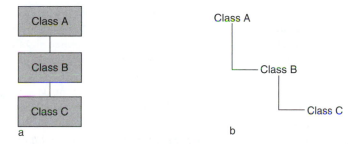

FIGURE 11.8   Sample Inheritance Diagrams

Figures 11.8a and 11.8b illustrate the relationship between three classes, which are named A, B, and C. In both cases, class A is the parent class to class B, which in turn is the parent class to class C. In Figure 11.8a, the relationship is indicated by level, with derived classes placed underneath base classes. In Figure 11.8b, a parent/child relationship is implied by location and indentation, with a child class always placed below and indented from its parent class.

As a practical example of an inheritance diagram, Figure 11.9 illustrates the relationship of the `DecimalFormat` Java class to the `java.lang.Object` class. As indicated in this

FIGURE 11.9   The `DecimalFormat` Inheritance Hierarchy

figure, this class' base class is the NumberFormat class. The figure also shows that the ChoiceFormat class is derived from this same base class.

EXERCISES 11.4

1. Define the following terms:
   a. inheritance
   b. base class
   c. derived class
   d. simple inheritance
   e. multiple inheritance
   f. class hierarchy
   g. polymorphism
   h. late binding
   i. dynamic binding
   j. early binding

2. What three features must a programming language provide for it to be classified as an object-oriented language?

3. a. Describe the two methods Java provides for implementing polymorphism.
   b. Which of the two methods listed in Exercise 3a qualifies a language to be a true object-oriented language and why is this the case?

4. Describe the difference between a private and a protected class member.

5. a. Modify Program 11.8 to include a derived class named Sphere from the base Circle class. The only additional class members of Sphere should be a constructor and a calcval() method that returns the volume of the sphere. (*Note: volume = 4/3 π radius³*)
   b. Include the class constructed for Exercise 5a in a working Java program. Have your program call all of the member methods in the Sphere class.

6. a. Create a base class named Point that consists of an x and y coordinate. From this class, derive a class named Circle having an additional data member named radius. For this derived class, the x and y data members represent the center coordinates of a circle. The method members of the first class should consist of a constructor, an area method named area that returns zero, and a distance() method that returns the distance between two points, where

   $$distance = \sqrt{(x2 - x1)^2 + (y2 - y1)^2}$$

   In addition, the derived class should have a constructor and an override method named area that returns the area of a circle.
   b. Include the classes constructed for Exercise 6a in a working Java program. Have your program call all of the member methods in each class. In addition, call the base class distance() method with two Circle objects and explain the result returned by the method.

7. a. Using the classes constructed for Exercise 6a, derive a class named Cylinder from the derived Circle class. The Cylinder class should have a constructor and a member method named area() that determines the surface area of the Cylinder. For this method, use the algorithm *surface area = 2πr (l + r)*, where *r* is the radius of the cylinder and *l* is the length.
   b. Include the classes constructed for Exercise 7a in a working Java program. Have your program call all of the member methods in the Cylinder class.

     c. What do you think might be the result if the base class `distance()` method was called using two `Cylinder` objects?

8. a. Create a base class named `Rectangle` that contains `length` and `width` data members. From this class, derive a class named `Box` having an additional data member named `depth`. The method members of the base `Rectangle` class should consist of a constructor and an `area()` method. The derived `Box` class should have a constructor and an override method named `area()` that returns the surface area of the box and a `volume()` method.

     b. Include the classes constructed for Exercise 8a in a working Java program. Have your program call all of the member methods in each class and explain the result when the `area()` method is called using two `Box` objects.

11.5 REFERENCE VARIABLES AS CLASS MEMBERS[3]

As you saw in Section 11.2, a class can contain any Java data type. Thus, the inclusion of a reference variable in a class should not seem surprising, and in many situations, it can be extremely useful. In some cases, however, using reference data members can result in seemingly strange behavior for the unwary.

For example, assume that we need to store a list of book titles, with each stored as a string. Such an arrangement appears in Figure 11.10, which shows two objects, `book1` and `book2`, each of which consists of a single reference data member. As depicted, object `book1`'s single data member references the title `Windows Primer`, and object `book2`'s data member references `A Brief History of Western Civilization`.

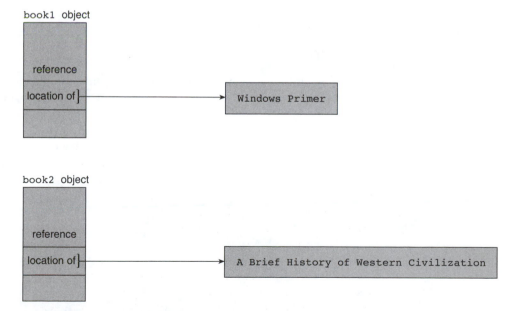

FIGURE 11.10   Two Objects Containing Reference Data Members

---

[3]This topic can be omitted on first reading with no loss of subject continuity.

A declaration for a class data member that stores a title, as illustrated in Figure 11.10, could be:

```
private String title;    // a reference to a book title
```

The definition of the constructor method, Book(), and the display method, showTitle(), are defined in the method definition section as:

```
// class method definition section
public Book(String booktitle)  // constructor
{
  title = booktitle;
}


public void showTitle()
{
  System.out.println("The title is " + title);
}
```

The body of the Book() constructor contains a single statement that initializes an object's title data member to the string provided when a Book object is instantiated. The showTitle() method is an accessor method that displays the string value stored in the title data member.

Program 11.9 illustrates this class within the context of a complete program. Notice that it is in the main() method that the book1 and book2 objects are instantiated.

The output displayed by Program 11.9 is:

```
The title is Windows Primer
The title is A Brief History of Western Civilization
```

Figure 11.11a illustrates the arrangement of references and allocated memory produced by Program 11.9 just before it completes execution. Now consider Program 11.10, which is essentially the same as Program 11.9 with one major modification: We have inserted the assignment statement book2 = book1; into the main() method. As we know from Section 11.1, this assignment produces a memberwise copy that copies the value in

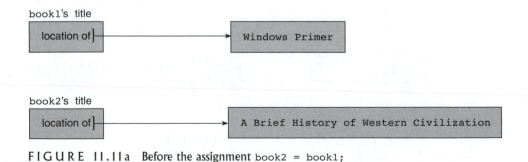

book1's title

location of ⊢ ——————→ Windows Primer

book2's title

location of ⊢ ——————→ A Brief History of Western Civilization

FIGURE 11.11a   Before the assignment book2 = book1;

PROGRAM 11.9

```java
public class Book
{
  // class variable declaration section
  private String title;


  // class method definition section
  public Book(String booktitle)  // constructor
  {
    title = booktitle;
  }

  public void showTitle()
  {
    System.out.println("The title is " + title);
  }

  public static void main(String[] args)
  {
    Book book1 = new Book("Windows Primer");
    Book book2 = new Book("A Brief History of Western Civilization");

    book1.showTitle();
    book2.showTitle();
  }
}
```

the `book1` reference variable into the `book2` reference variable. The consequence of this shallow copy is that both reference variables now reference the `Book` object that contains the string `Windows Primer`, and the reference to the title `A Brief History of Western Civilization` has been lost.[4] This situation is illustrated in Figure 11.11b.

FIGURE 11.11b   The Effect Produced by Assignment

---

[4]See Sections 8.2 and 11.1 for a review of shallow copies.

PROGRAM 11.10

```java
public class Book
{
  // class variable declaration section
  private String title;

  // class method definition section
  public Book(String booktitle)  // constructor
  {
    title = booktitle;
  }

  public void showTitle()
  {
    System.out.println("The title is " + title);
  }

  public static void main(String[] args)
  {
    Book book1 = new Book("Windows Primer");
    Book book2 = new Book("A Brief History of Western Civilization");

    book1.showTitle();
    book2.showTitle();

    book2 = book1;
    System.out.println("\nAfter assignment");
    book1.showTitle();
    book2.showTitle();
  }
}
```

The output produced by Program 11.10 is:

```
The title is Windows Primer
The title is A Brief History of Western Civilization

After assignment
The title is Windows Primer
The title is Windows Primer
```

This output is produced because both the book1.title and book2.title reference variables refer to the same string object (Figure 11.11b). Because the memberwise assignment illustrated in this figure results in the loss of the location of A Brief History of Western Civilization, the memory allocated to this string will ultimately be released by Java's automatic garbage collection system.

book1's title

book2's title

FIGURE 11.11c   The Desired Effect

Unlike the effect produced by Program 11.10, what is usually desired is that the book titles themselves be copied, as shown in Figure 11.11c, and that their references be left alone. Because String objects cannot be copied, we have two solutions to the problem. The easiest and preferred solution is to use StringBuffer class objects rather than String objects because the StringBuffer class does permit copying and overwriting of existing string values. The second method uses a work-around that essentially performs a deep copy. This is accomplished by first creating a new String object and then adjusting references so that the book2.title reference variable correctly points to the newly created string (as in Figure 11.11c) rather than pointing to the book1 string (as in Figure 11.11b). To achieve this desired assignment, we must explicitly write our own assignment method. A suitable definition for this method is:

```
public void setEqual(final Book oldbook)
{
  Book temp = new Book(oldbook.title);  // create a new Book object
  title = temp.title;
}
```

This definition first creates a new Book object having the same value as the object that is passed into it. The word final in the parameter list ensures that the method itself cannot alter the passed object. The method first instantiates a new Book object and then assigns the reference to this newly instantiated object to the reference of the object used in making the call. Thus, for example, a call such as book2.setEqual(book1) creates the arrangement in Figure 11.12. Here, as in Figure 11.12a, a new object is first created that contains the string Windows Primer. This object and its reference are created by the statement temp Book = new Book(book1.title). The statement title = temp.title then produces the situation in Figure 11.12b. Here the book2.title reference variable now correctly points to its own distinct string object. Program 11.11 includes this setEqual() method within the Book class and uses this class within the context of a complete program. The output produced by Program 11.11 is:

```
The title is Windows Primer
The title is A Brief History of Western Civilization

After assignment
The title is Windows Primer
The title is Windows Primer
```

book1

FIGURE 11.12a   Create a New Object and Reference

Although this output is the same as that produced by Program 11.10, it is now produced because each reference variable, book1.title and book2.title, points to its own distinct string object.

book1

FIGURE 11.12b   Adjust book2's Reference Value

PROGRAM 11.11

```
public class Book
{
  // class variable declaration section
  private String title;

   // class method definition section
  public Book(String booktitle)  // constructor
  {
    title = booktitle;
  }


  public void setEqual(final Book oldbook)
```

(Continued on next page)

(Continued from previous page)

```java
{
   Book temp = new Book(oldbook.title);   // create a new Book object
   title = temp.title;
}


public void showTitle()
{
   System.out.println("The title is " + title);
}


public static void main(String[] args)
{
   Book book1 = new Book("Windows Primer");
   Book book2 = new Book("A Brief History of Western Civilization");

   book1.showTitle();
   book2.showTitle();

   book2.setEqual(book1);
   System.out.println("\nAfter assignment");
   book1.showTitle();
   book2.showTitle();
}
}
```

EXERCISES 11.5

1. Compile and execute Program 11.9 and run the program to verify its operation.
2. **a.** Compile and execute Program 11.10 on your computer.
   b. Compile and execute Program 11.11 on your computer.
   c. Although Program 11.10 and Program 11.11 produce the same result, identify the difference between them.
3. **a.** Construct a class named Car that contains the following four data members: a double-precision variable named engineSize, a character variable named bodyStyle, an integer variable named colorCode, and a string named vinNum for a vehicle identification code. The method members should include a constructor and a display method that prints the engine size, body style, color code, and vehicle identification code.
   b. Include the class written for Exercise 3a in a working Java program that creates two Car objects and displays the object's values.
4. Modify the program written for Exercise 3 to include a method that assigns the values of one Car object to a second Car object. Your method should perform the assignment so that each reference variable refers to a distinct object in memory and not the same string value.
5. Using Program 11.9 as a start, write a program that creates five Book objects. The program should allow the user to enter the five book titles interactively and then display the entered titles.

6. Modify the program written in Exercise 5 so that it sorts the entered book titles in alphabetical order before it displays them. (*Tip:* You will have to define a sort routine for the titles.)

11.6 COMMON PROGRAMMING ERRORS

The more common programming errors associated with the class capabilities presented in this chapter are:

1. Forgetting to make class variables protected if you intend to use the class as a base class.
2. Using a user-defined assignment operator in a multiple assignment expression when the operator has not been defined to return an object.
3. Performing a memberwise copy of instance variables with a variable that is a reference when a deep copy of the item being referenced is desired. A memberwise copy produces a copy of the value in the reference and not a copy of the object being referenced.

11.7 CHAPTER SUMMARY

1. Each class has an associated *class scope*, which is defined by the brace pair, {}, that encloses the class. A class variable can be used anywhere within the class scope simply by using the variable's name.
2. A variable's scope and a method's scope are distinct from their visibility. *Visibility* determines whether a class member can be accessed from outside its class and is set using one or none of the following visibility modifiers: public, private, or protected. Data and method members declared as private can only be used by objects declared for the class. Data and member methods declared as public can be accessed external to the class. Data and member methods declared as protected are private to their class and can be extended into derived classes. All class variables and methods are accessible everywhere within their class regardless of their visibility modifiers.
3. In addition to the visibility of class members, a class itself has a visibility. When the keyword class is preceded by the keyword public, the class can be accessed by other classes. If the class is preceded by the keyword private, it can only be accessed by other classes within the same source file that it is located. Finally, if the class has no visibility modifier, it has *package visibility*.
4. Each created object receives its own set of data members, except those declared as static. A static data member is shared by all class objects and provides a means of communication between objects. A static data member must be declared as such within the class' data declaration section.
5. A static method member applies to the class as a whole rather than to individual objects. Thus, a static method member can access only static data members and other static method members.
6. For each class, only one copy of each member method is created, and each object uses the same method. The location of the object's data members is provided to the member method by passing a hidden reference argument named this. The this reference may be used explicitly by a member method to access a data member.
7. *Inheritance* is the capability of deriving one class from another class. The initial class used as the basis for the derived class is referred to as either the *base, parent,* or *superclass*. The derived class is referred to as either the *derived, child,* or *subclass*.
8. A *class hierarchy* is a description of the order in which one class is derived from another.

P A R T   4

Creating

Swing-Based

GUIs

C H A P T E R 1 2

Visual
Programming
Basics

In this chapter, we describe the fundamentals of event-based programming required in using a graphical user interface (GUI). This is followed by a very simple GUI using the Java 2.0-provided swing package of classes. Initially, we construct a simple window with no internal components from a single GUI class. Although a full understanding of this class requires the information on class construction provided in Part Two, this class can still be used as a basic model without this understanding. We then expand this GUI class to include a window-closing event, which forms the model structure for all subsequent component event handlers. Finally, we provide the GUI with an internal Command button component and an associated event handler that responds to the button being clicked.

12.1 EVENT-BASED PROGRAMMING

In all of the programs that we have examined so far, the sequence of events—that is, what happens when—is determined solely by the program. When such a program is executed, the user may be requested to enter input or select between choices, but *when* the requests are made is predetermined by the program's code. This does not mean that a graphical user interface (GUI) cannot be provided, but at best, the GUI is a dialog intended either to present information or to request specific input items as dictated by program code. When and where the dialog appears are entirely determined by the program.

A different programming model is an event-based one. **Event-based programs** provide a fully functioning GUI from which the user has a number of graphical components from which to choose. Although the program no longer controls which graphical component will be selected by the user, it is responsible for correctly reacting to whatever component is selected, if any, and in any order that selections are made.

The selection and activation of a specific graphical component by the user, such as clicking an on-screen button, are said to initiate an **event**. It is the responsibility of the program to correctly assess which specific event has occurred and then provide appropriate code to perform an action based on the identified event.

As an example of how an event-based program would be constructed in practice, consider the GUI shown in Figure 12.1. Here the user can click any of the internal buttons in any sequence. Additionally, the user can click any of the buttons on the top line

FIGURE 12.1   A Sample GUI

of the window itself. For the moment, let us only concern ourselves with the three internal buttons labeled Message, Clear, and Exit. The selection of any one of these buttons constitutes an event. As a practical matter, such an event can be triggered in one of the following three ways:

- Placing the mouse pointer over a button and clicking the left mouse button (clicking means pushing and releasing the left mouse button)

- Using the Tab key until the desired button is highlighted with a dotted line and then pushing the Enter key. The component that is highlighted with the dotted line is said "to have the focus" (as shown in Figure 12.1, the Message button has the focus)
- Pressing an accelerator key. An *accelerator key*, which is also referred to both as a *shortcut key* and *mnemonic key*, is any action that activates a GUI component through the keyboard

Once an event is triggered by a user, which in this case is done by selecting and activating one of the three button components in the window shown in Figure 12.1, program instructions take over. As illustrated in Figure 12.2, an event, such as clicking the mouse on a button, sets in motion a sequence of occurrences. If an event-handling object has been created and properly connected to an activating component, which is referred to as registering the event object, the event produces a specific result; otherwise, the event is ignored. This is, of course, the essence of a graphical user interface—the selection of which event object is executed depends on what event occurred, which ultimately depends on what the user does. The code from which the event-handling object is created, however, must still be written by the programmer. For the program in Figure 12.1, there are three events for which we will provide event code. If the user clicks the M̲essage button, the message `Hello There World!` will be displayed in the text field. Clicking the C̲lear button will result in the text field being cleared, and clicking the E̲xit button will result in termination of the program in the same manner as clicking the window's Close button.

Notice that the sequence of events—that is, which action is to be taken—is controlled by the user. The user can click any one of three buttons, in any order, or even run a different Windows program while the Java program that displays the GUI is executing. This user determination of which event will take place next, as the program is running, is quite a different approach than that used in Parts One and Two of this text. In the programs presented in these earlier parts, the decisions as to which actions are taken and in what order are determined by the program.

An event-based graphical user interface such as that illustrated in Figure 12.1 requires that the programmer provide the code both to create the GUI and then appropriately process the events triggered by activating the displayed GUI components.

The aspect of Java that makes programming a GUI so easy is that Java provides an extensive set of objects that can be placed on a GUI in a very simple manner. Prior to Version 2.0, these objects, which are formally referred to as **components** in Java and informally as **controls,** were available from a package called `java.awt`, where awt stands for

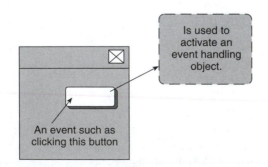

FIGURE 12.2 An Event "Triggers" the Initiation of an Event Object

TABLE 12.1 Generic GUI Objects

Component Type	Description
Top-Level Container	A basic window structure that includes such things as borders and resizing capabilities and can hold both intermediate containers and atomic components. Each GUI must have one of these components that ties the GUI into the operating system.
Intermediate Container	A graphical object displayed in a top-level container that itself can hold other intermediate containers and atomic components. Used to simplify placement and exact positioning of atomic components.
Atomic Components	Graphical objects used to accept and/or display individual items of information. Must be placed into a container using an `add()` method.

Abstract Window Toolkit. With Version 2.0, a package of components that was much simpler to use was available in the `javax.swing` package. Because the `swing` package is based on the older AWT package, the basic components in both packages are almost identical, but the names of the components were changed for the `swing` package. Table 12.1 lists the three generic types of objects used in creating a GUI, and Table 12.2 lists specific component types and their respective names under both AWT and swing. As can be seen in Table 12.2, the only difference between AWT and swing object names is that the equivalent Swing name is the same AWT component name prefixed by the letter J.

In this text, we will only create GUIs using the `swing` package of classes. Except for the Menu component, each of the atomic components in Table 12.2 is presented in detail and used in GUIs that are based on a top-level JFrame container. Using the `swing` package of classes and components means that we will not have to be concerned with writing the code for either producing the graphical objects listed in Tables 12.1 and 12.2 or for recognizing when certain events, such as "mouse was clicked," actually occur. Once the desired components are selected and coded into the program, Java takes care of creating the component and recognizing appropriate component events, such as clicking a button. What we will have to be concerned about is writing and including code to correctly processes events that can be triggered by a user's interaction with the GUI's components when a program is run.

The Event-Based Model

To gain a better understanding of how event-based programs are constructed, it is worthwhile comparing their structure to the procedure-driven programs that we have used until now. As you will see, the structures of these two types of programs are quite different.

A procedure-driven program is a carry-over from earlier times when the predominant operating system was DOS (disk operating system). DOS was a single-tasking operating system, where only a single program would execute at one time. Once DOS gave control to a program, the program took control of the computer. This situation is illustrated in Figure 12.3. Notice in this figure that DOS effectively relinquishes control over the computer's operation to the executing program. Specifically, if a Java program was being executed, control would be transferred to the start of the Java program, which is designated by the keyword `main`. Any operating system resources that the Java program needs, such as accessing data from a file, are initiated from within the Java program itself. Only after the Java program has finished executing would control pass from the program back to the operating system.

TABLE 12.2   AWT and Swing Components

Component Type	AWT Name	Swing Name
Top-Level Container	Frame	JFrame
Top-Level Container	Applet	JApplet
Top-Level Container	Dialog	JDialog
Top-Level Container	Window	JWindow
Intermediate Container	Panel	JPanel
Intermediate Container	InternalFrame	JInternalFrame
Intermediate Container	LayeredPane	JLayeredPane
Intermediate Container	RootPane	JRootPane
Atomic	Button	JButton
Atomic	Menu	JMenu
Atomic	Label	JLabel
Atomic	CheckBox	JCheckBox
Atomic	RadioButton	JRadioButton
Atomic	TextField	JTextField
Atomic	TextArea	JTextArea

The situation is quite different under a multitasking operating system such as Windows or UNIX. Since multiple programs can be executing, it is essential that the operating system retain primary control, at all times, in the management of the computer's resources. This control prevents any one program from effectively taking control and inhibiting other programs from running. It also is necessary to ensure that information destined for one application does not become lost or inadvertently accepted by another application. To see why, consider the following case.

Assume that two different programs are executing and have open windows on the screen. In this situation, a user could click controls in either application. If one of the applications were in total control of the computer, it would be responsible for determining on what object and in which program the user clicked the mouse. Clearly, the programmer who developed one of the executing programs would not be concerned or even be expected to know how to intercept and correctly route an event used by any of the other myriad of programs that the operating system was also executing. So if a mouse click in another program occurred, it would most likely be lost while any one of the other programs had control of the computer's resources.

The solution to this problem is to allow only the operating system, be it Windows, UNIX, or Linux, to have total control of the computer and never relinquish this control to any executing programs. Under this arrangement, most executing programs spend the

FIGURE 12.3   Program Control under DOS

majority of their time in a sleep type of mode. When the operating system, which is always running, detects an event such as a mouse click, it first determines what the event was and in which application window the event occurred. This type of operation is shown in Figure 12.4.

FIGURE 12.4 Program Control under a Multitasking Operating System

For the type of operation shown in Figure 12.4, it is the operating system's responsibility to first make a determination when the user does something as to what event actually occurred and in which application it took place. Once this is done, the operating system passes this event information, in the form of a specific message, to the appropriate application and only then permits the application to take action. The action, however, may be interrupted at any time if the operating system detects another event taking place.

The process in Figure 12.4 effectively standardizes the user interface provided by the operating system because the operating system determines how events are recognized and passed into an application. In this arrangement, an application only needs to know how to accept and then act on the information received from the operating system. Clearly, how the information is delivered depends on the operating system. Thus, every program being executed on a computer must have a standard interface to the specific operating system running the computer. You will now see how this interface is specifically handled in Java using the swing package of components and their associated methods.

Containment Hierarchy

Every GUI component created in Java has a placement level, with atomic components and containers logically placed within other appropriate containers. This hierarchy of component placement is referred to as a **containment hierarchy.** Each such hierarchy consists of one and only one top-level container and then any number of other intermediate containers and/or atomic components that are placed into it. The top-level container, which for a stand-alone Swing-based GUI is almost always a JFrame, forms the starting point for the hierarchy.[1] Because one of the primary functions of a top-level container is to interface with the operating system directly, earlier versions of Java referred to such containers as **heavyweight** components. This name derived from the fact that only top-level containers

---

[1]Although from its name you might think a JWindow would be used, this is actually a very restrictive container. It is rarely used in practice because it does not provide any controls or title bar and is always placed on top of all other windows.

TABLE 12.3   Layout Managers

Manager	Description	Use Type
FlowLayout	Components are added to the container from left to right and top to bottom, in a row-by-row manner, starting from the top left corner of the container.	Simple
GridLayout	All components are created equal in size and displayed in the requested number of rows and columns. Blank areas fill in unused columns.	Simple
BorderLayout	Up to five components can be placed in the container. The components are placed in positions denoted as north, south, west, east, and center. These positions correspond to the top, bottom, left side, right side, and center positions of the container.	Special Purpose
CardLayout	This layout permits implementation of an area that can contain different components at different times.	Special Purpose
BoxLayout	Components are placed into either a single row or column. Column components can be center, left-edge, or right-edge aligned.	Flexible
GridBagLayout	Components are placed in a spreadsheet type grid of cells, with components permitted to span across and down multiple cells.	Flexible

were effectively "weighed down" with the additional functionality required for interfacing with the operating system.

The next important level in a containment hierarchy is a **content pane.** This is an internal component provided by each top-level container into which all of the visible components displayed by a GUI must be placed. Optionally, a menu bar can also be added to a top-level container. When a menu bar is added to a GUI, it is positioned within the top-level container but is placed outside of the container's content pane. Figure 12.5 illustrates the most commonly used Swing-based containment hierarchy, which is the one that we will follow in constructing all of our Swing-based GUIs. As shown in the figure, the hierarchy starts with a JFrame. The JFrame automatically provides a root pane, which in turn contains the content pane. Because it is the content pane to which intermediate containers and atomic components are added, you generally will not need to be concerned with the root pane.[2] Notice in the figure that although all visible components must go through the JFrame's content pane, a menu bar is not attached to the content pane.

Each top-level and intermediate container has an associated default layout manager that defines how components are positioned and sized within the container's content pane. This default placement can always be changed by explicitly specifying another layout manager. Table 12.3 lists the six layout managers currently available and how they are typically categorized for ease of use. Table 12.4 lists the default layout manager associated with each top-level container type. Detailed use of layout managers is presented in the next chapter.

---

[2]The root pane and its internal components must explicitly be dealt with only in more advanced applications where, for example, mouse clicks must be intercepted or multiple components must be painted over.

TABLE 12.4   Top-Level Container Default Layout Managers

Container	Default Layout Manager
JFrame	BorderLayout
JDialog	BorderLayout
JPanel	BorderLayout
JWindow	FlowLayout

TABLE 12.5   Lightweight Atomic Components

Component	Description
JButton	A component that triggers an event when clicked.
JLabel	A displayed text or icon.
JTextField	A single line where text may be entered and displayed.
JTextArea	An area that can span multiple lines where text can be entered and displayed.
JPasswordField	Same as a JTextField, but entered characters are displayed as asterisks, *.
JCheckBox	A component that may be either checked or unchecked.
JRadioButton	A component consisting of one or more items, only one of which may be selected.

Finally, the lower levels of a containment hierarchy consist of intermediate containers and atomic components such as buttons, labels, and text areas. These intermediate containers and atomic components are frequently referred to as **lightweight** components. The implication of the term lightweight is that because these components are not directly anchored to the underlying operating system they do not need the heavyweight functionality provided by Java for interfacing with the operating system. Table 12.5 lists the lightweight atomic components that we will introduce and use in this text.

FIGURE 12.5   A Typical Swing-Based Containment Hierarchy

EXERCISES 12.1

1. What is the purpose of a GUI and what elements does a user see in a GUI?
2. What gets executed when an event occurs?
3. List the three ways that an event can be triggered by a user.
4. List the three component types that can create a GUI in Java.
5. What top-level container type is used, almost exclusively, to create stand-alone Java application GUIs?
6. What is a containment hierarchy and how it is used to create a GUI?
7. What is the internal component provided by each top-level container to which all visible GUI components must be added?
8. **a.** What is the purpose of a layout manager?
   b. What is the default layout manager for a JFrame container?

12.2 CREATING A SWING-BASED WINDOW

It is now time to construct our first functioning GUI window using the swing package of classes. Although there are numerous ways to create a GUI, all of the various techniques you will encounter are implemented within the context of the following two predominant approaches:

1. Construct the GUI as a separate class using Swing components. Then use a main() method to instantiate (i.e., create) an object of the class. When a specific GUI object is instantiated, the GUI will appear on the screen.
2. Construct a GUI object using Swing components from within a main() method without first creating a separate GUI class.

In general, the first approach is preferred because it adheres more closely to accepted object-oriented practice. Using this approach, all of the details of the GUI are encapsulated into a separate class, and then when a GUI is required, an object of the class is created. The second approach is sometimes used to introduce Swing components and to create extremely simple GUIs. This is how we will use both of these approaches in this text. Here our first example uses the second approach to introduce an extremely simple GUI using a Swing JFrame container. Consider Program 12.1.

PROGRAM 12.1

```java
import javax.Swing.*;
public class FirstGui
{
  public static void main(String[] args)
  {
    JFrame mainFrame; // declare a JFrame reference variable
    mainFrame = new JFrame("First GUI Window"); //instantiate a JFrame object

    mainFrame.setSize(300,150);
    mainFrame.show();
  }
}
```

The first statement in Program 12.1's `main()` method declares a variable named `mainFrame` to be of type `JFrame`. The next statement uses the `new` operator to create a JFrame object that will be referenced by the `mainFrame` variable. This statement also sets the title bar text for the JFrame, which in this case is the string `First GUI Window`. When this program is executed, the JFrame object becomes a window that is displayed on the screen with the designated title. Although we have used two statements to instantiate a JFrame object, the same effect can be achieved by the single statement

```
JFrame mainFrame = new JFrame("First GUI Window");
```

The next statement in `main()`

```
mainFrame.setSize(300,150);
```

uses a `setSize()` method to set the size of the frame in pixels.[3] The general syntax of the `setSize()` method is

```
objectReferenceName.setSize(width, height)
```

The *objectReferenceName* to the left of the required period identifies a specific object, and the name to the right of the period identifies the method. As you have seen previously, this is the standard object-oriented notation for applying a class method to a specific object.

The fourth line uses the `show()` method to make the JFrame object appear on the screen. An entirely equivalent method is `setVisible(true)`; you can therefore use these methods interchangeably. When Program 12.1 is compiled and executed, the JFrame creates the window in Figure 12.6. Because this window is controlled by the operating system, it can be manipulated using standard window techniques. Thus, we can click on the Maximize or Minimize buttons, move or resize the window, and close the window by

FIGURE 12.6   The Window Displayed by Program 12.1

clicking the Close button, X. Unfortunately, closing the window in Windows *does not* close the Java application. Thus, if you click the Close button, the underlying Java application, which in this case is Program 12.1, is still executing. To close the Java program, you must press the Ctrl and C keys at the same time. This is the "break" sequence recognized by most operating systems that causes the currently executing program to stop running.

---

[3]A pixel refers to a single position on a computer screen. For example, a screen area of 800 $\times$ 600 refers to a width of 800 pixels by a length of 600 pixels.

An event-handling method that will accept the close event from the operating system and correctly close the underlying Java program is presented in the next section. Before considering this event handler, however, we first modify Program 12.1 to encapsulate all of the functionality of the GUI into a basic GUI class. To see how this is done, consider Program 12.2.

PROGRAM 12.2

```
import javax.Swing.*;
public class FirstWindow extends JFrame
{
  private JFrame mainFrame;

  public FirstWindow() // a constructor
  {
    mainFrame = new JFrame("First GUI Window");

    mainFrame.setSize(300,150);
    mainFrame.show();
  }

  public static void main(String[] args)
  {
    new FirstWindow();
  }
}  // end of class
```

Notice that the class provided in Program 12.2 has been named FirstWindow, which has been defined as extending the class JFrame. This means that our FirstWindow class has access to all of the public and protected methods that are available to the JFrame class, such as setSize() and show(). Within our class, we have defined a single class variable named mainFrame to be of type JFrame. We have also defined a single constructor method. The three statements within this constructor are almost identical to those that we previously used within Program 12.1's main() method. The only difference is the first statement, where we do not have to declare mainFrame as being of type JFrame precisely because of its declaration as a class variable. Now look at the main() method. Here all that is required to produce the GUI is that a new instance of the class FirstWindow be created. This is accomplished by the statement new FirstWindow(). When this statement is executed, the constructor for the FirstWindow class is automatically called. This constructor performs the same task previously performed by Program 12.1's main() method and produces the same GUI created by Program 12.1, as shown in Figure 12.6. Because Program 12.2 would be stored on disk as FirstWindow.java, which is derived from its class name, it must be compiled and executed using the statements

```
javac FirstWindow.java
java FirstWindow
```

If you are not familiar with the construction of classes presented in Part Two, Program 12.2 will appear more complicated than Program 12.1. Nevertheless, Program 12.2 has very distinct advantages over Program 12.1. The main advantage is that all of the GUI components are encapsulated within a single well-defined class that isolates the GUI code from the application that uses it. This means that the same application can use different GUIs and that different parts of the overall system can be altered without affecting other parts, which is precisely the advantage provided by object-oriented languages. Thus, as more and more functionality is added to Program 12.2's GUI, its basic structure allows us to focus on the additional components and their relationship to the GUI as a whole and lets us consolidate these design elements into a single self-contained class. The `main()` method can then be used operationally for either independent testing of the GUI or inclusion of it within a larger context that uses the GUI for both user input and display. In practice, a more extensive `main()` method would be included in its own class, as was discussed in Part Two of this text. For our immediate purposes, however, Program 12.2's `FirstWindow` class will be the basic model upon which we will design all of our subsequent Swing-based GUIs.

Look and Feel

A GUI's **look and feel** refers to how the GUI appears on the screen and how a user interacts with it. Although we will always use the default look and feel named Java, the Swing package actually supports the four look and feel types listed in Table 12.6, three of which are illustrated in Figure 12.7. As can be seen from these examples, the differences in the displays are determined by the line thickness, shading, and the two- or three-dimensional look provided.

Also listed in Table 12.6 are the Java statements for explicitly selecting each look and feel type. In the absence of either an explicit look and feel selection or an invalid choice, the default Java look and feel is used. To implement a specific look and feel, the code in

(a) Java Default

(b) Windows

(c) UNIX

FIGURE 12.7   Look and Feel Examples

TABLE 12.6 Look and Feel GUI Types

Type	Code	Comment
Java	`setLookAndFeel("javax.Swing.plaf.metal.MetalLookAndFeel");`	Can be used on all systems.
Mac	`setLookAndFeel("javax.Swing.plaf.mac.MacLookAndFeel");`	Can only be used on Macintosh systems.
Windows	`setLookAndFeel("com.sun.java.Swing.plaf.windows.WindowsLookAndFeel");`	Can only be used on Windows systems.
UNIX	`setLookAndFeel("com.sun.java.Swing.plaf.motif.MotifLookAndFeel");`	Can be used on all systems.

Table 12.6 must be included in a `try` and `catch` block similar to the following, which sets a Windows look and feel:

```
try
{
  UIManager.setLookAndFeel("com.sun.java.Swing.plaf.windows.WindowsLookAndFeel");
  SwingUtilities.updateComponentTreeUI(mainFrame);
  mainFrame.pack();
}catch (Exception e){}
```

In this code, the identifier `mainFrame` is the name that has been consistently declared in all of our GUI-based programs as being of type JFrame. The `pack()` method will force the change to the selected look and feel even after the GUI has been displayed. Thus, this section of code can be placed either before or after a `show()` method has been invoked to display a GUI.

EXERCISES 12.2

1. Describe the two main approaches to constructing GUIs using Swing-based components.
2. **a.** Enter and execute Program 12.1 on your computer.
   b. What is a major problem with Program 12.1?
   c. After closing the window constructed by Program 12.1, how can the underlying Java program be halted and return provided to the operating system?
   d. How would Program 12.1 be named and stored on your computer?
3. **a.** Enter and execute Program 12.2 on your computer.
   b. What is a major problem with Program 12.2?
   c. After closing the window constructed by Program 12.2, how can the underlying Java program be halted and return provided to the operating system?
   d. How would Program 12.2 be named and stored on your computer?
4. Replace the statement `mainFrame.show()` in Program 12.2 with the statement `mainFrame.setVisible(true)` and execute the program to verify that it produces the same effect.

5. Modify Program 12.2 so that the size of the displayed GUI is 400 pixels wide $\times$ 200 pixels high.

6. Write a Java program that constructs a window having the title `The Hello Application - Ver. 1.0`.

7. Modify Program 12.2 so that the `main()` method is contained within a class named `TestFirstWindow`. The program should be stored under the name `TestFirstWindow.java`.

8. What is meant by a GUI's look and feel?

9. List the four look and feel types provided by Java's `swing` package.

10. Modify Program 12.2 so that it is displayed with a UNIX look and feel.

12.3 ADDING A WINDOW-CLOSING EVENT HANDLER

When creating a functioning GUI in Java, we will always use the following two-phase process:

Phase 1: Construct the component so that it appears visually
Phase 2: Provide an event handler for the component

We will adhere to this process no matter how many components we add into the GUI. For now, however, our GUI consists of a single JFrame component. Because we have completed phase 1 for this component, when Program 12.2 is executed, the component appears visually and a blank window is displayed. If you click the window's Close button, the window will close, but the underlying Java application is still running and must be stopped by pressing the Ctrl and C keys at the same time. In this section, we complete phase 2 for this graphical user interface by providing it with an event handler that closes the underlying Java application when the window's Close button is clicked. Formally, an **event handler** is an object that responds appropriately when an event occurs, such as clicking a window's Close button.

In creating a window-closing event handler, we will first provide a generic description of Java's event-handling methodology. This is followed by an in-depth presentation of the three predominant ways in which event handlers are constructed in practice. Thus, this section is a basic primer on creating event handlers in general, although we will apply each technique to a window-closing event. When you have completed this section, you will have all the tools needed to easily understand and construct event handlers for the atomic components presented in the next chapter.

The Event Delegation Model

Although creating a Java event handler is a rather cookbook affair once the underlying process is understood, it does requires a number of predefined steps. This is because Java implements event handling by what is known as an **event delegation model.** This model requires two basic elements: a component, such as a window or button, that can generate an event, and an event handler, which is a separate object that is formally referred to as a **listener object.** The component delegates responsibility to the listener object for doing something when an event is generated. The glue that attaches an event to a specific event handler (the listener object) is a *registration statement*. Only event handlers that have been correctly registered actually receive the news when a specific event has taken place. Thus, the complete set of steps for phase 2 of our GUI design procedure is:

Phase 2: Provide an event handler for a component
  Step 1: Write the code for an event handler class, which is known as the listener class
  Step 2: Create an instance of the event handler class (this means instantiating an object of the class using the new operator); the created object is known as a listener object
  Step 3: Register the listener object created in step 2

Each of these three steps for collectively constructing and activating an event handler is contained in Program 12.3, which implements a complete event handler for closing the GUI when the window's Close button is clicked. We have named the GUI class in Program 12.3 SecondWindow and delegated the event-handling method to a separate class named WinHandler, which is the listener class. Notice that we have also added the statement import java.awt.event.*; at the top of the program. It is the java.awt.event package that provides the underlying methods needed by a listener class.

Let us now examine how each of the three event delegation elements, which have been boldfaced for easy recognition, are provided by Program 12.3.

In Program 12.3, the event-handling (listener) class has been coded as a separate nonnested class. Doing so at this point permits us to concentrate specifically on all of the elements needed by an event-handling class. Later in this section, we will provide two useful techniques for significantly reducing the size of the event-handling code, but we will do this in stages. The reason is that you will encounter each version in your programming work. Thus, the discussion forms the basis for understanding all of the event-handling methods you will see in practice and will use for the atomic components that are added into our basic GUI in the next chapter. For now, however, consider Program 12.3's listener class by itself, which is reproduced here for convenience.

```
// Step 1 - define a listener class to handle window events
class WinHandler implements WindowListener
{
  public void windowClosing(WindowEvent e) {System.exit(0);}
  public void windowClosed(WindowEvent e) {}
  public void windowOpened(WindowEvent e) {}
  public void windowIconified(WindowEvent e) {}
  public void windowDeiconified(WindowEvent e) {}
  public void windowActivated(WindowEvent e) {}
  public void windowDeactivated(WindowEvent e) {}
} // end of listener class
```

First, notice the class' header line specifies that the WinHandler class implements a WindowListener interface. Except for the name that we have chosen for our class, WinHandler, which is a programmer-selectable identifier, the rest of this header is standard for creating a class that will perform as a WindowListener. Specifically, a

PROGRAM 12.3

```java
import javax.Swing.*;
import java.awt.event.*;   // this is needed for the event handlers
public class SecondWindow extends JFrame
{
  private JFrame mainFrame;

  public SecondWindow() // a constructor
  {
    mainFrame = new JFrame("Second GUI Window");

    mainFrame.setSize(300,150);
    mainFrame.show();

    WinHandler handler = new WinHandler();  // Phase 2 - Step 2: create an event handler
    mainFrame.addWindowListener(handler);   // Phase 2 - Step 3: register (activate) the handler
  }

  public static void main(String[] args)
  {
    new SecondWindow();
  }
}  // end of GUI class

  // Phase 2 - Step 1: define a listener class to handle window events
class WinHandler implements WindowListener
{
  public void windowClosing(WindowEvent e) {System.exit(0);}
  public void windowClosed(WindowEvent e) {}
  public void windowOpened(WindowEvent e) {}
  public void windowIconified(WindowEvent e) {}
  public void windowDeiconified(WindowEvent e) {}
  public void windowActivated(WindowEvent e) {}
  public void windowDeactivated(WindowEvent e) {}
}  // end of listener class
```

WindowListener is implemented because this interface is required by Java for handling window events. Table 12.7 presents the required interfaces for the components considered in this text. This table also lists, in the third column, all of the required methods for each event handler type. Java requires that if even one of these methods is implemented in a listener class, all of the listed methods must be implemented, even if they consist of empty bodies.

Now concentrate on the listener class' internal construction. Notice that the class consists of no declared variables and seven methods, only one of which has a nonempty body. This single nonempty method is the windowClosing() method, and the single

TABLE 12.7   GUI Component Events Types

Component	Required Interface Type	Required Methods	Available Adapter Class
Window	WindowListener	windowClosing( )	WindowAdapter
		windowClosed( )	
		windowOpened( )	
		windowActivated( )	
		windowDeactivated( )	
		windowIconified( )	
		windowDeiconified( )	
Mouse	MouseMotionListener	mouseDragged(MouseEvent)	MouseMotionAdapter
		mouseMoved(MouseEvent)	
	MouseListener	mousePressed(MouseEvent)	MouseAdapter
		mouseReleased(MouseEvent)	
		mouseClicked(MouseEvent)	
Keyboard	KeyListener	keyPressed(KeyEvent)	KeyAdapter
		keyReleased(KeyEvent)	
		keyTyped(KeyEvent)	
Button	ActionListener	actionPerformed(ActionEvent)	ActionAdapter
Text Field	TextListener	textValueChanged(TextEvent)	(none)
Check Box	ItemListener	itemStateChanged(ItemEvent)	(none)
Radio Box	ItemListener	itemStateChanged(ItemEvent)	(none)
Focus Events	FocusListener	focusGained(FocusEvent)	FocusAdapter
		focusLost(FocusEvent)	

statement constituting its body is System.exit(0). This statement should be familiar because it is the same statement that closed all of the programs in Part One that used the swing package to implement a dialog box. The other six methods are still required by any listener class that is implemented as a WindowListener, as listed in Table 12.7, even if we are not interested in using them. Because we are only concerned with the WindowClosing() method, these other methods are constructed as empty methods with no internal statements.

Having taken care of constructing the event-handling class (step 1), the two remaining steps must be completed. Step 2, instantiating an object of the listener class, is accomplished in Program 12.3 with the statement

```
WinHandler handler = new WinHandler();  // Phase 2 - Step 2: create an event handler
```

This statement should also look familiar because it is one of the standard ways that we have used throughout the text to instantiate (i.e., create) an object. In this particular case, the name `handler` is a programmer-selected reference variable that is declared to be of type `WinHandler`, which is the name of the `WindowListener` class that we constructed for step 1. As always, this single statement can be replaced by two statements, one of which first declares a reference variable and the second of which instantiates an object. Using two statements, step 2 can also be realized as:

```
WinHandler handler;
handler = new WinHandler();
```

The statement in Program 12.3 that performs step 3 and attaches the `WindowListener` object named `handler` created in step 2 to the desired component, which in our specific case is `mainFrame`, is:

```
mainFrame.addWindowListener(handler);   // Phase 2 - Step 3: register (activate) the handler
```

We will discuss `add()` methods in detail in the next section, so for now we simply use this statement as is. This statement activates the listener object created in step 2, and it is formally referred to as a **registration statement.**

When Program 12.3 is compiled and executed using the statements

```
javac SecondWindow.java
java SecondWindow
```

the GUI in Figure 12.8 is displayed. Except for the title bar, this is the same GUI created by Program 12.2 and previously shown in Figure 12.6. The central difference between these two GUIs is that clicking the Close button on the window constructed by Program 12.3 not only closes the window but shuts down the underlying Java program and returns control appropriately to the operating system.

FIGURE 12.8   The Window Displayed by Program 12.3

Adapter and Inner Classes

In Program 12.3, the listener class is constructed as a separate class, and it has two minor problems that can be easily rectified. The first of these problems is that, even though we only need to handle one event, the listener class is required to contain the seven event-handling methods in Table 12.7 for a `WindowListener`. The second problem is that the listener class code (step 1) is located after the GUI class code at the end of the program, when it would be preferable to have it closer to the code that instantiates (step 2) and registers (step 3) the listener. We will solve these problems one at a time.

First, Java provides a special set of classes, referred to as *adapter classes*, that declare empty event-handling methods for a given interface type, such as the `WindowListener` class in Table 12.7. Because an adapter class provides all of the method declarations for an interface, it can be used as the parent class for a listener class. By construction, all adapter classes are constructed in Java as abstract classes. An **abstract class** is a class from which objects cannot be directly instantiated but which can be used as a parent from which other classes can be derived. For example, as listed in Table 12.7, the adapter class provided in Java that can be used as a parent class to create a `WindowListener` is named `WindowAdapter`. Now consider the following listener class, which extends the adapter class named `WindowAdapter`:

```
// extend an adapter class to handle window events
class WinHandler extends WindowAdapter
{
  public void windowClosing(WindowEvent e) {System.exit(0);}
}  // end of listener class
```

Because we are extending an adapter class that provides declarations for all of the required window event methods, all we need to do is provide code for the event method that we are actually interested in. Our class' single `windowClosing()` method will override the method with the same name in the parent `WindowAdapter` class, and the six other required methods are provided for by the remaining empty methods declared in the adapter class.

Using our new `WinHandler` class in place of the longer version provided in Program 12.3 and renaming our basic GUI class as `ThirdWindow` result in Program 12.4. Here the new class is boldfaced so you can easily see where we have made the change. Also notice the boldfaced line in the basic GUI class, which is

```
mainFrame.addWindowListener(new WinHandler());
```

This line instantiates an object of the `WinHandler` listener class and registers the class in a single statement; it replaces the equivalent following two lines from Program 12.3:

```
WinHandler handler = new WinHandler();   // Phase 2 - Step 2: create an event handler
mainFrame.addWindowListener(handler);    // Phase 2 - Step 3: register (activate) the handler
```

Because you will see single-line and double-line statements for creating and registering an event handler object, you should be familiar with both styles. In your own work, select one of these two styles based either on preference, policy, or instruction and be consistent in its usage throughout all of your programs.

The output displayed when Program 12.4 is executed appears in Figure 12.9. Except for the window's title bar, this GUI is identical to that provided by Program 12.3. As with the prior program's operation, both the window and the underlying Java program will be correctly shut down when the Close button is pressed.

Notice that we have significantly reduced the size of the listener class using an adapter class. The next minor problem that we would like to address is to have the event-

PROGRAM 12.4

```
import javax.Swing.*;
import java.awt.event.*;
public class ThirdWindow extends JFrame
{
  private JFrame mainFrame;

  public ThirdWindow() // a constructor
  {
    mainFrame = new JFrame("Third GUI Window");

    mainFrame.setSize(300,150);
    mainFrame.show();

     // create and register the handler in one statement
    mainFrame.addWindowListener(new WinHandler());
  }

  public static void main(String[] args)
  {
    new ThirdWindow();
  }
}  // end of GUI class

  // extend an adapter class to handle window events
class WinHandler extends WindowAdapter
{
  public void windowClosing(WindowEvent e) {System.exit(0);}
}  // end of listener class
```

handling class placed closer to the point at which the event handler object is created and registered. Doing so centralizes all aspects of the event-handling mechanism in one place for easy reference.

Notice that in both Programs 12.3 and 12.4, the listener class is coded as a separate class that is located outside the class that constructs the GUI. Whenever the code for an event-handling class is significantly longer than the WinHandler class coded in Program

FIGURE 12.9 The Window Displayed by Program 12.4

12.3, it should be created in this manner. For small listener classes, however, which our `WinHandler` class has become, the code can easily be nested inside the main GUI class without unduly breaking up the code used to create the visual display of components. This is done by nesting the listener class into the main GUI class.

When one class is nested inside another class, it is referred to as an **inner class.** As an example of such a class, consider Program 12.5. Notice that this program's `WinHandler` class is identical to that in Program 12.4, but it is now located inside the GUI class. This is done precisely to move the event-handling class closer to where the creation and registration of the event-handling object is made.

PROGRAM 12.5

```java
import javax.Swing.*;
import java.awt.event.*;
public class FourthWindow extends JFrame
{
  private JFrame mainFrame;

  public FourthWindow() // a constructor
  {
    mainFrame = new JFrame("Fourth GUI Window");

    mainFrame.setSize(300,150);
    mainFrame.show();

     // create and register the handler in one statement
    mainFrame.addWindowListener(new WinHandler());
  }

    // an inner class to handle window events
  class WinHandler extends WindowAdapter
  {
    public void windowClosing(WindowEvent e) {System.exit(0);}
  }  // end of inner class

  public static void main(String[] args)
  {
    new FourthWindow();
  }
}  // end of GUI class
```

Figure 12.10 shows the window displayed by Program 12.5. Again, except for the title bar, this GUI is the same as that produced by Programs 12.3 and 12.4, and all three programs operationally shut down in the same way.

Although we have chosen in Program 12.5 to use Program 12.4's adapter class version of the listener class as an inner class within the defining GUI class, the same could have been done with the longer listener class provided in Program 12.3. You may also see

FIGURE 12.10   The Window Displayed by Program 12.5

a listener class nested within a separate class that includes the `main()` method if the instantiation of the event-handling object is performed within the `main()` method.

We are now almost finished with the various ways listener classes are constructed in practice. The overriding rule in all cases is that the listener class be made as short as possible, without sacrificing clarity, and that the code be placed as close as possible to where an object of the class is actually instantiated. For larger listener classes, this means creating a separate class that is placed outside the class that creates the GUI, and for smaller classes, it means using an inner class. If only one or two event methods are actually needed, an adapter class should be used to shorten the code, either as an inner or a separate class.

Anonymous Classes

The last extensively used variation for creating event-handling classes is provided by anonymous classes. As the term suggests, an **anonymous class** is a class without a name. The advantage of this type of class is that it permits placing the event-handling class code directly into the statement that creates an instance of the event-handling class. Such classes can only be used when the event instantiation and registration are accomplished using a single statement. This is because an individual instantiation statement first requires declaring an event object with the name of a specific class, which precludes a class having no name.

As a specific example of an anonymous class, consider the following code, which would qualify as a stand-alone class if it had a standard class header line. This missing header line qualifies the class as anonymous.

```
{
  public void windowClosing(WindowEvent e) {System.exit(0);}
}
```

Carefully compare this anonymous class to Program 12.5's `WinHandler` class, which is repeated here for convenience:

```
class WinHandler extends WindowAdapter
{
  public void windowClosing(WindowEvent e) {System.exit(0);}
}
```

Notice that except for the anonymous class' missing header line, these two classes are identical and that both classes have the same body and, therefore, perform the exact same function.

The question now becomes: Where is this anonymous class placed? The answer is that the class is placed wherever a listener class name would normally be used to create a new instance of the class. As a specific example of this placement, consider the creation and registration statement in Program 12.5, which is repeated here for convenience:

```
mainFrame.addWindowListener(new WinHandler());
```

We are now going to move the last parenthesis and closing semicolon from this statement down to provide space for three additional lines as follows:

```
mainFrame.addWindowListener(new WinHandler()



);
```

It is within these newly created empty lines that the anonymous class is placed, producing the following code:

```
mainFrame.addWindowListener(new WindowAdapter()
{   // anonymous class
  public void windowClosing(WindowEvent e) {System.exit(0);}
}
);
```

First, notice that the interface type, WindowAdapter, is specifically designated in the header line. Secondly, because whitespace does not count in Java, at a minimum, the last two lines in the code are usually placed together as });. Program 12.6 uses this code in our final version of creating a window-closing event handler. For convenience, we have bold-faced the statements that create and register the listener object using the anonymous class.

When Program 12.6 is compiled and executed, the GUI in Figure 12.11 is produced. Operationally, this window is closed in the same manner as all of the previous programs that provided window-closing event handling code.

FIGURE 12.11 The Window Displayed by Program 12.6

In addition to the version of the anonymous class that handles the window-closing event in Program 12.6, be prepared to see other space-saving versions of this code, such as:

```
mainFrame.addWindowListener(new WindowAdapter()
{public void windowClosing(WindowEvent e) {System.exit(0);}});
```

PROGRAM 12.6

```java
import javax.Swing.*;
import java.awt.event.*;
public class FifthWindow extends JFrame
{

  private JFrame mainFrame;

  public FifthWindow() // a constructor
  {
    mainFrame = new JFrame("Fifth GUI Window");

    mainFrame.setSize(300,150);
    mainFrame.show();

      // create and register the handler in one statement
      // using an anonymous inner class
    mainFrame.addWindowListener(new WindowAdapter()
    {   // anonymous class
      public void windowClosing(WindowEvent e) {System.exit(0);}
    });
  }

  public static void main(String[] args)
  {
    new FifthWindow();
  }
}  // end of GUI class
```

Anonymous classes should only be used when an event handler consists of a single method that is only one or two lines in length. Because our event handler class fits this description perfectly, it is an ideal candidate for implementation as an anonymous class. Also notice that an anonymous class is always used within a statement that creates an instance of the class. Because the creation statement must itself be contained within a class, the placement of an anonymous class will always force it to be an inner class.

Finally, be aware that in all of our event-handling code we have constructed a single listener object for a single event source, which in our particular case has been a window. This situation is shown in Figure 12.12a. For completeness, it should be mentioned that multiple listener objects can be registered to the same event source (Figure 12.12b) and that a single listener object can be registered to multiple event sources (Figure 12.12c). In the next chapter (Section 13.4), we will present a practical example of this last case where the same event handler is registered to two components. For this situation, the event handler must use its input argument to determine the component that triggered the event and then take appropriate action.

(a) One listener registered to one component

(b) Three listeners registered to one component

(c) One listener registered to three components

FIGURE 12.12 Various Registration Configurations

EXERCISES 12.3

1. **a.** Compile, execute, and run Program 12.3 on your computer.
   b. Repeat Exercise 1a but remove the registration statement

```
mainFrame.addWindowListener(handler);  // Phase 2 - Step 3: register (activate) the handler
```

   With this statement removed, determine what happens when you now close down the displayed window using the window's Close (X) button.

2. Modify Program 12.3 so that it displays a message box with the message The Underlying Java Program will now be closed when the Close button is clicked. Only when the user clicks the message box's OK button should the program be terminated.

3. **a.** Compile, execute, and run Program 12.4 on your computer.
   b. Make sure to first compile Program 12.3 and then change Program12.4's single main() method's statement from new FourthWindow(); to new ThirdWindow();. Now compile, execute, and run the modified Program 12.4. Determine what happened and why.

4. Define what is meant by an inner class.

5. **a.** Describe the purpose of an adapter class.
   b. Must an adapter class always be used as an inner class?

6. **a.** Describe the difference between an anonymous class and a nonanonymous class.
   b. Must an anonymous class always be used as an inner class?

7. Why do you think the TextListener and ItemListener classes have no equivalent adapter classes? (*Tip:* See Table 12.7.)

8. Write a Java program that constructs a window having the title `The Hello Application - Ver. 1.0`. Make sure that your program contains a window-closing event object that correctly closes the window when the Close button is pressed.

12.4 ADDING A BUTTON COMPONENT

Although the application presented in the previous section is a useful introduction to a `JFrame` container-based GUI and a window-closing event handler that we will use in all of our subsequent GUIs, it is not a very useful application in itself. To make it practical, we have to add lightweight components, such as buttons and data entry and display fields with their related event classes. The process that we will always follow in adding components to a GUI is the following two-phase procedure:

Phase 1: Construct the component so that it appears visually.
 Step 1: Create a specific component.
 Step 2: Add the component into a container.
Phase 2: Provide an event handler for the component
 Step 1: Write the code for an event handler class (a listener class).
 Step 2: Create an instance of the event handler class (a listener object).
 Step 3: Register the listener object.

In phase 1, the component is added into a container, which in our case will always be a `JFrame`. This creates the actual graphical interface that the user sees on the screen. By providing each component with an event handler (phase 2), the component comes "alive" so that when it is selected something actually happens.

In this section, we illustrate this two-phase process with a button component as a specific example. Thus, we will first create a GUI containing a button (phase 1) and then attach an event handler to the added component (phase 2). After constructing and activating one lightweight component into a GUI, you will have learned the method for placing and activating all other Java components, such as labels and data entry components, into a top-level container. Specific examples of each of these other components, however, are provided in the next chapter.

Adding a Button

A button component, which is also referred to as both a **push button** and a **command button,** is constructed from a `JButton` component. For our next GUI, we will use this component type to create the user interface shown in Figure 12.13.

FIGURE 12.13   The `ButtonGuiOne` Class' GUI

Phase 1: Construct the Component So That It Appears Visually

Specifically, when adding a lightweight component, be it an intermediate container or an atomic component, into a top-level container, the two steps in this phase become:

Step 1: Create a specific component.
Step 2: Add the component to the JFrame's content pane.

Numerous examples of step 1 have been provided throughout this chapter when we have used a top-level JFrame component to create a basic GUI window. When adding lightweight components into a top-level container, they must be added to the container's content pane. A container's **content pane** directly or indirectly holds all of the container's visible components. Thus, the really new step is step 2, which binds a component to the underlying top-level JFrame container. However, let's take these steps one by one to create and add a functioning button into our basic GUI.

Step 1: Create a Button Recall that an instance of a JFrame has been constructed throughout this chapter by first declaring a class variable to be of type JFrame using the statement

```
private JFrame mainFrame;
```

It is important to note that the variable name that we have chosen, in this case mainFrame, can be any valid variable name that satisfies Java's identifier rules. Once a variable is declared to be of type JFrame, an actual JFrame object was created using a statement similar to:

```
mainFrame = new JFrame("Example of a Gui with a Button");
```

In exactly the same manner, a button component, which is of type JButton, can be created. First, we will declare a class variable to be of type JButton using the statement

```
private JButton firstButton;
```

As with all class variable names, the specific name, which in this case is firstButton, is programmer selected. Next, to create an object of the desired JButton type, we will place the following statement within the class' constructor method:

```
firstButton = new JButton("Press me");   // create a button
```

Here the string in quotes provides the text that is displayed inside the button when the component is displayed as part of the GUI. This text is referred to as the button's **caption.**

Step 2: Add the Component to the JFrame's Content Pane Once a button object is created, it must be added to a container's content pane to be displayed. This can be accomplished using two statements: one for obtaining the content pane and the second for actually adding the component to the pane. For our specific example, in which we have a JFrame object named mainFrame, the statement

```
Container c = mainFrame.getContentPane();
```

defines a reference variable named c that has access to our `mainFrame` object's content pane. Although the name of the `Container` reference variable can be any valid Java identifier, the general syntax of this statement is standard and will be used throughout all of our remaining Swing-based programs. This syntax is

```
Container ContainerName = JFrameName.getContentPane();
```

Once the content pane is available, a component is added to it using one of the `Container` class' `add()` methods. At a minimum, all of the various `add()` methods require the name of the component that is to be added as an argument. An additional argument frequently can fine-tune the object's placement by overriding the layout manager's default placement. As a specific example, for the button object that was created and named `firstButton` in step 1, the statement

```
c.add(firstButton);
```

will add this button into our JFrame's content pane.

Although we have used a two-statement procedure of first getting a content pane and then adding a component to it, these two statements can be compressed into a single statement. For our particular components, the single-statement equivalent for step 2 is:

```
mainFrame.getContentPane().add(firstButton);
```

In practice, you will encounter both the one- and two-statement forms for adding a component to a JFrame's content pane (step 2).

Program 12.7 uses the four statements that we have described for creating and adding a JButton component into a basic JFrame GUI. For convenience, each of the statements we have introduced in this section has been boldfaced and annotated with a comment as to which step it specifically refers to. The rest of the code in this program should be familiar because it is the same basic code that we have used throughout this chapter to create a JFrame-based window with a window-closing event handler.

When Program 12.7 is compiled and executed, the displayed GUI will appear as in Figure 12.14. Although the GUI can be closed and the underlying Java application correctly shut down by clicking the window's Close button, clicking the JButton produces no effect. This is because we have not included and registered any button event handler. Before doing this, however, we will add both a ToolTip and an accelerator key to the button shown in Figure 12.14.

FIGURE 12.14 The GUI Displayed by Program 12.7

PROGRAM 12.7

```java
import javax.Swing.*;
import java.awt.event.*;
import java.awt.Container;  // need this to add controls
public class ButtonGuiOne extends JFrame
{
  private JFrame mainFrame;
  private JButton firstButton;                    // Phase 1 - Step 1: first statement

  public ButtonGuiOne() // a constructor
  {
    mainFrame = new JFrame("Example of a Gui with a Button");

      // create a button object
    firstButton = new JButton("Press me");   // Phase 1 - Step 1: second statement

      // get the content pane
    Container c = mainFrame.getContentPane(); // Phase 1 - Step 2: first statement

      // add the button to the ContentPane
    c.add(firstButton);                       // Phase 1 - Step 2: second statement

    mainFrame.setSize(300,150);

      // define and register window event handler
    mainFrame.addWindowListener(new WindowAdapter()
    {
      public void windowClosing(WindowEvent e) {System.exit(0);}
    });

    mainFrame.show();
  }

  public static void main(String[] args)
  {
    new ButtonGuiOne();  // instantiate a GUI object
  }

} // end of ButtonGuiOne class
```

Adding ToolTips and Accelerator Keys

The current Window's look and feel includes both ToolTips and accelerator keys. A **ToolTip** is any single line of text that appears when a user positions the mouse cursor over a GUI component. Its purpose is to provide a quick single-line documentation for the selected component. An **accelerator key,** which is referred to as a **mnemonic key** in Java, is any key that initiates an action by pressing the Alt key and a designated letter.

Both ToolTips and mnemonics are created using a `set()` method, which is inherited from Java's JComponent Swing class. Specifically, the general syntax to create a ToolTip is

```
objectName.setToolTipText("string value");
```

As a specific example, the statement

```
firstButton.setToolTipText("This is a button");
```

uses this syntax to create the ToolTip `This is a button` for a component object named firstButton.

In a similar manner, the general syntax for creating an accelerator key is

```
objectName.setMnemonic('letter');
```

For example, assuming that we have a button named `firstButton`, the statement

```
firstButton.setMnemonic('P');
```

creates the letter P as the mnemonic for the button. Within a button's caption, the first occurrence of the designated letter, if it exists, is underlined to indicate its status as the mnemonic for the button. If the letter is not contained in the button's caption, it will still act as an accelerator but will not be explicitly designated as such in the caption. In effect, the accelerator key then becomes a "hidden" hot-key sequence. Such hidden key sequences are studiously avoided by professional programmers because they generally serve to annoy users who accidentally activate the sequence or make an insecure user nervous about other unexpected features that can produce unanticipated results. Users of a program generally have all they can manage in learning how all documented features of a program work; providing hidden features that can surprise a user is almost always a sign of a very inexperienced programmer.

Program 12.8 illustrates the inclusion of both a ToolTip and mnemonic key for the button previously created in Program 12.7. The results of these two new features appear in Figure 12.15.

FIGURE 12.15 The ToolTip and Mnemonic Key Created by Program 12.8

PROGRAM 12.8

```java
import javax.Swing.*;
import java.awt.event.*;
import java.awt.Container;  // need this to add controls
public class ButtonGuiTwo extends JFrame
{
  private JFrame mainFrame;
  private JButton firstButton;                    // Phase 1 - Step 1: first statement

  public ButtonGuiTwo() // a constructor
  {
    mainFrame = new JFrame("Example of a Gui with a Button");

      // create a button object
    firstButton = new JButton("Press me");    // Phase 1 - Step 1: second statement

      // get the content pane
    Container c = mainFrame.getContentPane(); // Phase 1 - Step 2: first statement
      // add the button to the ContentPane
    c.add(firstButton);                           // Phase 1 - Step 2: second statement

    firstButton.setToolTipText("This is a button"); // create a ToolTip
    firstButton.setMnemonic('P');                   // create a Mnemonic key

    mainFrame.setSize(300,150);

      // define and register window event handler
    mainFrame.addWindowListener(new WindowAdapter()
    {
      public void windowClosing(WindowEvent e) {System.exit(0);}
    });

    mainFrame.show();
  }

  public static void main(String[] args)
  {
    new ButtonGuiTwo();  // instantiate a GUI object
  }

}  // end of ButtonGuiTwo class
```

Adding an Event Handler

An extremely important feature of our two-phase GUI development procedure is that it permits seeing how a GUI will appear before any event code has to be written. Thus, Program 12.8 can be executed to verify that its button component appears correctly without the necessity of first supplying it with event-handling code. Once the visual aspects of a component are satisfied, the second phase in the process, which is to create and register an event handler for the component, can be completed. We will now do this for the button component displayed by Program 12.8 so that an appropriate response occurs when the button is clicked.

An event handler for an atomic component, such as a button, is created and registered in the same way that the window-closing method was created and registered for a JFrame container in the last section. Specifically, for the button added into the GUI in Program 12.8, we will now apply phase 2 of the development process:

Phase 2: Provide an event handler for the component.
  Step 1: Write the code for an event handler class (a listener class).
  Step 2: Create an instance of the event handler class (a listener object).
Step 3: Register the listener object.

Providing the button with an event handler will make the component come alive so that something actually happens when it is selected. In our particular case, we will have the program display a message box when the button is clicked.

Step 1: Write the Code for an Event Handler Class (a Listener Class) Using Table 12.7, we see that the required event handler interface for a button is an `ActionListener` and that the class implementing this handler must define a single method named `actionPerformed()`. In addition, the same table provides the information that this method expects to receive an ActionEvent parameter type. Naming our class `ButEventHandler` and using the Java convention of naming the passed parameter e (both are programmer-selected names), the basic structure of our listener class is:

```
class ButEventHandler implements ActionListener
{
  public void actionPerformed(ActionEvent e)
  {
     // this is currently an empty method body
  }
}
```

For purposes of illustration, we will have our button display the message box shown in Figure 12.16 when the button is clicked. The required statement to produce this dialog is:

```
JOptionPane.showMessageDialog(null, "Button was Pressed",
   "Event Handler Message",JOptionPane.INFORMATION_MESSAGE);
```

FIGURE 12.16 Message Box Produced by Program 12.9

Placing this `showMessageDialog()` call into the body of the `actionPerformed()` method of our listener class completes the class definition as follows:

```
class ButEventHandler implements ActionListener
  {
    public void actionPerformed(ActionEvent e)
    {
      JOptionPane.showMessageDialog(null, "Button was Pressed",
        "Event Handler Message",JOptionPane.INFORMATION_MESSAGE);
    }
  }
```

Step 2: Create an Instance of the Event Handler Class (a Listener Object)
To create an instance of our listener class, which is named `ButEventHandler` (and recall this is a programmer-selected name), we can use the following statement:

```
ButEventHandler bhandler = new ButEventHandler();   // instantiate a handler
```

In this statement, the name of the reference variable, `bhandler`, is also a programmer-selected name. As always, this single-line declaration and instantiation statement can be constructed using a separate declaration followed by an instantiation. Thus, the statement can also be written as:

```
ButEventHandler bhandler; // declare a reference variable
bhandler = new ButEventHandler();   // instantiate the event handler
```

As has been stated, the instantiated event handler object is formally referred to as a listener object.

Step 3: Register the Listener Object
Once a listener object has been created, it still must be attached to one or more components for it to be invoked. Attaching a listener object to a component is accomplished by a registration statement using a variation of an `add()` method. For an event class that has been implemented as an `ActionListener`, the correct registration uses an `add ActionListener()` method. Specifically, because our listener object was instantiated using the reference variable named `bhandler` and we want to attach this listener to the component named `firstButton`, the following registration statement must be used:

```
firstButton.addActionListener(bhandler);   // register the handler
```

Program 12.9 includes all of the event-handling code that we have presented in this section within the context of the GUI created in Program 12.8. For convenience, this code has been boldfaced. In reviewing this code, notice that the event-handling class has been constructed as an inner class.

When Program 12.9 is executed, the GUI in Figure 12.15 is displayed, which is the same GUI displayed by Program 12.8. However, since we have now supplied the push button with event-handling code, when the button is clicked, the dialog in Figure 12.16 is displayed.

PROGRAM 12.9

```java
import javax.Swing.*;
import java.awt.event.*;
import java.awt.Container;  // need this to add controls
public class ButtonGuiThree extends JFrame
{
  private JFrame mainFrame;
  private JButton firstButton;

  public ButtonGuiThree() // a constructor
  {
    mainFrame = new JFrame("Example of a Gui with a Button");

      // create a button object
    firstButton = new JButton("Press me");

      // get the content pane
    Container c = mainFrame.getContentPane();

      // add the button to the ContentPane
    c.add(firstButton);

    firstButton.setToolTipText("This is a button");
    firstButton.setMnemonic('P');

    mainFrame.setSize(300,150);

      // define and register window event handler
    mainFrame.addWindowListener(new WindowAdapter()
    {
      public void windowClosing(WindowEvent e) {System.exit(0);}
    });

      // create and register the button event handler
    ButEventHandler bhandler = new ButEventHandler();  // instantiate a handler
    firstButton.addActionListener(bhandler);  // register the handler

    mainFrame.show();
  }

    // inner class for the button event handler
  class ButEventHandler implements ActionListener
  {
    public void actionPerformed(ActionEvent e)
    {
```

(Continued on next page)

(Continued from previous page)

```
        JOptionPane.showMessageDialog(null, "Button was Pressed",
          "Event Handler Message",JOptionPane.INFORMATION_MESSAGE);
    }
  } // end of inner class


  public static void main(String[] args)
  {
    new ButtonGuiThree();  // instantiate a GUI object
  }


} // end of ButtonGuiThree class
```

EXERCISES 12.4

1. **a.** To what top-level pane must all GUI components be added?
   b. What method obtains the internal component referred to in Exercise 1a?
   c. What method adds a component to the internal frame referred to in Exercise 1a?
2. Enter, compile, and execute Program 12.7 on your computer.
3. Create a Java program that has a single JButton object with the caption Message.
4. Modify the program written for Exercise 3 to include the M key as a keyboard accelerator key. Additionally, the button should be equipped with a ToolTip that displays the string Displays a message.
5. Enter, compile, and execute Program 12.8 on your computer.
6. Enter, compile, and execute Program 12.9 on your computer.
7. Modify Program 12.9 to display the message Hello World! when the button is clicked.
8. Write, compile, and execute a Java program that prints your name and address in a message box when the user clicks on a JButton object. The JButton's caption should be Name and Address. In addition, the button should use the letter N as a keyboard accelerator key and provide a ToolTip of your choosing.
9. Modify Program 12.9 so that the button's listener class is coded as an anonymous class.

12.5 COMMON PROGRAMMING ERRORS

The common programming errors related to creating Swing-based GUIs are:

1. Forgetting to include all of the following statements when creating a full-featured Swing-based GUI:

```
import javax.Swing.*; // needed for creating a Swing based GUI
import java.awt.event.*; // needed for event handling
import java.awt.Container;  // needed for adding atomic components
```

2. Mistyping the JButton keyword as Jbutton. Both the J and B must be capitalized. In general, spelling and letter case mistakes are one of the most common programming errors made in Java. If your GUI does not display a component or an event handler

does not seem to operate, you should first check that all component and method names are spelled correctly.

3. Creating an event handler and failing to register it. An event handler is not activated until both an object of the handler class is instantiated and the handler object is registered. If the event handler object is not registered, the expected event will not be handled, which is the same result that occurs if no handler were written for the event.

4. Incorrectly spelling the getContentPane() method name when adding a component, such as a JButton, into a top-level container. The only letters that must be capitalized in this method name are the C for Content and the P for Pane. This is just a variation on the spelling error listed in error 2.

5. Modifying a GUI class that has previously been compiled and changing its name but forgetting to change the name when an instance of the class is created in the main() method. The application runs but creates an object of the earlier GUI class. This happens because the previous compilation resulted in a .class file for the earlier GUI class, which is still stored and available to instantiate an object, even though the source code for the class may no longer exist in any source code file.

6. Creating a mnemonic key with a letter that is not contained as part of a button's caption. Although the designated key will act correctly as an accelerator key when it is pressed with the Alt key, a user will not know this because the letter will not be underlined in the button's caption.

12.6 CHAPTER SUMMARY

1. *Event-based* programs execute program code depending on what events occur, which in turn depend on what the user does. Thus, the order of events is determined by the user's actions and not predetermined by program code.

2. GUIs are graphical user interfaces that provide the user with components that recognize user actions, such as the clicking of a mouse, and generate events when a user-generated action takes place.

3. Java handles events triggered by GUI components using an *event delegation model*. This model distinguishes between the code that displays a GUI component from the code that handles events associated with the component. In effect, the component delegates event handling to a separate class. The class constructed to handle component-related events is referred to as a *listener class*.

4. The swing package of classes, which was introduced in Java 2.0, provides a relatively straightforward means of constructing GUIs. This package of classes provides three generic types of graphical components: top-level containers that connect a GUI to the underlying operating system, intermediate containers that can be used to simplify component placement, and atomic components such as buttons, labels, and text areas.

5. Graphical components are structured into a Swing-based GUI following a containment hierarchy. This hierarchy requires that atomic components must be placed into containers, the most basic of which is a top-level container. The most common top-level Swing container is the JFrame.

6. To be visible, a JFrame object must execute either a show() or setVisible(true) method. These two methods are interchangeable.

7. Functioning components are added into a JFrame container using the following two-phase process:

Phase 1: Construct the component so that it appears visually.
  Step 1: Instantiate a specific component.
  Step 2: Add the component to the JFrame's content pane.
Phase 2: Provide an event handler for the component.
  Step 1. Write the code for an event handler class, which is known as a listener class.
  Step 2. Create an instance of the event handler class (this means instantiating an object of the class using the new operator); the created object is known as a listener object.
 Step 3. Register the listener object created in Step 2.

8. An instantiated component is added to a JFrame's content pane (phase 1-step 2) using both a getContentPane() and add() method. For example, if a JFrame object named mainFrame has been instantiated, the statement

    `Container c = mainFrame.getContentPane();`

    defines a reference variable named c that has access to the mainFrame object's content pane. For an instantiated button object named firstButton , the statement

    `c.add(firstButton);`

    then adds this button into mainFrame's content pane.
        The two-statement procedure of first getting a content pane and then adding a component to it can always be combined into a single statement. Thus, the previous two statements can be replaced by the equivalent single statement:

    `mainFrame.getContentPane().add(firstButton);`

9. The size of a component can be set using a setSize() method. For example, if mainFrame is the name of a JFrame object, the method call mainFrame.setSize (300,150) will set the size of the displayed frame to 300 pixels wide × 150 pixels high.

10. The name of the listener class for each Swing component must be a Java-specified name. For the components presented in this text, if a listener class is provided for a component, the required listener class names are:

Component	Required Listener Class Name
Window	WindowListener
Mouse	MouseMotionListener
	MouseListener
Keyboard	KeyListener
Button	ActionListener
Text Field	TextListener
Check Box	ItemListener
Radio Box	ItemListener

11. Each implemented listener class requires a specific set of methods that must be included, even if this means creating empty method bodies. The required methods for the listener classes corresponding to the components presented in this text are:

Listener	Required Methods
WindowListener	windowClosing()
	windowClosed()
	windowOpened()
	windowActivated()
	windowDeactivated()
	windowIconified()
	windowDeiconified()
MouseMotionListener	mouseDragged(MouseEvent)
	mouseMoved(MouseEvent)
MouseListener	mousePressed(MouseEvent)
	mouseReleased(MouseEvent)
	mouseClicked(MouseEvent)
KeyListener	keyPressed(KeyEvent)
	keyReleased(KeyEvent)
	keyTyped(KeyEvent)
ActionListener	actionPerformed(ActionEvent)
TextListener	textValueChanged(TextEvent)
ItemListener	itemStateChanged(ItemEvent)

For example, the following class named `Winhandler` implements a `WindowListener` class in which only the window-closing event is actually handled. The remaining six methods required of a `WindowListener` are given empty bodies.

```
// A listener class to handle window events
class WinHandler implements WindowListener
{
  public void windowClosing(WindowEvent e) {System.exit(0);}
  public void windowClosed(WindowEvent e) {}
  public void windowOpened(WindowEvent e) {}
  public void windowIconified(WindowEvent e) {}
  public void windowDeiconified(WindowEvent e) {}
  public void windowActivated(WindowEvent e) {}
  public void windowDeactivated(WindowEvent e) {}
}  // end of listener class
```

12. Listener classes can be nested inside the class that instantiates and displays GUI components. Such nested classes are referred to as *inner classes*.

13. Certain listener classes can be constructed by extending Java-supplied adapter classes. An *adapter class* is a class that defines empty event-handling methods for a corresponding listener class. By construction, all adapter classes are constructed in Java as *abstract classes*, which means that objects cannot be directly instantiated from the class but that it can be used as a parent class from which other classes can be derived. The correspondence between listener classes and the adapter classes that can construct them are:

Listener Name	Available Adapter Class
WindowListener	WindowAdapter
MouseMotionListener	MouseMotionAdapter
MouseListener	MouseAdapter
KeyListener	KeyAdapter
ActionListener	ActionAdapter
TextListener	(none)
ItemListener	(none)

For example, the following extended class named `WinHandler` uses the adapter class named `WindowAdapter` to create a listener class that actively handles only the window-closing event:

```
// extend an adapter class to handle window events
class WinHandler extends WindowAdapter
{
  public void windowClosing(WindowEvent e) {System.exit(0);}
}  // end of listener class
```

14. Once a listener class has been defined, an object of the class type must be instantiated, and this object must be registered for the event handler to be activated. For example, the following two statements

```
WinHandler handler = new WinHandler(); // instantiate an event handler object
mainFrame.addWindowListener(handler);  // register the handler
```

first instantiate an object named `handler` from a listener class named `WinHandler` and then register the object. These two statements can be combined into the single statement

```
mainFrame.addWindowListener(new WinHandler());
```

15. An anonymous class can construct a listener class whenever a single-statement listener object instantiation and registration are employed. An anonymous class is a class that does not use a class header line to name the class and should only be used when a listener class' body consists of one or two statements. When used, the class definition is placed within the statement that instantiates a listener object. For example, the statement

```
mainFrame.addWindowListener(new WindowAdapter()
{ // anonymous class
  public void windowClosing(WindowEvent e) {System.exit(0);}
});
```

uses the anonymous (unnamed) class

```
{
  public void windowClosing(WindowEvent e) {System.exit(0);}
}
```

directly within the instantiation and registration statement.

CHAPTER 13

Additional
Components
and Event Handlers

In this chapter, we show how additional GUI components can be added to the basic JFrame GUI presented in Chapter 12. The procedure presented for adding components is illustrated using text fields, radio buttons, and check boxes. Providing a GUI with these components produces a rather complete graphical user interface that is more than adequate for the majority of Java programs you will write. It also provides you with the ability to add other components as you need them. In addition, we discuss layout managers that permit you to position the additional components in various configurations.

We also provide listener classes for each of the new components presented. We present a new type of listener class, referred to as a focus listener, for detecting and appropriately responding to focus events. Specifically, the focus events considered are when a component gains or loses focus. Finally, we present procedures for validating user input on a keystroke-by-keystroke basis, as each key is pressed.

13.1 ADDING MULTIPLE COMPONENTS

Adding components to a container uses the same procedure that was presented in the previous chapter for adding a single button. To review, this procedure consists of the following two phases:

Phase 1: Construct the component so that it appears visually.
Step 1: Instantiate a specific component.
Step 2: Add the component to the JFrame's content pane.
Phase 2: Provide an event handler for the component.
Step 1: Write the code for an event handler class (a listener class).
Step 2: Instantiate an instance of the event handler.
Step 3: Register the listener object.

The additional consideration, however, when adding more than one component, is the placement of each component within its container. As described in Section 12.1, each container—both top-level and intermediate—has an associated default layout manager. This default, which can be changed by explicitly indicating a different manager, determines how components are to be sized and positioned.

Layout Managers

The available layout managers, which were listed in Table 12.3 and are repeated in Table 13.1 for convenience, can be categorized as simple (FlowLayout and GridLayout), flexible (BoxLayout and GridBagLayout), and special purpose (BorderLayout and CardLayout). In this chapter, we show how to use FlowLayout and BorderLayout managers to position multiple components into a JFrame-based GUI. When not explicitly specified, the default manager for a JFrame container is BorderLayout.

For our first example, we will use a FlowLayout manager to create a GUI containing three buttons. Because a FlowLayout manager is not the default for a JFrame container, we will need to use a `setLayout()` method to explicitly set it as the defining layout manager. The general syntax for this method is

```
containerName.setLayout(new managerName());
```

TABLE 13.1 Layout Managers

Manager	Description	Use Type
FlowLayout	Components are added to the container from left to right and top to bottom, in a row-by-row manner, starting from the top left corner of the container.	Simple
GridLayout	All components are created equal in size and displayed in the requested number of rows and columns. Blank areas fill in unused columns.	Simple
BorderLayout	Up to five components can be placed in the container. The components are placed in positions denoted as north, south, west, east, and center. These positions correspond to the top, bottom, left side, right side, and center positions of the container.	Special Purpose
CardLayout	This layout permits implementation of an area that can contain different components at different times.	Special Purpose
BoxLayout	Components are placed into either a single row or column. Column components can be center, left-edge, or right-edge aligned.	Flexible
GridBagLayout	Components are placed in a spreadsheet type grid of cells, with components permitted to span across and down multiple cells.	Flexible

For example, if c is the name of a JFrame content pane container, and we want to explicitly declare the FlowLayout manager for positioning components within this container, the required statement is:[1]

```
c.setLayout(new FlowLayout());
```

Once set, either by default or explicit specification, the layout manager has complete control over the sizing and positioning of components. It is the sole determiner of how components are initially shaped and then reshaped and repositioned when their holding container is resized and moved about the screen. Table 13.2 provides three methods that can influence the sizing of a component, but these settings are generally only used by each manager as a guideline in its efforts to shape and position each component.

Program 13.1 explicitly sets a FlowLayout manager and then adds three buttons into a JFrame container. The statement setting the layout manager and the statements for creating and adding each button into the container are boldfaced. In reviewing this program, first notice that the statement import java.awt.*; is needed for our selection of layout managers. Also notice that each button component is individually created and

---

[1]It should be noted that this single-line specification is equivalent to the two-statement form

```
FlowLayout manager = new FlowLayout()
c.setLayout(manager);
```

where the name manager is any valid user-selected identifier.

TABLE 13.2 Component Sizing Methods

Method	Description
component.setPreferredSize(int pixels)	Sets the component's preferred size in pixels.
component.setMaximumSize(int pixels)	Sets the component's maximum size in pixels.
component.setMinimumSize(int pixels)	Sets the component's minimum size in pixels.

added into the container's content pane with a three-statement sequence similar to the following used for the first button:

```
   // declare a button to be of type JButton
private JButton messageButton;
   // create the button object
messageButton = new JButton("Message");
   // add the button to the ContentPane
c.add(messageButton);
```

Using a FlowLayout manager, each component is added into its designated container in the order that its add() method is encountered. The first component is added beginning at the top-left side of the container, and additional components are sequentially placed on the same row, continuing until the right edge of the container is reached. A new row is started if additional space is required. The GUI displayed when Program 13.1 is executed appears in Figure 13.1.

FIGURE 13.1 The GUI Displayed by Program 13.1

It is important to note that although Program 13.1 contains no event handlers for its atomic components, it can still be compiled and executed to produce the GUI in Figure 13.1.

PROGRAM 13.1

```
import javax.swing.*;
import java.awt.event.*;
import java.awt.Container;  // need this to add controls
import java.awt.*;  // need this for layout manager

public class MultiButtons extends JFrame
{
   private JFrame mainFrame;
```

(Continued on next page)

(Continued from previous page)

```java
    private JButton messageButton;
    private JButton clearButton;
    private JButton exitButton;

    public MultiButtons() // a constructor
    {
      mainFrame = new JFrame("The Hello Application - Ver. 1.0");

        // create the button objects
      messageButton = new JButton("Message");
      clearButton = new JButton("Clear");
      exitButton = new JButton("Exit");

        // get the content pane & specify layout manager
      Container c = mainFrame.getContentPane();
      c.setLayout(new FlowLayout());

        // add the button to the ContentPane
      c.add(messageButton);
      c.add(clearButton);
      c.add(exitButton);

        // create accelerator keys
      messageButton.setMnemonic('M');
      clearButton.setMnemonic('C');
      exitButton.setMnemonic('x');

      mainFrame.setSize(300,100);

        // define and register window event handler
      mainFrame.addWindowListener(new WindowAdapter()
      {
         public void windowClosing(WindowEvent e) {System.exit(0);}
      });

      mainFrame.show();
    }

    public static void main(String args[])
    {
      MultiButtons app;   // declare a MultiButtons variable
      app = new MultiButtons();  // instantiate a GUI object
    }

} // end of class
```

TABLE 13.3   Program 13.1's Initial Properties Table

Object	Property	Setting
JFrame	Name	mainFrame
	Caption	The Hello Application—Ver. 1.0
	Layout manager	FlowLayout
JButton	Name	messageButton
	Caption	Message
	Mnemonic	M
JButton	Name	clearButton
	Caption	Clear
	Mnemonic	C
JButton	Name	exitButton
	Caption	Exit
	Mnemonic	x

Properties Tables

Once you begin constructing GUIs with multiple components, it is very useful to create a table that contains all of the relevant data about the components that will be added to the interface. The table that performs this function is referred to as a **properties table.** This table becomes very useful for both documentation and programming purposes. As a programming tool, you should prepare the table before writing any code. Doing so provides you with all of the component names that you intend to use and initial settings that must be set. For example, the properties table for Program 13.1 at its current stage of development is listed in Table 13.3.

Adding the Event Handler

Adding event handlers constitutes the second phase of completing a graphical user interface. As we have repeatedly seen throughout the previous chapter, this phase consists of the following steps:

Phase 2: Provide an event handler for the component.
  Step 1: Write the code for an event handler class (a listener class).
  Step 2: Instantiate an instance of the event handler class.
  Step 3: Register the listener object.

The GUI constructed by Program 13.1 already contains our standard window-closing event handler, which we have constructed as an anonymous class. To complete the GUI, we will now provide each of the three buttons with an event handler. The names that we have selected for each handler are listed in Table 13.4, which is an expanded version of the original properties table.

The first two button event handlers in Table 13.4 will display a message box indicating that the button was clicked, and the third handler will close the application. The following code, which would be placed immediately before the constructor's closing brace—that is, after the `mainFrame.show();` statement—accomplishes this:

TABLE 13.4   Program 13.1's Expanded Properties Table

Object	Property	Setting	Listener Class	Listener Object
JFrame	Name	mainFrame	anonymous	
	Caption	The Hello Application— Ver. 1.0		
	Layout manager	FlowLayout		
JButton	Name	messageButton	MessageButtonHandler	mhandler
	Caption	Message		
	Mnemonic	M		
JButton	Name	clearButton	ClearButtonHandler	chandler
	Caption	Clear		
	Mnemonic	C		
JButton	Name	exitButton	ExitButtonHandler	ehandler
	Caption	Exit		
	Mnemonic	x		

```java
   // inner classes for the button event handlers
class MessageButtonHandler implements ActionListener
{
  public void actionPerformed(ActionEvent e)
  {
    JOptionPane.showMessageDialog(null, "Message Button was Clicked",
     "Event Handler Message",JOptionPane.INFORMATION_MESSAGE);
  }
}  // end of inner class

class ClearButtonHandler implements ActionListener
{
  public void actionPerformed(ActionEvent e)
  {
    JOptionPane.showMessageDialog(null, "Clear Button was Clicked",
     "Event Handler Message",JOptionPane.INFORMATION_MESSAGE);
  }
}  // end of inner class

class ExitButtonHandler implements ActionListener
{
  public void actionPerformed(ActionEvent e)
  {
    System.exit(0);
  }
}  // end of inner class
```

Once this code is included in Program 13.1, all that remains is to instantiate and register each event handler (steps 2 and 3 of phase 2). The following statements, which would be placed before the `mainFrame.show();` in Program 13.1, accomplish this:

```
// create and register the button event handlers
MessageButtonHandler mhandler = new MessageButtonHandler();  // instantiate a handler
messageButton.addActionListener(mhandler);  // register the handler

ClearButtonHandler chandler = new ClearButtonHandler();  // instantiate a handler
clearButton.addActionListener(chandler);  // register the handler

ExitButtonHandler ehandler = new ExitButtonHandler();  // instantiate a handler
exitButton.addActionListener(ehandler);  // register the handler
```

In creating our three button event handlers, we have followed the current Java convention of providing each atomic component with its individual event handler. An alternative, which you will encounter in your programming work, is to use a single-button handler class for all buttons in a GUI, in which the event handler determines which button was clicked. Then, depending on the selected button, appropriate processing is performed. Using this approach, the following single-button handler class, which we have named `ButtonsHandler`, can replace the three previously presented individual classes:

```
    // inner class for the button event handler
class ButtonsHandler implements ActionListener
{
  public void actionPerformed(ActionEvent e)
  {
    if (e.getSource() == messageButton)
      JOptionPane.showMessageDialog(null, "Message Button was Clicked",
        "Event Handler Message",JOptionPane.INFORMATION_MESSAGE);
    else if (e.getSource() == clearButton)
      JOptionPane.showMessageDialog(null, "Clear Button was Clicked",
        "Event Handler Message",JOptionPane.INFORMATION_MESSAGE);
    else if (e.getSource() == exitButton)
      System.exit(0);
  }
} // end of inner class
```

This single-listener class approach has the advantage of centralizing all button event handling. In reviewing this class, notice that a `getSource()` method determines which button was actually clicked. Here the argument that we have named e, which is passed into the method, provides the source of the `ActionEvent` that triggered the event handler. Using the `getSource()` method permits us to specifically identify this source as one of the three buttons. Once the button that triggered the event has been identified, the code provides the appropriate processing.

As with all event processing code, it still remains to instantiate and register an event-handling object. Here we need only instantiate the single-button event handler and then register the same object for each of the three buttons. The following code can be used:

```
                // create and register a single button event handler
ButtonsHandler bhandler = new ButtonsHandler();  // instantiate a handler
messageButton.addActionListener(bhandler);  // register the handler
clearButton.addActionListener(bhandler);      // register the handler
exitButton.addActionListener(bhandler);    // register the handler
```

Figure 13.2 shows the message boxes that are displayed when either forms of the event handlers we have presented are incorporated into Program 13.1 (which we leave for Exercises 2 and 3). Clicking the Exit button closes the application in the same manner as clicking the window's Close button.

Event Handler Message [×]	**Event Handler Message** [×]
(i) **Message Button was Clicked**	(i) **Clear Button was Clicked**
[OK]	[OK]

(a) The Message Button Display   (b) The Clear Button Display

FIGURE 13.2   Message Boxes Displayed by the Button Event Handlers

In the next section, we will complete Program 13.1 by adding a text display area and appropriate event handler for this new component. Before doing so, however, we can use Program 13.1 to introduce two important concepts connected with any GUI: keyboard focus and tab sequence.

Keyboard Focus and Tab Control

When an application is run and a user is looking at the container, only one of the container's controls will have **keyboard focus**, or the focus for short. The control with the focus is the object that will be affected by pressing a key or clicking the mouse. For example, when a button has the focus, its caption will be surrounded by either a solid or dotted rectangle (Figure 13.3). Similarly, when a text area has the focus, a solid cursor appears, indicating that the user can type data.

An object can only receive keyboard focus if it is capable of responding to user input through either the keyboard or mouse. Thus, such controls as labels and lines can never receive the focus. To get the focus, a visible control must be enabled. By enabling a visible object, you permit it to respond to user-generated events, such as pressing a key or clicking a mouse. As the default setting for a component is that it is enabled, you do not usually have to be concerned with this setting unless you want to disable it explicitly. A component capable of receiving focus, such as a button, can get the focus in one of four ways:

FIGURE 13.3   A Button With and Without Focus

1. A user clicks the mouse directly on the object.
2. A user presses the Tab key until the object gets the focus.
3. A user presses the accessor key for the object.
4. The code activates the focus.

To see how the first three methods operate, compile and execute Program 13.1. Once the program is executing, click any of the buttons. As you do, notice how the focus shifts. Now press the Tab key a few times and see how the focus shifts from component to component. Do the same pressing the accelerator key for each button. The sequence in which the focus shifts from component to component as the Tab key is pressed is called the **tab sequence.** This sequence is initially determined by the order in which components are placed on the container, but it can be explicitly modified using program code. For our specific example, focus shifts from the <u>M</u>essage button to the <u>C</u>lear button to the E<u>x</u>it button and then back again to the <u>M</u>essage button.

The default tab order obtained as a result of placing components on the container can be altered by invoking the setNextFocusableComponent() method. For example, the sequence of statements

```
messageButton.setNextFocusableComponent(exitButton);
exitButton.setNextFocusableComponent(clearButton);
clearButton.setNextFocusableComponent(messageButton);
```

would alter the focus sequence from the <u>M</u>essage button to the E<u>x</u>it button to the <u>C</u>lear button and then back to the <u>M</u>essage button. To explicitly set the first component that receives focus, you must either detect when the window itself gets the focus or use a focus listener to force the focus to switch when the first component receives focus. How to do this is presented at the end of Section 13.3.

EXERCISES 13.1

1. Enter, compile, and execute Program 13.1 on your computer.
2. Modify Program 13.1 to include the three individual listener classes presented in this section. Compile and execute your program to verify that it operates correctly.
3. Modify Program 13.1 to include the single listener class presented in this section. Compile and execute your program to verify that it operates correctly.
4. How is an accelerator key created for a JButton component?
5. What are the four ways that an atomic component can receive focus?
6. a. Write a Java program that creates a GUI having the following properties table:

Object	Property	Setting
JFrame	Name	mainFrame
	Caption	Messages
	Layout	FlowLayout
JButton	Name	cmdGood
	Caption	Good
	Mnemonic	G
JButton	Name	cmdBad
	Caption	Bad
	Mnemonic	B

    b. Add individual event handlers to the program written for Exercise 6a so that when a user clicks the <u>G</u>ood button, the message `Today is a good day!` appears in a dialog box, and when the <u>B</u>ad button is clicked, the message `I'm having a bad day today!` is displayed.

7. Write a Java application having three buttons. Clicking the first button should produce the message `See no evil`, clicking the second button should produce the message `Hear no evil`, and clicking the third button should produce the message `Speak no evil` in the text box.

8. Create a graphical interface that contains four buttons and two text fields. The names of these components should be `butOne`, `butTwo`, `butThree`, and `butFour`. These components should be added into a JFrame content pane in the order `butThree`, `butOne`, `butTwo`, and `butFour`. Using code, set the tab sequence so that tab control goes from `butThree` to `butFour` to `butTwo` to `butOne`.

13.2 TEXT COMPONENTS FOR DISPLAY

The three swing-provided text entry and display components are text fields, password fields, and text areas. Objects of these types are constructed from JTextField, JPassword-Field, and JTextArea component types. We consider each of these components in this section, with particular attention on the JTextField component.

Adding a JTextField Component

A JTextField component can be used for both entering data and displaying results on a single line. In our current application, we will add a JTextField component for displaying a message when the messageButton in Program 13.1 is clicked. The object instantiated from a JTextField component is referred to as a **text field.**

    Placing and activating a text field on a container are accomplished using the same two-phase procedure that we have used throughout this and the previous chapter—that is, by first instantiating and adding the text field object into a container and then by instantiating and registering an appropriate event handler. The statements that we will use for the first phase, which is instantiating and adding a text field to the container in Program 13.1, are:

```
private JTextField tField; // declare a class variable
tField = new JTextField("Hello World!"); // instantiate an object
c.add(tField,BorderLayout.NORTH);   // add the object to the container
```

    Except for the second statement

```
tField = new JTextField("Hello World!"); // instantiate an object
```

which is used to instantiate a new JTextField object, the first and third statements should be familiar. These statements are similar to those that were used in Section 13.1 to add the three buttons into the GUI in Figure 13.1. The second statement uses one of four possible constructors for instantiating a JTextField object. The four available constructors are:

```
JTextField(initial displayed string)
JTextField(initial displayed string, integer text field size)
JTextField(integer text field size)
JTextField()
```

When an initial string is included in the constructor, the string is displayed when the text field is visible. Similarly, when an integer field size is provided, it specifies a scale factor for determining the width of the field. The actual size of the field is internally determined by multiplying the integer argument by the width, in pixels, of the average character for the current text field's font. If the field size is not large enough to accommodate a displayed string, only the portion of the string that can fit in the specified size is displayed. The remaining part of the string can then be seen by scrolling throughout the field.

Program 13.2 includes the three statements for adding a text field into our GUI within the context of a complete program. For convenience, these three statements have been boldfaced. Also notice that we have used the default BorderLayout manager for placement of each component. Because we have placed the text field in the north, or topmost, position, the width of the field is determined by the width of the JFrame container. In this configuration, any size provided for the text field in its constructor is ignored by the layout manager.

PROGRAM 13.2

```java
import javax.swing.*;
import java.awt.event.*;
import java.awt.Container;  // need this to add controls
import java.awt.*;  // need this for layout manager
public class TextGuiOne extends JFrame
{
  private JFrame mainFrame;
  private JButton messageButton;
  private JButton clearButton;
  private JButton exitButton;
  private JTextField tField;

  public TextGuiOne() // a constructor
  {
    mainFrame = new JFrame("The Hello Application - Ver.2.0");

      // create all components
    messageButton = new JButton("Message");
    clearButton = new JButton("Clear");
    exitButton = new JButton("Exit");
    tField = new JTextField("Hello World!");

      // get the content pane
    Container c = mainFrame.getContentPane();
```

(Continued on next page)

(Continued from previous page)

```
          // add the components to the ContentPane
      c.add(tField,BorderLayout.NORTH);
      c.add(messageButton,BorderLayout.WEST);
      c.add(clearButton,BorderLayout.CENTER);
      c.add(exitButton,BorderLayout.EAST);


        // create accelerator keys
      messageButton.setMnemonic('M');
      clearButton.setMnemonic('C');
      exitButton.setMnemonic('x');


      mainFrame.setSize(300,150);


        // define and register window event handler
      mainFrame.addWindowListener(new WindowAdapter()
      {
        public void windowClosing(WindowEvent e) {System.exit(0);}
      });


        mainFrame.show();
    }

    public static void main(String args[])
    {
      new TextGuiOne();  // instantiate a GUI object
    }

}  // end of class
```

In reviewing Program 13.2, notice that, in the `main()` method, we have instantiated a `TextGuiOne` object without specifically declaring a `TextGuiOne` reference variable. This can be done because we have no later need within the method to access the GUI object by name. The GUI displayed when Program 13.2 is compiled and executed is shown in Figure 13.4.

At this point, we have assembled all of the components required for our application. Properties Table 13.5 provides a summary of the initial property settings for each

FIGURE 13.4   The GUI Displayed by Program 13.2

TABLE 13.5   Program 13.2's Initial Property Settings

Object	Property	Setting
JFrame	Name	mainFrame
	Caption	The Hello Application—Ver. 2.0
JButton	Name	messageButton
	Caption	Message
	Mnemonic	M
JButton	Name	clearButton
	Caption	Clear
	Mnemonic	C
JButton	Name	exitButton
	Caption	Exit
	Mnemonic	x
JTextField	Name	tField
	Text	Hello World!

component. Thus, within the context of a complete program development, we have completed the first phase in our two-phase process for each component that we want added into our JFrame-based GUI, which is

> *Phase 1: Construct the component so that it appears visually.*
> *Step 1: Instantiate a specific component.*
> *Step 2: Add the component to the JFrame's content pane.*

All that remains is to add the event-handling code so that each button performs its designated task when it is clicked.

Adding Event Handlers

Now that the physical appearance of our GUI is set (The Hello Application—Ver. 2.0 in Figure 13.4), we still need to supply the three buttons with event code. Because the text field is only for display purposes in response to clicking either the <u>M</u>essage or <u>C</u>lear button, this component will have no associated event code. Thus, we will initially create three mouse click event objects, each of which will be activated by clicking one of the three buttons. Two of these event procedures will change the text displayed in the text box, and the last will exit the program.

The listener classes for our button events are:

```
class MessageButtonHandler implements ActionListener
{
  public void actionPerformed(ActionEvent e)
  {
    tField.setText("Hello World Once Again!");
  }
}  // end of inner class

class ClearButtonHandler implements ActionListener
{
```

```
  public void actionPerformed(ActionEvent e)
  {
    tField.setText("");
  }
}  // end of inner class


class ExitButtonHandler implements ActionListener
{
  public void actionPerformed(ActionEvent e)
  {
    System.exit(0);
  }
}  // end of inner class
```

These event classes are fairly straightforward. The simplest of the three listener classes is the last one, which closes the application when the Exit button is clicked. This last event code thus operates exactly the same as the event code that closes the application when the window's Close button is clicked.

Both the code for the Message and Clear buttons use a setText() method to set the text into the text field. Specifically, the statement tField.setText("Hello World Once Again!"); is executed when the Message button is clicked. Notice that this statement changes a property of one object, the text displayed in a text field, using an event associated with another object, a button. Similarly, the statement tField.setText(""); forces display of an empty string when the Clear button is activated. An **empty string** is defined as a string with no characters. Setting the text displayed in the text field to this string value has the effect of clearing the text field of all text. Note that a value such as " ", which consists of one or more blank spaces, would also clear the text field. A string with one or more blank spaces, however, is not an empty string, which is defined as a string having *no* characters. Program 13.3 contains this event code, which is boldfaced for easier identification, within the context of a complete program. Also included in the program are the required statements to instantiate and register the three event handlers, which have also been boldfaced.

In reviewing Program 13.3, locate the inner listener classes, the statements that instantiate each listener object from these classes, and the listener object registration statements. When Program 13.3 is compiled and executed, the GUI in Figure 13.5 is displayed.

Notice that when the program is first run, focus is on the text field, which is indicated by the cursor at the start of the field. Focus is on this component because it was the first component added to the container. The initial string in this field was placed there by the constructor that was used to instantiate the field from the JTextField class.

FIGURE 13.5 The GUI Displayed by Program 13.3

PROGRAM 13.3

```java
import javax.swing.*;
import java.awt.event.*;
import java.awt.Container;  // need this to add controls
import java.awt.*;  // need this for layout manager
public class TextGuiTwo extends JFrame
{
  private JFrame mainFrame;
  private JButton messageButton;
  private JButton clearButton;
  private JButton exitButton;
  private JTextField tField;

  public TextGuiTwo() // a constructor
  {
    mainFrame = new JFrame("The Hello Application - Ver. 3.0");

      // create all components
    messageButton = new JButton("Message");
    clearButton = new JButton("Clear");
    exitButton = new JButton("Exit");
    tField = new JTextField("Hello World!");

      // get the content pane
    Container c = mainFrame.getContentPane();

      // add the components to the ContentPane
    c.add(tField,BorderLayout.NORTH);
    c.add(messageButton,BorderLayout.WEST);
    c.add(clearButton,BorderLayout.CENTER);
    c.add(exitButton,BorderLayout.EAST);

      // create accelerator keys
    messageButton.setMnemonic('M');
    clearButton.setMnemonic('C');
    exitButton.setMnemonic('x');

    mainFrame.setSize(300,150);

      // define and register window event handler
    mainFrame.addWindowListener(new WindowAdapter()
    {
      public void windowClosing(WindowEvent e) {System.exit(0);}
    });
```

(Continued on next page)

(Continued from previous page)

```
      // create and register the button event handlers
   MessageButtonHandler mhandler = new MessageButtonHandler(); // instantiate a handler
   messageButton.addActionListener(mhandler);  // register the handler

   ClearButtonHandler chandler = new ClearButtonHandler();  // instantiate a handler
   clearButton.addActionListener(chandler);  // register the handler

   ExitButtonHandler ehandler = new ExitButtonHandler();  // instantiate a handler
   exitButton.addActionListener(ehandler);  // register the handler

   mainFrame.show();
 }


    // inner classes for the button event handlers
 class MessageButtonHandler implements ActionListener
 {
   public void actionPerformed(ActionEvent e)
   {
     tField.setText("Hello World Once Again!");
   }
 }  // end of inner class

 class ClearButtonHandler implements ActionListener
 {
   public void actionPerformed(ActionEvent e)
   {
     tField.setText("");
   }
 }  // end of inner class

 class ExitButtonHandler implements ActionListener
 {
   public void actionPerformed(ActionEvent e)
   {
     System.exit(0);
   }
 }  // end of inner class

 public static void main(String args[])
 {
   new TextGuiTwo();  // instantiate a GUI object
 }

}  // end of class
```

Now click the Message button. Doing so will trigger this button's button click event handler and display the message shown in Figure 13.6.

F I G U R E   1 3 . 6   The GUI After the Message Button Is Clicked

Clicking the Clear button invokes the `chandler` event object, which clears the text field, and clicking the Exit button invokes the `ehandler()` listener object. This object terminates program execution.

Before leaving Program 13.3, one additional comment should be mentioned. Because we have constructed the program essentially to use the text field for output display purposes, we will explicitly alter the operation of the text field so that a user cannot enter data into the field. We do this with a `setEditable()` method. For example, the statement

```
tField.setEditable(false);  // don't allow user input
```

makes the `tField` component unavailable for user input. This statement can be placed anywhere following the instantiation of the `tField` reference variable and before the statement that adds `tField` into the content pane. If this is done, the uneditable test field will be shown with a default gray background in place of the default white background (Figure 13.6).

A JPasswordField component works in exactly the same manner as a JTextField with one exception. The exception is that each character sent to a JPasswordField, either because it is being entered at the keyboard or being sent under program control, will be displayed as a single asterisk, *. Data retrieved from a JPasswordField, however, are in a string format, exactly as if they were entered into a JTextField; it is only the display that disguises the actual data.

Setting Font and Color

In addition to the `setText()` and `setEditable()` methods presented in this section, there are a number of other very useful JComponent methods that can be used in conjunction with a text field. In addition, a number of these methods have a wider applicability and can be used with other swing-based components. Table 13. 6 lists these methods, including the two we have already encountered.

Font

In setting a component's font for its displayed text, such as a button's caption, a label's text, or the text presented within a text field, the `setFont()` method is used. This method uses a `Font` argument that is formally specified using a typeface, style, and point size. The desired typeface must be enclosed in double quotes, such as `"Arial"`, `"TimesRoman"`, or `"Courier"`. If you select a specific typeface that is not installed on the

TABLE 13.6 Common Set Methods

Method	Description	Example
object.setText(*string*)	Places the string into the designated object.	tField.setText("This is a test");
object.setEditable(boolean)	Enables or disables a text component for input.	tField.setEditable(false);
object.setFont(Font);	Sets font as to typeface, style, and point size.	tField.setFont(newFont("arial",Font.BOLD,10));
object.setEnable(boolean)	Enables or disables a component.	mButton.setEnable(false);
object.setForeground(color)	Sets a component's foreground color.	mButton.setForeground(red);
object.setBackground(color)	Sets a component's background color.	mButton.setBackground(gray);

computer executing the program, a substitute default font will be used. In addition, a generic typeface, such as "Serif", "MonoSpaced", or "SansSerif" can also be specified. Here Java will substitute a default, which is usually Times Roman for the serif font, Courier for the monospaced font, and either Helvetica or Arial for the sans-serif font.

For selecting a style, one or more of three symbolic constants are typically used. These constants, which are named Font.PLAIN, Font.BOLD, and Font.ITALIC, designate either a plain, bold, or italic presentation, respectively. In addition, the expression Font.BOLD + Font.ITALIC will yield a boldface and italic text style. The point size must be an integer value that sets the point size of the displayed type (there are 72 points in an inch). For example, the statement

```
tField.setFont(new Font("Courier", Font.BOLD, 12));
```

will set the text in the tField component to be displayed as 12-point Courier bold. It should be noted that the previous statement setting the font can be written in a number of other ways, including the following:

```
Font myFont = new Font("Courier", Font.BOLD, 12);
tField.setFont(myFont);
```

Regardless of the statements that set the font, a repaint() method must be used to apply the new font to text currently displayed in a component. For example, if we wish to have a newly set font applied to text currently displayed by a component named tField, the statement tField.repaint() should be used.

Color
The last two methods listed in Table 13.6 permit specification of a component's foreground and background colors. The foreground color determines the color of any displayed text or graphics, and the background color determines the color of the background. For example, the foreground color of this page is black, and its background color is white.

The vast majority of color monitors are of the RGB type, which means that they create their colors from combinations of red, green, and blue. Every color presented on the screen is defined by using three separate numbers: one for red, one for green, and one for blue. Individually, the red, green, and blue components of a color are represented by an integer number between 0 and 255. Table 13.7 lists the red, green, and blue content of a number of commonly used colors.

Although the color values in Table 13.7 specify the relative intensity of red, green, and blue in the final color, the actual displayed color depends on the color monitor. The `Color` class, which is provided as part of the `java.awt` package, provides a number of methods for both selecting and setting desired foreground and background colors. To get a clear understanding of the color codes, you can use the `Color()` method, which permits setting the color code by individually specifying the red, blue, and green content of the desired final color. The format of this method is:[2]

```
Color(red, green, blue)
```

where:

> *red* is an integer number in the range 0 to 255 that represents the color's red component
> *green* is an integer number in the range 0 to 255 that represents the color's green component
> *blue* is an integer number in the range 0 to 255 that represents the color's blue component

For example, the statements

```
Color myColor;
myColor = new Color(255,255,0);
```

or the single-line equivalent statement

```
Color myColor = new Color(255,255,0);
```

specifies that the variable `myColor` designates the color yellow (see Table 13.7). Using a value less than 0 or greater that 255 for a color component results in a compiler error message.

In addition to individually specifying the red, green, and blue content of a color, the `Color` class provides the symbolic color constants listed in Table 13.8 (see Table 13.7 for the individual red, green, and blue components provided by each of these constants).

For example, using the `magenta` constant, the statement

```
Color someColor = Color.magenta;
```

can replace the statement

```
Color someColor = new Color(255, 0, 255);
```

---

[2]Another form of this method is `Color(float red, float green, float blue)`, where each color component is represented as a floating-point value between 0.0f and 0.1f. The f suffix is required because, in its absence, the compiler will interpret the values as double-precision numbers.

TABLE 13.7   RGB Color Values

Color	Red Content	Green Content	Blue Content
Black	0	0	0
Blue	0	0	255
Cyan	0	255	255
Dark Gray	64	64	64
Gray	128	128	128
Green	0	255	0
Light Gray	192	192	192
Magenta	255	0	255
Orange	255	200	0
Pink	255	175	175
Red	255	0	0
Yellow	255	255	0
White	255	255	255

Once you have determined your desired colors, the `setForeground()` and `setBackground()` methods (see Table 13.6) can set the foreground and background colors, respectively, of any GUI component, including the content pane itself. For example, if c is the object name of the JFrame content pane, each of the following statements

```
c.setBackground(Color.blue);
c.setBackground(new Color(0, 0, 255)
```

sets the background color of the content pane to blue. Similarly, either of the following statements sets the foreground color to red:

```
c.setForeground(Color.red);
c.setForeground(new Color(255, 0, 0)
```

Because the first form of each of these statements clearly designates the color, it is the preferred statement. You should only use the second form whenever you are using a color that is not listed in Table 13.8, and then you should document what the intended color is, either as a comment or in a declaration statement with an identifier name that corresponds to the selected color. In like manner, both the foreground and background colors of any component can be specified. All that is required is that the appropriate `set()` method is prefixed with the name of the desired component.

JTextArea Components

For GUI output that requires a single displayed line, a JTextField component is the Swing component of choice. There are times, however, where you will need to display more than one line of text. For these situations, an object constructed from the JTextArea class can be used. In addition, as we will see in the next section, JTextField, JPasswordField, and JTextArea components can also be used for input.[3]

---

[3]However, as noted earlier, the JPasswordField component will display an asterisk for each entered character.

TABLE 13.8   Color Constants

Class	Constant	Color
Color	static final black	black
Color	static final blue	blue
Color	static final cyan	cyan
Color	static final darkGray	dark gray
Color	static final gray	gray
Color	static final green	green
Color	static final lightGray	light gray
Color	static final magenta	magenta
Color	static final orange	orange
Color	static final pink	pink
Color	static final red	red
Color	static final white	white
Color	static final yellow	yellow

A JTextArea component is constructed in almost the same manner as a JTextField, but the JTextArea constructor requires two arguments: one to indicate the number of rows for the text area and one to indicate the number of columns. For example, the expression new JTextArea(10,30) will create a text area that consists of 10 rows and 30 columns.

Once a text area is instantiated, text can be displayed in it using an append() method. For example, if we have already constructed a JTextArea component named outArea, the statement outArea.append("This is a test"); will display the string argument in the text area. Each additional append() invocation adds text to the end of the string already displayed. For example, the code

```
outArea.setFont(new Font("Courier", Font.PLAIN, 10));    // set the font
for (num = 1; num < 11; num++)
  outArea.append("The number is now" + num + '\n');
```

first sets the display font to Courier and then causes the following display in the text area object named outArea:

```
The number is now 1
The number is now 2
The number is now 3
The number is now 4
The number is now 5
The number is now 6
The number is now 7
The number is now 8
The number is now 9
The number is now 10
```

Notice that to produce this display we have placed a newline escape sequence within the argument passed to append(). This escape sequence is very common and almost always necessary when using a text area for display purposes. If either the row or column size specified for a text area is too small to accommodate the displayed string, the appropriate specification is ignored and the text area is automatically expanded to accommodate the output string.

Program 13.4 uses a text area to display a table of 10 numbers, including their squares and cubes. The actual code for creating a table is contained in the class method named createTable(). Except for the use of an append() method rather than a print() method, this code is almost identical to Program 5.10, and it is instructive to compare these two programs. For convenience, the three statements that create the text area object have been boldfaced in Program 13.4. These boldfaced statements should be extremely familiar because they are the same types of statements that have created all of our swing-based GUI components.

PROGRAM 13.4

```java
import javax.swing.*;
import java.awt.event.*;
import java.awt.Container;  // need this to add controls
import java.awt.*;   // need this for layout manager
import java.text.*;  // need this for formatting
public class ShowTextArea extends JFrame
{
  private JFrame mainFrame;
  private JTextArea outArea;

  public ShowTextArea() // a constructor
  {
    mainFrame = new JFrame("Example of a Text Area for Output");

      // create all components
    outArea = new JTextArea(10, 28);

      // get the content pane
    Container c = mainFrame.getContentPane();
    c.setLayout(new FlowLayout());

      // add the components to the ContentPane
    c.add(outArea);

    mainFrame.setSize(300,250);

      // define and register window event handler
    mainFrame.addWindowListener(new WindowAdapter()
```

(Continued on next page)

```
(Continued from previous page)
    {
       public void windowClosing(WindowEvent e) {System.exit(0);}
    });

    mainFrame.show();
}

public void createTable()
{
  int num;
  DecimalFormat df = new DecimalFormat("0000");

  outArea.setFont(new Font("Courier", Font.BOLD, 10));
  outArea.append("  NUMBER     SQUARE     CUBE\n");
  outArea.append("  ------     ------     ----\n");

  outArea.setFont(new Font("Courier", Font.PLAIN, 10));
  for (num = 1; num < 11; num++)
  {
    outArea.append("    " + df.format(num));
    outArea.append("       " + df.format(num*num));
    outArea.append("      " + df.format(num * num * num) +'\n');
  }

  return;
}

public static void main(String args[])
{

  ShowTextArea app;  // declare an object of type ShowTextArea
  app = new ShowTextArea();  // instantiate a GUI object

  app.createTable();
}

} // end of class
```

After reviewing how a text area is constructed, you should notice the use of the `append()` method for displaying text within the text area object. Finally, pay particular attention to the invocation of the `createTable()` method within the `main()` method. Because `createTable()` is a nonconstructor class method, it must be invoked with a specific class object for it to operate on. The output created when Program 13.4 is executed is shown in Figure 13.7.

FIGURE 13.7   The GUI Produced by Program 13.4

EXERCISES 13.2

1. Compile and execute Program 13.3 on your computer.

2. Create a graphical interface that contains two buttons and two text fields. The names of these components should be butOne, butTwo, txtFirst, and txtSecond. These components should be added into a JFrame content pane in the order txtFirst, butOne, butTwo, and txtSecond. Using code, set the tab sequence so that tab control goes from txtFirst to txtSecond to butTwo to butOne.

3. a. Write a Java program that creates a GUI having the following properties table:

Object	Property	Setting
JFrame	Name	mainFrame
	Caption	Messages
	Layout	FlowLayout
JButton	Name	cmdGood
	Caption	Good
	Mnemonic	G
JButton	Name	cmdBad
	Caption	Bad
	Mnemonic	B
JTextField	Name	txtMessage
	Text	(none)

   b. Add individual event handlers to the program written for Exercise 3a so that when a user clicks the Good button, the message Today is a good day! appears in the text field, and when the Bad button is clicked, the message I'm having a bad day today! is displayed in the text field.

4. Write a Java application having three buttons and a text field. Clicking the first button should produce the message See no evil in the text field, clicking the second button should produce the message Hear no evil, and clicking the third button should produce the message Speak no evil in the text field.

5. a. Create a text field component that has a red foreground color and a blue background color. The initial text displayed in the field should be Welcome to Java.

   b. Add a text field component to the GUI created for Exercise 5a that has a white foreground color and a red background color. The initial text displayed in the field should be `Object-oriented language`.

6. Write, compile, and execute a Java program than contains a text field and three buttons. The text field should initially contain the text `This is a test`. When the first button is clicked, the text in the text field should change to Helvetica font, when the second button is clicked, the text should change to Garamond font (if your system does not have Garamond, select a font that you do have), and when the third button is clicked, the text should change to Courier font.

7. a. Write a Java program that creates a GUI having the following properties table:

Object	Property	Setting
JFrame	Name	mainFrame
	Caption	TypeFace Example
	Layout	FlowLayout
JButton	Name	cmdBold
	Caption	Bold
	Mnemonic	B
JButton	Name	cmdItalic
	Caption	Italic
	Mnemonic	I
JTextField	Name	txtMessage
	Text	This is a test

   By clicking the text field, the user should be able to enter any desired text in nonboldface and nonitalic font. When the user clicks the Bold button, the text in the text field should change to boldface, and when the user clicks the Italic button, the text should change to italic.

   b. From a user's viewpoint, what is the problem with the program as it is written?

8. Add two more buttons to the program written for Exercise 7a. One of the additional buttons, when clicked, should change the text displayed in the text field to a nonbold state. When the second button is clicked, the text should be displayed in nonitalic state. (*Tip:* See Exercise 6.)

9. Compile and execute Program 13.4 on your computer.

10. Modify Program 13.4's JTextArea to be 5 rows by 10 columns and verify that the program ignores both dimensions when it is executed.

11. Add three command buttons to Program 13.4. Clicking the first button should produce the table shown in Figure 13.7, clicking the second button should clear the text area, and clicking the third button should cause the program to close. (*Tip:* Move the code in the current `createTable()` to the first button's event handler class.)

13.3 TEXT COMPONENTS FOR DATA ENTRY

Although we have only used a JTextField component for output, it is also the most versatile and common atomic component for interactive user input. This control permits the user to enter a string at the terminal, which can easily be retrieved and processed.

TABLE 13.9 Program 13.5's Properties Table

Object	Property	Setting	Listener Class	Listener Object
JFrame	Name	mainFrame	anonymous	
	Caption	Temperature Conversion		
	Layout manager	FlowLayout		
JLabel	Name	fahrLabel		
	Caption	Enter a Fahrenheit temperature:		
JLabel	Name	celsLabel		
	Caption	The corresponding Celsius value is:		
JTextField	Name	fahrField		
	Size	5		
JTextField	Name	celsField		
	Size	5		
JButton	Name	convertButton	`ConvertButtonHandler`	chandler
	Caption	Convert		
	Mnemonic	C		
JButton	Name	exitButton	`ExitButtonHandler`	ehandler
	Caption	Exit		
	Mnemonic	x		

When used for input, a JTextField component is almost always used in conjunction with a label control, where the label provides a prompt and the text field provides the actual means for the user to input data. For example, consider the properties table for Program 13.5, which is listed in Table 13.9. The GUI corresponding to this table is shown in Figure 13.8. In the GUI shown in the figure, the label is `Enter a Fahrenheit temperature:` and the corresponding text field provides an input area for the user to enter data.

Label objects are constructed from JLabel atomic components, and a label is created in the same manner as in constructing buttons and text fields. For example, the first label in Figure 13.8 was constructed using the following statements, which are the same type of statements that have added atomic components to all of the GUIs illustrated in this and the previous chapter:

```
private JLabel fahrLabel;   // declare a class variable
fahrLabel = new JLabel("Enter a Fahrenheit temperature:"); //instantiate an object
c.add(fahrLabel); // add the object to the content pane
```

The `fahrField` text field listed in Table 13.9 will be used for data input while the program is executing. All data entered into a text field are assumed by Java to be string data. This means that if numbers are to be input, the entered string must be explicitly converted to numerical data. It also means that some data validation is typically required to ensure that a user does not enter data that will cause the application to crash.

FIGURE 13.8   The User Interface Corresponding to Table 13.9

Consider again the interface in Figure 13.8 where the user is prompted to enter a temperature in degrees Fahrenheit. Once a user enters a Fahrenheit temperature, the program will compute the corresponding temperature in degrees Celsius and display the calculated value in the second text field.

Now consider Program 13.5, which implements the GUI defined by Properties Table 13.9, paying particular attention to the `ConvertButtonHandler` listener class code, which has been boldfaced for easier identification.

The actual calculation and display of a Celsius temperature are performed whenever the Convert button is activated. This conversion is accomplished using the three statements

```
instring = fahrField.getText();  // read the input value
invalue = Double.parseDouble(instring);  // convert to a double
outvalue = 5.0/9.0 * (invalue - 32.0);
```

which is followed by a call to a `setText()` method to display the calculated result.

Notice that a `getText()` method retrieves the string contained in the `fahrField` text field. The `getText()` method is the input equivalent to the `setText()` method, which sends a string to a text field. Here the retrieved string is stored into the `instring` string. In the next statement, this string value is converted to a double-precision number by passing the string as an argument to the `ParseDouble()` method if necessary (review Section 3.3 for an explanation of this method). Finally, the third statement converts the input value into an equivalent Celsius temperature. Figure 13.9 illustrates a sample run of Program 13.5.

Before leaving Program 13.5, we point out a number of minor but important problems that can occur with it. These problems will be corrected at the end of this section and Section 13.5. First, reconsider the conversion statement

```
invalue = Double.parseDouble(instring);
```

This statement operates correctly when a user enters any string that can be considered as a number, such as 212 or 187.45. If a user inadvertently types in a string such as 212a,

FIGURE 13.9   A Sample Run of Program 13.5

PROGRAM 13.5

```java
import java.text.*;  // need this for formatting
import javax.swing.*;
import java.awt.event.*;
import java.awt.Container;  // need this to add controls
import java.awt.*;  // need this for layout manager

public class ConvertTempOne extends JFrame
{
  private JFrame mainFrame;
  private JButton convertButton;
  private JButton exitButton;
  private JTextField fahrField;
  private JTextField celsField;
  private JLabel fahrLabel;
  private JLabel celsLabel;

  public ConvertTempOne() // a constructor
  {
    mainFrame = new JFrame("Temperature Conversion");

      // create all components
    convertButton = new JButton("Convert to Celsius");
    exitButton = new JButton("Exit");
    fahrLabel = new JLabel("Enter a Fahrenheit temperature:");
    celsLabel = new JLabel("The corresponding Celsius value is:");
    fahrField = new JTextField(5);
    celsField = new JTextField(5);

      // get the content pane
    Container c = mainFrame.getContentPane();
      // set the layout manager
    c.setLayout(new FlowLayout());

      // add the components to the ContentPane
    c.add(fahrLabel);
    c.add(fahrField);
    c.add(celsLabel);
    c.add(celsField);
    c.add(convertButton);
    c.add(exitButton);

      // create accelerator keys
    convertButton.setMnemonic('C');
    exitButton.setMnemonic('x');

    mainFrame.setSize(350,150);
```

(Continued on next page)

(Continued from previous page)

```
        // define and register window event handler
    mainFrame.addWindowListener(new WindowAdapter()
    {
      public void windowClosing(WindowEvent e) {System.exit(0);}
    });

      // create and register the button event handlers
    ConvertButtonHandler chandler = new ConvertButtonHandler();  // instantiate a handler
    convertButton.addActionListener(chandler);  // register the handler

    ExitButtonHandler ehandler = new ExitButtonHandler();  // instantiate a handler
    exitButton.addActionListener(ehandler);  // register the handler

    mainFrame.show();
  }

    // inner classes for the button event handlers
  class ConvertButtonHandler implements ActionListener
  {
    public void actionPerformed(ActionEvent e)
    {
      DecimalFormat num = new DecimalFormat(",###.##");
      String instring;
      double invalue, outvalue;

      instring = fahrField.getText();  // read the input value
      invalue = Double.parseDouble(instring);  // convert to a double
      outvalue = 5.0/9.0 * (invalue - 32.0);
      celsField.setText(num.format(outvalue));
    }
  }  // end of inner class

  class ExitButtonHandler implements ActionListener
  {
    public void actionPerformed(ActionEvent e)
    {
      System.exit(0);
    }
  }  // end of inner class

  public static void main(String args[])
  {
    new ConvertTempOne();  // instantiate a GUI object
  }
}  // end of class
```

TABLE 13.10 Required `FocusListener` Event Methods

Method	Description
`public void focusGained(FocusEvent e)`	This method is triggered when a component receives keyboard focus.
`public void focusLost(FocusEvent e)`	This method is triggered when a component loses keyboard focus.

however, the program will crash. This is because the `ParseDouble()` method is not equipped to handle invalid numerical characters. In addition, `parseDouble()` is not equipped to convert an empty string, which is produced whenever the user clicks the Convert button without first entering any data into the input text field. To handle this latter problem, we can check for an empty string before performing the conversion calculation. The detection of invalid characters, however, is typically handled by inspecting each key as it is pressed. A data-input validation technique that accomplishes this using keyboard event handling is presented in Section 13.5.

A second set of problems is that, due to the event driven nature of the program, a user could inadvertently attempt to enter a Celsius rather than a Fahrenheit temperature. Similarly, after having one Fahrenheit temperature converted, the user could then enter a second such temperature, which would overwrite the first temperature that was correctly converted. At that point, the interface would show the new Fahrenheit temperature alongside the Celsius temperature that corresponded to the previously entered value. In creating GUIs, it is the programmer's responsibility to forestall this type of operation. Doing so requires constructing special event handler classes known as *focus listeners*.

Constructing Focus Listeners

In Section 13.1, we introduced the concept of keyboard focus. Whenever a component receives the focus, it automatically triggers a focus-gained event, and whenever it loses focus, it triggers a focus-lost event. The sequence is that the component that loses focus triggers a focus-lost event before the next component that receives focus triggers a focus-gained event.[4] A listener class that is constructed to handle these events must be implemented as a `FocusListener` class and, as listed in Table 13.10, must contain two required methods. Optionally, a `FocusAdapter` class may also be used as the parent class for a `FocusListener`.

One of the first requirements of a `FocusListener` class is to determine the component that triggered the focus event. Consider the following skeleton code for a listener class that we have named `FocusHandler`. This class implements a `FocusListener` for detecting when two components named `fahrField` and `celsField` receive and lose focus. First notice that the class correctly includes a `focusGained()` and `focusLost()` method, and each method uses an if-else statement to detect which specific component triggered the focus event. This is accomplished by using the `FocusEvent` argument, which we have named `e`, and a `getSource()` method to determine the source of each event with the individual components of interest.

[4]The terms "fires an event" and "triggers an event" are synonyms.

```
class FocusHandler implements FocusListener
{
  public void focusGained(FocusEvent e) // this detects when a component gets
  {                                      // the focus
    if(e.getSource() == fahrField)    // this detects that the fahrField component
    {                                 // got the focus
      // do something
    }
    else if(e.getSource() == celsField) // this detects that the celsField
    {                                   // component got the focus
      // do something
    }
  }
  public void focusLost(FocusEvent e)   // this detects when a component loses
  {                                     // the focus
    if(e.getSource() == fahrField)     // this detects that the fahrField component
    {                                  // lost the focus
      // do something
    }
    else if(e.getSource() == celsField) // this detects that the celsField
    {                                   // component lost the focus
      // do something
    }
  }
}  // end of focus listener class
```

We will use this skeleton FocusListener class to correctly handle two of the user-related problems that were identified for Program 13.5 and make the program respond in a "reasonable" manner. To understand what reasonable means, recall that the purpose of Program 13.5 is to permit a user to enter a Fahrenheit temperature and then, by clicking the Convert button, have the program calculate and display the corresponding Celsius temperature. As it stands, however, a user can inadvertently enter a Celsius rather than a Fahrenheit temperature. Similarly, after a Fahrenheit temperature has been correctly converted, entry of a second Fahrenheit temperature would put the GUI in a state where the newly entered Fahrenheit value is displayed alongside the Celsius temperature corresponding to the previously entered value.

To forestall such program operation, the new event handlers that will be provided and a commentary on why we have chosen the specified actions for each handler follow:

Event Handler for the Fahrenheit Text Field Listener
When this box gets the focus:
    Set the value in the Fahrenheit text field to a blank.
    Set the value in the Celsius text field to a blank.
Commentary on this event handler:
    This will set up the Fahrenheit text field to receive a new input value and prevents display of an incorrect Celsius value while the user is entering a new Fahrenheit temperature.

Event Handler for the Celsius Text Field Listener

When this box gets the focus:

Set the focus to the Fahrenheit text field.

Commentary on this event handler:

This will prevent a user from entering a value into the Celsius text field because this box can only get the focus if the user tabs to it or clicks it. Under these conditions, our event handler will automatically set the focus on the Fahrenheit box, which is where users should be if they are trying to enter a value. Once the focus gets shifted to the Fahrenheit box, that box's focus-gained event will clear the Celsius text field and disable it.

Event Handler for the Convert Button Listener

When this button is clicked:

Retrieve the Fahrenheit text field's data value.

If no input has been entered, set the input to "0".

Convert the Fahrenheit data to a Celsius value using the formula

$Celsius = 5/9 * (Fahrenheit - 32)$

Enable the Celsius text field.

Display the calculated Celsius value.

Commentary on this event handler:

This is a straightforward task of converting the input value to an output value and enabling the Celsius text field so that the displayed value is not shadowed. The check for an empty string will detect the case where the user clicks the Convert button without having entered any data into the Fahrenheit text field.

Event Handler for the Exit Button Listener

When this button is clicked:

Close down the application.

Commentary on this event handler:

This is the standard closing event handler.

Although the actions taken by our event handler methods are straightforward and typical of the types of actions that a reasonably simple Windows program must take, we will need some help from the JComponent class to perform them. Table 13.11 lists a number of extremely useful JComponent methods, the first and last of which complete our skeleton FocusListener class. The methods are used for both setting and determining the next component to receive focus under normal circumstances and for forcing focus onto a different component under program control. One of these methods, setNextFocusableComponent(), was presented and used in Section 13.1.

The required event handlers, which were previously described, can now be written using the methods listed in Table 13.11, and are presented as ConvertTempOne's Focus-Listener class' code.[5]

---

[5]It should be noted that the statement `fahrField.grabFocus();` in this code can be replaced by the two statements:

`fahrField.setRequestFocusEnabled(true);`

`fahrField.requestFocus();`

Typically, before using these statements, a test would be made using the `isRequestFocusEnabled()` method. We use the `grabFocus()` unconditionally here because we know that the `fahrField` component can always accept the focus.

TABLE 13.11   Useful Focus Control Methods

Method	Description
grabFocus(Component)	Sets the focus on its component argument if it does not already have it. Although it will set focus on a component that has been setEnabled() to false, in this case it will not be useful because the component has been disabled. Another approach is to use an isRequestFocusEnabled(), setRequestFocusEnabled(), and requestFocus() sequence.
requestFocus(Component)	Sets the focus on its component argument only if the component's setRequestFocusEnabled() has been set to true and the component does not already have the focus.
setRequestFocusEnabled(boolean)	Sets whether the receiving component can obtain the focus when requestFocus() is called.
isRequestFocusEnabled(Component)	Returns a boolean value of true or false, indicating whether the component can receive focus using requestFocus().
setNextFocusableComponent(Component)	Specifies the next component to receive focus but does not shift focus to this component.

ConvertTempOne Event Handler
Focus Listener Class' Event Code

```
class FocusHandler implements FocusListener
{
  public void focusGained(FocusEvent e)
  {
    if(e.getSource() == fahrField)
    {
      fahrField.setText("");   // blank input textfield
      celsField.setText("");   // blank Celsius textfield
    }
    else if(e.getSource() == celsField)
    {

      celsField.setNextFocusableComponent(fahrField);
      fahrField.grabFocus();
    }
  }
  public void focusLost(FocusEvent e)
  {
    if(e.getSource() == fahrField)
    {
      fahrField.setNextFocusableComponent(convertButton);
```

```
        }
    }
}   // end of focus listener class


class ConvertButtonHandler implements ActionListener
{
   public void actionPerformed(ActionEvent e)
   {
      DecimalFormat num = new DecimalFormat(",###.##");
      String instring;
      double invalue, outvalue;

      celsField.setEnabled(true); //enable Celsius text field
      instring = fahrField.getText();  // read the input value
        // prevent entry of an empty string
      if (instring.equals(""))
      {
         instring = "0";
         fahrField.setText("0");
      }
      invalue = Double.parseDouble(instring);  // convert to a double
      outvalue = 5.0/9.0 * (invalue - 32.0);
      celsField.setText(num.format(outvalue));
   }
}


class ExitButtonHandler implements ActionListener
{
   public void actionPerformed(ActionEvent e)
   {
      System.exit(0);
   }
}
```

Having defined the required Focus Listener class' event handlers, all that remains is to enter them as part of the application. Listener objects for the last two event classes, ConvertButtonHandler and ExitButtonHandler, can be instantiated and registered as previously listed in the code for Program 13.5. A listener object of the FocusHandler class can then be instantiated and registered using the following statements:

```
FocusHandler fhandler = new FocusHandler();
fahrField.addFocusListener(fhandler);
celsField.addFocusListener(fhandler);
```

Notice that the last two statements register the same listener object to both the fahrField and celsField components. We leave the insertion of these statements into Program 13.5 as Exercise 7b.

Input Validation Revisited

The event code for the `ConvertTempTwo` class retouches on the necessity of validating user input by employing one of the more common techniques associated with text field input, which is to explicitly test for an empty string. This conversion can be done either immediately after the user has entered the data, in which case it will be triggered by the component's focus-lost event, or it can be done immediately before the data are used or stored, as in our previous example. Clearly, both places ensure that invalid data will not enter the system and corrupt any results derived by it.

Another very important type of validation occurs while the user is entering data on a keystroke-by-keystroke basis. This type of front-end key-by-key validation is made using a `KeyListener` class, which detects keyboard events triggered by a keystroke. This permits action to be taken that rejects an invalid keystroke before the key's value is accepted into the input string. Keyboard events return both the Unicode value of each key as well as detecting if the Function, Arrow, and Control keys have been pressed. Using these events for data validation is based on selecting the desired characters and rejecting undesirable characters from entering the final string. The methods for performing a keystroke-by-keystroke validation using a `KeyListener` class are presented in Section 13.5.

EXERCISES 13.3

1. Enter and execute Program 13.2 on your computer.

2. Enter and execute Program 13.3 on your computer.

3. Modify Program 13.3 so that the user cannot enter any text into the text field component (*Tip:* Use a `setEditable(false)` method.)

4. Enter and execute Program 13.4 on your computer.

5. Modify Program 13.5 to include the `ConvertTempOne Class'` FocusListener developed in this section.

6. Rewrite the `ConvertTempOne Class'` FocusListener developed in this section as two FocusListeners—one for the `fahrField` component and one for the `celsField` component. Name these classes `FahrFocusListener` and `CelsFocusListener`, respectively.

7. **a.** What statements are needed to instantiate listener objects for the classes written for Exercise 6 and to have these objects correctly registered. Assume the listener object for the `FahrFocusListener` class is named `fahrhandler` and the listener object for the `CelsFocusListener` class is named `celshandler`.

   b. Enter and execute Program 13.5 using the focus handler classes written for Exercise 6 and the instantiation and registration statements written for Exercise 7a.

8. **a.** Write by hand a Java program that uses a JLabel component to display the following prompt:

   `Enter the amount of the bill:`

   After accepting a value for the amount of the bill in a text field, your program, upon the click of a <u>C</u>alculate button, should calculate the sales tax, assuming a tax rate of 6 percent. The display of the sales tax, as a dollar amount, should appear in a text field named taxShow when the <u>C</u>alculate button is clicked. A second button should be provided to terminate the application.

b. Include the event procedure written for Exercise 8a in a working program. For testing purposes, verify your program using an initial amount of $36.00. After manually checking that the result produced by your program is correct, use your program to complete the following table:

```
Amount          Sales Tax
(dollars)       (dollars)
  36.00
  40.00
  52.60
  87.95
 125.00
 182.93
```

9. a. Write a Java program that converts Celsius temperatures to their equivalent Fahrenheit values. Use a label to display the following prompt:

```
Enter the temperature in degrees Celsius:
```

After accepting a value entered from the keyboard into a text field, the program should convert the entered temperature to degrees Fahrenheit using the equation *Fahrenheit = (9.0 / 5.0) * Celsius + 32.0*. The program should then display the temperature in degrees Fahrenheit in a clearly labeled text field. A JButton button should be provided to terminate the application.

b. Verify the program written for Exercise 9a by first calculating the Fahrenheit equivalent of the following test data by hand and then using your program to see if it produces the correct results.

Test data set 1: 0 degrees Celsius
Test data set 2: 50 degrees Celsius
Test data set 3: 100 degrees Celsius

When you are sure your procedure is working correctly, use it to complete the following table:

```
Celsius         Fahrenheit
   45
   50
   55
   60
   65
   70
```

10. Write and execute a Java program that displays the following prompts using two label components:

```
Enter the length of the office:
Enter the width of the office:
```

Have your program accept the user input in two text fields. When a button is clicked, your program should calculate the area of the office and display the area in a text field. This display should be cleared whenever the input text fields receive the focus. A second button should be provided to terminate the application. Verify your procedure with the following test data:

Test data set 1: length = 12.5, width = 10
Test data set 2: length = 12.4, width = 0
Test data set 3: length = 0, width = 10

11. **a.** Write and execute a Java program that displays the following prompts and uses two text fields to receive the input data:

```
Enter the miles driven:
Enter the gallons of gas used:
```

Your program should calculate and display the miles per gallon in a text field when a button is clicked. Use the equation *miles per gallon = miles / gallons used*. The display should be cleared whenever one of the text fields gets the focus. A second button should be provided to terminate the application. Verify your procedure with the following test data:

Test data set 1: miles = 276, gas = 10 gallons
Test data set 2: miles = 200, gas = 15.5 gallons

When you have completed your verification, use your procedure to complete the following table:

Miles Driven	Gallons Used	mpg
250	16.00	
275	18.00	
312	19.54	
296	17.39	

b. For the procedure written for Exercise 11a, determine how many verification runs are required to ensure the procedure is working correctly and give a reason supporting your answer.

12. Write a Java program that displays the following prompts:

```
Enter the length of the swimming pool:
Enter the width of the swimming pool:
Enter the average depth of the swimming pool:
```

Have your program accept the user input in three text fields. When a button is clicked, your program should calculate the volume of the swimming pool and display the volume in a fourth text field. This display should be cleared whenever the input text fields receive the focus. A second button should be provided to terminate the application. In calculating the volume, use the equation *volume = length * width * average depth*.

13. Write and execute a Java program that provides three text fields for the input of three user-input numbers. There should be a single label prompt that tells the user to enter three numbers in the text fields. When the user clicks a button, the program should calculate the average of the numbers and then display the average in a clearly labeled fourth text field. The displayed value should be cleared whenever one of the text fields receives the focus. A second button should be provided to terminate the application. Verify your procedure with the following test data:

Test data set 1: 100, 100, 100
Test data set 2: 100, 50, 0

When you have completed your verification, use your program to complete the following table:

```
Numbers              Average
92, 98, 79
86, 84, 75
63, 85, 74
```

14. Write a Java program that prompts the user to input two numbers, each accepted by a text field, and that has a button with the caption Swap. When this button is clicked, the values in the two text fields should be switched.

13.4 ADDING CHECK BOX, RADIO BUTTON, AND GROUP COMPONENTS

Check box and radio button components are extremely useful in presenting users with a set of defined choices from which they must make a selection. The difference between the two types of components is in the nature of the selection that must be made. In a radio button group, the user can select only one choice from a mutually exclusive set of choices—for example, selecting a category of either being single, married, divorced, or widowed. Here the user is presented with a list of choices from which one and only one selection can be made. In a check box control, the user is also presented with a list of one or more choices, but each choice can be selected or not independently of any other selection. An example is providing a list of style choices for displaying text, such as bold and italic. The user can select one, both, or neither choice. As these two types of components are closely related, we present both in this section.

Check Boxes

The check box control provides a user with a simple yes or no type of option. For example, the interface in Figure 13.10 has two check boxes. The properties table for this interface is listed in Table 13.12.

As illustrated in Figure 13.10, both check boxes are unchecked. This is the default setting when a JCheckBox component is added to a container and can be altered using a setSelected() method. For example, the statement chkItalic.setSelected(true); would cause the Italic check box in Figure 13.10 to be checked. In addition, whether a check box is checked or not may be altered by the user at run time by either clicking the

FIGURE 13.10   An Interface with Two Check Boxes

TABLE 13.12   The Properties Table for Figure 13.10

Object	Property	Setting
JFrame	Name	mainFrame
	Caption	Check Box Example
JLabel	Name	lblPrompt
	Caption	Enter Some Text:
JTextField	Name	txtBox1
	Text	(Blank)
	Font	SansSerif
	Style	Font.PLAIN
JCheckBox	Name	chkItalic
	Caption	Italic
	Mnemonic	I
JCheckBox	Name	chkBold
	Caption	Bold
	Mnemonic	B
JButton	Name	exitButton
	Caption	Exit
	Mnemonic	x

box, pressing the Space key when the box is in focus, or pressing the accelerator key specified for the box. It can also be changed at run time using the `setSelected()` method within executing program code.

Each check box in an application is independent of any other check box. This means that the choice made in one box has no effect on, and does not depend on, the choice made in another box. Thus, check boxes are useful for providing a set of one or more options that can be in effect at the same time, provided that each option is individually of the yes-no, on-off, or true-false type. For example, in the interface shown in Figure 13.10, the check box options consist of a set of two check boxes that permit independent selection of how the text is to be displayed. Selecting or deselecting Bold has no effect on the choice for italic or nonitalic.

Because of their on-off nature, check boxes are also known as toggle selections, where a user can effectively toggle, or switch back and forth, between a check mark and no check mark. If no check mark appears in a box, clicking it changes its selected state to `true` and causes a check to appear; otherwise, if the box has a check, clicking it changes its selected state to `false` and causes the check to be cleared.

Program 13.6 provides the code for constructing the interface shown in Figure 13.10. The statements that create and display the check box components are boldfaced for easy reference.

Adding a Check Box Listener Class

Having provided the user interface for making a selection, it still remains to provide the code to determine the selection and then to act appropriately based on the selection. The event code to do this follows on page 644:

PROGRAM 13.6

```java
import javax.swing.*;
import java.awt.event.*;
import java.awt.Container;  // need this to add controls
import java.awt.*;  // need this for layout manager
public class CheckBoxOne extends JFrame
{
  private JFrame mainFrame;
  private JButton exitButton;
  private JLabel inLabel;
  private JTextField tinField;
  private JCheckBox boxItalic;
  private JCheckBox boxBold;

  public CheckBoxOne() // a constructor
  {
    mainFrame = new JFrame("Check Box Example");

      // create all components

    exitButton = new JButton("Exit");
    inLabel = new JLabel("Enter Some Text:");
    tinField = new JTextField(20);
    boxItalic = new JCheckBox("Italic");
    boxBold = new JCheckBox("Bold");

      // get the content pane
    Container c = mainFrame.getContentPane();
      // set the layout manager
    c.setLayout(new FlowLayout());

      // add the components to the ContentPane
    c.add(inLabel);
    c.add(tinField);
    c.add(boxItalic);
    c.add(boxBold);
    c.add(exitButton);

      // create accelerator keys
    boxItalic.setMnemonic('I');
    boxBold.setMnemonic('B');
    exitButton.setMnemonic('x');
```

(Continued on next page)

(Continued from previous page)

```
    mainFrame.setSize(250,150);

      // define and register window event handler
    mainFrame.addWindowListener(new WindowAdapter()
    {
      public void windowClosing(WindowEvent e) {System.exit(0);}
    });

      // create and register the exit button event handler

    ExitButtonHandler ehandler = new ExitButtonHandler();  // instantiate a handler
    exitButton.addActionListener(ehandler);  // register the handler

    mainFrame.show();
  }

    // inner class for the Exit button event handler
  private class ExitButtonHandler implements ActionListener
  {
    public void actionPerformed(ActionEvent e)
    {
      System.exit(0);
    }
  }  // end of inner class

  public static void main(String args[])
  {
    new CheckBoxOne();  // instantiate a GUI object
  }

}  // end of class
```

Program 13.6's Check Box Listener Class' Event Code

```
/// Check Box listener class code
 class ChkBoxHandler implements ItemListener
 {
   private int italicFont;
   private int boldFont;

   public void itemStateChanged(ItemEvent e)
   {

     if (e.getSource() == boxBold)
```

```
      if (e.getStateChange() == e.SELECTED)
        boldFont = Font.BOLD;
      else
        boldFont = Font.PLAIN;
    else
      if (e.getStateChange() == e.SELECTED)
        italicFont = Font.ITALIC;
      else
        italicFont = Font.PLAIN;

    tinField.setFont( new Font( "Courier", italicFont + boldFont, 14));
    tinField.repaint();
  }
} // end of Check box listener class
```

Notice in this event code that the `itemStateChanged()` methods for both the Italic and Bold check boxes use an `if` statement to determine which box triggered the event. Within each `if` statement is a further `if` statement to determine whether the box has been selected or not. Based on this determination, the respective text field style property, `Font.ITALIC` and `Font.BOLD`, is either set or the `Font.PLAIN` is used. If we had needed to, a statement such as `boxBold.setSelected(true);` can force the `boxBold` check box to be checked under program control.

Once the `ItemListener` class is written, the last step is to instantiate an instance of this class and register it to each individual check box in the interface. This is accomplished by the following statements:

```
ChkBoxHandler chandler = new ChkBoxHandler();
boxItalic.addItemListener(chandler);
boxBold.addItemListener(chandler);
```

To have our `ItemListener` class integrated into Program 13.6 requires placing the foregoing instantiation and registration statements either immediately before or after the similar statements used for the `exitButton` and placing the `ItemListener` class as an inner class either before or after the `exitButton`'s inner listener class. We leave this as Exercise 3. Figure 13.11 illustrates how text entered into the text area appears when the listener class has been implemented and both check boxes have been checked.

FIGURE 13.11 A Sample Display with Both Boxes Checked

Radio Buttons

A group of radio button controls provide a user with a set of one or more choices, only one of which can be selected. The radio buttons in a designated group operate together, where selecting one radio button in the group immediately deselects and clears all the other buttons in the group. Thus, the choices in a radio button group are mutually exclusive. The term *radio button* was selected for these components because they operate in the same manner as the channel selector buttons provided on radios, where selecting one channel automatically deselects all other channels.

As an example of using radio buttons, consider a form that requires information on the marital status of an employee. As the employee can be either single, married, divorced, or widowed, selection of one category automatically means the other categories are not selected. This type of choice is ideal for a radio button group, as shown in Figure 13.12, where the group consists of four individual radio buttons.

FIGURE 13.12   A Radio Button Group

Each radio button placed in a container, by default, forms its own group of one. To group a number of radio buttons together, you must add them into a ButtonGroup. The ButtonGroup is not an object that is displayed on the GUI, and it has no effect on how the radio buttons are displayed; it does, however, keep track of the internal relationship between buttons in the group. Thus, the ButtonGroup ensures only one button at a time can be selected. As an example of how a button group is created, assume that we have three radio button objects named rdbutCourier, rdbutSansSerif, and rdbutSerif. The following statements instantiate a ButtonGroup object named rgroup and assign each component to this group:

```
   // instantiate a ButtonGroup object
ButtonGroup rgroup = new ButtonGroup();
   // add buttons into this group
rgroup.add(rdbutCourier);
rgroup.add(rdbutSansSerif);
rgroup.add(rdbutSerif);
```

Now let's see how to create the three buttons that we have just grouped together. As an example, consider the interface shown in Figure 13.13. This interface consists of three radio buttons with the captions C̲ourier, S̲ansSerif, and Seri̲f, respectively. We will use these buttons to select the style of print that is displayed in the text field. Since these

TABLE 13.13   Properties Table for Figure 13.13's Interface

Object	Property	Setting
Form	Name	mainFrame
	Caption	Radio Button Example
JFrame	Name	lblPrompt
	Caption	Enter Some Text:
JTextField	Name	tinField
	Text	(Blank)
	Font	Courier
	Style	Font.PLAIN
	Size	12
JRadioButton	Name	rdbutCourier
	Caption	Courier
	Mnemonic	C
	Selected	true
JRadioButton	Name	rdbutSansSerif
	Caption	SansSerif
	Mnemonic	S
	Selected	false
JRadioButton	Name	rdbutSerif
	Caption	Serif
	Mnemonic	f
	Selected	false
JButton	Name	exitButton
	Caption	Exit
	Mnemonic	false

FIGURE 13.13   An Interface Containing a Radio Button Group

styles are mutually exclusive in that only one style can be operational at a given time, the choice of radio buttons for this selection is appropriate. The properties table for this interface appears in Table 13.13.

Notice in Properties Table 13.13 that only one of the radio buttons has been selected. If an attempt is made to select more than one button in a group, only the last selection is activated. Radio buttons are constructed from JRadioButton components following the same procedure as we have used throughout this chapter for instantiating all of our Swing-based components. The specific statements that create the interface in Figure 13.13 are included in Program 13.7 and are boldfaced for easy referencing.

PROGRAM 13.7

```
import java.text.*;  // need this for formatting
import javax.swing.*;
import java.awt.event.*;
import java.awt.Container;  // need this to add controls
import java.awt.*;  // need this for layout manager
public class RadioButtons extends JFrame
{
  private JFrame mainFrame;
  private JButton exitButton;
  private JLabel inLabel;
  private JTextField tinField;
  private JRadioButton rdbutCourier;
  private JRadioButton rdbutSansSerif;
  private JRadioButton rdbutSerif;

  public RadioButtons() // a constructor
  {
    mainFrame = new JFrame("Radio Button Example");

      // create all components

    exitButton = new JButton("Exit");
    inLabel = new JLabel("Enter Some Text:");
    tinField = new JTextField(20);
    rdbutCourier = new JRadioButton("Courier");
    rdbutSansSerif = new JRadioButton("SansSerif");
    rdbutSerif = new JRadioButton("Serif");

      // put the buttons into a single group
    ButtonGroup rgroup = new ButtonGroup();
    rgroup.add(rdbutCourier);
    rgroup.add(rdbutSansSerif);
    rgroup.add(rdbutSerif);

      // get the content pane
    Container c = mainFrame.getContentPane();
      // set the layout manager
    c.setLayout(new FlowLayout());

      // add the components to the ContentPane
    c.add(inLabel);
    c.add(tinField);
    c.add(rdbutCourier);
```

(Continued on next page)

(Continued from previous page)

```
    c.add(rdbutSansSerif);
    c.add(rdbutSerif);
    c.add(exitButton);

        // create accelerator keys
    rdbutCourier.setMnemonic('C');
    rdbutSansSerif.setMnemonic('S');
    rdbutSerif.setMnemonic('f');
    exitButton.setMnemonic('x');

      // set the initial button and corresponding font
    rdbutCourier.setSelected(true);
    tinField.setFont(new Font("Courier", Font.PLAIN, 12));

    mainFrame.setSize(300,150);

        // define and register window event handler
    mainFrame.addWindowListener(new WindowAdapter()
    {
      public void windowClosing(WindowEvent e) {System.exit(0);}
    });

        // create and register the event handlers
    ExitButtonHandler ehandler = new ExitButtonHandler();  // instantiate a handler
    exitButton.addActionListener(ehandler);  // register the handler

    mainFrame.show();
  }

      // inner class for the Exit button event handler
  class ExitButtonHandler implements ActionListener
  {
    public void actionPerformed(ActionEvent e)
    {
      System.exit(0);
    }
  }  // end of inner class

  public static void main(String args[])
  {
    new RadioButtons();  // instantiate a GUI object
  }

}  // end of class
```

In reviewing the code within Program 13.7 that specifically relates to creating the three radio buttons, the additional steps needed for radio buttons that are not common to most other components are:

- Their inclusion into a single ButtonGroup
- Use of a setSelect() method to initially select one of the buttons

If a setSelect() method were not used to initially select one of the radio buttons, none of the buttons would be selected when the GUI is first displayed. Similarly, if the buttons were not placed together into a single group, each button would individually constitute its own group and be independent of any other button. This would, of course, defeat the purpose of providing three mutually exclusive choices.

Adding a Radio Button Listener Class

As always, once a Swing-based component has been placed on a GUI, all that remains is to provide it with an appropriate listener class. The radio button listener class for Program 13.7 is listed here:

PROGRAM 13.7'S RADIO BUTTON LISTENER CLASS' EVENT CODE

```
   // Listener class for the Radio button handlers
  private class RButHandler implements ItemListener
  {
    public void itemStateChanged(ItemEvent e)
    {

      if (e.getSource() == rdbutCourier)
          tinField.setFont(new Font("Courier", Font.PLAIN, 12));
      else if (e.getSource() == rdbutSansSerif)
          tinField.setFont(new Font("SansSerif", Font.PLAIN, 12));
      else if (e.getSource() == rdbutSerif)
          tinField.setFont(new Font("Serif", Font.PLAIN, 12));

      tinField.repaint();
    }
  }  // end of inner class
```

The primary function of this listener class code is to determine which button in a group was actually selected and then to use this information appropriately. Thus, the first task handled by the listener class is to determine which button was selected. This is accomplished using a getSource() method and comparing the returned value to each radio button object's name. Once the selected button is identified, the code sets the font to the selected choice.

The last step in providing our GUI with a working version of the listener code is to instantiate a listener object from the class and then register it to each radio button. This can be accomplished by the following statements:

```
RButHandler rhandler = new RButHandler();
rdbutCourier.addItemListener(rhandler);
rdbutSansSerif.addItemListener(rhandler);
rdbutSerif.addItemListener(rhandler);
```

These statements should be placed either immediately before or after the exitButton's registration statements. Similarly, the ItemListener class itself should be placed, as an inner class, either before or after the exitButton's inner listener class. The integration of the listener class and activation statements into Program 13.7 is left as Exercise 6. Assuming this is done, Figure 13.14 provides an example of how user-entered text looks when the Serif radio button has been selected.

FIGURE 13.14   An Example of User-Entered Text

The text in Figure 13.14 and any subsequently entered text can now be changed by the user with the radio buttons. While the program is executing, a radio button can be selected in one of the following ways:

- Clicking the mouse on the desired button
- Using the accelerator keys
- Using a setSelected() method under program control, as for example,
  butCourier.set.Selected(true);

For example, if the user clicks the Courier radio button, the text will appear as in Figure 13.15.

FIGURE 13.15   The Text in Courier Font

Before leaving Program 13.7, one further comment is in order. Notice that, unlike the check box event code, no selection statement is required once the selected button has been identified. This is because a selected check box can be in one of two states, checked or unchecked, but a selected radio button, by definition, must be checked. Thus, once a radio button is selected and triggers an event, the event can be acted upon immediately, with no further processing needed to determine the button's state.

EXERCISES 13.4

1. Determine whether the following choices should be presented on a GUI with check boxes or with radio buttons:
   a. The choice of air conditioning or not on a new automobile order form.
   b. The choice of automatic or manual transmission on a new automobile order form.
   c. The choice of AM/FM, AM/FM tape, or AM/FM CD radio on a new automobile order form.
   d. The choice of tape backup system or no tape backup system on a new computer order form.
   e. The choice of a 17-, 19-, or 21-inch color monitor on a new computer order form.
   f. The choice of CD-ROM drive or not on a new computer order form.
   g. The choice of a 4-, 6-, or 8-speed CD-ROM drive on a new computer order form.
   h. The choice of a 800-, 900-, or 1000-MHz Pentium processor on a new computer order form.

2. Enter and run Program 13.6 on your computer to verify that it correctly produces the GUI shown in Figure 13.10.

3. Add the appropriate listener class provided in this section to Program 13.6. Compile and execute your program to verify that it operates correctly.

4. a. Modify the Program written for Exercise 3 so that the choices presented by the check box are replaced by two radio buttons.
   b. Based on your experience with Exercise 4a, determine what type of input choice is best presented using a check box rather than radio buttons.

5. Enter and run Program 13.7 on your computer to verify that it correctly produces the GUI shown in Figure 13.13.

6. Add the appropriate listener class provided in this section to Program 13.7. Compile and execute your program to verify that it operates correctly.

7. a. Modify Program 13.6 so that the choices presented by the check boxes are replaced by radio buttons.
   b. Based on your experience with Exercise 7a, determine what type of input choice is best presented using a check box rather than a radio button.

8. a. Modify the GUI produced by Program 13.7 so that the user can additionally specify the point size for the text field. The default point size should be 10, with the user capable of choosing among 8, 10, and 12 points.
   b. Add event code to the program written for Exercise 8a to correctly handle the selection of point size.

9. Modify Program 13.7 so that rather than selecting font type, a user can select whether to make the displayed text uppercase or lowercase using a radio button group consisting of two buttons. Make sure to include event code so that the displayed text corresponds to a user's selection. (*Tip:* Use the `String` class' `toUpperCase()` and `toLowerCase()` methods. For example, the expression `"abcd".toUpperCase()` creates the string `"ABCD"`.)

13.5 KEYSTROKE INPUT VALIDATION

Validating user input is an essential part of a professionally written program. For example, a professional program would not permit the input of a date such as 5/33/02, which contains an obviously invalid day. Similarly, division of any number by zero within a program, such as 14 / 0, should not be allowed. Both examples illustrate the need for input validation in which program code checks for improper input data before an attempt is made to process them further. We now have most of the tools to supply keystroke-by-keystroke input data validation to programs such as the temperature conversion in Program 13.5.

Clearly, Program 13.5 expects that the user will enter a number and not a text string into the text field. If the data entered cannot be converted to numerical data, the program will crash when it attempts to convert this quantity to a Celsius temperature. In Section 13.3, an input validation technique was presented that was used just prior to using the input data within a calculation. Ideally, however, it is preferable to validate the input data either on a character-by-character basis, as each character is being entered, or immediately after the input component loses focus. This latter verification is in fact one of the primary uses of the `focusLost()` method: to validate the data before they are passed into the system for further processing or storage. If the data do not pass their required validation, a suitable error message can be displayed, and focus immediately shifts back to the input component until valid data are entered.

In a keystroke-by-keystroke validation, each character is verified as the user enters it. Typically, this type of validation is made using either `keyPressed()`, `keyReleased()`, or `keyTyped()` event methods. How to perform this type of validation is presented in this section.

The three methods that can be employed in a keystroke-by-keystroke validation are listed in Table 13.14. Each of the event methods in the table provides information about the key being activated by a user. The difference between these event methods is the amount of information provided. The `keyTyped()` method can only be used to supply the Unicode character of a character key, whereas the `keyPressed()` and `keyReleased()` methods can detect and process the Function, Cursor, Enter, and Shift keys in addition to the printable character keys. Because we will need to detect when noncharacter keys, such as the Enter, Backspace, and Function keys, have been entered, we will need either the `keyPressed()` or `keyReleased()` methods.

As a specific example, consider the GUI shown in Figure 13.16. The properties table for this interface is listed in Table 13.15 on page 656, and the class corresponding to this GUI and table is named `Validation`. As provided in Program 13.8, the code for this class also includes event handler objects for both the Window Closing button and the internal Exit button.

FIGURE 13.16   The GUI Corresponding to Table 13.16

TABLE 13.14   Required `KeyListener` Event Methods

Method	Description
public void keyPressed(KeyEvent e)	This method is invoked when a key is pressed.
public void keyReleased(KeyEvent e)	This method is invoked when a key is released.
public void keyTyped(KeyEvent e)	This method is invoked when a key is typed.

PROGRAM 13.8

```java
import javax.swing.*;
import java.awt.event.*;
import java.awt.Container;  // need this to add controls
import java.awt.*;  // need this for layout manager

public class Validation extends JFrame
{
  private JFrame mainFrame;
  private JButton exitButton;
  private JTextField inputField;
  private JTextField messageField;
  private JLabel inputLabel;

  public Validation() // a constructor
  {
    mainFrame = new JFrame("Input Validation");

      // create all components
    exitButton = new JButton("Exit");
    inputLabel = new JLabel("Enter an integer number:");
    inputField = new JTextField(5);
    messageField = new JTextField(20);

      // get the content pane
    Container c = mainFrame.getContentPane();
      // set the layout manager
    c.setLayout(new FlowLayout());

      // add the components to the ContentPane
    c.add(inputLabel);
    c.add(inputField);
    c.add(exitButton);
    c.add(messageField);

      // create accelerator keys
```

(Continued on next page)

(Continued from previous page)

```
    exitButton.setMnemonic('x');


    mainFrame.setSize(250,125);


        // define and register window event handler
    mainFrame.addWindowListener(new WindowAdapter()
    {
      public void windowClosing(WindowEvent e) {System.exit(0);}
    });


        // create and register the button event handler
    ExitButtonHandler ehandler = new ExitButtonHandler();  // instantiate a handler
    exitButton.addActionListener(ehandler);  // register the handler


    mainFrame.show();
  }


    // inner class for the exit button event handler
  class ExitButtonHandler implements ActionListener
  {
    public void actionPerformed(ActionEvent e)
    {
      System.exit(0);
    }
  }  // end of button listener class


  public static void main(String args[])
  {
    new Validation();  // instantiate a GUI object
  }


}  // end of class
```

For the GUI illustrated in Figure 13.16, the entered data must be an integer, which means each key pressed should either be the Enter key, the Backspace key, or correspond to a character between 0 and 9. To ensure that only numerical data are entered, we can validate each typed character and reject any keystrokes that do not result in one of the characters 0 through 9. This can be done by adding a key listener to the inputField which monitors all key press events. Using the `keyReleased()` method and implementing the key listener class using an adapter class provide the following class and event header lines:

```
class InputFieldKeyHandler extends KeyAdapter
{
  public void keyReleased(KeyEvent e)
  {
```

T A B L E 1 3 . 1 5   Initial Properties Table for the `validation` Class

Object	Property	Setting
Form	Name	mainFrame
	Caption	Input Validation
JFrame	Name	inputLabel
	Caption	Enter an integer number:
JTextField	Name	inputField
	Text	(Blank)
	Size	5
JTextField	Name	messageField
	Text	(Blank)
	Size	20
JButton	Name	exitButton
	Caption	Exit
	Mnemonic	x

Notice that, like all listener classes, the name we have selected for our class, `InputFieldKeyHandler`, is a programmer-selected name. It is now time to determine the validation code that is to be executed after each key is released.

The `KeyEvent` argument, which we have named e, that is passed into `keyReleased()` provides both the character value of all printable keys as well as the codes corresponding to the nonprintable keys. The two methods needed to extract the character and code information are listed in Table 13.16.

On a very superficial plane, an invalid integer character is one that falls outside the range of 0 to 9 and can be detected by the following code:

```
keyChar = e.getChar(); // get the character
If e.getChar() < '0' || e.getChar() > '9' // see if an invalid key was pressed
```

Having detected an invalid key, however, we are still left with removing it from the entered string. Because our validation procedure involves directly manipulating the displayed text field string, we must also be concerned with removing a character when the user presses the Backspace key. Thus, we will have to detect the Backspace key and make adjustments to the displayed string by removing a character each time this key is released.

Finally, for completeness, there is one additional verification that we should make. Most users expect that pressing the Enter key will terminate data input. This, of course, is not the case for text fields, where the user must either press the Tab key, click another object, or use accelerator keys to move off the field. We can, however, check the value of the key just pressed to determine if it was the Enter key.

Java provides named constants for each key, both character and noncharacter, available on a keyboard. A list of the more common named constants appears in Table 13.17. It is to these constants that the key code of the last key pressed can be compared, which permits determining exactly which nonprintable key was pressed. The information in Tables 13.16 and 13.17 permits us to create a statement such as

TABLE 13.16　Retrieving Keystroke Character and Code Information

Method	Description	Example
getKeyChar()	Returns the character for the key typed, pressed, or released.	e.getKeyChar()
getKeyCode()	Returns a code for the key pressed or released.	e.getKeyCode()

```
if(e.getKeyCode() == VK_ENTER)
   exitButton.grabFoucs();
```

This statement will cause the focus to shift to the `exitButton` component whenever the last key detected was the Enter key. We will use this statement in our final validation routine.

We now have all of the pieces assembled, except for one, to create a key listener that will provide the appropriate validation that only a valid integer has been entered into the text field box for the GUI in Figure 13.16. The algorithm for this validation is:

> *Upon detection of a key release event*
> *1. Clear any previous error messages*
> *2. Read in the string from the text field*
> *3. Process the last key detected as follows*
>   *If the key pressed was the Enter key*
>   *shift focus to the next component*
>   *Else If the key pressed was the Backspace key*
>   *remove the last character from the string*
>   *Else If the key is not a valid integer character*
>   *remove the last character from the string*
> *4. Display the string in the text field*

The last remaining piece is how to correctly remove the last entered character from the input string. We do this with one of string methods presented in Chapter 7. This is the `substring()` method, which has the syntax

stringObject.substring(*starting index number, ending index number*)

The first argument to the `substring()` method specifies the starting index from which characters are to be extracted (recall that the first character in a string has an index value of 0), and the ending index specifies the index that is one beyond the last character to be extracted. For example, the expression `"123a".substring(0,3)` yields the string value `"123"`. This result is obtained as follows: The first argument specifies extraction is to start at index position 0, which contains the character '1'. Extraction of characters stops at one less than index position 3, which is the second argument. Thus, the extraction of characters ends at index position 2, which contains the character '3'. Hence, using the `substring()` method, we can remove the last entered character. This is done either because the Backspace key was pressed, indicating the user's explicit desire to erase the last entered character, or because the validation code has determined that the last character is not a valid integer digit. Understanding that the method name, InputFieldHandler, is a programmer-selected name and that we have chosen to construct the `KeyListener` using its corresponding `KeyAdapter` class, the completed integer validation routine is:

T A B L E   1 3 . 1 7   Java Key Named Constants

Named Constants	Key
VK_0 to VK_9	0 to 9
VK_A to VK_Z	A to Z
VK_BACK_SPACE	Backspace
VK_F1-VK_F12	Function keys F1 to F12
VK_UP	Up arrow key
VK_DOWN	Down arrow key
VK_ENTER	Enter key
VK_TAB	Tab key
VK_SPACE	Space key
VK_PAGE_UP	PgUp key
VK_PAGE_DOWN	PgDn key
VK_SHIFT	Shift key
VK_ADD	+ key
VK_SUBTRACT	- key
VK_HOME	Home key

```java
  // key stroke validation written as a key listener
class InputFieldKeyHandler extends KeyAdapter
{
  public void keyReleased(KeyEvent e)
  {
    int keyCode, length;
    char keyChar;
    String inputGood;

    keyCode = e.getKeyCode();   // get the integer code of the last key pressed
    keyChar = e.getKeyChar();   // get the character code of the last key pressed
                                // when a character key is pressed

    messageField.setText("");  // clear last error message

    inputGood = inputField.getText(); // get the current string
    length = inputGood.length();
      // process the last key pressed
    if (keyCode == KeyEvent.VK_ENTER)  // shift focus
    {
      System.out.println("Enter key was pressed");
      exitButton.grabFocus();
    }
    else if (keyCode == KeyEvent.VK_BACK_SPACE) // erase last character
    {
      System.out.println("Backspace key was pressed");
      length = inputGood.length();
      inputGood = inputGood.substring(0, length);
```

```
      System.out.println("length = " + length + "  input = " + inputGood);
   }
   else if (keyChar < '0' || keyChar > '9')
   {
      messageField.setText("     Invalid Character - Not Accepted");
      inputGood = inputGood.substring(0, length - 1);
      System.out.println("length = " + length + "  input = " + inputGood);
   }


      // display the validated string
      inputField.setText(inputGood);
   }
} // end of key listener class
```

Having constructed a `KeyListener` class, the last step is to instantiate an instance of this class and register it to the `inputField` text field that we are monitoring. The following statements do this:

```
// instantiate and register the input field's key listener
InputFieldKeyHandler khandler = new InputFieldKeyHandler();
inputField.addKeyListener(khandler);
```

To integrate our `KeyListener` class into Program 13.8 requires placing the foregoing instantiation and registration statements either immediately before or after the similar statements used for the `exitButton` and placing the `KeyListener` class as an inner class either before or after the `exitButton`'s inner listener class. We leave this as Exercise 2.

EXERCISES 13.5

1. Enter, compile, and execute Program 13.8 on your computer.
2. Add the `KeyListener` class developed in this section to Program 13.8, including the statements to instantiate a listener object, and have it registered to Program 13.8's input text field.
3. a. Modify the program written for Exercise 2 so that the error message text field is disabled whenever the field is cleared of any message.
   b. Modify the program written for Exercise 3a so that the error message field has a red background and a white foreground whenever an error message is written to it.
4. a. Rewrite the `KeyListener` presented in this section so that the validation routine is provided in a public method named `checkInteger(char keyChar, int keyCode)` that can be used by any other `KeyListener` object. This method should be called each time a key pressed event is triggered, and the call to the method should come from the `KeyListener` code.
   b. From a practical viewpoint, why shouldn't the code for shifting focus when the Enter key is detected be included in the method written for Exercise 4a?
5. Modify the `KeyListener` class developed in this section to verify that a valid real number is being input. Such a number consists of the digits 0 through 9 and at most a single decimal point.

6. **a.** Rewrite the KeyListener written for Exercise 5 so that the validation part of the listener is provided in a public method named `checkInteger(char keyChar, int keyCode)` that can be used by any other KeyListener object. Your method should be called each time a key pressed event is triggered, and the call to your method should come from the KeyListener code.

   b. From a practical viewpoint, why shouldn't the code for shifting focus when the Enter key is detected be included in the method written for Exercise 6a?

13.6 COMMON PROGRAMMING ERRORS

The common programming errors related to the swing-based components presented in this chapter are:

1. Mistyping the JTextField keyword as JTextfield and making a similar error with both the JPasswordField and JTextArea components. If your GUI does not display a component or an event handler does not seem to operate, you should first check that all component and method names are spelled correctly.

2. Forgetting to include a radio button into a ButtonGroup object. By default, each radio button forms its own group of one.

3. Creating an event handler and failing to register it. An event handler is not activated until both an object of the listener class is instantiated and the listener object is registered. If the listener object is not registered, the expected event will not be handled, which is the same result that occurs if no handler were written for the event.

13.7 CHAPTER SUMMARY

1. The swing package provides a number of atomic components that can be added into a swing-based GUI. The most common are command buttons, labels, text areas, check boxes, and radio buttons.

2. Text area components include JTextField, JPasswordField, and JTextArea controls. The first two of these components permit entry and display of a single line of text, with the JPasswordField component displaying each character as an asterisk for password protection. The JTextArea component permits entry and display of multiple lines of text.

3. In most cases, a text field has an associated label component. This is a read-only field that is created from a JLabel component.

4. A check box is a control that appears as a square box with an attached label and provides a yes-no type of selection. If multiple check boxes are used, the choice supplied by each box can be selected or not, independent of any other selection. Thus, a user can select one, all, or no boxes.

5. In a radio button group, the user can select only one choice from a mutually exclusive set of choices. Here the user is presented with a list of choices from which one and only one selection can be made.

6. The placement of atomic components is determined by a container's layout managers. The default layout manager for a JFrame container is the BorderLayout. In this layout, up to five components can be placed in positions corresponding to

the top, bottom, left side, right side, and middle of the container. Another layout manager can be specified using a `setLayout()` method. The other available layout managers consist of FlowLayout, GridLayout, CardLayout, BoxLayout, and GridBagLayout.

7. Once an atomic component has been placed on a GUI, it should be provided with an event handler. The steps for adding an event handler are:

   Step 1: Write the code for an event handler class (a listener class).
   Step 2: Instantiate an instance of the listener class.
   Step 3: Register the listener object.

8. A *properties table* lists all of the components in a GUI and their associated listeners. This table is very helpful both in documenting the objects on a GUI and in providing a programmer's quick reference to the names and properties of each component.

9. When an application is run and a user is looking at the container, only one of the container's controls will have *keyboard focus*, or the focus for short. The control with the focus is the object that will be affected by pressing a key or clicking the mouse.

10. A focus listener is an event-handling class that responds to focus-generated events. Such events are triggered whenever a component receives or loses focus.

PART 5

Additional Programming Topics

CHAPTER 14

File I/O

The data for the programs we have seen so far have either been assigned internally within the programs or entered interactively during program execution. This type of data entry is fine for small amounts of data.

In this chapter, we present how to store data outside a program using Java's object-oriented capabilities. This external data storage permits a program to use the data without the user having to re-create them interactively each time the program is executed. This also provides the basis for sharing data between programs so that the data output by one program can be input directly to another program.

14.1 FILES AND STREAMS

To store and retrieve data on a file in Java, two items are required:

- A file
- A file stream object

Files

Any collection of data that is stored together under a common name on a storage medium other than the computer's main memory is called a **data file.** Typically, data files are stored on a disk, magnetic tape, or CD-ROM. For example, the Java programs that you store on disk are examples of files. The stored data in this particular form of a file are referred to as a **program file** and consist of the program code that becomes input data to the Java compiler.

A file is physically stored on an external medium, such as a disk, using a unique file name referred to as the **external file name.** The external file name is the name of the file as it is known by the operating system. It is the external name that is displayed when the operating system displays the contents of a directory.

Each computer operating system has its own specification as to the maximum number of characters permitted for an external file name. Table 14.1 lists these specifications for the more common operating systems.

To ensure that the examples presented in this text are compatible with all of the operating systems in Table 14.1, we will generally, but not exclusively, adhere to the more restrictive DOS and VMX specifications. If you are using an operating system that permits longer names, you should take advantage of the increased length specification to create more descriptive file names. The selected name, however, should always be a manageable length, which is typically considered to be no more than 12 to 14 characters, with an outside maximum of 25 characters. Very long file names should be avoided. Although such names can be extremely descriptive, they take more time to type and are prone to typing errors.

Using the DOS convention, the following are all valid computer data file names:

```
prices.dat     records        info.txt
exper1.dat     scores.dat     math.mem
```

Computer file names should be chosen to indicate both the type of data in the file and the application for which it is used. Frequently, the first eight characters describe the data themselves, and an extension (the characters after the decimal point) describes

TABLE 14.1   Maximum Allowable File Name Characters

Operating System	Maximum Length
DOS	8 characters plus an optional period and 3-character extension
VMX	8 characters plus an optional period and 3-character extension
Windows 95, 98, 2000	255 characters
UNIX	
Early versions	14 characters
Current versions	255 characters

the application. For example, the Lotus 123 spreadsheet program automatically applies an extension of wk3 to all spreadsheet files, Microsoft's Word and the WordPerfect word processing programs use the extensions doc and wpx (where x refers to the version number), respectively, and Java compilers require a program file to have the extension java. When creating your own file names, you should adhere to this practice. For example, using the DOS convention, the name exper1.dat is appropriate in describing a file of data corresponding to experiment number 1.

File Stream Objects

A **file stream** is a one-way transmission path that is used to connect a file stored on a physical device, such as a disk or CD-ROM, to a program. Each file stream has its own mode, which determines the direction of data on the transmission path—that is, whether the path will move data from a file into a program or whether the path will move data from a program to a file. A file stream that receives or reads data from a file into a program is referred to as an **input file stream.** A file stream that sends or writes data to a file is referred to as an **output file stream.** Notice that the direction, or mode, is always defined in relation to the program and not the file; data that go into a program are considered input data, and data sent out from the program are considered output data. Figure 14.1 illustrates the data flow from and to a file using input and output streams.

For each file that your program uses, a distinct file stream object must be created. If you are going to read and write to a file, both an input and output file stream object are required. Depending on where the file is stored and whether data in the file are stored as character-based or byte-based values, the specific stream objects will be created from different classes. Table 14.2 lists the most common file stream classes for input and output

FIGURE 14.1   Input and Output File Streams

TABLE 14.2 Basic I/O Stream Classes Usage

Mode	For a Character-Based File	For a Byte-Based File
Input	Use a `FileReader` class	Use a `FileInputStream` class
Output	Use a `FileWriter` class	Use a `FileOutputStream` class

from both **character-based,** which are also known as **text files,** and b**yte-based** files. A detailed description of these two file types is provided in Section 14.9. Briefly, however, the characters and numbers stored in a byte-based file use the same binary code as specified by Java for its primitive data types, while character-based files store each individual letter, digit, and special symbols such as the decimal point and dollar sign using an individual character code. This permits such files to be read by either a word processing program or text editor.

For example, if you need to read data from a character-based file, the information in Table 14.2 indicates that you would use Java's `FileReader` class to create an input stream object. Similarly, for writing to a byte-stream file, the appropriate output stream object should be created from Java's `FileOutputStream` class.

Creating a file stream object is almost a cookbook procedure. In creating a file stream object, a physical communications path is established between a program and an external data file. This path defines both the direction of data transfer and the capabilities provided by the stream for data conversions and the buffering of data between a program and a file.

An input file stream object automatically attempts to open its associated file in read mode. This means that data in the file can be read by the program, and the file is referred to as an **input file.** An explicit check is usually always made, using techniques presented in Section 14.6, to ensure that a file intended for reading actually exists before an input stream attempts to open it.

An output file stream can open its associated file in one of two ways: write or append. When the output stream opens a file for writing, which is the default, the file is made available for accepting data from the program, and the file is referred to as an **output file.** If a file exists with the same name as a file opened for writing, the old file is erased. It is for this reason that an explicit check is usually made, again using techniques presented in Section 14.6, to alert the user to this possibility before a file is opened.

A file opened for appending makes an existing file available for data to be added to the end of the file. If the file opened for appending does not exist, a new file with the designated name is created and made available to receive output from the program. The only difference between a file opened in write mode and one opened in append mode is where the data are physically placed in the file. In write mode, the data are written starting at the beginning of the file, whereas in append mode, the data are written starting at the end of the file. For a new file, the two modes are identical.

As a specific example, let's take a moment to see how an object stream is created in practice. Assume that we wish to read data from an existing character-based file named `prices.txt`. Figure 14.2 illustrates the structure of the input stream necessary for reading the file. The complete stream begins at the file and ends at the program.

Using the information in Table 14.2, we see that to read data from a character-based file we can construct the basic input stream object to connect the file to the program from the `FileReader` class. Arbitrarily selecting the reference variable name `fr` for our input stream object, the following code creates the necessary input file stream object:

POINT OF INFORMATION

INPUT AND OUTPUT STREAMS

A *stream* is a one-way transmission path between a source and a destination. What gets sent down this transmission path is a stream of bytes. A good analogy to this "stream of bytes" is a stream of water that provides a one-way transmission path of water from a source to a destination.

Two stream objects that we have already used extensively are the input stream object named `System.in` and the output stream object named `System.out`. The `System.in` object provides a transmission path from keyboard to program, whereas the `System.out` **object** provides a transmission path from program to terminal screen. The `System.in` stream object is an instance of `java.io.BufferedInputStream`, which is a subclass of `java.io.InputStream`. The `System.out` object is an instance of `java.io.PrintStream`, which is a subclass of `java.io.OutputStream`. These two stream objects are automatically declared and instantiated by the Java compiler for use by the compiled program.

File stream objects provide essentially the same capabilities as the `System.in` and `System.out` objects, except they connect a program to a file rather than the keyboard or terminal screen. Also file stream objects must be explicitly instantiated.

```
    // set up the basic input stream
FileReader fr = new FileReader("prices.txt");
```

Notice that this declaration statement both creates an input stream and causes the `prices.txt` file to be opened for reading. Because the specific details of establishing this physical communications link between the program and data file are handled by Java and the operating system and are transparent to the program, the programmer need not consider them except for ensuring that the link is successfully established. In practice, you will frequently see this declaration statement written over two lines as

```
FileReader fr =
    new FileReader("prices.txt");
```

and we will use both the single-line and double-line form throughout this chapter.

FIGURE 14.2 A FileReader Input Stream

Besides establishing the actual physical connection between a program and a data file, the instantiated file stream created by this declaration equates the file's external computer name to the reference variable name used internally by the program. From a programming perspective, this is of primary importance because once the `fr` stream object has been created, the program will access the file using the reference variable name `fr`, while the computer's operating system continues to know the file by the name `prices.txt`. As an object created from the `FileReader` class, the program can now use this class' methods to read data from the file. For example, the statement

```
fr.read()
```

causes the next character from the `prices.txt` file to be read.

In a similar manner, character-based output stream objects can be created from the `FileWriter` class. For example, the statement

```
FileWriter fw =
    new FileWriter("backup.txt");
```

creates a character-based output stream object to a file named `backup.txt`. When an output stream object is created, a file with the given external name is automatically created by the operating system, whether or not such a file name already exists. If a file with the given external name does exist, *it will be erased* and a new empty file with the same name is created in its stead. Thus, any data in the original file are automatically lost. It is precisely to prevent erasing an existing file that you should always check if a file exists before opening it for output. Once the new file is created, any data written by the program to the output stream are automatically placed in the new file. For the preceding instantiation statement, the program accesses this file using the reference variable name `fw`. For example, a statement such as

```
fw.write('a');
```

will cause the appropriate code for the lowercase letter a to be placed on the `backup.txt` file.

It should be noted that character-based streams created from the `FileReader` and `FileWriter` classes always transmit characters as 16-bit data. For the majority of current computers that use 8-bit file systems, however, which are typically based on the ASCII code, these 16-bit data are encoded and stored as 8-bit ASCII characters using the computer's default character-encoding scheme (this is explained more fully in Section 14.9).

Because the stream objects created from the basic I/O classes listed in Table 14.2 (for both character-based and byte-based files) are restricted to byte processing capabilities, the basic input and output stream objects created from these classes are almost always enclosed into other stream objects that provide expanded capabilities. These expanded streams are referred to as **processing streams** because of the additional processing capabilities that they provide. Processing stream objects that are created from FileReader and FileWriter stream objects are presented in Section 14.2, where character-based file processing is described in detail. Similarly, processing stream objects that are created from FileInputStream and FileOutputStream stream objects are presented in Section 14.3, where byte-based file processing is described in detail. In all cases, the construction of an expanded processing stream object requires that a basic stream object is first created from one of the classes listed in Table 14.2.

Closing a Stream Object

A file stream object is closed using its class' `close()` method. This method closes the basic I/O stream object and all processing streams created from it. For example, the statement

```
fw.close();
```

closes the object stream named `fw`. As indicated, the `close()` method takes no argument.

Since all operating systems have a limit on the maximum number of files that can be accessed at one time, closing stream objects that are no longer needed makes good sense. Any open streams existing at the end of normal program execution are automatically closed.

Buffering

Every time a byte or sequence of bytes is written to or read from a file, a call to the underlying operating system is required. Because the number of accesses to a file storage medium, such as a disk, and the resulting operating system calls can be significantly reduced by buffering, this type of transfer is used for almost all file transfers. How buffering is conceptually constructed for transferring data between a program and a data file is illustrated in Figure 14.3.

As illustrated in Figure 14.3, when transferring data between a program and a file using a buffered stream, the buffered stream provides a storage area that is used by the data as they are transferred between the program and the file. In most cases, a buffered stream will provide enhanced I/O speed and performance.

From its side, the program either writes a set of data bytes to the buffered stream or reads a set of data bytes from the stream. On the file side of the stream, the transfer of data between the device storing the actual data file (usually a tape, disk, or CD-ROM drive) and the stream is handled by special operating system programs that are referred to as **device drivers.**[1] Typically, a disk device driver will only transfer data between the disk and stream buffer in fixed sizes, such as 1,024 bytes at a time. Thus, the stream buffer provides a convenient means of permitting a device driver to transfer data in blocks of one size while the program can access them using a different size (typically as individual characters or as a fixed number of characters per line).

Buffered object streams are created from buffered stream classes. The creation of a buffered stream, however, always requires the prior creation of a basic I/O stream object from one of the stream classes listed in Table 14.2. That is, you cannot create a buffered stream object without first creating a basic I/O stream object. Except for one case used to illustrate unbuffered file I/O presented at the end of Section 14.2, all of the file examples

---

[1]Device drivers are not stand-alone programs but are an integral part of the operating system. Essentially, the device driver is a section of operating system code that accesses a hardware device, such as a disk unit, and handles the data transfer between the device and the computer's memory. Thus, it must correctly synchronize the speed of the data transferred between the computer and the device sending or receiving the data. This is because the computer's internal data transfer rate is generally much faster than any device connected to it.

Computer

Disk or Tape

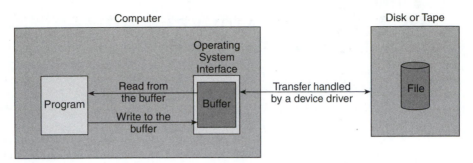

FIGURE 14.3 The Data Transfer Mechanism

in this chapter will use buffered streams. The actual construction of such streams is presented in Section 14.2 for character-based files and Section 14.3 for byte-based files.

EXERCISES 14.1

1. Using the reference manuals provided with your computer's operating system, determine the maximum number of characters that can be used to name a file for storage by your computer system.

2. Would it be appropriate to call a saved Java program a file? Why or why not?

3. **a.** What are the basic input and output stream classes used for constructing input and output stream objects for use with a character-based file?

   b. What are the basic input and output stream classes used for constructing input and output stream objects for use with a byte-based file?

4. Write suitable Java statements to create individual input streams named `fr` for each of the following character-based files: `inData.txt`, `prices.txt`, `coupons.dat`, and `results.mem`.

5. Write suitable Java statements to create individual output streams named `fw` for each of the following character-based files: `outData.txt`, `prices.txt`, `coupons.dat`, and `results.mem`.

6. Write suitable Java statements to create individual input streams named `fis` for each of the following byte-based files: `inData`, `distance`, `rates.dat`, and `coupons.dat`.

7. Write suitable Java statements to create individual output streams named `fos` for each of the following byte-based files: `outData`, `distance`, `rates.dat`, and `coupons.dat`.

8. Write individual statements to create appropriate stream objects for the following external data files.

External Name	File Type	Stream Name	Mode
`coba.mem`	text	memo	input
`book.let`	text	letter	input
`coupons.bnd`	text	coups	output
`yield.bnd`	byte-based	yield	input
`test.dat`	byte-based	inFile	output
`rates.dat`	byte-based	outFile	output

9. Write `close()` statements for each of the file stream objects created in Exercise 8.

14.2 WRITING AND READING CHARACTER-BASED FILES

Reading and writing character-based files involve almost the identical operations used for reading input from a keyboard and writing data to a display screen. For writing to a character-based file, a FileWriter stream object (see Table 14.2) provides the basic stream object that connects a file to a program.

As you have seen in Section 14.1, however, FileWriter input stream objects are extremely restrictive in that they only provide the capability to read a character at a time from a file. For this reason, the additional processing stream classes listed in Table 14.3 are provided. Each of these classes provides extensions to a FileWriter stream object that can be used both to enhance performance and improve data transfer capabilities. It is important to realize, however, that an expanded output stream object cannot be created without first constructing a basic FileWriter input stream object. This is because all expanded character-based output streams are built around and based on a FileWriter stream object. So this basic stream object must always be created first. As this is the first time we will be creating an expanded set of stream objects, we will individually present and explain each required declaration. For a specific example, assume that we want to open an output stream to a text file named `prices.txt`. For this, the following code can initially be used:

```
// set up the basic output stream
FileWriter fw =
    new FileWriter("prices.txt");
```

Notice that we have selected `fw` as the reference variable name to reference a FileWriter object that will be connected to the external file named `prices.txt`. Once this statement is executed, we can use the `FileWriter` class' `write()` method to write individual characters to the `prices.txt` file, as was illustrated in Section 14.1.

At this point, we should mention that a basic FileWriter output stream can be created in a manner that opens its associated file in append mode. For example, the statement

```
// set up the basic output stream and open a file in append mode
FileWriter fw =
    new FileWriter("prices.txt", true);
```

opens the file named `prices.txt` and makes it available for data to be appended to the end of the file. It is the second argument in the preceding statement, the boolean value `true`, that causes the file to be opened in append mode.

Regardless of the way the file connected to a basic FileWriter output stream object is opened, the associated stream methods restrict output to a character at a time. To create an output stream object that can directly handle character representations of numerical data, such as integers and double-precision numbers, and sequences of character data stored as strings, we must expand the basic output stream object.

To accomplish this, the first enhancement is almost always to make the output stream into a buffered stream. This permits the Java program to write characters to the buffered stream without forcing a call to the underlying operating system for each character that is written. What happens with a buffered stream is that all the data are first written into an

TABLE 14.3   Character-Based Output Stream Classes

Class	Type	Comments	Common Methods
FileWriter	Basic Output	Basic stream used for character-based input.	write(), flush(), close()
BufferedWriter	Buffering	Provides output buffering, which typically improves performance.	write(), flush(), close()
PrintWriter	Processing	Provides a number of useful output methods.	flush(), close(), print(char), print(String), print(int), print(float), print(double), print(boolean), and corresponding println() methods

internal buffer, which is then written to the actual file only if the buffer reaches its capacity, the buffer stream is closed, or the buffer stream is flushed using a flush() method.

Assuming that a FileWriter object named fw has already been created using one of the previous declaration statements, a buffered output stream can now be created using the fw reference variable as follows:

```
// buffer the stream for faster output
BufferedWriter bw =
    new BufferedWriter(fw);
```

In this statement, the reference variable name bw is programmer selected, and any valid Java variable name can be used instead. Because buffering almost always provides improved performance, it is recommended that you use it for all file I/O. Unfortunately, even though buffered byte streams improve I/O performance, these streams are still restricted to the byte or string output methods provided by the BufferedWriter class. For example, assuming that our BufferedWriter object is referenced by the variable named bw, the statement

```
bw.write('a');
```

causes the code for the lowercase letter to be placed into the buffer. Similarly, the sequence of statements

```
bw.write("This is a test");
bw.newLine();
```

causes the string This is a test followed by a newline separator to be written to the output buffer.

The output buffer can be flushed, which forces a write to the corresponding file, at any time using the statement bw.flush(). It should be noted that since we now have two file stream objects, we could write to the file using references to each stream. Although this is possible, good programming practice indicates that you use the methods applicable

to the last object stream created. It should also be noted that the final instantiation of a
BufferedWriter object using the two executable statements

```
FileWriter fw =
    new FileWriter("prices.txt");
BufferedWriter bw =
    new BufferedWriter(fw);
```

can be identically created using the single statement

```
BufferedWriter bw =
            new BufferedWriter(new FileWriter("prices.txt"));
```

In your programming career, you will see both single- and double-statement instantiations, with individual statements themselves placed over one or two lines, so you should become familiar with each approach.

The last enclosing stream object that we will need to create is a PrintWriter object. The reason is that the PrintWriter class contains a number of extremely useful class methods that will permit us to write the character representations of strings, doubles, floats, integers, and boolean data to a file. Although we can construct a PrintWriter stream from either a FileWriter stream or a BufferedWriter stream, we will always use a buffered stream. Doing so provides us with the inherent performance advantages associated with buffering. Thus, the complete set of statements for creating the output streams that we will use throughout this chapter to construct character-based files is:[2]

```
    // set up the basic output stream
FileWriter fw =
    new FileWriter("prices.txt");

    // buffer it for faster output
BufferedWriter bw =
    new BufferedWriter(fw);

    // this provides a set of useful methods
PrintWriter pw =
    new PrintWriter(bw);
```

As always, this set of three statements can be implemented with a single-statement. For our particular example, a single-statement equivalent that you should be prepared to encounter in your programming career (with variations on white space) is:

```
PrintWriter pw =
        new PrintWriter(new BufferedWriter(new FileWriter("prices.txt")));
```

Once the last stream has been created, we can use the methods provided by the PrintWriter class (see Table 14.3) for actually writing data to the file.

---

[2]As you might imagine, a similar set is required for writing to a byte-based file. The byte-based equivalents are presented in Section 14.3.

No matter which methods we use, however, it is always a sequence of one or more characters that will be output to a text file. For example, if pw is declared as a PrintWriter stream object, each of the following output statements places one or more characters onto the file connected to the pw stream.

```
pw.print('a');
pw.print("Hello World!");
pw.print(22);      // print an integer as a string
pw.print(39.95); // print a double as a string
pw.println("Have a Good Day"); // print a string and a newline sequence
```

The file stream name pw in each of these statements, in place of the System.out you have been using directs the output stream to a specific file instead of to the standard display device. Program 14.1 illustrates the use of the PrintWriter methods to write a list of descriptions and prices to a file named prices.txt. In examining this program, notice that the main() header line uses the phrase throws java.io.IOException. Because we are not providing main() with any I/O exception handling capabilities, we must instruct it to throw any such exceptions that might occur up to the next level (this is the same reasoning as described in Section 3.3 for keyboard input). If an I/O exception does occur and main() passes it up, the program stops execution and an error message is displayed.

PROGRAM 14.1

```java
import java.io.*;
public class WriteTextPrices
{
  public static void main(String[] args)
    throws java.io.IOException
  {
      // set up the basic output stream
    FileWriter fw =
        new FileWriter("prices.txt");
      // buffer it for faster output
    BufferedWriter bw =
        new BufferedWriter(fw);
      // this provides a set of useful methods
    PrintWriter pw =
        new PrintWriter(bw);

    pw.println("Mats 39.95");
    pw.println("Bulbs 3.22");
    pw.println("Fuses 1.08");

    pw.close();
  }
}
```

When Program 14.1 is executed, a file named `prices.txt` is created and saved by the computer. The file is a sequential file that, after it is opened, is written with the following data:

```
Mats 39.95
Bulbs 3.22
Fuses 1.08
```

The actual storage of characters in the file depends on the character codes used by the computer. Although only 30 characters appear to be stored in the file, corresponding to the descriptions, blanks, and prices written to the file, the file actually contains 36 characters. The extra characters consist of the carriage return and line feed at the end of each line that is created by the `println()`'s newline escape sequence. Assuming characters in the file are stored using the ASCII code, the `prices.txt` file is physically stored as illustrated in Figure 14.4. For convenience, the character corresponding to each hexadecimal code is listed below the code. A code of 20 represents the blank character. In addition, your particular system may append an end of file marker as the last byte stored in the file.

```
4D 61 74 73 20 33 39 2E 39 35 0D 0A 42 75 6C 62 73 20
 M  a  t  s     3  9  .  9  5 cr lf  B  u  l  b  s
```

```
33 2E 32 32 0D 0A 46 75 73 65 73 20 31 2E 30 38 0D 0A
 3  .  2  2 cr lf  F  u  s  e  s     1  .  0  8 cr lf
```

FIGURE 14.4 The `test.dat` File as Stored by the Computer

Embedded and Interactive File Names

Although Program 14.1 provides the basics of creating and storing data into a character-based file, there are three practical problems with the program as it stands:

1. The external file name is embedded within the program code.
2. There is no provision for a user to enter the desired file name while the program is executing.
3. There is no checking to see that a file of the existing name does not already exist.

Techniques to correct the third problem, file checking, are presented in detail in Section 14.6. Here we present techniques that appropriately deal with the first two problems.

The first problem, embedding a file's name within the code, can be alleviated by assigning the file name to a string variable at the top of the program. As you will see, this solution also makes it easy to correct the second problem because once a string variable is used for the name, this variable can be assigned to an external name either by explicit assignment of a string value or by interactively reading in a file's name when the program is executing.

To see how this is done, first consider Program 14.2, where we have assigned the string value `prices.dat` to the string variable named `fileName`. The output file produced by Program 14.2 is identical to that produced by Program 14.1.

PROGRAM 14.2

```java
import java.io.*;
public class WriteTextPrices2
{
  public static void main(String[] args)
    throws java.io.IOException
  {
    String fileName = "prices.txt";

      // set up the basic output stream
    FileWriter fw = new FileWriter(fileName);
      // buffer it for faster output
    BufferedWriter bw = new BufferedWriter(fw);
      // this provides a set of useful methods
    PrintWriter pw = new PrintWriter(bw);

    pw.println("Mats 39.95");
    pw.println("Bulbs 3.22");
    pw.println("Fuses 1.08");

    pw.close();
  }
}
```

Once a string variable is declared to store a file's name, it can be used in one of two ways. First, as in Program 14.2, it can be placed at the top of a program to clearly identify a file's external name rather than be embedded within one or more statements throughout the program, as in Program 14.1. Next, we can use the string variables to permit the user to enter the file name as the program is executing. Doing so eliminates the need to recompile the program each time the file name has to be changed. For example, the code

```java
  // set up a basic keyboard input stream
InputStreamReader isr = new
    InputStreamReader(System.in);

  // buffer it so we can use a readLine()
BufferedReader br = new
    BufferedReader(isr);

String fileName;

System.out.print("\nEnter the file's name: ");
fileName = br.readLine();
```

allows a user to enter a file's external name at run time using the keyboard input techniques presented in Section 3.3. The only restriction in this code is that the user must not

POINT OF INFORMATION

A WAY TO CLEARLY IDENTIFY A FILE'S NAME AND LOCATION

During program development, data files are usually placed in the same directory as the program. Therefore, an expression such as `File inFile = new File("test.dat");` causes no problem in locating the file. In production systems, however, it is not uncommon for data files to reside in one directory and program files reside in another. In this situation, you would include the full pathname of any file you are using. When a full pathname is used, however, a double delimiter, \\, must separate file names. The double backslashes provide an escape sequence where the first backslash tells the compiler to correctly consider the next character as a backslash.

Another important convention is to list all file names at the top of a program instead of embedding the names deep within the code. This is easily accomplished by assigning each file name to a string variable. For example, if a declaration such as

```
String inputFile = "C:\\jdk\\test.dat"
```

is placed at the top of a program file, both the name of the file and its location are clearly visible. Then, if some other file is to be used, all that is required is a simple one-line change at the top of the program.

Using a string variable for the file's name is also useful for any subsequent file checks and display messages. For example, consider the statement

```
System.out.println("The file " + inputFile + " is not available for input.");
```

Here the name of the offending file is printed as part of the message without explicitly rewriting the full pathname a second time.

enclose the entered string value in double quotes, which is a plus, and that the entered string value cannot contain any blanks. The reason is that the compiler will terminate the string when it encounters a blank. We leave it as Exercise 3 to include this code in Program 14.2.

Reading from a Text File

Reading data from a character-based file is almost identical to reading data from a standard keyboard, except that the `System.in` object is replaced by the file stream object declared in the program. The same problem that we had with keyboard input, however, still remains, which means that the basic input from a text file will be either a character or a string. This is reinforced by referring to Table 14.4, which lists the two main file stream classes available for text file input. As is seen in the table, the two methods that we will have to rely on are the character input method `read()` and the string input method `readLine()`. Thus, from the point of view of reading a text file, it is useful

TABLE 14.4 Character-Based Input Stream Classes

Class	Type	Comments	Common Methods
FileReader	Basic Input	Basic stream used for character-based input. Supplies character-by-character input.	read()
BufferedReader	Processing	Provides buffering, which typically improves performance.	read()
		Supplies character-by-character and line-by-line input and typically uses a FileInputStream object argument.	readLine()

to consider each line in the file as a string. Using this approach, each line can first be input and then separated into constituent pieces using the StringTokenizer methods presented in Section 9.3.

Program 14.3 illustrates reading the prices.txt file that was created in Program 14.1. Each line is input one at a time using a readLine() method. In effect, the program

PROGRAM 14.3

```java
import java.io.*;
public class ReadTextPrices
{
  public static void main(String[] args)
    throws java.io.IOException
  {
    String fileName = "prices.txt";
    int i;
    String inLine;

      // set up the basic input stream
    FileReader fr =
        new FileReader(fileName);
      // buffer the input stream
    BufferedReader br =
        new BufferedReader(fr);

      // read and display three lines
    for(i = 0; i < 3; i++)
    {
      inLine = br.readLine();  // read a line
      System.out.println(inLine);  // display the line
    }

    br.close();
  }
}
```

is really a line-by-line text-copying program, reading a line of text from the file and then displaying it on the terminal. The display produced by Program 14.3 is:

```
Mats 39.95
Bulbs 3.22
Fuses 1.08
```

Although Program 14.3 uses a fixed-count `for` loop to read in exactly three lines, it is frequently more convenient to have the program keep reading lines until there are no more data left in the file. This is easily accomplished because the BufferedReader method `readLine()` used in the program automatically returns a `null` when the input stream contains no more lines. Thus, in place of the `for` loop in Program 14.3, the following `while` loop can be substituted:

```
while ( (inLine = br.readLine()) != null)
{
    System.out.println(inLine);  // display the line
}
```

It should be noted that the parentheses surrounding the expression (`inLine = br.readLine()`) are necessary to ensure that a line is first read and assigned to the reference variable named `inLine` before this reference is compared to the `null` reference value. In their absence, the complete expression would be `inLine = br.readLine() != null`. Due to the precedence of operations, the relational expression `br.readLine() != null` would be executed first. Because this is a relational expression, its result is either a boolean `true` or `false` based on the data retrieved by the `br.readLine()` method. Attempting to assign this boolean result to the string referenced by `inLine` is an invalid conversion across an assignment operator and results in a compiler error.

Finally, if it were necessary to obtain the description and price as individual variables, the string returned by `readLine()` in Program 14.3 can be processed further to extract the individual data items. This is typically accomplished using a StringTokenizer object in the same manner as for multiple value keyboard input (see Section 3.3). For example, assuming that the variable `st` has been declared as a StingTokenizer object, `desc` as a String object, and `price` as a precision variable, the statements

```
st = new StringTokenizer(inLine);
desc = st.nextToken();
price = Double.parseDouble(st.nextToken());
```

can be used to extract description and price values from the `inLine` string read within Program 14.3's `for` loop. These statements, which are boldfaced for easier recognition, are used within the context of a complete program in Program 14.4. Notice also that a single-line declaration is used in Program 14.4 to open the buffered output stream in place of the two-line declaration employed in Program 14.3. Either style of declaration is acceptable, and both are found in practice.

PROGRAM 14.4

```java
import java.io.*;
import java.util.*;    // needed for StringTokenizer
public class ReadTextPrices2
{
  public static void main(String[] args)
    throws java.io.IOException
  {
    String fileName = "prices.txt";
    int i;
    double price;
    String inLine, desc;
    StringTokenizer st;

       // set up a buffered input stream - notice the single statement used
    BufferedReader br = new BufferedReader(new FileReader(fileName));

       // read and display three lines
    for (i = 0; i < 3; i++)
    {
      inLine = br.readLine();
      st = new StringTokenizer(inLine);     // here is where the string is
      desc = st.nextToken();                // parsed into individual values
      price = Double.parseDouble(st.nextToken());
      System.out.println("Description: " + desc + '\t'
                        + "Price: " + price);
    }

    br.close();
  }
}
```

The output produced by Program 14.4 is:

```
Description: Mats    Price: 39.95
Description: Bulbs   Price: 3.22
Description: Fuses   Price: 1.08
```

Although we have not used Program 14.7's numerical values in a numerical calculation, the program does illustrate the process of converting text-based file data into numerical data types. Clearly, once string values have been converted into numerical values, these values can subsequently be used in appropriate numerical calculations. Finally, it should be noted that the stripping of individual values requires that the programmer knows how the data are placed within each line of the file.

Unbuffered I/O[3]

The examples illustrating text file input and output in this section have all used buffered streams. There are cases, however, where it is useful to read and write individual characters in an unbuffered manner. To show how this can be done, we present an extremely simple application that performs a file copy one character at a time.

Specifically, for our example, assume that we wish to read the data from a character-based file named info.txt one character at a time and write these data out to a file named backup.txt. Essentially, this application is a file copy program that reads the data from one file in a character-by-character manner and writes them to a second file. For purposes of illustration, assume that the characters stored in the input file are as shown in Figure 14.5.

```
Now is the time for all good people
  to come to the aid of their party.
Please call (555) 888-6666 for
  further information.
```

FIGURE 14.5 The Data Stored in info.txt

Figure 14.6 illustrates the structure of the streams that are necessary for producing our file copy. In this figure, the input stream object referenced by the variable fr will read data from the info.txt file, and the output stream object referenced by the variable fw will write data to the backup.txt file.

Because we are dealing with character-based files, we must construct our basic input and output stream objects from the stream classes FileReader and FileWriter, respectively (refer to Table 14.2). Arbitrarily using the reference variable names fr and fw, the following statements create the appropriate file stream objects:

```
    // set up the basic input stream
FileReader fr =
    new FileReader("info.txt");
    // set up the basic output stream
FileWriter fw =
    new FileOutputStream("backup.txt");
```

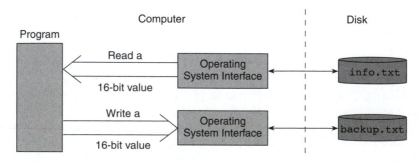

FIGURE 14.6 File Copy Stream Structure

[3]This topic can be omitted on first reading without loss of subject continuity.

Streams created from either the `FileReader` and `FileWriter` classes always transmit characters as 16-bit data regardless of how the characters are actually stored in a file (and most file systems currently store characters as 8-bit ASCII data—see Section 14.9). Thus, the character read into a Java program using a FileReader `read()` method will return a 16-bit Unicode value rather than an 8-bit ASCII character code. In addition to its intended purpose of accommodating Unicode data, the return of a 16-bit value permits the `read()` method to alert us to the fact that the end of a stream has been reached and no more data are available. This is accomplished by `read()` returning a -1 value whenever the end of a stream is reached. Because -1 has no character representation, it ensures that when this value is detected, it can never be confused with any legitimate character that could be encountered as normal data in the file.

Now consider Program 14.5, which is a bare-bones program that omits all file checking and stream buffering before performing its file copy. It does, however, illustrate the unbuffered reading and writing of a text file. When it has completed executing, a file named `backup.txt` will be an exact duplicate of the `prices.txt` file created in Program 14.3.

PROGRAM 14.5

```java
import java.io.*;
public class CopyTextPrices
{
  static final int EOF = -1;
  public static void main(String[] args)
    throws java.io.IOException
  {
      // open a basic input stream
    FileReader fr = new FileReader("info.txt");
     // open a basic output stream
    FileWriter fw = new FileWriter("backup.txt");

    int c;
    while ((c = fr.read()) != EOF)
      fw.write(c);

    fr.close();
    fw.close();
  }
}
```

In reviewing Program 14.5, notice that we are using unbuffered FileReader and FileWriter stream objects and their associated `read()` and `write()` methods. We are also using a named constant EOF that has been equated to the value -1. The reason for creating this value as a named constant is that the `read()` method returns a -1 when it locates the end of the input stream.

Within Program 14.5, the statement

```java
while( (c = fr.read()) != EOF)
```

continually reads a value from the `fr` input stream until the EOF value is detected. As long as the returned value does not equal the EOF value, the value is written out to the unbuffered `fw` object stream. It should be noted that the parentheses surrounding the expression `(c = fr.read())` are necessary to ensure that a value is first read and assigned to the variable `c` before the retrieved value is compared to the EOF value. In their absence, the complete expression would be `c = fr.read() != EOF`. Due to the precedence of operations, the relational expression `fr.read() != EOF` would be executed first. Because this is a relational expression, its result is either a boolean `true` or `false` value based on the data retrieved by the `read()` method. Attempting to assign this boolean result to the variable `c` is an invalid conversion across an assignment operator and results in a compiler error.

EXERCISES 14.2

1. Enter and execute Program 14.1 on your computer.
2. Enter and execute Program 14.2 on your computer.
3. Modify Program 14.2 to permit the user to interactively enter the name of a file.
4. Enter and execute Program 14.3 on your computer.
5. a. Write a Java program that accepts five lines of text from the keyboard and writes each line to a file named `text.dat`.
   b. Modify Program 14.3 to read and display the data stored in the `text.dat` file created in Exercise 5a.
6. Determine the operating system command or procedures provided by your computer to display the contents of a saved file. Compare its operation to the program developed for Exercise 5b.
7. Write, compile, and run a Java program that writes the four real numbers 92.65, 88.72, 77.46, and 82.93 to a text file named `results.txt`. After writing the data to the file, your program should read the data from the file, determine the average of the four numbers read, and display the average. Verify the output produced by your program by manually calculating the average of the four input numbers.
8. a. Write, compile, and execute a Java program that creates a text file named `points` and writes the following three lines of data to the file:

   ```
    6.3   8.2   18.25   24.32
    4.0   4.0   10.0    -5.0
   -2.0   5.0    4.0     5.0
   ```

   b. Using the data in the `points` file created in Exercise 8a, write, compile, and run a Java program that reads each line and interprets the first and second numbers in the line as the coordinates of one point and the third and fourth numbers as the coordinates of a second point. Have your program compute and display the slope and midpoint of each pair of entered points.
9. a. Write, compile, and run a Java program that creates a text file named `grades.txt` and writes the following five lines of data to the file:

   ```
   90.3   92.7   90.3   99.8
   85.3   90.5   87.3   90.8
   93.2   88.4   93.8   75.6
   82.4   95.6   78.2   90.0
   93.5   80.2   92.9   94.4
   ```

b. Using the data in the `grades.txt` file created in Exercise 9a, write, compile, and run a Java program that reads each line in the file, computes the average for each line, and displays the average.

10. a. Create a file containing the following car numbers, number of miles driven, and number of gallons of gas used by each car:

Car No.	Miles Driven	Gallons Used
54	250	19
62	525	38
71	123	6
85	1,322	86
97	235	14

b. Write a Java program that reads the data in the file created in Exercise 10a and displays the car number, miles driven, gallons used, and the miles per gallon for each car. The output should additionally contain the total miles driven, total gallons used, and average miles per gallon for all the cars. These totals should be displayed at the end of the output report.

11. a. A file named `polar.txt` contains the polar coordinates needed in a graphics program. Currently, this file contains the following data:

Distance (inches)	Angle (degrees)
--------	----------
2.0	45.0
6.0	30.0
10.0	45.0
4.0	60.0
13.0	55.0
8.0	15.0

Write a Java program to create the data in this file on your computer system (without the header lines).

b. Using the `polar.txt` file created in Exercise 11a, write a Java program that reads this file and creates a second file named `xycord.dat`. The entries in the new file should contain the rectangular coordinates corresponding to the polar coordinates in the `polar.txt` file. Polar coordinates are converted to rectangular coordinates using the equations

$$x = r \cos \theta$$
$$y = r \sin \theta$$

where r is the distance coordinate and θ is the radian equivalent of the angle coordinate in the `polar.txt` file.

12. a. Store the following data in a file: 5 96 87 78 93 21 4 92 82 85 87 6 72 69 85 75 81 73

b. Write a Java program to calculate and display the average of each group of numbers in the file created in Exercise 12.a. The data are arranged in the file so that each group of numbers is preceded by the number of data items in the group. Thus, the first number in the file, 5, indicates that the next five numbers should be grouped together. The number 4 indicates that the following four numbers are a group, and the 6 indicates that the last six numbers are a group. (*Tip:* Use a nested loop.)

13. Enter the data shown in Figure 14.5 into a character-based file named `info.txt`.

14. Enter and execute Program 14.5 on your computer. When the program has completed execution, verify that a file named `backup.txt` exists and contains the data created for the `info.txt` file created in Exercise 13.

15. Rewrite Program 14.5 so that it uses buffered input and output streams in place of the unbuffered FileReader and FileWriter streams.

16. Modify Program 14.5 so that the input file is read using a `readLine()` method and the output file is written using a `println()` method. (*Tip:* You will have to add processing streams to the existing FileReader and FileWriter streams. See Exercise 15.)

14.3 WRITING AND READING BYTE-BASED FILES

An alternative to text files, where each character in the file is represented by a unique code, is byte-based files. The advantage of a byte-based file is that Java's primitive data types, such as `ints` and `doubles`, are written, stored, and read directly in their binary representation. This means that there is no number-to-string conversion required when writing a number and no string-to-number conversion required when a value is read back from the file. For files consisting predominantly of numerical data, this is a distinct advantage and can improve program efficiency. The disadvantage is that the ability to easily inspect the file using either a word processing or text editing program and to see the numerical values as textual information is lost. In this section, we first present the creation of a byte-based file using an output stream and then show how to read the file using a byte-based input stream.

Table 14.5 lists the common byte-based output file streams. Like their character-based counterparts, a basic byte-based output stream is typically wrapped into other streams that provide additional processing capabilities.

For output, the set of stream objects typically instantiated from the classes in Table 14.5 is:

```
// set up the basic output stream
FileOutputStream fos =
    new FileOutputStream(outFile);

// buffer it for faster output
BufferedOutputStream bos =
    new BufferedOutputStream(fos);

// this provides a set of useful methods
DataOutputStream dos =
    new DataOutputStream(bos);
```

T A B L E 14.5 Common Byte-Based File Output Stream Classes

Class	Mode	Comments	Typical Object Name
FileOutputStream	Output	Basic stream used for byte-based output. Supplies character-by-character output.	fos
BufferedOutputStream	Output	Provides buffering, which improves performance. Supplies character-by-character and line-by-line output. Typically uses a FileOutputStream object argument.	bos
DataOutputStream	Output	Supplies additional output methods. Typically uses either an FileOutputStream object or BufferedOutputStream object argument.	dos

In this set of instantiations, the terms fos, bos, and dos are common programmer-selected names for their respective stream types. The outFile argument in the creation of the first stream can be either a string variable, string constant, or file object name, as described in Section 14.6.

The primary reasons for the first wrapping, which results in the creation of a BufferedOutputStream object, are that this stream provides for writing complete lines rather than just single bytes, as provided by a FileOutputStream, and that buffered output is generally more efficient than unbuffered byte-by-byte output.

The primary reason for the second wrapping, which results in the creation of a DataOutputStream, is that this stream provides a rich set of methods for writing both string and numerical data. Table 14.6 lists the common class methods provided by the DataOutputStream class. As is evident from this table, we now have a rather large set of methods from which to choose when writing various types of data to a byte-based file.

In a similar manner, an output stream can be created that opens its associated file in append mode. If the file opened for appending does not exist, a new file with the designated name is created and made available to the output stream to receive data from the program. Connecting an output stream to a file opened in append mode is accomplished by adding a boolean argument to the first stream object created. For our example, the statement

```
// set up the basic output stream and open the file in append mode
FileOutputStream fos =
    new FileOutputStream(outFile, true);
```

opens the outFile and makes it available for data to be appended to the end of the file.

As a specific example of creating a byte-based file, consider Program 14.6 on page 689.

The byte-based file created by Program 14.6 is illustrated in Figure 14.7, which uses hexadecimal values to indicate the equivalent binary values.[4] Although the figure separates the file's data into three individual lines, with bars, |, used to distinguish individual items, in actuality the file is stored as a consecutive sequence of bytes. As indicated

---

[4]The specific byte patterns shown are those obtained using the real number storage specification presented in Appendix I.

TABLE 14.6 `DataOutputStream` Class Methods

Method	Description
`flush()`	Flushes the stream, which forces any buffered output bytes to be written to the file.
`close()`	Closes the file output stream.
`writeByte(int b)`	Writes a byte to the underlying output stream as a 1-byte value.
`writeBoolean(boolean v)`	Writes a boolean to the underlying stream as a 1-byte value. The value `true` is written as the cast value `(byte)` `1`, and the value `false` is written as the cast value `(byte)` `0`.
`writeBytes(String s)`	Writes the String `s` to the underlying output stream as a sequence of bytes. The higher 8 bits of each character are discarded (not written).
`writeChar(int v)`	Writes a `char` to the underlying output stream as a 2-byte Unicode value, with the high byte written first.
`writeChars(String s)`	Writes the String `s` to the underlying output stream as a sequence of characters. Writes each character to the underlying output stream as a 2-byte Unicode value.
`writeDouble(double v)`	Converts the `double` value `v` to a `long` and then writes the `long` value to the underlying output stream using 8 bytes, with the high byte written first.
`writeFloat(float v)`	Converts the `float` value `v` to an `int` and then write the `int` value to the underlying output stream using 4 bytes, with the high byte written first.
`writeInt(int v)`	Writes an `int` to the underlying output stream using 4 bytes, with the high byte written first.
`writeLong(long v)`	Writes a `long` to the underlying output stream using 8 bytes, with the high byte written first.
`writeShort(int v)`	Writes a `short` to the underlying output stream using 2 bytes, with the high byte written first.

in the figure, each value consists of 8 bytes, which is the size of a double-precision number specified in Java.

```
|40 43 F9 99 99 99 99 9A| <--- corresponds to 39.95
|40 09 C2 8F 5C 28 F5 C3| <--- corresponds to 3.22
|3F F1 47 AE 14 7A E1 48| <--- corresponds to 1.08
```

FIGURE 14.7 The Stored Binary Data in the `prices.dat` File
and Their Decimal Equivalent

Reading a byte-based file, such as that illustrated in Figure 14.7, requires constructing an input byte-based stream and then using appropriate stream methods for data input. Table 14.7 lists the common byte-based input file streams.

As with all stream objects, the purpose of creating an initial basic stream, in this case using the `FileInputStream` class, and then wrapping this initial object into other streams,

TABLE 14.7 Common Byte-Based File Input Stream Classes

Class	Mode	Comments	Typical Object Name
FileInputStream	Input	Basic stream used for byte-based input. Supplies character-by-character input.	fis
BufferedInputStream	Input	Provides buffering, which improves performance. Supplies character-by-character and line-by-line input. Typically uses a FileInputStream object argument.	bis
DataInputStream	Input	Supplies additional input methods. Typically uses either a FileInputStream object or BufferedInputStream object argument.	dis

PROGRAM 14.6

```java
import java.io.*;
public class WritePrices
{
  public static void main(String[] args)
    throws java.io.IOException
  {
    String fileName = "prices.dat";

      // set up the basic output stream
    FileOutputStream fos =
        new FileOutputStream(fileName);

      // buffer it for faster output
    BufferedOutputStream bos =
        new BufferedOutputStream(fos);

      // this provides a set of useful methods
    DataOutputStream dos =
        new DataOutputStream(bos);

    dos.writeDouble(39.95);
    dos.writeDouble(3.22);
    dos.writeDouble(1.08);

    dos.close();

    System.out.println("A new " + fileName + " file has been written.");
  }
}
```

PROGRAM 14.7

```java
import java.io.*;
public class ReadPrices
{
  public static void main(String[] args)
    throws java.io.IOException
  {
    String fileName = "prices.dat";

      // set up the basic input stream
    FileInputStream fis =
        new FileInputStream(fileName);

      // buffer it for faster input
    BufferedInputStream bis =
        new BufferedInputStream(fis);

      // this provides a set of useful methods
    DataInputStream dis =
        new DataInputStream(bis);

    System.out.println("The values read from the " + fileName
                        + " file are:");
    System.out.println(dis.readDouble());
    System.out.println(dis.readDouble());
    System.out.println(dis.readDouble());

    dis.close();
  }
}
```

is to obtain the additional features, such as buffering, and the additional methods provided by each subsequent stream. For byte-based streams, the `DataInputStream` class provides the methods listed in Table 14.8. A comparison of these methods to those of Table 14.6 reveals that the DataInputStream methods are the input counterparts to the output methods provided by the `DataOutputStream` class. These input methods permit reading primitive data types directly from a file into a program without the need for any intermediate conversions.

Program 14.7 illustrates the opening of a byte-based input stream object, the input of the data stored in the file created in Program 14.6, and the display of these data. By now, the construction of the input stream objects should be familiar to you. In reviewing the actual input of the data, notice that the individual data items are read directly as double-precision values using the `readDouble()` method. Although we have chosen to display the input values directly, in a more typical application, the input values would be assigned to double-precision variables for further numerical processing.

TABLE 14.8   `DataInputStream` Class Methods

Method	Description
`close()`	Closes the input stream.
`readBoolean()`	Reads a `boolean` from the input stream.
`readByte()`	Reads a `byte` from the input stream.
`readChar()`	Reads a `char` (16-bits) from the input stream
`readDouble()`	Reads a `double` (64-bits) from the input stream.
`readFloat()`	Reads a `float` (32-bits) from the input stream.
`readInt()`	Reads an `int` (32-bits) from the input stream.
`readLong()`	Read a `long` (64-bits) from the input stream.
`readShort()`	Reads a `short` (16-bits) from the input stream.
`readLine()`	replaced by `BufferedReader.readLine()`.

The output produced by Program 14.7 is:

The values read from the `prices.dat` file are:
```
39.95
3.22
1.08
```

Caution

Table 14.8 lists a `readLine()` method provided by the `DataInputStream` class. This method has been deprecated in Java 2.0, which means that it may not be supported in some future release.

The reason for deprecating the DataInputStream's `readLine()` method is that it can cause programs to pause indefinitely when reading files that are either sent over a network or input via the keyboard. This occurs because this particular method uses a carriage return line feed sequence (\r\n) to determine when to stop reading. For locally stored files, this pair of codes is typically created whenever a line has been written, so `readLine()` rarely causes a problem for this type of file. However, if your program uses this method and a file is sent over a network that does not specify the \r\n sequence as an end of line (the HTTP protocol does specify this pair as a required line termination), your program can go into a permanent pause state.

Before this problem became known, `readLine()` was widely and conveniently used to read byte-based files that contained string data as the last item on a line. For example, if a line consisted of a sequence of numerical data and then string data, the numerical data would have been read using the primitive data type read methods listed in Table 14.8, followed by a `readLine()`. This technique is now replaced by reading and appending individual characters to a StringBuffer variable (see Section 7.3) until a known end of line character is encountered. A typical implementation of this replacement approach would appear as follows, where `inchar` has been declared as a character variable, `dis` as a DataInputStream object, and `sbvar` as a StringBuffer variable:

```
while( (inchar = dis.inChar()) != '\r')
   sbvar.append(inchar);
```

In this example, it is assumed that each line is terminated by a single carriage return code.

EXERCISES 14.3

1. Enter and execute Program 14.6 on your computer.

2. Enter and execute Program 14.7 on your computer.

3. Write, compile, and run a Java program that writes the numbers 92.65, 88.72, 77.46, and 82.93 as double-precision values to a byte-based file named `results.dat`. After writing the data to the file, your program should read the data from the file, determine the average of the four numbers read, and display the average. Verify the output produced by your program by manually calculating the average of the four input numbers.

4. **a.** Write, compile, and execute a Java program that creates a byte-based file named `points` and writes the following numbers to the file:

    ```
     6.3   8.2   18.25   24.32
     4.0   4.0   10.0    -5.0
    -2.0   5.0    4.0     5.0
    ```

    b. Using the data in the `points` file created in Exercise 4a, write, compile, and run a Java program that reads four numbers using a `for` loop and interprets the first and second numbers in each record as the coordinates of one point and the third and fourth numbers as the coordinates of a second point. Have your program compute and display the slope and midpoint of each pair of entered points.

5. **a.** Write, compile, and run a Java program that creates a byte-based file named `grades.bin` and writes the following data to the file:

    ```
    90.3   92.7   90.3   99.8
    85.3   90.5   87.3   90.8
    93.2   88.4   93.8   75.6
    82.4   95.6   78.2   90.0
    93.5   80.2   92.9   94.4
    ```

    b. Using the data in the `grades.bin` file created in Exercise 5a, write, compile, and run a Java program that reads, computes, and displays the average of each group of four grades.

6. **a.** Create a byte-based file containing the following car numbers, number of miles driven, and number of gallons of gas used by each car:

Car No.	Miles Driven	Gallons Used
54	250	19
62	525	38
71	123	6
85	1,322	86
97	235	14

    b. Write a Java program that reads the data in the file created in Exercise 6a and displays the car number, miles driven, gallons used, and the miles per gallon for each car. The output should additionally contain the total miles driven, total gallons used, and average miles per gallon for all the cars. These totals should be displayed at the end of the output report.

7. a. A byte-based file named `polar.dat` contains the polar coordinates needed in a graphics program. Currently, this file contains the following data:

Distance (inches)	Angle (degrees)
--------	----------
2.0	45.0
6.0	30.0
10.0	45.0
4.0	60.0
13.0	55.0
8.0	15.0

Write a Java program to create the data in this file on your computer system (without the header lines).

b. Using the `polar.dat` file created in Exercise 7a, write a Java program that reads this file and creates a second byte-based file named `xycord.dat`. The entries in the new file should contain the rectangular coordinates corresponding to the polar coordinates in the `polar.dat` file. Polar coordinates can be converted to rectangular coordinates using the equations

$$x = r \cos \theta$$
$$y = r \sin \theta$$

where r is the distance coordinate and θ is the radian equivalent of the angle coordinate in the `polar.dat` file.

14.4 APPLICATIONS

In this section, two applications are presented. The first application uses a file storing the 10 most recent pollen counts, which are used in the summer as allergy "irritability" measures. As a new reading is obtained, it is added to the file, and the oldest stored reading is deleted.

The second application presents an expanded file update procedure. In this application, a file containing inventory data, consisting of book identification numbers and quantities in stock, is updated by information contained in a second file. This application requires that identification numbers in the two files be matched before a record is updated.

Application 1: Pollen Counts

Pollen count readings, which are taken from August through September in the northeastern region of the United States, measure the number of ragweed pollen grains in the air. Pollen counts in the range of 10 to 200 grains per cubic meter of air are typical during this time of year. Pollen counts above 10 begin to affect a small percentage of hay fever sufferers, counts in the range of 30 to 40 will noticeably bother approximately 30 percent of hay fever sufferers, and counts between 40 and 50 adversely affect more than 60 percent of all hay fever sufferers.

A program is to be written that updates a file containing the 10 most recent pollen counts. As a new count is obtained, it is to be added to the end of the file, and the oldest count is to be deleted from the file. (This type of data storage is formally referred to as a first-in first-out, FIFO, list, which is also called a **queue.** If the list is maintained in last-in first-out order, LIFO, it is called a **stack.**) Additionally, the averages of the old and new files' data must be calculated and displayed. For purposes of illustration, assume that a file name `Pollen.dat`, containing the data shown in Figure 14.8, has already been created.

```
30  ← — —  Oldest pollen count (to be deleted)
60
40
80
90
120
150
130
160
170 ← — —  Last pollen count
```

FIGURE 14.8   Data Currently in the `Pollen.dat` File

The pseudocode for the file update program is:

Display a message indicating what the program does
Request the name of the data file
Request a new pollen count reading
Open the data file
Do for 10 data items
    Read a value into an array
    Add the value to a total
EndDo
Calculate and display the old 10-day average
Calculate and display the new 10-day average
Write the nine most recent pollen counts from the array to the file
Write the new pollen count to the file
Close the file

In reviewing this algorithm, notice that an array temporarily stores the contents of the file. Thus, when the file is initially read, the first pollen count in the file is stored in the first array element, the second pollen count in the second array element, and so on (Figure 14.9). Once the data are "captured" in the array, the data file can be overwritten with the latest 10 counts. As further illustrated in Figure 14.9, the first nine values written to the file are taken from array elements 2 through 10, respectively. Finally, the last count written to the file is the most recent value. Program 14.8 expresses this algorithm in Java. Following is a sample run using Program 14.8:

```
Enter the pollen count file name: Pollen.dat
Enter the new pollen count reading: 200
    The old 10 average is: 103.0
    The new 10 average is: 120.0
    An updated data file has been written.
```

FIGURE 14.9   The Update Process

PROGRAM 14.8

```java
import java.io.*;
public class PollenUpdate
{
    // This method updates the pollen count file
    // and calculates the latest count average
  public static void main(String[] args)
  throws java.io.IOException
  {
    final int PCOUNT = 10;
    int a[] = new int[PCOUNT];
    int sum = 0;

    String fileName, inLine, s1;
    String inFile, outFile;
    int i, newCount;

      // set up the basic keyboard input stream
      // needed for conversion capabilities
    InputStreamReader isr = new InputStreamReader(System.in);
      // needed to use readLine()
    BufferedReader br = new BufferedReader(isr);

      // obtain the input data
    System.out.print("Enter the pollen count file name: ");
    fileName = br.readLine();
    System.out.print("Enter the new pollen count reading: ");
```

(Continued on next page)

(Continued from previous page)

```
   s1 = br.readLine();
   newCount= Integer.parseInt(s1);
   br.close();

   // set up the basic file input stream
   BufferedReader fi = new BufferedReader(new FileReader(fileName));

   // read the existing data
   for(i = 0; i < 10; i++)
   {
     inLine = fi.readLine();  // read a line
     a[i] = Integer.parseInt(inLine);
     sum = sum + a[i];
   }
   fi.close();

   // compute and display the old and new averages
   System.out.println("    The old " + PCOUNT + " average is: " + (double)(sum)/ 10.0);
   sum = sum - a[0] + newCount;
   System.out.println("    The new " + PCOUNT + " average is: " + (double)(sum)/ 10.0);

   // set up the basic file output stream
   PrintWriter pw =
         new PrintWriter(new BufferedWriter(new FileWriter(fileName)));

   // write the updated data to the file
   for(i = 1; i < 10; i++)
     pw.println(a[i]);
   pw.println(newCount);
   System.out.println("    An updated data file has been written.");
   pw.close();
 }
}
```

The updated file created by Program 14.8 is illustrated in Figure 14.10. In reviewing the contents of this file, notice that the most current reading has been added to the end of the file and that the other counts are obtained from the original file shown in Figure 14.8 but moved up one position in the file.

Application 2: Master/Transactions File Update

A common form of file update occurs when the update data are themselves contained in a file. Here the file to be updated is referred to as a master file, and the file containing the update data is referred to as a transactions file.

```
 60  ← — — Oldest count
 40
 80
 90
120
150
130
160
170
200  ← — — Most recent reading
```

FIGURE 14.10 The Updated `Pollen.dat` File

As a specific example of this type of update, assume that the current master file, named `OldBookMaster.dat`, contains the book identification numbers and quantities in stock in Table 14.9.

A transactions file, named `BookTransactions.dat`, contains the quantities of each book bought, sold, or returned to stock each day. For purposes of illustration, assume that the `BookTransactions.dat` file is sorted by ID number at the end of each month and contains the data in Table 14.10.

There are two methods of updating a master file once a transactions file has been created. The direct access method, where any record in the master file can be read, updated, and written back to the file directly, is presented in Section 14.5. For the type of files we have been using, each record in the file must be read in the order it is located in the file. Additionally, a record can only be written to the end of the file because writing a record automatically erases all records from that point to the end of the file. This constraint effectively prohibits updating a record within an existing file because an update, by definition, requires that an existing record be rewritten.

The solution to this problem is to use an update algorithm in which all records that need to be are updated at the same time so that a completely new and updated master file is created when the update is completed. The key to creating this new updated master file is that the records in the transactions file be sorted by ID number to correspond to the order of ID numbers in the master file. Notice in Tables 14.9 and 14.10 that this is indeed the case for the data in the `BookTransactions.dat` and `OldBookMaster.dat` files.

Once the two files are in the same ID number order, the procedure for creating an updated master file consists of reading one master record from the existing master file and one record from the transactions file. If the ID numbers of the two records match, the

TABLE 14.9   Data Contained in the `OldBookMaster.dat` File

Book ID No.	Quantity in Stock
125	98
289	222
341	675
467	152
589	34
622	125

TABLE 14.10   Data Contained in the Transactions File Named `BookTransactions.dat`

ID No.	Date	Sold	Returned	Bought
289	1/10/03	125	34	50
341	1/10/03	300	52	0
467	1/15/03	50	20	200
467	1/20/03	225	0	160
589	1/31/03	75	10	55

transaction record's information is applied to the data in the master record, and another transaction record is read. As long as the transaction record's ID number matches the master record's ID number, the update of the master record continues. When the transaction record's ID number does not match the master record's ID number, indicating that there is no further update data to be applied to the master record, an updated record is written to the new master file. Let's see how this procedure works with the two files shown in Tables 14.9 and 14.10.

The first record read from the master file has ID number 125, and the first transaction record has ID number 289. Since the ID numbers do not match, the update of this first master record is complete (in this case, there is no update information), and the existing master record is written, without modification, to the new master file. Then the next master record, which has an ID number of 289, is read. Since this ID number matches the transaction ID number, the inventory balance for book number 289 is updated, yielding a new balance of 181 books. Because the transaction file can contain multiple update records for the same ID number (notice the two records for ID number 467), the next transaction record is read and checked before writing an updated record to the new master file. Since the ID number of the next transaction record is not 289, the update of this book number is complete and an updated master record is written to the new master file.

This algorithm continues, record by record, until the last master record has been updated. Should the end of the transactions file be encountered before the last master record is read from the existing master file, the remaining records in the existing master file are written directly to the new master file with no need to check for update information.

Because this update procedure uses two master files, a notation must be established to clearly distinguish between them. By convention, the existing master file is always referred to as the old master file, and the updated master file is called the new master file. Using these terms, the pseudocode description of the update procedure is:

```
Open the old master file
Open the transactions file
Open the new master file (initially blank)
Read the first old master record
For all records in the transactions file
    Read a transaction record
    While the transaction ID does not match the old master ID
        Write an updated master record to the new master file
        Read the next master record
    EndWhile
    If the ID numbers do match, calculate a new balance
```

(Continued on next page)

EndFor
 // To get here the last transaction record has just been read
Write the last updated master to the new master file
While there are any remaining records in the old master file
   Read an old master record
   Write a new master record
EndWhile
Close all files

In Java, this update procedure is described by Program 14.9.

PROGRAM 14.9

```java
import java.io.*;
import java.util.*;  // needed for StringTokenizer class
public class BookUpdate
{
  // This method updates a master file of book
  // inventory data using a transactions file
  public static void main(String[] args)
    throws java.io.IOException
  {
    String OldMasterFile = "OldBook.mas";
    String NewMasterFile = "NewBook.mas";
    String TransactionsFile = "Book.trn";

    String inmaster, date, intrans;
    String idmaster, idtrans, outData;
    StringTokenizer sm, st;
    int n, balance, sold, returned, bought;

      // set up the basic file input streams
    BufferedReader om =
            new BufferedReader(new FileReader(OldMasterFile));
    BufferedReader tr =
            new BufferedReader(new FileReader(TransactionsFile));
    PrintWriter pw =
            new PrintWriter(new BufferedWriter(new FileWriter(NewMasterFile)));

      // read the first master record
    inmaster = om.readLine();
    sm = new StringTokenizer(inmaster);
    idmaster = sm.nextToken();    // get the master id
    balance = Integer.parseInt(sm.nextToken());
    outData = inmaster;
      // read the first transaction record
```

(Continued on next page)

(Continued from previous page)

```
    intrans = tr.readLine();

    do
    {
        st = new StringTokenizer(intrans);
        idtrans = st.nextToken();  // get the transaction id
        n = idmaster.compareTo(idtrans);   // compare ids
        if (n < 0) // idmaster is less than idtrans
        {    // write out the current master record
             // and get a new master
            pw.println(outData);  // write new master
            inmaster = om.readLine();
            sm = new StringTokenizer(inmaster);
            idmaster = sm.nextToken();    // get the master id
            balance = Integer.parseInt(sm.nextToken());
            outData = idmaster + "     " + balance;
        }
        else  // update the current master and read another transaction
        {
            date = st.nextToken();
            sold =  Integer.parseInt(st.nextToken());
            returned =  Integer.parseInt(st.nextToken());
            bought =  Integer.parseInt(st.nextToken());
            balance = balance + bought - sold + returned;
            outData = idmaster + "     " + balance;
              // read the next transaction
            if( (intrans = tr.readLine()) == null )
             break;  // hit end of transaction file
        }
    } while(true);
        // write out the last updated master record
    pw.println(outData);
        // read and display the remaining old master records
    while( (inmaster = om.readLine()) != null )
        pw.println(inmaster);

    System.out.println("...The File Update is complete...");
    System.out.println("... A new master file named " + NewMasterFile
                    +" has been written ...");
        // close all files
    om.close();
    tr.close();
    pw.close();
    }
}
```

The output displayed by Program 14.9 is:

```
...The File Update is complete...
... A new master file named NewBook.mas has been written ...
```

The data in the new master file created by the program are:

```
125     98
289    181
341    427
467    257
589     24
622    125
```

EXERCISES 14.4

1. Write a Java program to create the `Pollen.dat` file illustrated in Figure 14.8.

2. An alternate update algorithm to the one in Program 14.8 is to use two files: The first file is the `Pollen.dat` file illustrated in Figure 14.8, and the second file is the updated file. Using two files, the update algorithm becomes:

   Open both files
   Read and add the first pollen count in the file to a total
   For the next nine pollen counts
       Read a pollen count from the file
       Add the new count to the total
       Write the count to the new file
   EndFor
   Input a new pollen count from the keyboard
   Write the current pollen count to the new file
   Close both files
   Calculate and display the previous 10-day average
   Calculate and display the current 10-day average

   Write a Java file update program using this algorithm.

3. a. A file named `Polar.dat` contains the polar coordinates needed in a graphics program. Currently, this file contains the following data:

Distance (inches)	Angle (degrees)
2	45
6	30
10	45
4	60
12	55
8	15

   Write a Java program to create this file on your computer system.

b. Using the `Polar.dat` file created in Exercise 3a, write a Java program that accepts distance and angle data from the user and adds the data to the end of the file.

c. Using the `Polar.dat` file created in Exercise 3a, write a Java program that reads this file and creates a second file named `XYcoord.dat`. The entries in the new file should contain the rectangular coordinates corresponding to the polar coordinates in the `Polar.dat file`. Polar coordinates are converted to rectangular coordinates using the equations:

$$x = r\cos(\Theta)$$
$$y = r\sin(\Theta)$$

where r is the distance coordinate and Θ is the radian equivalent of the angle coordinate in the `Polar.dat file`.

4. a. Write a Java program to create both the `OldBookMaster.dat` file in Table 14.9 and the `BookTransactions.dat file` in Table 14.10. (*Note:* Do not include the column headings in the file.)

b. Using the files created in Exercise 4a, enter and run Program 14.9 to verify its operation.

c. Modify Program 14.9 to prompt the user for the names of the old master file, the new master file, and the transactions file. The modified program should accept these file names as input while the program is executing.

d. Using the `BookTransactions.dat` file created in Exercise 4a, write a Java program that reads this file and displays the transaction data in it, including the heading records shown in Table 14.10.

5. a. Write a Java program to create a data file containing the following information, where a component type of R denotes a resistor, an I denotes an inductor, and a C denotes a capacitor:

Circuit Number	Component Type	Component Value	Component Voltage
-------	---------	---------	---------
3496	R1	56.1	34.6
3496	I1	12.2	12.4
3496	C1	22×10^{-6}	6.2
3496	R2	68.2	13.7
1476	R1	150.6	2.4
1476	R2	21.9	18.7
1476	R3	47.4	5.0
1476	I1	33.0	30.4
1476	R4	17.5	10.7
5678	R1	220.8	175.9
5678	C1	12×10^{-6}	12.8
5678	R2	148.1	13.1

b. Using the file created in Exercise 5a, and assuming that all resistences are in ohms, inductances in henrys, and capacitances in farads, write a Java program that calculates the power taken by each circuit and displays it in the format shown below. Note that only the resistors take power. This power is in watts and is given by the expression E^2/R, where E is the voltage across the resistance, R. For example, the display for the first circuit should be:

```
Circuit Number: 3496

Resistor
 Number        Power
--------       -----

   R1           21.4
   R2           12.6


Total Power:   34.0
```

6. a. Write a Java program to create a data file containing the following information:

Student ID Number	Student Name	Course Code	Course Credits	Course Grade
2333021	Bokow, R.	NS201	3	A
2333021	Bokow, R.	MG342	3	A
2333021	Bokow, R.	FA302	1	A
2574063	Fustil, D.	MK106	3	C
2574063	Fustil, D.	MA208	3	B
2574063	Fustil, D.	CM201	3	C
2574063	Fustil, D.	CP101	2	B
2663628	Kingsley, M.	QA140	3	A
2663628	Kingsley, M.	CM245	3	B
2663628	Kingsley, M.	EQ521	3	A
2663628	Kingsley, M.	MK341	3	A
2663628	Kingsley, M.	CP101	2	B

b. Using the file created in Exercise 6a, write a Java program that creates student grade reports. The grade report for each student should contain the student's name and identification number, a list of courses taken, the credits and grade for each course, and a semester grade point average. For example, the grade report for the first student should be:

```
Student Name: Bokow, R.
Student ID Number: 2333021

Course     Course     Course
Code       Credits    Grade
-------    -------    ------
NS201         3          A
MG342         3          A
FA302         1          A


Total Semester Course Credits Completed: 7
Semester Grade Point Average: 4.0
```

The semester grade point average is computed in two steps. First, each course grade is assigned a numerical value (A = 4, B = 3, C = 2, D = 1,

$F = 0$), and the sum of each course's grade value times the credits for each course is computed. This sum is then divided by the total number of credits taken during the semester.

7. **a.** Write a Java program to create a data file containing the following information:

Student ID Number	Student Name	Course Credits	Cumulative Grade Point Average (GPA)
----------	------------	-------	-------------
2333021	Bokow, R.	48	4.0
2574063	Fustil, D.	12	1.8
2663628	Kingsley, M.	36	3.5

b. Using the file created in Exercise 7a as a master file and the file created in Exercise 6a as a transactions file, write a file update program to create an updated master file.

8. Enter and execute Program 14.9. To do this, you will either have to create the two files used by the program or copy them from the Web site provided for this text (see Appendix J). You can also obtain the source code for Program 14.9 from the same Web site.

9. To shorten Program 14.9, a student wrote the following program. Determine why this program does not produce the same result as Program 14.9.

```java
import java.io.*;
import java.util.*;  // needed for StringTokenizer class
public class BookUpdate2
{
  // This method updates a master file of book
  // inventory data using a transactions file
  public static void main(String[] args)
    throws java.io.IOException
  {
    String OldMasterFile = "OldBook.mas";
    String TransactionsFile = "Book.trn";
    String NewMasterFile = "NewBook.mas";

    String inmaster, date, intrans;
    String idmaster, idtrans, outData;
    StringTokenizer sm, st;
    int n, balance, sold, returned, bought;

      // set up the basic file input streams
    BufferedReader om =
          new BufferedReader(new FileReader(OldMasterFile));
    BufferedReader tr =
          new BufferedReader(new FileReader(TransactionsFile));
    PrintWriter pw =
      new PrintWriter(new BufferedWriter(new FileWriter(NewMasterFile)));
```

```
   // read the first master record
 inmaster = om.readLine();
 sm = new StringTokenizer(inmaster);
 idmaster = sm.nextToken();   // get the master id
 balance = Integer.parseInt(sm.nextToken());
 outData = inmaster;
   // read the first transaction record
 intrans = tr.readLine();

 do
 {
    st = new StringTokenizer(intrans);
    idtrans = st.nextToken();  // get the transaction id
    n = idmaster.compareTo(idtrans);   // compare ids
    if (n < 0) // idmaster is less than idtrans
    {   // write out the current master record
        // and get a new master
      System.out.println(outData);  // to console
      pw.println(outData);  // write new master
      inmaster = om.readLine();
      sm = new StringTokenizer(inmaster);
      idmaster = sm.nextToken();   // get the master id
      balance = Integer.parseInt(sm.nextToken());
      outData = idmaster + "    " + balance;
    }
    else  // update the current master and read another transaction
    {
      date = st.nextToken();
      sold =  Integer.parseInt(st.nextToken());
      returned =  Integer.parseInt(st.nextToken());
      bought =  Integer.parseInt(st.nextToken());
      balance = balance + bought - sold + returned;
      outData = idmaster + "    " + balance;
        // read the next transaction
      if( (intrans = tr.readLine()) == null )
       break;  // hit end of transaction file
    }
 } while(true);
     // write out the last updated master record
 System.out.println(outData);
 pw.println(outData);
   // read and display the remaining old master records
 while( (inmaster = om.readLine()) != null )
   System.out.println(inmaster);
   pw.println(inmaster);
 pw.close();
  }
}
```

10. Modify Program 14.9 to display the contents of the newly created master file.
11. Modify Program 14.9 to accept the names of each file from the keyboard.

14.5 RANDOM ACCESS FILES

The manner in which data in a file are written and retrieved is called **file access**. All of the files created so far have used **sequential access**, which means that data in the file are accessed sequentially, one item after another. Thus, for example, the fourth item in a sequentially accessed file cannot be read without first reading the first three items in the file, and the last item in the file cannot be read without first reading all of the previous items. Because data within a sequential file cannot be replaced, updating a sequential access file requires a file update procedure in which a completely new file is created for each update (e.g., see the second application in the previous section). For applications in which the majority of the data in a file must be read and updated, such as updating a monthly payroll file, sequential access conforms to the way the file must be updated and is not a restriction.

In many applications, random access to data in the file, where individual data in the middle of the file can be retrieved, modified, and rewritten without reading or writing any other data, is preferable. **Random access** files, also referred to as **direct access** files, provide this capability. In this section, you will see how to create and use random access files. In Java, random access files are typically created as byte-based files using methods almost identical to those provided by the `DataInputStream` and `DataOutputStream` presented in Section 14.3.

The key to creating and using random access files is imposing a structure on the file so that specific items can be located and updated in place. The most common structure consists of fixed-length records that themselves consist of a set of fixed-length items. This permits locating any specific record and any specific item in a record by skipping over a fixed number of bytes. For example, Figure 14.11 illustrates a record consisting of an integer product identification code, an integer number representing the quantity in stock, and a double-precision number representing the item's selling price. Using a byte-based file, each integer value requires 4 bytes of storage and the double-precision value requires 8 bytes. Thus, each record in the file requires 16 bytes of storage, and the identification code, quantity, and price are stored in the same positions in every record.

FIGURE 14.11 Fixed-Length Record Consisting of 16 Bytes

A random access file is created as an object of the class `RandomAccessFile`. The basic stream object needed for creating and using a random access file requires a file name, either as a string variable, string constant, or `File` object, and a mode. The mode can be either an "r" for read only or "rw", which permits reading and writing to the same file. For example, the statement

```
RandomAccessFile raf =
    new RandomAccessFile("products.dat", "rw");
```

creates a random access file stream to the file named products.dat, on the current directory, that can be read from and written to. If this file exists, it will be opened; otherwise, it will be created.

Once a random access file stream has been opened in read-write mode, reading and writing the file are almost identical to reading and writing a byte-based file. That is, the RandomAccessFile methods are similar to those of the DataInputStream and DataOutputStream classes in that they permit primitive data values to be read from and written to the file. Table 14.11 lists the methods provided by the RandomAccessFile class.

The key to providing random access to a file is that each random access stream establishes an internal file position pointer. This pointer keeps track of where the next byte is to be read from, written to, or skipped over. The two member methods that are used to access and change the file position marker are the first two listed in Table 14.11, seek() and getFilePointer().

The seek() method permits the programmer to move to any byte position in the file, whether for reading, writing, or skipping over. To understand this method fully, you must first understand how data are referenced in the file using the file position pointer.

Each byte in a random access file can be accessed by its position in the file. The first byte in the file is located at position 0, the next byte at position 1, and so on. A byte's position is also referred to as its offset from the start of the file. The first byte has an offset of 0, the second byte has an offset of 1, and so on for each byte in the file.

The seek() method requires a single argument: an offset, as a long integer, into the file. The offset is always calculated from the beginning of the file. Using this argument, the seek() method sets the current value of the file's internal position pointer. All subsequent read, write, or skip operations then operate on the file starting at the position indicated by this file pointer. As a specific example, assume that a data file named test.dat consists of the data illustrated in Figure 14.12.

Notice that each character stored in the file in Figure 14.12 consists of 2 bytes. This is because the file was created using the DataOutputStream's writeChar() method, which writes characters using 2-bytes per character. In practice, the file can be constructed either as a byte-based file or as a random access file because the output streams that create both of these files use the same type of output methods. (The creation of this file is left as Exercise 1.)

For the file shown in Figure 14.12, the length of the file is 8 bytes, and a statement such as raf.seek(4) places an internal file position pointer at the start of the 2-byte sequence that stores the letter x in the file. Now, if the expression raf.readChar() is executed, the

FIGURE 14.12 The Data in the test.dat File

TABLE 14.11   `RandomAccessFile` Member Methods

Name	Type	Description
seek()	Access	Moves the file pointer.
getFilePointer()	Access	Retrieves the current file pointer.
length	Information	Returns the number of bytes in the file.
getFD()	Information	Retrieves the file descriptor.
close()	Close	Closes the file.
read()	Input	Reads bytes.
readBoolean()	Input	Reads a boolean value.
readByte()	Input	Reads an 8-bit byte.
readChar()	Input	Reads a 16-bit char.
readDouble()	Input	Reads a 64-bit double.
readFloat()	Input	Reads a 16-bit float.
readFully()	Input	Reads the requested number of bytes, using blocking until the read is complete.
readInt()	Input	Reads a 32-bit int.
readLine()	Input	Reads a line.
readLong()	Input	Reads a 64-bit long.
readShort()	Input	Reads a 16-bit short.
readUnsignedByte()	Input	Reads an unsigned 8-bit byte.
readUnsignedShort()	Input	Reads an unsigned 8-bit short.
readUTF()	Input	Reads using UTF code.
skipBytes()	Input	Skips bytes.
writeBoolean()	Output	Writes a boolean value.
writeByte()	Output	Writes an 8-bit byte.
writeChar()	Output	Writes a 16-bit char.
writeDouble()	Output	Writes a 64-bit double.
writeFloat()	Output	Writes a 16-bit float.
writeInt()	Output	Writes a 32-bit int.
writeLine()	Output	Writes a line.
writeLong()	Output	Writes a 64-bit long.
writeShort()	Output	Writes a 16-bit short.
writeUTF()	Output	Writes using UTF code.

next 2 bytes of storage will be read and the file's position pointer is automatically moved to byte position 6. This type of automatic adjustment to the file pointer is made whenever a read, skip, or write is encountered.

Program 14.10 illustrates the `seek()` method to read the characters in a byte-based file named `test.dat` in reverse order, from the last character to the first. As each character is read, it is also displayed. Assuming the file `test.dat` contains the data in Figure 14.12, the output displayed by Program 14.10 is:

```
t | x | e | N |
```

Program 14.10 initially goes to the last character in the file. The position of this last character is obtained as the length of the file, which is 8 bytes minus 2. If we had simply

PROGRAM 14.10

```java
import java.io.*;
public class DisplayReversed
{
  static final int SIZEOFCHAR = 2;    // there are 2 bytes per char

  public static void main(String[] args)
    throws java.io.IOException
  {
    String fileName = "test.dat";
    char ch;
    long last, position, setbytepos;

      // set up the basic random access input/output stream
    RandomAccessFile raf =
      new RandomAccessFile(fileName, "rw");

    last = raf.length();  // get length of the file
    position = last - SIZEOFCHAR; // starting position of last char
    while(position >= 0)
    {
      raf.seek(position);    // move to the character
      ch = raf.readChar();
      System.out.print(ch + " | ");
      position = position - SIZEOFCHAR;  // position of prior char
    }

    raf.close();
  }
}
```

set the file's position pointer to eight, we would be pointing to the end of the last character, but we want to start at the beginning of the last character. The position of this last character, as seen in Figure 14.12, is at byte position 6, which is 2 bytes before the end of the file. The first invocation of the `seek()` method positions the internal file pointer value to correctly locate the start of this last character. As each character is read, the character is displayed and the position is adjusted to access the next character.

While the `seek()` method moves the file pointer's value, the `getFilePointer()` method returns the value in the file position pointer. For example, after the first `readChar()` is executed in Program 14.10, the method call

```java
raf.getFilePointer()
```

would return the `long` integer value 8. In Program 14.10, the `getFilePointer()` method is not used. The important point illustrated by Program 14.10 is that accessing files randomly does require knowing exactly how the data in the file are stored and having

TABLE 14.12   Product Information to Be Stored in a Random Access File

Identification Code	Quantity in Stock	Selling Price
1001	476	28.35
1002	348	32.56
1003	517	51.27
1004	284	23.75
1005	165	35.25

some means for precisely locating the byte position of each data item in the file. In practice, this is typically accomplished by aggregating data items into fixed-length records, which is presented next.

Using Fixed-Length Records[5]

Because random access of data in a random access file is by byte position, applications that use random access files must provide a known means of locating each data item in the file. In practice, this is accomplished by ensuring that the data items are assembled into fixed-length records and providing each record with an identification number or account code that can be converted, either directly or indirectly, into a byte offset.

For example, assume that a random access file containing the data in Table 14.12 is to be created. This is accomplished by writing five records to the file. Each record in the file stores a product identification number, the quantity of the product in stock, and the product's selling price, with each data item stored in numerical form and not as strings. Specifically, the product identification number has been selected as a four-digit integer so that subtracting 1000 from the identification number yields the correct record number. Thus, the data for product identification number 1001 will be stored in record number 1, the data for product identification number 1002 will be stored in record number 2, and so on. (Converting an identification code to a record number is formally called **hashing**.) Program 14.11 creates the required file.

In reviewing Program 14.11, notice that most of the coding is concerned with inputting data from the keyboard and converting the entered data into numerical form. The actual writes of the numerical data to the random access file are handled by the following three statements contained within the `for` loop:

```
raf.writeInt(acct);
raf.writeInt(amt);
raf.writeDouble(price);
```

When Program 14.11 is executed, and assuming that the data in Table 14.12 are entered correctly, the byte-based file created by the program is illustrated in Figure 14.13. Hexadecimal values are used in the figure to indicate the equivalent binary values. Although the figure separates the file's records into individual lines, with bars, |, used to distinguish individual items in each record, in actuality the file is stored as a consecutive sequence of bytes. The file will be exactly 80 bytes in length, which corresponds to five records of 16 bytes each. Figure 14.14 lists the data in the file converted into a decimal

---

[5]This topic can be omitted on first reading with no loss of subject continuity.

PROGRAM 14.11

```java
import java.io.*;

public class WriteRandom
{
  public static void main(String[] args)
    throws java.io.IOException
  {
    String fileName = "products.dat";
    String acctstring, amtstring, pricestring;
    int acct, amt;
    double price;

      // set up the keyboard for string input
    InputStreamReader isr =
        new InputStreamReader(System.in);
    BufferedReader br =
        new BufferedReader(isr);

      // set up the basic random access input/output stream
    RandomAccessFile raf =
        new RandomAccessFile(fileName, "rw");

      // enter and store data for five records
    for(int i = 1; i <= 5; i++)
    {
      System.out.print("Enter the identification number: ");
      acctstring = br.readLine();
      acct = Integer.parseInt(acctstring);
      raf.writeInt(acct);
      System.out.print("Enter the quantity in stock: ");
      amtstring = br.readLine();
      amt = Integer.parseInt(amtstring);
      raf.writeInt(amt);
      System.out.print("Enter the price: ");
      pricestring = br.readLine();
      price = Double.parseDouble(pricestring);
      raf.writeDouble(price);
    }

    System.out.println("The file " + fileName
                    + " has been written.");
    System.out.println("The length of the file is "
                    + raf.length() + " bytes.");
    raf.close();

  }
}
```

```
|00 00 03 E9|00 00 01 DC|40 3C 59 99 99 99 99 9A|  <-- 1st record of 16 bytes
|00 00 03 EA|00 00 01 5C|40 40 47 AE 14 7A E1 48|  <-- 2nd record of 16 bytes
|00 00 03 EB|00 00 02 05|40 49 A2 8F 5C 28 F5 C3|  <-- 3rd record of 16 bytes
|00 00 03 EC|00 00 01 1C|40 37 C0 00 00 00 00 00|  <-- 4th record of 16 bytes
|00 00 03 ED|00 00 00 A5|40 41 A0 00 00 00 00 00|  <-- 5th record of 16 bytes
|<-4 bytes->|<-4 bytes->|<------ 8 bytes ------>|
```

FIGURE 14.13 The Data in the File Produced by Program 14.11

format. To check these values, you would first have to convert the hexadecimal values in
Figure 14.13 to their binary equivalent. Then, for the first two integer values in each
record, you can use the techniques presented in Section 1.9 to convert from binary to
decimal. To convert the double-precision data in the last 8 bytes of each record, you will
need the information presented on real number storage in Appendix I.

```
|1001|  476|   28.35|  <-- 1st record
|1002|  348|   32.56|  <-- 2nd record
|1003|  517|   51.27|  <-- 3rd record
|1004|  284|   23.75|  <-- 4th record
|1005|  165|   35.25|  <-- 5th record
```

FIGURE 14.14 The Decimal Equivalent of the Data in Figure 14.13

Program 14.12 illustrates using the numerical methods `readInt()` and `readDouble()`
to directly input the numerical data in the random access file created by Program 14.11.
Notice that because we are sequentially reading all of the data in the file, starting with
the first identification number, the program does not yet directly make use of random access features of the file. The output produced by Program 14.12 is:

```
ID. No.    Quantity    Price

           In Stock

-------    --------    ------
  1001        476      $28.35
  1002        348      $32.56
  1003        517      $51.27
  1004        284      $23.75
  1005        165      $35.25
```

PROGRAM 14.12

```java
import java.io.*;
public class ReadRandom
{
  public static void main(String[] args)
    throws java.io.IOException
  {
    String fileName = "products.dat";
    int acct, amt;
    double price;
```

(Continued on next page)

(Continued from previous page)

```
        // set up the basic random access input/output stream
      RandomAccessFile raf =
        new RandomAccessFile(fileName, "rw");


        // print the headings
      System.out.println("          Quantity");
      System.out.println("ID. No.   In Stock    Price");
      System.out.println("-------   --------   ------");


        // read and print the data
      for(int i = 1; i <= 5; i++)
      {
        acct = raf.readInt();
        amt = raf.readInt();
        price = raf.readDouble();
        System.out.println(" " + acct
                              + "           " + amt
                              + "        $" + price);
      }


      raf.close();
   }
}
```

The real advantage to random access files is that records in the file can be read and written in any order. This permits the lookup of a single record anywhere in the file and the capability to update each accessed record. To illustrate this, consider Program 14.13, which requests a user to enter an identification number. If the record corresponding to the desired identification number is located, the user is requested to enter a new quantity and the updated data are written to the existing record; otherwise, the user is informed that no record exists for the entered identification number.

Following is a sample run of Program 14.13 in which two existing records have been successfully updated and one incorrectly entered identification number has been correctly detected.

```
Enter the identification number (999 to stop): 1003
The current quantity in stock is: 517
Enter the new quantity: 436
The record has been updated.
Enter a new identification number (999 to stop): 1008
There is no record for this id number
Please recheck and reenter the identification number (999 to stop): 1005
The current quantity in stock is: 165
Enter the new quantity: 196
The record has been updated.
```

PROGRAM 14.13

```java
import java.io.*;
public class UpdateRandom
{

  static final int RECLEN = 16;    // record length in bytes
  static final int BASEREC = 1000;

  public static void main(String[] args)
    throws java.io.IOException
  {
    String fileName = "products.dat";
    String acctstring, amtstring, pricestring;
    int acct, amt;
    int recnum;
    double price;
    long filelen, position, setbytepos;

      // set up the keyboard for string input
    InputStreamReader isr =
      new InputStreamReader(System.in);
    BufferedReader br =
      new BufferedReader(isr);

      // set up the basic random access input/output stream
    RandomAccessFile raf =
      new RandomAccessFile(fileName, "rw");

    filelen = raf.length();  // get length of the file
    System.out.print("Enter the identification number (999 to stop): ");
    acctstring = br.readLine();

    while (!acctstring.equals("999"))
    {
        // calculate the record number for this id number
      recnum = Integer.parseInt(acctstring) - BASEREC;
        // calculate the starting byte position for this record
      position = (recnum - 1) * RECLEN;
        // make sure this is a valid byte position
      if (position < 0 || position > (filelen - 1))
      {
        System.out.println("There is no record for this id number");
        System.out.print("Please recheck and reenter the identification "
                      + "number (999 to stop): ");
        acctstring = br.readLine();
```

(Continued on next page)

```
(Continued from previous page)
        continue;
    }
    raf.seek(position);  // move to the record
    acct = raf.readInt();
    setbytepos = raf.getFilePointer();
    amt = raf.readInt();
    System.out.println("The current quantity in stock is: " + amt);
    System.out.print("Enter the new quantity: ");
    amtstring = br.readLine();
    amt = Integer.parseInt(amtstring);
    raf.seek(setbytepos);  // reset position to the amt field
    raf.writeInt(amt);
    System.out.println("The record has been updated.");
    System.out.print("Enter a new identification number (999 to stop): ");
    acctstring = br.readLine();
  }

  raf.close();
 }
}
```

EXERCISES 14.5

1. Either by copying the file from the Web site associated with this text or writing a Java program, create a byte-based file named test.dat that stores the following four letters as individual characters (see Figure 14.12):

   Next

   The file can be created in Java using either DataOutputStream or RandomAccess-File methods.

2. Enter and execute Program 14.10 to read and display the data in the file created in Exercise 1a in reverse order.

3. Assume that a text editor created the file test.dat for Exercise 1 or the file was created as a text-based file using methods from the PrintWriter class. In this case:
   a. How would the stored characters differ from those shown in Figure 14.12?
   b. What modification would you have to make to Program 14.10 to read and display the characters in the file?

4. Write and execute a Java program that reads and displays every second character in the test.dat file created for Exercise 1.

5. Write a method named findChars() that returns the total number of characters in a byte-based file. Assume that the file consists of character data only.

6. a. Write a method named readBytes() that reads and displays n characters starting from any position in a byte-based file that consists of stored characters only. The method should accept three arguments: a file name, the position of the first character to be read, and the number of characters to be read. The character position argument should be in characters, not in bytes. Thus,

if the letters An unusual opportunity are stored in the file, the first u in unusual would be designated as character number 4.

   b. Modify the readBytes() method written for Exercise 6a to store the characters read as either a String or StringBuffer object. The method should return the String or StringBuffer object that is created.

7. Enter and execute Program 14.11 on your computer.

8. Enter and execute Program 14.12 on your computer.

9. Enter and execute Program 14.13 on your computer.

14.6 THE File CLASS

Before attempting to read from or write to a file, good programming practice requires that you check the status of the desired file that will be attached to a file stream. These checks can be done using the methods of a Java class named File. It should be noted that the methods of this class do not let you perform any file input or output; for this, you need to establish appropriate file stream objects. What the File class does provide is a number of useful methods that permit you to perform relevant checks on a file's status. Table 14.13 on page 718 lists the methods provided by this class.

Program 14.14 illustrates a number of the File class' methods within the context of a complete program.

PROGRAM 14.14

```
import java.io.*;
public class CheckFile
{
  public static void main(String[] args)
    throws java.io.IOException
  {

    String fileName = "C:\\jdk\\prices.dat";  // note that a full pathname
                                              // requires two delimiters
    String nextName = "backup.dat";   // a relative pathname can also be used

    File inFile = new File(fileName);
    File newName = new File(nextName);

    if (inFile.exists())
    {
      System.out.println("The file " + fileName + " exists");

        // check the type of file
      if (inFile.isDirectory())
        System.out.println("  This is a directory");
```
(Continued on next page)

(Continued from previous page)

```java
    else if (inFile.isFile())
      System.out.println("  This is a regular file");

      // check if file is readable
    if (inFile.canRead())
      System.out.println("  The file can be read");
    else
      System.out.println("  The file is not readable");

      // check if file is writeable
    if (inFile.canWrite())
    System.out.println("  The file can be written to");
    else
      System.out.println("  The file is not writeable");

    // report the file's length
    System.out.println("The file length is " + inFile.length() + " bytes.");

    // report the file's directory path
  System.out.println("The pathname of this file's parent is "
                    + inFile.getParent());

    // rename the file
  inFile.renameTo(newName);
  System.out.println("The file has been renamed " + newName);
  System.out.println("The full pathname for this file is "
                    + newName.getAbsolutePath());
  }
  else
   System.out.println("The file " + fileName + " does not exist.");
  }
}
```

The output produced by Program 14.14 is:

```
The file prices.dat exists
  This is a regular file
  The file can be read
  The file can be written to
The file length is 24 bytes.
The pathname of this file's parent is C:\jdk
The file has been renamed backup.dat
The full pathname for this file is C:\jdk\backup.dat
```

TABLE 14.13 Common `File` Class Methods

Method	Description
canRead()	Returns a boolean true if the file can be read from.
canWrite()	Returns a boolean false if the file exists and can be written to.
delete()	Deletes the designated file and returns a boolean true if successful.
exists()	Returns a boolean true if the designated file exists.
getAbsolutePath()	Generates the full pathname of this file from system directory information.
getName()	Returns the file name of this file from the given pathname.
getParent()	Returns the pathname of the parent directory of the file from the given pathname.
isDirectory()	Returns a boolean true if the designated file is a directory.
isFile()	Returns true if the file is a regular (nondirectory) file.
length()	Returns the size of the file, in bytes, as provided by the operating system.
renameTo()	Renames the file.

Although the display produced by Program 14.14 is rather straightforward, a few items in this output should be mentioned. First, the pathname returned by the `getParent()` method is obtained from the pathname provided in the program. If a relative pathname is provided, `getParent()` will return a null value. If you want the program to generate the full pathname of a file from system information, you must use the `getAbsolutePath()` method, as is illustrated by the last displayed line. Additionally, the `renameTo()` method will only rename a file if the new name is not already in use. Once a file is renamed, however, the previous name is no longer valid. Finally, a practical notational consideration needs to be explained. In practice, as is done in Program 14.4, the expression if (inFile.exists()) is used in preference to the longer expression if(inFile.exists() == true). It is important to become familiar with the shorter notation because it is preferred by most professional programmers. Similarly, an expression such as if (inFile.exists() == false) would be coded by a professional Java programmer as if (!inFile.exists()).

File Checking

One of the most important uses of the `File` class is to check that files intended for input exist and are readable. Similarly, if you intend to write to a file, you should first check that a file with the given name does not already exist. If it does, all of the data in the file will be erased at the moment that an output stream is connected to the file.

Program 14.15 illustrates two typical checks that should be made before any file is opened for reading. First, the program checks that the file exists. Next, if the file does exist, the program checks that it can be read. Such checks are especially important for UNIX-based systems, where read privileges can be easily turned off.

Assuming that the `prices.dat` file does not exist on the directory where Program 14.15 is stored, the following message is displayed:

```
The file prices.dat does not exist - please check and rerun.
```

Similarly, if the file does exist but does not have read privileges, the following message is displayed:

PROGRAM 14.15

```java
import java.io.*;
public class CheckForRead
{
  public static void main(String[] args)
    throws java.io.IOException
  {
    String fileName = "prices.dat";

    File inFile = new File(fileName);

      // check that the file exists and can be read
    if (inFile.exists() == false)
    {
      System.out.println("The file " + fileName
                          + " does not exist - please check and rerun.");
      System.exit(1);
    }
    else if(inFile.canRead() == false)
    {
      System.out.println("The file " + fileName
            + " exists but does not have read permission - please check.");
      System.exit(1);
    }

      // set up the input stream and read the file

    System.out.println("The file " + fileName + " exists and can be read.");

  }
}
```

```
The file prices.dat exists but does not have read permission - please check.
```

In both of these cases, the System.exit() method will terminate program execution. If the file does exist and can be read, the message

```
The file prices.dat exists and can be read.
```

is displayed. In practice, this statement would be replaced by statements that read and process the data in the file as presented in the previous sections.

On the output side, whenever data are to be written to a file, you should always check if a file with the desired name already exists on the system. If it does, you can then either choose not to open an output stream to the file or give the user the choice as to whether the output stream should be opened. This is an important decision because once an output stream is opened for writing, the data in the existing file are automatically lost,

PROGRAM 14.16

```java
import java.io.*;
public class CheckForWrite
{
  public static void main(String[] args)
    throws java.io.IOException
  {
    String fileName = "prices.dat";
    char response;

    File outFile = new File(fileName);

      // check that the file does not already exist
    if (outFile.exists())
    {
      System.out.println("The file " + fileName + "currently exists.");
      System.out.print("Are you sure you want to write to it? Enter y or n:");
      response = (char) System.in.read();
      if (response == 'n')
        System.exit(1);
    }

      // set up the output stream and write to the file
    System.out.println("The file " + fileName + " can be written to.");
  }
}
```

unless the existing file is opened in append mode. How this type of check is accomplished in practice is illustrated in Program 14.16. Assuming that a file named `prices.dat` is available on the current directory, a sample run of Program 14.16 will display the following output lines:

```
The file prices.dat currently exists.
Are you sure you want to write to it? Enter y or n:
```

Depending on how the user responds, the file will either be erased and written over or the program will terminate. In practice, the severity of the message presented to the user and whether or not the user is even given a choice to delete an existing file depend on the application and the importance of the file being considered.

EXERCISES 14.6

1. **a.** Describe the difference between numbers stored in a character-based file and numbers stored in byte-based file.

   b. Describe the difference between letters stored in a character-based file and letters stored in a byte-based file.

2. Enter and execute Program 14.14 on your computer.
3. Modify Program 14.14 so that the file name can be interactively entered by a user.
4. Modify Program 14.1 to include the file checks provided by Program 14.14.
5. Enter and execute Program 14.15 on your computer.
6. Enter and execute Program 14.16 on your computer.
7. Modify Program 14.1 to include the input file check provided by Program 14.16.

14.7 COMMON PROGRAMMING ERRORS

The following programming errors are common when using files:

1. Using a file's external name in place of the internal file stream object reference variable when accessing the file. The only stream method that uses the data file's external name is the first stream used to open the file.
2. Not realizing that a file opened when an output stream is instantiated is, by default, in write mode. This automatically erases all file data. If data are to be added to an existing file, the file should be opened for appending.
3. Testing for the end of file in an incorrect way. In general, a `null` value is returned when a read beyond the end of a character-based file is attempted, and an EOF exception is generated when reading beyond the end of a byte-based file is attempted. When an incorrect end of file test is made, a program will generally either terminate abnormally or go into an infinite loop.
4. Forgetting to surround the expression `c = fr.read()` in a loop such as `while( (c = fr.read()) != EOF)`, used to read bytes from a file stream, in parentheses. The parentheses are necessary to ensure that a byte is first read and assigned to the variable c before the retrieved value is compared to the EOF value. In their absence, the complete expression would be `c = fr.read() != EOF`. Due to the precedence of operations, the relational expression `fr.read() != EOF` would be executed first. Because this is a relational expression, its result is either a boolean `true` or `false` value based on the data retrieved by the `c.read()` method. Attempting to assign this boolean result to the variable c is an invalid conversion across an assignment operator and results in a compiler error. This same error occurs when the parentheses surrounding the expression `(inLine = br.readLine())` in a loop such as `while ((inLine = br.readLine()) != null)`, used to read lines from a file, are omitted.

14.8 CHAPTER SUMMARY

1. A *data file* is any collection of data stored together on an external storage medium under a common name.
2. A *character-based file* is one in which each data item in the file is stored using a character-based code, such as ASCII. A character-based file is also referred to as a *text file*. Java imposes no structure on a character-based file, which means that what data are stored is determined by the application and the placement of the character data created by the programmer.
3. A *byte-based file* is one in which each data item in the file is stored using the computer's internal binary code. A byte-based file is also referred to as a *binary file*.

Java imposes no structure on a byte-based file, which means that what data are stored is determined by the application and the placement of the data created by the programmer.

4. Character-based and byte-based files can be opened for reading, writing, or appending. A file opened for writing creates a new file or erases any existing file having the same name as the opened file. A file opened for appending makes an existing file available for data to be added to the end of the file. If the file does not exist, it is created. A file opened for reading makes an existing file's data available for input.

5. The file stream classes that are used to create input and output streams for character-based files are:

Class	Type	Comments	Methods
Reader	Abstract	Abstract class for byte-based input.	–
FileReader	Basic input	Basic stream used for byte-based input. Supplies character-by-character input.	read()
BufferedReader	Input processing	Provides buffering, which typically improves performance.	read() readLine()
Writer	Abstract	Abstract class for byte-based output.	
BufferedWriter	Output	Provides buffering, which typically improves performance.	write(int c) write(String s, int start, int end)
PrintWriter	Output	Provides a number of useful output methods.	flush(), close(), print(char), print(String), print(int), print(float), print(double), print(boolean), and corresponding println() methods

6. For writing to a character-based file, an output stream must be instantiated. A commonly used output stream is created using the following instantiations:

```
// set up the basic output stream
FileWriter fw =
    new FileWriter(fileName); // The fileName can be a File argument,
                              // String variable, or String constant
// buffer it for faster output
BufferedWriter bw =
    new BufferedWriter(fw);

// this provides a set of useful methods
PrintWriter pw =
    new PrintWriter(bw);
```

This set of individual instantiations can also be implemented using the single statement

```
PrintWriter pw =
    new PrintWriter(new BufferedWriter(new FileWriter(fileName)));
```

     The first instantiation in this sequence of statements opens the associated file in write mode. To open it in append mode, this instantiation should be written as:

```
FileWriter fw =
    new FileWriter(fileName, true);
```

7. The `PrintWriter` class contains the following methods for writing numerical values in character-based form:

```
        print(char), println(char)
        print(String), println(String)
        print(int), println(int)
print(float), println(float)
        print(double), println(double)
print(boolean), println(boolean)
```

8. For reading from a character-based file, an input stream must be instantiated. A commonly used input stream is created using the following instantiations:

```
  // set up the basic input stream
FileReader fr =
    new FileReader(fileName);  // The fileName can be a File argument,
                               // String variable, or String constant
  // buffer the input stream
BufferedReader br =
    new BufferedReader(fr);
```

     This set of individual instantiations can also be implemented using the single statement

```
BufferedReader br =
    new BufferedReader(new FileReader(fileName));
```

9. The `BufferedReader` class permits reading character-based file data either as individual bytes using a `read()` method or complete lines using a `readLine()` method. A line is considered any sequence of bytes terminated by a carriage return (\r), line feed (\n), carriage return and line feed (\r\n), or end of stream marker. Generally, character-based files are read using `readLine()`, and then individual data items are parsed from the line using StringTokenizer methods.

10. The file stream classes that are used to create byte-based files are:

Class	Mode	Comments	Typical Object Name
InputStream	Input	Abstract class for byte-based input.	—
FileInputStream	Input	Basic stream used for byte-based input. Supplies character-by-character input.	fis
BufferedInputStream	Input	Provides buffering, which improves performance. Supplies character-by-character and line-by-line input. Typically uses a FileInputStream object argument	bis
DataInputStream	Input	Supplies additional input method. Typically uses either a FileInputStream object or BufferedInputStream object argument.	dis

(Continued on next page)

(Continued from previous page)

OutputStream	Output	Abstract class for byte-based output.	–
FileOutputStream	Output	Basic stream used for byte-based output. Supplies character-by-character output.	fos
BufferedOutputStream	Output	Provides buffering, which improves performance. Supplies character-by-character and line-by-line output. Typically uses a FileOutputStream object argument.	bos
DataOutputStream	Output	Supplies additional output methods. Typically uses either an FileOutputStream object or BufferedOutputStream object argument.	dos

11. For writing to a byte-based file, an output file stream must be instantiated. For opening the file in write mode, the following set of statements is typically used:

```
// set up the basic output stream
FileOutputStream fos =
    new FileOutputStream(outFile);

// buffer it for faster output
BufferedOutputStream bos =
    new BufferedOutputStream(fos);

// this provides a set of useful methods
DataOutputStream dos =
    new DataOutputStream(bos);
```

The first instantiation in this sequence of statements opens the associated file in write mode. To open it in append mode, this instantiation should be written as:

```
FileOutputStream fos =
    new FileOutputStream(outFile, true);
```

12. For reading from a byte-based file, an input stream object must be instantiated. This is typically accomplished using the following set of statements:

```
// set up the basic input stream
FileInputStream fis =
    new FileInputStream(inFile);

// buffer it for faster input
BufferedInputStream bis =
    new BufferedInputStream(fis);

// this provides a set of useful methods
DataInputStream dis =
    new DataInputStream(bis);
```

13. Input and output streams and random access files are formally closed using a `close()` method. The syntax of this method is

```
streamName.close()
```

All streams and files are automatically closed when the program they are opened in finishes executing.

14. The manner in which data are written to and read from a file is called the file's *access method*.

    a. In a *sequential access file*, data are accessed in a sequential manner. This means that the second data item in the file cannot be read until the first data item has been read, the third data item cannot be read until the first and second data items have been read, and so on, until the last data item is read. Similarly, a data item cannot be written until all previous data items have been written.

    b. In a *random access file*, any data item can be read, written, or replaced without affecting any other data item in the file. Typically, data in a random access file are stored in a fixed-length record format, where each record contains a value that can be translated into a record position value.

15. The `RandomAccessFile` class is used to create random access file streams.

16. For reading and writing to a random access file, a file stream must be instantiated. This is typically accomplished using a statement of the form

```
// set up the basic random access input/output stream
RandomAccessFile raf =
     new RandomAccessFile(fileName, "rw");
```

If the last argument in this instantiation is "r" rather than "rw", the file can only be used for input and cannot be written to using the instantiated file stream.

17. The `seek()` method provides the capability to set a random access file's internal file pointer at any byte position in the file. Subsequent read, write, or skip operations all commence from the position indicated by the internal file pointer.

18. Although files created as character-based and byte-based can be read as a random access file, the class methods used for a random access file stream most closely match those methods used for byte-based streams. Thus, random access is most closely associated with byte-based files.

19. If a file is to be read, a check, using the `File` class' methods, should be made to ensure that the file exists.

20. If a file is to be written, a check, using the `File` class' methods, should be made that a file of the same name *does not* already exist.

14.9 CHAPTER SUPPLEMENT: CHARACTER AND BYTE FILE STORAGE

The files in which we have stored our Java programs are referred to as text or character-based (the designations are synonymous) files. This means that each character in the files is stored using a character code, which is typically ASCII. This code assigns a specific code to each letter in the alphabet, to each of the digits 0 through 9, and to special symbols such as the period and dollar sign. Table 14.14 lists the correspondence between the characters 0 through 9 and their ASCII and Unicode representations in both binary and hexadecimal notation. Additionally, the ASCII and Unicode codes for a period, blank space, carriage return, tab, and line feed character are included in the table. In all cases, notice that the lower 8 bits in the Unicode representation are identical to the ASCII bit

TABLE 14.14   Selected ASCII Codes and Unicodes

Character	ASCII Binary Value	ASCII Hex. Value	Unicode Binary Value	Unicode Hex. Value
0	00110000	30	00000000 00110000	0030
1	00110001	31	00000000 00110001	0031
2	00110010	32	00000000 00110010	0032
3	00110011	33	00000000 00110011	0033
4	00110100	34	00000000 00110100	0034
5	00110101	35	00000000 00110101	0035
6	00110110	36	00000000 00110110	0036
7	00110111	37	00000000 00110111	0037
8	00111000	38	00000000 00111000	0038
9	00111001	39	00000000 00111001	0039
.	00101110	2E	00000000 00101110	002E
Tab	00001001	09	0000000000001001	0009
Blank space	00100000	20	00000000 00100000	0020
Carriage Ret.	00001101	0D	00000000 00001101	000D
Line Feed	00001010	0A	00000000 00001010	000A

code and that the upper 8 bits are all 0s. This correspondence is true for the first 128 codes; thus, the Unicodes for these first 128 characters are identical to the ASCII codes (the upper bytes of these Unicodes are all 0s), except that the extra Unicode byte is a 0. Because of this correspondence, the ASCII uppercase and lowercase letter codes can be obtained from the Unicode letter codes previously provided in Table 2.3.

Using Table 14.14, we can determine how the decimal number 67432.83, for example, is stored in a data file using the ASCII code. In ASCII, this sequence of digits and decimal point require eight character storage locations and are stored using the codes in Figure 14.15.

36 37 34 33 32 2E 38 33

FIGURE 14.15   The Number *67432.83* Represented in ASCII Code

The advantage of using character codes for data files is that the file can be read and displayed by any word processing or editor program that is provided by your computer system. Such word processing and editor programs are called text editors because they are designed to process alphabetical text. The word processing program can read the character code in the data file and display the letter, symbol, or digit corresponding to the code. This permits a data file created in Java to be examined and changed by other than Java text editor programs.

An alternative to character-based files, where each character in the file is represented by a unique code, is **byte-based** or **binary** files (the terms are synonymous). Byte-based files store numerical values using the program's internal numerical code.[6] For example, assume that the program stores integer numbers internally using Java's 32-bit designation in the format described in Section 1.9. Using this format, the decimal number 8 is

---

[6]This topic assumes that you are familiar with the computer storage concepts presented in Section 1.9.

represented as the 32-bit binary number 00000000 00000000 00000000 00001000, the decimal number 12 as 00000000 00000000 00000000 00001100, and the decimal number 497 as 00000000 00000000 00000001 11110001. As hexadecimal numbers, these are 00 00 00 08, 00 00 00 0C, and 00 00 01 F1, respectively. Figure 14.16 shows how these three numbers are stored using byte-based codes.

00 00 00 08 00 00 00 0C 00 00 01 F

FIGURE 14.16 The Numbers 8, 12, and 497 Stored as Bytecodes

The advantages of using this format are that no intermediary conversions are required for storing or retrieving the data (since the external storage codes match the Java program's internal storage representation), and for files consisting of large double-precision numbers, the resulting file usually requires less storage space than its character-based counterpart. The primary disadvantage is that the file can no longer be visually inspected using a text editing program.

Notice that the term byte-based can be misleading because both byte-based and character-based files store data using bytes. It is the interpretation of what the byte stream represents when applied to numbers that distinguishes the two file types. In character-based files, all numbers are stored as a sequence of individual digits, each one of which is represented by the character symbols 0 through 9, including a possible decimal point. In byte-based files, numbers are stored as a fixed sequence of bytes that represents the binary equivalent of the number.

For alphabetical characters, both byte-based and character-based files use the same individual character codes, but in a text-based file, a character is typically represented using its ASCII code, stored as 8 bits, while a byte-based code stores characters as the 16-bit character data type specified in Java's Unicode format. As an example, Figures 14.17a and 14.17b show how the characters Hello World are stored in character- and byte-based formats, respectively, using a hexadecimal representation.

FIGURE 14.17a Hello World Stored as an ASCII Text File

The individual character codes in Figures 14.17a and 14.17b can be obtained from both Table 2.3 and Table 14.14. In comparing these figures, notice that the byte-based file shown in Figure 14.17b uses 2 bytes for each character where the upper byte consists of zeros and the lower byte is the same as the byte code used in the ASCII text file shown in Figure 14.17a.

FIGURE 14.17b Hello World Stored as a Byte-Based File

CHAPTER 15

Numerical

Methods

One of the most common tasks in science and engineering is finding the roots of equations—that is, given a function f(x), finding values of x such that f(x) = 0.0. This type of problem also includes determining the points of intersection of two curves. If the curves are represented by functions f(x) and g(x), respectively, the intersection points correspond to the roots of the function F(x) = f(x) − g(x).

A second important task is numerical integration in which approximation methods are used to determine the integral's value when exact solutions do not exist. In this chapter, we first present and apply several programming techniques for finding the roots of equations. This is followed by techniques commonly employed in numerical integration.

15.1 INTRODUCTION TO ROOT FINDING

Root-solving techniques are important for a number of reasons. They are useful, easy to understand, and usually easy to carry out. Thus, with a minimum of instruction, you are able to solve genuine problems in engineering. A vital element in numerical analysis is appreciating what can or cannot be solved and clearly understanding the accuracy of the answers obtained. Since this appreciation and understanding come mostly from experience, you need to begin solving numerical problems immediately. Besides, you will find that root-solving problems are fun.

Some examples of the types of functions that are encountered in root-solving problems are

$$ax^2 + bx + c = 0 \tag{Eq. 15.1}$$
$$2x^4 - 7x^3 + 4x^2 + 7x - 6 = (x-1)(x+1)(2x-3) = 0 \tag{Eq. 15.2}$$
$$x^5 - 2x^3 - 5x^2 + 2 = 0 \tag{Eq. 15.3}$$
$$\sin^5(x) + \sin^3(x) + 5\cos(x) - 7 = 0 \tag{Eq. 15.4}$$
$$100e - x - \sin(2\pi x) = 0 \tag{Eq. 15.5}$$

The general quadratic equation, Equation 15.1, can be solved easily and exactly by using the quadratic formula:

$$r = \frac{-b \pm \sqrt{(b^2 - 4ac)}}{2a}$$

Equation 15.2 can be solved exactly by factoring the polynomial. The roots are then clearly 1, −1, 2, 3/2. However, most polynomials cannot be factored so easily, and other more general techniques are required. There are formulas for the exact solution of general cubic or quartic equations, but they are cumbersome and thus seldom used. No exact formula is possible for a polynomial like Equation 15.3, in which the highest power of *x* is greater than 4. For these polynomials, numerical means must generally be used to determine the roots.

You will recall from high school algebra that a polynomial of degree *n* (i.e., the highest power of x^n) has precisely *n* roots, of which some may be complex numbers and others may be multiple roots. Thus, Equation 15.3 has three real roots,

$r_1 = -0.712780744625\ldots$
$r_2 = 0.57909844162\ldots$
$r_3 = 2.0508836199\ldots$

and two complex roots,

$$r_4 = 0.757225433526 + i(0.57803468208)$$
$$r_5 = 0.757225433526 + i(0.57803468208)$$

The equation

$$x^2 - 2x + 1 = 0$$

can be factored as

$$(x - 1)^2 = 0$$

and has two real roots, both of which happen to be the same. In this case, the root is said to be a multiple root with multiplicity 2.

Equations 15.4 and 15.5 are called **transcendental equations** and represent an entirely different class of functions. Transcendental equations typically involve trigonometric, exponential, or logarithmic functions and cannot be reduced to any polynomial equation in x. The real roots of polynomials are usually classified as being either rational numbers (i.e., a simple fraction) or irrational (e.g., $\sqrt{2}$). The roots of transcendental equations are often transcendental numbers like π or e. Irrational numbers and transcendental numbers are represented by nonrepeating decimal fractions and cannot be expressed as simple fractions. These numbers are important to mathematics because they are responsible for the real number system being dense or continuous. Thus, the classification of equations as polynomials or transcendental and the roots of these equations as rational or irrational is vital to traditional mathematics; however, the distinction is of less consequence to the computer. In fact, not only is the number system available to the computer not continuous, but it is also a finite set.

At any rate, when finding the roots of equations, the distinction between polynomials and transcendental equations is unnecessary, and the same numerical procedures are applied to both. The distinction between the two types of functions is, however, important in other regards. For example, many of the theorems you learned concerning roots of polynomials do not apply to transcendental equations. Thus, both Equations 15.4 and 15.5 have an infinite number of real roots.

All of the root-solving techniques discussed in this chapter are interactive; that is, you specify an interval that is known to contain a root or simply an initial guess for the root, and the various recipes will return a more limited interval or a better guess. Some of the techniques we discuss will be guaranteed to find a root eventually but may take considerable computer time to arrive at the answer. Others may converge to a root much faster but are more susceptible to problems of divergence; that is, they come with no guarantees.

The common ingredient in all root-solving recipes is that potential computational difficulties of any nature are best avoided by mastering as much intelligence as possible in the initial choice of the method used and the accompanying initial guess. This part of the problem is often the most difficult and time consuming. The art involved in numerical analysis consists in balancing time spent optimizing the solution of the problem before computation against time spent correcting unforeseen errors during computation. If at all possible, the function should be roughly sketched before root solving is attempted either by using graphing routines or by generating a table of function values that are then graphed by hand. These graphs are extremely useful to the programmer not only in estimating the first guess for the root but also in anticipating potential difficulties. If a sketch is not feasible, some method of monitoring the function must be utilized to arrive at some understanding of what the function is doing before the actual computation is initiated. As an example of the general procedure we will follow, consider the transcendental function

$$f(x) = e^{-x} - \sin(\tfrac{1}{2}\pi x)$$

This equation, as you will shortly see, has an infinite number of positive roots. For the moment, we will concentrate on obtaining an initial guess for the first root and then use this initial guess to find a more precise root value.

We begin by gathering as much information as possible before trying to construct a Java program. This step almost always involves making a rough sketch of the function being considered. The preceding equation can be written as

$$e^{-x} = \sin(\tfrac{1}{2}\pi x)$$

A root of this equation then corresponds to any value of x such that the left side and right side are equal. If the left and right sides are plotted independently, the roots of the original equation are then given by the points of intersection of the two curves (Figure 15.1). From the sketch, we see that the roots are

Roots 0.4, 1.9, 4.0, . . .

Because the sine oscillates, there will be an infinite number of positive roots. We will concentrate first on improving the estimate of the first root near 0.4. We begin by establishing a procedure, or algorithm, that is based on the most obvious method of attack when using a pocket calculator; that is, we begin at some value of x just before the root (say, 0.3) and step along the x axis, carefully watching the magnitude and particularly the sign of the function.

Step	x	e^{-x}	$\sin(\tfrac{1}{2}\pi x)$	$f(x) = e^{-x} - \sin(\tfrac{1}{2}\pi x)$
0	0.3	0.741	0.454	0.297
1	0.4	0.670	0.588	0.082
2	0.5	0.606	0.707	−0.101

Notice that the function has changed sign between 0.4 and 0.5, indicating a root between these two x values. Thus, for the next approximation, we will use the midpoint value, $x = 0.45$, for our next step:

3	0.45	0.638	0.649	−0.012

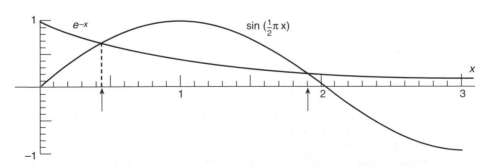

FIGURE 15.1 Graph of e^{-x} and $\sin(\tfrac{1}{2}\pi x)$ for Locating the Intersection Points

The function is again negative at 0.45, indicating that the root is between 0.4 and 0.45. The next approximation will, therefore, be the midpoint of this interval, 0.425. In this way, we can proceed systematically to a computation of the root to any desired degree of accuracy.

4	0.425	0.654	0.619	0.0347
5	0.4375	0.6456	0.6344	0.01126
6	0.44365	0.6417	0.6418	−0.00014

The key element in the procedure is the monitoring of the sign of the function. When the sign changes, specific action is taken to refine the estimate of the root. This change in sign of the function, indicating the vicinity of a root has been located, forms the key element in the computer code for locating roots. We now consider a number of root-finding methods that use this procedure as their basis.

EXERCISES 15.1

1. Use the iterative technique presented in this section to find a root of the equation

    $f(x) = \sin x - x/3 = 0$ (x is in radians)

    To do this, first rewrite the equation as

    $\sin x = x/3$

    and plot the left and right sides independently on the same graph.

15.2 THE BISECTION METHOD

The root-solving procedure illustrated in the preceding section is suitable for hand calculations; however, a slight modification will make it more "systematic" and easier to adapt to computer coding.

Suppose we already know that there is a root between $x = a$ and $x = b$; that is, the function changes sign in this interval. For simplicity, we will assume that there is only one root between $x = a$ and $x = b$ and that the function is continuous in this interval. The function might then resemble the sketch in Figure 15.2. If we next define $x_1 = a$ and $x_3 = b$ as the left and right ends of the interval, respectively, and $x_2 = \frac{1}{2}(x_1 + x_3)$ as the midpoint, in which half-interval does the function cross the x-axis? In the figure, the crossing is on the right, so we replace the full interval by the right half-interval. Thus,

x_2 now becomes x_1
x_3 remains as it is
x_2 is recalculated as the value $\frac{1}{2}(x_1 + x_3)$

and the question is again posed: In which half-interval does the function cross the x axis? After determining a second time whether the left half or the right half contains the root, the interval is once more replaced by either the left or right half-interval. This process continues until we narrow in on the root to within some previously assigned accuracy. Each step halves the interval, and so after n iterations, the size of the interval that contains the root will be $(b - a)/2^n$. If we are required to find a root to within a tolerance δ (i.e., $|x - \text{root}| < \delta$), the number of iterations n required can be determined from

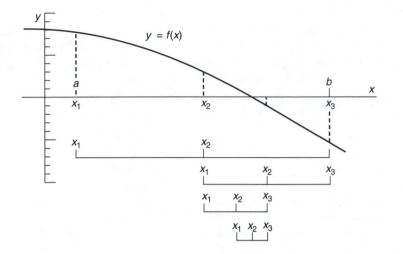

FIGURE 15.2   Root Determination by the Bisection Method

```
b - a
----- < δ
 2ⁿ
```

For example, the initial search interval in the example presented in the previous section was $(b - a) = 0.1$. If the root was required to an accuracy of $\delta = 10^{-5}$, then

```
0.1
--- < 10⁻⁵
 2ⁿ
```

or

```
2ⁿ > 10⁴
```

This can be solved for n as follows:

```
      log(10⁴)
n > -------- > 13
       log(2)
```

Thus, the calculation reveals that the desired degree of accuracy is achieved after the 13th application of the interval halving procedure. The only element of the method that has been omitted is how the computer is to determine which half of the interval contains the axis crossing. To that end, consider the product of the function evaluated at the left, $f_1 = f(x_1)$, and the function evaluated at the midpoint, $f_2 = f(x_2)$.

If	Then
$f_1 f_2 > 0.0$	f_1 and f_2 are both positive or both negative. In either case, there is no crossing between x_1 and x_2, and no root lies within the interval.
$f_1 f_2 < 0.0$	$f(x)$ has changed sign between x_1 and x_2. In this case, there is a root within the interval bounded by x_1 and x_2.

A program to compute the roots of an equation using this procedure is illustrated by Program 15.1. In reviewing this program, the following features should be especially noted:

- In each iteration after the first, there is only one function evaluation. It would be highly inefficient to reevaluate $f(x_1)$, $f(x_2)$, and $f(x_3)$ for each iteration since two of them are already known. If the function were extremely complicated, redundant computations like this would be a serious problem. A great deal of computer time can be wasted by unnecessary function evaluations.

- The program contains several checks for potential problems along with diagnostic messages (e.g., excessive iteration, no roots in interval, etc.) even though the programmer may think these possibilities are remote. Generally, the more of these checks a program contains, the better. They take only a few minutes to code and can save hours of debugging.

- The criterion for success is based on the size of the interval. Thus, even if the function were not close to zero at a point, x is changing very little, and continuing would not substantially improve the accuracy of the root.

PROGRAM 15.1

```java
import java.io.*;   // needed to access input stream classes
import java.text.*; // needed for formatting
public class BiSection
{
  public static void main (String[] args)
  throws java.io.IOException
  {
    String s1;
    int imax;        // maximum number of iterations
    double a, b;     // left and right ends of the original interval
    double epsilon;  // convergence criterion


      // set up the basic input stream
      // needed for conversion capabilities
    InputStreamReader isr = new InputStreamReader(System.in);
      // needed to use readLine()
    BufferedReader br = new BufferedReader(isr);


      // obtain the input data
    System.out.print("Enter the lower limit of the original search interval: ");
    s1 = br.readLine();
```

(Continued on next page)

(Continued from previous page)

```java
    a = Double.parseDouble(s1);
    System.out.print("Enter the upper limit of the original search interval: ");
    s1 = br.readLine();
    b = Double.parseDouble(s1);
    System.out.print("Enter the convergence criteria: ");
    s1 = br.readLine();
    epsilon = Double.parseDouble(s1);
    System.out.print("Enter the maximum number of iterations allowed: ");
    s1 = br.readLine();
    imax = Integer.parseInt(s1);

    bisection(a, b, epsilon, imax);
}


    // A bisection method that finds roots of a function
    // The interval a < x < b is known to contain a root of f(x). The estimate
    // of the root is successively improved by finding in which half
    // of the interval the root lies and then replacing the original
    // interval by that half-interval.
 public static void bisection(double a, double b, double epsilon, int imax)
 {
    int i;              // current iteration counter
    double x1, x2, x3;  // left, right, and midpoint of current interval
    double f1, f2, f3;  // function evaluated at these points
    double width;       // width of original interval = (b - a)
    double curwidth;    // width of current interval = (x3 - x1)

    DecimalFormat df = new DecimalFormat("0.000000");

       // echo back the passed input data
    System.out.println("\nThe original search interval is from " + a
                    + " to " + b );
    System.out.println("The convergence criterion is: interval < "  + epsilon );
    System.out.println("The maximum number of iterations allowed is " + imax );

       // calculate the root
    x1 = a;
    x3 = b;
    f1 = f(x1);
    f3 = f(x3);
    width = (b - a);

       // verify there is a root in the interval
```

(Continued on next page)

(Continued from previous page)

```
    if (f1 * f3 > 0.0)
      System.out.println("\nNo root in the original interval exists" );
    else
    {
      for (i = 1; i <= imax; i++)
      {
          // find which half of the interval contains the root
        x2 = (x1 + x3) / 2.0;
        f2 = f(x2);
        if (f1 * f2 <= 0.0)  // root is in left half interval
        {
          curwidth = (x2 - x1) / 2.0;
          f3 = f2;
          x3 = x2;
        }
        else  // root is in right half interval
        {
          curwidth = (x3 - x2) / 2.0;
          f1 = f2;
          x1 = x2;
        }
        if (curwidth < epsilon)
        {
        System.out.println("\nA root at x = " + df.format(x2) + " was found "
                      + "in " + i + " iterations" );
        System.out.println("The value of the function is " + f2 );
        return;
        }
      }
    }
    System.out.println("\nAfter " + imax + " iterations, no root was found "
                  + "within the convergence criterion" );

    return;
  }


    // method to evaluate f(x)
  public static double f(double x)
  {
      final double PI = Math.acos(-1.0);  // value of pi

      return (Math.exp(-x) - Math.sin(0.5 * PI * x));
  }
}
```

A sample run of Program 15.1 produced the following:

```
Enter the lower limit of the original search interval: .4
Enter the upper limit of the original search interval: .5
Enter the convergence criteria: .00001
Enter the maximum number of iterations allowed: 25


The original search interval is from 0.4 to 0.5
The convergence criterion is: interval < 1.0E-5
The maximum number of iterations allowed is 25


A root at x = 0.443567 was found in 13 iterations
The value of the function is 1.2259482798926413E-5
```

Although Program 15.1 is used to evaluate the roots of the equation $f(x) = e^{-x} - \sin(\pi x/2)$, by changing the calculation in the return statement, this program can be used for any function.

One final comment: The bisection method in Program 15.1 is an example of a so-called brute-force method; that is, it possesses a minimum of finesse. Although it illustrates fundamental Java techniques, much more powerful and clever numerical procedures are available. These techniques are presented next.

EXERCISES 15.2

1. Use the bisection procedure for finding the roots of an equation. First construct a table of the following form:

Step	x_1	x_2	x_3	$f(x_1)$	$f(x_2)$	$f(x_3)$	Crossing Left	Right
0	a	$\frac{1}{2}(a+b)$	b					
1								

Next use the bisection procedure and a pocket calculator to obtain the roots of the following functions to an accuracy of five significant figures.

a. $f(x) = x^2 + 2x - 15$ (Use $a = 2.8$, $b = 3.1$. The exact answer $= 3.0$.)
b. $g(x) = \frac{1}{2}\sin(x)(e^x - e^{-x})$ (This is the elliptic gear equation, with x in radians. Use $a = 1$, $b = 4$.)
c. $e(x) = \sqrt{(R^2 - x^2)} - x\tan(x)$ (Equation for quantum energies of a particle in a box. Use $R = 10$, $a = 4.0$, $b = 4.7$.)
d. Predict the number of steps needed to obtain the answer to the specified accuracy of five significant figures in parts a through c.

2. a. Modify Program 15.1 to solve for the indicated roots of each of the functions of Exercise 1.
   b. Modify Program 15.1 to produce a table similar to the one required in Exercise 1 for each of the functions listed in Exercise 1.

3. Write a Java program to find the maximum of a function $f(x)$ over an interval $a \leq x \leq b$ by starting at $x = a$ with a step size Δx. Evaluate $f_1 = f(x)$ and $f_2 = f(x + \Delta x)$. If $f_1 < f_2$, replace x with $x + \Delta x$ and continue; otherwise, reduce the step size by half and repeat the comparison. The program should terminate successfully when $\Delta < 10^{-6}$.

15.3 REFINEMENTS TO THE BISECTION METHOD

The bisection method described in the previous section presents the basics upon which most root-finding methods are constructed. It is a so-called brute-force method that is rarely used in practice, since for almost any problem an alternative method that is faster, more accurate, and only slightly more complex is available. All of the refinements of the bisection method that might be devised are based on attempts to use as much information as is available about the behavior or the function at each iteration. In the ordinary bisection method, the only feature of the function that is monitored is its sign. Thus, if we were searching for roots of the function

$$f(x) = e^{-x} - \sin(\tfrac{1}{2}\pi x)$$

we would begin the search, as described in Section 15.1, by stepping along the x axis and watching for a change in sign of the function as follows:

```
i    x_i       f(x_i)
0    0.0       2.0
1    0.1       1.33
2    0.2       0.75
3    0.3       0.29
4    0.4      -.05
```

The next step in the bisection procedure is to reduce the step size by half; that is, try, $x_5 = 0.35$. However, from the magnitude of the numbers listed, we would expect the root be closer to 0.4 than to 0.3. Thus, by using information about the size of the functional value in addition to its sign, we may be able to speed up the convergence. In the present case, we might interpolate the root to be approximately

```
  0.29 - 0.0            f_3 - 0
--------------    =    -------    =    0.853
0.29 - (-0.05)         f_3 - f_4
```

of the distance from $x_3 = 0.3$ to $x_4 = 0.4$, or $x_5 = 0.3853$. Continuing in this manner and interpolating at each step, we would obtain the following results:

```
i    x_i         f(x_i)
3    0.30        0.29
4    0.40       -0.05
5    0.385      -0.0083
```

```
6    0.3823      -0.0013
7    0.3819      -0.00019
8    0.38185     -0.000028
9    0.38184     -0.000004
```

Comparing these results with the bisection method applied to a similar function in the previous section, we see that the convergence rate for the present method is significantly faster. The next task is to formalize this procedure into a method suitable for a general function.

Regula Falsi Method

The basic idea in the first refinement of the bisection algorithm is that the new method will be essentially the same as bisection except that in place of the midpoint of the interval at each step of the calculation, an interpolated value for the root is used. The method is illustrated in Figure 15.3. In the figure, a root is known to exist in the interval $(x_{XL} \leftrightarrow x_3)$, and in the drawing, f_1 is negative whereas f_3 is positive. The interpolated position of the root is x_2. Since the two triangles ABC and CDE are similar, the lengths of the sides are related by

```
DE     CD
-- =  --
AB     BC
```

or

```
0.0 - f₁     x₂ - x₁
-------- =  -------
f₃ - f₁     x₃ - x₁
```

which may be solved for the unknown position x_2 to yield

```
                        f₁
x₂ = x₁ - (x₃ - x₁)  ------
                      f₃ - f₁
```

This value of x_2 then replaces the midpoint used in the bisection algorithm, and the rest of the procedure remains exactly the same. Thus, the next step would be to determine whether the actual root is to the left or to the right of x_2. As before,

If $f_1 \times f_2 < 0$, then the root is on the left
If $f_2 \times f_3 < 0$, then the root is on the right

In the figure, the root is to the left of x_2, so the interval used for the next iteration would be

$$x_3 = x_2$$
$$f_3 = f_2$$

$$x_2 = x_1 - (x_3 - x_1) \ \frac{f_1}{f_3 - f_1}$$

$$f_2 = f(x_2)$$

In other words, to employ this slightly faster algorithm, the only change that has to be made to the previous bisection code is to replace statements of the form

$$x_2 = (x_1 + x_3) \ / \ 2$$

by a statement of the form

$$x_2 = x_1 - (x_3 - x_1) \ \frac{f_1}{f_3 - f_1}$$

This method is still guaranteed to obtain a root eventually and will almost always converge faster than the conventional bisection algorithm. We do, however, pay a small price. The values of f_1 and f_3 used in solving for x_2 may be very nearly equal, and we could be plagued by round-off errors in their difference. Also, in the bisection algorithm, we could predict with some precision the number of iterations required to obtain the root to a desired accuracy (see Section 15.1). This prediction is no longer possible if we use the interpolated values, and the code must now include a check for excessive iterations.

This method illustrates that an almost trivial change in the algorithm, which is based on more intelligent monitoring of the function, can reap considerable rewards in more

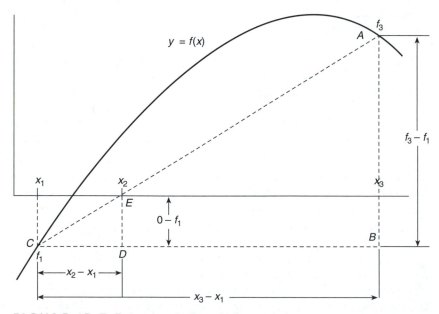

F I G U R E 1 5 . 3 Estimating the Root by Interpolation

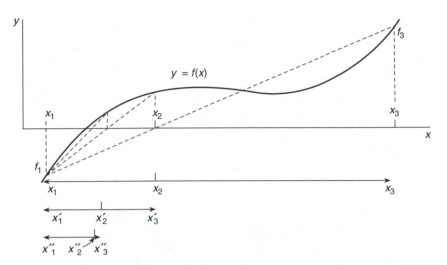

FIGURE 15.4 Graphical Illustration of Several Iterations of the Regula Falsi Algorithm

rapid convergence. The formal name of the method just described is the *regula falsi method* (the method of false position).

Are there any additional improvements in the basic bisection algorithm that can be easily implemented? To answer this question, we must examine in more detail the manner in which the regula falsi method arrives at a solution. This is best done graphically. The calculation begun in Figure 15.3 continues in Figure 15.4. Notice that in this example, in which the function is concave downward near the root, the value of the left limit of the search interval near the root, x_l, never changes. The actual root always remains in the left segment in each iteration. The right segment of the interval, $x_3 - x_2$, shrinks quite rapidly, but the left segment, $x_2 - x_1$, does not. If the function were concave upward, the converse would be true. Thus, a drawback in the regula falsi method is that even though the method converges more rapidly to a value of x that results in a "small" $|f(x)|$, the interval containing the root does *not* diminish significantly.

Modified Regula Falsi Method

Perhaps the procedure can be made to converge more rapidly if the interval can somehow be made to collapse from both directions. One way to accomplish this is demonstrated in Figure 15.5. The idea is as follows:

```
If the root is determined to lie in the left segment (x₂ - x₁)
        The interpolation line is drawn between the points (x₁,¹/₂f₁) and (x₃, f₃)
Elseif the root is in the right segment
        The interpolation line is drawn between the points (x₁, f₁) and (x₃,¹/₂f₃)
EndIf
```

Using this algorithm, the slope of the line is *artificially* reduced. The effect of this reduction is that if the root is in the left of the original interval, it will eventually turn up in the right segment of a later interval and subsequently will alternate between left and right. The last modification to the bisection method in combination with the regula falsi method is known as the *modified regula falsi method*, and it is a very powerful and popular

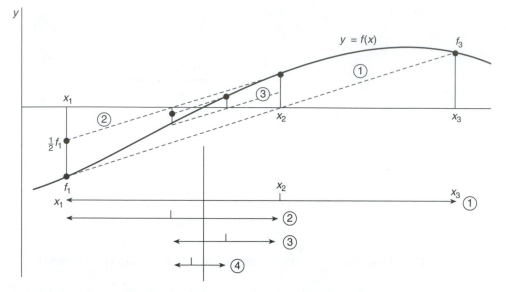

FIGURE 15.5 Graphical Illustration of the Modified Regula Falsi Method

procedure for finding roots of equations. The alternatives to the original bisection code presented in Program 15.1 are quite trivial and are incorporated within Program 15.2.

The Java code in Program 15.2 requires some explanation:

I.   The function $f(x)$ is evaluated only once per cycle. If the function is complicated and therefore costly to compute, this measure of efficiency can be attractive, even decisive, in choosing the appropriate method of solution.

II. The code can terminate in only three ways:

A. One success path: If the current fractional size of the search interval—that is, (current interval)/(original interval)—is less than the user-supplied convergence criterion, the original aim of the program, to narrowly bracket a root, has been achieved. There is no guarantee that this criterion will result in a value of $f(x)$ that is "small." The point is, however, that successive iterations have resulted in only small changes in the interval containing the root, and so continuing the process is not necessary or productive.

B. There are two failure paths:

1. If the number of iterations is greater than I_{max}, then the process is stopped. This test allows the programmer to specify the maximum cost that will be accepted for an attempted solution. Since in the regula falsi and modified regula falsi methods the number of iterations is not predictable, this form of safeguard is essential. It is also a prudent precaution against unforeseen errors in the construction of the problem that could cause the program to cycle forever and not obtain a solution. Statements of this type are required in any program in which there is a danger of infinite looping.

2. If the function does not change sign ($f_1 \times f_3 > 0$), then the process is stopped. Since the original interval was known to contain a root, the only way this condition can arise is by error. Usually, the error is in the code for the function $f(x)$; that is, you are attempting to find a root of a function different from the one intended.

PROGRAM 15.2

```java
import java.io.*;    // needed to access input stream classes
import java.text.*; // needed for formatting
public class ModRegulaFalsi
{
  public static void main (String[] args)
  throws java.io.IOException
  {
    String s1;
    int imax;        // maximum number of iterations
    double a, b;     // left and right ends of the original interval
    double epsilon;  // convergence criterion

      // set up the basic input stream
      // needed for conversion capabilities
    InputStreamReader isr = new InputStreamReader(System.in);
      // needed to use readLine()
    BufferedReader br = new BufferedReader(isr);

      // obtain the input data
    System.out.print("Enter the lower limit of the original search interval: ");
    s1 = br.readLine();
    a = Double.parseDouble(s1);
    System.out.print("Enter the upper limit of the original search interval: ");
    s1 = br.readLine();
    b = Double.parseDouble(s1);
    System.out.print("Enter the convergence criteria: ");
    s1 = br.readLine();
    epsilon = Double.parseDouble(s1);
    System.out.print("Enter the maximum number of iterations allowed: ");
    s1 = br.readLine();
    imax = Integer.parseInt(s1);

    modregfalsi(a, b, epsilon, imax);
  }

    // A modified regula falsi method that finds roots of a function
    // The maximum number of iterations permitted is imax. The convergence
    // criterion is the fractional size of the search interval (x3 - x1) / (b - a)
    // is less than epsilon. A relaxation factor RELAX is used
  public static void modregfalsi(double a, double b, double epsilon, int imax)
  {
    final double RELAX = 0.9;  // the relaxation factor

    int i;                // current iteration counter
```

(Continued on next page)

(Continued from previous page)

```java
    double x1, x2, x3; // left, right, and midpoint of current interval
    double f1, f2, f3; // function evaluated at these points
    double width;      // width of original interval = (b - a)
    double curwidth;   // width of current interval = (x3 - x1)

    DecimalFormat df = new DecimalFormat("0.000000");

      // echo back the passed input data
    System.out.println("\nThe original search interval is from " + a + " to " + b
                  + "\nThe convergence criterion is: interval < "  + epsilon
                  + "\nThe maximum number of iterations allowed is " + imax );

      // calculate the root
    x1 = a;
    x3 = b;
    f1 = f(x1);
    f3 = f(x3);
    width = Math.abs(b - a);

      // iterations
    for (i = 1; i <= imax; i++)
    {
      curwidth = (x3 - x1) / width;
      x2 = x1 - width * curwidth * f1 / (f3 - f1);
      f2 = f(x2);
      if (Math.abs(curwidth) < epsilon) // root is found
      {
        System.out.println("\nA root at x = " + df.format(x2) + " was found "
                      + "in " + i + " iterations" );
        System.out.println("The value of the function is " + f2 );
        return;
      }
      else  // check for left and right crossing
      {
        if(f1 * f2 < 0.0) // check for crossing on the left
        {
          x3 = x2;
          f3 = f2;
          f1 = RELAX * f1;
        }
        else if (f2 * f3 < 0.0)  // check for crossing on the right
        {
          x1 = x2;
          f1 = f2;
```

(Continued on next page)

(Continued from previous page)

```
          f3 = RELAX * f3;

      }
      else  // no crossing in the interval
      {
        System.out.println(
                "The search for a root has failed due to no root in the interval\n"
                + "In step " + i
                + " of the iteration the function does not change sign");

      }
    }
  }
  System.out.println("\nAfter " + imax + " iterations, no root was found "
                 + "within the convergence criterion\n"
                 + "The search for a root has failed due to excessive iterations\n"
                 + "after the maximum number of " + imax + " iterations" );


  return;
}


  // method to evaluate f(x)
  public static double f(double x)
  {
      final double PI = Math.acos(-1.0);  // value of pi
      return (Math.exp(-x) - Math.sin(0.5 * PI * x));

  }
}
```

A sample run using Program 15.2 produced the following:

```
Enter the lower limit of the original search interval: .4
Enter the upper limit of the original search interval: .5
Enter the convergence criteria: .00001
Enter the maximum number of iterations allowed: 25

The original search interval is from 0.4 to 0.5
The convergence criterion is: interval < 1.0E-5
The maximum number of iterations allowed is 25

A root at x = 0.443574 was found in 7 iterations
The value of the function is -2.2537445243386856E-9
```

In comparing the results from the sample run of Program 15.2 to those of Program 15.1, notice that a more exact root was located by the modified regula falsi function in five fewer iterations (7 as opposed to 13). The exactness of the root is indicated by the functional value at the root, which is closer to 0.0 in the output produced by Program

TABLE 15.1 Comparison of Root-Finding Methods Using the Function $f(x) = e^{-x} - \sin(\frac{1}{2}\pi x)$

i	Bisection x_2	Regula Bisection x_2	Modified Regula Bisection x_2
1	0.35	0.385	0.385
2	0.375	0.3823	0.3820
3	0.3875	0.3819	0.38183
4	0.38125	0.38185	0.381843
5	0.38438	0.381844	0.38184267
6	0.38281	0.381843	0.38184276
7	0.38203	0.3818428	0.38184275
8	0.38164	0.38184275	0.38184275

15.2. A more complete comparison of the rate of convergence for all three root-finding methods presented so far, as these methods applied to the function

$$f(x) = e^{-x} - \sin(\tfrac{1}{2}\pi x)$$

is presented in Table 15.1.

A slope-reduction factor of one-half was used in constructing the drawing in Figure 15.5 and is an example of what is called a **relaxation factor,** a number used to alter the results of one iteration before inserting them into the next. Determining the optimum relaxation factor is almost always an extremely complex problem in any calculation and is well beyond the scope of this text. However, in this instance, a little trial and error shows that a less drastic decrease in the slope will result in improved convergence. Using a reduction factor of 0.9 should be adequate for most problems; this factor generated the values in Table 15.1.

Summary of the Algorithms Based on Bisection

The characteristic features of the three methods discussed in this and the previous section are as follows:

Bisection	Success based on size of interval
	Slow convergence
	Predictable number of iterations
	Interval halved in each iteration
	Guaranteed to bracket a root
Regula falsi	Success based on size of function
	Faster convergence
	Unpredictable number of iterations
	Interval containing root is not small
	Monitors size of function as well as its sign
Modified regula falsi	Success based on size of interval
	Faster convergence
	Unpredictable number of iterations

Of the three methods, the modified regula falsi is probably the most efficient for common problems and is the recommended algorithm whenever the only information available is that the function changes sign between x_1 and x_3.

The requirement that the initial search interval be one in which the function changes sign (only once) can occasionally be troublesome. For example, the problem of finding the root of the function

$$f(x) = x^2 - 2x + 1 = (x - 1)^2$$

is not suited to any of the algorithms based on bisection because the function never changes sign. This difficulty occurs whenever the root of the function is a multiple root of even multiplicity. A method that overcomes this limitation is the secant method, which is the topic of the next section.

EXERCISES 15.3

1. Roughly reproduce the sketch in Figure 15.6 and then graphically apply the regula falsi method for three iterations.

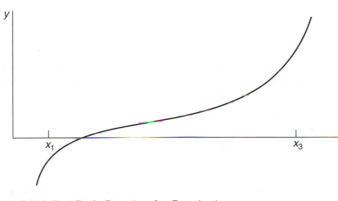

FIGURE 15.6 Function for Exercise 1

2. Using a pocket calculator, apply the regula falsi procedure for three iterations to the following functions:
   a. $f(x) = xe^{-x^2} - \cos(x)$ $a = 0$, $b = 2$; exact root $= 1.351491185 \ldots$
   b. $g(x) = x^2 - 2x - 3$ $a = 0$, $b = 4$; exact root $= 3.0$
   c. $h(x) = e^x - (1 + x + x^2/2)$ $a = -1$, $b = 1$; exact root $= 0.0$
   d. $F(x) = x^3 - 2x - 5$ $a = 1$, $b = 3$; exact root $= 2.0945514815 \ldots$
   e. $G(x) = 10 \ln(x) - x$ $a = 1$, $b = 2$; exact root $= 1.1183255916 \ldots$
3. Roughly reproduce Figure 15.6 and then graphically apply the modified regula falsi method for three iterations.
4. a. Execute Program 15.2.
   b. Use Program 15.2 to find the root of one of the functions in Exercise 2 to an accuracy of 10^{-5}.
   c. Change the relaxation factor from 0.9 to 0.75 and rerun the program. Comment on the difference between the two calculations.

15.4 THE SECANT METHOD

The secant method is identical to the method of false position (regula falsi method) except that the sign of $f(x)$ need not be checked at each iteration. As in the regula falsi method, the values of x_0 and x_1 are required to start the procedure, but then the following algorithm is employed to obtain an improvement for the next value of x:

Start with the interval defined by (x_0, x_1)
Compute the next value of x as

```
          f(x₀)
x₂ = ------------- (x₁ - x₀)
      f(x₀) - f(x₁)
```

Replace the pair of values (x_0, x_1) by the pair (x_1, x_2)
Repeat steps 2 and 3 until the value of f(x) is within an acceptable limit of zero

The secant method can be shown (see Exercise 2) to be equivalent to repeatedly replacing the function by straight lines drawn through the points $(x_0, f(x_0))$ and $(x_1, f(x_1))$—that is, secant lines. The Java code for a function implementing the secant method is included within Program 15.3.

PROGRAM 15.3

```java
import java.io.*;   // needed to access input stream classes
import java.text.*; // needed for formatting
public class Secant
{
  public static void main (String[] args)
  throws java.io.IOException
  {
    String s1;
    int imax;          // maximum number of iterations
    double a, b;       // left and right ends of the original interval
    double epsilon;    // convergence criterion

      // set up the basic input stream
      // needed for conversion capabilities
    InputStreamReader isr = new InputStreamReader(System.in);
      // needed to use readLine()
    BufferedReader br = new BufferedReader(isr);

      // obtain the input data
    System.out.print("Enter the lower limit of the original search interval: ");
    s1 = br.readLine();
    a = Double.parseDouble(s1);
    System.out.print("Enter the upper limit of the original search interval: ");
```

(Continued on next page)

(Continued from previous page)

```java
      s1 = br.readLine();
      b = Double.parseDouble(s1);
      System.out.print("Enter the convergence criteria: ");
      s1 = br.readLine();
      epsilon = Double.parseDouble(s1);
      System.out.print("Enter the maximum number of iterations allowed: ");
      s1 = br.readLine();
      imax = Integer.parseInt(s1);

      secant(a, b, epsilon, imax);
   }


   // This method implements the secant method for finding
   // a root of a function
   public static void secant(double a, double b, double epsilon, int imax)
   {

      int i;              // current iteration counter
      double x0, x1;      // left and right x values of current interval
      double f0, f1;      // function evaluated at these points
      double dx0;         // delta x0
      double dx1;         // delta x1



      DecimalFormat df = new DecimalFormat("0.000000");

         // echo back the passed input data
      System.out.println("\nThe original search interval is from " + a + " to " + b
                    + "\nThe convergence criterion is: interval < "  + epsilon
                    + "\nThe maximum number of iterations allowed is " + imax );

         // determine the root
      x0 = a;
      f0 = f(x0);
      dx0 = Math.abs(b - a);
      dx1 = 0;

         // iterations
      for (i = 1; i <= imax; i++)
      {
         x1 = x0 + dx0;
         f1 = f(x1);
         if (Math.abs(f1) < epsilon) // root is found
         {
```

(Continued on next page)

(Continued from previous page)

```
      System.out.println("\nA root at x = " + df.format(x1 + dx1) + " was found "
                  + "in " + i + " iterations" );
      System.out.println("The value of the function is " + f1 );
      return;
    }
    else  // do next iteration
    {
      dx1 = ( f1/(f0 - f1) ) * dx0;
      x0 = x1;
      dx0 = dx1;
      f0 = f1;
    }
  }
  System.out.println("\nAfter " + imax + " iterations, no root was found "
                  + "within the convergence criterion\n"
                  + "The search for a root has failed due to excessive iterations\n"
                  + "after the maximum number of " + imax + " iterations" );

  return;
}


  // method to evaluate f(x)
 public static double f(double x)
 {
   final double PI = Math.acos(-1.0);   // value of pi
   return (Math.exp(-x) - Math.sin(0.5 * PI * x));
 }
}
```

A sample run using Program 15.3 produced the following:

```
Enter the lower limit of the original search interval: .4
Enter the upper limit of the original search interval: .5
Enter the convergence criteria: .00001
Enter the maximum number of iterations allowed: 25

The original search interval is from 0.4 to 0.5
The convergence criterion is: interval < 1.0E-5
The maximum number of iterations allowed is 25

A root at x = 0.443628 was found in 4 iterations
The value of the function is -9.014170276877564E-8
```

Although the secant method is probably the most popular method to find the root of a function, it does possess divergence problems. Thus, a check should be built into the

Java code for this method that detects when successive intervals start to become larger rather than smaller.

EXERCISES 15.4

1. a. Execute Program 15.3 on your computer.

   b. Use Program 15.3 to find the root of the function $f(x) = x^2 - 2x + 0.9$ starting with an initial guess of $x_0 = 0.6$ and $x_1 = 0.9$.

2. The method secant of Program 15.3 was used to find a root of the function $f(x) = x^2 - 2x + 0.9$ starting with an initial guess of $x_0 = 0.6$, $x_1 = 1.0$, and the values of x_0 and $x_1 - x_0$ were printed for each iteration. The results are:

Step	x_0	$x_1 - x_0$
0	0.600	0.300
1	0.900	−0.180
2	0.720	−0.057
3	0.663	0.022
4	0.685	−0.001

Carefully graph the function for $0.5 \le x \le 1.0$ and use the foregoing numbers to graphically demonstrate how the secant method arrives at a root of the function.

3. Use Program 15.3 to find a root of the function $f(x) = x^2 - 2x - 3$.

15.5 INTRODUCTION TO NUMERICAL INTEGRATION

The integration of a function of a single variable can be thought of as either the opposite of differentiation (i.e., the antiderivative) or as the area under a curve. Antiderivatives are ordinarily discussed in depth in a calculus course. Here we will concentrate instead on the less analytic, more visual approach of interpreting a definite integral as an area. That is, the integral of the function $f(x)$ from $x = a$ to $x = b$, designated as

$$I = \int_a^b f(x)\,dx$$

will be evaluated by devising techniques for measuring the area under the graph of the function over this interval (Figure 15.7). This method of evaluating an integral lends itself so naturally to numerical computation that the most effective way to understand the process of integration is to learn the numerical approach first and later have these ideas reinforced by the more formal concepts of the antiderivative.

Another reason for studying numerical integration at this stage is that it is a so-called stable process; it almost always works. This is because numerical integration consists of expressing the area as the sum of areas of smaller segments, a procedure that is relatively safe from problems such as division by zero or round-off error caused by subtracting numbers of approximately the same magnitude.

Finally, it is unfortunately true that many, perhaps most, of the integrals that occur in actual engineering or science problems cannot be expressed in any closed form. For example, an integral as innocent appearing as

$$I = \int_a^b f(x)\,dx$$

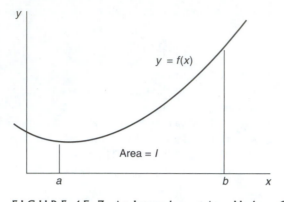

FIGURE 15.7 An Integral as an Area Under a Curve

is of this type, and the only way that it can be evaluated is numerically. To formally integrate a function—that is, to obtain a closed expression for the answer—often takes considerable training and experience. Dozens of "tricks" must be learned and understood. On the other hand, the procedures of numerical integration are few in number, and all are quite easy to understand and remember. As in many earlier numerical procedures, we begin by replacing the function over a limited range by straight-line segments.

The interval $x = a$ to $x = b$ is divided into subintervals or panels of size Δx, the function is replaced by line segments over each subinterval, and the area under the function is then approximated by the area under the line segments. This is the trapezoidal rule approximation for an integral and is described in the next section. The next order approximation is to replace the function by parabolic segments and is known as Simpson's rule, which is presented in Section 15.7.

15.6 THE TRAPEZOIDAL RULE

An approximation to the area under a complicated curve is obtained by assuming that the function can be replaced by simpler functions over a limited range. A straight line, the simplest approximation to a function, is the first to be considered and leads to what is called the **trapezoidal rule.**

The area under the curve $f(x)$ from $x = a$ to $x = b$ is approximated by the area beneath a straight line drawn between the points $[xa, f(a)]$ and $[xb, f(b)]$ (Figure 15.8). The shaded area is then the approximation to the integral and is the area of a trapezoid, which is

$I =$ (average value of f over interval) (width of interval)

or

$$I = \tfrac{1}{2}[f(a) + f(b)]\,(b - a) = T_0 \qquad\qquad \text{(Eq. 15.6)}$$

This is the trapezoidal rule for one panel, identified as T_0.

To improve the accuracy of the approximation to the area under a curve, the interval is next divided in half and the function approximated by straight-line segments over each half. The area in this case is approximated by the area of two trapezoids, as illustrated in Figure 15.9.

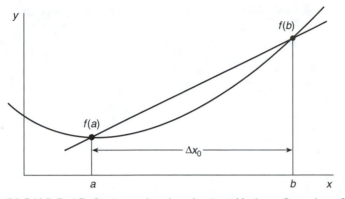

FIGURE 15.8 Approximating the Area Under a Curve by a Single Trapezoid

$$I \propto T_1 = [\tfrac{1}{2}(f(a) + f_1)\Delta x_L] + [\tfrac{1}{2}(f_1 + f(b)\Delta x_L]$$

or

$$T_1 = \frac{\Delta x_L}{2} [f(a) + 2f_1 + f(b)] \qquad\qquad (Eq. \ 15.7)$$

where

$$\Delta x_L = \frac{(b - a)}{2}$$

$$f_1 = f(x = a + \Delta x_L)$$

Notice that when adding the areas of the trapezoids, the sides at $f(a)$ and $f(b)$ are sides of only the first and last trapezoid, whereas the side at f_1 is a side of two trapezoids and thus "counts twice," explaining the factor of 2 in Equation 15.7.

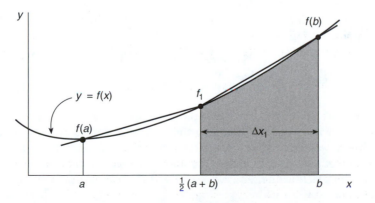

FIGURE 15.9 Two-panel Approximation to the Area

Furthermore, the two-panel approximation, T_1, can be related to the one-panel results, T_0, as

$$T_1 = \frac{T_0}{2} + \Delta x_1 f_1 \qquad \text{(Eq. 15.8)}$$

To increase the accuracy further, the interval is simply subdivided into a large number of panels. The result for n panels is clearly

$$I \propto T_n = \tfrac{1}{2}\,\Delta x_n \left(f(a) + 2\sum_{i=1}^{n-1} f_i + f(b) \right) \qquad \text{Trapezoidal Rule} \qquad \text{(Eq. 15.9)}$$

where $\Delta x_n = (b - a)/n$ and f_i is the function evaluated at each of the interior points,

$$f_i = f(x = a + i\,\Delta x_n)$$

The reason for the extra factor of 2 in Equation 15.9 is the same as in the two-panel example.

Computational Form of the Trapezoidal Rule Equation

Equation 15.9 was derived assuming that the widths of all the panels are the same and equal to Δx_n. However, equal panel widths are not required in the derivation, and the equation can easily be generalized to a partition of the interval into unequal panels of width Δx_i, $i = 1, \ldots, n - 1$. However, for reasons to be explained a bit later, we will not only restrict the panel widths to be equal but the number of panels to be a power of 2—that is,

$$n = 2^k$$

The number of panels is n, the order of the calculation will be called k, and the corresponding trapezoidal rule approximation will be labeled as T_k. Thus, T_0 is the result for $n = 2^0 = 1$ panel. The situation for $k = 2$ or $2^2 = 4$ panels is illustrated in Figure 15.10. In the figure, the width of a panel is $\Delta x_2 = (b - a)/2^2$, and the value of the $k = 2$ trapezoidal rule approximation is

$$T_2 = (\Delta x_2/2)[f(a) + 2f(a + \Delta x_2) + 2f(a + \Delta x_2) + 2f(a + 3\,\Delta x_2) + f(b)] \qquad \text{(Eq. 15.10)}$$

However, since $2\Delta x_2 = \Delta x_1$, we see that

$$f(a + 2\,\Delta x_2) = f(a + x_1)$$

and $f(a + \Delta x_1)$ was already determined in the previous calculation of T_1 (Equation 15.8). The point is that by successively doubling the number of panels in each stage, the only new information we require to proceed to the next order trapezoidal rule approximation is the evaluation of the function at the midpoints of the current intervals.

To exploit this fact further, Equations 15.7 and 15.8 can be used to rewrite Equation 15.10 in the form

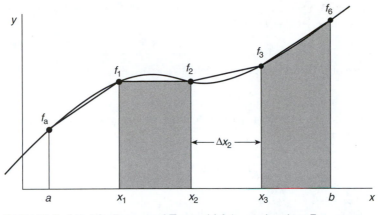

FIGURE 15.10 Four-panel Trapezoidal Approximation, T_2

$$T_2 = (\Delta x_1/4)[f(a) + 2f(a + \Delta x_1) + f(b)] + \Delta x_2[f(a + \Delta x_2) + f(a + 3\,\Delta x_2)]$$
$$= T_1/2 + \Delta x_2[f(a + \Delta x_2) + f(a + 3\,\Delta x_2)]$$

This equation can easily be generalized to yield

$$T_k = \tfrac{1}{2}T_{k-1} + \Delta x_k \sum_{\substack{i=1 \\ \text{odd only}}}^{n-1} f(a + i\,\Delta x_k) \qquad\qquad \text{(Eq. 15.11)}$$

where

$$\Delta x_k = \frac{b - a}{2^k}$$

The procedure for using Equation 15.11 to approximate an integral by the trapezoidal rule is then:

1. Compute T_0 by using Equation 15.6.
2. Repeatedly apply Equation 15.11 for $k = 1, 2, \ldots$ until sufficient accuracy is obtained.

Example of a Trapezoidal Rule Calculation

To illustrate the ideas of this section, we use the integral

$$I = \int_1^2 (1/x)\,dx$$

The function $f(x) = 1/x$ can of course be integrated analytically to give $ln(x)$, and since $ln(1) = 0$, the value of the integral is $ln(2) = 0.69314718$. The trapezoidal rule approximation to the integral with $a = 1$ and $b = 2$ begins with Equation 15.6 to obtain T_0.

$$T_0 = \frac{1}{2}\left(\frac{1}{1} + \frac{1}{2}\right)(2 - 1) = 0.75$$

Repeated use of Equation 15.11 then yields

$k = 1$ $\Delta x_1 = {}^1/_2$
    $T_1 = T_0/2 + {}^1/_2[f(1 + {}^1/_2)] = 0.75/2 + {}^1/_2(1/1.5)$
    $= 0.708333$

$k = 2$ $\Delta x_2 = {}^1/_4$
    $T_2 = T_1/2 + {}^1/_4(1/1.25 + 1/1.75)$
    $= 0.6970238$

$k = 3$ $\Delta x_3 = {}^1/_8$
    $T_3 = T_2/2 + {}^1/_8(1/1.125 + 1/1.375 + 1/1.625 + 1/1.875)$
    $= 0.69412185$

Continuing the calculation through $k = 5$ yields

k	T_k
0	0.75
1	0.70833
2	0.69702
3	0.69412
4	0.69339
5	0.693208
.	.
.	.
. .	
Exact	0.693147 . . .

The convergence of the computed values of the trapezoidal rule is not particularly fast, but the method is quite simple.

EXERCISES 15.6

1. Evaluate the following integrals by using the trapezoidal rule in the following way:

a. Evaluate T_0 for one panel by using Equation 15.6.

b. Compute T_1 using the value of T_0 and Equation 15.11.

c. Continue the calculation through T_4.

Collect your results in the form of a table. (Be careful: Errors in one step will carry over into the next.)

Exact Result

a. $\int_0^8 x^2\, dx$ 170.667

b. $\int_0^8 x^4\, dx$ 6553.6

c. $\displaystyle\int_0^1 x e^{-x}\,dx$ $1 - 2/e = 0.2642411175\ldots$

d. $\displaystyle\int_0^{\pi/2} x\sin(x)\,dx$ 1.0

e. $\displaystyle\int_0^1 (1 + x^2)^{3/2}\,dx$ $1.567951962\ldots$

f. $\displaystyle\int_0^1 e^{-x2}\,dx$ $0.74682404\ldots$

15.7 SIMPSON'S RULE

The trapezoidal rule is based on approximating the function by straight-line segments. To improve the accuracy and the convergence rate of the method, an obvious direction to take would be to approximate the function by parabolic segments in place of straight lines. This idea results in an approximation for the integral known as **Simpson's rule,** the simplest example of which is illustrated in Figure 15.11. To uniquely specify a parabola requires three points, and so the lowest order Simpson's rule has two panels.

To proceed, we need to know the area under a parabola drawn through three points. Note that the corresponding step in the derivation of the trapezoidal rule was trivial: The area under a line through two points is simply $\Delta x[f(a) + f(b)]/2$.

If the curve $f(x)$ drawn in Figure 15.11 is approximated by a parabola drawn through the three points $f(a)$, $f(b)$, and the value of $f(x)$ at the midpoint of the interval f_{mid}, it can be shown using calculus that the shaded area under the parabola, denoted as S_1, is

$$S_1 = {}^{1}\!/_3 \Delta x_1 [f(a) + 4f(a + \Delta x_1) + f(b)]$$

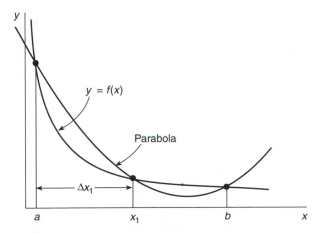

FIGURE 15.11 Two Panel Simpson's Rule Approximation to an Integral

where

$$\Delta x_1 = \frac{b - a}{2}$$

This is the first order Simpson's rule approximation where $k = 1$ and $n = 2^1$ panels. The next level of approximation is to halve the interval width and partition the interval into four panels (Figure 15.12). The area under the function $f(x)$ is then approximated as the area under the two parabolas shown in the figure. Again, using calculus, it can be shown that the area under the two parabolas is

```
S₂ = ¹/₃Δx₂{[f(a)+ 4f(x₁) + f(x₂)] + [f(x₂) + 4f(x₃) + f(b)]}
   = ¹/₃Δx₂{f(a)+ 4[f(x₁) + f(x₃)] + 2f(x₂) + f(b)}          (Eq. 15.12)
```

where

$$\Delta x_2 = \frac{b - a}{2^2}$$

and

$$f_i = f(x = a + i\,\Delta x_2)$$

FIGURE 15.12 Second-order Simpson's Rule Approximation
Is the Area Under Two Parabolas

This procedure can be extended to 8, 16, 32, and so on panels. The result is a rather simple generalization of Equation 15.12 and for $n = 2^k$ panels is:

$$S_k = \frac{1}{3}\Delta x_k [f(a) + 4 \sum_{\substack{i=1 \\ \text{odd only}}}^{n-1} f(a + i\Delta x_k) + 2 \sum_{\substack{i=2 \\ \text{even only}}}^{n-2} f(a + i\Delta x_k) + f(b)] \qquad \text{(Eq. 15.13)}$$

where

$$\Delta x_k = \frac{b - a}{2^k}$$

Equation 15.13, which is known as Simpson's rule, is an extremely popular method of evaluating integrals of functions that are smooth, and rightly so. As you will see later in the chapter, Simpson's rule converges nicely in most instances and is relatively easy to use. Also, Equation 15.13 can easily be adapted to handle an odd number of unevenly spaced points and is the most common method for estimating the integral of experimentally obtained data.

Example of Simpson's Rule as an Approximation to an Integral

Again consider the integral

$$I = \int_1^2 (1/x)\,dx$$

Using Equation 15.13, first for $k = 1$ yields

$$k = 1 \qquad n = 2^1 = 2 \qquad \Delta x_1 = \frac{b - a}{2^2} = \frac{1}{2}$$

```
S₁ = ¹/₃ (¹/₂)[1 + 4(1/1.5) + ¹/₂]
   = 0.6944444
```

Repeating for $k = 2$

$$k = 2 \qquad n = 2^2 = 4 \qquad \Delta x_2 = \frac{1}{4}$$

```
S₂ = ¹/₃ (¹/₄) [1 + 4(1/1.25 + 1/1.75) + 2(1/1.5) + ¹/₂]
   = 0.69325397
```

Continuing the calculation, we obtain the values listed in Table 15.2. For comparison, results are also included for the same integral obtained in the previous section using the trapezoidal rule. Clearly, Simpson's rule converges much faster than the trapezoidal rule, at least for this example.

TABLE 15.2 Trapezoidal and Simpson's Rule Results for the Integral $\int_1^2 (1/x)\,dx$

Order k	Number of Panels n	T_k	S_k
0	1	0.75	—
1	2	0.7083	0.6944
2	4	0.69702	0.69325
3	8	0.69412	0.69315
4	16	0.69339	0.6931466
5	32	0.693208	0.6931473
6	64	0.693162	0.6931472

EXERCISES 15.7

1. Using Equation 15.13, calculate the two-panel and the four-panel Simpson's rule results, S_1 and S_2, for the following integrals.

		Exact Result
a.	$\int_0^8 x^2\,dx$	170.667
b.	$\int_0^8 x^4\,dx$	6553.6
c.	$\int_0^1 xe^{-x}\,dx$	$1 - 2/e = 0.2642411175\ldots$
d.	$\int_0^{\pi/2} x \sin(x)\,dx$	1.0
e.	$\int_0^1 (1 + x^2)^{3/2}\,dx$	$1.567951962\ldots$
f.	$\int_0^1 e^{-x^2}\,dx$	$0.74682404\ldots$

2. Using Equation 15.13, calculate S_1 through S_4 for the integrals listed in Exercise 1.

15.8 COMMON PROGRAMMING ERRORS

In using the modified bisection root-finding method, two problems can occur:

1. Round-off error, which can occur whenever the values of $f(x_1)$ and $f(x_3)$ used in the computation are very nearly equal.
2. A prediction of the exact number of iterations required to achieve a desired accuracy is not available. To successfully counter these two problems, the code in these two methods must detect their occurrence to prevent excessive and possibly infinite iterations.

With respect to numerical integration,

3. Excessive computation times can also be a problem. This typically occurs whenever the number of iterations exceeds 50. Frequently, it is possible to significantly reduce run time by carefully inspecting each program loop to ensure that only those

calculations that must be iteritively computed are included within the loop and moving all other calculations to be computed either before or after the loop is completed.

15.9 CHAPTER SUMMARY

1. All of the root-solving methods described in this chapter are of an iterative nature and can be categorized within two classes of root-finding algorithms depending on whether you are starting with an interval containing a root or with an initial estimate of the root. The bisection-based procedures begin with an interval that is known to contain a root and are guaranteed to converge to within a prescribed tolerance bracketing of the root. Of the bisection methods, the modified regula falsi is the fastest converging and is recommended.

2. In algorithms based on the bisection method, the initial interval is refined by repeatedly evaluating the function at points within the interval and then, by monitoring the sign of the function, determining in which subinterval the root lies. If the left and right ends of the current interval are x_1 and x_3, respectively, the standard bisection method uses the function evaluated at the midpoint, $x_2 = \frac{1}{2}(x_1 + x_3)$. The sign of the function at x_2 is compared with that at either end of the interval to determine which half of the interval contains the root. The full interval is then replaced by this half and the process repeated. After n iterations, the root will be contained in an interval of size $(x_3 - x_1)/2^n$.

3. In the regula falsi method, the conditions are the same as for the bisection method. But instead of using the midpoint of the interval, a straight line connecting the points at the ends of the interval is used to interpolate the position of the root. The intersection of this line with the x axis determines the value of x_2 to be used in the next step. This value of x_2 is given by the equation

```
             f(x₁)
x2 = x1 - (x3 - x1) ------------
             f(x₃) - f(x₁)
```

in place of the equation for the midpoint. Convergence is faster than with the bisection method. However, it is likely that the interval will collapse down to the root from one side only.

4. The modified regula falsi method is the same as the regula falsi method except for the following change: In each iteration, when the full interval is replaced by the subinterval containing the root, a relaxation factor is used to first modify the value of the function at the fixed end of the subinterval. A relaxation factor of approximately 0.9 is suggested. This additional feature will cause the interval to collapse from both ends, and convergence is then based on interval size. This method is the preferred procedure for finding a root of a function that is not too expensive to evaluate and that is known to have a root in a specified interval.

5. The secant method replaces the function by a secant line through two points and then finds the point of intersection of the line with the x axis. The algorithm requires two input numbers, x_0 and Δx_0, corresponding to initial guesses for the root and for an interval containing the root. This pair of values is then replaced by the pair $(x_1, \Delta x_1)$, where

$$x_1 = x_0 + \Delta x_0$$

and

$$\Delta x_1 = \frac{f(x_1)}{f(x_0) - f(x_1)} \; \Delta x_0$$

and the process is continued until the new interval Δx is sufficiently small.

6. Root-solving methods are amenable to Java coding. However, the success of a program to find the root of a function usually depends on the quality of the information supplied by the user—that is, how accurate the initial guess or search interval is and how well the method chosen matches the circumstances of the problem. Execution-time problems are most frequently traceable to errors in coding the function or to inadequate user-supplied diagnostics for potential problems.

7. The integral of $f(x)$ from $x = a$ to $x = b$, written as

$$I = \int_a^b f(x)\,dx$$

is evaluated numerically by computing the area under the curve $f(x)$ over the specified range of x. The procedures for estimating this area consist of partitioning the interval $a \le x \le b$ into n panels of width $\Delta x_i (i = 1, n)$ and approximating the function $f(x)$ over each panel by a simpler function.

8. The trapezoidal rule results from replacing the function $f(x)$ by straight-line segments over the panels Δx_i. The approximate value for the integral is then given by the following formula, which is known as the trapezoidal rule:

$$\int_a^b f(x)\,dx \approx \tfrac{1}{2}\,\Delta x_n \left(f(a) + 2\sum_{i=1}^{n-1} f_i + f(b) \right)$$

If the panels are of equal size *and* the number of panels is $n = 2^k$, where k is a positive integer, the trapezoidal rule approximation is then labeled as T_k and satisfies the equation

$$T_k = \tfrac{1}{2} T_{k-1} + \Delta x_k \sum_{\substack{i=1 \\ \text{odd only}}}^{n-1} f(a + i\,\Delta x_k)$$

where

$$\Delta x_k = \frac{b - a}{2^k}$$

In the next level of approximation, the function $f(x)$ is replace by $n/2$ parabolic segments over pairs of equally sized panels, $\Delta x = (b - a)/n$ and results in the formula for the area known as Simpson's rule:

$$\int_a^b f(x)\,dx \approx \tfrac{1}{3}\Delta x_k [f(a) + 4 \sum_{\substack{i=1 \\ \text{odd only}}}^{n-1} f(a + i\Delta x_k) + 2 \sum_{\substack{i=2 \\ \text{even only}}}^{n-2} f(a + i\Delta x_k) + f(b)]$$

CHAPTER 16

Additional

Capabilities

Previous chapters have presented Java's basic structure, statements, and capabilities. This chapter presents additional capabilities that you may require or find useful as you progress in your understanding and use of Java. None of these are advanced features, but their usage is typically rather restricted. The features described in Sections 16.1 and 16.2 are almost never used to the extent of the topics presented in the prior chapters. Unlike the other topics, command-line arguments, the topic of Section 16.3, are used extensively by some programmers. The topic is included in this chapter because it can be introduced almost at any point within your study of Java.

16.1 ADDITIONAL FEATURES

This section presents a number of additional Java features and statements.

Other Number Bases

In addition to explicitly specifying integer literals as decimal numbers, such values can also be specified as either octal or hexadecimal numbers. Any integer having a leading 0 is taken to be an octal value, while any integer beginning with a leading 0x or 0X is considered a hexadecimal number. Thus, for example, the value 0347 is considered an octal integer number in Java, whereas the number 0x467adf is considered a hexadecimal value. Appending the letter L to either of these two values would make them `long` integer literals.

The `flush()` Statement

Whenever you have used a `print()` or `println()` method, what actually happens is that the arguments placed within the parentheses are sequentially put in a temporary holding area called a **buffer.** For example, if the statement `System.out.print("This");` is executed, the letters `T`, `h`, `i`, and `s` are placed in the buffer, as illustrated in Figure 16.1. This buffer is continually used until it is forced to send its contents to an output stream. This forced sending of the buffer's contents to an output stream is referred to as **flushing the buffer,** or **flushing** for short.

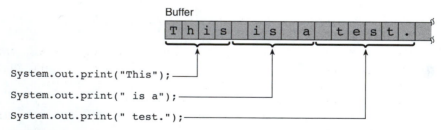

FIGURE 16.1 Displayed Characters Are First Stored in a Buffer

Flushing occurs whenever a line terminator character is encountered, the end of the program is reached, or an explicit `flush()` method is called.[1] For example, the following three statements cause the buffer to be filled with the characters `This is a test`.

---

[1]Flushing to `System.out` is automatic when a line terminator is encountered because this stream is, by default, an autoflush stream.

```
System.out.print("This");
System.out.print(" is a");
System.out.print(" test.");
```

The contents of the buffer will automatically be flushed and sent to the screen when the program containing these statements has completed executing. However, by using a `flush()` method, which has the syntax `System.out.flush();`, you can force the contents of the buffer to be immediately displayed and the buffer cleared. Adding the statement after the previous three `print()` statements will force an immediate display of the buffer's contents and clear the buffer.

The following section of code produces the same single-line message, `This is a test.`, as the previous lines of code:

```
System.out.print("This");
System.out.flush()
System.out.print(" is a");
System.out.flush()
System.out.print(" test.");
System.out.flush()
```

This last section of code forces each set of characters to be output immediately after they have been placed in the buffer. Notice that both sets of statements leave the cursor at the end of the displayed line because clearing the buffer does not cause a new line to be started. Only a newline character, \n, will force the display to start on a new line. The appending of a newline character to the data it placed in the buffer by the `println()` method both causes the buffer to be flushed and the cursor moved to the start of the next line as part of displaying the current buffer contents.

Conditional Expressions

A conditional expression uses the conditional operator, `?:`, and provides an alternative way of expressing a simple `if-else` statement. The syntax of a conditional expression is:

```
condition ? expression1 : expression2
```

If the value of the condition is true, *expression1* is evaluated; otherwise, *expression2* is evaluated. The value for the complete conditional expression is the value of either *expression1* or *expression2* depending on which expression was evaluated. As always, the value of the expression may be assigned to a variable.

Conditional expressions are most useful in replacing simple `if-else` statements. For example, the `if-else` statement

```
if (hours > 40)
  rate = .045;
else
  rate = .02;
```

can be replaced with the one-line statement

```
rate = (hours > 40) ? .045 : .02;
```

Here the complete conditional expression

```
(hours > 40) ? .045 : .02
```

is evaluated before any assignment is made to `rate` because the conditional operator, `?:`, has a higher precedence than the assignment operator. Within the conditional expression, the expression `hours > 40` is evaluated first. If this expression is true, the value of the complete conditional expression is set to .045; otherwise, the conditional expression has a value of .02. Finally, the value of the conditional expression, either .045 or .02, is assigned to the variable `rate`.

The conditional operator, `?:`, is unique in Java in that it is a ternary operator. This means that the operator connects three operands. The first operand is always a relational or logical expression that is evaluated first. The next two operands are other valid expressions of the same or compatible data types, which can be single constants, variables, or more general expressions. The complete conditional expression consists of all three operands connected by the conditional operator symbols, `?` and `:`.

In general, conditional expressions tend to be unclear and are best avoided. They are only useful in replacing `if-else` statements when the expressions in the equivalent `if-else` statement are not long or complicated. For example, the statement

```
maxValue = a > b ? a : b;
```

is a one-line statement that assigns the maximum value of the variables `a` and `b` to `maxValue`. A longer, equivalent form of this statement is:

```
if (a > b)
  maxValue = a;
else
  maxValue = b;
```

Because of the length of the expressions involved, a conditional expression *would not* be useful in replacing the following `if-else` statement:

```
if (amount > 20000)
  taxes = .025(amount - 20000) + 400;
else
  taxes = .02 * amount;
```

16.2 BIT OPERATORS

Java operates with data entities that are stored as one or more bytes, such as character, integer, and double-precision constants and variables. In addition, Java provides for the manipulation of individual bits of character and integer constants and variables. The operators that perform bit manipulations are called bit operators. The bit operators presented in this section are listed in Table 16.1.

TABLE 16.1   Bit Operators

Operator	Description
&	Bitwise AND
|	Bitwise inclusive OR
^	Bitwise exclusive OR
~	Bitwise NOT
<<	Bitwise left shift with zero fill
>>	Bitwise right shift with sign fill
>>>	Bitwise right shift with zero fill

All of the operators in Table 16.1, except ~, are binary operators, which means they require two operands. For these bit operators, each operand is considered as a binary number consisting of a series of individual 1s and 0s. The respective bits in each operand are then compared on a bit-by-bit basis, and the result is determined based on the selected operation.

The bit operations listed in Table 16.1 can also be used on boolean data. When operating on boolean values, the & and | operators perform the same function as the && and || operators but always evaluate both operands. That is, they do not use the short-circuited evaluation performed by the boolean operators && and || (see Section 4.1). Because this is generally not desirable, you should use the short-circuit && and || operators for boolean operations unless a specific result is required, or you must logically compare two integer operands.

The AND Operator

The bitwise AND operator causes a bit-by-bit AND comparison between its two operands. The result of each bit-by-bit comparison is 1 only when both bits being compared are 1s; otherwise, the result of the AND operation is 0. For example, assume that the following two 8-bit numbers are to be ANDed:

```
1 0 1 1 0 0 1 1
1 1 0 1 0 1 0 1
---------------
```

To perform an AND operation, each bit in one operand is compared to the bit occupying the same position in the other operand. Figure 16.2 illustrates the correspondence between bits for these two operands. Bitwise AND comparisons are determined by the following rule: *The result of an AND comparison is 1 when both bits being compared are 1s; otherwise, the result is 0.* The result of each comparison is, of course, independent of any other bit comparison.

```
  1 0 1 1 0 0 1 1
& 1 1 0 1 0 1 0 1
-------------------
  1 0 0 1 0 0 0 1
```

FIGURE 16.2   A Sample AND Operation

AND operations are extremely useful in masking, or eliminating, selected bits from an operand. This is a direct result of the fact that ANDing any bit (1 or 0) with a 0 forces the resulting bit to be 0, whereas ANDing any bit (1 or 0) with a 1 leaves the original bit unchanged. For example, assume that the variable op1 has the arbitrary bit pattern x x x x x x x x, where each x can be either 1 or 0, independent of any other x in the number. The result of ANDing this binary number with the binary number 0 0 0 0 1 1 1 1 is:

```
   op1 =    x x x x x x x x
   op2 =    0 0 0 0 1 1 1 1
           ----------------
Result =    0 0 0 0 x x x x
```

As can be seen from this example, the 0s in op2 effectively mask, or eliminate, the respective bits in op1, and the 1s in op2 filter, or pass, the respective bits in op1 through with no change in their values. In this example, the variable op2 is called a `mask`. By choosing the mask appropriately, any individual bit in an operand can be selected, or filtered, out of an operand for inspection. For example, ANDing the variable op1 with the mask 0 0 0 0 0 1 0 0 forces all the bits of the result to be 0, except for the third bit. The third bit of the result will be a copy of the third bit of op1. Thus, if the result of the AND is 0, the third bit of op1 must have been 0, and if the result of the AND is a nonzero number, the third bit must have been 1.

The Inclusive OR Operator

The inclusive bitwise OR operator, |, performs a bit-by-bit comparison of its two operands in a similar fashion to the bit-by-bit AND. The result of the bitwise OR comparison, however, is determined by the following rule: *The result of the comparison is 1 if either bit being compared is 1; otherwise, the result is 0.*

Figure 16.3 illustrates an OR operation. As shown in the figure, when either of the two bits being compared is 1, the result is 1; otherwise, the result is 0. As with all bit operations, the result of each comparison is independent of any other comparison.

```
     1 0 1 1 0 0 1 1
   | 1 1 0 1 0 1 0 1
   ---------------------
     1 1 1 1 0 1 1 1
```

FIGURE 16.3   A Sample OR Operation

Inclusive OR operations are extremely useful in forcing selected bits to take on a 1 value or for passing through other bit values unchanged. This is a direct result of the fact that ORing any bit (1 or 0) with a 1 forces the resulting bit to be 1, and ORing any bit (1 or 0) with a 0 leaves the original bit unchanged. For example, assume that the variable op1 has the arbitrary bit pattern x x x x x x x x, where each x can be either 1 or 0, independent of any other x in the number. The result of ORing this binary number with the binary number 1 1 1 1 0 0 0 0 is:

```
op1 =    x x x x x x x x
op2 =    1 1 1 1 0 0 0 0
         ----------------
Result = 1 1 1 1 x x x x
```

As can be seen from this example, the 1s in op2 force the resulting bits to 1, and the 0s in op2 filter, or pass, the respective bits in op1 through with no change in their values. Thus, using an OR operation, a similar masking operation can be produced as with an AND operation, except the masked bits are set to 1s rather than cleared to 0s. Another way of looking at this is to say that ORing with a 0 has the same effect as ANDing with a 1.

The Exclusive OR Operator

The exclusive OR operator, ^, performs a bit-by-bit comparison of its two operands. The result of the comparison is determined by the following rule: *The result of the comparison is 1 if one and only one of the bits being compared is 1; otherwise, the result is 0.*

Figure 16.4 illustrates an exclusive OR operation. As shown in the figure, when both bits being compared are the same value (both 1 or both 0), the result is 0. Only when both bits have different values (one bit 1 and the other 0) the result is 1. Again, each pair or bit comparison is independent of any other bit comparison.

```
  1 0 1 1 0 0 1 1
^ 1 1 0 1 0 1 0 1
---------------------
  0 1 1 0 0 1 1 0
```

FIGURE 16.4 A Sample Exclusive OR Operation

An exclusive OR operation can create the opposite value, or complement, of any individual bit in a variable. This is a direct result of the fact that exclusive ORing any bit (1 or 0) with a 1 forces the resulting bit to be of the opposite value of its original state, while exclusive ORing any bit (1 or 0) with a 0 leaves the original bit unchanged. For example, assume that the variable op1 has the arbitrary bit pattern x x x x x x x x, where each x can be either 1 or 0, independent of any other x in the number. Using the notation that x̄ is the complement (opposite) value of x, the result of exclusive ORing this binary number with the binary number 0 1 0 1 0 1 0 1 is:

```
op1 =    x x x x x x x x
op2 =    0 1 0 1 0 1 0 1
         ----------------
              _   _   _   _
Result = x x x x x x x x
```

As can be seen from this example, the 1s in op2 force the resulting bits to be the complement of their original bit values, and the 0s in op2 filter, or pass, the respective bits in op1 through with no change in their values.

The COMPLEMENT Operator

The bitwise COMPLEMENT operator, ~, is a unary operator that changes each 1 bit in its operand to 0 and each 0 bit to 1. For example, if the variable op1 contains the binary number 11001010, ~op1 replaces this binary number with the number 00110101. The complement operator can force any bit in an operand to 0, independent of the actual number of bits used to store the number. For example, the statement

```
op1 = op1 & ~07;    // 07 is an octal number
```

or its shorter form,

```
op1 &= ~07;     // 07 is an octal number
```

both set the last three bits of op1 to 0. Either of these two statements can, of course, be replaced by ANDing the last three bits of op1 with 0s if the number of bits used to store op1 is known. If op1 is a 16-bit short integer, the appropriate AND operation is

```
op1 = op1 & 0177770;     // in octal
```

or

```
op1 = op1 & 0xFFF8;     // in hexadecimal
```

For a 32-bit integer value, the foregoing AND sets the leftmost or higher order 16 bits to 0 also, which is an unintended result. The correct statement for a 32-bit integer is:

```
op1 = op1 & 027777777770;     // in octal
```

or

```
op1 = op1 & 0xFFFFFFF8;      // in hexadecimal
```

Using the bitwise NOT operator in this situation frees the programmer from having to consider the storage size of the operand.

The Shift Operators

The left shift operator, <<, causes the bits in an operand to be shifted to the left by a given amount. For example, the statement

```
op1 = op1 << 4;
```

causes the bits in op1 to be shifted 4 bits to the left, filling any vacated bits with a 0. Figure 16.5 illustrates the effect of shifting the binary number 1111100010101011 to the left by 4 bit positions.

For unsigned integers, each left shift corresponds to multiplication by 2. This is also true for signed numbers using two's complement representation as long as the leftmost bit does not switch values. Since a change in the leftmost bit of a two's complement num-

FIGURE 16.5   An Example of a Left Shift

ber represents a change in both the sign and magnitude represented by the bit, such a shift does not represent a simple multiplication by 2.

The right shift operator, >>, causes the bits in an operand to be shifted to the right by a given amount. For example, the statement

```
op2 = op1 >> 3;
```

causes the bits in op1 to be shifted to the right by 3 bit positions. Figure 16.6a illustrates the right shift of the unsigned binary number 1111100010101011 by 3 bit positions. As illustrated, the three rightmost bits are shifted "off the end" and are lost, and the sign bit is reproduced in the vacated bits. Figure 16.6b illustrates the right shift of a negative

FIGURE 16.6a   An Unsigned Arithmetic Right Shift

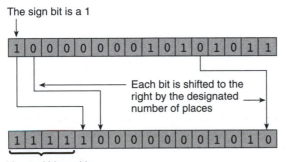

FIGURE 16.6b   The Right Shift of a Negative Binary Number

The sign bit is a 0

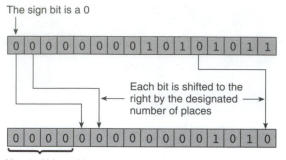

Each bit is shifted to the right by the designated number of places

Vacated bit positions are filled with 0s

FIGURE 16.6c   The Right Shift of a Positive Binary Number

binary number by 4 bit positions, where the sign bit is reproduced in the vacated bits. Figure 16.6c illustrates the equivalent right shift of a positive signed binary number.

The type of fill illustrated in Figures 16.6b and 16.6c, where the sign bit is reproduced in vacated bit positions, is called an arithmetic right shift. In an arithmetic right shift, each single shift to the right corresponds to a division by 2.

Instead of reproducing the sign bit in right-shifted signed numbers, the right shift operator, >>>, automatically fills the vacated bits with 0s. This type of shift is called a logical shift. For positive signed numbers, where the leftmost bit is 0, both arithmetic and logical right shifts produce the same result. The results of these two shifts are only different when negative numbers are involved.

16.3 COMMAND-LINE ARGUMENTS

Arguments can be passed to any method in a program, including the main() method. In this section, we describe the procedures for passing arguments to main() when a program is initially invoked and having main() correctly receive and store the arguments passed to it. Both the sending and receiving sides of the transaction must be considered. Fortunately, the interface for transmitting arguments to a main() method has been standardized in Java, so both sending and receiving arguments can be done almost mechanically.

All the programs that have been run so far have been invoked by typing the words Java and a class name, which is the same as the class that contains the main() method to be executed. The line on which these two items are typed is formally referred to as the **command line.** This line always starts with the operating system prompt, which for the UNIX operating system is usually the $ symbol and for a DOS window is typically a C>.

Assuming that you are using a DOS window that uses a C> prompt, the complete command line for executing a main() method within a class named CommandLineArgs is

```
C> java CommandLineArgs
```

As illustrated in Figure 16.7, this command line causes the CommandLineArgs bytecode program to begin execution with its main() method, but no arguments are passed to main().

Now assume that we want to pass the five separate string arguments three blind mice showed up directly into CommandLineArgs's main() function. Sending arguments into a

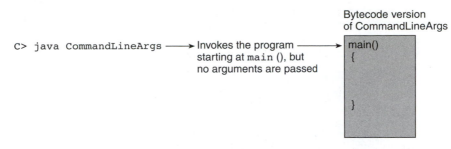

FIGURE 16.7   Invoking the `CommandLineArgs` Bytecode Program

`main()` method is extremely easy. It is accomplished by including the arguments on the command line used to begin program execution. Because the arguments are typed on the command line, they are, naturally, called **command-line arguments.** To pass the arguments `three blind mice showed` up directly into the `main()`method of the `CommandLineArgs` program, we only need to add the desired words after the program name on the command line:

`C> java CommandLineArgs three blind mice showed up`

Upon encountering the command line `CommandLineArgs three blind mice showed` up, the operating system automatically passes the sequence of five strings after the program's name into `main()`.

Sending command-line arguments to `main()` is always this simple. The arguments are typed on the command line, and the operating system passes them into `main()` as a sequence of separate strings. Now let's see how `main()` stores and accesses these arguments.

Arguments passed to `main()`, like all method arguments, must be declared as part of the method's definition. To standardize argument passing to a `main()` function, only one type of argument is allowed, which is an array of strings. This array is named `args` and is declared as `String[] args`. Notice that this declaration has been included in the header line that we have been using throughout this text for `main()`, which is

`public static void main(String[] args)`

Thus, all of the programs in this text have been constructed to receive command-line arguments. The `args` array declared in the header line is actually an array of references, where each reference can be used to access one of the string arguments passed to `main()`. Thus, if any arguments are passed to `main()`,`args[0]` refers to the first argument, `args[1]` to the second argument, and so on. Figure 16.8 illustrates how the arguments `three blind mice showed` up are stored and referenced using the `args` array. Notice that the number of command-line arguments is determined using the expression `args.length`, which is the number of references stored in the `args` array. For the arrangement shown in Figure 16.7, `args.length` is five.

Once command-line arguments are passed to a Java program, they can be used like any other Java strings. Program 16.1 causes its command-line arguments to be displayed from within `main()`. The output of this program for the command line

`C> Java CommandLineArgs three blind mice showed up`

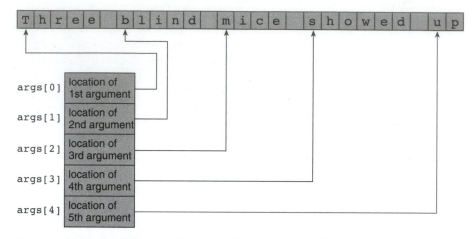

FIGURE 16.8   Accessing Command-Line Arguments Using the `args` Array

is:

```
The number of command line arguments is 5
These are the arguments that were passed to main():
three
blind
mice
showed
up
```

PROGRAM 16.1

```java
// A program that displays command line arguments
public class CommandLineArgs
{
  public static void main(String[] args)
  {
    int i, numOfArgs;

    numOfArgs = args.length;
    System.out.println("The number of command line arguments is " + numOfArgs);
    System.out.println("These are the arguments that were passed to main():");
    for (i = 0; i < numOfArgs; i++)
      System.out.println(args[i]);
    System.out.println();
  }
}
```

As illustrated by this output, the term `args.length` correctly determines that the number of command-line arguments is five. Also notice that each command-line argument is referenced using an `args` array element.

Two final comments about command-line arguments are in order. Any argument typed on a command-line is considered a string. If you want numerical data passed to main(), it is up to you to convert the passed string into its numerical counterpart. This is seldom an issue because most command-line arguments are used as string flags to pass appropriate processing control signals to an invoked program. Second, it is interesting to note that there is nothing inherently special about the parameter name args. By convention, however, it is the name that is used and understood by Java programmers to refer to command-line arguments passed to main().

EXERCISES FOR CHAPTER 16

1. Rewrite each of the following if-else statements using a conditional expression:

   a. ```
   if (a < b);
       minimumValue = a;
   else
       minimumValue = b;
   ```

   b. ```
   if (num < 0)
       sign = -1;
   else
       sign = 1;
   ```

   c. ```
   if (flag == 1)
       value = num;
   else
       value = num * num;
   ```

   d. ```
   if (credit == plus)
       rate = prime;
   else
       rate = prime + delta;
   ```

   e. ```
   if (!bond)
       coupon = .075;
   else
       coupon = 1.1;
   ```

2. Determine the results of the following operations:

   | a. | | b. | | c. | |
   |---|---|---|---|---|---|
   | | 11001010 | | 11001010 | | 11001010 |
   | & | 10100101 | \| | 10100101 | ^ | 10100101 |
   | | ---------- | | ---------- | | ---------- |

3. Write the octal representations of the binary numbers given in Exercise 2.

4. a. Assume that the arbitrary bit pattern xxxxxxxx, where each x can represent either 1 or 0, is stored in the integer variable flag. Determine the octal value of a mask that can be ANDed with the bit pattern to reproduce the third and fourth bits of flag and set all other bits to 0. The rightmost bit in flag is considered bit 0.

   b. Determine the octal value of a mask that can be inclusively ORed with the bit pattern in flag to reproduce the third and fourth bits of flag and set all other bits to 1. Again, consider the rightmost bit in flag to be bit 0.

   c. Determine the octal value of a mask that can be used to complement the values of the third and fourth bits of flag and leave all other bits unchanged.
   ```

Determine the bit operation that should be used with the mask value to produce the desired result.

5. Enter and execute Program 16.1 on your computer.

6. Write a program that accepts two integer values as command-line arguments. The program should multiply the two values entered and display the result. (*Tip:* The command line must be accepted as string data and converted to numerical values before multiplication.)

7. **a.** Write a program that accepts the name of a data file as a command-line argument. Have your program open the data file and display its contents, line by line, on the screen.

   b. Would the program written for Exercise 7a work correctly for a program file?

8. Modify the program written for Exercise 15a so that each line displayed is preceded by a line number.

16.4 CHAPTER SUMMARY

1. The `print()` method simply places its text input into a buffer, and the buffer's contents are then displayed either when the program is finished executing or a `flush()` method is invoked. The input to a `println()` method is automatically flushed from the buffer, with a terminating newline escape sequence added, as part of the `println()` method call.

2. A conditional expression provides an alternative way of expressing a simple `if-else` statement. The general form of a conditional expression is:

```
condition ? expression1 : expression2
```

The equivalent `if-else` statement for this is:

```
if (condition)
   expression1;
else
   expression2;
```

3. Individual bits of character and integer variables and constants can be manipulated using Java's bit operators. These are the AND, inclusive OR, exclusive OR, NOT, and shift operators.

4. The AND and inclusive OR operators are useful in creating masks. These masks can be used to pass or eliminate individual bits from the selected operand. The exclusive OR operator is useful in complementing an operand's bits.

5. The NOT operator changes each 1 bit in its operand to 0 and each 0 bit to 1.

6. The shift operators permit all of the bits in an operand to be shifted left or right by a specified amount. Left shifts fill vacated bit positions with 0s, whereas the fill character for right shift can be specified as filling the vacated bit positions with 0s by replication of the sign bit.

7. Arguments passed to `main()` are termed command-line arguments. Java provides a standard argument-passing procedure in which `main()` can accept any number of arguments passed to it. Each argument passed to `main()` is considered a string and is stored using an array of references named `args`. The total number of arguments on the command line can be determined as `args.length`.

APPENDIX A

Operator

Precedence

Table

Table A.1 presents the symbols, precedence, descriptions, and associativity of Java's operators. Operators toward the top of the table have a higher precedence than those toward the bottom. Operators within each section have the same precedence and associativity.

TABLE A.1 Summary of Java Operators

Operator	Description	Associativity
( )	Function call	Left to right
[ ]	Array element	
.	Member reference	
++	Postfix increment	Left to right
--	Postfix decrement	
++	Prefix increment	Right to left
--	Prefix decrement	
-	Unary minus	
!	Logical negation	
~	One's complement	
new	Object instantiation	
(type)	Type conversion (cast)	Right to left
*	Multiplication	Left to right
/	Division	
%	Remainder (modulus)	
+	Addition	Left to right
+	String concatenation	
-	Subtraction	
<<	Left shift	Left to right
>>	Right shift with sign	
>>>	Right shift with zero fill	
<	Less than	Left to right
<=	Less than or equal to	
>	Greater than	
>=	Greater than or equal to	
==	Equal to	Left to right
!=	Not equal to	
&	Bitwise AND	Left to right
^	Bitwise exclusive OR	Left to right
|	Bitwise inclusive OR	Left to right
&&	Logical AND	Left to right
||	Logical OR	Left to right
?:	Conditional expression	Right to left
=	Assignment	Right to left
+= -= *=	Assignment	
/= %=	Assignment	
<<= >>= >>>=	Assignment	
&= ^= |=	Assignment	

APPENDIX B

Unicode

Character Set

Unicode provides 65,536 different codes, with each code using 2 bytes (16 bits). The following are the first 256 characters in the Unicode character set. The first 128 of these characters are the same as the ASCII character set, except that ASCII characters are stored using 8 bits and thus do not store the leading 8 bits of zeros in the corresponding Unicode character. Characters having decimal values of 0 through 31, except for codes 13 and 27, are referred to as control characters because they are created by pressing the Control key and a letter key at the same time.

Key(s)	Dec	Hex	Key	Dec	Hex	Key	Dec	Hex	Key	Dec	Hex
Ctrl 1	0	0000	Space	32	0020	@	64	0040	`	96	0060
Ctrl A	1	0001	!	33	0021	A	65	0041	a	97	0061
Ctrl B	2	0002	"	34	0022	B	66	0042	b	98	0062
Ctrl C	3	0003	#	35	0023	C	67	0043	c	99	0063
Ctrl D	4	0004	$	36	0024	D	68	0044	d	100	0064
Ctrl E	5	0005	%	37	0025	E	69	0045	e	101	0065
Ctrl F	6	0006	&	38	0026	F	70	0046	f	102	0066
Ctrl G	7	0007	'	39	0027	G	71	0047	g	103	0067
Ctrl H	8	0008	(	40	0028	H	72	0048	h	104	0068
Ctrl I	9	0009	)	41	0029	I	73	0049	i	105	0069
Ctrl J	10	000A	*	42	002A	J	74	004A	j	106	006A
Ctrl K	11	000B	+	43	002B	K	75	004B	k	107	006B
Ctrl L	12	000C	,	44	002C	L	76	004C	l	108	006C
Ctrl M	13	000D	-	45	002D	M	77	004D	m	109	006D
Ctrl N	14	000E	.	46	002E	N	78	004E	n	110	006E
Ctrl O	15	000F	/	47	002F	O	79	004F	o	111	006F
Ctrl P	16	0010	0	48	0030	P	80	0050	p	112	0070
Ctrl Q	17	0011	1	49	0031	Q	81	0051	q	113	0071
Ctrl R	18	0012	2	50	0032	R	82	0052	r	114	0072
Ctrl S	19	0013	3	51	0033	S	83	0053	s	115	0073
Ctrl T	20	0014	4	52	0034	T	84	0054	t	116	0074
Ctrl U	21	0015	5	53	0035	U	85	0055	u	117	0075
Ctrl V	22	0016	6	54	0036	V	86	0056	v	118	0076
Ctrl W	23	0017	7	55	0037	W	87	0057	w	119	0077
Ctrl X	24	0018	8	56	0038	X	88	0058	x	120	0078
Ctrl·Y	25	0019	9	57	0039	Y	89	0059	y	121	0079
Ctrl Z	26	001A	:	58	003A	Z	90	005A	z	122	007A
Esc	27	001B	;	59	003B	[	91	005B	{	123	007B
Ctrl <	28	001C	<	60	003C	\	92	005C	|	124	007C
Ctrl /	29	001D	=	61	003D	]	93	005D	}	125	007D
Ctrl =	30	001E	>	62	003E	^	94	005E	~	126	007E
Ctrl -	31	001F	?	63	003F	_	95	005F	del	127	007F

Key	Dec	Hex	Key	Dec	Hex	Key	Dec	Hex	Key	Dec	Hex
**	128	0080	(space)	160	0100	À	192	0120	à	224	0140
**	129	0081	¡	161	0101	Á	193	0121	á	225	0141
**	130	0082	¢	162	0102	Â	194	0122	â	226	0142
**	131	0083	£	163	0103	Ã	195	0123	ã	227	0143
**	132	0084	¤	164	0104	Ä	196	0124	ä	228	0144
**	133	0085	¥	165	0105	Å	197	0125	å	229	0145
**	134	0086	¦	166	0106	Æ	198	0126	æ	230	0146
**	135	0087	§	167	0107	Ç	199	0127	ç	231	0147
**	136	0088	¨	168	0108	È	200	0128	è	232	0148
**	137	0089	©	169	0109	É	201	0129	é	233	0149
**	138	008A	ª	170	010A	Ê	202	012A	ê	234	014A
**	139	008B	«	171	010B	Ë	203	012B	ë	235	014B
**	140	008C	¬	172	010C	Ì	204	012C	ì	236	014C
**	141	008D	-	173	010D	Í	205	012D	í	237	014D
**	142	008E	®	174	010E	Î	206	012E	î	238	014E
**	143	008F	¯	175	010F	Ï	207	012F	ï	239	014F
**	144	0090	°	176	0110	Ð	208	0130	∂	240	0150
**	145	0091	±	177	0111	Ñ	209	0131	ñ	241	0151
**	146	0092	²	178	0112	Ò	210	0132	ò	242	0152
**	147	0093	³	179	0113	Ó	211	0133	ó	243	0153
**	148	0094	´	180	0114	Ô	212	0134	ô	244	0154
**	149	0095	µ	181	0115	Õ	213	0135	õ	245	0155
**	150	0096	¶	182	0116	Ö	214	0136	ö	246	0156
**	151	0097	·	183	0117	×	215	0137	÷	247	0157
**	152	0098	¸	184	0118	Ø	216	0138	ø	248	0158
**	153	0099	¹	185	0119	Ù	217	0139	ù	249	0159
**	154	009A	º	186	011A	Ú	218	013A	ú	250	015A
**	155	009B	»	187	011B	Û	219	013B	û	251	015B
**	156	009C	¼	188	011C	Ü	220	013C	ü	252	015C
**	157	009D	½	189	011D	Ý	221	013D	ý	253	015D
**	158	009E	¾	190	011E	Þ	222	013E	þ	254	015E
**	159	009F	¿	191	011F	ß	223	013F	ÿ	255	015F

**These characters have no Unicode-specified meaning.

APPENDIX C

Compiling and

Executing a

Java Program

Using a Sun-based compiler, the simplest syntax of the command to compile a program stored as *name*.java, where *name* is the name of a specific program and .java is the required extension that the program was saved with, is:

```
javac name.java
```

The line on which this command is typed is formally referred to as the **command line.** This line always starts with the operating system prompt, which for computers that use the UNIX operating system is usually the $ symbol and for Windows-based systems is typically c>.

Assuming that you have a Windows-based computer that uses a C> prompt, this command would appear as

```
C> javac name.java
```

As a specific example of this format, the command line

```
C> javac DisplayHelloWorld.java
```

will compile the program named DisplayHelloWorld.java. The output of the compilation, assuming it was successful, is automatically named and saved in the file named DisplayHelloWorld.class. It should be noted that the javac compiler is pronounced ja-vack and not ja-va-see.

In addition to performing a simple compilation, the javac compiler also provides for a number of useful output options, which appear in Table C.1. As shown in this table, the general syntax of the compilation command line is:

```
C> javac <options> <source files>
```

where c> is provided by the operating system, <options> means select any or none of options listed in Table C.1, and <source files> means a list of zero or more source files (supplying no source files brings up the information in Table C.1).

As a specific example of selecting a number of options, assume you want the compiler both to tell you how it is progressing and to provide debugging information as compilation is taking place for the program named DisplayHelloWorld.java. The following command accomplishes this.

```
javac -verbose -g DisplayHelloWorld.java
```

Here the -verbose option, which is formally referred to as a command-line argument, instructs the compiler to output messages indicating what the compiler is doing, and the -g option tells the compiler to generate debugging information for any compiler-detected error.

The output of a successful compilation is automatically saved with the same name as the source file, but with a .class extension instead of the .java extension. The compiled version of the source code with the .class extension is an encoded set of bytes that can only be run on a Java Virtual Machine. If this code contains a main() method, execution of the code can be initiated using the command line

```
C> java name
```

where name is the class name used to save the program initially. For example, if the program named DisplayHelloWorld.java has been successfully compiled to yield the DisplayHelloWorld.class, the command line

```
C> java DisplayHelloWorld
```

will initiate execution of the compiled program.

TABLE C.1 javac Compiler Options

Usage: `javac <options> <source files>`

where `<options>` includes:

`-g`	Generates all debugging information.
`-g:`	Generates no debugging information.
`-g:{lines, vars, source}`	Generates some debugging information.
`-O`	Optimizes: May hinder debugging or enlarge class files.
`-nowarn`	Generates no warnings.
`-verbose`	Outputs messages about what the compiler is doing.
`-deprecation`	Outputs source locations where deprecated APIs are being used.
`-classpath <path>`	Specifies where to find user class files.
`-sourcepath <path>`	Specifies where to find input source files.
`-bootclasspath <path>`	Overrides location of bootstrap class files.
`-extdirs <dirs>`	Overrides location of installed extensions.
`-d <directory>`	Specifies where to place generated class files.
`-encoding <encoding>`	Specifies character encoding used by source files.
`-target<release>`	Generates class files for a specific Virtual Machine version.

APPENDIX D

Obtaining

Locales

The locales available on your computer system can be obtained using the following program:

```java
import java.util.*;  // needed for Locale
import java.text.*;  // needed for NumberFormat
public class DisplayLocales
{
  public static void main(String[] args)
  {
    int i, number;

    Locale availableLocales[] = NumberFormat.getAvailableLocales();
    System.out.println("The available locales are:");
    number = availableLocales.length;

    for (i = 0; i < number; i++)
    System.out.println(availableLocales[i].getDisplayName());
  }
}
```

The following are the first 30 lines displayed when this program was run on the author's computer:

```
The available locales are:
English
English (United States)
Arabic
Arabic (United Arab Emirates)
Arabic (Bahrain)
Arabic (Algeria)
Arabic (Egypt)
Arabic (Iraq)
Arabic (Jordan)
Arabic (Kuwait)
Arabic (Lebanon)
Arabic (Libya)
Arabic (Morocco)
Arabic (Oman)
Arabic (Qatar)
Arabic (Saudi Arabia)
Arabic (Sudan)
Arabic (Syria)
Arabic (Tunisia)
Arabic (Yemen)
Byelorussian
Byelorussian (Belarus)
Bulgarian
Bulgarian (Bulgaria)
Catalan
Catalan (Spain)
Czech
Czech (Czech Republic)
Danish (Denmark)
```

APPENDIX E

Creating

Leading

Spaces

As described in Section 3.2, one potentially annoying problem associated with formatting integers using the `setMinimumIntegerDigits()` method is that leading unfilled digit positions are padded with zeros (as an example of this effect, review the output produced by Program 3.8). Following is a method named `addSpaces()` that can create leading blank spaces. This method requires the number of desired leading spaces, which is accepted as the parameter n, and returns a string consisting of exactly n spaces. It is to this string that the desired integer number must then be concatenated.

```
   // this method creates a string with n space characters
public static String addSpaces(int n)
{
   StringBuffer temp = new StringBuffer(n);
   int i;
     // modify temp to contain the desired number of spaces
   for(i = 0; i < n; i++)
   temp.append(' ');      // append a blank

   return temp.toString();    // convert to a string and return it
}
```

To use this method in practice, first determine the number of digits in the integer part of the number being output using the `String` class' `length()` method. This value is then subtracted from the desired display field width to determine the number of required leading spaces. It is this value that is passed as an argument into addSpaces(). After addSpaces() returns a string with the designated number of spaces, the number to be displayed is then appended to this blank string. This yields a final string with the desired number of leading spaces.

To see how this is realized, consider Program E.1, which displays the number 6 in a total field width of eight. Because the value being displayed consists of one digit, we will need to add seven leading spaces to this number before displaying it.

This leading space technique also works with floating-point and double-precision numbers, with one additional step. Because the leading number of blank spaces is determined by the number of digits in the integer part of a number, if a number with a fractional part is to be displayed, the integer portion of the number must first be extracted for correct computation of the needed spaces. In all cases, however, this technique will only align multiple rows of numbers correctly when a monospaced font, such as Courier, is used.

PROGRAM E.1

```
public class PadWithSpaces
{
  public static void main(String[] args)
  {
    final int WIDTH = 8;  // this sets the size of the output field
    int n, numlength;
    String outstr = "";
    int testNumber;

    testNumber = 6;  // this is the number we will output
    outstr += testNumber;  // convert to a string
    numlength = outstr.length();  // get the number of integer digits

    n = WIDTH - numlength;  // determine number of spaces needed
    outstr = addSpaces(n) + outstr;
    System.out.println(outstr);
  }

    // this method creates a string with n space characters
  public static String addSpaces(int n)
  {
    StringBuffer temp = new StringBuffer(n);
    int i;

    for(i = 0; i < n; i++)
    temp.append(' ');     // append a blank

    return temp.toString();
  }
}
```

Creating
and Using
Packages

A **package** consists of one or more individual class files that are stored in the same directory and have been assigned a package name. Using an appropriate `import` statement, this package name then provides a simple and convenient way of permitting access to all of the classes in the package to any Java program that might wish to use them.

As a specific example of a package, consider Figure F.1, which consists of two classes named `ClassOne` and `ClassTwo`. As required by Java, each of these classes has been stored in a separate file, with each file having the same name as its class followed by the `.java` extension. Thus, as shown in Figure F.1, the file containing `ClassOne` is stored as `ClassOne.java` and the file containing `ClassTwo` is stored as `ClassTwo.java`. To make each of these classes a member

file: `ClassOne.java`

```
package foobar.utilities;
public class ClassOne
{
        .
        .
        .
}
```

file: `ClassTwo.java`

```
package foobar.utilities;
public class ClassTwo
{
        .
        .
        .
}
```

These specify
the package

FIGURE F.1 Creating a Package Consisting of Two Class Files of the same package, which for illustration purposes we will name foobar.utilities, requires that the statement package foobar.utilities; be included as the first line in each file. Notice that this is the case for the two files shown in Figure F.1.

Once a package has been created, an import statement is used to make the classes in the file available to any Java program that needs access to one or more of the classes in the package. For example, if a Java program needed to access a class in the foobar.utilities package, the import statement

```
import foobar.utilities.*;
```

would make both classes in this package available for use by the new Java program. The new Java program need not be in the same directory as the package because the package name tells the compiler where to look for the classes. Thus, the name selected for a package is not arbitrary but must be a pathname containing the directory in which all of the classes in the package are stored. An additional option with the import statement is that it need not make all of the classes in a package available to a new Java program. For example, if only the ClassOne file is needed in the new Java program, the statement

```
import foobar.utilities.ClassOne;
```

can be used. Generally, however, since an import statement only notifies the compiler of the location of the files, the more general syntax import packageName.*; is used. The compiler ultimately will include only the classes in a package that it needs.

It should also be noted that a package name always separates directories using a period rather than either a backward, \, or a forward slash, /, used by the Windows and UNIX operating systems, respectively. Finally, because package names are generally relative and not full pathnames, the root directory of the full pathname must be set in the CLASSPATH variable of your operating system. For example, if the full pathname of the foobar.utilities directory is c:\java\programs\foobar\utilities, then the system CLASSPATH variable must be set using a statement similar to

```
CLASSPATH=c:\java\programs      <--- this is for a Windows-based system
CLASSPATH /usr/java/programs    <--- this is for a UNIX-based system
```

The setting of the CLASSPATH variable should only be done by someone familiar with setting system-dependent variables.[1]

Fully Qualified Names

Because an import statement provides the compiler with enough information to locate the desired class, this statement relieves the programmer of listing the complete path-

[1] In a Windows-based system, the CLASSPATH variable is typically set in the autoexec.bat file, while in a UNIX-based system, the variable is set in a shell file. If an existing path is already set, append the new setting to the existing one with a preceding semicolon. Additionally, either a SET or setenv keyword may be required with the CLASSPATH statement.

name of the desired file when a class is being accessed. However, an `import` statement is not strictly required. For example, if the `ClassOne` class shown in Figure F.1 contains a `public` method named `sample()`, this method can be accessed as `java.programs.foobar.utilites.sample()` without the program using it having an `import` statement for the package in which `sample()` is located. This is because the statement itself provides the compiler with complete location information for `sample()`. When the package name is included in this manner, the method name is referred to as **fully qualified.** With one exception, a fully qualified name is always required whenever an `import` statement *is not included* for the named package. The one exception is when the `java.lang` package is involved. Because this package of classes is used in almost every Java program, the compiler will automatically import this package with or without an explicit `import` statement for this package. This permits us to use a statement such as `System.out.println("Hello");`, for example, rather than the fully qualified name `java.lang.System.out.println("Hello");`, even though the program containing this statement does not contain the statement `import java.lang.*:`.

APPENDIX G

A Keyboard

Input Class

Section 3.4 presented the Java-provided statements required to set up input streams for reading data entered at the keyboard. In place of the techniques described in that section, you can use the read methods provided in the class named KBR, which is presented in this appendix. The code for this class, whose name is derived from the term *keyboard read,* is listed at the end of this appendix and is available on this text's Web site. This appendix explains how to access and use the methods in the KBR class. This class provides the following five methods:

```
readChar()
readInt()
readLong()
readFloat()
readDouble()
```

Each of these is a general-purpose method that can read a single character, integer, long, float, or double value, respectively, that is entered at the keyboard. Each of these methods automatically sets up the necessary input streams, described in Section 3.4, for reading data entered at the keyboard, and all of the methods are used in essentially the same manner. For example, a statement such as

```
number = KBR.readInt();
```

will read data entered at the keyboard. If the data represent a valid integer value, the number is accepted and stored in the variable named number. Here number can be any programmer-selected variable that has been declared as an integer data type. If the entered data do not correspond to a valid integer value, the method will display an error message and request that the user reenter an integer value. Program G.1 illustrates all of the KBR read() methods within the context of a complete program.

PROGRAM G.1

```
public class KeyBoardReadTest
{
  public static void main (String[] args)
  throws java.io.IOException
  {
    char key;
    int num1;
    long num2;
    float num3;
    double num4;

    System.out.print("Enter a character: ");
    key = KBR.readChar();
    System.out.println("The character entered is " + key);

    System.out.print("Enter an integer value: ");
    num1 = KBR.readInt();
    System.out.println("The integer entered is " + num1);

    System.out.print("Enter a long integer value: ");
    num2 = KBR.readLong();
    System.out.println("The long integer entered is " + num2);

    System.out.print("Enter a float value: ");
    num3 = KBR.readFloat();
    System.out.println("The floating point value entered is " + num3);

    System.out.print("Enter a double value: ");
    num4 = KBR.readDouble();
    System.out.println("The double value entered is " + num4);
  }
}
```

As seen in Program G.1, all of the KBR read() methods are called in the same manner by preceding the desired method with the class name, KBR, and a period and assigning the entered value to a variable of the appropriate data type. Also notice in Program G.1 that no input streams have been declared. The reason is that the required streams are constructed from within the KBR class.

All that is required to use the methods in this class is that this complete class code be copied from the Web site associated with this text into the directory (folder) that you use for your Java programs. Once the class code is copied into your programming directory, you must compile it using the statement

```
javac KBR.java
```

After the class has been compiled, the corresponding class file will be available for use in all of your programs, and the methods can be used as shown in Program G.1.

KBR CLASS CODE

```java
// This class can be used to enter single character and numerical
// values at the Keyboard, as described in Appendix G of the text.

import java.io.*;    // needed to access input stream classes
public class KBR
{

  // This method sets up the basic Keyboard input streams
  // and reads a line of characters from the Keyboard.
  // It returns all characters entered as a string, with any
  // entered whitespace included.
  public static String readData()
  throws java.io.IOException
  {
      // set up the first input stream, which is
      // needed for conversion capabilities
    InputStreamReader isr = new InputStreamReader(System.in);
      // set up a buffered stream, which is
      // needed to access readLine()
    BufferedReader br = new BufferedReader(isr);

    return br.readLine();  // read and return the entered data
  }

  // This method captures and returns the first character entered
  // at the keyboard. If no characters are entered, it will return
  // the code for the Enter key.
  public static char readChar()
  throws java.io.IOException
  {
    String inString = null;
    char key;

    inString = readData();
    if (inString.length() == 0)
      key = 0x000D;   // Unicode value for the Enter key
    else
```

```java
        key = inString.charAt(0);  // 1st character entered
    return key;


}


// This method attempts to convert the characters entered at the
// keyboard to an integer value. If the conversion cannot
// be done, an error message is displayed and the read is
// continued until a valid integer is entered.
public static int readInt()
throws java.io.IOException
{
  int inValue = 0;  // must initialize the variable
  boolean validNumber = false;
  String inString = null;

  while(!validNumber)
  {
    try
    {
      inString = readData();
      inValue = Integer.parseInt(inString.trim());
      validNumber = true;
    }
    catch(NumberFormatException e)
    {
      System.out.println("  The value you entered is not valid. ");
      System.out.println("  Please enter only numeric digits.");
      System.out.print("Enter an integer value: ");
    }
  }
  return inValue;
}


// This method attempts to convert the characters entered at the
// keyboard to a long integer value. If the conversion cannot
// be done, an error message is displayed and the read is
// continued until a valid long integer is entered.
public static long readLong()
throws java.io.IOException
{
  long inValue = 0L;  // must initialize the variable
  boolean validNumber = false;
  String inString = null;

  while(!validNumber)
```

(Continued on next page)

(Continued from previous page)

```java
      {
        try
        {
          inString = readData();
          inValue = Long.parseLong(inString.trim());
          validNumber = true;
        }
        catch(NumberFormatException e)
        {
          System.out.println("  The value you entered is not valid. ");
          System.out.println("  Please enter only numeric digits.");
          System.out.print("Enter a long integer value: ");
        }
      }
      return inValue;
  }


  // This method attempts to convert the characters entered at the
  // keyboard to a float value. If the conversion cannot
  // be done, an error message is displayed and the read is
  // continued until a valid float is entered.
  public static float readFloat()
  throws java.io.IOException
  {
    float inValue = 0F;  // must initialize the variable
    boolean validNumber = false;
    String inString = null;

     while(!validNumber)
     {
       try
       {
         inString = readData();
         inValue = Float.parseFloat(inString.trim());
         validNumber = true;
       }
       catch(NumberFormatException e)
       {
         System.out.println("  The value you entered is not valid. ");
         System.out.println("  Please enter only numeric digits");
         System.out.println("  and, at most, a single decimal point.");
         System.out.print("Enter a float value: ");
       }
     }
     return inValue;
  }
```

```java
// This method attempts to convert the characters entered at the
// keyboard to a double value. If the conversion cannot
// be done, an error message is displayed and the read is
// continued until a valid double is entered.
public static double readDouble()
throws java.io.IOException
{
  double inValue = 0;  // must initialize the variable
  boolean validNumber = false;
  String inString = null;

   while(!validNumber)
  {
    try
    {
      inString = readData();
      inValue = Double.parseDouble(inString.trim());
      validNumber = true;
    }
    catch(NumberFormatException e)
    {
      System.out.println("  The value you entered is not valid. ");
      System.out.println("  Please enter only numeric digits");
      System.out.println("  and, at most, a single decimal point.");
      System.out.print("Enter a double value: ");
    }
  }
  return inValue;
}
}
```

APPENDIX H

Applets

This appendix may be downloaded from the Brooks/Cole Web site located at www.Brookscole.com. To obtain this appendix, go to the Web site at www.Brookscole.com and select the Disciplines category. From this category, select Computer Science and then select Java. Locate the text *Java for Engineers and Scientists* and click DownLoad Appendix H.

APPENDIX I

Real Number

Storage

The two's complement binary code to store integer values was presented in Section 1.9. In this appendix, the binary storage format to store single-precision and double-precision numbers is presented. Collectively, both single- and double-precision values are commonly referred to as both *real* and *floating-point* values, respectively, with the two terms considered synonymous.

Like their decimal number counterparts that separate the integer and fractional parts of a number with a decimal point, floating-point numbers are represented in a conventional binary form using a binary point for the same purpose. For example, consider the binary number 1011.11. The digits to the left of the binary point (1011) represent the integer part of the number, and the digits to the right of the binary point (11) represent the fractional part.

To store a floating-point binary number, a code similar to decimal scientific notation is used. To obtain this code, the conventional binary number format is separated into a mantissa and exponent. The following examples illustrate floating-point numbers expressed in this scientific notation:

Conventional Binary Notation	Binary Scientific Notation
1010.0	1.01 exp 011
−10001.0	−1.0001 exp 100
0.001101	1.101 exp −011
−0.000101	−1.01 exp −100

In binary scientific notation, exp stands for exponent. The binary number in front of exp is referred to as the mantissa, and the binary number following exp is the exponent value. Except for the number 0, the mantissa always has a single leading 1 followed immediately by a binary point. The exponent represents a power of 2 and indicates the number of places the binary point should be moved in the mantissa to obtain the conventional binary notation. If the exponent is positive, the binary point is moved to the right. If the exponent is negative, the binary point is moved to the left. For example, the exponent `011` in the number `1.01 exp 011` means move the binary point three places to the right so that the number becomes `1010`. The `-011` exponent in the number `1.101 exp -011` means move the binary point three places to the left so that the number becomes `0.001101`.

In storing floating-point numbers, the sign, mantissa, and exponent are stored individually within separate fields. The number of bits in each field determines the precision of the number. Single-precision (32-bit) and double-precision (64-bit) data formats are defined by the Institute of Electrical and Electronics Engineers (IEEE) Standard 754-1985 to have the characteristics given in Table I.1. The format for a single-precision real number is illustrated in Figure I.1.

FIGURE I.1   Single-Precision Real Number Storage Format

The sign bit shown in Figure I.1 refers to the sign of the mantissa. A sign bit of 1 represents a negative number, and a bit value of 0 represents a positive value. Since all mantissas, except for the number 0, have a leading 1 followed by their binary points, these two items are never stored explicitly. The binary point implicitly resides immediately to the left of mantissa bit 22, and a leading 1 is always assumed. The binary number 0 is specified by setting all mantissa and exponent bits to 0. For this case only, the implied leading mantissa bit is also 0.

The exponent field contains an exponent that is biased by 127. For example, an exponent of 5 would be stored using the binary equivalent of the number 132 (127 + 5). Using eight exponent bits, this is coded as 10000100. The addition of 127 to each exponent allows negative exponents to be coded within the exponent field without the need for an explicit sign bit. For example, the exponent −011, which corresponds to −3, would be stored using the binary equivalent of +124 (127 − 3).

Figure I-2 illustrates the encoding and storage of the decimal number 59.75 as a 32-bit single-precision binary number. The sign, exponent, and mantissa are determined as follows:

The conventional binary equivalent of

   `-59.75`

is

   `-111011.11`

Expressed in binary scientific notation, this becomes

   `-1.1101111 exp 101`

The minus sign is signified by setting the sign bit to 1. The mantissa's leading 1 and binary point are omitted, and the 23-bit mantissa field is encoded as

   `11011110000000000000000`

TABLE I.1   IEEE Standard 754-1985 Floating-Point Specification

Data Format	Sign Bits	Mantissa Bits	Exponent Bits
Single-precision	1	23	8
Double-precision	1	52	11

The exponent field encoding is obtained by adding the exponent value of 101 to 1111111, which is the binary equivalent of the 127_{10} bias value.

$$
\begin{array}{lll}
1\ 1\ 1\ 1\ 1\ 1\ 1 & = & 127_{10} \\
+\ 1\ 0\ 1 & = & +5_{10} \\
\hline
1\ 0\ 0\ 0\ 0\ 1\ 0\ 0 & = & 132_{10}
\end{array}
$$

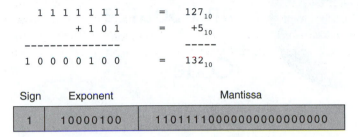

Sign	Exponent	Mantissa
1	10000100	11011110000000000000000

FIGURE I.2   The Encoding and Storage of a Binary Number

APPENDIX J

Solutions and Source Code

Solutions to selected odd-numbered exercises and source code for all programs listed in the text may be downloaded from the Brooks/Cole Web site located at www.Brookscole.com.

To Obtain Solutions

To obtain solutions to selected odd-numbered exercises, go to the Web site at www.Brookscole.com and select the Disciplines category. From this category, select Computer Science and then select Java. Locate the text *Java for Engineers and Scientists* and click DownLoad Java Solutions.

To Obtain Source Code

To obtain the source code for the programs listed in the text, go to the Web site at www.Brookscole.com and select the Disciplines category. From this category, select Computer Science and then select Java. Locate the text *Java for Engineers and Scientists* and click DownLoad Java Source files.

INDEX